Delight in Thinking

AN INTRODUCTION TO PHILOSOPHY READER

Delight in Thinking

AN INTRODUCTION TO PHILOSOPHY READER

Steven D. Hales

Bloomsburg University

Scott C. Lowe

Bloomsburg University

Boston Burr Ridge, IL Dubuque, IA Madison, WI New York
San Francisco St. Louis Bangkok Bogotá Caracas Kuala Lumpur
Lisbon London Madrid Mexico City Milan Montreal New Delhi
Santiago Seoul Singapore Sydney Taipei Toronto

The McGraw-Hill Companies

Published by McGraw-Hill, an imprint of The McGraw-Hill Companies, Inc., 1221 Avenue of the Americas, New York, NY 10020.

This book is printed on acid-free paper.

1 2 3 4 5 6 7 8 9 0 FGR/FGR 0 9 8 7 6

ISBN-13: 978-0-07-312936-5
ISBN-10: 0-07-312936-4

Editor in Chief: *Emily Barrosse*
Publisher: *Lyn Uhl*
Sponsoring Editor: *Jon-David Hague*
Signing Sales Representative: *Daniel Pello*
Marketing Manager: *Suzanna Ellison*
Project Managers: *Stacy Shearer and Carey Eisner*
Senior Designer: *Kim Menning*
Text Designer: *Caroline McGowan*
Cover Designer: *Ross Carron*
Production Supervisor: *Randy Hurst*
Composition: *10/12 Bembo by International Typesetting & Composition*
Printing: *45# New Era Matte, Quebecor World*

Credits: The credits section for this book begins on page 444 and is considered an extension of the copyright page.

Library of Congress Cataloging-in-Publication Data

Delight in thinking : an introduction to philosophy reader / [edited by] Scott C. Lowe, Steven D. Hales.
p. cm.
Includes bibliographical references.
ISBN-13: 978-0-07-312936-5
ISBN-10: 0-07-312936-4
1. Philosophy—Textbooks. I. Lowe, Scott C. II. Hales, Steven D.
B74.D45 2007
100—dc22 2005058400

www.mhhe.com

For my daughter Holly

—SDH

For J.I.A.R.

—SCL

Contents

God and Religious Belief 159

Free Will 233

Philosophy of Mind 273

Personal Identity 331

Preface for Instructors

Can you remember what first got you hooked on philosophy? It probably wasn't parsing Wittgenstein or digging through Duns Scotus—the pleasures of scholarship came later. For us, in any case, it was reading something exciting, a book or article or short story that had real philosophical content in it. It was that sense of being confronted with a philosophical puzzle, or iconoclastic idea, wrapped in accessible, stimulating prose. In our first philosophy classes there was the sense of the mind awakening to grand possibilities, the recognition that great thinkers actually believed things that, were we to voice them at home, would bring laughter or scorn from our families. Philosophy, as Plato wrote, begins in wonder. Furthermore, we would humbly add, it begins with a sense of delight when we turn away from the shadows and into the sun, when the door to the life of the mind is first kicked open. That is what we want for our students too: a delight in thinking.

One of the main challenges of teaching an introductory philosophy course is that the great majority of students have not had one in high school. Since few high schools offer a course in philosophy, or anything like it, most students have not had a lot of practice reading a sustained argument presented over several pages, identifying premises, or drawing conclusions and analyzing them. Nor are they likely to have encountered philosophical ideas outside of religious training or articles on applied ethics in the newspaper. So, when you ask students at the beginning of the semester what they think their philosophy course will be about, most of them understandably have only a vague idea. Indeed, even after handing out a syllabus with a list of topics, students may still be rather unsure of what is to come. Add to that the fact that the topics taken up in a philosophy course are rather abstract, and you've got a double problem: for most students, philosophy is both unfamiliar and abstract.

So how can we, as conscientious professors, find a way to introduce students to the discipline that will get them excited about philosophy? Unfortunately, many books currently on the market designed for Introduction to Philosophy are heavy on the classics—loads of Plato, Aquinas, Locke, Kant, and so forth. To be sure, students ought to be exposed to the great thinkers of history. The problem is that these readings are often too difficult for someone new to the discipline to get a lot out of. From our experiences, students will begin to read lengthy selections from The Great Dead Heroes, get frustrated, and (we fear) give up. One solution is to assign single-author textbooks where traditional philosophical topics have been simplified and presented through that one author's voice. Most of us resist this approach, however, feeling that a college course in philosophy *has* to include a bit of Plato and the others, and not just in a predigested and regurgitated form. Too many times professors are then stumped, with no other solution in view, and spend their days in the Sisyphean task of rolling out the classics and hoping for the best.

Delight in Thinking is a solution to this conundrum. It is designed to be the sole text for an Introduction to Philosophy course, a course that introduces students to the vibrant living issues and puzzles in philosophy, not just the pantheon of the ancient dead. The book is organized thematically and includes readings from all the major sub-disciplines of philosophy. Without pretending to be all-inclusive, there are readings on essential topics in ethics and political philosophy, a wide range of issues concerning religious belief, classic and contemporary readings on free will, philosophy of mind and personal identity, as well as core readings in epistemology. With a wide variety of topics to work with, instructors can structure a course in the way that best serves their needs.

In addition, the carefully selected and edited readings in this anthology bridge the gap between the popular presentation of philosophical ideas and the real meat of the great works of the past. We have purposely picked readings that try to address students on their own terms, selecting them from general-readership magazines like *Harper's, Lingua Franca,* and *Scientific American.* These readings stimulate students' interest in the existence of God, the nature of the mind, or what makes a rational belief. Then, once students have gotten interested in a topic and prepped a bit, they are presented with a classic. A student who is fascinated by a strange neurological case study by Oliver Sacks is more willing to make a real effort to read Locke's thoughts on personal identity. There are pedagogical tools to help the students along: brief introductions to each section explain what the upcoming topics are and how they are related to each other, reading questions precede each of the selections to help students master the readings, and biographies of each of the authors make them seem like real human beings who care and think and write about such unusual things.

It is our fervent hope that students will be excited by the topics of this book and that they, like their professors, will find delight in thinking.

Acknowledgments

Between us, we have over 30 years of teaching Introduction to Philosophy. We thank our 4000-plus students for honing our understanding of how best to get across the excitement of philosophy.

Our colleagues in the philosophy department have been helpful interlocutors in discussing articles and pedagogical strategies. We are also grateful to Bloomsburg University for granting us the time to work on this book and the following reviewers for their insightful commentary:

Robert Almeder—*Georgia State University*
Eric M. Cave—*Arkansas State University*

Bill Hartmann—*St. Louis Community College, Forest Park*
Michael Pelt—*Oakland City University*
Evelyn Pluhar—*Pennsylvania State University, Fayette Campus*
Kathleen Squadrito—*Purdue University*

We would also like to thank the following reviewers for their valuable feedback:

John Barton—*Rochester College*
Panayot Butchvarov—*University of Iowa*
Robert J. Caputi—*Trocaire College*
Vernon Caston—*Crown College*
Anthony J. Celano—*Stonehill College*
Steven B. Cowan—*Southeastern Bible College*
Christoph Cox—*Hampshire College*
John Culp—*Azusa Pacific University*
Robert Cummins—*University of California, Davis*
Deane Curtin—*Gustavus Adolphus College*
John D'Adamo—*Archbishop Curley High School*
Christian Early—*Eastern Mennonite University*
Paul A. Fideler—*Lesley University*
Catherine Ludlum Foos—*Indiana University, East*
Stewart C. Goetz—*Ursinus College*
Anthony Graybosch—*California State University, Chico*
Samuel Oluoch Imbo—*Hamline University*
Barbara Kauffmann—*Carnegie Mellon University*
Jean Kazez—*Southern Methodist University*
Robert Knollman—*Mt. Notre Dame High School*
William Krieger—*California State Polytechnic University, Pomona*
Abigail Levin—*University of Alaska, Southeast*
Hilde Lindemann—*Michigan State University*
James C. Manley—*California State Polytechnic University, Pomona*
Don W. Melander—*New England College*
Diane Morgan—*Wilson College*
Mark C. E. Peterson—*University of Wisconsin, Washington County*
Naomi Reshotko—*University of Denver*
Thomas Rickards—*Episcopal Academy*
Michael Roe—*Rancho Verde High School*
Tony Rosenberger—*River Valley High School*
James M. Stinespring—*Alderson-Broaddus College*
C. Michael Stinson—*Southside Virginia Community College*
Paul C. Taylor—*University of Washington*
Noëlle Vahanian—*Lebanon Valley College*
Harry van der Linden—*Butler University*
Xinli Wang—*Juniata College*

Clodagh Weldon—*Dominican University*
Keith D. Wyma—*Whitworth College*
John Zavodny—*Unity College*

Finally, we thank Dan Pellow, our local McGraw-Hill representative, who first saw the merits in this project, and Jon-David Hague, the wise and foresighted McGraw-Hill editor who saw *Delight in Thinking* to its completion.

Welcome to Philosophy

What are you doing here, anyway? If you're reading this textbook, it's likely that you're taking a college-level Introduction to Philosophy course. As you will see, asking difficult, sometimes unusual questions and coming up with careful answers is important to doing philosophy. So let's start with one of the most immediate questions we might raise: what are you doing? Out of all the possible things you could be doing, you've chosen to attend college. Why? You must view attending college and getting a degree as being valuable, but how? One kind of value is fiscal; having a college degree is likely to help you get a better job. Is that the only value though? Lots of people would say that there are other, perhaps even more important, values to a college education, like becoming literate and informed about the world, becoming a better citizen, becoming a better, more moral person. These values are benefits to you, but they are also benefits to the broader society. And after all, it is the broader society that has created colleges and universities and which continues to put resources (lots of resources!) into maintaining them so that you can attend. What does our society get out of your going to college? Well, one might suggest they get a more skilled worker, a more active citizen, a more engaged neighbor, parent, friend, etc. Colleges are clearly pretty important, so it seems fair to ask, what ought colleges teach in order to accomplish their important role in society? Jacques Barzun, historian and former provost of Columbia University, has some interesting and provocative suggestions in answer to that question. He argues that colleges ought to focus much more on educating students in the liberal arts and much less on training them for work. In that way, he suggests, colleges will better serve their students and society.

One of the liberal arts is philosophy. But why study philosophy instead of history, anthropology, or languages? What is the value of *this* class? That's a hard question and one that philosophers themselves disagree about. Certainly philosophers are interested in looking at some big issues, topics like the nature of truth or justice, right and wrong, and the existence of God, all of which are taken up in this book. Further, equally important to the activity of doing philosophy is bringing an intellectually honest, open, and critical attitude to examining these important topics. Without adopting such an attitude while thinking about these topics, you risk missing one of the central values of studying philosophy: learning to carefully examine your own beliefs and, after critical reflection, deciding which, if any of them, are defensible. Without intellectual honesty and self-examination, you will get little out of this class. One of the greatest exemplars of this critical attitude was the ancient Greek philosopher, Socrates, the subject of Plato's *The Apology*. Socrates devoted his entire life to critical reflection on beliefs commonly held in his day. He engaged people in conversation and challenged them to explain what they were doing and why. (You can imagine how popular that made him.) And in the end, his life of inquiry led to his death. Carefully examining your own ideas is not without risks, probably not death, but it is scary, difficult, and painful. Yet, without questioning and doubt, it's not clear how one can ever claim to have beliefs of one's *own*.

Finally, one of the hallmarks of philosophy, and of critical inquiry in general, is questioning authority. Part of having beliefs that are one's own is having beliefs that you can defend and not just accept *on authority,* whatever that authority is. Admittedly, sometimes accepting beliefs on authority doesn't turn out badly. Remember when you were little and your parents told you (in no uncertain terms) that whacking your brother with a baseball bat was *wrong,* and you believed them just because they are your parents? Yet, on the whole, doing or believing something just because someone in authority says to has a pretty bad track record. Some of the worst examples of human behavior—slavery, terrorism, the Holocaust, the Inquisition—were in large part the result of people doing terrible things to others because those with power and authority said it was acceptable to do so. One of the more frightening aspects of these periods in history is the degree to which atrocities were carried out by ordinary people like you and your classmates, not by monsters or the deranged. "Yeah, but I'm not like that; I know better," you say to yourself. We would all like to think that of ourselves, but unfortunately the evidence doesn't back us up (just think about the last time you gave in to "peer pressure"). Stanley Milgram presents an account of experiments in which average people like you and me were willing to inflict significant pain on others just because the experimenter, someone posing as a scientist in a white lab coat, *asked* them to. In light of Milgram's experiments, we would all do well to renew our efforts to think more carefully and to think for ourselves.

Trim the College?—A Utopia!

JACQUES BARZUN (1907–) was born in France and moved to the United States as a teenager. He attended Columbia University where he earned his BA and PhD and then taught cultural history for many decades. He was dean of faculties and provost at Columbia from 1958 to 1967. Barzun is a prolific writer and author of more than 10 books, including *The Teacher in America* (1945), *The American University* (1968), and most recently *From Dawn to Decadence: 500 Years of Western Cultural Life, 1500 to the Present* (2000).

THINKING QUESTIONS

Jacques Barzun, *Trim the College?—A Utopia!*

1. What does "utopia" mean in the title of this article?
2. Which disciplines does Barzun include among the liberal arts?
3. What do you hope to gain by getting a college degree?
4. According to Barzun, why should studying the liberal arts be the core of a college education?
5. What needlessly drives up the cost of college, according to Barzun?

IT IS AGREED THAT ALL who can read and write and want to go to college should be able to. Lack of money should not be a hindrance. But as to what a college is, there is no agreement. It is not even discussed. Yet look at the facts. The undergraduate unit of a large Ivy League university with 40 majors and hundreds of electives differs widely from a liberal-arts college, and both differ from a small institution that started as a denominational college—or from the typical Roman Catholic university. The college of a huge state university is another thing again, and so are the scattered parts of a state system that were originally teachers' colleges or normal schools.

This variety, it is said, gives everybody a chance to find the place that suits his or her talents and tastes. That is pious nonsense. The young have no idea what they are getting into, and they often have no choice. Selection is determined by geography, cost, and the luck of admission or rejection.

What further complicates this catch-as-catch-can is the price of the longed-for boon of a "college experience." The strain on the budget is notorious. If a family has more than one child to educate, the cost can be a quarter of a million dollars. To be sure, some students can qualify for scholarships or loans, but not all, and one who goes to graduate or professional school may enter the job market with a massive debt. Is anybody prepared to deny that this state of affairs, although tamely accepted, is sheer unreason? All to college, but the hurdles are a mile high.

This social lunacy makes up the first argument for rediscovering what a college is and for trimming today's institutions to fit. The nature of education makes up the second. What is the basic college? History suggests some answers. When the cathedral school of the 12th century decided that more advanced teaching should be available, the medieval university was born. It took three directions, two of them professional: theology and law. The third was "letters," the liberal arts that we call the humanities, with mathematics included. We have duly retained the term "liberal arts." We even apply it to certain colleges. But the real thing is rarely found.

Two other models of the college developed next. First, the English universities at Oxford and Cambridge took the form of small colleges. Those were financed by royalty, prelates, and statesmen and specialized in the interests of their patrons. But all were intent on introducing the young to contemporary knowledge, rather than to a profession. And all were small enough to provide students the attention they needed to acquire that knowledge. The second model arose in the 16th century, when the Society of Jesus began to cover Europe with colleges designed to strengthen the Catholic faith as Protestantism grew. That goal was to be achieved by making well-educated minds. Proof of success: nearly all great European thinkers of the next two centuries, from Descartes to Voltaire, went to Jesuit colleges (and repaid their mentors by successfully combating religious dogma).

The Jesuit institutions, like the English and the Continental universities, taught the liberal arts and the numerical sciences. Certain subjects, such as logic and rhetoric, may no longer appeal to us, but the lesson for the present is that the core of an all-purpose higher education consists of these "arts."

Even if, nowadays, students attend college who are older than was once the norm, the goals of college education remain the same. The arts are fit for all minds, endowing them with particular and general abilities: to think, to speak simply and clearly, to express views rationally, to own and use a body of facts and ideas that are widely known, to detect errors and fallacies, resolve intellectual problems, and possibly make discoveries in some branch of learning. To this armament of powers, the last five centuries have supplied new areas to exploit: history and the social sciences and the hugely expanded substance of the physical and life sciences. Those have broadened the curriculum of the basic college, but they do not change its character and role.

Nor does the deplorable state of American public schools justify fundamentally changing the core purpose of college, but the failure of high schools to impart the techniques of study and a modicum of subject matter does interfere with the integrity of college work by creating the necessity to make students go through remedial courses in reading, writing, grammar, mathematical reasoning, or other skills needed to go on in the liberal arts.

In these conditions, what must the college be and do? 1. Devote its energies and resources to the liberal arts as here defined. 2. Run remedial programs until no longer needed. 3. For health, safety, and recreation, provide modest facilities for physical exercise, intramural sports, and some extracurricular activities, as well for medical care. But if the extras are for "enrichment," it is better to make sure there is something to enrich.

Nothing has been said so far about intercollegiate athletics. Nothing can abate the national passion for such sports. Yet, only some of the 3,500 institutions of higher learning in our country are truly burdened by the incubus. Let them call on their alumni to bear the cost; it is they who demand the sport.

For the college as such, concentrating on the liberal arts is not enough. They must be introduced as a required group, in the first two years of college. A free choice of electives may lead to four years of freshman work, which evades the purpose of an organized curriculum. In the last two years of college, a guided choice of courses in two or three subjects can then satisfy a student's developing sense of direction. The young *discover* where their abilities lie rather than know their vocation as freshmen.

To be of any worth, the liberal arts must not only figure in the catalog, they must also be taught as arts, not as scholarly disciplines—and that must be done by teachers. The present system, which favors faculty research over teaching, turns the liberal arts into professional subjects. Indeed, one may hear the teacher of an introductory course assert that he hopes to attract some students into his field. The course, thereby, ceases to be a *college* subject. "Liberal" in liberal arts means precisely "free" of professionalism and pedantry.

But what of the student whose interest lies in an area like film and theater, art and music, photography and television, and who wants to "qualify" for a job the day after graduation? Let there be a School of Applied Arts on campus or at the nearest university, similar to business and journalism schools. The applied arts are not college work; the very scheduling of long hours of practice makes for conflicts with other studies.

What, then, are college youths to carry away from their studies as they are swallowed up by career, parenthood, or civic obligations? Much will be buried, but the innumerable portions of purport, reasoning, and significance will still be there for instant recognition and application to the uses of life. It is this "apperceptive mass" that makes college graduates educated instead of ignorant.

Besides fulfilling its indicated purpose, the college so conceived would yield results measurable in money. First savings: The college offers only courses that serve the liberal arts. Like the catalog, the faculty is correspondingly small. By seeking teachers, the college need not pay an extraordinary sum to obtain the transcendent researcher for whom all are bidding. Limiting campus amenities within reason similarly disburdens the budget. The endowment might even begin to suffice.

Colleges will also save money by pruning the many offices that have grown up to oversee things that form no part of their role—offices devoted to community service, mental health, development, government relations, public relations, and alumni affairs. Together, those have planted a bureaucracy at the heart of the institution. A college should not advertise: Prospective students cannot compare places until they have been on campus for a year. As for entertainment, students profit from providing it for themselves.

Students should also help teach one another. For that reason, the true college must remain of modest size; large numbers prevent familiar conversation, jollity, or camaraderie in anything but small cliques. College matures through the sense of belonging to a common society. That sense begins through the required core in the first two years; it is sustained by the unspecialized handling of all subjects, which leads to comparing notes and discussing matters with teachers. These, by the way, feel no need to seek popularity by inflating grades, the present counterpart of student cheating.

One last provision: Student aid is to free the recipient to be a student. He or she should not have to work for money, especially when classmates don't. For one thing, it skews an individual's academic record by handicapping the worker, who is also deprived of the leisure and the beneficial companionship just cited.

With the nature of a basic college understood and respected, the cost of tuition comes down to a point where those middle-class families now ineligible for help will not have to go heavily into debt. By the same economy, the full subsidy of the less well off becomes possible. Seeing reason return to the academy, many people whose exchequer is now drained by tuition will be grateful to give money for scholarships.

Of course, none of what has been described here is possible. Too many vested interests oppose any such sensible transformation of what we indiscriminately call colleges. The bureaucracy is entrenched on the campus as firmly as anywhere, and so is the faculty, with its specialist bent and overextended offerings. Very possibly, even the beneficiaries of the change—hypnotized parents of the college-bound—might shy away from supporting it, vaguely afraid of some unforeseen disaster. Let them start saving for college with the birth of each child (early marriage and childbearing is recommended), and with compound interest over 17 years, that quarter of a million dollars is not unattainable.

The Apology

PLATO (427–347 BCE), along with his student, Aristotle, is regarded as the greatest thinker of the ancient world. Born into a wealthy family in Athens, as a young man he came under the influence of Socrates, about whom the dialogues, including *The Apology,* are written. The dialogues are breathtaking in their scope, covering topics in metaphysics, epistemology, ethics, philosophy of religion, political philosophy, and logic. In 387 BCE Plato founded the Academy, the first institution of formal learning in the Western world.

THINKING QUESTIONS

Plato, *The Apology*

1. Why is this work called *The Apology* since Socrates isn't apologizing? What *is* Socrates doing?
2. What is the Oracle at Delphi and what did the oracle say that got Socrates started on his life of inquiry?
3. Why do you suppose that Socrates sought out the poets, politicians, and artisans to help him understand what the oracle meant? Who would you consult if you faced a similar challenge?
4. What is Socrates accused of that he is on trial for?
5. What does Socrates mean by the "unexamined life"?
6. Why does Socrates think that a life "inquiring after the virtues" is valuable?
7. Why doesn't Socrates fear death?

I. THE SPEECH

Introduction

To what degree, Gentlemen of Athens, you have been affected by my accusers, I do not know. I, at any rate, was almost led to forget who I am—so convincingly did they speak. Yet hardly anything they have said is true. Among their many falsehoods, I was especially surprised by one; they said you must be on guard lest I deceive you, since I am a clever speaker. To have no shame at being directly refuted by facts when I show myself in no way clever with words—that, I think, is the very height of shamelessness. Unless, of course, they call a man a clever speaker if he speaks the truth. If that is what they mean, why, I would even admit to being an orator—though not after *their* fashion.

These men, I claim, have said little or nothing true. But from me, Gentlemen, you will hear the whole truth. It will not be prettily tricked out in elegant speeches like theirs, words and phrases all nicely arranged. To the contrary: you will hear me speak naturally in the words which happen to occur to me. For I believe what I say to be just, and let no one of you expect otherwise. Besides, it would hardly be appropriate in a man of my age, Gentlemen, to come before you making up speeches like a boy. So I must specifically ask one thing of you, Gentlemen. If you hear me make my defense in the same words I customarily use at the tables in the Agora, and other places where many of you have heard me, please do not be surprised or make a disturbance because of it. For things stand thus: I am now come into court for the first time; I am seventy years old; and I am an utter stranger to this place. If I were a foreigner, you would unquestionably make allowances if I spoke in the dialect and manner in which I was raised. In just the same way, I specifically ask you now, and justly so, I think, to pay no attention to my manner of speech—it may perhaps be poor, but then perhaps an improvement—and look strictly to this one thing, whether or not I speak justly. For that is the virtue of a judge, and the virtue of an orator is to speak the truth.

Statement

First of all, Gentlemen, it is right for me to defend myself against the first false accusations lodged against me, and my first accusers; and next, against later accusations and later accusers. For the fact is that many accusers have risen before you against me; at this point they have been making accusations for many years, and they have told no truth. Yet I fear them more than I fear Anytus and those around him—though they too are dangerous. Still, the others are more dangerous. They took hold of most of you in childhood, persuading you of the truth of accusations which were in fact quite false: "There is a certain Socrates . . . Wise man . . . Thinker on things in the Heavens . . . Inquirer into all things beneath Earth . . . Making the weaker argument stronger. . . . " Those men, Gentlemen of Athens, the men who spread that report, are my dangerous accusers; for their hearers believe that those who inquire into such things acknowledge no gods.

Again, there have been many such accusers, and they have now been at work for a long time; they spoke to you at a time when you were especially trusting—some of you children, some only a little older—and they lodged their accusations quite by default, no one appearing in defense. But the most absurd thing is that one cannot even know or tell their names—unless perhaps in the case of a comic poet. But those who use malicious slander to persuade you, and those who, themselves persuaded, persuade others—all are most difficult to deal with. For it is impossible to bring any one of them forward as a witness and cross-examine him. I must rather, as it were, fight with shadows in making my defense, and question where no one answers.

Please grant, then, as I say, that two sets of accusers have risen against me: those who now lodge their accusations, and those who lodged accusations long since. And please accept the fact that I must defend myself against the latter first. For in fact, you heard their accusations earlier, and with far greater effect than those which came later.

Very well then. A defense is to be made, Gentlemen of Athens. I am to attempt to remove from you this short time that prejudice which you have been long in acquiring. I might wish that this should come to pass, if it were in some way better for you and for me, wish that I might succeed in my defense. But I think the thing difficult, and its nature hardly escapes me. Still, let that go as pleases the God; the law must be obeyed, and a defense conducted.

Refutation of the Old Accusers

Let us then take up from the beginning the charges which have given rise to the prejudice—the charges on which Meletus in fact relied in lodging his indictment. Very well, what do those who slander me say? It is necessary to read, as it were, their sworn indictment: "Socrates is guilty of needless curiosity and meddling interference, inquiring into things beneath Earth and in the Sky, making the weaker argument stronger, and teaching others the same." The charge is something like that. Indeed, you have seen it for yourselves in a comedy by Aristophanes—a certain Socrates being carried around on the stage, talking about walking on air and babbling a great deal of other nonsense, of which I understand neither much nor little. Mark you, I do not mean to disparage such knowledge, if anyone in fact has it—let me not be brought to trial by Meletus on such a charge as that! But Gentlemen, I have no share of it. Once again, I offer the majority of you as witnesses, and ask those of you who have heard me in conversation—there are many among you—inform each other, please, whether any of you ever heard anything of the sort. From that you will recognize the nature of the other things the multitude says about me.

The fact is that there is nothing in these accusations. And if you have heard from anyone that I undertake to educate men, and make money doing it, that is false too. Once again, I think it would be a fine thing to be able to educate men, as Gorgias of Leontini does, or Prodicus of Ceos, or Hippias of Elis. For each of them, Gentlemen, can enter any given city and convince the youth—who might freely associate with any of their fellow citizens they please—to drop those associations and associate with them, to pay money for it, and give thanks in the bargain. As a matter of fact, there is a man here right now, a Parian, and a wise one, who as I learn has just come to town. For I happened to meet a person who has spent more money on Sophists than everyone else put together, Callias, son of Hipponicus. So I asked him—for he has two sons—"Callias," I said, "if your two sons were colts or calves, we could get an overseer for them and hire him, and his business would be to make them excellent in their appropriate virtue. He would be either a horse-trainer or a farmer. But as it is, since the two of them are men, whom do you intend to get as an overseer? Who has knowledge of that virtue which belongs to a man and a citizen? Since you have sons, I'm sure you have considered this. Is there such a person," I said, "or not?"

"To be sure," he said.

"Who is he?" I said. "Where is he from, and how much does he charge to teach?"

"Evenus, Socrates," he said. "A Parian. Five minae."

And I count Evenus fortunate indeed, if he really possesses that art, and teaches it so modestly. For my own part, at any rate, I would be puffed up with vanity and pride if I had such knowledge. But I do not, Gentlemen.

Perhaps one of you will ask, "But Socrates, what is this all about? Whence have these slanders against you arisen? You must surely have been busying yourself with something out of the ordinary; so grave a report and rumor would not have arisen had you not been doing something rather different from most folk. Tell us what it is, so that we may not take action in your case unadvisedly." That, I think, is a fair request, and I shall try to indicate what it is that has given me the name I have. Hear me, then. Perhaps some of you will think I joke; be well assured that I shall be telling the whole truth.

Gentlemen of Athens, I got this name through nothing but a kind of wisdom. What kind? The kind which is perhaps peculiarly human, for it may be I am really wise in that. And perhaps the men I just mentioned are wise with a wisdom greater than human—either that, or I cannot say what. In any case, I have no knowledge of it, and whoever says I do is lying and speaks to my slander.

Please, Gentlemen of Athens. Do not make a disturbance, even if I seem to you to boast. For it will not be my own words I utter; I shall refer you to the speaker, as one worthy of credit. For as witness to you of my wisdom—whether it is wisdom of a kind, and what kind of wisdom it is—I shall call the God at Delphi.

You surely knew Chaerephon. He was my friend from youth, and a friend of your democratic majority. He went into exile with you, and with you he returned. And you know what kind of a man he was, how eager and impetuous in whatever he rushed into. Well, he once went to Delphi and boldly asked the oracle—as I say, Gentlemen, please do not make a disturbance—he asked whether anyone is wiser than I. Now, the Pythia replied that no one is wiser. And to this his brother here will testify, since Chaerephon is dead.

Why do I mention this? I mention it because I intend to inform you whence the slander against me has arisen. For when I heard it, I reflected: "What does the God mean? What is the sense of this riddling utterance? I know that I am not wise at all; what then does the God mean by saying I am wisest? Surely he does not speak falsehood; it is not permitted to him." So I puzzled for a long time over what was meant, and then, with great reluctance, I turned to inquire into the matter in some such way as this.

I went to someone with a reputation for wisdom, in the belief that there if anywhere I might test the meaning of the utterance and declare to the oracle that, "This man is wiser than I am, and you said I was wisest." So I examined him—there is no need to mention a name, but it was someone in political life who produced this effect on me in discussion, Gentlemen of Athens—and I concluded that though he seemed wise to many other men, and most especially to himself, he was not. I tried to show him this; and thence I became hated, by him and by many who were present. But I left thinking to myself, "I am wiser than that man. Neither of us probably knows anything worthwhile; but he thinks he does and does not, and I do not and do not think I do. So it seems at any rate that I am wiser in this one small respect: I do not think I know what I do not." I then went to another man who was reputed to be even wiser, and the same thing seemed true again; there too I became hated, by him and by many others.

Nevertheless, I went on, perceiving with grief and fear that I was becoming hated, but still, it seemed necessary to put the God first—so I had to go on, examining what the oracle meant by testing everyone with a reputation for knowledge. And by the Dog, Gentlemen—I must tell you the truth—I swear that I had some such experience as this: it seemed to me that those most highly esteemed for wisdom fell little short of being most deficient, as I carried on inquiry in behalf of the God, and that others reputedly inferior were men of more discernment.

But really, I must display my wanderings to you; they were like those of a man performing labors—all to the end that I might not leave the oracle untested. From the politicians I went to the poets—tragic, dithyrambic, and the rest—thinking that there I would discover myself manifestly less wise by comparison. So I took up poems over which I thought they had taken special pains, and asked them what they meant, so as also at the same time to learn from them. Now, I am ashamed to tell you the truth, Gentlemen, but still, it must be told. There was hardly anyone present who could not give a better account than they of what they had themselves produced. So presently I came to realize that poets do not make what they make by wisdom, but by a kind of native disposition or divine inspiration, exactly like seers and prophets. For the latter also utter many fine things, but know nothing of the things of which they speak. That is how the poets also appeared to me, while at the same time I realized that because of their poetry they thought themselves the wisest of men in other matters—and were not. Once again, I left thinking myself superior to them in just the way I was to the politicians.

Finally I went to the craftsmen. I was aware that although I knew scarcely anything, I would find that they knew many things, and fine ones. In this I was not mistaken: they knew things that I did not, and in that respect were wiser. But Gentlemen of Athens, it seemed to me that the poets and our capable public craftsmen had exactly the same failing: because they practiced their own arts well, each deemed himself wise in other things, things of great importance. This mistake quite obscured their wisdom. The result was that I asked myself on behalf of the oracle whether I would accept being such as I am, neither wise with their wisdom nor foolish with their folly, or whether I would accept wisdom and folly together and become such as they are. I answered, both for myself and the oracle, that it was better to be as I am.

From this examination, Gentlemen of Athens, much enmity has risen against me, of a sort most harsh and heavy to endure, so that many slanders have arisen, and the name is put abroad that I am 'wise'. For on each occasion those present think I am wise in the things in which I test others. But very likely, Gentlemen, it is really the God who is wise, and by his oracle he means to say that, "Human nature is a thing of little worth, or none." It appears that he does not mean this fellow Socrates, but uses my name to offer an example, as if he were saying that, "He among you, Gentlemen, is wisest who, like Socrates, realizes that he is truly worth nothing in respect to wisdom." That is why I still go about even now on behalf of the God, searching and inquiring among both citizens and strangers, should I think some one of them is wise; and when it seems he is not, I help the God and prove it. Due to this pursuit, I have no leisure worth mentioning either for the affairs of the City or for my own estate; I dwell in utter poverty because of my service to the God.

Then too the young men follow after me—especially the ones with leisure, namely, the richest. They follow of their own initiative, rejoicing to hear men tested, and often they imitate me and undertake to test others; and next, I think, they find an ungrudging plenty of people who think they have some knowledge but know little or nothing. As a result, those whom they test become angry at me, not at themselves, and say that, "This fellow Socrates is utterly polluted, and corrupts the youth." And when someone asks them what it is he does, what it is he teaches, they cannot say because they do not know; but so as not to seem at a loss, they mutter the kind of thing that lies ready to hand against anyone who pursues wisdom: "Things in the Heavens and beneath the Earth," or, "Not acknowledging gods," or, "Making the weaker argument stronger." The truth, I suppose, they would not wish to state, namely, that it is become quite clear that they pretend to knowledge and know nothing. And because they are concerned for their pride, I think, and zealous, and numerous, and speak vehemently and persuasively about me, they have long filled your ears with zealous slander. It was on the strength of this that Meletus attacked me, along with Anytus and Lycon—Meletus angered on behalf of the poets, Anytus on behalf of the public craftsmen and the politicians, Lycon on behalf of the orators. So the result is, as I said to begin with, that I should be most surprised were I able to remove from you in this short time a slander which has grown so great. There Gentlemen of Athens, you have the truth, and I have concealed or misrepresented nothing in speaking it, great or small. Yet I know quite well that it is just for this that I have become hated—which is in fact an indication of the truth of what I say, and that this is the basis of the slander and charges against me. Whether you inquire into it now or hereafter you will find it to be so.

Refutation of Meletus

Against the charges lodged by my first accusers, let this defense suffice. But for Meletus—the good man who loves his City, so he says—and for my later accusers, I shall attempt a further defense. Once more then, as before a different set of accusers, let us take up their sworn indictment. It runs something like this: it says that Socrates is guilty of corrupting the youth, and of not acknowledging the gods the City acknowledges, but other new divinities. Such is the charge. Let us examine its particulars.

It claims I am guilty of corrupting the youth. But I claim, Gentlemen of Athens, that it is Meletus who is guilty—guilty of jesting in earnest, guilty of lightly bringing men to trial, guilty of pretending a zealous concern for things he never cared about at all. I shall try to show you that this is true.

Come here, Meletus. Now tell me. Do you count it of great importance that the young should be as good as possible?

"I do."

Then come and tell the jurors this: who improves them? Clearly you know, since it is a matter of concern to you. Having discovered, so you say, that I am the man who is corrupting them, you bring me before these judges to accuse me. But now come and say who makes them better. Inform the judges who he is.

You see, Meletus. You are silent. You cannot say. And yet, does this not seem shameful to you, and a sufficient indication of what I say, namely, that you never cared at all? Tell us, my friend. Who improves them?

"The laws."

But I did not ask you that, dear friend. I asked you what man improves them—whoever it is who in the first place knows just that very thing, the laws.

"These men, Socrates. The judges."

Really Meletus? These men here are able to educate the youth and improve them?

"Especially they."

All of them? Or only some?

"All."

By Hera, you bring good news. An ungrudging plenty of benefactors! But what about the audience here. Do they improve them, or not?

"They too."

And members of the Council?

"The Councillors too."

Well then Meletus, do the members of the Assembly, the Ecclesiasts, corrupt the young? Or do they all improve them too?

"They too."

So it seems that every Athenian makes them excellent except me, and I alone corrupt them. Is that what you are saying?

"That is exactly what I am saying."

You condemn me to great misfortune. But tell me, do you think it is so with horses? Do all men improve them, while some one man corrupts them? Or quite to the contrary, is it some one man or a very few, namely horse-trainers, who are able to improve them, while the majority of people, if they handle horses and use them, corrupt them? Is that not true, Meletus, both of horses and all other animals? Of course it is, whether you and Anytus affirm or deny it. It would be good fortune indeed for the youth if only one man corrupted them and the rest benefited. But the fact is, Meletus, that you sufficiently show that you never gave thought to the youth; you clearly indicate your own lack of concern, indicate that you never cared at all about the matters in which you bring action against me.

But again, dear Meletus, tell us this: is it better to dwell among fellow citizens who are good, or wicked? Do answer, dear friend; surely I ask nothing hard. Do not wicked men do evil things to those around them, and good men good things?

"Of course."

Now, is there anyone who wishes to be harmed rather than benefited by those with whom he associates? Answer me, dear friend, for the law requires you to answer. Is there anyone who wishes to be harmed?

"Of course not."

Very well then, are you bringing action against me here because I corrupt the youth intentionally, or unintentionally?

"Intentionally, I say."

How can that be, Meletus? Are you at your age so much wiser than I at mine that you recognize that evil men always do evil things to those around them, and good men do good, while I have reached such a pitch of folly that I am unaware that if I do some evil to those with whom I associate, I shall very likely receive some evil at their hands, with the result that I do such great evil intentionally, as you claim? I do not believe you, Meletus, and I do not think anyone else does either. On the contrary: either I do not corrupt the youth, or if I do, I do so unintentionally. In either case, you lie. And if I corrupt them unintentionally, it is not the law to bring action here for that sort of mistake, but rather to instruct and admonish in private; for clearly, if I once learn, I shall stop what I unintentionally do. You, however, were unwilling to associate with me and teach me; instead, you brought action here, where it is law to bring those in need of punishment rather than instruction.

Gentlemen of Athens, what I said is surely now clear: Meletus was never concerned about these matters, much or little. Still, Meletus, tell us this: how do you say I corrupt the youth? Or is it clear from your indictment that I teach them not to acknowledge gods the City acknowledges, but other new divinities? Is this what you mean by saying I corrupt by teaching?

"Certainly. That is exactly what I mean."

Then in the name of these same gods we are now discussing, Meletus, please speak a little more plainly still, both for me and for these gentlemen here. Do you mean that I teach the youth to acknowledge that there are gods, and thus do not myself wholly deny gods, and am not in that respect guilty—though the gods are not those the City acknowledges, but different ones? Or are you claiming that I do not myself acknowledge any gods at all, and teach this to others?

"I mean that. You acknowledge no gods at all."

Ah, my dear Meletus, why do you say such things? Do I not at least acknowledge Sun and Moon as gods, as other men do?

"No, no, Gentlemen and Judges, not when he says the Sun is a stone and the Moon earth."

My dear Meletus! Do you think it is Anaxagoras you are accusing? Do you so despise these judges here and think them so unlettered that they do not know it is the books of Anaxagoras of Clazomenae which teem with such statements? Are young men to learn these things specifically from me, when they can buy them sometimes in the Orchestra for a drachma, if the price is high, and laugh at Socrates if he pretends they are his own—especially since they are so absurd? Well, dear friend, is that what you think? I acknowledge no gods at all?

"No, none whatever."

You cannot be believed, Meletus—even, I think, by yourself. Gentlemen of Athens, I think this man who stands here before you is insolent and unchastened, and has brought this suit precisely out of insolence and unchastened youth. He seems to be conducting a test by propounding a riddle: "Will Socrates, the wise man, realize how neatly I contradict myself, or will I deceive him and the rest of the audience?" For certainly it seems clear that he is contradicting himself in his indictment. It is as though he were saying, "Socrates is guilty of not acknowledging gods, and acknowledges gods." Yet surely this is to jest.

Please join me, Gentlemen, in examining why it appears to me that this is what he is saying. And you answer us, Meletus. The rest of you will please remember what I asked you at the beginning, and make no disturbance if I fashion arguments in my accustomed way.

Is there any man, Meletus, who acknowledges that there are things pertaining to men, but does not acknowledge that there are men? Let him answer for himself, Gentlemen—and let him stop interrupting. Is there any man who does not acknowledge that there are horses, but acknowledges things pertaining to horsemanship? Or does not acknowledge that there are flutes, but acknowledges things pertaining to flute playing? There is not, my good friend. If you do not wish to answer, I'll answer for you and for the rest of these people here. But do please answer my next question, at least: Is there any man who acknowledges that there are things pertaining to divinities, but does not acknowledge that there are divinities?

"There is not."

How obliging of you to answer—reluctantly, and under compulsion from these gentlemen here. Now, you say that I acknowledge and teach things pertaining to divinities—whether new or old, still at least I acknowledge them, by your account; indeed, you swore to that in your indictment. But if I acknowledge that there are things pertaining to divinities, must I surely not also acknowledge that there are divinities? Isn't that so? Of course it is—since you do not answer, I count you as agreeing. And divinities, we surely believe, are either gods or children of gods? Correct?

"Of course."

So if I believe in divinities, as you say, and if divinities are a kind of god, there is the jesting riddle I attributed to you: you are saying that I do not believe in gods, and again that I do believe in gods because I believe in divinities. On the other hand, if divinities are children of gods, some born illegitimately of nymphs, or others of whom this is also told, who could possibly believe that there are children of gods, but not gods? It would be as absurd as believing that there are children of horses and asses, namely, mules, without believing there are horses and asses. Meletus, you could not have brought this indictment except in an attempt to test us—or because you were at a loss for any true basis of prosecution. But as to how you are to convince anyone of even the slightest intelligence that one and the same man can believe that there are things pertaining to divinities and gods, and yet believe that there are neither divinities nor heroes—there is no way.

Digression: Socrates' Mission to Athens

Gentlemen of Athens, I do not think further defense is needed to show that, by the very terms of Meletus' indictment, I am not guilty; this, surely, is sufficient. But as I said before, a great deal of enmity has risen against me among many people, and you may rest assured this is true. And that is what will convict me, if I am convicted—not Meletus, not Anytus, but the grudging slander of the multitude. It has convicted many another good and decent man; I think it will convict me; nor is there reason to fear that with me it will come to a stand.

Perhaps someone may say, "Are you not ashamed, Socrates, at having pursued such a course that you now stand in danger of being put to death?" To him I would make a just reply: You are wrong, Sir, if you think that a man worth anything at all should take thought for danger in living or dying. He should look when he acts to one thing: whether what he does is just or unjust, the work of a good man or a bad one. By your account, those demigods and heroes who laid down their lives at Troy would be of little worth—the rest of them, and the son of Thetis too; Achilles so much despised danger instead of submitting to disgrace that when he was intent on killing Hector his goddess mother told him, as I recall, "My son, if you avenge the slaying of your comrade Patroclus with the death of Hector, you yourself shall die; for straightway with Hector is his fate prepared for you." Achilles heard, and thought little of the death and danger. He was more afraid to live as a bad man, with friends left unavenged. "Straightway let me die," he said, "exacting right from him who did the wrong, that I may not remain here as a butt of mockery beside the crook-beaked ships, a burden to the earth." Do you suppose that he gave thought to death and danger?

Gentlemen of Athens, truly it is so: wherever a man stations himself in belief that it is best, wherever he is stationed by his commander, there he must I think remain and run the risks, giving thought to neither death nor any other thing except disgrace. I should indeed have wrought a fearful thing, Gentlemen of Athens, if, when the commanders you chose stationed me at Potidaea and Amphipolis and Delium, I there remained as others did, and ran the risk of death; but then, when the God stationed me, as I thought and believed, obliging me to live in the pursuit of wisdom, examining myself and others—if then, at that point, through fear of death or any other thing, I left my post. That would have been dreadful indeed, and then in truth might I be justly brought to court for not acknowledging the existence of gods, for willful disobedience to the oracle, for fearing death, for thinking myself wise when I am not.

For to fear death, Gentlemen, is nothing but to think one is wise when one is not; for it is to think one knows what one does not. No man knows death, nor whether it is not the greatest of all goods; and yet men fear it as though they well knew it to be the worst of evils. Yet how is this not folly most to be reproached, the folly of believing one knows what one does not? I, at least, Gentlemen, am perhaps superior to most men here and just in this, and if I were to claim to be wiser than anyone else it would be in this: that as I have no satisfactory knowledge of things in the Place of the Dead, I do not think I do. I do know that to be guilty of disobedience to a superior, be he god or man, is shameful evil.

So as against evils I know to be evils, I shall never fear or flee from things which for aught I know may be good. Thus, even if you now dismiss me, refusing to do as Anytus bids—Anytus, who said that either I should not have been brought to trial to begin with or, since brought, must be put to death, testifying before you that if I were once acquitted your sons would pursue what Socrates teaches and all be thoroughly corrupted—if with this in view you were to say to me, "Socrates, we shall not at this time be persuaded by Meletus, and we dismiss you. But on this condition: that you no longer pass time in that inquiry of yours, or pursue philosophy. And if you are again taken doing it, you die." If, as I say, you were to dismiss me on that condition, I would reply that I hold you in friendship and regard, Gentlemen of Athens, but I shall obey the God rather than you, and while I have breath and am able I shall not cease to pursue wisdom or to exhort you, charging any of you I happen to meet in my accustomed manner. "You are the best of men, being an Athenian, citizen of a city honored for wisdom and power beyond all others. Are you then not ashamed to care for the getting of money, and reputation, and public honor, while yet having no thought or concern for truth and understanding and the greatest possible excellence of your soul?" And if some one of you disputes this, and says he does care, I shall not immediately dismiss him and go away. I shall question him and examine him and test him, and if he does not seem to me to possess virtue, and yet says he does, I shall rebuke him for counting of more importance things which by comparison are worthless. I shall do this to young and old, citizen and stranger, whomever I happen to meet, but I shall do it especially to citizens, in as much as they are more nearly related to me. For the God commands this, be well assured, and I believe that you have yet to gain in this City a greater good than my service to the God. I go about doing nothing but persuading you, young and old, to care not for body or money in place of, or so much as, excellence of soul. I tell you that virtue does not come from money, but money and all other human goods both public and private from virtue. If in saying this I corrupt the youth, that would be harm indeed. But anyone who claims I say other than this speaks falsehood. In these matters, Gentlemen of Athens, believe Anytus, or do not. Dismiss me, or do not. For I will not do otherwise, even if I am to die for it many times over.

Please do not make a disturbance, Gentlemen. Abide in my request and do not interrupt what I have to say, but listen. Indeed, I think you will benefit by listening. I am going to tell you certain things at which you may perhaps cry out; please do not do it. Be well assured that if you kill me, and if I am the sort of man I claim, you will harm me less than you harm yourselves. There is no harm a Meletus or Anytus can do me; it is not possible, for it does not, I think, accord with divine law that a better man be harmed by a worse. Meletus perhaps can kill me, or exile me, or disenfranchise me; and perhaps he and others too think those things great evils. I do not. I think it a far greater evil to do what he is now doing, attempting to kill a man unjustly. And so, Gentlemen of Athens, I am far from making a defense for my own sake, as some might think; I make it for yours, lest you mistake the gift the God has given you and cast your votes against me. If you kill me, you will not easily find such another man as I, a man who—if I may put it a bit absurdly—has been fastened as it were to the City by the God as to a large and well-bred horse, a horse grown sluggish because of its size, and in need of being roused by a kind of gadfly. Just so, I think, the God has fastened me to the City. I rouse you. I persuade you. I upbraid you. I never stop lighting on each one of you, everywhere, all day long. Such another will not easily come to you again, Gentlemen, and if you are persuaded by me, you will spare me. But perhaps you are angry, as men roused from sleep are angry, and perhaps you will swat me, persuaded by Meletus that you may lightly kill. Then will you continue to sleep out your lives, unless the God sends someone else to look after you.

That I am just that, a gift from the God to the City, you may recognize from this: it scarcely seems a human matter merely, that I should take no thought for anything of my own and endure the neglect of my house and its affairs for these long years now, and ever attend to yours, going to each of you in private like a father or elder brother, persuading you to care for virtue. If I got something from it, if I took pay for this kind of exhortation, that would explain it. But as things are, you can see for yourselves that even my accusers, who have accused me so shamefully of everything else, could not summon shamelessness enough to provide witnesses to testify that I ever took pay or asked for it. For it is enough, I think, to provide my poverty as witness to the truth of what I say.

Perhaps it may seem peculiar that I go about in private advising men and busily inquiring, and yet do not enter your Assembly in public to advise the City. The reason is a thing you have heard me mention many times in many places, that something divine and godlike comes to me—which Meletus, indeed, mocked in his indictment. I have had it from childhood. It comes as a kind of voice, and when it comes, it always turns me away from what I am about to do, but never toward it. That is what opposed my entering political life, and I think it did well to oppose. For be well assured, Gentlemen of

Athens, that had I attempted long since to enter political affairs, I should long since have been destroyed—to the benefit of neither you nor myself.

Please do not be angry at me for telling the simple truth. It is impossible for any man to be spared if he legitimately opposes you or any other democratic majority, and prevents many unjust and illegal things from occurring in his city. He who intends to fight for what is just, if he is to be spared even for a little time, must of necessity live a private rather than a public life.

I shall offer you a convincing indication of this—not words, but what you respect, deeds. Hear, then, what befell me, so that you may know that I will not through fear of death give way to any man contrary to what is right, even if I am destroyed for it. I shall tell you a thing which is tedious—it smacks of the law courts—but true. Gentlemen of Athens, I never held other office in the City, but I was once a member of the Council. And it happened that our Tribe, Antiochis, held the Prytanate when you decided to judge as a group the cases of the ten generals who had failed to gather up the bodies of the slain in the naval battle,—illegally, as later it seemed to all of you. But at the time, I alone of the Prytanies opposed doing a thing contrary to law, and cast my vote against it. And when the orators were ready to impeach me and have me arrested—you urging them on with your shouts—I thought that with law and justice on my side I must run the risk, rather than concur with you in an unjust decision through fear of bonds or death. Those things happened while the City was still under the Democracy. But when Oligarchy came, the Thirty in turn summoned me along with four others to the Rotunda and ordered us to bring back Leon the Salamanian from Salamis so that he might be executed, just as they ordered many others to do such things, planning to implicate as many people as possible in their own guilt. But I then showed again, not by words but deeds, that death, if I may be rather blunt, was of no concern whatever to me; to do nothing unjust or unholy—that was my concern. Strong as it was, that oligarchy did not so frighten me as to do a thing unjust, and when we departed the Rotunda, the other four went into Salamis and brought back Leon, and I left and went home. I might have been killed for that, if the oligarchy had not shortly afterward been overthrown. And of these things you will have many witnesses.

Now, do you think I would have lived so many years if I had been in public life and acted in a manner worthy of a good man, defending what is just and counting it, as is necessary, of first importance? Far from it, Gentlemen of Athens. Not I, and not any other man. But through my whole life I have shown myself to be that sort of man in public affairs, the few I've engaged in; and I have shown myself the same man in private. I never gave way to anyone contrary to what is just—not to others, and certainly not to those slanderously said to be my pupils. In fact, I have never been teacher to anyone. If, in speaking and tending my own affairs, anyone wished to hear me, young or old, I never begrudged him; nor do I discuss for a fee and not otherwise. To rich and poor alike I offer myself as a questioner, and if anyone wishes to answer, he may hear what I have to say. And if any of them turned out to be useful men, or any did not, I cannot justly be held responsible. To none did I promise instruction, and none did I teach; if anyone says that he learned from me or heard in private what others did not, you may rest assured he is not telling the truth.

Why is it, then, that some people enjoy spending so much time with me? You have heard, Gentlemen of Athens: I told you the whole truth. It is because they enjoy hearing people tested who think they are wise and are not. After all, it is not unamusing. But for my own part, as I say, I have been ordered to do this by God—in oracles, in dreams, in every way in which other divine apportionment ever ordered a man to do anything.

These things, Gentlemen of Athens, are both true and easily tested. For if I am corrupting some of the youth, and have corrupted others, it must surely be that some among them, grown older, if they realize that I counseled them toward evil while young, would now come forward to accuse me and exact a penalty. And if they were unwilling, then some of their relatives—fathers, brothers, other kinsmen—if their own relatives had suffered evil at my hands, would now remember, and exact a penalty. Certainly there are many such men I see present. Here is Crito, first, of my own age and deme, father of Critobulus; then there is Lysanias of Sphettos, father of Aeschines here. Next there is Antiphon of Cephisus, father of Epigenes. Then there are others whose brothers engaged in this pastime. There is Nicostratus, son of Theozotides, brother of Theodotus—and Theodotus is dead, so he could not have swayed him—and Paralus here, son of Demodocus, whose brother was Theages. And here is Adeimantus, son of Ariston, whose brother is Plato there; and Aeantodorus, whose brother is Apollodorus here. I could name many others, some of whom at least Meletus ought certainly have provided in his speech as witnesses. If he forgot it then, let him do it now—I yield the floor—and let him say whether he has any witnesses of the sort. You will find that quite to the contrary, Gentlemen, every one of these men is ready to help me—I, who corrupt their relatives, as Meletus and Anytus claim. Those who are themselves corrupted might perhaps have reason to help me; but their relatives are older men who have not been corrupted. What reason could they have for supporting me except that it is right and just, because they know Meletus is lying and I am telling the truth?

Peroration

Very well then, Gentlemen. This, and perhaps a few other things like it, is what I have to say in my defense. Perhaps some of you will remember his own conduct and be offended, if when brought to trial on a lesser charge than this, he begged his judges with tearful supplication, and caused his children to come forward so that he might be the more pitied, along with other relatives and a host of friends; whereas I shall do none of these things, even though I am, as it would seem at least, in the extremity of danger. Perhaps someone with this in mind may become hardened against me; angered by it, he may cast his vote in anger. If this is true of any of you—not that I expect it, but if it is—I think it might be appropriate to say, "I too have relatives, my friend; for as Homer puts it, I am not 'of oak and rock,' but born of man, so I have relatives—yes, and sons too, Gentlemen of

Athens, three of them, one already a lad and two of them children. Yet not one of them have I caused to come forward here, and I shall not beg you to acquit me." Why not? Not out of stubbornness, Gentlemen of Athens, nor disrespect for you. Whether or not I am confident in the face of death is another story; but I think that my own honor, and yours, and that of the whole City would suffer, if I were to behave in this way, I being of the age I am and having the name I have—truly or falsely, it being thought that Socrates is in some way superior to most men. If those of you reputed to be superior in wisdom or courage or any other virtue whatever are to be men of this sort, it would be disgraceful; I have often seen such people behave surprisingly when put on trial, even though they had a reputation to uphold, because they were persuaded that they would suffer a terrible thing if they were put to death—as though they would be immortal if you did not kill them. I think they cloak the City in shame, so that a stranger might think that those among the Athenians who are superior in virtue, and whom the Athenians themselves judge worthy of office and other honors, are no better than women. These are things, Gentlemen of Athens, which those of you who have a reputation to uphold ought not to do; nor if we defendants do them, ought you permit it. You ought rather make it clear that you would far rather cast your vote against a man who stages these pitiful scenes, and makes the City a butt of mockery, than against a man who shows quiet restraint.

But apart from the matter of reputation, Gentlemen, it does not seem to me just to beg a judge, or to be acquitted by begging; it is rather just to teach and persuade. The judge does not sit to grant justice as a favor, but to render judgment; he has sworn no oath to gratify those whom he sees fit, but to judge according to law. We ought not accustom you, nor ought you become accustomed, to forswear yourselves; it is pious in neither of us. So do not expect me, Gentlemen of Athens, to do such things in your presence as I believe to be neither honorable nor just nor holy, especially since, by Zeus, it is for impiety that I am being prosecuted by this fellow Meletus here. For clearly, if I were to persuade and compel you by supplication, you being sworn as judges, I would teach you then indeed not to believe that there are gods, and in making my defense I would in effect accuse myself of not acknowledging them. But that is far from so; I do acknowledge them, Gentlemen of Athens, as no one of my accusers does, and to you and to the God I now commit my case, to judge in whatever way shall be best both for me and for you. *(Socrates is found guilty by a vote of 281 to 220.)*

II. THE COUNTERPENALTY

I am not distressed, Gentlemen of Athens, at what has happened, nor angered that you have cast your votes against me. Many things contribute to this, among them the fact that I expected it. I am much more surprised at the number of votes either way: I did not think it would be by so little, but by more. As it is, it seems, if only thirty votes had fallen otherwise, I would have been acquitted. And so far as Meletus at least is concerned, it seems to me, I am already acquitted—and more than acquitted, since it is clear that if Anytus and Lycon had not come forward to accuse me, Meletus would have been fined a thousand drachmas for not obtaining a fifth part of the vote.

The man demands death for me. Very well. Then what counterpenalty shall I propose to you, Gentlemen of Athens? Clearly something I deserve, but what? What do I deserve to pay or suffer because I did not through life keep quiet, and yet did not concern myself, as the multitude do, with money or property or military and public honors and other office, or the secret societies and political clubs which keep cropping up in the City, believing that I was really too reasonable and temperate a man to enter upon these things and survive. I did not go where I could benefit neither you nor myself; instead, I went to each of you in private, where I might perform the greatest service. I undertook to persuade each of you not to care for any thing which belongs to you before first caring for yourselves, nor to care for anything which belongs to the City before caring for the City itself, and so too with everything else. Now, what do I deserve to suffer for being this sort of man? Some good thing, Gentlemen of Athens, if penalty is really to be assessed according to desert. What then is fitting for a poor man who has served his City well, and needs leisure to exhort you? Why, Gentlemen of Athens, nothing is more fitting for such a man than to be fed in the Prytaneum, at the common table of the City—yes, and far more fitting than for one of you who has been an Olympic victor in the single-horse or two- or four-horse chariot races. For he makes you seem happy, whereas I make you happy in truth, and he does not need subsistence, and I do. If then I must propose a penalty I justly deserve, I propose that, public subsistence in the Prytaneum.

Perhaps some of you will think that in saying this I speak much as I spoke of tears and pleading, out of stubborn pride. That is not so, Gentlemen of Athens, though something of this sort is: I am persuaded that I have not intentionally wronged any man, but I cannot persuade you of it; we have talked so short a time. Now, I believe if you had a law, as other people do, that cases involving death shall not be decided in a single day, that you would be persuaded; but as things are, it is not easy in so short a time to do away with slanders grown so great. Being persuaded, however, that I have wronged no one, I am quite unwilling to wrong myself, or claim that I deserve some evil and propose any penalty of the kind. What is there to fear? That I may suffer the penalty Meletus proposes, when as I say, I do not know whether it is good or evil? Shall I choose instead a penalty I know very well to be evil? Imprisonment, perhaps? But why should I live in prison, a slave to men who happen to occupy office as the Eleven? A fine, then, and imprisonment till I pay it? But that comes to the same thing, since I have no money to pay it. Shall I then propose exile? Perhaps you would accept that. But I must indeed love life and cling to it dearly, Gentlemen, if I were so foolish as to think that, although you, my own fellow-citizens, cannot bear my pursuits and discussions, which have become so burdensome and hateful that you now seek to be rid of them, others will bear them lightly. No, Gentlemen. My life would be fine indeed, if at my age I went to live in exile, always moving from city to city, always driven out. For be well assured that wherever I go, the young men will listen to what I say as they do here; if I turn them away they will themselves drive me out, appealing to their elders; if I do not turn them away, their fathers and relations will drive me out in their behalf.

Perhaps someone may say, "Would it not be possible for you to live in exile, Socrates, if you were silent and kept quiet?" But this is the hardest thing of all to make some of you believe. If I say that to do so would be to disobey the God, and therefore I cannot do it, you will not believe me because you will think that I am being sly and dishonest. If on the other hand I say that the greatest good for man is to fashion arguments each day about virtue and the other things you hear me discussing, when I examine myself and others, and that the unexamined life is not for man worth living, you will believe what I say still less. I claim these things are so, Gentlemen; but it is not easy to convince you. At the same time, I am not accustomed to think myself deserving of any evil. If I had money, I would propose a fine as great as I could pay—there would be no harm in that. But as things stand, I have no money, unless the amount I can pay is the amount you are willing to exact of me. I might perhaps be able to pay a mina of silver. So I propose a penalty in that amount. But Plato here, Gentlemen of Athens, and Crito and Critobulus and Apollodorus bid me propose thirty minas, and they will stand surety. So I propose that amount. You have guarantors sufficient for the sum. *(Socrates is condemned to death.)*

III. EPILOGUE

For the sake of only a little time, Gentlemen of Athens, you are to be accused by those who wish to revile the City of having killed Socrates, a wise man—for those who wish to reproach you will say I am wise even if I am not. And if you had only waited a little, the thing would have come of its own initiative. You see my age. You see how far spent my life already is, how near to death.

I say this, not to all of you, but to those of you who voted to condemn me. To them I also say this. Perhaps you think, Gentlemen of Athens, that I have been convicted for lack of words to persuade you, had I thought it right to do and say anything to be acquitted. Not so. It is true I have been convicted for a lack; not a lack of words, but lack of bold shamelessness, unwillingness to say the things you would find it pleasant to hear—weeping and wailing, saying and doing many things I claim to be unworthy of me, but things of the sort you are accustomed to hear from others. I did not then think it necessary to do anything unworthy of a free man because of danger; I do not now regret so having conducted my defense; and I would far rather die with that defense than live with the other. Neither in court of law nor in war ought I or any man contrive to escape death by any means possible. Often in battle it becomes clear that a man may escape death by throwing down his arms and turning in supplication to his pursuers; and there are many other devices for each of war's dangers, so that one can avoid dying if he is bold enough to say and do anything at all. It is not difficult to escape death, Gentlemen; it is more difficult to escape wickedness, for wickedness runs faster than death. And now I am old and slow, and I have been caught by the slower runner. But my accusers are clever and quick, and they have been caught by the faster runner, namely Evil. I now take my leave, sentenced by you to death; they depart convicted by Truth for injustice and wickedness. I abide in my penalty, and they in theirs. That is no doubt as it should be, and I think it is fit.

I desire next to prophesy to you who condemned me. For I have now reached that point where men are especially prophetic, when they are about to die. I say to you who have decreed my death that to you there will come hard on my dying a thing far more difficult to bear than the death you have visited upon me. You have done this thing in the belief that you would be released from submitting to examination in your lives. I say that it will turn out otherwise. Those who come to examine you will be more numerous, and I have up to now restrained them, though you perceived it not. They will be more harsh inasmuch as they are younger, and you will be the more troubled. If you think by killing to hold back the reproach due you for not living rightly, you are profoundly mistaken. That release is neither possible nor honorable. The release which is both most honorable and most easy is not to cut down others, but to so prepare yourselves that you will be as good as possible. This I utter as prophecy to you who voted for my condemnation, and take my leave.

But with you who voted for my acquittal, I should be glad to discuss the nature of what has happened, now, while the authorities are busy and I am not yet gone where, going, I must die. Abide with me, Gentlemen, this space of time; nothing prevents our talking with each other while we still can. To you, as my friends, I wish to display the meaning of what has now fallen to my lot. A remarkable thing has occurred, Gentlemen and Judges—and I am correct in calling you Judges. My accustomed oracle, which is divine, always came quite frequently before in everything, opposing me even in trivial matters if I was about to err. And now a thing has fallen to my lot which you also see yourselves, a thing which some might think, and do in fact believe, to be ultimate among evils. But the sign of the God did not oppose me early this morning when I left my house, nor when I came up to the court room here, nor at any point in my argument in anything I was about to say. And yet in many places, in other arguments, it has checked me right in the middle of speaking; but today it has not opposed me in any way, in none of my deeds, in none of my words. What do I take to be the reason? I will tell you. Very likely what has fallen to me is good, and those among us who think that death is an evil are wrong. There has been convincing indication of this. For the accustomed sign would surely have opposed me, if I were not in some way acting for good.

Let us also consider a further reason for high hope that death is good. Death is one of two things. Either to be dead is not to exist, to have no awareness at all, or it is, as the stories tell, a kind of alteration, a change of abode for the soul from this place to another. And if it is to have no awareness, like a sleep when the sleeper sees no dream, death would be a wonderful gain; for

I suppose if someone had to pick out that night in which he slept and saw no dream, and put the other days and nights of his life beside it, and had to say after inspecting them how many days and nights he had lived in his life which were better and sweeter, I think that not only any ordinary person but even the Great King himself would find them easily numbered in relation to other days, and other nights. If death is that, I say it is gain; for the whole of time then turns out to last no longer than a single night. But if on the contrary death is like taking a journey, passing from here to another place, and the stories told are true, and all who have died are there—what greater good might there be, my Judges? For if a man once goes to the place of the dead, and takes leave of those who claim to be judges here, he will find the true judges who are said to sit in judgment there—Minos, Rhadamanthus, Aeacus, Triptolemus, and the other demigods and heroes who lived just lives. Would that journey be worthless? And again, to meet Orpheus and Musaeus, Hesiod and Homer—how much would any of you give? I at least would be willing to die many times over, if these things are true. I would find a wonderful pursuit there, when I met Palamedes, and Ajax, son of Telemon, and any others among the ancients done to death by unjust verdicts, and compared my experiences with theirs. It would not, I think, be unamusing. But the greatest thing, surely, would be to test and question there as I did here—who among them is wise? Who thinks he is and is not? How much might one give, my Judges, to examine the man who led the great army against Troy, or Odysseus, or Sisyphus, or a thousand other men and women one might mention—to converse with them, to associate with them, to examine them—why, it would be inconceivable happiness. Especially since they surely do not kill you for it there. For they are happier there than men are here in other ways, and they are already immortal for the rest of time, if the stories told are true.

But you too, my Judges, must be of good hope concerning death. You must recognize that this one thing is true: that there is no evil for a good man either in living or in dying, and that the gods do not neglect his affairs. What has now come to me did not come of its own initiative. It is clear to me that to die now and be released from my affairs is better for me. That is why the sign did not turn me back, and I bear no anger whatever toward those who voted to condemn me, or toward my accusers. And yet, it was not with this in mind that they accused and convicted me. They thought to do harm, and for that they deserve blame. But this much would I ask of them: when my sons are grown, Gentlemen, exact a penalty of them: give pain to them exactly as I gave pain to you, if it seems to you that they care more for wealth or anything else than they care for virtue. And if they seem to be something and are nothing, rebuke them as I rebuked you, because they do not care for what they ought, because they think themselves something and are worth nothing. And should you do that, both I and my sons will have been justly dealt with at your hands.

But it is already the hour of parting—I to die and you to live. Which of us goes to the better is unclear to all but the God.

Obedience to Authority

STANLEY MILGRAM (1933–1984) was a psychologist at Harvard, Yale, and The Graduate Center at the City University of New York. When he was 28 years old, he developed his most famous experiment: the study of obedience to authority in human beings. He proved that average people will torture others merely because some legitimate authority has told them to do so. Disturbingly, the "authority" need be no more than a nerdy actor in a lab coat, who has no real power or command over the subjects who carry out his orders. Although Milgram's obedience experiments made him a famous young researcher, they were so controversial that Harvard denied him tenure. While Milgram went on to do other important social-scientific studies, his work on obedience remains his most lasting legacy.

THINKING QUESTIONS

Stanley Milgram, *Obedience to Authority*

1. How do you think you would have performed in the role of the teacher? Why?
2. How high a shock do you think you would have given? Consider the protocol in which the learner grunts at 75 volts, and asks to be let out at 150 volts. In that setup, 50 percent of the subjects went all the way to 450 volts. If you would have let them out earlier, what makes you different?
3. Afterward, the subjects insisted that they weren't sadistic monsters. Do you think they were? If so, do you think you are?
4. What do you think is worse, that you don't know how you would behave in a similar circumstance or that, secretly, you do know?
5. Why do you think the teachers kept going? After all, this wasn't war or self-defense. The teachers did what they were told on the nominal authority of an experimenter in the name of an experiment in which they had no stake. Why did they obey?
6. Would you have predicted that half of your classmates would torture someone in the name of science?
7. Some of the subjects said that they didn't want to accept responsibility for what happened to the learner, and they went on with the experiment when the experimenter said that the responsibility was all his. Do you think that the teachers were responsible anyway?
8. In what ways do you obey authority without really questioning it?

9. If obedience to authority is the problem, what is the solution? If there weren't obedience, wouldn't there be anarchy and chaos? How do you know when to obey and when to defy authority?

OBEDIENCE IS AS BASIC an element in the structure of social life as one can point to. Some system of authority is a requirement of all communal living, and it is only the man dwelling in isolation who is not forced to respond, through defiance or submission, to the commands of others. Obedience, as a determinant of behavior, is of particular relevance to our time. It has been reliably established that from 1933 to 1945 millions of innocent people were systematically slaughtered on command. Gas chambers were built, death camps were guarded, daily quotas of corpses were produced with the same efficiency as the manufacture of appliances. These inhumane policies may have originated in the mind of a single person, but they could only have been carried out on a massive scale if a very large number of people obeyed orders.

Obedience is the psychological mechanism that links individual action to political purpose. It is the dispositional cement that binds men to systems of authority. Facts of recent history and observation in daily life suggest that for many people obedience may be a deeply ingrained behavior tendency, indeed, a prepotent impulse overriding training in ethics, sympathy, and moral conduct. C. P. Snow (1961) points to its importance when he writes:

> When you think of the long and gloomy history of man, you will find more hideous crimes have been committed in the name of obedience than have ever been committed in the name of rebellion. If you doubt that, read William Shirer's *Rise and Fall of the Third Reich*. The German Officer Corps were brought up in the most rigorous code of obedience . . . in the name of obedience they were party to, and assisted in, the most wicked large scale actions in the history of the world. (p. 24)

The Nazi extermination of European Jews is the most extreme instance of abhorrent immoral acts carried out by thousands of people in the name of obedience. Yet in lesser degree this type of thing is constantly recurring: ordinary citizens are ordered to destroy other people, and they do so because they consider it their duty to obey orders. Thus, obedience to authority, long praised as a virtue, takes on a new aspect when it serves a malevolent cause; far from appearing as a virtue, it is transformed into a heinous sin. Or is it?

The moral question of whether one should obey when commands conflict with conscience was argued by Plato, dramatized in *Antigone,* and treated to philosophic analysis in every historical epoch. Conservative philosophers argue that the very fabric of society is threatened by disobedience, and even when the act prescribed by an authority is an evil one, it is better to carry out the act than to wrench at the structure of authority. Hobbes stated further that an act so executed is in no sense the responsibility of the person who carries it out but only of the authority that orders it. But humanists argue for the primacy of individual conscience in such matters, insisting that the moral judgments of the individual must override authority when the two are in conflict.

The legal and philosophic aspects of obedience are of enormous import, but an empirically grounded scientist eventually comes to the point where he wishes to move from abstract discourse to the careful observation of concrete instances. In order to take a close look at the act of obeying, I set up a simple experiment at Yale University. Eventually, the experiment was to involve more than a thousand participants and would be repeated at several universities, but at the beginning, the conception was simple. A person comes to a psychological laboratory and is told to carry out a series of acts that come increasingly into conflict with conscience. The main question is how far the participant will comply with the experimenter's instructions before refusing to carry out the actions required of him.

But the reader needs to know a little more detail about the experiment. Two people come to a psychology laboratory to take part in a study of memory and learning. One of them is designated as a "teacher" and the other a "learner." The experimenter explains that the study is concerned with the effects of punishment on learning. The learner is conducted into a room, seated in a chair, his arms strapped to prevent excessive movement, and an electrode attached to his wrist. He is told that he is to learn a list of word pairs; whenever he makes an error, he will receive electric shocks of increasing intensity.

The real focus of the experiment is the teacher. After watching the learner being strapped into place, he is taken into the main experimental room and seated before an impressive shock generator. Its main feature is a horizontal line of thirty switches, ranging from 15 volts to 450 volts, in 15-volt increments. There are also verbal designations which range from SLIGHT SHOCK to DANGER—SEVERE SHOCK. The teacher is told that he is to administer the learning test to the man in the other room. When the learner responds correctly, the teacher moves on to the next item; when the other man gives an incorrect answer, the teacher is to give him an electric shock. He is to start at the lowest shock level (15 volts) and to increase the level each time the man makes an error, going through 30 volts, 45 volts, and so on.

The "teacher" is a genuinely naïve subject who has come to the laboratory to participate in an experiment. The learner, or victim, is an actor who actually receives no shock at all. The point of the experiment is to see how far a person will proceed in a concrete and measurable situation in which he is ordered to inflict increasing pain on a protesting victim. At what point will the subject refuse to obey the experimenter?

Conflict arises when the man receiving the shock begins to indicate that he is experiencing discomfort. At 75 volts, the "learner" grunts. At 120 volts he complains verbally; at 150 he demands to be released from the experiment. His protests continue as the shocks escalate, growing increasingly vehement and emotional. At 285 volts his response can only be described as an agonized scream.

Observers of the experiment agree that its gripping quality is somewhat obscured in print. For the subject, the situation is not a game; conflict is intense and obvious. On one hand, the manifest suffering of the learner presses him to quit. On the other, the experimenter, a legitimate authority to whom the subject feels some commitment, enjoins him to continue. Each time the subject hesitates to administer shock, the experimenter orders him to continue. To extricate himself from the situation, the subject must make a clear break with authority. The aim of this investigation was to find when and how people would defy authority in the face of a clear moral imperative.

There are, of course, enormous differences between carrying out the orders of a commanding officer during times of war and carrying out the orders of an experimenter. Yet the essence of certain relationships remain, for one may ask in a general way: How does a man behave when he is told by a legitimate authority to act against a third individual? If anything, we may expect the experimenter's power to be considerably less than that of the general, since he has no power to enforce his imperatives, and participation in a psychological experiment scarcely evokes the sense of urgency and dedication engendered by participation in war. Despite these limitations, I thought it worthwhile to start careful observation of obedience even in this modest situation, in the hope that it would stimulate insights and yield general propositions applicable to a variety of circumstances.

A reader's initial reaction to the experiment may be to wonder why anyone in his right mind would administer even the first shocks. Would he not simply refuse and walk out of the laboratory? But the fact is that no one ever does. Since the subject has come to the laboratory to aid the experimenter, he is quite willing to start off with the procedure. There is nothing very extraordinary in this, particularly since the person who is to receive the shocks seems initially cooperative, if somewhat apprehensive. What is surprising is how far ordinary individuals will go in complying with the experimenter's instructions. Indeed, the results of the experiment are both surprising and dismaying. Despite the fact that many subjects experience stress, despite the fact that many protest to the experimenter, a substantial proportion continue to the last shock on the generator.

Many subjects will obey the experimenter no matter how vehement the pleading of the person being shocked, no matter how painful the shocks seem to be, and no matter how much the victim pleads to be let out. This was seen time and again in our studies and has been observed in several universities where the experiment was repeated. It is the extreme willingness of adults to go to almost any lengths on the command of an authority that constitutes the chief finding of the study and the fact most urgently demanding explanation.

A commonly offered explanation is that those who shocked the victim at the most severe level were monsters, the sadistic fringe of society. But if one considers that almost two-thirds of the participants fall into the category of "obedient" subjects, and that they represented ordinary people drawn from working, managerial, and professional classes, the argument becomes very shaky. Indeed, it is highly reminiscent of the issue that arose in connection with Hannah Arendt's 1963 book, *Eichmann in Jerusalem*. Arendt contended that the prosecution's effort to depict Eichmann as a sadistic monster was fundamentally wrong, that he came closer to being an uninspired bureaucrat who simply sat at his desk and did his job. For asserting these views, Arendt became the object of considerable scorn, even calumny. Somehow, it was felt that the monstrous deeds carried out by Eichmann required a brutal, twisted, and sadistic personality, evil incarnate. After witnessing hundreds of ordinary people submit to the authority in our own experiments, I must conclude that Arendt's conception of the *banality of evil* comes closer to the truth than one might dare imagine. The ordinary person who shocked the victim did so out of a sense of obligation—a conception of his duties as a subject—and not from any peculiarly aggressive tendencies.

This is, perhaps, the most fundamental lesson of our study: ordinary people, simply doing their jobs, and without any particular hostility on their part, can become agents in a terrible destructive process. Moreover, even when the destructive effects of their work become patently clear, and they are asked to carry out actions incompatible with fundamental standards of morality, relatively few people have the resources needed to resist authority. A variety of inhibitions against disobeying authority come into play and successfully keep the person in his place.

Sitting back in one's armchair, it is easy to condemn the actions of the obedient subjects. But those who condemn the subjects measure them against the standard of their own ability to formulate high-minded moral prescriptions. That is hardly a fair standard. Many of the subjects, at the level of stated opinion, feel quite as strongly as any of us about the moral requirement of refraining from action against a helpless victim. They, too, in general terms know what ought to be done and can state their values when the occasion arises. This has little, if anything, to do with their actual behavior under the pressure of circumstances.

If people are asked to render a moral judgment on what constitutes appropriate behavior in this situation, they unfailingly see disobedience as proper. But values are not the only forces at work in an actual, ongoing situation. They are but one narrow band of causes in the total spectrum of forces impinging on a person. Many people were unable to realize their values in action and found themselves continuing in the experiment even though they disagreed with what they were doing.

The force exerted by the moral sense of the individual is less effective than social myth would have us believe. Though such prescriptions as "Thou shalt not kill" occupy a pre-eminent place in the moral order, they do not occupy a correspondingly intractable position in human psychic structure. A few changes in newspaper headlines, a call from the draft board, orders from a man with epaulets, and men are led to kill with little difficulty. Even the forces mustered in a psychology experiment will go a long way toward removing the individual from moral controls. Moral factors can be shunted aside with relative ease by a calculated restructuring of the informational and social field.

What, then, keeps the person obeying the experimenter? First, there is a set of "binding factors" that lock the subject into the situation. They include such factors as politeness on his part, his desire to uphold his initial promise of aid to the experimenter, and the awkwardness of withdrawal. Second, a number of adjustments in the subject's thinking occur that undermine his resolve to break with the authority. The adjustments help the subject maintain his relationship with the experimenter, while at the same time reducing the strain brought about by the experimental conflict. They are typical of thinking that comes about in obedient persons when they are instructed by authority to act against helpless individuals.

One such mechanism is the tendency of the individual to become so absorbed in the narrow technical aspects of the task that he loses sight of its broader consequences. The film *Dr. Strangelove* brilliantly satirized the absorption of a bomber crew in the exacting technical procedure of dropping nuclear weapons on a country. Similarly, in this experiment, subjects become immersed in the procedures, reading the word pairs with exquisite articulation and pressing the switches with great care. They want to put on a competent performance, but they show an accompanying narrowing of moral concern. The subject entrusts the broader tasks of setting goals and assessing morality to the experimental authority he is serving.

The most common adjustment of thought in the obedient subject is for him to see himself as not responsible for his own actions. He divests himself of responsibility by attributing all initiative to the experimenter, a legitimate authority. He sees himself not as a person acting in a morally accountable way but as the agent of external authority. In the postexperimental interview, when subjects were asked why they had gone on, a typical reply was: "I wouldn't have done it by myself. I was just doing what I was told." Unable to defy the authority of the experimenter, they attribute all responsibility to him. It is the old story of "just doing one's duty" that was heard time and time again in the defense statements of those accused at Nuremberg. But it would be wrong to think of it as a thin alibi concocted for the occasion. Rather, it is a fundamental mode of thinking for a great many people once they are locked into a subordinate position in a structure of authority. The disappearance of a sense of responsibility is the most far-reaching consequence of submission to authority.

Although a person acting under authority performs actions that seem to violate standards of conscience, it would not be true to say that he loses his moral sense. Instead, it acquires a radically different focus. He does not respond with a moral sentiment to the actions he performs. Rather, his moral concern now shifts to a consideration of how well he is living up to the expectations that the authority has of him. In wartime, a soldier does not ask whether it is good or bad to bomb a hamlet; he does not experience shame or guilt in the destruction of a village: rather he feels pride or shame depending on how well he has performed the mission assigned to him.

Another psychological force at work in this situation may be termed "counteranthropomorphism." For decades psychologists have discussed the primitive tendency among men to attribute to inanimate objects and forces the qualities of the human species. A countervailing tendency, however, is that of attributing an impersonal quality to forces that are essentially human in origin and maintenance. Some people treat systems of human origin as if they existed above and beyond any human agent, beyond the control of whim or human feeling. The human element behind agencies and institutions is denied. Thus, when the experimenter says, "The experiment *requires* that you continue," the subject feels this to be an imperative that goes beyond any merely human command. He does not ask the seemingly obvious question, "Whose experiment? Why should the designer be served while the victim suffers?" The wishes of a man—the designer of the experiment—have become part of a schema which exerts on the subject's mind a force that transcends the personal. "It's *got* to go on. It's *got* to go on," repeated one subject. He failed to realize that a man like himself wanted it to go on. For him the human agent had faded from the picture, and "The Experiment" had acquired an impersonal momentum of its own.

No action of itself has an unchangeable psychological quality. Its meaning can be altered by placing it in particular contexts. An American newspaper recently quoted a pilot who conceded that Americans were bombing Vietnamese men, women, and children but felt that the bombing was for a "noble cause" and thus was justified. Similarly, most subjects in the experiment see their behavior in a larger context that is benevolent and useful to society—the pursuit of scientific truth. The psychological laboratory has a strong claim to legitimacy and evokes trust and confidence in those who come to perform there. An action such as shocking a victim, which in isolation appears evil, acquires a totally different meaning when placed in this setting. But allowing an act to be dominated by its context, while neglecting its human consequences, can be dangerous in the extreme.

At least one essential feature of the situation in Germany was not studied here—namely, the intense devaluation of the victim prior to action against him. For a decade and more, vehement anti-Jewish propaganda systematically prepared the German population to accept the destruction of the Jews. Step by step the Jews were excluded from the category of citizen and national, and finally were denied the status of human beings. Systematic devaluation of the victim provides a measure of psychological justification for brutal treatment of the victim and has been the constant accompaniment of massacres, pogroms, and wars. In all likelihood, our subjects would have experienced greater ease in shocking the victim had he been convincingly portrayed as a brutal criminal or a pervert.

Of considerable interest, however, is the fact that many subjects harshly devalue the victim *as a consequence* of acting against him. Such comments as,

"He was so stupid and stubborn he deserved to get shocked," were common. Once having acted against the victim, these subjects found it necessary to view him as an unworthy individual, whose punishment was made inevitable by his own deficiencies of intellect and character.

Many of the people studied in the experiment were in some sense against what they did to the learner, and many protested even while they obeyed. But between thoughts, words, and the critical step of disobeying a malevolent authority lies another ingredient, the capacity for transforming beliefs and values into action. Some subjects were totally convinced of the wrongness of what they were doing but could not bring themselves to make an open break with authority. Some derived satisfaction from their thoughts and felt that—within themselves, at least—they had been on the side of the angels. What they failed to realize is that subjective feelings are largely irrelevant to the moral issue at hand so long as they are not transformed into action. Political control is effected through action. The attitudes of the guards at a concentration camp are of no consequence when in fact they are allowing the slaughter of innocent men to take place before them. Similarly, so-called "intellectual resistance" in occupied Europe—in which persons by a twist of thought felt that they had defied the invader—was merely indulgence in a consoling psychological mechanism. Tyrannies are perpetuated by diffident men who do not possess the courage to act out their beliefs. Time and again in the experiment people disvalued what they were doing but could not muster the inner resources to translate their values into action.

A variation of the basic experiment depicts a dilemma more common than the one outlined above: the subject was not ordered to push the trigger that shocked the victim, but merely to perform a subsidiary act (administering the word-pair test) before another subject actually delivered the shock. In this situation, 37 of 40 adults from the New Haven area continued to the highest shock level on the generator. Predictably, subjects excused their behavior by saying that the responsibility belonged to the man who actually pulled the switch. This may illustrate a dangerously typical situation in complex society: it is psychologically easy to ignore responsibility when one is only an intermediate link in a chain of evil action but is far from the final consequences of the action. Even Eichmann was sickened when he toured the concentration camps, but to participate in mass murder he had only to sit at a desk and shuffle papers. At the same time the man in the camp who actually dropped Cyclon-B into the gas chambers was able to justify *his* behavior on the grounds that he was only following orders from above. Thus there is a fragmentation of the total human act; no one man decides to carry out the evil act and is confronted with its consequences. The person who assumes full responsibility for the act has evaporated. Perhaps this is the most common characteristic of socially organized evil in modern society.

The problem of obedience, therefore, is not wholly psychological. The form and shape of society and the way it is developing have much to do with it. There was a time, perhaps, when men were able to give a fully human response to any situation because they were fully absorbed in it as human beings. But as soon as there was a division of labor among men, things changed. Beyond a certain point, the breaking up of society into people carrying out narrow and very special jobs takes away from the human quality of work and life. A person does not get to see the whole situation but only a small part of it, and is thus unable to act without some kind of over-all direction. He yields to authority but in doing so is alienated from his own actions.

George Orwell caught the essence of the situation when he wrote:

> As I write, highly civilized human beings are flying overhead, trying to kill me. They do not feel any enmity against me as an individual, nor I against them. They are only "doing their duty," as the saying goes. Most of them, I have no doubt, are kind-hearted law abiding men who would never dream of committing murder in private life. On the other hand, if one of them succeeds in blowing me to pieces with a well-placed bomb, he will never sleep any the worse for it.

Moral Philosophy

"Murder is wrong." It's a pretty safe bet that you agree with that one. "Abortion is wrong." You might or might not agree with that one, or you might agree if it was modified in some way, or . . . What are we doing when we make claims about right and wrong? To whom do they apply and how might we settle difficult questions about what we ought to do? These are just some of the questions that are part of the study of moral theory. When we focus on the *theory* end of moral philosophy, we look at the nature of moral judgments and the kind of principles we might use to defend the moral judgments we make. We are then not so much concerned with the different positions one might take on particular moral issues, like abortion or capital punishment, which are the subject matter of *applied* ethics.

The debate between utilitarian ethics and Kantian, or deontological, ethics has been the central issue in moral philosophy for well over a century. As daunting as words like "utilitarianism" and "deontological" might sound, they are simply the terms we use to describe some pretty familiar ideas. The theory of utilitarianism is presented by the 19th-century English philosophers Jeremy Bentham and John Stuart Mill. Utilitarians believe that right actions are those which maximize the overall happiness of everyone affected by the act. Think about situations in which you have had to make a decision. One familiar way to decide between the options open to you is to consider how much better or worse off each person touched by that action will be made, and then do the action that will produce the greatest balance of happiness over unhappiness. Certainly considering the *consequences* of our actions is one important, and familiar, feature of our moral reasoning. Another important feature of moral reasoning is the idea of doing our duty and respecting the rights of others. Acting out of duty is the central idea in deontological ethics, presented to us by the 18th-century German philosopher, Immanuel Kant. Kant argues that the most important feature of human beings is that we are rational beings with free will. Showing respect for the dignity and worth of such beings is what ethics is all about for Kant. Therefore, right actions are those which fulfill our obligations and duties and respect the rights of valuable beings like you and me. So, for Kant, the consequences of actions—the happiness or pleasure produced—is at best of secondary concern.

But utilitarianism and Kantianism are not the only moral theories out there for us to consider. Alternative views of ethics suggest that the key to right or wrong action is found in some other principle or basic idea. The view called *cultural relativism* is discussed and critiqued by Mary Midgely. Cultural relativism is the idea that right actions are the ones that a culture says are right, based on its traditions and beliefs. Midgely offers an example from medieval Japanese Samurai culture to challenge the view that relativism is correct. Another commonly held view is called *ethical egoism*. Egoism is the idea that right actions are ones that best serve the overall interests of the person acting. According to egoism, we have no duty to consider the interests of others in deciding what to do, one's own interests are all that count. James Rachels elaborates ethical egoism for us and offers his own criticism of it. One very old view of morality holds that right actions are simply the ones that God or the gods want us to do, wrong actions are the ones they don't want us to do. Discussion of this view goes all the way back to the ancient Greeks. In the selection from Plato we meet Socrates on the way to his own trial, engaged in a conversation with his friend Euthyphro. In the course of their dialogue they discuss several different ways to understand piety (love of the gods) but can't come to any resolution about what makes an act pious or good. Plato starts a long-standing tradition that holds that religion and morality are separable topics, and actions are good (or bad) not simply because God says so.

Not all discussion in ethics is about principles that are supposed to guide action. Another important topic in moral philosophy takes us into questions about the nature of moral judgments themselves. How do we make moral judgments, what are they based on? Both Jonathan Bennett and Friedrich Nietzsche discuss the balance between reason and sentiment or conscience in making and defending moral judgments. Bennett uses literary and historical examples to argue that sound moral decisions must fit with both conscience and our reasoned principles about ethics. Nietzsche, on the other hand, rejects altogether the role of conscience, while also rejecting traditional (especially Kantian) principles; both are equally irrational. Instead, Nietzsche argues that reason, properly used, will lead us in a very different direction in deciding what each of us ought to be. Finally, Carol Gilligan offers yet another critique of the traditional, principle-based approach to ethics, this one from a feminist perspective. She argues that traditional perspectives on ethics, with their emphasis on justice, miss an important aspect of our everyday experience—the special relationships we have with the friends and family who are closest to us. Gilligan advocates an "ethics of care" to stand in contrast to the traditional perspective, and suggests that the long-standing neglect of caring personal relationships in the study of ethics may be due to differences between men and women.

The Conscience of Huckleberry Finn

JONATHAN BENNETT (1930–) was educated at Oxford University and taught at Cambridge University, the University of British Columbia, and then at Syracuse University for more than two decades. He is the author of numerous articles and books on the history of philosophy, philosophy of language, and ethics including *Locke, Berkeley, Hume: Central Themes* (1971), *The Act Itself* (1995), and *A Philosophical Guide to Conditionals* (2003).

THINKING QUESTIONS

Jonathan Bennett, *The Conscience of Huckleberry Finn*

1. What distinction does Bennett draw between *sympathy* and *bad morality*? Is it the same distinction as the one between *feelings* and *moral judgments*?
2. How does the story of Huck and Jim help illustrate the conflict between sympathy and moral judgment? Why do you think sympathy wins in Huck's case?
3. Bennett characterizes Himmler as someone acting on principle. How is Himmler's case the opposite of Huck's? What is Himmler's view of the role of sympathy in his decision to kill Jews?
4. How is Jonathan Edwards's attitude toward sympathy different from either Huck's or Himmler's?
5. How does Bennett think we ought to balance principle and sympathy in deciding what we ought to do?

IN THIS PAPER, I shall present not just the conscience of Huckleberry Finn but two others as well. One of them is the conscience of Heinrich Himmler. He became a Nazi in 1923; he served drably and quietly, but well, and was rewarded with increasing responsibility and power. At the peak of his career he held many offices and commands, of which the most powerful was that of leader of the S.S.—the principal police force of the Nazi regime. In this capacity, Himmler commanded the whole concentration-camp system, and was responsible for the execution of the so-called 'final solution of the Jewish problem'. It is important for my purposes that this piece of social engineering should be thought of not abstractly but in concrete terms of Jewish families being marched to what they think are bath-houses, to the accompaniment of loud-speaker renditions of extracts from *The Merry Widow* and *Tales of Hoffman,* there to be choked to death by poisonous gases. Altogether, Himmler succeeded in murdering about four and a half million of them, as well as several million gentiles, mainly Poles and Russians.

The other conscience to be discussed is that of the Calvinist theologian and philosopher Jonathan Edwards. He lived in the first half of the eighteenth century, and has a good claim to be considered America's first serious and considerable philosophical thinker. He was for many years a widely-renowned preacher and Congregationalist minister in New England; in 1748 a dispute with his congregation led him to resign (he couldn't accept their view that unbelievers should be admitted to the Lord's Supper in the hope that it would convert them); for some years after that he worked as a missionary, preaching to Indians through an interpreter; then in 1758 he accepted the presidency of what is now Princeton University, and within two months died from a smallpox inoculation. Along the way he wrote some first-rate philosophy: his book attacking the notion of free will is still sometimes read. Why I should be interested in Edwards' *conscience* will be explained in due course.

I shall use Heinrich Himmler, Jonathan Edwards and Huckleberry Finn to illustrate different aspects of a single theme, namely the relationship between *sympathy* on the one hand and *bad morality* on the other.

★ ★ ★

All that I can mean by a 'bad morality' is a morality whose principles I deeply disapprove of. When I call a morality bad, I cannot prove that mine is better; but when I here call any morality bad, I think you will agree with me that it is bad; and that is all I need.

There could be dispute as to whether the springs of someone's actions constitute a *morality.* I think, though, that we must admit that someone who acts in ways which conflict grossly with our morality may nevertheless have a morality of his own—a set of principles of action which he sincerely assents to, so that for him the problem of acting well or rightly or in obedience to conscience is the problem of conforming to *those* principles. The problem of conscientiousness can arise as acutely for a bad morality as for any other: rotten principles may be as difficult to keep as decent ones.

As for 'sympathy': I use this term to cover every sort of fellow-feeling, as when one feels pity over someone's loneliness, or horrified compassion over his pain, or when one feels a shrinking reluctance to act in a way which will bring misfortune to someone else. These *feelings* must not be confused with *moral judgments.* My sympathy for someone in distress may lead me to help him, or even to think that I ought to help him; but in itself it is not a judgment about what I ought to do but just a *feeling* for him in his plight. We shall get some light on the difference between feelings and moral judgments when we consider Huckleberry Finn.

Obviously, feelings can impel one to action, and so can moral judgments; and in a particular case sympathy and morality may pull in opposite directions. This can happen not just with bad moralities, but also with good ones like yours and mine. For example, a small child, sick and miserable, clings tightly to his mother and screams in terror when she tries to pass him over to the doctor to be examined. If the mother gave way to her sympathy, that is to her feeling for the child's misery and fright, she would hold it close and not let the doctor come near; but don't we agree that it might be wrong for her to act on such a feeling? Quite generally, then, anyone's moral principles may apply to a particular situation in a way which runs contrary to the particular thrusts of fellow-feeling that he has in that situation. My immediate concern is with sympathy in relation to bad morality, but not because such conflicts occur only when the morality is bad.

Now, suppose that someone who accepts a bad morality is struggling to make himself act in accordance with it in a particular situation where his sympathies pull him another way. He sees the struggle as one between doing the right, conscientious thing, and acting wrongly and weakly, like the mother who won't let the doctor come near her sick, frightened baby. Since we don't accept this person's morality, we may see the situation very differently, thoroughly disapproving of the action he regards as the right one, and endorsing the action which from his point of view constitutes weakness and backsliding.

Conflicts between sympathy and bad morality won't always be like this, for we won't disagree with every single dictate of a bad morality. Still, it can happen in the way I have described, with the agent's right action being our wrong one, and vice versa. That is just what happens in a certain episode in chapter 16 of *The Adventures of Huckleberry Finn,* an episode which brilliantly illustrates how fiction can be instructive about real life.

★ ★ ★

Huck Finn has been helping his slave friend Jim to run away from Miss Watson, who is Jim's owner. In their raft-journey down the Mississippi river, they are near to the place at which Jim will become legally free. Now let Huck take over the story:

> Jim said it made him all over trembly and feverish to be so close to freedom. Well, I can tell you it made me all over trembly and feverish, too, to hear him, because I begun to get it through my head that he *was* most free—and who was to blame for it? Why, *me.* I couldn't get that out of my conscience, no how nor no way. . . . It hadn't ever come home to me, before, what this thing was that I was doing. But now it did; and it stayed with me, and scorched me more and more. I tried to make out to myself that *I* warn't to blame, because *I* didn't run Jim off from his rightful owner; but it warn't no use, conscience up and say, every time: 'But you knowed he was running for his freedom, and you could

> a paddled ashore and told somebody.' That was so—I couldn't get around that, no way. That was where it pinched. Conscience says to me: 'What had poor Miss Watson done to you, that you could see her nigger go off right under your eyes and never say one single word? What did that poor old woman do to you, that you could treat her so mean? . . .' I got to feeling so mean and so miserable I most wished I was dead.

Jim speaks of his plan to save up to buy his wife, and then his children, out of slavery; and he adds that if the children cannot be bought he will arrange to steal them. Huck is horrified:

> Thinks I, this is what comes of my not thinking. Here was this nigger which I had as good as helped to run away, coming right out flat-footed and saying he would steal his children—children that belonged to a man I didn't even know; a man that hadn't ever done me no harm.
>
> I was sorry to hear Jim say that, it was such a lowering of him. My conscience got to stirring me up hotter than ever, until at last I says to it: 'Let up on me—it ain't too late, yet—I'll paddle ashore at first light, and tell.' I felt easy, and happy, and light as a feather, right off. All my troubles was gone.

This is bad morality all right. In his earliest years Huck wasn't taught any principles, and the only ones he has encountered since then are those of rural Missouri, in which slave-owning is just one kind of ownership and is not subject to critical pressure. It hasn't occurred to Huck to question those principles. So the action, to us abhorrent, of turning Jim in to the authorities presents itself *clearly* to Huck as the right thing to do.

For us, morality and sympathy would both dictate helping Jim to escape. If we felt any conflict, it would have both these on one side and something else on the other—greed for a reward, or fear of punishment. But Huck's morality conflicts with his sympathy, that is, with his unargued, natural feeling for his friend. The conflict starts when Huck sets off in the canoe towards the shore, pretending that he is going to reconnoitre, but really planning to turn Jim in:

> As I shoved off, [Jim] says: 'Pooty soon I'll be a-shout'n for joy, en I'll say, it's all on accounts o' Huck I's free man . . . Jim won't ever forgit you, Huck; you's de bes' fren' Jim's ever had; en you's de *only* fren' old Jim's got now.'
>
> I was paddling off, all in a sweat to tell on him; but when he says this, it seemed to kind of take the tuck all out of me. I went along slow then, and I warn't right down certain whether I was glad I started or whether I warn't. When I was fifty yards off, Jim says:
>
> 'Dah you goes, de ole true Huck; de on'y white genlman dat ever kep' his promise to ole Jim.' Well, I just felt sick. But I says, I *got* to do it—I can't get *out* of it.

In the upshot, sympathy wins over morality. Huck hasn't the strength of will to do what he sincerely thinks he ought to do. Two men hunting for runaway slaves ask him whether the man on his raft is black or white:

> I didn't answer up prompt. I tried to, but the words wouldn't come. I tried, for a second or two, to brace up and out with it, but I warn't man enough—hadn't the spunk of a rabbit. I see I was weakening; so I just give up trying, and up and says: 'He's white.'

So Huck enables Jim to escape, thus acting weakly and wickedly—he thinks. In this conflict between sympathy and morality, sympathy wins.

One critic has cited this episode in support of the statement that Huck suffers 'excruciating moments of wavering between honesty and respectability'. That is hopelessly wrong, and I agree with the perceptive comment on it by another critic, who says:

> The conflict waged in Huck is much more serious: he scarcely cares for respectability and never hesitates to relinquish it, but he does care for honesty and gratitude—and both honesty and gratitude require that he should give Jim up. It is not, in Huck, honesty at war with respectability but love and compassion for Jim struggling against his conscience. His decision is for Jim and hell: a right decision made in the mental chains that Huck never breaks. His concern for Jim is and remains *irrational.* Huck finds many reasons for giving Jim up and none for stealing him. To the end Huck sees his compassion for Jim as a weak, ignorant, and wicked felony.

That is precisely correct—and it can have that virtue only because Mark Twain wrote the episode with such unerring precision. The crucial point concerns *reasons,* which all occur on one side of the conflict. On the side of conscience we have principles, arguments, considerations, ways of looking at things:

> 'It hadn't ever come home to me before what I was doing'
> 'I tried to make out that I warn't to blame'
> 'Conscience said "But you knowed . . ."—I couldn't get around that'
> 'What had poor Miss Watson done to you?'
> 'This is what comes of my not thinking'
> '. . . children that belonged to a man I didn't even know'.

On the other side, the side of feeling, we get nothing like that. When Jim rejoices in Huck, as his only friend, Huck doesn't consider the claims of friendship or have the situation 'come home' to him in a different light. All that happens is: 'When he says this, it seemed to kind of take the tuck all out of me. I went along slow then, and I warn't right down certain whether I was glad I started or whether I warn't.' Again, Jim's words about Huck's 'promise' to him don't give Huck any *reason* for changing his plan: in his morality promises to slaves probably don't count. Their effect on him is of a different kind: 'Well, I just felt sick.' And when the moment for final decision comes, Huck doesn't weigh up pros and cons: he simply *fails* to do what he believes to be right—he isn't strong enough, hasn't 'the spunk of a rabbit'. This passage in the novel is notable not just for its finely wrought irony, with Huck's weakness of will leading him to do the right thing, but also for its masterly handling of the difference between general moral principles and particular unreasoned emotional pulls.

* * *

Consider now another case of bad morality in conflict with human sympathy the case of the odious Himmler. Here, from a speech he made to some S.S. generals, is an indication of the content of his morality:

> What happens to a Russian, to a Czech, does not interest me in the slightest. What the nations can offer in the way of good blood of our type, we will take, if necessary by kidnapping their children and raising them here with us. Whether nations live in prosperity or starve to death like cattle interests me only in so far as we need them as slaves to our *Kultur;* otherwise it is of no interest to me. Whether 10,000 Russian females fall down from exhaustion while digging an antitank ditch interests me only in so far as the antitank ditch for Germany is finished.

But has this a moral basis at all? And if it has, was there in Himmler's own mind any conflict between morality and sympathy? Yes there was. Here is more from the same speech:

> . . . I also want to talk to you quite frankly on a very grave matter . . . I mean . . . the extermination of the Jewish race. . . . Most of you must know what it means when 100 corpses are lying side by side, or 500, or 1,000. To have stuck it out and at the same time—apart from exceptions caused by human weakness—to have remained decent fellows, that is what has made us hard. This is a page of glory in our history which has never been written and is never to be written.

Himmler saw his policies as being hard to implement while still retaining one's human sympathies—while still remaining a 'decent fellow'. He is saying that only the weak take the easy way out and just squelch their sympathies, and is praising the stronger and more glorious course of retaining one's sympathies while acting in violation of them. In the same spirit, he ordered that when executions were carried out in concentration camps, those responsible 'are to be influenced in such a way as to suffer no ill effect in their character and mental attitude'. A year later he boasted that the S.S. had wiped out the Jews

> without our leaders and their men suffering any damage in their minds and souls. The danger was considerable, for there was only a narrow path between the Scylla of their becoming heartless ruffians unable any longer to treasure life, and the Charybdis of their becoming soft and suffering nervous breakdowns.

And there really can't be any doubt that the basis of Himmler's policies was a set of principles which constituted his morality—a sick, bad, wicked *morality.* He described himself as caught in 'the old tragic conflict between will and obligation'. And when his physician Kersten protested at the intention to destroy the Jews, saying that the suffering involved was 'not to be contemplated', Kersten reports that Himmler replied:

> He knew that it would mean much suffering for the Jews. . . . 'It is the curse of greatness that it must step over dead bodies to create new life. Yet we must . . . cleanse the soil or it will never bear fruit. It will be a great burden for me to bear.'

This, I submit, is the language of morality.

So in this case, tragically, bad morality won out over sympathy. I am sure that many of Himmler's killers did extinguish their sympathies, becoming 'heartless ruffians' rather than 'decent fellows'; but not Himmler himself. Although his policies ran against the human grain to a horrible degree, he did not sandpaper down his emotional surfaces so that there was no grain there, allowing his actions to slide along smoothly and easily. He did, after all, bear his hideous burden, and even paid a price for it. He suffered a variety of nervous and physical disabilities, including nausea and stomach-convulsions, and Kersten was doubtless right in saying that these were 'the expression of a psychic division which extended over his whole life'.

This same division must have been present in some of those officials of the Church who ordered heretics to be tortured so as to change their theological opinions. Along with the brutes and the cold careerists, there must have been some who cared, and who suffered from the conflict between their sympathies and their bad morality.

★ ★ ★

In the conflict between sympathy and bad morality, then, the victory may go to sympathy as in the case of Huck Finn, or to morality as in the case of Himmler.

Another possibility is that the conflict may be avoided by giving up, or not ever having, those sympathies which might interfere with one's principles. That seems to have been the case with Jonathan Edwards. I am afraid that I shall be doing an injustice to Edwards' many virtues, and to his great intellectual energy and inventiveness; for my concern is only with the worst thing about him—namely his morality, which was worse than Himmler's.

According to Edwards, God condemns some men to an eternity of unimaginably awful pain, though he arbitrarily spares others—'arbitrarily' because none deserve to be spared:

> Natural men are held in the hand of God over the pit of hell; they have deserved the fiery pit, and are already sentenced to it; and God is dreadfully provoked, his anger is as great towards them as to

> those that are actually suffering the executions of the fierceness of his wrath in hell . . . ; the devil is waiting for them, hell is gaping for them, the flames gather and flash about them, and would fain lay hold on them . . . ; and . . . there are no means within reach that can be any security to them. . . . All that preserves them is the mere arbitrary will, and uncovenanted unobliged forebearance of an incensed God.

Notice that he says 'they have deserved the fiery pit.' Edwards insists that men *ought* to be condemned to eternal pain; and his position isn't that this is right because God wants it, but rather that God wants it because it is right. For him, moral standards exist independently of God, and God can be assessed in the light of them (and of course found to be perfect). For example, he says:

> They deserve to be cast into hell; so that . . . justice never stands in the way, it makes no objection against God's using his power at any moment to destroy them. Yea, on the contrary, justice calls aloud for an infinite punishment of their sins.

Elsewhere, he gives elaborate arguments to show that God is acting justly in damning sinners. For example, he argues that a punishment should be exactly as bad as the crime being punished; God is infinitely excellent; so any crime against him is infinitely bad; and so eternal damnation is exactly right as a punishment—it is infinite, but, as Edwards is careful also to say, it is 'no more than infinite.'

Of course, Edwards himself didn't torment the damned; but the question still arises of whether his sympathies didn't conflict with his *approval* of eternal torment. Didn't he find it painful to contemplate any fellow-human's being tortured for ever? Apparently not:

> The God that holds you over the pit of hell, much as one holds a spider or some loathsome insect over the fire, abhors you, and is dreadfully provoked; . . . he is of purer eyes than to bear to have you in his sight; you are ten thousand times so abominable in his eyes as the most hateful venomous serpent is in ours.

When God is presented as being as misanthropic as that, one suspects misanthropy in the theologian. This suspicion is increased when Edwards claims that 'the saints in glory will . . . understand how terrible the sufferings of the damned are; yet . . . will not be sorry for [them].' He bases this partly on a view of human nature whose ugliness he seems not to notice:

> The seeing of the calamities of others tends to heighten the sense of our own enjoyments. When the saints in glory, therefore, shall see the doleful state of the damned, how will this heighten their sense of the blessedness of their own state. . . . When they shall see how miserable others of their fellow-creatures are . . . ; when they

> shall see the smoke of their torment, . . . and hear their dolorous shrieks and cries, and consider that they in the mean time are in the most blissful state, and shall surely be in it to all eternity; how they will rejoice!

I hope this is less than the whole truth! His other main point about why the saints will rejoice to see the torments of the damned is that it is *right* that they should do so:

> The heavenly inhabitants . . . will have no love nor pity to the damned. . . . [This will not show] a want of a spirit of love in them . . . for the heavenly inhabitants will know that it is not fit that they should love [the damned] because they will know then, that God has no love to them, nor pity for them.

The implication that *of course* one can adjust one's feelings of pity so that they conform to the dictates of some authority—doesn't this suggest that ordinary human sympathies played only a small part in Edwards' life?

⋆ ⋆ ⋆

Huck Finn, whose sympathies are wide and deep, could never avoid the conflict in that way; but he is determined to avoid it, and so he opts for the only other alternative he can see—to give up morality altogether. After he has tricked the slave-hunters, he returns to the raft and undergoes a peculiar crisis:

> I got aboard the raft, feeling bad and low, because I knowed very well I had done wrong, and I see it warn't no use for me to try to learn to do right; a body that don't get *started* right when he's little, ain't got no show—when the pinch comes there ain't nothing to back him up and keep him to his work, and so he gets beat. Then I thought a minute, and says to myself, hold on—s'pose you'd a done right and give Jim up; would you feel better than what you do now? No, says I, I'd feel bad—I'd feel just the same way I do now. Well, then, says I, what's the use you learning to do right, when it's troublesome to do right and ain't no trouble to do wrong, and the wages is just the same? I was stuck. I couldn't answer that. So I reckoned I wouldn't bother no more about it, but after this always do whichever come handiest at the time.

Huck clearly cannot conceive of having any morality except the one he has learned—too late, he thinks—from his society. He is not entirely a prisoner of that morality, because he does after all reject it; but for him that is a decision to relinquish morality as such; he cannot envisage revising his morality, altering its content in face of the various pressures to which it is subject, including pressures from his sympathies. For example, he does not begin to approach the thought that slavery should be rejected on moral grounds, or the thought that what he is doing is not theft because a person cannot be owned and therefore cannot be stolen.

The basic trouble is that he cannot or will not engage in abstract intellectual operations of any sort. In chapter 33 he finds himself 'feeling to blame, somehow' for something he knows he had no hand in; he assumes that this feeling is a deliverance of conscience; and this confirms him in his belief that conscience shouldn't be listened to:

> It don't make no difference whether you do right or wrong, a person's conscience ain't got no sense, and just goes for him *anyway.* If I had a yaller dog that didn't know no more than a person's conscience does, I would pison him. It takes up more room than all the rest of a person's insides, and yet ain't no good, nohow.

That brisk, incurious dismissiveness fits well with the comprehensive rejection of morality back on the raft. But this is a digression.

On the raft, Huck decides not to live by principles, but just to do whatever 'comes handiest at the time'—always acting according to the mood of the moment. Since the morality he is rejecting is narrow and cruel, and his sympathies are broad and kind, the results will be good. But moral principles are good to have, because they help to protect one from acting badly at moments when one's sympathies happen to be in abeyance. On the highest possible estimate of the role one's sympathies should have, one can still allow for principles as embodiments of one's best feelings, one's broadest and keenest sympathies. On that view, principles can help one across intervals when one's feelings are at less than their best, i.e. through periods of misanthropy or meanness or self-centredness or depression or anger.

What Huck didn't see is that one can live by principles and yet have ultimate control over their content. And one way such control can be exercised is by checking of one's principles in the light of one's sympathies. This is sometimes a pretty straightforward matter. It can happen that a certain moral principle becomes untenable—meaning literally that one cannot hold it any longer—because it conflicts intolerably with the pity or revulsion or whatever that one feels when one sees what the principle leads to. One's experience may play a large part here: experiences evoke feelings, and feelings force one to modify principles. Something like this happened to the English poet Wilfred Owen, whose experiences in the First World War transformed him from an enthusiastic soldier into a virtual pacifist. I can't document his change of conscience in detail; but I want to present something which he wrote about the way experience can put pressure on morality.

The Latin poet Horace wrote that it is sweet and fitting (or right) to die for one's country—*dulce et decorum est pro patria mori*—and Owen wrote a fine poem about how experience could lead one to relinquish that particular moral principle. He describes a man who is too slow donning his gas mask during a gas attack—'As under a green sea I saw him drowning,' Owen says. The poem ends like this:

In all my dreams before my helpless sight
He plunges at me, guttering, choking, drowning.
If in some smothering dreams, you too could pace
Behind the wagon that we flung him in,
And watch the white eyes writhing in his face,
His hanging face, like a devil's sick of sin;
If you could hear, at every jolt, the blood
Come gargling from the froth-corrupted lungs,
Bitter as the cud
Of vile, incurable sores on innocent tongues,—
My friend, you would not tell with such high zest
To children ardent for some desperate glory,
The old Lie: Dulce et decorum est
Pro patria mori.

★ ★ ★

There is a difficulty about drawing from all this a moral for ourselves. I imagine that we agree in our rejection of slavery, eternal damnation, genocide, and uncritical patriotic self-abnegation; so we shall agree that Huck Finn, Jonathan Edwards, Heinrich Himmler, and the poet Horace would all have done well to bring certain of their principles under severe pressure from ordinary human sympathies. But then we can say this because we can say that all those are bad moralities, whereas we cannot look at our own moralities and declare them bad. This is not arrogance: it is obviously incoherent for someone to declare the system of moral principles that he *accepts* to be *bad,* just as one cannot coherently say of anything that one *believes* it but it is *false.*

Still, although I can't point to any of my beliefs and say 'That is false', I don't doubt that some of my beliefs *are* false; and so I should try to remain open to correction. Similarly, I accept every single item in my morality—that is inevitable—but I am sure that my morality could be improved, which is to say that it could undergo changes which I should be glad of once I had made them. So I must try to keep my morality open to revision, exposing it to whatever valid pressures there are—including pressures from my sympathies.

I don't give my sympathies a blank cheque in advance. In a conflict between principle and sympathy, principles ought sometimes to win. For example, I think it was right to take part in the Second World War on the allied side; there were many ghastly individual incidents which might have led someone to doubt the rightness of his participation in that war; and I think it would have been right for such a person to keep his sympathies in a subordinate place on those occasions, not allowing them to modify his principles in such a way as to make a pacifist of him.

Still, one's sympathies should be kept as sharp and sensitive and aware as possible, and not only because they can sometimes affect one's principles or one's conduct or both. Owen, at any rate, says that feelings and sympathies are vital even when they can do nothing but bring pain and distress. In another poem he speaks of the blessings of being numb in one's feelings: 'Happy are the men who yet before they are killed/Can let their veins run cold,' he says. These are the ones who do not suffer from any compassion which, as Owen puts it, 'makes their feet/Sore on the alleys cobbled with their brothers.' He contrasts these 'happy' ones, who 'lose all imagination', with himself and others 'who with a thought besmirch/Blood over all our soul.' Yet the poem's verdict goes against the 'happy' ones. Owen does not say that they will act worse than the others whose souls are besmirched with blood because of their keen awareness of human suffering. He merely says that they are the losers because they have cut themselves off from the human condition:

By choice they made themselves immune
To pity and whatever moans in man
Before the last sea and the hapless stars;
Whatever mourns when many leave these shores;
Whatever shares
The eternal reciprocity of tears.

EUTHYPHRO

PLATO (427–347 BCE), along with his student, Aristotle, is regarded as the greatest thinker of the ancient world. Born into a wealthy family in Athens, as a young man he came under the influence of Socrates, about whom the dialogues, including *Euthyphro,* are written. The dialogues are breathtaking in their scope, covering topics in metaphysics, epistemology, ethics, philosophy of religion, political philosophy, and logic. In 387 BCE Plato founded the Academy, the first institution of formal learning in the Western world.

THINKING QUESTIONS

Plato, *Euthyphro*

1. Euthyphro has come to the court to prosecute his father. What did his father do? Why does Euthyphro think his father was wrong? Why does Euthyphro think that he is right to bring the case against his father to court?
2. What is Euthyphro's first definition of "piety"? Why does Socrates reject this definition as inadequate?
3. What is Euthyphro's second definition of "piety"? How is it an improvement on his first attempt? Why does Socrates reject this one too?
4. What is Euthyphro's final definition of "piety"?
5. Assume that a pious, or good, act is one that all the gods love. Socrates notes that this question still remains: (1) Is a thing good because the gods love it, or (2) do the gods love it because it is good? What is the difference between (1) and (2)?
6. Socrates defends the idea that the gods love things because they are pious or good. What is his reasoning?
7. Why does Socrates' view imply that morality and religion are logically separate?

EUTHYPHRO: What in the world are you doing here in the king's hall, Socrates? Why have you left your haunts in the Lyceum? You surely cannot have a suit before him, as I have.

SOCRATES: The Athenians, Euthyphro, call it an indictment, not a suit.

EUTHYPHRO: What? Do you mean that someone is prosecuting you? I cannot believe that you are prosecuting anyone yourself.

SOCRATES: Certainly I am not.

EUTHYPHRO: Then is someone prosecuting you?

SOCRATES: Yes.

EUTHYPHRO: Who is he?

SOCRATES: I scarcely know him myself, Euthyphro; I think he must be some unknown young man. His name, however, is Meletus, and his district Pitthis, if you can call to mind any Meletus of that district—a hook-nosed man with lanky hair and rather a scanty beard.

EUTHYPHRO: I don't know him, Socrates. But tell me, what is he prosecuting you for?

SOCRATES: What for? Not on trivial grounds, I think. It is no small thing for so young a man to have formed an opinion on such an important matter. For he, he says, knows how the young are corrupted, and who are their corrupters. He must be a wise man who, observing my ignorance, is going to accuse me to the state, as his mother, of corrupting his friends. I think that he is the only one who begins at the right point in his political reforms; for his first care is to make the young men as good as possible, just as a good farmer will take care of his young plants first, and, after he has done that, of the others. And so Meletus, I suppose, is first clearing us away who, as he says, corrupt the young men growing up; and then, when he has done that, of course he will turn his attention to the older men, and so become a very great public benefactor. Indeed, that is only what you would expect when he goes to work in this way.

EUTHYPHRO: I hope it may be so, Socrates, but I fear the opposite. It seems to me that in trying to injure you, he is really setting to work by striking a blow at the foundation of the state. But how, tell me, does he say that you corrupt the youth?

SOCRATES: In a way which sounds absurd at first, my friend. He says that I am a maker of gods; and so he is prosecuting me, he says, for inventing new gods and for not believing in the old ones.

EUTHYPHRO: I understand, Socrates. It is because you say that you always have a divine guide. So he is prosecuting you for introducing religious reforms; and he is going into court to arouse prejudice against you, knowing that the multitude are easily prejudiced about such matters. Why, they laugh even at me, as if I were out of my mind, when I talk about divine things in the assembly and tell them what is going to happen; and yet I have never foretold anything which has not come true. But they are resentful of all people like us. We must not worry about them; we must meet them boldly.

SOCRATES: My dear Euthyphro, their ridicule is not a very serious matter. The Athenians, it seems to me, may think a man to be clever without paying him much attention, so long as they do not think that he teaches his wisdom to others. But as soon as they think that he makes other people clever, they get angry, whether it be from resentment, as you say, or for some other reason.

EUTHYPHRO: I am not very anxious to test their attitude toward me in this matter.

SOCRATES: No, perhaps they think that you are reserved, and that you are not anxious to teach your wisdom to others. But I fear that they may think that I am; for my love of men makes me talk to everyone whom I meet quite freely and unreservedly, and without payment. Indeed, if I could I would gladly pay people myself to listen to me. If then, as I said just now, they were only going to laugh at me, as you say they do at you, it would not be at all an unpleasant way of spending the day—to spend it in court, joking and laughing. But if they are going to be in earnest, then only prophets like you can tell where the matter will end.

EUTHYPHRO: Well, Socrates, I dare say that nothing will come of it. Very likely you will be successful in your trial, and I think that I shall be in mine.

SOCRATES: And what is this suit of yours, Euthyphro? Are you suing, or being sued?

EUTHYPHRO: I am suing.

SOCRATES: Whom?

EUTHYPHRO: A man whom people think I must be mad to prosecute.

SOCRATES: What? Has he wings to fly away with?

EUTHYPHRO: He is far enough from flying; he is a very old man.

SOCRATES: Who is he?

EUTHYPHRO: He is my father.

SOCRATES: Your father, my good man?

EUTHYPHRO: He is indeed.

SOCRATES: What are you prosecuting him for? What is the accusation?

EUTHYPHRO: Murder, Socrates.

SOCRATES: Good heavens, Euthyphro! Surely the multitude are ignorant of what is right. I take it that it is not everyone who could rightly do what you are doing; only a man who was already well advanced in wisdom.

EUTHYPHRO: That is quite true, Socrates.

SOCRATES: Was the man whom your father killed a relative of yours? But, of course, he was. You would never have prosecuted your father for the murder of a stranger?

EUTHYPHRO: You amuse me, Socrates. What difference does it make whether the murdered man were a relative or a stranger? The only question that you have to ask is, did the murderer kill justly or not?

If justly, you must let him alone; if unjustly, you must indict him for murder, even though he share your hearth and sit at your table. The pollution is the same if you associate with such a man, knowing what he has done, without purifying yourself, and him too, by bringing him to justice. In the present case the murdered man was a poor laborer of mine, who worked for us on our farm in Naxos. While drunk he got angry with one of our slaves and killed him. My father therefore bound the man hand and foot and threw him into a ditch, while he sent to Athens to ask the priest what he should do. While the messenger was gone, he entirely neglected the man, thinking that he was a murderer, and that it would be no great matter, even if he were to die. And that was exactly what happened; hunger and cold and his bonds killed him before the messenger returned. And now my father and the rest of my family are indignant with me because I am prosecuting my father for the murder of this murderer. They assert that he did not kill the man at all; and they say that, even if he had killed him over and over again, the man himself was a murderer, and that I ought not to concern myself about such a person because it is impious for a son to prosecute his father for murder. So little, Socrates, do they know the divine law of piety and impiety.

SOCRATES: And do you mean to say, Euthyphro, that you think that you understand divine things and piety and impiety so accurately that, in such a case as you have stated, you can bring your father to justice without fear that you yourself may be doing something impious?

EUTHYPHRO: If I did not understand all these matters accurately, Socrates, I should not be worth much—Euthyphro would not be any better than other men.

SOCRATES: Then, my dear Euthyphro, I cannot do better than become your pupil and challenge Meletus on this very point before the trial begins. I should say that I had always thought it very important to have knowledge about divine things; and that now, when he says that I offend by speaking carelessly about them, and by introducing reforms, I have become your pupil. And I should say, "Meletus, if you acknowledge Euthyphro to be wise in these matters and to hold the correct belief, then think the same of me and do not put me on trial; but if you do not, then bring a suit, not against me, but against my master, for corrupting his elders—namely, myself whom he corrupts by his teaching, and his own father whom he corrupts by admonishing and punishing him." And if I did not succeed in persuading him to release me from the suit or to indict you in my place, then I could repeat my challenge in court.

EUTHYPHRO: Yes, by Zeus! Socrates, I think I should find out his weak points if he were to try to indict me. I should have a good deal to say about him in court long before I spoke about myself.

SOCRATES: Yes, my dear friend, and knowing this I am anxious to become your pupil. I see that Meletus here, and others too, seem not to notice you at all, but he sees through me without difficulty and at once prosecutes me for impiety. Now, therefore, please explain to me what you were so confident just now that you knew. Tell me what are righteousness and sacrilege with respect to murder and everything else. I suppose that piety is the same in all actions, and that impiety is always the opposite of piety, and retains its identity, and that, as impiety, it always has the same character, which will be found in whatever is impious.

EUTHYPHRO: Certainly, Socrates, I suppose so.

SOCRATES: Tell me, then, what is piety and what is impiety?

EUTHYPHRO: Well, then, I say that piety means prosecuting the unjust individual who has committed murder or sacrilege, or any other such crime, as I am doing now, whether he is your father or your mother or whoever he is; and I say that impiety means not prosecuting him. And observe, Socrates, I will give you a clear proof, which I have already given to others, that it is so, and that doing right means not letting off unpunished the sacrilegious man, whosoever he may be. Men hold Zeus to be the best and the most just of the gods; and they admit that Zeus bound his own father, Cronos, for wrongfully devouring his children; and that Cronos, in his turn, castrated his father for similar reasons. And yet these same men are incensed with me because I proceed against my father for doing wrong. So, you see, they say one thing in the case of the gods and quite another in mine.

SOCRATES: Is not that why I am being prosecuted, Euthyphro? I mean, because I find it hard to accept such stories people tell about the gods? I expect that I shall be found at fault because I doubt those stories. Now if you who understand all these matters so well agree in holding all those tales true, then I suppose that I must yield to your authority. What could I say when I admit myself that I know nothing about them? But tell me, in the name of friendship, do you really believe that these things have actually happened?

EUTHYPHRO: Yes, and more amazing things, too, Socrates, which the multitude do not know of.

SOCRATES: Then you really believe that there is war among the gods, and bitter hatreds, and battles, such as the poets tell of, and which the great painters have depicted in our temples, notably in the pictures which cover the robe that is carried up to the Acropolis at the great Panathenaic festival? Are we to say that these things are true, Euthyphro?

EUTHYPHRO: Yes, Socrates, and more besides. As I was saying, I will report to you many other stories about divine matters, if you like, which I am sure will astonish you when you hear them.

SOCRATES: I dare say. You shall report them to me at your leisure another time. At present please try to give a more definite answer to the question which I asked you just now. What I asked you, my friend, was, What is piety? and you have not explained it to me to my satisfaction. You only tell me that what you are doing now, namely, prosecuting your father for murder, is a pious act.

EUTHYPHRO: Well, that is true, Socrates.

SOCRATES: Very likely. But many other actions are pious, are they not, Euthyphro?

EUTHYPHRO: Certainly.

SOCRATES: Remember, then, I did not ask you to tell me one or two of all the many pious actions that there are; I want to know what is characteristic of piety which makes all pious actions pious. You said, I think, that there is one characteristic which makes all pious actions pious, and another characteristic which makes all impious actions impious. Do you not remember?

EUTHYPHRO: I do.

SOCRATES: Well, then, explain to me what is this characteristic, that I may have it to turn to, and to use as a standard whereby to judge your actions and those of other men, and be able to say that whatever action resembles it is pious, and whatever does not, is not pious.

EUTHYPHRO: Yes, I will tell you that if you wish, Socrates.

SOCRATES: Certainly I do.

EUTHYPHRO: Well, then, what is pleasing to the gods is pious, and what is not pleasing to them is impious.

SOCRATES: Fine, Euthyphro. Now you have given me the answer that I wanted. Whether what you say is true, I do not know yet. But, of course, you will go on to prove that it is true.

EUTHYPHRO: Certainly.

SOCRATES: Come, then, let us examine our statement. The things and the men that are pleasing to the gods are pious, and the things and the men that are displeasing to the gods are impious. But piety and impiety are not the same; they are as opposite as possible—was not that what we said?

EUTHYPHRO: Certainly.

SOCRATES: And it seems the appropriate statement?

EUTHYPHRO: Yes, Socrates, certainly.

SOCRATES: Have we not also said, Euthyphro, that there are quarrels and disagreements and hatreds among the gods?

EUTHYPHRO: We have.

SOCRATES: But what kind of disagreement, my friend, causes hatred and anger? Let us look at the matter thus. If you and I were to disagree as to whether one number were more than another, would that make us angry and enemies? Should we not settle such a dispute at once by counting?

EUTHYPHRO: Of course.

SOCRATES: And if we were to disagree as to the relative size of two things, we should measure them and put an end to the disagreement at once, should we not?

EUTHYPHRO: Yes.

SOCRATES: And should we not settle a question about the relative weight of two things by weighing them?

EUTHYPHRO: Of course.

SOCRATES: Then what is the question which would make us angry and enemies if we disagreed about it, and could not come to a settlement? Perhaps you have not an answer ready; but listen to mine. Is it not the question of the just and unjust, of the honorable and the dishonorable, of the good and the bad? Is it not questions about these matters which make you and me and everyone else quarrel, when we do quarrel, if we differ about them and can reach no satisfactory agreement?

EUTHYPHRO: Yes, Socrates, it is disagreements about these matters.

SOCRATES: Well, Euthyphro, the gods will quarrel over these things if they quarrel at all, will they not?

EUTHYPHRO: Necessarily.

SOCRATES: Then, my good Euthyphro, you say that some of the gods think one thing just, the others another; and that what some of them hold to be honorable or good, others hold to be dishonorable or evil. For there would not have been quarrels among them if they had not disagreed on these points, would there?

EUTHYPHRO: You are right.

SOCRATES: And each of them loves what he thinks honorable, and good, and just; and hates the opposite, does he not?

EUTHYPHRO: Certainly.

SOCRATES: But you say that the same action is held by some of them to be just, and by others to be unjust; and that then they dispute about it, and so quarrel and fight among themselves. Is it not so?

EUTHYPHRO: Yes.

SOCRATES: Then the same thing is hated by the gods and loved by them; and the same thing will be displeasing and pleasing to them.

EUTHYPHRO: Apparently.

SOCRATES: Then, according to your account, the same thing will be pious and impious.

EUTHYPHRO: So it seems.

SOCRATES: Then, my good friend, you have not answered my question. I did not ask you to tell me what action is both pious and impious; but it seems that whatever is pleasing to the gods is also displeasing to them. And so, Euthyphro, I should not be surprised if what you are doing now in punishing your father is an action well pleasing to Zeus, but hateful to Cronos and Uranus, and acceptable to Hephaestus, but hateful to Hera; and if any of the other gods disagree about it, pleasing to some of them and displeasing to others.

EUTHYPHRO: But on this point, Socrates, I think that there is no difference of opinion among the gods: they all hold that if one man kills another unjustly, he must be punished.

SOCRATES: What, Euthyphro? Among mankind, have you never heard disputes whether a man ought to be punished for killing another man unjustly, or for doing some other unjust deed?

EUTHYPHRO: Indeed, they never cease from these disputes, especially in courts of justice. They do all manner of unjust things; and then there is nothing which they will not do and say to avoid punishment.

SOCRATES: Do they admit that they have done something unjust, and at the same time deny that they ought to be punished, Euthyphro?

EUTHYPHRO: No, indeed, that they do not.

SOCRATES: Then it is not the case that there is nothing which they will not do and say. I take it, they do not dare to say or argue that they must not be punished if they have done something unjust. What they say is that they have not done anything unjust, is it not so?

EUTHYPHRO: That is true.

SOCRATES: Then they do not disagree over the question that the unjust individual must be punished. They disagree over the question, who is unjust, and what was done and when, do they not?

EUTHYPHRO: That is true.

SOCRATES: Well, is not exactly the same thing true of the gods if they quarrel about justice and injustice, as you say they do? Do not some of them say that the others are doing something unjust, while the others deny it? No one, I suppose, my dear friend, whether god or man, dares to say that a person who has done something unjust must not be punished.

EUTHYPHRO: No, Socrates, that is true, by and large.

SOCRATES: I take it, Euthyphro, that the disputants, whether men or gods, if the gods do disagree, disagree over each separate act. When they quarrel about any act, some of them say that it was just, and others that it was unjust. Is it not so?

EUTHYPHRO: Yes.

SOCRATES: Come, then, my dear Euthyphro, please enlighten me on this point. What proof have you that all the gods think that a laborer who has been imprisoned for murder by the master of the man whom he has murdered, and who dies from his imprisonment before the master has had time to learn from the religious authorities what he should do, dies unjustly? How do you know that it is just for a son to indict his father and to prosecute him for the murder of such a man? Come, see if you can make it clear to me that the gods necessarily agree in thinking that this action of yours is just; and if you satisfy me, I will never cease singing your praises for wisdom.

EUTHYPHRO: I could make that clear enough to you, Socrates; but I am afraid that it would be a long business.

SOCRATES: I see you think that I am duller than the judges. To them, of course, you will make it clear that your father has committed an unjust action, and that all the gods agree in hating such actions.

EUTHYPHRO: I will indeed, Socrates, if they will only listen to me.

SOCRATES: They will listen if they think that you are a good speaker. But while you were talking, it occurred to me to ask myself this question: suppose that Euthyphro were to prove to me as clearly as possible that all the gods think such a death unjust, how has he brought me any nearer to understanding what piety and impiety are? This particular act, perhaps, may be displeasing to the gods, but then we have just seen that piety and impiety cannot be defined in that way; for we have seen that what is displeasing to the gods is also pleasing to them. So I will let you off on this point, Euthyphro; and all the gods shall agree in thinking your father's action wrong and in hating it, if you like. But shall we correct our definition and say that whatever all the gods hate is impious, and whatever they all love is pious; while whatever some of them love, and others hate, is either both or neither? Do you wish us now to define piety and impiety in this manner?

EUTHYPHRO: Why not, Socrates?

SOCRATES: There is no reason why I should not, Euthyphro. It is for you to consider whether that definition will help you to teach me what you promised.

EUTHYPHRO: Well, I should say that piety is what all the gods love, and that impiety is what they all hate.

SOCRATES: Are we to examine this definition, Euthyphro, and see if it is a good one? Or are we to be content to accept the bare statements of other men or of ourselves without asking any questions? Or must we examine the statements?

EUTHYPHRO: We must examine them. But for my part I think that the definition is right this time.

SOCRATES: We shall know that better in a little while, my good friend. Now consider this question. Do the gods love piety because it is pious, or is it pious because they love it?

EUTHYPHRO: I do not understand you, Socrates.

SOCRATES: I will try to explain myself: we speak of a thing being carried and carrying, and being led and leading, and being seen and seeing; and you understand that all such expressions mean different things, and what the difference is.

EUTHYPHRO: Yes, I think I understand.

SOCRATES: And we talk of a thing being loved, of a thing loving, and the two are different?

EUTHYPHRO: Of course.

SOCRATES: Now tell me, is a thing which is being carried in a state of being carried because it is carried, or for some other reason?

EUTHYPHRO: No, because it is carried.

SOCRATES: And a thing is in a state of being led because it is led, and of being seen because it is seen?

EUTHYPHRO: Certainly.

SOCRATES: Then a thing is not seen because it is in a state of being seen: it is in a state of being seen because it is seen; and a thing is not led because it is in a state of being led: it is in a state of being led because it is led; and a thing is not carried because it is in a state of being carried: it is in a state of being carried because it is carried. Is my meaning clear now, Euthyphro? I mean this: if anything becomes or is affected, it does not become because it is in a state of becoming: it is in a state of becoming because it becomes; and it is not affected because it is in a state of being affected: it is in a state of being affected because it is affected. Do you not agree?

EUTHYPHRO: I do.

SOCRATES: Is not that which is being loved in a state either of becoming or of being affected in some way by something?

EUTHYPHRO: Certainly.

SOCRATES: Then the same is true here as in the former cases. A thing is not loved by those who love it because it is in a state of being loved; it is in a state of being loved because they love it.

EUTHYPHRO: Necessarily.

SOCRATES: Well, then, Euthyphro, what do we say about piety? Is it not loved by all the gods, according to your definition?

EUTHYPHRO: Yes.

SOCRATES: Because it is pious, or for some other reason?

EUTHYPHRO: No, because it is pious.

SOCRATES: Then it is loved by the gods because it is pious; it is not pious because it is loved by them?

EUTHYPHRO: It seems so.

SOCRATES: But, then, what is pleasing to the gods is pleasing to them, and is in a state of being loved by them, because they love it?

EUTHYPHRO: Of course.

SOCRATES: Then piety is not what is pleasing to the gods, and what is pleasing to the gods is not pious, as you say, Euthyphro. They are different things.

EUTHYPHRO: And why, Socrates?

SOCRATES: Because we are agreed that the gods love piety because it is pious, and that it is not pious because they love it. Is not this so?

EUTHYPHRO: Yes.

SOCRATES: And that what is pleasing to the gods because they love it, is pleasing to them by reason of this same love, and that they do not love it because it is pleasing to them.

EUTHYPHRO: True.

SOCRATES: Then, my dear Euthyphro, piety and what is pleasing to the gods are different things. If the gods had loved piety because it is pious, they would also have loved what is pleasing to them because it is pleasing to them; but if what is pleasing to them had been pleasing to them because they loved it, then piety, too, would have been piety because they loved it. But now you see that they are opposite things, and wholly different from each other. For the one is of a sort to be loved because it is loved, while the other is loved because it is of a sort to be loved. My question, Euthyphro, was, What is piety? But it turns out that you have not explained to me the essential character of piety; you have been content to mention an effect which belongs to it—namely, that all the gods love it. You have not yet told me what its essential character is. Do not, if you please, keep from me what piety is; begin again and tell me that. Never mind whether the gods love it, or whether it has other effects: we shall not differ on that point. Do your best to make clear to me what is piety and what is impiety.

EUTHYPHRO: But, Socrates, I really don't know how to explain to you what is in my mind. Whatever statement we put forward always somehow moves round in a circle, and will not stay where we put it.

SOCRATES: I think that your statements, Euthyphro, are worthy of my ancestor Daedalus. If they had been mine and I had set them down, I dare say you would have made fun of me, and said that it was the consequence of my descent from Daedalus that the statements which I construct run away, as his statues used to, and will not stay where they are put. But, as it is, the statements are yours, and the joke would have no point. You yourself see that they will not stay still.

EUTHYPHRO: Nay, Socrates, I think that the joke is very much in point. It is not my fault that the statement moves round in a circle and will not stay still. But you are the Daedalus, I think; as far as I am concerned, my statements would have stayed put.

SOCRATES: Then, my friend, I must be a more skillful artist than Daedalus; he only used to make his own works move, while I, you see, can make other people's works move, too. And the beauty of it is that I am wise against my will. I would rather that our statements had remained firm and immovable than have all the wisdom of Daedalus and all the riches of Tantalus to boot. But enough of this. I will do my best to help you to explain to me what piety is, for I think that you are lazy. Don't give in yet. Tell me, do you not think that all piety must be just?

EUTHYPHRO: I do.

SOCRATES: Well, then, is all justice pious, too? Or, while all piety is just, is a part only of justice pious, and the rest of it something else?

EUTHYPHRO: I do not follow you, Socrates.

SOCRATES: Yet you have the advantage over me in your youth no less than your wisdom. But, as I say, the wealth of your wisdom makes you complacent. Exert yourself, my good friend: I am not asking you a difficult question. I mean the opposite of what the poet [Stasinus] said, when he wrote:

> "You shall not name Zeus the creator, who made all
> things: for where there is fear there also is reverence."

Now I disagree with the poet. Shall I tell you why?

EUTHYPHRO: Yes.

SOCRATES: I do not think it true to say that where there is fear, there also is reverence. Many people who fear sickness and poverty and other such evils seem to me to have fear, but no reverence for what they fear. Do you not think so?

EUTHYPHRO: I do.

SOCRATES: But I think that where there is reverence there also is fear. Does any man feel reverence and a sense of shame about anything, without at the same time dreading and fearing the reputation of wickedness?

EUTHYPHRO: No, certainly not.

SOCRATES: Then, though there is fear wherever there is reverence, it is not correct to say that where there is fear there also is reverence. Reverence does not always accompany fear; for fear, I take it, is wider than reverence. It is a part of fear, just as the odd is a part of number, so that where you have the odd you must also have number, though where you have number you do not necessarily have the odd. Now I think you follow me?

EUTHYPHRO: I do.

SOCRATES: Well, then, this is what I meant by the question which I asked you. Is there always piety where there is justice? Or, though there is always justice where there is piety, yet there is not always piety where there is justice, because piety is only a part of justice? Shall we say this, or do you differ?

EUTHYPHRO: No, I agree. I think that you are right.

SOCRATES: Now observe the next point. If piety is a part of justice, we must find out, I suppose, what part of justice it is? Now, if you had asked me just now, for instance, what part of number is the odd, and what number is an odd number, I should have said that whatever number is not even is an odd number. Is it not so?

EUTHYPHRO: Yes.

SOCRATES: Then see if you can explain to me what part of justice is piety, that I may tell Meletus that now that I have been adequately instructed by you as to what actions are righteous and pious, and what are not, he must give up prosecuting me unjustly for impiety.

EUTHYPHRO: Well, then, Socrates, I should say that righteousness and piety are that part of justice which has to do with the careful attention which ought to be paid to the gods; and that what has to do with the careful attention which ought to be paid to men is the remaining part of justice.

SOCRATES: And I think that your answer is a good one, Euthyphro. But there is one little point about which I still want to hear more. I do not yet understand what the careful attention is to which you refer. I suppose you do not mean that the attention which we pay to the gods is like the attention which we pay to other things. We say, for instance, do we not, that not everyone knows how to take care of horses, but only the trainer of horses?

EUTHYPHRO: Certainly.

SOCRATES: For I suppose that the skill that is concerned with horses is the art of taking care of horses.

EUTHYPHRO: Yes.

SOCRATES: And not everyone understands the care of dogs, but only the huntsman.

EUTHYPHRO: True.

SOCRATES: For I suppose that the huntsman's skill is the art of taking care of dogs.

EUTHYPHRO: Yes.

SOCRATES: And the herdsman's skill is the art of taking care of cattle.

EUTHYPHRO: Certainly.

SOCRATES: And you say that piety and righteousness are taking care of the gods, Euthyphro?

EUTHYPHRO: I do.

SOCRATES: Well, then, has not all care the same object? Is it not for the good and benefit of that on which it is bestowed? For instance, you see that horses are benefited and improved when they are cared for by the art which is concerned with them. Is it not so?

EUTHYPHRO: Yes, I think so.

SOCRATES: And dogs are benefited and improved by the huntsman's art, and cattle by the herdsman's, are they not? And the same is always true. Or do you think care is ever meant to harm that which is cared for?

EUTHYPHRO: No, indeed; certainly not.

SOCRATES: But to benefit it?

EUTHYPHRO: Of course.

SOCRATES: Then is piety, which is our care for the gods, intended to benefit the gods, or to improve them? Should you allow that you make any of the gods better when you do a pious action?

EUTHYPHRO: No indeed; certainly not.

SOCRATES: No, I am quite sure that that is not your meaning, Euthyphro. It was for that reason that I asked you what you meant by the careful attention which ought to be paid to the gods. I thought that you did not mean that.

EUTHYPHRO: You were right, Socrates. I do not mean that.

SOCRATES: Good. Then what sort of attention to the gods will piety be?

EUTHYPHRO: The sort of attention, Socrates, slaves pay to their masters.

SOCRATES: I understand; then it is a kind of service to the gods?

EUTHYPHRO: Certainly.

SOCRATES: Can you tell me what result the art which serves a doctor serves to produce? Is it not health?

EUTHYPHRO: Yes.

SOCRATES: And what result does the art which serves a ship-wright serve to produce?

EUTHYPHRO: A ship, of course, Socrates.

SOCRATES: The result of the art which serves a builder is a house, is it not?

EUTHYPHRO: Yes.

SOCRATES: Then tell me, my good friend: What result will the art which serves the gods serve to produce? You must know, seeing that you say that you know more about divine things than any other man.

EUTHYPHRO: Well, that is true, Socrates.

SOCRATES: Then tell me, I beg you, what is that grand result which the gods use our services to produce?

EUTHYPHRO: There are many notable results, Socrates.

SOCRATES: So are those, my friend, which a general produces. Yet it is easy to see that the crowning result of them all is victory in war, is it not?

EUTHYPHRO: Of course.

SOCRATES: And, I take it, the farmer produces many notable results; yet the principal result of them all is that he makes the earth produce food.

EUTHYPHRO: Certainly.

SOCRATES: Well, then, what is the principal result of the many notable results which the gods produce?

EUTHYPHRO: I told you just now, Socrates, that accurate knowledge of all these matters is not easily obtained. However, broadly I say this: if any man knows that his words and actions in prayer and sacrifice are acceptable to the gods, that is what is pious; and it preserves the state, as it does private families. But the opposite of what is acceptable to the gods is sacrilegious, and this it is that undermines and destroys everything.

SOCRATES: Certainly, Euthyphro, if you had wished, you could have answered my main question in far fewer words. But you are evidently not anxious to teach me. Just now, when you were on the very point of telling me what I want to know, you stopped short. If you had gone on then, I should have learned from you clearly enough by this time what piety is. But now I am asking you questions, and must follow wherever you lead me; so tell me, what is it that you mean by piety and impiety? Do you not mean a science of prayer and sacrifice?

EUTHYPHRO: I do.

SOCRATES: To sacrifice is to give to the gods, and to pray is to ask of them, is it not?

EUTHYPHRO: It is, Socrates.

SOCRATES: Then you say that piety is the science of asking of the gods and giving to them?

EUTHYPHRO: You understand my meaning exactly, Socrates.

SOCRATES: Yes, for I am eager to share your wisdom, Euthyphro, and so I am all attention; nothing that you say will fall to the ground. But tell me, what is this service of the gods? You say it is to ask of them, and to give to them?

EUTHYPHRO: I do.

SOCRATES: Then, to ask rightly will be to ask of them what we stand in need of from them, will it not?

EUTHYPHRO: Naturally.

SOCRATES: And to give rightly will be to give back to them what they stand in need of from us? It would not be very skillful to make a present to a man of something that he has no need of.

EUTHYPHRO: True, Socrates.

SOCRATES: Then piety, Euthyphro, will be the art of carrying on business between gods and men?

EUTHYPHRO: Yes, if you like to call it so.

SOCRATES: But I like nothing except what is true. But tell me, how are the gods benefited by the gifts which they receive from us? What they give is plain enough. Every good thing that we have is their gift. But how are they benefited by what we give them? Have we the advantage over them in these business transactions to such an extent that we receive from them all the good things we possess, and give them nothing in return?

EUTHYPHRO: But do you suppose, Socrates, that the gods are benefited by the gifts which they receive from us?

SOCRATES: But what *are* these gifts, Euthyphro, that we give the gods?

EUTHYPHRO: What do you think but honor and praise, and, as I have said, what is acceptable to them.

SOCRATES: Then piety, Euthyphro, is acceptable to the gods, but it is not profitable to them nor loved by them?

EUTHYPHRO: I think that nothing is more loved by them.

SOCRATES: Then I see that piety means that which is loved by the gods.

EUTHYPHRO: Most certainly.

SOCRATES: After that, shall you be surprised to find that your statements move about instead of staying where you put them? Shall you accuse me of being the Daedalus that makes them move, when you yourself are far more skillful than Daedalus was, and make them go round in a circle? Do you not see that our statement has come round to where it was before? Surely you remember that we have already seen that piety and what is pleasing to the gods are quite different things. Do you not remember?

EUTHYPHRO: I do.

SOCRATES: And now do you not see that you say that what the gods love is pious? But does not what the gods love come to the same thing as what is pleasing to the gods?

EUTHYPHRO: Certainly.

SOCRATES: Then either our former conclusion was wrong or, if it was right, we are wrong now.

EUTHYPHRO: So it seems.

SOCRATES: Then we must begin again and inquire what piety is. I do not mean to give in until I have found out. Do not regard me as unworthy; give your whole mind to the question, and this time tell me the truth. For if anyone knows it, it is you; and you are a Proteus whom I must not let go until you have told me. It cannot be that you would ever have undertaken to prosecute your aged father for the murder of a laboring man unless you had known exactly what piety and impiety are. You would have feared to risk the anger of the gods, in case you should be doing wrong, and you would have been afraid of what men would say. But now I am sure that you think that you know exactly what is pious and what is not; so tell me, my good Euthyphro, and do not conceal from me what you think.

EUTHYPHRO: Another time, then, Socrates, I am in a hurry now, and it is time for me to be off.

SOCRATES: What are you doing, my friend! Will you go away and destroy all my hopes of learning from you what is pious and what is not, and so of escaping Meletus?

I meant to explain to him that now Euthyphro has made me wise about divine things, and that I no longer in my ignorance speak carelessly about them or introduce reforms. And then I was going to promise him to live a better life for the future.

Trying Out One's New Sword

MARY MIDGELY (1919–) was born in London and educated at Oxford University. She taught at the University of Newcastle upon Tyne for many years. She has written on a variety of philosophical topics in ethics, especially on the connection between humans and nonhuman animals. She is the author of more than 50 books and articles, including *Heart and Mind* (1984), from which this selection is taken, *Science and Poetry* (2001), and *The Myths We Live By* (2004).

THINKING QUESTIONS

Mary Midgely, *Trying Out One's New Sword*

1. What is the view that Midgely calls "moral isolationism"? Why do people hold this view?
2. What does Midgely mean by "judging"? What are you doing when you judge the practices of another culture?
3. If it is not OK to make a negative judgment about another culture, is it OK to make a positive judgment about it? What do you need to know about the other culture in either case?
4. What is moral skepticism? What is Midgely's argument against it?
5. If someone accepts cultural relativism, what could he say about the example of the Samurai slicing the passerby in half? What couldn't he say?

ALL OF US ARE, MORE OR LESS, in trouble today about trying to understand cultures strange to us. We hear constantly of alien customs. We see changes in our lifetime which would have astonished our parents. I want to discuss here one very short way of dealing with this difficulty, a drastic way which many people now theoretically favour. It consists in simply denying that we can ever understand any culture except our own well enough to make judgements about it. Those who recommend this hold that the world is sharply divided into separate societies, sealed units, each with its own system of thought. They feel that the respect and tolerance due from one system to another forbids us ever to take up a critical position to any other culture. Moral judgement, they suggest, is a kind of coinage valid only in its country of origin.

I shall call this position 'moral isolationism'. I shall suggest that it is certainly not forced upon us, and indeed that it makes no sense at all. People usually take it up because they think it is a respectful attitude to other cultures. In fact, however, it is not respectful. Nobody can respect what is entirely unintelligible to them. To respect someone, we have to know enough about him to make a *favourable* judgement, however general and tentative. And we do understand people in other cultures to this extent. Otherwise a great mass of our most valuable thinking would be paralysed.

To show this, I shall take a remote example, because we shall probably find it easier to think calmly about it than we should with a contemporary one, such as female circumcision in Africa or the Chinese Cultural Revolution. The principles involved will still be the same. My example is this. There is, it seems, a verb in classical Japanese which means 'to try out one's new sword on a chance wayfarer'. (The word is *tsujigiri,* literally 'crossroads-cut'.) A samurai sword had to be tried out because, if it was to work properly, it had to slice through someone at a single blow, from the shoulder to the opposite flank. Otherwise, the warrior bungled his stroke. This could injure his honour, offend his ancestors, and even let down his emperor. So tests were needed, and wayfarers had to be expended. Any wayfarer would do—provided, of course, that he was not another Samurai. Scientists will recognize a familiar problem about the rights of experimental subjects.

Now when we hear of a custom like this, we may well reflect that we simply do not understand it; and therefore are not qualified to criticize it at all, because we are not members of that culture. But we are not members of any other culture either, except our own. So we extend the principle to cover all extraneous cultures, and we seem therefore to be moral isolationists. But this is, as we shall see, an impossible position. Let us ask what it would involve.

We must ask first: Does the isolating barrier work both ways? Are people in other cultures equally unable to criticize *us*? This question struck me sharply when I read a remark in *The Guardian* by an anthropologist about a South American Indian who had been taken into a Brazilian town for an operation, which saved his life. When he came back to his village, he made several highly critical remarks about the white Brazilians' way of life. They may very well have been justified. But the interesting point was that the anthropologist called these remarks 'a damning indictment of Western civilization'. Now the Indian had been in that town about two weeks. Was he in a position to deliver a damning indictment? Would we ourselves be qualified to deliver such an indictment on the Samurai, provided we could spend two weeks in ancient Japan? What do we really think about this?

My own impression is that we believe that outsiders can, in principle, deliver perfectly good indictments—only, it usually takes more than two weeks to make them damning. Understanding has degrees. It is not a slapdash yes-or-no matter. Intelligent outsiders can progress in it, and in some ways will be at an advantage over the locals. But if this is so, it must clearly apply to ourselves as much as anybody else.

Our next question is this: Does the isolating barrier between cultures block praise as well as blame? If I want to say that the Samurai culture has many virtues, or to praise the South American Indians, am I prevented from doing *that* by my outside status? Now, we certainly do need to praise other societies in this way. But it is hardly possible that we could praise them effectively if we could not, in principle, criticize them. Our praise would be worthless if it rested on no definite grounds, if it did not flow from some understanding. Certainly we may need to praise things which we do not *fully* understand. We say 'there's something very good here, but I can't quite make out what it is yet'. This happens when we want to learn from strangers. And we can learn from strangers. But to do this we have to distinguish between those strangers who are worth learning from and those who are not. Can we then judge which is which?

This brings us to our third question: What is involved in judging? Now plainly there is no question here of sitting on a bench in a red robe and sentencing people. Judging simply means forming an opinion, and expressing it if it is called for. Is there anything wrong about this? Naturally, we ought to avoid forming—and expressing—*crude* opinions, like that of a simple-minded missionary, who might dismiss the whole Samurai culture as entirely bad, because non-Christian. But this is a different objection. The trouble with crude opinions is that they are crude, whoever forms them, not that they are formed by the wrong people. Anthropologists, after all, are outsiders quite as much as missionaries. Moral isolationism forbids us to form *any* opinions on these matters. Its ground for doing so is that we don't understand them. But there is much that we don't understand in our own culture too. This brings us to our last question: If we can't judge other cultures, can we really judge our own? Our efforts to do so will be much damaged if we are really deprived of our opinions about other societies, because these provide the range of comparison, the spectrum of alternatives against which we set what we want to understand. We would have to stop using the mirror which anthropology so helpfully holds up to us.

In short, moral isolationism would lay down a general ban on moral reasoning. Essentially, this is the programme of immoralism, and it carries a distressing logical difficulty. Immoralists like Nietzsche are actually just a rather specialized sect of moralists. They can no more afford to put moralizing out of business than smugglers can afford to abolish customs regulations. The power of moral judgement is, in fact, not a luxury, not a perverse indulgence of the self-righteous. It is a necessity. When we judge something to be bad or good, better or worse than something else, we are taking it as an example to aim at or avoid. Without opinions of this sort, we would have no framework of comparison for our own policy, no chance of profiting by other people's insights or mistakes. In this vacuum, we could form no judgements on our own actions.

Now it would be odd if Homo sapiens had really got himself into a position as bad as this—a position where his main evolutionary asset, his brain, was so little use to him. None of us is going to accept this sceptical diagnosis. We cannot do so, because our involvement in moral isolationism does not flow from apathy, but from a rather acute concern about human hypocrisy and other forms of wickedness. But we polarize that concern around a few selected moral truths. We are rightly angry with those who despise, oppress or steamroll other cultures. We think that doing these things is actually *wrong.* But this is itself a moral judgement. We could not condemn oppression and insolence if we thought that all our condemnations were just a trivial local quirk of our own culture. We could still less do it if we tried to stop judging altogether.

Real moral scepticism, in fact, could lead only to inaction, to our losing all interest in moral questions, most of all in those which concern other societies. When we discuss these things, it becomes instantly clear how far we are from doing this. Suppose, for instance, that I criticize the bisecting Samurai, that I say his behaviour is brutal. What will usually happen next is that someone will protest, will say that I have no right to make criticisms like that of another culture. But it is most unlikely that he will use this move to end the discussion of the subject. Instead, he will justify the Samurai. He will try to fill in the background, to make me understand the custom, by explaining the exalted ideals of discipline and devotion which produced it. He will probably talk of the lower value which the ancient Japanese placed on individual life generally. He may well suggest that this is a healthier attitude than our own obsession with security. He may add, too, that the wayfarers did not seriously mind being bisected, that in principle they accepted the whole arrangement.

Now an objector who talks like this is implying that it *is* possible to understand alien customs. That is just what he is trying to make me do. And he implies, too, that if I do succeed in understanding them, I shall do something better than giving up judging them. He expects me to change my present judgement to a truer one—namely, one that is favourable. And the standards I must use to do this cannot just be Samurai standards. They have to be ones current in my own culture. Ideals like discipline and devotion will not move anybody unless he himself accepts them. As it happens, neither discipline nor devotion is very popular in the West at present. Anyone who appeals to them may well have to do some more arguing to make *them* acceptable, before he can use them to explain the Samurai. But if he does succeed here, he will have persuaded us, not just that there was something to be said for them in ancient Japan, but that there would be here as well.

Isolating barriers simply cannot arise here. If we accept something as a serious moral truth about one culture, we can't refuse to apply it—in however different an outward form—to other cultures as well, wherever circumstance admit it. If we refuse to do this, we just are not taking the other culture seriously. This becomes clear if we look at the last argument used by my objector—that of justification by consent of the victim. It is suggested that sudden bisection is quite in order, *provided* that it takes place between consenting adults. I cannot now discuss how conclusive this justification is. What I am pointing out is simply that it can only work if we believe that *consent* can make such a transaction respectable—and this is a thoroughly modern and

Western idea. It would probably never occur to a Samurai; if it did, it would surprise him very much. It is *our* standard. In applying it, too, we are likely to make another typically Western demand. We shall ask for good factual evidence that the wayfarers actually do have this rather surprising taste—that they are really willing to be bisected. In applying Western standards in this way, we are not being confused or irrelevant. We are asking the questions which arise *from where we stand,* questions which we can see the sense of. We do this because asking questions which you can't see the sense of is humbug. Certainly we can extend our questioning by imaginative effort. We can come to understand other societies better. By doing so, we may make their questions our own, or we may see that they are really forms of the questions which we are asking already. This is not impossible. It is just very hard work. The obstacles which often prevent it are simply those of ordinary ignorance, laziness and prejudice.

If there were really an isolating barrier, of course, our own culture could never have been formed. It is no sealed box, but a fertile jungle of different influences—Greek, Jewish, Roman, Norse, Celtic and so forth, into which further influences are still pouring—American, Indian, Japanese, Jamaican, you name it. The moral isolationist's picture of separate, unmixable cultures is quite unreal. People who talk about British history usually stress the value of this fertilizing mix, no doubt rightly. But this is not just an odd fact about Britain. Except for the very smallest and most remote, all cultures are formed out of many streams. All have the problem of digesting and assimilating things which, at the start, they do not understand. All have the choice of learning something from this challenge, or, alternatively, of refusing to learn, and fighting it mindlessly instead.

This universal predicament has been obscured by the fact that anthropologists used to concentrate largely on very small and remote cultures, which did not seem to have this problem. These tiny societies, which had often forgotten their own history, made neat, self-contained subjects for study. No doubt it was valuable to emphasize their remoteness, their extreme strangeness, their independence of our cultural tradition. This emphasis was, I think, the root of moral isolationism. But, as the tribal studies themselves showed, even there the anthropologists were able to interpret what they saw and make judgements—often favourable—about the tribesmen. And the tribesmen, too, were quite equal to making judgements about the anthropologists—and about the tourists and CocaCola salesmen who followed them. Both sets of judgements, no doubt, were somewhat hasty, both have been refined in the light of further experience. A similar transaction between us and the Samurai might take even longer. But that is no reason at all for deeming it impossible. Morally as well as physically, there is only one world, and we all have to live in it.

Ethical Egoism

JAMES RACHELS (1941–2003) was an undergraduate at Mercer University and earned his doctorate at the University of North Carolina. He taught philosophy at Duke University, the University of Richmond, New York University, the University of Miami and, for the last 25 years of his life, at the University of Alabama-Birmingham. Dr. Rachels wrote numerous books and articles, including several widely used philosophy textbooks. His work in both theoretical and applied ethics, especially on topics such as euthanasia and the treatment of animals, remains influential.

THINKING QUESTIONS

James Rachels, *Ethical Egoism*

1. What is ethical egoism? How is egoism different from our traditional views about ethics?
2. Why wouldn't ethical egoists lie, steal, and cheat, even though they don't believe that they have an obligation to others not to do so?
3. What does Ayn Rand mean by "the ethics of altruism"? Why do the ethics of altruism demand "sacrificing one's life"?
4. Rachels claims that the most serious problem with egoism is that it is arbitrary. What does he mean by this, and why is arbitrariness a bad thing for an ethical theory?

IS THERE A DUTY TO HELP STARVING PEOPLE?

Each year millions of people die of malnutrition and related health problems. A common pattern among children in poor countries is death from dehydration caused by diarrhea brought on by malnutrition. The executive director of the United Nations Children's Fund (UNICEF) has estimated that about 15,000 children die in this way every day. That comes to 5,475,000 children annually. If we add those who die from other preventable causes, the number goes over 10 million. Even if this estimate is too high, the number that die is staggering.

For those of us in the affluent countries, this poses an acute problem. We spend money on ourselves, not only for the necessities of life but for countless luxuries—for fine automobiles, fancy clothes, stereos, sports, movies, and so on. In our country, even people with modest incomes enjoy such things. The problem is that we could forgo our luxuries and give the money for famine relief instead. The fact that we don't suggests that we regard our luxuries as more important than their lives.

Why do we allow people to starve when we could save them? Few of us actually believe our luxuries are that important. Most of us, if asked the question directly, would probably be a bit embarrassed, and we would say that we probably should do more to help. The explanation of why we do not is, at least in part, that we hardly ever think of the problem. Living our own comfortable lives, we are insulated from it. The starving people are dying at some distance from us; we do not see them and we can avoid even thinking of them. When we do think of them, it is only abstractly, as statistics. Unfortunately for the hungry, statistics do not have much power to move us.

We respond differently when there is a "crisis," when a great mass of people in one place are starving, as in Ethiopia in 1984 or Somalia in 1992. Then, it is front-page news and relief efforts are mobilized. But when the needy are scattered, the situation does not seem so pressing. The 5,475,000 children are unfortunate that they are not all gathered in, say, Chicago.

But leaving aside the question of why we behave as we do, what is our duty? What *should* we do? We might think of this as the "commonsense" view of the matter: Morality requires that we balance our own interests against the interests of others. It is understandable, of course, that we look out for our own interests, and no one can be faulted for attending to their own basic needs. But at the same time the needs of others are also important, and when we can help others—especially at little cost to ourselves—we should do so. So, if you have an extra 10 dollars, and giving it to a famine-relief agency would help to save the life of a child, then commonsense morality would say that you should give the money.

This way of thinking involves a general assumption about our moral duties: It is assumed that we have moral duties to other people, and not merely duties that we create, such as by making a promise or incurring a debt. We have "natural" duties to others *simply because they are people who could be helped or harmed by what we do.* If a certain action would benefit (or harm) other people, then that is a reason why we should (or should not) do that action. The commonsense assumption is that other people's interests *count,* for their own sakes, from a moral point of view.

But one person's common sense is another person's naive platitude. Some thinkers have maintained that, in fact, we have no "natural" duties to other people. Ethical Egoism is the idea that each person ought to pursue his or her own self-interest exclusively. It is different from Psychological Egoism, which is a theory of human nature concerned with how people *do* behave. Psychological Egoism says that people do in fact always pursue their own interests. Ethical Egoism, by contrast, is a normative theory—that is, a theory about how we *ought* to behave. Regardless of how we do behave, Ethical Egoism says that our only duty is to do what is best for ourselves.

It is a challenging theory. It contradicts some of our deepest moral beliefs—beliefs held by most of us, at any rate—and it is not easy to refute.

We will examine the most important arguments for and against it. If it turns out to be true, then of course that is immensely important. But even if it turns out to be false, there is still much to be learned from examining it, for we may gain some insight into the reasons why we *do* have obligations to other people.

But before looking at the arguments, we should be a little clearer about exactly what this theory says and what it does not say. In the first place, Ethical Egoism does not say that one should promote one's own interests *as well as* the interests of others. That would be an ordinary, commonsensical view. Ethical Egoism is the radical view that one's *only* duty is to promote one's own interests. According to Ethical Egoism, there is only one ultimate principle of conduct, the principle of self-interest, and this principle sums up all of one's natural duties and obligations.

However, Ethical Egoism does not say that you should *avoid* actions that help others. It may happen in many instances that your interests coincide with the interests of others, so that in helping yourself you will be helping them willy-nilly. Or it may happen that aiding others is an effective means for creating some benefit for yourself. Ethical Egoism does not forbid such actions; in fact, it may recommend them. The theory insists only that in such cases the benefit to others is not what makes the act right. What makes the act right is, rather, the fact that it is to one's own advantage.

Finally, Ethical Egoism does not imply that in pursuing one's interests one ought always to do what one wants to do, or what gives one the most pleasure in the short run. Someone may want to drink a lot or smoke cigarettes or take drugs or waste his best years at the racetrack. Ethical Egoism would frown on all this, regardless of the momentary pleasure it brings. Ethical Egoism says that a person ought to do what really is in his or her own best interests, over the long run. It endorses selfishness, but it doesn't endorse foolishness. . . .

IN SUPPORT OF ETHICAL EGOISM: AYN RAND'S ARGUMENT

Ayn Rand is not much read by philosophers, largely because the leading ideas associated with her name—that capitalism is a morally superior economic system, and that morality demands absolute respect for the rights of individuals—are developed more rigorously by other writers. Nevertheless, she was a charismatic figure who attracted a devoted following during her lifetime, and today, two decades after her death, the Ayn Rand industry is still going strong. Among 20th-century writers, the idea of Ethical Egoism is probably more closely associated with her than with anyone else.

Ayn Rand regarded the ethics of "altruism" as a totally destructive idea, both in society as a whole and in the lives of individuals taken in by it. Altruism, to her way of thinking, leads to a denial of the value of the individual. It says to a person: Your life is merely something that may be sacrificed. "If a man accepts the ethics of altruism," she writes, "his first concern is not how to live his life, but how to sacrifice it." Those who promote the ethics of altruism are beneath contempt—they are parasites who, rather than working to build and sustain their own lives, leech off those who do. She writes:

> Parasites, moochers, looters, brutes and thugs can be of no value to a human being—nor can he gain any benefit from living in a society geared to *their* needs, demands and protections, a society that treats him as a sacrificial animal and penalizes him for his virtues in order to reward *them* for their vices, which means: a society based on the ethics of altruism.

By "sacrificing one's life" Rand does not mean anything so dramatic as dying. A person's life consists, in part, of projects undertaken and goods earned and created. Thus to demand that a person abandon his projects or give up his goods is an effort to "sacrifice his life."

Rand also suggests that there is a metaphysical basis for egoistic ethics. Somehow, it is the only ethics that takes seriously the *reality* of the individual person. She bemoans "the enormity of the extent to which altruism erodes men's capacity to grasp . . . the value of an individual life; it reveals a mind from which the reality of a human being has been wiped out."

What, then, of the hungry children? It might be argued that Ethical Egoism itself "reveals a mind from which the reality of a human being has been wiped out"—namely, the human being who is starving. But Rand quotes with approval the answer given by one of her followers: "Once, when Barbara Brandon was asked by a student: 'What will happen to the poor . . . ?' she answered: 'If *you* want to help them, you will not be stopped.' "

All these remarks are, I think, part of one continuous argument that can be summarized like this:

1. A person has only one life to live. If we value the individual—that is, if the individual has moral worth—then we must agree that this life is of supreme importance. After all, it is all one has, and all one is.
2. The ethics of altruism regards the life of the individual as something one must be ready to sacrifice for the good of others. Therefore, the ethics of altruism does not take seriously the value of the human individual.
3. Ethical Egoism, which allows each person to view his or her own life as being of ultimate value, does take the human individual seriously—it is, in fact, the only philosophy that does so.
4. Thus, Ethical Egoism is the philosophy that we ought to accept.

One problem with this argument, as you may already have noticed, is that it assumes we have only two choices: Either we accept the "ethics of altruism" or we accept Ethical Egoism. The choice is then made to look obvious by picturing "the ethics of altruism" as an insane doctrine that only an idiot would accept—"the ethics of altruism" is said to be the view that one's own interests have *no* value, and that one must be ready to sacrifice oneself *totally* any time *anybody* asks it. If this is the alternative, then any other view, including Ethical Egoism, will look good by comparison.

But that is hardly a fair picture of the choices. What we called the commonsense view stands between the two extremes. It says that one's own interests and the interests of others are *both* important and must be balanced against one another. Sometimes, when the balancing is done, it will turn out that one should act in the interests of others; at other times, it will turn out that one should take care for oneself. So even if we should reject the extreme "ethics of altruism," it does not follow that we must accept the other extreme of Ethical Egoism, because there is a middle way available. . . .

AGAINST ETHICAL EGOISM

Ethical Egoism haunts moral philosophy. It is not a popular doctrine; the most important philosophers have rejected it outright. But it has never been very far from their minds. Although no thinker of consequence has defended it, almost everyone has felt it necessary to explain why he was rejecting it, as though the very possibility that it might be correct was hanging in the air, threatening to smother their other ideas. As the merits of the various "refutations" have been debated, philosophers have returned to it again and again.

Curiously, philosophers have not paid much attention to what you might think is the most obvious argument against Ethical Egoism, namely that it would endorse wicked actions—provided, of course, that those actions benefit the person who does them. Here are some examples, taken from various newspapers: To increase his profits, a pharmacist filled prescriptions for cancer-patients using watered-down drugs. A nurse raped two patients while they were unconscious. A paramedic gave emergency patients injections of sterile water rather than morphine, so that he could sell the morphine. Parents fed a baby acid so that they could fake a lawsuit, claiming the baby's formula was tainted. A 13-year-old girl was kidnapped by a neighbor and kept shackled in an underground bomb-shelter for 181 days, while she was sexually abused.

Suppose that, by doing such things, someone could actually gain some benefit for himself. Of course, this means that he would have to avoid being caught. But if he could get away with it, wouldn't Ethical Egoism have to say that such actions are permissible? This seems enough by itself to discredit the doctrine. I believe this is a valid complaint; nonetheless, one might think that it begs the question against Ethical Egoism, because in saying that these actions are wicked, we are appealing to a nonegoistic conception of wickedness. So we might ask if there isn't some further problem with Ethical Egoism, that doesn't beg the question. . . .

The Argument That Ethical Egoism Is Unacceptably Arbitrary. . . . we come to the argument that I think comes closest to an outright refutation of Ethical Egoism. It is also the most interesting of the arguments, because it provides some insight into why the interests of other people *should* matter to us. But before presenting this argument, we need to look briefly at a general point about moral values. So let us set Ethical Egoism aside for a moment and consider this related matter.

There is a whole family of moral views that have this in common: They all involve dividing people into groups and saying that the interests of some groups count for more than the interests of other groups. Racism is the most conspicuous example; racism divides people into groups according to race and assigns greater importance to the interests of one race than to others. The practical result is that members of one race are treated better than the others. Anti-Semitism works the same way, and so can nationalism. People in the grip of such views will think, in effect: "*My* race counts for more," or "Those who believe in *my* religion count for more," or "*My* country counts for more," and so on.

Can such views be defended? The people who accept such views are usually not much interested in argument—racists, for example, rarely try to offer rational grounds for their beliefs. But suppose they did. What could they say?

There is a general principle that stands in the way of any such defense, namely: *We can justify treating people differently only if we can show that there is some factual difference between them that is relevant to justifying the difference in treatment.* For example, if one person is admitted to law school while another is rejected, this might be justified by pointing out that the first graduated from college with honors and scored well on the admissions test, while the second dropped out of college and never took the test. However, if both graduated with honors and did well on the entrance examination—if they are in all relevant respects equally well qualified—then it is merely arbitrary to admit one but not the other.

So, we must ask: Can a racist point to any differences between, say, white people and black people that would justify treating them differently? In the past, racists have sometimes attempted to do this by picturing blacks as stupid, lacking in ambition, and the like. If this were true, then it might justify treating them differently, in at least some circumstances. (This is the deep purpose of racist stereotypes, to provide the "relevant differences" needed to justify differences in treatment.) But of course it is not true, and in fact there are no such general differences between the races. Thus racism is an arbitrary doctrine, in that it advocates treating people differently even though there are no differences between them to justify it.

Ethical Egoism is a moral theory of the same type. It advocates that each of us divide the world into two categories of people—ourselves and all the rest—and that we regard the interests of those in the first group as more important than the interests of those in the second group. But each of us can ask, what is the difference between me and everyone else that justifies placing myself in this special category? Am I more intelligent? Do I enjoy my life more? Are my accomplishments greater? Do I have needs or abilities that are so different from the needs or abilities of others? In short, *what makes me so special?* Failing an answer, it turns out that Ethical Egoism is an arbitrary doctrine, in the same way that racism is arbitrary. And this, in addition to explaining why Ethical Egoism is unacceptable, also sheds some light on the question of why we should care about others.

We should care about the interests of other people for the same reason we care about our own interests; for their needs and desires are comparable to our own. Consider, one last time, the starving children we could feed by giving up some of our luxuries. Why should we care about them? We care about ourselves, of course—if we were starving, we would go to almost any lengths to get food. But what is the difference between us and them? Does hunger affect them any less? Are they somehow less deserving than we? If we can find no relevant difference between us and them, then we must admit that if our needs should be met, so should theirs. It is this realization, that we are on a par with one another, that is the deepest reason why our morality must include some recognition of the needs of others, and why, then, Ethical Egoism fails as a moral theory.

The Principle of Utility

JEREMY BENTHAM (1748–1832) was born in London and educated at Queen's College, Oxford University. An outspoken advocate of political and social reform, Bentham wrote widely on economics, politics, and political philosophy. His most famous work was *An Introduction to the Principles of Morals and Legislation* published in 1789. He is regarded as the founder of the utilitarian view in ethics and political philosophy, and greatly influenced the work of John Stuart Mill. In his will, Bentham directed that his body be preserved, dressed in his clothes, and made available for public display. You can see a picture of Bentham's "auto-icon" at http://www.ucl.ac.uk/Bentham-Project/info/jb.htm.

THINKING QUESTIONS

Jeremy Bentham, *The Principle of Utility*

1. What does Bentham mean by the "principle of utility"?
2. What does it mean to say that an action "ought to be done" according to Bentham?
3. Bentham offers a method by which the happiness, pleasure, or utility that results from an action can be summed up, the so-called "hedonistic calculus." Why does utilitarianism need such a calculus?
4. What are the seven elements of the hedonistic calculus? How do they work together to give a total amount of happiness?
5. Is adding up the happiness or pleasure that results from your actions really possible? What would you have to know about others to accomplish it?

I. Nature has placed mankind under the governance of two sovereign masters, *pain* and *pleasure*. It is for them alone to point out what we ought to do, as well as to determine what we shall do. On the one hand the standard of right and wrong, on the other the chain of causes and effects, are fastened to their throne. They govern us in all we do, in all we say, in all we think: every effort we can make to throw off our subjection, will serve but to demonstrate and confirm it. In words a man may pretend to abjure their empire: but in reality he will remain subject to it all the while. The *principle of utility* recognizes this subjection, and assumes it for the foundation of that system, the object of which is to rear the fabric of felicity by the hands of reason and of law.

Systems which attempt to question it, deal in sounds instead of sense, in caprice instead of reason, in darkness instead of light.

But enough of metaphor and declamation: it is not by such means that moral science is to be improved.

II. The principle of utility is the foundation of the present work: it will be proper therefore at the outset to give an explicit and determinate account of what is meant by it. By the principle of utility is meant that principle which approves or disapproves of every action whatsoever, according to the tendency it appears to have to augment or diminish the happiness of the party whose interest is in question: or, what is the same thing in other words to promote or to oppose that happiness. I say of every action whatsoever, and therefore not only of every action of a private individual, but of every measure of government.

III. By utility is meant that property in any object, whereby it tends to produce benefit, advantage, pleasure, good, or happiness, (all this in the present case comes to the same thing) or (what comes again to the same thing) to prevent the happening of mischief, pain, evil, or unhappiness to the party whose interest is considered: if that party be the community in general, then the happiness of the community: if a particular individual, then the happiness of that individual.

IV. The interest of the community is one of the most general expressions that can occur in the phraseology of morals: no wonder that the meaning of it is often lost. When it has a meaning, it is this. The community is a fictitious *body,* composed of the individual persons who are considered as constituting as it were its *members.* The interest of the community then is, what is it?—the sum of the interests of the several members who compose it.

V. It is in vain to talk of the interest of the community, without understanding what is the interest of the individual. A thing is said to promote the interest, or to be *for* the interest, of an individual, when it tends to add to the sum total of his pleasures: or, what comes to the same thing, to diminish the sum total of his pains.

VI. An action then may be said to be conformable to the principle of utility, or, for shortness sake, to utility, (meaning with respect to the community at large) when the tendency it has to augment the happiness of the community is greater than any it has to diminish it.

VALUE OF A LOT OF PLEASURE OR PAIN, HOW TO BE MEASURED

I. Pleasures then, and the avoidance of pains, are the *ends* that the legislator has in view; it behooves him therefore to understand their *value.* Pleasures and pains are the instruments he has to work with: it behooves him therefore to understand their force, which is again, in other words, their value.

II. To a person considered by *himself,* the value of a pleasure or pain considered *by itself,* will be greater or less, according to the four following circumstances:

1. Its *intensity.*
2. Its *duration.*
3. Its *certainty* or *uncertainty.*
4. Its *propinquity* or *remoteness.*

III. These are the circumstances which are to be considered in estimating a pleasure or a pain considered each of them by itself. But when the value of any pleasure or pain is considered for the purpose of estimating the tendency of any *act* by which it is produced, there are two other circumstances to be taken into the account; these are,

5. Its *fecundity,* or the chance it has of being followed by sensations of the *same* kind: that is, pleasures, if it be a pleasure: pains, if it be a pain.
6. Its *purity,* or the chance it has of not being followed by sensations of the *opposite* kind: that is, pains, if it be a pleasure: pleasures, if it be a pain.

These two last, however, are in strictness scarcely to be deemed properties of the pleasure or the pain itself; they are not, therefore, in strictness to be taken into the account of the value of that pleasure or that pain. They are in strictness to be deemed properties only of the act, or other event, by which such pleasure or pain has been produced; and accordingly are only to be taken into the account of the tendency of such act or such event.

IV. To a *number* of persons, with reference to each of whom to the value of a pleasure or a pain is considered, it will be greater or less, according to seven circumstances: to wit, the six preceding ones; viz.

1. Its *intensity.*
2. Its *duration.*
3. Its *certainty* or *uncertainty.*
4. Its *propinquity* or *remoteness.*
5. Its *fecundity.*
6. Its *purity.*

And one other; to wit:

7. Its *extent;* that is, the number of persons to whom it *extends;* or (in other words) who are affected by it.

V. To take an exact account then of the general tendency of any act, by which the interests of a community are affected, proceed as follows. Begin with any one person of those whose interests seem most immediately to be affected by it: and take an account,

1. Of the value of each distinguishable *pleasure* which appears to be produced by it in the *first* instance.

2. Of the value of each *pain* which appears to be produced by it in the *first* instance.
3. Of the value of each pleasure which appears to be produced by it *after* the first. This constitutes the *fecundity* of the first *pleasure* and the *impurity* of the first *pain.*
4. Of the value of each *pain* which appears to be produced by it after the first. This constitutes the *fecundity* of the first *pain,* and the *impurity* of the first pleasure.
5. Sum up all the values of all the *pleasures* on the one side, and those of all the pains on the other. The balance, if it be on the side of pleasure, will give the *good* tendency of the act upon the whole, with respect to the interests of that *individual* person; if on the side of pain, the *bad* tendency of it upon the whole.
6. Take an account of the *number* of persons whose interests appear to be concerned; and repeat the above process with respect to each. *Sum up* the numbers expressive of the degrees of *good* tendency, which the act has, with respect to each individual, in regard to whom the tendency of it is *good* upon the whole: do this again with respect to each individual, in regard to whom the tendency of it is *good* upon the whole: do this again with respect to each individual, in regard to whom the tendency of it is *bad* upon the whole. Take the *balance* which if on the side of *pleasure,* will give the general *good tendency* of the act, with respect to the total number or community of individuals concerned; if on the side of pain, the general *evil tendency,* with respect to the same community.

VI. It is not to be expected that this process should be strictly pursued previously to every moral judgment, or to every legislative or judicial operation. It may, however, be always kept in view: and as near as the process actually pursued on these occasions approaches to it, so near will such process approach to the character of an exact one.

VII. The same process is alike applicable to pleasure and pain, in whatever shape they appear: and by whatever denomination they are distinguished: to pleasure, whether it be called *good* (which is properly the cause or instrument of pleasure) or *profit* (which is distant pleasure, or the cause or instrument of, distant pleasure,) or *convenience,* or *advantage, benefit, emolument, happiness,* and so forth: to pain, whether it be called *evil,* (which corresponds to *good*) or *mischief,* or *inconvenience,* or *disadvantage,* or *loss,* or *unhappiness,* and so forth.

VIII. Nor is this a novel and unwarranted, any more than it is a useless, theory. In all this there is nothing but what the practice of mankind, wheresoever they have a clear view of their own interest, is perfectly conformable to. An article of property, an estate in land, for instance, is valuable, on what account? On account of the pleasures of all kinds which it enables a man to produce, and what comes to the same thing the pains of all kinds which it enables him to avert. But the value of such an article of property is universally understood to rise or fall according to the length or shortness of the time which a man has in it: the certainty or uncertainty of its coming into possession: and the nearness or remoteness of the time at which, if at all, it is to come into possession. As to the *intensity* of the pleasures which a man may derive from it, this is never thought of, because it depends upon the use which each particular person may come to make of it; which cannot be estimated till the particular pleasures he may come to derive from it, or the particular pains he may come to exclude by means of it, are brought to view. For the same reason, neither does he think of the *fecundity* or *purity* of those pleasures.

Utilitarianism

JOHN STUART MILL (1806–1873) was one of the most important philosophers of the 19th century, especially in the areas of ethics and political philosophy. Recognized as a prodigy at a very young age, Mill could read Latin and Greek by the age of seven. Having received a thorough education at home, Mill never attended university and instead started to work at the East India Company at the age of 17, working there all his professional life. Among Mill's most famous works are *On Liberty* (1859), *Utilitarianism* (1863), and *The Subjection of Women* (1869) in which he argues for equal civil rights for women, a very radical view at the time. Mill was one of the main proponents of the utilitarian view of ethics. Leaving England for France, he died at Avignon in 1873.

THINKING QUESTIONS

John Stuart Mill, *Utilitarianism*

1. What does Mill give as the "Greatest Happiness Principle"?
2. What is the fundamental value which we are supposed to maximize in all of our actions, according to utilitarianism?
3. In any situation of choice, which action ought I do, according to utilitarianism?
4. What is the distinction between higher and lower pleasures, according to Mill? Why does he think he needs to make this distinction?
5. How does Mill defend the claim that the higher pleasures are better? Do you think that his appeal to "competent judges" is a good argument?
6. What does Mill mean when he says that utilitarianism is accused of setting a standard "too high for humanity"? How does he respond to this criticism?

WHAT UTILITARIANISM IS

. . . Those who know anything about the matter are aware that every writer, from Epicurus to Bentham, who maintained the theory of utility, meant by it, not something to be contradistinguished from pleasure, but pleasure itself, together with exemption from pain; and instead of opposing the useful to the agreeable or the ornamental, have always declared that the useful means these, among other things. . . .

The creed which accepts as the foundation of morals, Utility, or the Greatest Happiness Principle, holds that actions are right in proportion as they tend to promote happiness, wrong as they tend to produce the reverse of happiness. By happiness is intended pleasure, and the absence of pain; by unhappiness, pain, and the privation of pleasure. To give a clear view of the moral standard set up by the theory, much more requires to be said; in particular, what things it includes in the ideas of pain and pleasure; and to what extent this is left an open question. But these supplementary explanations do not affect the theory of life on which this theory of morality is grounded—namely, that pleasure, and freedom from pain, are the only things desirable as ends; and that all desirable things (which are as numerous in the utilitarian as in any other scheme) are desirable either for the pleasure inherent in themselves, or as means to the promotion of pleasure and the prevention of pain.

Now, such a theory of life excites in many minds, and among them in some of the most estimable in feeling and purpose, inveterate dislike. To suppose that life has (as they express it) no higher end than pleasure—no better and nobler object of desire and pursuit—they designate as utterly mean and groveling; as a doctrine worthy only of swine, to whom the followers of Epicurus were, at a very early period, contemptuously likened; and modern holders of the doctrine are occasionally made the subject of equally polite comparisons by its German, French, and English assailants.

When thus attacked, the Epicureans have always answered, that it is not they, but their accusers, who represent human nature in a degrading light; since the accusation supposes human beings to be capable of no pleasures except those of which swine are capable. . . . Human beings have faculties more elevated than the animal appetites, and when once made conscious of them, do not regard anything as happiness which does not include their gratification. . . . It is quite compatible with the principle of utility to recognize the fact, that some *kinds* of pleasure are more desirable and more valuable than others. It would be absurd that while, in estimating all other things, quality is considered as well as quantity, the estimation of pleasures should be supposed to depend on quantity alone.

If I am asked, what I mean by difference of quality in pleasures, or what makes one pleasure more valuable than another, merely as a pleasure, except its being greater in amount, there is but one possible answer. Of two pleasures, if there be one to which all or almost all who have experience of both give a decided preference, irrespective of any feeling of moral obligation to prefer it, that is the more desirable pleasure. If one of the two is, by those who are competently acquainted with both, placed so far above the other that they prefer it, even though knowing it to be attended with a greater amount of discontent, and would not resign it for any quantity of the other pleasure which their nature is capable of, we are justified in ascribing to the preferred enjoyment a superiority in quality, so far outweighing quantity as to render it, in comparison, of small account.

Now it is an unquestionable fact that those who are equally acquainted with, and equally capable of appreciating and enjoying, both, do give a most marked preference to the manner of existence which employs their higher faculties. Few human creatures would consent to be changed into any of the lower animals, for a promise of the fullest allowance of a beast's pleasures; no intelligent human being would consent to be a fool, no instructed person would be an ignoramus, no person of feeling and conscience would be selfish and base, even though they should be persuaded that the fool, the dunce, or the rascal is better satisfied with his lot than they are with theirs. They would not resign what they possess more than he for the most complete satisfaction of all the desires which they have in common with him. If they ever fancy they would, it is only in cases of unhappiness so extreme, that to escape from it they would exchange their lot for almost any other, however undesirable in their own eyes. A being of higher faculties requires more to make him happy, is capable probably of more acute suffering, and certainly accessible to it at more points, than one of an inferior type; but in spite of these liabilities, he can never really wish to sink into what he feels to be a lower grade of existence. . . . It is indisputable that the being whose capacities of enjoyment are low, has the greatest chance of having them fully satisfied; and a highly endowed being will always feel that any happiness which he can look for, as the world is constituted, is imperfect. But he can learn to bear its imperfections, if they are at all bearable; and they will not make him envy the being who is indeed unconscious of the imperfections, but only because he feels not at all the good which those imperfections qualify. It is better to be a human being dissatisfied than a pig satisfied; better to be Socrates dissatisfied than a fool satisfied. And if the fool, or the pig, are a different opinion, it is because they only know their own side of the question. The other party to the comparison knows both sides.

It may be objected, that many who are capable of the higher pleasures, occasionally, under the influence of temptation, postpone them to the lower. But this is quite compatible with a full appreciation of the intrinsic superiority of the higher. Men often, from infirmity of character, make their election for the nearer good, though they know it to be the less valuable; and this no less when the choice is between two bodily pleasures, than when it is between bodily and mental. They pursue sensual indulgences to the injury of health, though perfectly aware that health is the greater good. It may be further objected, that many who begin with youthful enthusiasm for everything noble, as they advance in years sink into indolence and selfishness. But I do not believe that those who undergo this very common change, voluntarily choose the lower description of pleasures in preference to the higher. I believe that before they devote themselves exclusively to the one, they have already become incapable of the other. Capacity for the nobler feelings is in most natures a very tender plant, easily killed, not only by hostile influences, but by mere want of sustenance; and in the majority of young persons it speedily dies away if the occupations to which their position in life has devoted them, and the society into which it has thrown them, are not favourable to keeping that higher capacity in exercise. Men lose their high aspirations as they lose their intellectual tastes, because they have not time or opportunity for indulging them; and they addict themselves to inferior pleasures, not because they deliberately prefer them, but because they are either the only ones to which they have access, or the only ones which they are any longer capable of enjoying. It may be questioned whether any one who has remained equally susceptible to both classes of pleasures, ever knowingly and calmly preferred the lower; though many, in all ages, have broken down in an ineffectual attempt to combine both.

From this verdict of the only competent judges, I apprehend there can be no appeal. On a question which is the best worth having of two pleasures, or which of two modes of existence is the most grateful to the feelings, apart from its moral attributes and from its consequences, the judgment of those who are qualified by knowledge of both, or, if they differ, that of the majority among them, must be admitted as final. And there needs be the less hesitation to accept this judgment respecting the quality of pleasures, since there is no other tribunal to be referred to even on the question of quantity. What means are there of determining which is the acutest of two pains, or the intensest of two pleasurable sensations, except the general suffrage of those who are familiar with both? Neither pains nor pleasures are homogeneous, and pain is always heterogeneous with pleasure. What is there to decide whether a particular pleasure is worth purchasing at the cost of a particular pain, except the feelings and judgment of the experienced? When, therefore, those feelings and judgment declare the pleasures derived from the higher faculties to be preferable *in kind,* apart from the question of intensity, to those of which the animal nature, disjoined from the higher faculties, is susceptible, they are entitled on this subject to the same regard.

According to the Greatest Happiness Principle, as above explained, the ultimate end, with reference to and for the sake of which all other things are desirable (whether we are considering our own good or that of other people), is an existence exempt as far as possible from pain, and as rich as possible in enjoyments, both in point of quantity and quality; the test of quality, and the rule for measuring it against quantity, being the preference felt by those who in their opportunities of experience, to which must be added their habits of self-consciousness and self-observation, are best furnished with the means of comparison. This, being, according to the utilitarian opinion, the end of human action, is necessarily also the standard of morality; which may accordingly be defined, the rules and precepts for human conduct, by the observance of which an existence such as has been described might be, to the greatest extent possible, secured to all mankind; and not to them only, but, so far as the nature of things admits, to the whole sentient creation. . . .

Against this doctrine, however, arises another class of objectors, who say that happiness, in any form, cannot be the rational purpose of human life and action; because, in the first place, it is unattainable. . . .

The first of these objections would go to the root of the matter were it well founded; for if no happiness is to be had at all by human beings, the attainment of it cannot be the end of morality, or of any rational conduct. . . . When, however, it is thus positively asserted to be impossible that human life should be happy, the assertion, if not something like a verbal quibble, is at least an exaggeration. If by happiness be meant a continuity of highly pleasurable excitement, it is evident enough that this is impossible. A state of exalted pleasure lasts only moments, or in some cases, and with some intermissions, hours or days, and is the occasional brilliant flash of enjoyment, not its permanent and steady flame. Of this the philosophers who have taught that happiness is the end of life were as fully aware as those who taunt them. The happiness which they meant was not a life of rapture; but moments of such, in an existence made up of few and transitory pains, many and various pleasures, with a decided predominance of the active over the passive, and having as the foundation of the whole, not to expect more from life than it is capable of bestowing. A life thus composed, to those who have been fortunate enough to obtain it, has always appeared worthy of the name of happiness. And such an existence is even now the lot of many, during some considerable portion of their lives. The present wretched education, and wretched social arrangements, are the only real hindrance to its being attainable by almost all. . . .

I must again repeat, what the assailants of utilitarianism seldom have the justice to acknowledge, that the happiness which forms the utilitarian standard of what is right in conduct, is not the agent's own happiness, but that of all concerned. As between his own happiness and that of others, utilitarianism requires him to be as strictly impartial as a disinterested and benevolent spectator. In the golden rule of Jesus of Nazareth, we read the complete spirit of the ethics of utility. To do as you would be done by, and to love your neighbour as yourself, constitute the ideal perfection of utilitarian morality. As the means of making the nearest approach to this ideal, utility would enjoin, first, that laws and social arrangements should place the happiness, or (as speaking practically it may be called) the interest, of every individual, as nearly as possible in harmony with the interest of the whole; and secondly, that education and opinion, which have so vast a power over human character, should so use that power as to establish in the mind of every individual an indissoluble association between his own happiness and the good of the whole; especially between his own happiness and the practice of such modes of conduct, negative and positive, as regard for the universal happiness prescribes; so that not only he may be unable to conceive the possibility of happiness to himself, consistently with conduct opposed to the general good, but also that a direct impulse to promote the general good may be in every individual one of the habitual motives of action, and the sentiments connected therewith may fill a large and prominent place in every human being's sentient existence. If the impugners of the utilitarian morality represented it to their own minds in this its true character, I know not what recommendation possessed by any other morality they could possibly affirm to be wanting to it; what more beautiful or more exalted developments of human nature any other ethical system can be supposed to foster, or what springs of action, not accessible to the utilitarian, such systems rely on for giving effect to their mandates.

The objectors to utilitarianism cannot always be charged with representing it in a discreditable light. On the contrary, those among them who entertain anything like a just idea of its disinterested character, sometimes find fault with its standard as being too high for humanity. They say it is exacting too much to require that people shall always act from the inducement of promoting the general interests of society. But this is to mistake the very meaning of a standard of morals, and confound the rule of action with the motive of it. It is the business of ethics to tell us what are our duties, or by what test we may know them; but no system of ethics requires that the sole motive of all we do shall be a feeling of duty; on the contrary, ninety-nine hundredths of all our actions are done from other motives, and rightly so done, if the rule of duty does not condemn them. It is the more unjust to utilitarianism that this particular misapprehension should be made a ground of objection to it, inasmuch as utilitarian moralists have gone beyond almost all others in affirming that the motive has nothing to do with the morality of the action, though much with the worth of the agent. He who saves a fellow creature from drowning does what is morally right, whether his motive be duty, or the hope of being paid for his trouble; he who betrays the friend that trusts him, is guilty of a crime, even if his object be to serve another friend to whom he is under greater obligations. But to speak only of actions done from the motive of duty, and in direct obedience to principle: it is a misapprehension of the utilitarian mode of thought, to conceive it as implying that people should fix their minds upon so wide a generality as the world, or society at large. The great majority of good actions are intended not for the benefit of the world, but for that of individuals, of which the good of the world is made up; and the thoughts of the most virtuous man need not on these occasions travel beyond the particular persons concerned, except so far as is necessary to assure himself that in benefiting them he is not violating the rights, that is, the legitimate and authorized expectations, of any one else. . . .

Again, defenders of utility often find themselves called upon to reply to such objections as this—that there is not time, previous to action, for calculating and weighing the effects of any line of conduct on the general happiness. This is exactly as if any one were to say that it is impossible to guide our conduct by Christianity, because there is not time, on every occasion on which anything has to be done, to read through the Old and New Testaments. The answer to the objection is, that there has been ample time, namely, the whole past duration of the human species. During all that time, mankind have been learning by experience the tendencies of actions; on which experience all the prudence, as well as all the morality of life, are dependent. People talk as if the commencement of this course of experience had hitherto been put off, and as if, at the moment when some man feels tempted to meddle with the property or life of another, he had to begin considering for the first time whether murder and theft are injurious to human happiness. Even then I do not think that he would find the question very puzzling; but, at all events, the matter is now done to his hand. It is truly a whimsical supposition that, if mankind were agreed in considering utility to be the test of morality, they would remain without any agreement as to what is useful, and would take no measures for having their notions on the subject taught to the young, and enforced by law and opinion. There is no difficulty in proving any ethical standard whatever to work ill, if we suppose universal idiocy to be conjoined with it. . . .

The Categorical Imperative

IMMANUEL KANT (1724–1804) is universally considered to be among the most important and influential thinkers in the history of the Western world. The son of a saddle maker, Kant was born in Königsberg, East Prussia (now part of Poland), and lived there most of his life. Educated at the University of Königsberg, he taught there for over 40 years starting in 1755. Kant's most important works include the metaphysical treatise, *Critique of Pure Reason* (1781) and his brief, but very influential work on ethics, *Foundations of the Metaphysics of Morals* (1785). Kant is one of the main proponents of the deontological view of ethics.

THINKING QUESTIONS

Immanuel Kant, *The Categorical Imperative*

1. What does Kant mean by a "good will"?
2. What is the difference between hypothetical imperatives and categorical imperatives? How do they "command" us differently?
3. What does Kant mean by "universal law" in the first formulation of the categorical imperative? How is treating moral rules as universal similar to some of our everyday moral beliefs?
4. What does it mean to treat others as an "end in itself" as stated in the second formulation of the categorical imperative?
5. Read the two formulations of the categorical imperative that Kant gives. How are they alike? (Kant thought that they were identical.) How are they different?

THE GOOD WILL AS GOOD IN ITSELF

Nothing in the world—indeed nothing even beyond the world—can possibly be conceived which could be called good without qualification except a *good will*. Intelligence, wit, judgment, and the other talents of the mind, however they may be named, or courage, resoluteness, and perseverence as qualities of temperament are doubtless in many respects good and desirable. But they can become extremely bad and harmful if the will, which is to make use of these gifts of nature and which in its special constitution is called character, is not good. It is the same with the gifts of fortune. Power, riches, honor, even health, general well-being, and the contentment with one's condition which is called happiness make for pride and even arrogance if there is not a good will to correct their influence on the mind and on its principles of action, so as to make it universally conformable to its end. It need hardly be mentioned that the sight of a being adorned with no feature of a pure and good will yet enjoying uninterrupted prosperity can never give pleasure to a rational impartial observer. Thus the good will seems to constitute the indispensable condition even of worthiness to be happy.

Some qualities seem to be conducive to this good will and can facilitate its action, but, in spite of that, they have no intrinsic unconditional worth. They rather presuppose a good will, which limits the high esteem which one otherwise rightly has for them and prevents their being held to be absolutely good. Moderation in emotions and passions, self-control, and calm deliberation not only are good in many respects but even seem to constitute a part of the inner worth of the person. But however unconditionally they were esteemed by the ancients, they are far from being good without qualification. For, without the principles of a good will, they can become extremely bad, and the coolness of a villain makes him not only far more dangerous but also more directly abominable in our eyes than he would have seemed without it.

The good will is not good because of what it effects or accomplishes or because of its adequacy to achieve some proposed end; it is good only because of its willing, i.e., it is good of itself. And, regarded for itself, it is to be esteemed incomparably higher than anything which could be brought about by it in favor of any inclination or even of the sum total of all inclinations. Even if it should happen that, by a particularly unfortunate fate or by the niggardly provision of a stepmotherly nature, this will should be wholly lacking in power to accomplish its purpose, and if even the greatest effort should not avail it to achieve anything of its end, and if there remained only the good will (not as a mere wish but as the summoning of all the means in our power), it would sparkle like a jewel with its own light, as something that had its full worth in itself. Usefulness or fruitlessness can neither diminish nor augment this worth. Its usefulness would be only its setting, as it were, so as to enable us to handle it more conveniently in commerce or to attract the attention of those who are not yet connoisseurs, but not to recommend it to those who are experts or to determine its worth.

But there is something so strange in this idea of the absolute worth of the will alone, in which no account is taken of any use, that, notwithstanding the agreement even of common sense, the suspicion must arise that perhaps only high-flown fancy is its hidden basis, and that we may have misunderstood the purpose of nature in its appointment of reason as the ruler of our will. We shall therefore examine this idea from this point of view.

In the natural constitution of an organized being, i.e., one suitably adapted to life, we assume as an axiom that no organ will be found for any purpose which is not the fittest and best adapted to that purpose. Now if its preservation, welfare—in a word, its happiness—were the real end of nature in a being having reason and will, then nature would have hit upon a very poor arrangement in appointing the reason of the creature to be the executor of this purpose. For all the actions which the creature has to perform with this intention, and the entire rule of its conduct, would be dictated much more exactly by instinct, and that end would be far more certainly attained by instinct than it ever could be by reason. And if, over and above this, reason should have been granted to the favored creature, it would have served only to let it contemplate the happy constitution of its nature, to admire it, to rejoice in it, and to be grateful for it to its beneficent cause. But reason would not have been given in order that the being should subject its faculty of desire to that weak and delusive guidance and to meddle with the purpose of nature. In a word, nature would have taken care that reason did not break forth into practical use nor have the presumption, with its weak insight, to think out for itself the plan of happiness and the means of attaining it. Nature would have taken over not only the choice of ends but also that of the means and with wise foresight would have intrusted both to instinct alone.

And, in fact, we find we find that the more a cultivated reason deliberately devotes itself to the enjoyment of life and happiness, the more the man falls short of true contentment. From this fact there arises in many persons, if only they are candid enough to admit it, a certain degree of misology, hatred of reason. This is particularly the case with those who are most experienced in its use. After counting all the advantages which they draw—I will not say from the invention of the arts of common luxury—from the sciences (which in the end seem to them to be also a luxury of the understanding), they nevertheless find that they have actually brought more trouble on their shoulders instead of gaining in happiness; they finally envy, rather than despise, the common run of men who are better guided by mere natural instinct and who do not permit their reason much influence on their conduct. . . .

Thus the moral worth of an action does not lie in the effect which is expected from it or in any principle of action which has to borrow its motive from this expected effect. For all these effects (agreeableness of condition, indeed even the promotion of the happiness of others) could be brought about through other causes and would not require the will of a rational being, while the highest and unconditional good can be found only in such a will. Therefore, the pre-eminent good can consist only in the conception of the law in itself (which can be present only in a rational being) so far as this conception and not the hoped-for effect is the determining ground of the will. This pre-eminent good, which we call moral, is already present in the person who acts according to this conception, and we do not have to expect it first in the result.

But what kind of a law can that be, the conception of which must determine the will without reference to the expected result? Under this condition alone the will can be called absolutely good without qualification. Since I have robbed the will of all impulses which could come to it from obedience to any law, nothing remains to serve as a principle of the will except universal conformity of its action to law as such. That is, I should never act in such a way that I could not will that my maxim should be a universal law. Mere conformity to law as such (without assuming any particular law applicable to certain actions) serves as the principle of the will, and it must serve as such a principle if duty is not to be a vain delusion and chimerical concept. The common reason of mankind in its practical judgments is in perfect agreement with this and has this principle constantly in view. . . .

ALL ACTION IS RULE GOVERNED

Everything in nature works according to laws. Only a rational being has the capacity of acting according to the conception of laws, i.e., according to principles. This capacity is will. Since reason is required for the derivation of actions from laws, will is nothing else than practical reason. If reason infallibly determines the will, the actions which such a being recognizes as objectively necessary are also subjectively necessary. That is, the will is a faculty of choosing only that which reason, independently of inclination, recognizes as practically necessary, i.e., as good. But if reason of itself does not sufficiently determine the will, and if the will is subjugated to subjective conditions (certain incentives) which do not always agree with objective conditions; in a word, if the will is not of itself in complete accord with reason (the actual case of men), then the actions which are recognized as objectively necessary are subjectively contingent, and the determination of such a will according to objective laws is constraint. That is, the relation of objective laws to a will which is not completely good is conceived as the determination of the will of a rational being by principles of reason to which this will is not by nature necessarily obedient.

The conception of an objective principle, so far as it constrains a will, is a command (of reason), and the formula of this command is called an *imperative*.

All imperatives are expressed by an "ought" and thereby indicate the relation of an objective law of reason to a will which is not in its subjective constitution necessarily determined by this law. This relation is that of constraint. Imperatives say that it would be good to do or to refrain from doing something, but they say it to a will which does not always do something simply because it is presented to it as a good thing to do. Practical good is what determines the will by means of the conception of reason and hence not by subjective causes but, rather, objectively, i.e., on grounds which are valid for every rational being as such. It is distinguished from the pleasant, as that which has an influence on the will only by means of a sensation from merely subjective causes, which hold only for the senses of this or that person and not as a principle of reason which holds for everyone.

A perfectly good will, therefore, would be equally subject to objective laws (of the good), but it could not be conceived as constrained by them to act in accord with them, because, according to its own subjective constitution, it can be determined to act only through the conception of the good. Thus no imperatives hold for the divine will or, more generally, for a holy will. The "ought" is here out of place, for the volition of itself is necessarily in unison with the law. Therefore imperatives are only formulas expressing the relation of objective laws of volition in general to the subjective imperfection of the will of this or that rational being, e.g., the human will.

All imperatives command either hypothetically or categorically. The former present the practical necessity of a possible action as a means to achieving something else which one desires (or which one may possibly desire). The categorical imperative would be one which presented an action as of itself objectively necessary, without regard to any other end. . . .

THE MORAL LAW EXPRESSED AS A CATEGORICAL IMPERATIVE

There is, therefore, only one categorical imperative. It is: Act only according to that maxim by which you can at the same time will that it should become a universal law.

Now if all imperatives of duty can be derived from this one imperative as a principle, we can at least show what we understand by the concept of duty and what it means, even though it remain undecided whether that which is called duty is an empty concept or not.

The universality of law according to which effects are produced constitutes what is properly called nature in the most general sense (as to form), i.e., the existence of things so far as it is determined by universal laws. [By analogy], then, the universal imperative of duty can be expressed as follows: Act as though the maxim of your action were by your will to become a universal law of nature.

We shall now enumerate some duties, adopting the usual division of them into duties to ourselves and to others and into perfect and imperfect duties.

1. A man who is reduced to despair by a series of evils feels a weariness with life but is still in possession of his reason sufficiently to ask whether it would not be contrary to his duty to himself to take his own life. Now he asks whether the maxim of his action could become a universal law of nature. His maxim, however, is: For love of myself, I make it my principle to shorten my life when by a longer duration it threatens more evil than satisfaction. But it is questionable whether this principle of self-love could become a universal law of nature. One immediately sees a contradiction in a system of nature, whose law would be to destroy life by the feeling whose special office is to impel the improvement of life. In this case it would not exist as nature; hence that maxim cannot obtain as a law of nature, and thus it wholly contradicts the supreme principle of all duty.

2. Another man finds himself forced by need to borrow money. He well knows that he will not be able to repay it, but he also sees that nothing will be loaned him if he does not firmly promise to repay it at a certain time. He

desires to make such a promise, but he has enough conscience to ask himself whether it is not improper and opposed to duty to relieve his distress in such a way. Now, assuming he does decide to do so, the maxim of his action would be as follows: When I believe myself to be in need of money, I will borrow money and promise to repay it, although I know I shall never do so. Now this principle of self-love or of his own benefit may very well be compatible with his whole future welfare, but the question is whether it is right. He changes the pretension of self-love into a universal law and then puts the question: How would it be if my maxim became a universal law? He immediately sees that it could never hold as a universal law of nature and be consistent with itself; rather it must necessarily contradict itself. For the universality of a law which says that anyone who believes himself to be in need could promise what he pleased with the intention of not fulfilling it would make the promise itself and the end to be accomplished by it impossible; no one would believe what was promised to him but would only laugh at any such assertion as vain pretense.

3. A third finds in himself a talent which could, by means of some cultivation, make him in many respects a useful man. But he finds himself in comfortable circumstances and prefers indulgence in pleasure to troubling himself with broadening and improving his fortunate natural gifts. Now, however, let him ask whether his maxim of neglecting his gifts, besides agreeing with his propensity to idle amusement, agrees also with what is called duty. He sees that a system of nature could indeed exist in accordance with such a law, even though man (like the inhabitants of the South Sea Islands) should let his talents rust and resolve to devote his life merely to idleness, indulgence, and propagation—in a word, to pleasure. But he cannot possibly will that this should become a universal law of nature or that it should be implanted in us by a natural instinct. For, as a rational being, he necessarily wills that all his faculties should be developed, inasmuch as they are given to him for all sorts of possible purposes.

4. A fourth man, for whom things are going well, sees that others (whom he could help) have to struggle with great hardships, and he asks, "What concern of mine is it? Let each one be as happy as heaven wills, or as he can make himself; I will not take anything from him or even envy him; but to his welfare or to his assistance in time of need I have no desire to contribute." If such a way of thinking were a universal law of nature, certainly the human race could exist, and without doubt even better than in a state where everyone talks of sympathy and good will or even exerts himself occasionally to practice them while, on the other hand, he cheats when he can and betrays or otherwise violates the rights of man. Now although it is possible that a universal law of nature according to that maxim could exist, it is nevertheless impossible to will that such a principle should hold everywhere as a law of nature. For a will which resolved this would conflict with itself, since instances can often arise in which he would need the love and sympathy of others, and in which he would have robbed himself, by such a law of nature springing from his own will, of all hope of the aid he desires.

The foregoing are a few of the many actual duties, or at least of duties we hold to be real, whose derivation from the one stated principle is clear. We must be able to will that a maxim of our action become a universal law; this is the canon of the moral estimation of our action generally. Some actions are of such a nature that their maxim cannot even be *thought* as a universal law of nature without contradiction, far from it being possible that one could will that it should be such. In others this internal impossibility is not found, though it is still impossible to *will* that their maxim should be raised to the universality of a law of nature, because such a will would contradict itself. We easily see that the former maxim conflicts with the stricter or narrower (imprescriptable) duty, the latter with broader (meritorious) duty. Thus all duties, so far as the kind of obligation (not the object of their action) is concerned, have been completely exhibited by these examples in their dependence on the one principle.

When we observe ourselves in any transgression of a duty, we find that we do not actually will that our maxim should become a universal law. That is impossible for us; rather, the contrary of this maxim should remain as a law generally, and we only take the liberty of making an exception to it for ourselves or for the sake of our inclination, and for this one occasion. Consequently, if we weighed everything from one and the same standpoint, namely, reason, we would come upon a contradiction in our own will, viz., that a certain principle is objectively necessary as a universal law and yet subjectively does not hold universally but rather admits exceptions. . . .

But suppose that there were something the existence of which in itself had absolute worth, something which, as an end in itself, could be a ground of definite laws. In it and only in it could lie the ground of a possible categorical imperative, i.e., of a practical law.

Now, I say, man and, in general, every rational being exists as an end in himself and not merely as a means to be arbitrarily used by this or that will. In all his actions, whether they are directed to himself or to other rational beings, he must always be regarded at the same time as an end. All objects of inclinations have only a conditional worth, for if the inclinations and the needs founded on them did not exist, their object would be without worth. The inclinations themselves as the sources of needs, however, are so lacking in absolute worth that the universal wish of every rational being must be indeed to free themselves completely from them. Therefore, the worth of any objects to be obtained by our actions is at all times conditional. Beings whose existence does not depend on our will but on nature, if they are not rational beings, have only a relative worth as means and are therefore called "things"; on the other hand, rational beings are designated "persons," because their nature indicates that they are ends in themselves, i.e., things which may not be used merely as means. Such a being is thus an object of respect and, so far, restricts all [arbitrary] choice. Such beings are not merely subjective ends whose existence as a result of our action has a worth for us but are objective ends, i.e., beings whose existence in itself is an end. Such an end is one for which no other end can be substituted, to which these beings should serve merely as means. For, without them, nothing of absolute worth could be found, and if all worth is conditional and thus contingent, no supreme practical principle for reason could be found anywhere. . . .

Thus the principle of every human will as a will giving universal laws in all its maxims is very well adapted to being a categorical imperative, provided it is otherwise correct. Because of the idea of universal lawgiving, it is based on no interest, and, thus of all possible imperatives, it alone can be unconditional. Or, better, converting the proposition: if there is a categorical imperative (a law for the will of every rational being), it can only command that everything be done from the maxim of its will as one which could have as its object only itself considered as giving universal laws. For only in this case are the practical principle and the imperative which the will obeys unconditional, because the will can have no interest as its foundation.

If we now look back upon all previous attempts which have ever been undertaken to discover the principle of morality, it is not to be wondered at that they all had to fail. Man was seen to be bound to laws by his duty, but it was not seen that he is subject only to his own, yet universal, legislation, and that he is only bound to act in accordance with his own will, which is, however, designed by nature to be a will giving universal laws. For if one thought of him as subject only to a law (whatever it may be), this necessarily implied some interest as a stimulus or compulsion to obedience because the law did not arise from his will. Rather, his will was constrained by something else according to a law to act in a certain way. By this strictly necessary consequence, however, all the labor of finding a supreme ground for duty was irrevocably lost, and one never arrived at duty but only at the necessity of action from a certain interest. This might be his own interest or that of another, but in either case the imperative always had to be conditional and could not at all serve as a moral command. This principle I will call the principle of *autonomy* of the will in contrast to all other principles which I accordingly count under *heteronomy*.

The concept of each rational being as a being that must regard itself as giving universal law through all the maxims of its will, so that it may judge itself and its actions from this standpoint, leads to a very fruitful concept, namely, that of a *realm of ends*.

By "realm" I understand the systematic union of different rational beings through common laws. Because laws determine ends with regard to their universal validity, if we abstract from the personal difference of rational beings and thus from all content of their private ends, we can think of a whole of all ends in systematic connection, a whole of rational beings as ends in themselves as well as of the particular ends which each may set for himself. This is a realm of ends, which is possible on the aforesaid principles. For all rational beings stand under the law that each of them should treat himself and all others never merely as means but in every case also as an end in himself. Thus there arises a systematic union of rational beings through common objective laws. This is a realm which may be called a realm of ends (certainly only an ideal), because what these laws have in view is just the relation of these beings to each other as ends and means.

A rational being belongs to the realm of ends as a member when he gives universal laws in it while also himself subject to these laws. He belongs to it as sovereign when he, as legislating, is subject to the will of no other. The rational being must regard himself always as legislative in a realm of ends possible through the freedom of the will, whether he belongs to it as member or as sovereign. He cannot maintain the latter position merely through the maxims of his will but only when he is a completely independent being without need and with power adequate to his will.

Morality, therefore, consists in the relation of every action to that legislation through which alone a realm of ends is possible. This legislation, however, must be found in every rational being. It must be able to arise from his will, whose principle then is to do no action according to any maxim which would be inconsistent with its being a universal law and thus to act only so that the will through its maxims could regard itself at the same time as universally lawgiving. If now the maxims do not by their nature already necessarily conform to this objective principle of rational beings as universally lawgiving, the necessity of acting according to that principle is called practical constraint, i.e., duty. Duty pertains not to the sovereign in the realm of ends, but rather to each member, and to each in the same degree.

Criticisms of Conventional Morality

FRIEDRICH NIETZSCHE (1844–1900) is one of the most notorious philosophers ever. He was also a brilliant aphorist, who declared that "God is dead," "what does not kill me makes me stronger," and called for the übermensch, or superman, whose existence would justify humanity. Nietzsche was a wide-ranging critic who had something to say about nearly every field of philosophy, as well as many of the social issues of his day. And he would go where reason led him—his youthful enthusiasm for the music of Richard Wagner turned to intense dislike in the light of Wagner's anti-Semitism, German nationalism, and (in Nietzsche's view) Christian pandering. Tragically, Nietzsche suffered from a profound insanity the final eleven years of his life, and was essentially unable to communicate. After Nietzsche's death his sister Elizabeth twisted his ideas so as to make them palatable to the Nazis, who latched onto him as their paradigm of a philosopher. Of course, Elizabeth also made sure that her vehemently anti-Christian brother received a proper Lutheran funeral.

THINKING QUESTIONS

Friedrich Nietzsche, *Criticisms of Conventional Morality*

1. What is your conscience? Could it be no more than the collection of prejudices that you were taught growing up? Why do you trust your conscience? Is it only because doing so "has brought you sustenance and honors," as Nietzsche suggests?
2. Kant claims that the moral law—his categorical imperative—is to act only according to those maxims or principles of action that one could will to be a universal law of nature. That is, only act in ways that you would want everyone to act. What are Nietzsche's criticisms of this idea?
3. Nietzsche maintains that every action is unique. What does he mean by this? How does this claim contribute to his critique of Kant?
4. Nietzsche recommends that we create our own values and our own moral laws. How can we accomplish these things?
5. According to Nietzsche, different moral codes are designed to achieve different purposes, that is, different practical aims. Is there any reason, then, to think that there is a moral code that is uniquely *true*?

6. Nietzsche claims to have "discovered two basic types" of morality. What are they? How do they differ from each other?
7. According to which type of morality does one have duties only to one's peers? Do you think this kind of moral code underwrites nationalism and patriotism?
8. What does Nietzsche see as the difference between good versus bad and good versus evil?
9. Nietzsche claims that there are no moral facts whatsoever, that morality is merely symptomatology. What can he mean by this? Morality is a symptom of what?

FROM *THE GAY SCIENCE* (ORIGINALLY PUBLISHED 1882)

§335. Why do you *listen* to the voice of your conscience? And what gives you the right to consider such a judgment true and infallible? For this *faith*—is there no conscience for that? Have you never heard of an intellectual conscience? A conscience behind your "conscience"? Your judgment "that is right" has a prehistory in your instincts, likes, dislikes, experiences, and lack of experiences. "*How* did it originate there?" you must ask, and then also: "*What* is it that impels me to listen to it?" You can listen to its commands like a good soldier who hears his officer's command. Or like a woman who loves the man who commands. Or like a flatterer and coward who is afraid of the commander. Or like a dunderhead who obeys because no objection occurs to him. In short, there are a hundred ways in which you can listen to your conscience. But *that* you take this or that judgment for the voice of conscience, in other words, *that* you feel something to be right, may be due to the fact that you have never thought much about yourself and simply have accepted blindly that what you had been told ever since your childhood was *right:* or it may be due to the fact that what you call your duty has up to this point brought you sustenance and honors,—and you consider it "right" because it appears to you as your *own* "condition of existence" (and that you have a *right* to existence seems irrefutable to you!).

For all that, the *firmness* of your moral judgment could be evidence of your personal abjectness, of impersonality, your "moral strength" might have its source in your stubbornness—or in your inability to envisage a new ideal! And, briefly: if you had thought more subtly, observed better, and learned more, you certainly would not go on calling this "duty" of yours and this "conscience" of yours duty and conscience: your understanding *of the manner in which moral judgments have originated* would spoil these grand words,—for example, "sin," "salvation of the soul," "redemption" have been spoiled for you.—And now don't cite the categorical imperative, my friend!—this term tickles my ear and makes me laugh despite your serious presence: it makes me think of old Kant who had obtained the "thing in itself" by *stealth*—another very ridiculous thing!—and was punished for this when the "categorical imperative" crept stealthily into his heart and *led him astray* back to "God," "soul," "freedom," and "immortality," like a fox who loses his way and goes astray back into his cage:—yet it had been *his* strength and cleverness that had *broken open* the cage!

What? You admire the categorical imperative within you? This "firmness" of your so-called moral judgment? This "unconditional" feeling that "here everyone must judge as I do"? Rather admire your *selfishness* at this point! And the blindness, pettiness, and frugality of your selfishness! For it is selfish to experience one's *own* judgment as a universal law; and this selfishness is blind, petty, and frugal because it betrays that you have not yet discovered yourself nor created for yourself an ideal of your own, your very own:—for that could never belong to somebody else and much less to all, to all!

Anyone who still judges "in this case everybody would have to act like this" has not yet taken five steps toward self-knowledge: otherwise he would know that there neither are nor can be actions that are the same,—that every action that has ever been done was done in an altogether unique and irretrievable way, and that this will be true of every future action,—that all regulations about actions relate only to their coarse exterior (and even the most inward and subtle regulations of all moralities so far),—that these regulations may lead to some semblance of sameness, *but really only to some semblance,*—that as one contemplates or looks back upon *any* action at all, it is and remains impenetrable,—that our opinions about "good," "noble," "great" can never be *proved true* by our actions because every action is unknowable,—that our opinions, valuations, and tables of what is good certainly belong among the most powerful levers in the involved mechanism of our actions, but that in any particular case the law of their mechanism is indemonstrable.

Let us therefore *limit* ourselves to the purification of our opinions and valuations and to the *creation of our own new tables of values:*—and let us stop brooding about the "moral value of our actions"! Yes, my friends, regarding all the moral chatter of some about others it is time to feel nauseous! Sitting in moral judgment should offend our taste! Let us leave such chatter and such bad taste to those who have nothing else to do but drag the past a few steps further through time and who never live in the present,—which is to say the many, the great majority! We, however, *want to become who we are,*—the new, unique, incomparable ones, who give themselves their own laws, who create themselves! And to that end we must become the best learners and discoverers of everything that is lawful and necessary in the world: we must become *physicists* in order to be able to be *creators* in this sense,—while hitherto all valuations and ideals have been based on *ignorance* of physics or were constructed so as to *contradict* it. Therefore: long live physics! And even more so that which *compels* us to turn to physics,—our honesty!

FROM *BEYOND GOOD AND EVIL* (ORIGINALLY PUBLISHED 1886)

§187. Even apart from the value of such claims as "there is a categorical imperative in us," one can still always ask: what does such a claim tell us about the man who makes it? There are moralities which are meant to justify their creator before others. Other moralities are meant to calm him and lead him to be satisfied with himself. With yet others he wants to crucify himself and humiliate himself. With others he wants to wreak revenge, with others conceal himself, with others transfigure himself and place himself way up, at a distance. This morality is used by its creator to forget, that one to have others forget him or something about him. Some moralists want to vent their power and creative whims on humanity; some others, perhaps including Kant, suggest with their morality: "What deserves respect in me is that I can obey—and you *ought* not to be different from me."—In short, moralities are also merely a *sign language of the affects.*

§260. Wandering through the many subtler and coarser moralities which have so far been prevalent on earth, or still are prevalent, I found that certain features recurred regularly together and were closely associated—until I finally discovered two basic types and one basic difference.

There are *master morality* and *slave morality*—I add immediately that in all the higher and more mixed cultures there also appears attempts at mediation between these two moralities, and yet more often the interpenetration and mutual misunderstanding of both, and at times they occur directly alongside each other—even in the same human being, within a single soul. The moral discrimination of value has originated either among a ruling group whose consciousness of its difference from the ruled group was accompanied by delight—or among the ruled, the slaves and dependents of every degree.

In the first case, when the ruling group determines what is "good," the exalted, proud states of the soul are experienced as conferring distinction and determining the order of rank. The noble human being separates from himself those in whom the opposite of such exalted, proud states find expression: he despises them. It should be noted immediately that in this first type of morality the opposition of "good" and "bad" means approximately the same as "noble" and "contemptible." (The opposition of "good" and "*evil*" has a different origin.) One feels contempt for the cowardly, the anxious, the petty, those intent on narrow utility; also for the suspicious with their unfree glances, those who humble themselves, the doglike people who allow themselves to be maltreated, the begging flatterers, above all the liars: it is part of the fundamental faith of all aristocrats that the common people lie. "We truthful ones"—thus the nobility of ancient Greece referred to itself.

It is obvious that moral designations were everywhere first applied to *human beings* and only later, derivatively, to *actions*. Therefore it is a gross mistake when historians of morality start from such questions as: why was the compassionate act praised? The noble type of man experiences *itself* as determining values; it does not need approval; it judges, "what is harmful to me is harmful in itself"; it knows itself to be that which first accords honor to things; it is *value-creating*. Everything it knows as part of itself it honors: such a morality is self-glorification. In the foreground there is the feeling of fullness, of power that seeks to overflow, the happiness of high tension, the consciousness of wealth that would give and bestow: the noble human being, too, helps the unfortunate, but not, or almost not, from pity, but prompted more by an urge begotten by excess of power. The noble human being honors himself as one who is powerful, also as one who has power over himself, who knows how to speak and be silent, who delights in being severe and hard with himself and respects all severity and hardness. "A hard heart Wotan put into my breast," says an old Scandinavian saga: a fitting poetic expression, seeing that it comes from the soul of a proud Viking. Such a type of man is actually proud of the fact that he is *not* made for pity, and the hero of the saga therefore adds as a warning: "If the heart is not hard in youth it will never harden." Noble and courageous human beings who think that way are furthest removed from that morality which finds the distinction of morality precisely in pity, or in acting for others, or *désintéressement* [disinterestedness] in faith in oneself, pride in oneself, a fundamental hostility and irony against "selflessness" belong just as definitely to noble morality as does a slight disdain and caution regarding compassionate feelings and a "warm heart."

It is the powerful who *understand* how to honor; this is their art, their realm of invention. The profound reverence for age and tradition—all law rests on this double reverence—the faith and prejudice in favor of ancestors and disfavor of those yet to come are typical of the morality of the powerful; and when the men of "modern ideas," conversely, believe almost instinctively in "progress" and "the future" and more and more lack respect for age, this in itself would sufficiently betray the ignoble origin of these "ideas."

A morality of the ruling group, however, is most alien and embarrassing to the present taste in the severity of its principle that one has duties only to one's peers; that against beings of a lower rank, against everything alien, one may behave as one pleases or "as the heart desires," and in any case "beyond good and evil"—here pity and like feelings may find their place. The capacity for, and the duty of, long gratitude and long revenge—both only among one's peers—refinement in repaying, the sophisticated concept of friendship, a certain necessity for having enemies (as it were, as drainage ditches for the affects of envy, quarrelsomeness, exuberance—at bottom, in order to be capable of being good *friends*): all these are typical characteristics of noble morality which, as suggested, is not the morality of "modern ideas" and therefore is hard to empathize with today, also hard to dig up and uncover.

It is different with the second type of morality, *slave morality*. Suppose the violated, oppressed, suffering, unfree, who are uncertain of themselves and weary, moralize: what will their moral valuations have in common? Probably, a pessimistic suspicion about the whole condition of man will find expression, perhaps a condemnation of man along with his condition. The slave's eye is not favorable to the virtues of the powerful: he is skeptical and suspicious, *subtly* suspicious, of all the "good" that is honored there—he would like to persuade himself that even their happiness is not genuine. Conversely, those qualities are brought out and flooded with light to serve to ease existence for those who suffer: here pity, the complaisant and obliging hand, the warm heart, patience, industry, humility and friendliness are honored—for here these are the most useful qualities and almost the only means for enduring the pressure of existence. Slave morality is essentially a morality of utility.

Here is the place for the origin of that famous opposition of "good" and "evil": into evil one's feelings project power and dangerousness, a certain terribleness, subtlety, and strength that does not permit contempt to develop. According to slave morality, those who are "evil" thus inspire fear; according to master morality it is precisely those who are "good" that inspire, and wish to inspire, fear, while the "bad" are felt to be contemptible.

The opposition reaches its climax when, as a logical consequence of slave morality, a touch of disdain is associated also with the "good" of this morality—this may be slight and benevolent—because the good human being has to be *undangerous* in the slave's way of thinking: he is good-natured, easy to deceive, a little stupid perhaps, *un bonhomme* [a simple man]. Wherever slave morality becomes preponderant, language tends to bring the words "good" and "stupid" closer together.

One last fundamental difference: the longing for *freedom,* the instinct for happiness and the subtleties of the feeling of freedom belong just as necessarily to slave morality and morals as artful and enthusiastic reverence and devotion are the regular symptoms of an aristocratic way of thinking and evaluating.

This makes plain why love *as passion*—which is our European specialty—simply must be of noble origin: as is well known, its invention must be credited to the Provençal knight-poets, those magnificent and inventive human beings of the "*gai saber*" to whom Europe owes so many things and almost owes itself.—

FROM *TWILIGHT OF THE IDOLS* (ORIGINALLY PUBLISHED 1889)

The "Improvers" of Mankind, §1. My demand upon the philosopher is known, that he take his stand *beyond* good and evil and leave the illusion of moral judgment *beneath* himself. This demand follows from an insight which I was the first to formulate: *that there are altogether no moral facts.* Moral judgments agree with religious ones in believing in realities which are not realities. Morality is merely an interpretation of certain phenomena—more precisely, a *mis*interpretation. Moral judgments, like religious ones, belong to a stage of ignorance at which the very concept of the real, and the distinction between what is real and imaginary, are still lacking: thus "truth," at this stage, designates all sorts of things which we today call "imaginings." Moral judgments are therefore never to be taken literally: so understood, they always contain mere absurdity. *Semeiotically,* however, they remain invaluable: they reveal, at least for those who know, the most valuable realities of cultures and inwardnesses which did not *know* enough to "understand" themselves. Morality is mere sign language, mere symptomatology: one must know what it is all *about* to be able to profit from it.

Gender and Moral Development

CAROL GILLIGAN (1936–) currently teaches at the New York University School of Law. Prior to holding this position she was Patricia Albjerg Graham chair in gender studies at the Harvard Graduate School of Education, where she taught for 30 years. Her main area of research is on gender differences in moral development. Author of dozens of articles and seven books, her most well-known work, *In a Different Voice* (1982), offers a feminist critique of the work of the prominent moral psychologist, Lawrence Kohlberg.

THINKING QUESTIONS

Carol Gilligan, *Gender and Moral Development*

1. What is the difference between a "justice perspective" on morality and a "care perspective" on morality? What is Gilligan saying about this distinction with the analogy of the duck-rabbit figure?
2. Gilligan mentions two famous studies by Piaget and Kohlberg of how people, both children and adults, make moral decisions. What does she think was wrong with the way those studies were done?
3. To illustrate her central theme, Gilligan uses the example of teenagers explaining changes in their religious views to their parents. "I have a right to my religious opinions," says one person. "I understand their fear of my new religious ideas," says another. How do these statements represent different approaches to morally justifying one's actions?
4. In the case of the medical student who broke school rules by drinking alcohol, would you turn him in? Why or why not? What *kind* of reasons would you offer for your decision?
5. If there are differences between men and women in the way that they tend to approach moral issues, *why* do you think that there is a difference?

WHEN ONE LOOKS AT AN AMBIGUOUS FIGURE like the drawing that can be seen as a young or old woman, or the image of the vase and the faces, one initially sees it in only one way. Yet even after seeing it in both ways, one way often seems more compelling. This phenomenon reflects the laws of perceptual organization that favor certain modes of visual grouping. But it also suggests a tendency to view reality as unequivocal and thus to argue that there is one right or better way of seeing.

The experiments of the Gestalt psychologists on perceptual organization provide a series of demonstrations that the same proximal pattern can be organized in different ways so that, for example, the same figure can be seen as a square or a diamond, depending on its orientation in relation to a surrounding frame. Subsequent studies show that the context influencing which of two possible organizations will be chosen may depend not only on the features of the array presented but also on the perceiver's past experience or expectation. Thus, a bird-watcher and a rabbit-keeper are likely to see the duck-rabbit figure in different ways; yet this difference does not imply that one way is better or a higher form of perceptual organization. It does, however, call attention to the fact that the rabbit-keeper, perceiving the rabbit, may not see the ambiguity of the figure until someone points out that it can also be seen as a duck.

This paper presents a similar phenomenon with respect to moral judgment, describing two moral perspectives that organize thinking in different ways. The analogy to ambiguous figure perception arises from the observation that although people are aware of both perspectives, they tend to adopt one or the other in defining and resolving moral conflict. Since moral judgments organize thinking about choice in difficult situations, the adoption of a single perspective may facilitate clarity of decision. But the wish for clarity may also imply a compelling human need for resolution or closure, especially in the face of decisions that give rise to discomfort or unease. Thus, the search for clarity in seeing may blend with a search for justification, encouraging the position that there is one right or better way to think about moral problems. This question, which has been the subject of intense theological and philosophical debate, becomes of interest to the psychologist not only because of its psychological dimensions—the tendency to focus on one perspective and the wish for justification—but also because one moral perspective currently dominates psychological thinking and is embedded in the most widely used measure for assessing the maturity of moral reasoning.

In describing an alternative standpoint, I will reconstruct the account of moral development around two moral perspectives, grounded in different dimensions of relationship that give rise to moral concern. The justice perspective, often equated with moral reasoning, is recast as one way of seeing moral problems and a care perspective is brought forward as an alternate vision or frame. The distinction between justice and care as alternative perspectives or moral orientations is based empirically on the observation that a shift in the focus of attention from concerns about justice to concerns about care changes the definition of what constitutes a moral problem, and leads the same situation to be seen in different ways. Theoretically, the distinction between justice and care cuts across the familiar divisions between thinking and feeling, egoism and altruism, theoretical and practical reasoning. It calls attention to the fact that all human relationships, public and private, can be characterized *both* in terms of equality and in terms of attachment, and that both inequality and detachment constitute grounds for moral concern. Since everyone is vulnerable both to oppression and to abandonment, two moral visions—one of justice and one of care—recur in human experience. The moral injunctions, not to act unfairly toward others, and not to turn away from someone in need, capture these different concerns.

The conception of the moral domain as comprised of at least two moral orientations raises new questions about observed differences in moral judgment and the disagreements to which they give rise. Key to this revision is the distinction between differences in developmental stage (more or less adequate positions within a single orientation) and differences in orientation (alternative perspectives or frameworks). The findings reported in this paper of an association between moral orientation and gender speak directly to the continuing controversy over sex differences in moral reasoning. In doing so, however, they also offer an empirical explanation for why previous thinking about moral development has been organized largely within the justice framework.

My research on moral orientation derives from an observation made in the course of studying the relationship between moral judgment and action. Two studies, one of college students describing their experiences of moral conflict and choice, and one of pregnant women who were considering abortion, shifted the focus of attention from the ways people reason about hypothetical dilemmas to the ways people construct moral conflicts and choices in their lives. This change in approach made it possible to see what experiences people define in moral terms, and to explore the relationship between the understanding of moral problems and the reasoning strategies used and the actions taken in attempting to resolve them. In this context, I observed that women, especially when speaking about their own experiences of moral conflict and choice, often define moral problems in a way that eludes the categories of moral theory and is at odds with the assumptions that shape psychological thinking about morality and about the self. This discovery, that a different voice often guides the moral judgments and the actions of women, called attention to a major design problem in previous moral judgment research: namely, the use of all-male samples as the empirical basis for theory construction.

The selection of an all-male sample as the basis for generalizations that are applied to both males and females is logically inconsistent. As a research strategy, the decision to begin with a single-sex sample is inherently problematic, since the categories of analysis will tend to be defined on the basis of the initial data gathered and subsequent studies will tend to be restricted to these categories. Piaget's work on the moral judgment of the child illustrates these problems since he defined the evolution of children's consciousness and practice of rules on the basis of his study of boys playing marbles, and then undertook a study of girls to assess the generality of his findings. Observing a series of differences both in the structure of girls' games and "in the actual mentality of little girls," he deemed these differences not of interest because "it was not this contrast which we proposed to study." Girls, Piaget found, "rather complicated our interrogatory in relation to what we know about boys," since the changes in their conception of rules, although following the same sequence observed in boys, did not stand in the same relation to social experience. Nevertheless, he concluded that "in spite of these differences in the structure of the game and apparently in the players' mentality, we find the same process at work as in the evolution of the game of marbles."

Thus, girls were of interest insofar as they were similar to boys and confirmed the generality of Piaget's findings. The differences noted, which included greater tolerance, a greater tendency toward innovation in solving conflicts, a greater willingness to make exceptions to rules, and a lesser concern with legal elaboration, were not seen as germane to "the psychology of rules," and therefore were regarded as insignificant for the study of children's moral judgment. Given the confusion that currently surrounds the discussion of sex differences in moral judgment, it is important to emphasize that the differences observed by Piaget did not pertain to girls' understanding of rules *per se* or to the development of the idea of justice in their thinking, but rather to the way girls structured their games and their approach to conflict resolution—that is, to their use rather than their understanding of the logic of rules and justice.

Kohlberg, in his research on moral development, did not encounter these problems since he equated moral development with the development of justice reasoning and initially used an all-male sample as the basis for theory and test construction. In response to his critics, Kohlberg has recently modified his claims, renaming his test a measure of "justice reasoning" rather than of "moral maturity" and acknowledging the presence of a care perspective in people's moral thinking. But the widespread use of Kohlberg's measure as a measure of moral development together with his own continuing tendency to equate justice reasoning with moral judgment leaves the problem of orientation differences unsolved. More specifically, Kohlberg's efforts to assimilate thinking about care to the six-stage developmental sequence he derived and refined by analyzing changes in justice reasoning (relying centrally on his all-male longitudinal sample) underscores the continuing importance of the points raised in this paper concerning (1) the distinction between differences in developmental stage within a single orientation and differences in orientation, and (2) the fact that the moral thinking of girls and women was not examined in establishing either the meaning or the measurement of moral judgment within contemporary psychology.

An analysis of the language and logic of men's and women's moral reasoning about a range of hypothetical and real dilemmas underlies the distinction elaborated in this paper between a justice and a care perspective. The empirical association of care reasoning with women suggests that discrepancies observed between moral theory and the moral judgments of girls and women may reflect a shift in perspective, a change in moral orientation. Like the figure-ground shift in ambiguous figure perception, justice and care as moral perspectives are not opposites or mirror-images of one another, with justice uncaring and care unjust. Instead, these perspectives denote different ways of organizing the basic elements of moral judgment: self, others, and the relationship between them. With the shift in perspective from justice to care, the organizing dimension of relationship changes from inequality/equality to attachment/detachment, reorganizing thoughts, feelings, and language so that words connoting relationship like "dependence" or "responsibility" or even moral terms such as "fairness" and "care" take on different meanings. To organize relationships in terms of attachment rather than in terms of equality changes the way human connection is imagined, so that the images or metaphors of relationship shift from hierarchy or balance to network or web. In addition, each organizing framework leads to a different way of imagining the self as a moral agent.

From a justice perspective, the self as moral agent stands as the figure against a ground of social relationships, judging the conflicting claims of self and others against a standard of equality or equal respect (the Categorical Imperative, the Golden Rule). From a care perspective, the relationship becomes the figure, defining self and others. Within the context of relationship, the self as a moral agent perceives and responds to the perception of need. The shift in moral perspective is manifest by a change in the moral question from "What is just?" to "How to respond?"

For example, adolescents asked to describe a moral dilemma often speak about peer or family pressure in which case the moral question becomes how to maintain moral principles or standards and resist the influence of one's parents or friends. "I have a right to my religious opinions," one teenager explains, referring to a religious difference with his parents. Yet, he adds, "I respect their views." The same dilemma, however, is also construed by adolescents as a problem of attachment, in which case the moral question becomes: how to respond both to oneself and to one's friends or one's parents, how to maintain or strengthen connection in the face of differences in belief. "I understand their fear of my new religious ideas," one teenager explains, referring to her religious disagreement with her parents, "but they really ought to listen to me and try to understand my beliefs."

One can see these two statements as two versions of essentially the same thing. Both teenagers present self-justifying arguments about religious disagreement; both address the claims of self and of others in a way that honors both. Yet each frames the problem in different terms, and the use of moral language points to different concerns. The first speaker casts the problem in terms of individual rights that must be respected within the relationship. In other words, the figure of the considering is the self looking on the disagreeing selves in relationship, and the aim is to get the other selves to acknowledge the right to disagree. In the case of the second speaker, figure and ground shift. The relationship becomes the figure of the considering, and relationships are seen to require listening and efforts at understanding differences in belief. Rather than the right to disagree, the speaker focuses on caring to hear and to be heard. Attention shifts from the grounds for agreement (rights and respect) to the grounds for understanding (listening and speaking, hearing and being heard). This shift is marked by a change in moral language from the stating of separate claims to rights and respect ("I have a right . . . I respect their views.") to the activities of relationship—the injunction to listen and try to understand ("I understand . . . they ought to listen . . . and try to understand."). The metaphor of moral voice itself carries the terms of the care perspective and reveals how the language chosen for moral theory is not orientation neutral.

The language of the public abortion debate, for example, reveals a justice perspective. Whether the abortion dilemma is cast as a conflict of rights or in terms of respect for human life, the claims of the fetus and of the pregnant woman are balanced or placed in opposition. The morality of abortion decisions thus construed hinges on the scholastic or metaphysical question as to whether the fetus is a life or a person, and whether its claims take precedence over those of the pregnant woman. Framed as a problem of care, the dilemma posed by abortion shifts. The connection between the fetus and the pregnant woman becomes the focus of attention and the question becomes whether it is responsible or irresponsible, caring or careless, to extend or to end this connection. In this construction, the abortion dilemma arises because there is no way not to act, and no way of acting that does not alter the connection between self and others. To ask what actions constitute care or are more caring directs attention to the parameters of connection and the costs of detachment, which become subjects of moral concern.

Finally, two medical students, each reporting a decision not to turn in someone who has violated the school rules against drinking, cast their decision in different terms. One student constructs the decision as an act of mercy, a decision to override justice in light of the fact that the violator has shown "the proper degrees of contrition." In addition, this student raises the question as to whether or not the alcohol policy is just, i.e., whether the school has the right to prohibit drinking. The other student explains the decision not to turn in a proctor who was drinking on the basis that turning him in is not a good way to respond to this problem, since it would dissolve the relationship between them and thus cut off an avenue for help. In addition, this student raises the question as to whether the proctor sees his drinking as a problem.

This example points to an important distinction, between care as understood or construed within a justice framework and care as a framework or a perspective on moral decision. Within a justice construction, care becomes the mercy that tempers justice; or connotes the special obligations or supererogatory duties that arise in personal relationships; or signifies altruism freely chosen—a decision to modulate the strict demands of justice by considering equity or showing forgiveness; or characterizes a choice to sacrifice the claims of the self. All of these interpretations of care leave the basic assumptions of a justice framework intact: the division between the self and others, the logic of reciprocity or equal respect.

As a moral perspective, care is less well elaborated, and there is no ready vocabulary in moral theory to describe its terms. As a framework for moral decision, care is grounded in the assumption that self and other are interdependent, an assumption reflected in a view of action as responsive and, therefore, as arising in relationship rather than the view of action as emanating from within the self and, therefore, "self governed." Seen as responsive, the self is by definition connected to others, responding to perceptions, interpreting events, and governed by the organizing tendencies of human interaction and human language. Within this framework, detachment, whether from self or from others, is morally problematic, since it breeds moral blindness or indifference—a failure to discern or respond to need. The question of what responses constitute care and what responses lead to hurt draws attention to the fact that one's own terms may differ from those of others. Justice in this context becomes understood as respect for people in their own terms.

The medical student's decision not to turn in the proctor for drinking reflects a judgment that turning him in is not the best way to respond to the drinking problem, itself seen as a sign of detachment or lack of concern. Caring for the proctor thus raises the question of what actions are most likely to ameliorate this problem, a decision that leads to the question of what are the proctor's terms.

The shift in organizing perspective here is marked by the fact that the first student does not consider the terms of the other as potentially different but instead assumes one set of terms. Thus the student alone becomes the arbiter of what is *the* proper degree of contrition. The second student, in turn, does not attend to the question of whether the alcohol policy itself is just or fair. Thus each student discusses an aspect of the problem that the other does not mention.

These examples are intended to illustrate two cross-cutting perspectives that do not negate one another but focus attention on different dimensions of the situation, creating a sense of ambiguity around the question of what is the problem to be solved. Systematic research on moral orientation as a dimension of moral judgment and action initially addressed three questions: (1) Do people articulate concerns about justice and concerns about care in discussing a moral dilemma? (2) Do people tend to focus their attention on one set of concerns and minimally represent the other? and (3) Is there an association between moral orientation and gender? Evidence from studies that included a common set of questions about actual experiences of moral conflict and matched samples of males and females provides affirmative answers to all three questions.

When asked to describe a moral conflict they had faced, 55 out of 80 (69 percent) educationally advantaged North American adolescents and adults raised considerations of both justice and care. Two-thirds (54 out of 80), however, focused their attention on one set of concerns, with focus defined as 75 percent or more of the considerations raised pertaining either to justice or to care. Thus the person who presented, say, two care considerations in discussing a moral conflict was more likely to give a third, fourth, and fifth than to balance care and justice concerns—a finding consonant with the assumption that justice and care constitute organizing frameworks for moral decision. The men and the women involved in this study (high school students, college students, medical students, and adult professionals) were equally likely to demonstrate the focus phenomenon (two-thirds of both sexes fell into the outlying focus categories). There were, however, sex differences in the direction of focus. With one exception, all of the men who focused, focused on justice. The women divided, with roughly one third focusing on justice and one third on care.

These findings clarify the different voice phenomenon and its implications for moral theory and for women. First, it is notable that if women were eliminated from the research sample, care focus in moral reasoning would virtually disappear. Although care focus was by no means characteristic of all women, it was almost exclusively a female phenomenon in this sample of educationally advantaged North Americans. Second, the fact that the women were advantaged means that the focus on care cannot readily be attributed to educational deficit or occupational disadvantage—the explanation Kohlberg and others have given for findings of lower levels of justice reasoning in women. Instead, the focus on care in women's moral reasoning draws attention to the limitations of a justice-focused moral theory and highlights the presence of care concerns in the moral thinking of both women and men. In this light, the Care/Justice group composed of one third of the women and one third of the men becomes of particular interest, pointing to the need for further research that attends to the way people organize justice and care in relation to one another—whether, for example, people alternate perspectives, like seeing the rabbit and the duck in the rabbit-duck figure, or integrate the two perspectives in a way that resolves or sustains ambiguity.

Third, if the moral domain is comprised of at least two moral orientations, the focus phenomenon suggests that people have a tendency to lose sight of one moral perspective in arriving at moral decision—a liability equally shared by both sexes. The present findings further suggest that men and women tend to lose sight of different perspectives. The most striking result is the virtual absence of care-focused reasoning among men. Since the men raised concerns about care in discussing moral conflicts and thus presented care concerns as morally relevant, a question is why they did not elaborate these concerns to a greater extent.

In summary, it becomes clear why attention to women's moral thinking led to the identification of a different voice and raised questions about the place of justice and care within a comprehensive moral theory. It also is clear how the selection of an all-male sample for research on moral judgment fosters an equation of morality with justice, providing little data discrepant with this view. In the present study, data discrepant with a justice-focused moral theory comes from a third of the women. Previously, such women were seen as having a problem understanding "morality." Yet these women may also be seen as exposing the problem in a justice-focused moral theory. This may explain the decision of researchers to exclude girls and women at the initial stage of moral judgment research. If one begins with the premise that "all morality consists in respect for rules," or "virtue is one and its name is justice," then women are likely to appear problematic within moral theory. If one begins with women's moral judgments, the problem becomes how to construct a theory that encompasses care as a focus of moral attention rather than as a subsidiary moral concern.

Political Philosophy

You don't murder, you don't steal. You pay your taxes and would go to war for your country if called upon. But why? Well, because the government says you have to. True, but why *ought* you do what the government says to, why are you obligated to follow the laws of your country? Further, how ought we arrange our political institutions so that our government and laws are just? These related questions are the central questions of political philosophy. The starting point for answers to these questions comes in the idea of consent. Surely if you *agree* to something you are obligated to follow through and do it. The idea that the authority of the state comes from the will of the governed, and that the obligation of the citizen to obey comes from his or her consent, finds one of its earliest expressions in the work of the 17th-century English philosopher, John Locke. Locke asks us to imagine a "state of nature," a world before anyone is in authority, before "civil society." What would it be like to live in the state of nature? Although it would be a world in which you had great freedom, it would also be a life where nothing was safe, not you or your possessions. Without a government, with its courts and police, how could you protect yourself, but by your own skill and strength, no match against the rest of the world. Locke argues that the conditions in the state of nature would be sufficiently bad that each of us would leave it if we could. How? By *consenting* to obey the rules of a group, a civil society, organized for our mutual protection. With this appeal to government based on the agreement of the governed, Locke began a tradition of social contract theory that continues to this day.

The most influential contract theorist of the 20th century was the Harvard philosopher John Rawls. Where Locke argued that we have literally agreed to obey the government, Rawls's version of the social contract is strictly hypothetical. Nonetheless, he argues that if we imagine *fair* circumstances for choosing the basic principles for building a society, then the principles selected under those fair conditions will yield a fair and just society. The original position is what Rawls calls the fair circumstances under which we imagine contractors choosing the basic principles, and the principles that he believes would be chosen, he calls the two principles of justice. Those two principles are the key ideas of his theory of "justice as fairness." One of Rawls's harshest critics was another Harvard philosopher, Robert Nozick. The alternative view Nozick defends is called libertarianism. The libertarian view can also be traced back to the work of Locke, but focuses on Locke's defense of individual rights, especially property rights. Nozick offers an ingenious example involving the great Los Angeles Lakers center, Wilt Chamberlain. Imagine that everybody who comes to see Chamberlain play must pay an extra fee to be given directly to him. After the end of the season Chamberlain has a considerable amount of money that he has earned by free exchange. He freely chose to use his talents to play basketball, the fans freely chose to pay extra to see him play. By what right then does the government take money away from Chamberlain (in the form of taxes) in order to benefit others? Libertarians argue that the only legitimate function of government is to protect individual rights, so the only legitimate reason to limit people's liberty (or their pocketbooks) is to pay for the government protections necessary to preserve individual rights.

Another contemporary view on organizing a just society is the deliberative model of democracy. The deliberative model shares some features of Rawls's justice as fairness theory, especially its emphasis on using fair procedures for deciding social policy issues. Instead of the original position, the deliberative model uses the idea of equal participation in a collective conversation to decide what the rules and policies of government should be for those who are governed by them. The basis of the deliberative model is the assumption that if you are going to be governed by a set of rules, then you ought to have a voice in shaping and deciding those rules. Turkish-born political theorist Seyla Benhabib explains the theory behind the deliberative model and how the model would work in the real world. How ought we educate children to be citizens in such a democracy? That's the question asked by political theorist and president of the University of Pennsylvania, Amy Gutmann. Gutmann argues that such an education cannot be "value neutral." Rather, there are values appropriate to "democratic character," understanding of science, history and literature, appreciation of appeals to reason, tolerance of difference, which it is appropriate for the schools to promote as part of citizenship in a participatory democracy.

Approaching democratic theory from a different direction, British political theorist Susan Mendus discusses feminist criticisms of democracy. Mendus argues that feminists have "lost the faith" that democratic institutions can bring equality for women. The problem lies not just in the way that democracies have developed over the last two hundred years—it's not just a "practical" problem that can be solved by making democracies more fully live up to their ideals. Rather, she argues, it is democratic theory itself that is flawed and must be changed.

From the State of Nature to Civil Society

JOHN LOCKE (1632–1704) was a British philosopher, captain of horse in the parliamentary army during the Glorious Revolution, physician, advisor to the Earl of Shaftesbury, and student and fellow of Christ Church College, Oxford for nearly 30 years. His philosophical writings are characterized by anti-authoritarianism and an advocacy of reason as the tool for gaining the truth. Although he did not start writing much until age 57, he then produced many important works, including *Letters Concerning Toleration* and *Two Treatises of Government,* as well as his masterpiece, *An Essay Concerning Human Understanding.*

THINKING QUESTIONS

John Locke, *From the State of Nature to Civil Society*

1. What does Locke mean by the "state of nature"? What rights do people have in the state of nature?
2. What is the central difference between the state of nature and civil society?
3. What are the advantages of living in the state of nature? What are the disadvantages?
4. In the state of nature, how do we gain property rights to things not previously owned by anyone else?
5. Why would people want to abandon the state of nature and form a civil society? What do we all have to give up in order to make civil society work?
6. What is the central role of government, according to Locke?

OF THE STATE OF NATURE

Sect. 4. To understand political power right, and derive it from its original, we must consider, what state all men are naturally in, and that is, a *state of perfect freedom* to order their actions, and dispose of their possessions and persons, as they think fit, within the bounds of the law of nature, without asking leave, or depending upon the will of any other man.

A *state* also *of Equality* wherein all the Power and Jurisdiction is reciprocal, no one having more than another; there being nothing more evident, than that the creatures of the same species and rank, promiscuously born to all the same advantages of nature, and the use of the same faculties, should also be equal one amongst another without subordination or subjection, unless the lord and master of them all should, by any manifest declaration of his will, set one above another, and confer on him, by an evident and clear appointment, an undoubted right to dominion and sovereignty. . . .

Sect. 6. But though this be a *state of liberty,* yet it is *not a state of licence*: though man in that state have an uncontrollable liberty to dispose of his person or possessions, yet he has not liberty to destroy himself, or so much as any creature in his possession, but where some nobler use than its bare preservation calls for it. The *state of nature* has a law of nature to govern it, which obliges every one: and reason, which is that law, teaches all mankind, who will but consult it, that being all *equal and independent,* no one ought to harm another in his life, health, liberty, or possessions: for men being all the workmanship of one omnipotent, and infinitely wise maker; all the servants of one sovereign master, sent into the world by his order, and about his business; they are his property, whose workmanship they are, made to last during his, not one another's pleasure: and being furnished with like faculties, sharing all in one community of nature, there cannot be supposed any such *subordination* among us, that may authorize us to destroy one another, as if we were made for one another's uses, as the inferior ranks of creatures are for ours. Every one, as he is *bound to preserve himself,* and not to quit his station wilfully, so by the like reason, when his own preservation comes not in competition, ought he, as much as he can, *to preserve the rest of mankind,* and may not, unless it be to do justice on an offender, take away, or impair the life, or what tends to the preservation of the life, the liberty, health, limb, or goods of another.

Sect. 7. And that all men may be restrained from invading others' rights, and from doing hurt to one another, and the law of nature be observed, which willeth the peace and *preservation of all mankind,* the *execution* of the law of nature is, in that state, put into every man's hands, whereby every one has a right to punish the transgressors of that law to such a degree, as may hinder its violation: for the *law of nature* would, as all other laws that concern men in this world, be in vain, if there were no body that in the state of nature had a *power to execute* that law, and thereby preserve the innocent and restrain offenders. And if any one in the state of nature may punish another for any evil he has done, every one may do so: for in that *state of perfect equality,* where naturally there is no superiority or jurisdiction of one over another, what any may do in prosecution of that law, every one must needs have a right to do.

Sect. 8. And thus, in the state of nature, *one man comes by a power over another;* but yet no absolute or arbitrary power, to use a criminal, when he has got him in his hands, according to the passionate heats, or boundless extravagancy of his own will; but only to retribute to him, so far as calm reason and conscience dictate, what is proportionate to his transgression, which is so much as may serve for *reparation* and *restraint:* for these two are the only reasons, why one man may lawfully do harm to another, which is that we call *punishment*. In transgressing the law of nature, the offender declares himself to live by another rule than that of reason and common equity, which is that measure God has set to the actions of men, for their mutual security; and so he becomes dangerous to mankind, the tye, which is to secure them from injury and violence, being slighted and broken by him. Which being a trespass against the whole species, and the peace and safety of it, provided for by the law of nature, every man upon this score, by the right he hath to preserve mankind in general, may restrain, or where it is necessary, destroy things noxious to them, and so may bring such evil on any one, who hath transgressed that law, as may make him repent the doing of it, and thereby deter him, and by his example others, from doing the like mischief. And in the case, and upon this ground, *every man hath a right to punish the offender, and be executioner of the law of nature. . . .*

Sect. 13. To this strange doctrine, viz. That *in the state of nature every one has the executive power* of the law of nature, I doubt not but it will be objected, that it is unreasonable for men to be judges in their own cases, that self-love will make men partial to themselves and their friends: and on the other side, that ill nature, passion and revenge will carry them too far in punishing others; and hence nothing but confusion and disorder will follow, and that therefore God hath certainly appointed government to restrain the partiality and violence of men. I easily grant, that *civil government* is the proper remedy for the inconveniencies of the state of nature, which must certainly be great, where men may be judges in their own case, since it is easy to be imagined, that he who was so unjust as to do his brother an injury, will scarce be so just as to condemn himself for it: but I shall desire those who make this objection, to remember, that *absolute monarchs* are but men; and if government is to be the remedy of those evils, which necessarily follow from men's being judges in their own cases, and the state of nature is therefore not to be endured, I desire to know what kind of government that is, and how much better it is than the state of nature, where one man, commanding a multitude, has the liberty to be judge in his own case, and may do to all his subjects whatever he pleases, without the least liberty to any one to question or controle those who execute his pleasure? And in whatsoever he doth, whether led by reason, mistake or passion, must be submitted to? Much better it is in the state of nature, wherein men are not bound to submit to the unjust will of another: and if he that judges, judges amiss in his own, or any other case, he is answerable for it to the rest of mankind.

Sect. 14. It is often asked as a mighty objection, *where are,* or ever were there any *men in such a state of nature?* To which it may suffice as an answer at present, that since all princes and rulers of *independent* governments all through the world, are in a state of nature, it is plain the world never was, nor ever will be, without numbers of men in that state. I have named all governors of *independent communities,* whether they are, or are not, in league with others: for it is not every compact that puts an end to the state of nature between men, but only this one of agreeing together mutually to enter into one community, and make one body politic; other promises, and compacts, men may make one with another, and yet still be in the state of nature. The promises and bargains for truck, &c.; between the two men in the desert island, mentioned by *Garcilasso de la Vega,* in his history of *Peru;* or between a *Swiss* and an *Indian,* in the woods of *America,* are binding to them, though they are perfectly in a state of nature, in reference to one another: for truth and keeping of faith belongs to men, as men, and not as members of society. . . .

OF THE STATE OF WAR

Sect. 16. The *state of war* is a state of *enmity* and *destruction:* and therefore declaring by word or action, not a passionate and hasty, but a sedate settled design upon another man's life, *puts him in a state of war* with him against whom he has declared such an intention, and so has exposed his life to the other's power to be taken away by him, or any one that joins with him in his defence, and espouses his quarrel; it being reasonable and just, I should have a right to destroy that which threatens me with destruction: for, *by the fundamental law of nature, man being to be preserved* as much as possible, when all cannot be preserved, the safety of the innocent is to be preferred: and one may destroy a man who makes war upon him, or has discovered an enmity to his being, for the same reason that he may kill a *wolf* or a *lion;* because such men are not under the ties of the commonlaw of reason, have no other rule, but that of force and violence, and so may be treated as beasts of prey, those dangerous and noxious creatures, that will be sure to destroy him whenever he falls into their power. . . .

Sect. 19. And here we have the plain *difference between the state of nature and the state of war,* which however some men have confounded, are as far distant, as a state of peace, good will, mutual assistance and preservation, and a state of enmity, malice, violence and mutual destruction, are one from another. Men living together according to reason, without a common superior on earth, with authority to judge between them, is *properly the state of nature.* But force, or a declared design of force, upon the person of another, where there is no common superior on earth to appeal to for relief, *is the state of war:* and it is the want of such an appeal gives a man the right of war even against an *aggressor,* tho' he be in society and a fellow subject. Thus *a thief,* whom I cannot harm, but by appeal to the law, for having stolen all that I am worth, I may kill, when he sets on me to rob me but of my horse or coat; because the law, which was made for my preservation, where it cannot interpose to secure my life from present force, which, if lost, is capable of no reparation, permits me my own defence, and the right of war, a liberty to kill the aggressor, because the aggressor allows not time to appeal to our common judge, nor the decision of the law, for remedy in a case where the mischief may be irreparable. Want of a common judge with authority, puts all men in a state of nature:

force without right, upon a man's person, makes a state of war, both where there is, and is not, a common judge. . . .

Sect. 21. To avoid this *state of war* (wherein there is no appeal but to heaven, and wherein every the least difference is apt to end, where there is no authority to decide between the contenders) is one great reason of men's putting themselves into society, and quitting the state of nature: for where there is an authority, a power on earth, from which relief can be had by *appeal,* there the continuance of the *state of war* is excluded, and the controversy is decided by that power. . . .

OF PROPERTY

Sect. 26. God, who hath given the world to men in common, hath also given them reason to make use of it to the best advantage of life, and convenience. The earth, and all that is therein, is given to men for the support and comfort of their being. And tho' all the fruits it naturally produces, and beasts it feeds, belong to mankind in common, as they are produced by the spontaneous hand of nature; and no body has originally a private dominion, exclusive of the rest of mankind, in any of them, as they are thus in their natural state: yet being given for the use of men, there must of necessity be *a means to appropriate* them some way or other, before they can be of any use, or at all beneficial to any particular man. The fruit, or venison, which nourishes the *wild Indian,* who knows no enclosure, and is still a tenant in common, must be his, and so his, i.e. a part of him, that another can no longer have any right to it, before it can do him any good for the support of his life.

Sect. 27. Though the earth, and all inferior creatures, be common to all men, yet every man has a *property* in his own *person:* this no body has any right to but himself. The *labour* of his body, and the *work* of his hands, we may say, are properly his. Whatsoever then he removes out of the state that nature hath provided, and left it in, he hath mixed his *labour* with, and joined to it something that is his own, and thereby makes it his *property.* It being by him removed from the common state nature hath placed it in, it hath by this *labour* something annexed to it, that excludes the common right of other men: for this *labour* being the unquestionable property of the labourer, no man but he can have a right to what that is once joined to, at least where there is enough, and as good, left in common for others.

Sect. 28. He that is nourished by the acorns he picked up under an oak, or the apples he gathered from the trees in the wood, has certainly appropriated them to himself. No body can deny but the nourishment is his. I ask then, when did they begin to be his? when he digested? or when he eat? or when he boiled? or when he brought them home? or when he picked them up? and it is plain, if the first gathering made them not his, nothing else could. That *labour* put a distinction between them and common: that added something to them more than nature, the common mother of all, had done; and so they became his private right. And will any one say, he had no right to those acorns or apples, he thus appropriated, because he had not the consent of all mankind to make them his? Was it a robbery thus to assume to himself what belonged to all in common? If such a consent as that was necessary, man had starved, notwithstanding the plenty God had given him. We see in *commons,* which remain so by compact, that it is the taking any part of what is common, and removing it out of the state nature leaves it in, which *begins the property;* without which the common is of no use. And the taking of this or that part, does not depend on the express consent of all the commoners. Thus the grass my horse has bit; the turfs my servant has cut; and the ore I have digged in any place, where I have a right to them in common with others, become my *property,* without the assignation or consent of any body. The *labour* that was mine, removing them out of that common state they were in, hath *fixed my property in them. . . .*

Sect. 31. It will perhaps be objected to this, that if gathering the acorns, or other fruits of the earth, &c.; makes a right to them, then any one may *ingross* as much as he will. To which I answer, Not so. The same law of nature, that does by this means give us property, does also *bound* that *property* too. *God has given us all things richly,* 1 Tim. vi. 12. is the voice of reason confirmed by inspiration. But how far has he given it us? *To enjoy.* As much as any one can make use of to any advantage of life before it spoils, so much he may by his labour fix a property in: whatever is beyond this, is more than his share, and belongs to others. Nothing was made by God for man to spoil or destroy. And thus, considering the plenty of natural provisions there was a long time in the world, and the few spenders; and to how small a part of that provision the industry of one man could extend itself, and ingross it to the prejudice of others; especially keeping within the *bounds,* set by reason, of what might serve for his *use;* there could be then little room for quarrels or contentions about property so established.

Sect. 32. But the *chief matter of property* being now not the fruits of the earth, and the beasts that subsist on it, but *the earth itself;* as that which takes in and carries with it all the rest; I think it is plain, that *property* in that too is acquired as the former. As *much land* as a man tills, plants, improves, cultivates, and can use the product of, so much is his *property.* He by his labour does, as it were, inclose it from the common. Nor will it invalidate his right, to say every body else has an equal title to it; and therefore he cannot appropriate, he cannot inclose, without the consent of all his fellow-commoners, all mankind. God, when he gave the world in common to all mankind, commanded man also to labour, and the penury of his condition required it of him. God and his reason commanded him to subdue the earth, i.e. improve it for the benefit of life, and therein lay out something upon it that was his own, his labour. He that in obedience to this command of God, subdued, tilled and sowed any part of it, thereby annexed to it something that was his *property,* which another had no title to, nor could without injury take from him.

Sect. 33. Nor was this *appropriation* of any parcel of land, by improving it, any prejudice to any other man, since there was still enough, and as good left;

and more than the yet unprovided could use. So that, in effect, there was never the less left for others because of his enclosure for himself: for he that leaves as much as another can make use of, does as good as take nothing at all. No body could think himself injured by the drinking of another man, though he took a good draught, who had a whole river of the same water left him to quench his thirst: and the case of land and water, where there is enough of both, is perfectly the same. . . .

OF POLITICAL OR CIVIL SOCIETY

Sect. 87. Man being born, as has been proved, with a Title to perfect Freedom, and an uncontrolled enjoyment of all the rights and privileges of the law of nature, equally with any other man, or number of men in the world, hath by nature a power, not only to preserve his property, that is, his life, liberty and estate, against the injuries and attempts of other men; but to judge of, and punish the breaches of that law in others, as he is persuaded the offence deserves, even with death itself, in crimes where the heinousness of the fact, in his opinion, requires it. But because no political society can be, nor subsist, without having in itself the power to preserve the property, and in order thereunto, punish the offences of all those of that society; there, and there only is political society, where every one of the members hath quitted this natural power, resigned it up into the hands of the community in all cases that exclude him not from appealing for protection to the law established by it. And thus all private judgment of every particular member being excluded, the community comes to be umpire, by settled standing rules, indifferent, and the same to all parties; and by men having authority from the community, for the execution of those rules, decides all the differences that may happen between any members of that society concerning any matter of right; and punishes those offences which any member hath committed against the society, with such penalties as the law has established: whereby it is easy to discern, who are, and who are not, in *political society* together. Those who are united into one body, and have a common established law and judicature to appeal to, with authority to decide controversies between them, and punish offenders, are in *civil society* one with another: but those who have no such common appeal, I mean on earth, are still in the state of nature, each being, where there is no other, judge for himself, and executioner; which is, as I have before shewed it, the perfect *state of nature*. . . .

Sect. 89. Where-ever therefore any number of men are so united into one society, as to quit every one his executive power of the law of nature, and to resign it to the public, there and there only is a *political,* or *civil society*. And this is done, where-ever any number of men, in the state of nature, enter into society to make one people, one body politic, under one supreme government; or else when any one joins himself to, and incorporates with any government already made: for hereby he authorizes the society, or which is all one, the legislative thereof, to make laws for him, as the public good of the society shall require; to the execution whereof, his own assistance (as to his own decrees) is due. And this *puts men* out of a state of nature *into* that of a *common-wealth,* by setting up a judge on earth, with authority to determine all the controversies, and redress the injuries that may happen to any member of the commonwealth; which judge is the legislative, or magistrates appointed by it. And where-ever there are any number of men, however associated, that have no such decisive power to appeal to, there they are still in *the state of nature.*

Sect. 90. Hence it is evident, that *absolute monarchy,* which by some men is counted the only government in the world, is indeed *inconsistent with civil society,* and so can be no form of civil-government at all: for the *end of civil society,* being to avoid, and remedy those inconveniencies of the state of nature, which necessarily follow from every man's being judge in his own case, by setting up a known authority, to which every one of that society may appeal upon any injury received, or controversy that may arise, and which every one of the society ought to obey; where-ever any persons are, who have not such an authority to appeal to, for the decision of any difference between them, there those persons are still *in the state of nature;* and so is every *absolute prince,* in respect of those who are under his *dominion.* . . .

OF THE BEGINNING OF POLITICAL SOCIETIES

Sect. 95. Men being, as has been said, by nature, all free, equal, and independent, no one can be put out of this estate, and subjected to the political power of another, without his own consent. The only way whereby any one divests himself of his natural liberty, and puts on the *bonds of civil society,* is by agreeing with other men to join and unite into a community for their comfortable, safe, and peaceable living one amongst another, in a secure enjoyment of their properties, and a greater security against any, that are not of it. This any number of men may do, because it injures not the freedom of the rest; they are left as they were in the liberty of the state of nature. When any number of men have so *consented to make one community or government,* they are thereby presently incorporated, and make *one body politic,* wherein the *majority* have a right to act and conclude the rest. . . .

Sect. 99. Whosoever therefore out of a state of nature unite into a *community,* must be understood to give up all the power, necessary to the ends for which they unite into society, to the *majority* of the community, unless they expressly agreed in any number greater than the majority. And this is done by barely agreeing to *unite into one political society,* which is *all the compact* that is, or needs be, between the individuals, that enter into, or make up a *commonwealth.* And thus that, which begins and actually *constitutes any political society,* is nothing but the consent of any number of freemen capable of a majority to unite and incorporate into such a society. And this is that, and that only, which did, or could give beginning to any *lawful government* in the world.

Contract Theory

JOHN RAWLS (1921–2002) was one of the most influential philosophers of the 20th century. Educated at Princeton, he was the John Cowles Professor of Philosophy at Harvard University where he started teaching in 1962. He was the author of several influential articles. His book, *A Theory of Justice,* published in 1971, generated a decades long, and ongoing, debate about the nature of the just state.

THINKING QUESTIONS

John Rawls, *Contract Theory*

1. What is the central value in a just society according to Rawls?
2. Rawls asks us to imagine that we are picking the principles that will guide society in an "original position." What are the conditions of the original position?
3. Why does Rawls think that principles chosen in the original position will be fair?
4. In what sense do the members of the society that results from the choices in the original position voluntarily accept the laws of that society?
5. What are the two principles of justice that Rawls thinks will come out of the original position? How do these principles guarantee that everyone is treated fairly?

MY AIM IS TO PRESENT a conception of justice which generalizes and carries to a higher level of abstraction the familiar theory of the social contract as found, say, in Locke, Rousseau, and Kant. In order to do this we are not to think of the original contract as one to enter a particular society or to set up a particular form of government. Rather, the guiding idea is that the principles of justice for the basic structure of society are the object of the original agreement. They are the principles that free and rational persons concerned to further their own interests would accept in an initial position of equality as defining the fundamental terms of their association. These principles are to regulate all further agreements; they specify the kinds of social cooperation that can be entered into and the forms of government that can be established. This way of regarding the principles of justice I shall call justice as fairness.

Thus we are to imagine that those who engage in social cooperation choose together, in one joint act, the principles which are to assign basic rights and duties and to determine the division of social benefits. Men are to decide in advance how they are to regulate their claims against one another and what is to be the foundation charter of their society. Just as each person must decide by rational reflection what constitutes his good, that is, the system of ends which it is rational for him to pursue, so a group of persons must decide once and for all what is to count among them as just and unjust. The choice which rational men would make in this hypothetical situation of equal liberty, assuming for the present that this choice problem has a solution, determines the principles of justice.

In justice as fairness the original position of equality corresponds to the state of nature in the traditional theory of the social contract. This original position is not, of course, thought of as an actual historical state of affairs, much less as a primitive condition of culture. It is understood as a purely hypothetical situation characterized so as to lead to a certain conception of justice. Among the essential features of this situation is that no one knows his place in society, his class position or social status, nor does any one know his fortune in the distribution of natural assets and abilities, his intelligence, strength, and the like. I shall even assume that the parties do not know their conceptions of the good or their special psychological propensities. The principles of justice are chosen behind a veil of ignorance. This ensures that no one is advantaged or disadvantaged in the choice of principles by the outcome of natural chance or the contingency of social circumstances. Since all are similarly situated and no one is able to design principles to favor his particular condition, the principles of justice are the result of a fair agreement or bargain. For given the circumstances of the original position, the symmetry of everyone's relations to each other, this initial situation is fair between individuals as moral persons, that is, as rational beings with their own ends and capable, I shall assume, of a sense of justice. The original position is, one might say, the appropriate initial status quo, and thus the fundamental agreements reached in it are fair. This explains the propriety of the name "justice as fairness": it conveys the idea that the principles of justice are agreed to in an initial situation that is fair. The name does not mean that the concepts of justice and fairness are the same, any more than the phrase "poetry as metaphor" means that the concepts of poetry and metaphor are the same.

Justice as fairness begins, as I have said, with one of the most general of all choices which persons might make together, namely, with the choice of the first principles of a conception of justice which is to regulate all subsequent criticism and reform of institutions. Then, having chosen a conception of justice, we can suppose that they are to choose a constitution and a legislature to enact laws, and so on, all in accordance with the principles of justice initially agreed upon. Our social situation is just if it is such that by this sequence of hypothetical agreements we would have contracted into the general system of rules which defines it. Moreover, assuming that the original position does determine a set of principles (that is, that a particular conception of justice would be chosen), it will then be true that whenever social institutions satisfy these principles those engaged in them can say to one another that they are cooperating on terms to which they would agree if they were free and equal persons whose relations with respect to one another were fair. They could all view their arrangements as meeting the stipulations which they would acknowledge in an initial situation that embodies widely accepted and reasonable constraints on the choice of principles. The general recognition of this fact would provide the basis for a public acceptance of the corresponding principles of justice. No society can, of course, be a scheme of cooperation which men enter voluntarily in a literal sense; each person finds himself placed at birth in some particular position in some particular society, and the nature of this position materially affects his life prospects. Yet a society satisfying the principles of justice as fairness comes as close as a society can to being a voluntary scheme, for it meets the principles which free and equal persons would assent to under circumstances that are fair. In this sense its members are autonomous and the obligations they recognize self-imposed.

One feature of justice as fairness is to think of the parties in the initial situation as rational and mutually disinterested. This does not mean that the parties are egoists, that is, individuals with only certain kinds of interests, say in wealth, prestige, and domination. But they are conceived as not taking an interest in one another's interests. They are to presume that even their spiritual aims may be opposed, in the way that the aims of those of different religions may be opposed. Moreover, the concept of rationality must be interpreted as far as possible in the narrow sense, standard in economic theory, of taking the most effective means to given ends. I shall modify this concept to some extent, as explained later, but one must try to avoid introducing into it any controversial ethical elements. The initial situation must be characterized by stipulations that are widely accepted.

In working out the conception of justice as fairness one main task clearly is to determine which principles of justice would be chosen in the original position. To do this we must describe this situation in some detail and formulate with care the problem of choice which it presents. These matters I shall take up in the immediately succeeding chapters. It may be observed, however, that once the principles of justice are thought of as arising from an original agreement in a situation of equality, it is an open question whether the principle of utility would be acknowledged. Offhand it hardly seems likely that persons who view themselves as equals, entitled to press their claims upon one another, would agree to a principle which may require lesser life prospects for some simply for the sake of a greater sum of advantages enjoyed by others. Since each desires to protect his interests, his capacity to advance his conception of the good, no one has a reason to acquiesce in an enduring loss for himself in order to bring about a greater net balance of satisfaction. In the absence of strong and lasting benevolent impulses, a rational man would not accept a basic structure merely because it maximized the algebraic sum of advantages irrespective of its permanent effects on his own basic rights and interests. Thus it seems that the principle of utility is incompatible with the conception of social cooperation among equals for mutual advantage. It appears to be inconsistent with the idea of reciprocity implicit in the notion of a well-ordered society. Or, at any rate, so I shall argue.

I shall maintain instead that the persons in the initial situation would choose two rather different principles: the first requires equality in the assignment of basic rights and duties, while the second holds that social and economic inequalities, for example inequalities of wealth and authority, are just only if they result in compensating benefits for everyone, and in particular for the least advantaged members of society. These principles rule out justifying institutions on the grounds that the hardships of some are offset by a greater good in the aggregate. It may be expedient but it is not just that some should have less in order that others may prosper. But there is no injustice in the greater benefits earned by a few provided that the situation of persons not so fortunate is thereby improved. The intuitive idea is that since everyone's well-being depends upon a scheme of cooperation without which no one could have a satisfactory life, the division of advantages should be such as to draw forth willing cooperation of everyone taking part in it, including those less well situated. Yet this can be expected only if reasonable terms are proposed. The two principles mentioned seem to be a fair agreement on the basis of which those better endowed, or more fortunate in their social position, neither of which we can be said to deserve, could expect the willing cooperation of others when some workable scheme is a necessary condition of the welfare of all. Once we decide to look for a conception of justice that nullifies the accidents of natural endowment and the contingencies of social circumstance as counters in quest for political and economic advantage, we are led to these principles. They express the result of leaving aside those aspects of the social world that seem arbitrary from a moral point of view. . . .

TWO PRINCIPLES OF JUSTICE

I shall now state in a provisional form the two principles of justice that I believe would be chosen in the original position. In this section I wish to make only the most general comments, and therefore the first formulation of these principles is tentative. As we go on I shall run through several formulations and approximate step by step the final statement to be given much later. I believe that doing this allows the exposition to proceed in a natural way.

The first statement of the two principles reads as follows.

> First: each person is to have an equal right to the most extensive basic liberty compatible with a similar liberty for others.
>
> Second: social and economic inequalities are to be arranged so that they are both (a) reasonably expected to be to everyone's advantage, and (b) attached to positions and offices open to all. . . .

By way of general comment, these principles primarily apply, as I have said, to the basic structure of society. They are to govern the assignment of rights and duties and to regulate the distribution of social and economic advantages. As their formulation suggests, these principles presuppose that the social structure can be divided into two more or less distinct parts, the first principle applying to the one, the second to the other. They distinguish between those aspects of the social system that define and secure the equal liberties of citizenship and those that specify and establish social and economic inequalities. The basic liberties of citizens are, roughly speaking, political liberty (the right to vote and to be eligible for public office) together with freedom of speech and assembly; liberty of conscience and freedom of thought; freedom of the person along with the right to hold (personal) property; and freedom from arbitrary arrest and seizure as defined by the concept of the rule of law. These liberties are all required to be equal by the first principle, since citizens of a just society are to have the same basic rights.

The second principle applies, in the first approximation, to the distribution of income and wealth and to the design of organizations that make use of differences in authority and responsibility, or chains of command. While the distribution of wealth and income need not be equal, it must be to everyone's advantage, and at the same time, positions of authority and offices of command must be accessible to all. One applies the second principle by holding positions open, and then, subject to this constraint, arranges social and economic inequalities so that everyone benefits.

These principles are to be arranged in a serial order with the first principle prior to the second. This ordering means that a departure from the institutions of equal liberty required by the first principle cannot be justified by, or compensated for, by greater social and economic advantages. The distribution of wealth and income, and the hierarchies of authority, must be consistent with both the liberties of equal citizenship and equality of opportunity.

How Liberty Upsets Patterns

ROBERT NOZICK (1938–2002) was University Professor of Philosophy at Harvard University until his tragic death from cancer. Writing on a wide variety of topics, Nozick was the author of numerous books and articles, including his most famous work, *Anarchy, State, and Utopia* (1974). In that work, Nozick defends political libertarianism, the view that the only legitimate function of government is to protect citizens' basic rights.

THINKING QUESTIONS

Robert Nozick, *How Liberty Upsets Patterns*

1. What does Nozick mean by "justice in holdings"? How does justice in holdings determine what each person is *entitled* to?
2. Nozick says that *liberty* upsets set patterns of distribution of wealth—liberty to do what?
3. What point is Nozick making with the example about Wilt Chamberlain? How does it help illustrate his view on justice in holdings?
4. What's so bad about violations of justice in holdings? Why is it wrong for the government to redistribute wealth, according to Nozick?

THE SUBJECT OF JUSTICE in holdings consists of three major topics. The first is the *original acquisition of holdings,* the appropriation of unheld things. This includes the issues of how unheld things may come to be held, the process, or processes, by which unheld things may come to be held, the things that may come to be held by these processes, the extent of what comes to be held by a particular process, and so on. We shall refer to the complicated truth about this topic, which we shall not formulate here, as the principle of justice in acquisition. The second topic concerns the *transfer of holdings* from one person to another. By what processes may a person transfer holdings to another? How may a person acquire a holding from another who holds it? Under this topic come general descriptions of voluntary exchange, and gift and (on the other hand) fraud, as well as reference to particular conventional details fixed upon in a given society. The complicated truth about this subject (with placeholders for conventional details) we shall call the principle of justice in transfer. (And we shall suppose it also includes principles governing how a person may divest himself of a holding, passing it into an unheld state.)

If the world were wholly just, the following inductive definition would exhaustively cover the subject of justice in holdings.

1. A person who acquires a holding in accordance with the principle of justice in acquisition is entitled to that holding.
2. A person who acquires a holding in accordance with the principle of justice in transfer, from someone else entitled to the holding, is entitled to the holding.
3. No one is entitled to a holding except by (repeated) applications of 1 and 2.

The complete principle of distributive justice would say simply that a distribution is just if everyone is entitled to the holdings they possess under the distribution. . . .

It is not clear how those holding alternative conceptions of distributive justice can reject the entitlement conception of justice in holdings. For suppose a distribution favored by one of these non-entitlement conceptions is realized. Let us suppose it is your favorite one and let us call this distribution D_1; perhaps everyone has an equal share, perhaps shares vary in accordance with some dimension you treasure. Now suppose that Wilt Chamberlain is greatly in demand by basketball teams, being a great gate attraction. (Also suppose contracts run only for a year, with players being free agents.) He signs the following sort of contract with a team: In each home game, twenty-five cents from the price of each ticket of admission goes to him. (We ignore the question of whether he is "gouging" the owners, letting them look out for themselves.) The season starts, and people cheerfully attend his team's games; they buy their tickets, each time dropping a separate twenty-five cents of their admission price into a special box with Chamberlain's name on it. They are excited about seeing him play; it is worth the total admission price to them. Let us suppose that in one season one million persons attend his home games, and Wilt Chamberlain winds up with $250,000, a much larger sum than the average income and larger even than anyone else has. Is he entitled to this income? Is this new distribution, D_2, unjust? If so, why? There is *no* question about whether each of the people was entitled to the control over the resources they held in D_1; because that was the distribution (your favorite) that (for the purposes of argument) we assumed was acceptable. Each of these persons *chose* to give twenty-five cents of their money to Chamberlain. They could have spent it on going to the movies, or on candy bars, or on copies of *Dissent* magazine, or of *Monthly Review*. But they all, at least one million of them, converged on giving it to Wilt Chamberlain in exchange for watching him play basketball. If D_1 was a just distribution, and people voluntarily moved from it to D_2, transferring parts of their shares they were given under D_1 (what was it for if not to do something with?), isn't D_2 also just? If the people were entitled to dispose of the resources to which they were entitled (under D_1), didn't this include their being entitled to give it to, or exchange it with, Wilt Chamberlain? Can anyone else complain on grounds of justice? Each other person already has his legitimate share under D_1. Under D_1, there is nothing that anyone has that anyone else has a claim of justice against. After someone transfers something to Wilt Chamberlain, third parties *still* have their legitimate shares; *their* shares are not changed. By what process could such a transfer among two persons give rise to a legitimate claim of distributive justice on a portion of what was transferred, by a third party who had no claim of justice on any holding of the others *before* the transfer? To cut off objections irrelevant here, we might imagine the exchanges occurring in a socialist society, after hours. After playing whatever basketball he does in his daily work, or doing whatever other daily work he does, Wilt Chamberlain decides to put in *overtime* to earn additional money. (First his work quota is set; he works time over that.) Or imagine it is a skilled juggler people like to see, who puts on shows after hours.

Why might someone work overtime in a society in which it is assumed their needs are satisfied? Perhaps because they care about things other than needs. I like to write in books that I read, and to have easy access to books for browsing at odd hours. It would be very pleasant and convenient to have the resources of Widener Library in my back yard. No society, I assume, will provide such resources close to each person who would like them as part of his regular allotment (under D_1). Thus, persons either must do without some extra things that they want, or be allowed to do something extra to get some of these things. On what basis could the inequalities that would eventuate be forbidden? Notice also that small factories would spring up in a socialist society, unless forbidden. I melt down some of my personal possessions (under D_1) and build a machine out of the material. I offer you, and others, a philosophy lecture once a week in exchange for your cranking the handle on my machine, whose products I exchange for yet other things, and so on. (The raw materials used by the machine are given to me by others who possess them under D_1, in exchange for hearing lectures.) Each person might participate to gain things over and above their allotment under D_1. Some persons even might want to leave their job in socialist industry and work full time in this private sector. I shall say something more about these issues in the next chapter. Here I wish merely to note how private property even in means of production would occur in a socialist society that did not forbid people to use as they wished some of the resources they are given under the socialist distribution D_1. The socialist society would have to forbid capitalist acts between consenting adults.

The general point illustrated by the Wilt Chamberlain example and the example of the entrepreneur in a socialist society is that no end-state principle or distributional patterned principle of justice can be continuously realized without continuous interference with people's lives. Any favored pattern would be transformed into one unfavored by the principle, by people choosing to act in various ways; for example, by people exchanging goods and services with other people, or giving things to other people, things the transferrers are entitled to under the favored distributional pattern. To maintain a pattern one must either continually interfere to stop people from transferring resources as they wish to, or continually (or periodically) interfere to take from some persons resources that others for some reason chose to transfer to them. (But if some time limit is to be set on how long people may keep resources others voluntarily transfer to them, why let them keep these resources for *any* period of time? Why not have immediate confiscation?) It might be objected that all persons voluntarily will choose to refrain from actions which would upset the pattern. This presupposes unrealistically (1) that all will most want to maintain the pattern (are those who don't, to be "reeducated" or forced to undergo "self-criticism"?), (2) that each can gather enough information about his own actions and the ongoing activities of others to discover which of his actions will upset the pattern, and (3) that diverse and far-flung persons can coordinate their actions to dovetail into the pattern. Compare the manner in which the market is neutral among persons' desires, as it reflects and transmits widely scattered information via prices, and coordinates persons' activities.

It puts things perhaps a bit too strongly to say that every patterned (or end-state) principle is liable to be thwarted by the voluntary actions of the individual parties transferring some of their shares they receive under the principle. For perhaps some *very* weak patterns are not so thwarted. Any distributional pattern with any egalitarian component is overturnable by the voluntary actions of individual persons over time; as is every patterned condition with sufficient content so as actually to have been proposed as presenting the central core of distributive justice. Still, given the possibility that some weak conditions or patterns may not be unstable in this way, it would be better to formulate an explicit description of the kind of interesting and contentful patterns under discussion, and to prove a theorem about their instability. Since the weaker the patterning, the more likely it is that the entitlement system itself satisfies it, a plausible conjecture is that any patterning either is unstable or is satisfied by the entitlement system.

A Deliberative Model of Democracy

SEYLA BENHABIB (1950–) was born in Istanbul, Turkey, and educated in Turkey and the United States, receiving her PhD from Yale University. Having taught previously at Harvard University, she is currently Eugene Meyer Professor of Political Science and Philosophy at Yale. The author of numerous books and articles, Dr. Benhabib's research explores issues of multiculturalism and feminism in political theory.

THINKING QUESTIONS

Seyla Benhabib, *A Deliberative Model of Democracy*

1. What is "legitimacy" in regard to democratic governments? Why is it necessary to the survival of a democratic society?
2. What is the "deliberative model of democracy"? What are the rules for deliberation that are built into it?
3. What are the advantages of the deliberative process to helping form and rank people's preferences? How is deliberation connected with the legitimacy of government?
4. Benhabib describes the deliberative model of democracy as "proceduralist." What does she mean by this? What are the procedures supposed to bring about?
5. The deliberative model is criticized for being dependent upon "the fiction of a mass assembly carrying out its deliberations in public and collectively." How does Benhabib respond to this criticism? How is it possible for there to be a real public conversation?

COMPLEX MODERN DEMOCRATIC SOCIETIES since the Second World War face the task of securing three public goods. These are legitimacy, economic welfare, and a viable sense of collective identity. These are "goods" in the sense that their attainment is considered worthy and desirable by most members of such societies; furthermore, not attaining one or a combination thereof would cause problems in the functioning of these societies such as to throw them into crises. . . .

According to the deliberative model of democracy, it is a necessary condition for attaining legitimacy and rationality with regard to collective decision-making processes in a polity, that the institutions of this polity are so arranged that what is considered in the common interest of all results from processes of collective deliberation conducted rationally and fairly among free and equal individuals. The more collective decision-making processes approximate this model the more increases the presumption of their legitimacy and rationality. Why?

The basis of legitimacy in democratic institutions is to be traced back to the presumption that the instances which claim obligatory power for themselves do so because their decisions represent an impartial standpoint said to be equally in the interests of all. This presumption can be fulfilled only if such decisions are in principle open to appropriate public processes of deliberation by free and equal citizens.

The discourse model of ethics formulates the most *general principles* and *moral intuitions* behind the validity claims of a deliberative model of democracy. The basic idea behind the model is that only those norms (i.e., general rules of action and institutional arrangements) can be said to be valid (i.e., morally binding), which would be agreed to by all those affected by their consequences, if such agreement were reached as a consequence of a process of deliberation that had the following features: 1) participation in such deliberation is governed by the norms of equality and symmetry; all have the same chances to initiate speech acts, to question, to interrogate, and to open debate; 2) all have the right to question the assigned topics of conversation; and 3) all have the right to initiate reflexive arguments about the very rules of the discourse procedure and the way in which they are applied or carried out. There are no prima facie rules limiting the agenda of the conversation, or the identity of the participants, as long as each excluded person or group can justifiably show that they are relevantly affected by the proposed norm under question. In certain circumstances this would mean that citizens of a democratic community would have to enter into a practical discourse with noncitizens who may be residing in their countries, at their borders, or in neighboring communities if there are matters that affect them all. Ecology and environmental issues in general are a perfect example of such instances when the boundaries of discourses keep expanding because the consequences of our actions expand and affect increasingly more people.

The procedural specifics of those special argumentation situations called "practical discourses" are not automatically transferable to a macro-institutional level, nor is it necessary that they should be so transferable. A theory of democracy, as opposed to a general moral theory, would have to be concerned with the question of institutional specifications and practical feasibility. Nonetheless, the procedural constraints of the discourse model can act as test cases for critically evaluating the criteria of membership and the rules for agenda setting, and for the structuring of public discussions within and among institutions. . . .

According to the deliberative model, procedures of deliberation generate legitimacy as well as assure some degree of practical rationality. But what are the claims to practical rationality of such deliberative democratic processes?

Deliberative processes are essential to the rationality of collective decision-making processes for three reasons. First, as Bernard Manin has observed in an excellent article "On Legitimacy and Deliberation," deliberative processes are also processes that impart information. New information is imparted because 1) no single individual can anticipate and foresee all the variety of perspectives through which matters of ethics and politics would be perceived by different individuals; and 2) no single individual can possess all the information deemed relevant to a certain decision affecting all. Deliberation is a procedure for being informed.

Furthermore, much political theory under the influence of economic models of reasoning in particular proceeds from a methodological fiction: this is the methodological fiction of an individual with an ordered set of coherent preferences. This fiction does not have much relevance in the political world. On complex social and political issues, more often than not, individuals may have views and wishes but no ordered set of preferences, since the latter would imply that they would be enlightened not only about the preferences but about the consequences and relative merits of each of their preferred choices in advance. It is actually the deliberative process itself that is likely to produce such an outcome by leading the individual to further critical reflection on his already held views and opinions; it is incoherent to assume that individuals can start a process of public deliberation with a level of conceptual clarity about their choices and preferences that can actually result only from a successful process of deliberation. Likewise, the formation of coherent preferences cannot precede deliberation; it can only succeed it. Very often individuals' wishes as well as views and opinions conflict with one another. In the course of deliberation and the exchange of views with others, individuals become more aware of such conflicts and feel compelled to undertake a coherent ordering.

More significantly, the very procedure of articulating a view in public imposes a certain reflexivity on individual preferences and opinions. When presenting their point of view and position to others, individuals must support them by articulating good reasons in a public context to their codeliberators. This process of *articulating good reasons in public* forces the individual to think of what would count as a good reason for all others involved. One is thus forced to think from the standpoint of all involved for whose agreement one is "wooing." Nobody can convince others in public of her point of view without being able to state why what appears good, plausible, just, and expedient to her can also be considered so from the standpoint of all involved. Reasoning from the standpoint of all involved not only forces a certain coherence upon one's own views but also forces one to adopt a standpoint that Hannah Arendt, following Kant, had called the "enlarged mentality."

A deliberative model of democracy suggests a necessary but not sufficient condition of practical rationality, because, as with any procedure, it can be misinterpreted, misapplied, and abused. Procedures can neither dictate outcomes nor define the quality of the reasons advanced in argumentation nor control the quality of the reasoning and rules of logic and inference used by participants.

Procedural models of rationality are underdetermined. Nonetheless, the discourse model makes some provisions against its own misuses and abuses in that the reflexivity condition built into the model allows abuses and misapplications at the first level to be challenged at a second, metalevel of discourse. Likewise, the equal chance of all affected to initiate such discourse of deliberation suggests that no outcome is prima facie fixed but can be revised and subjected to reexamination. Such would be the normative justification of majority rule as a decision procedure following from this model: in many instances the majority rule is a fair and rational decision procedure, not because legitimacy resides in numbers but because if a majority of people are convinced at one point on the basis of reasons formulated as closely as possible as a result of a process of discursive deliberation that conclusion A is the right thing to do, then this conclusion can remain valid until challenged by good reasons by some other group. It is not the sheer numbers that support the rationality of the conclusion, but the presumption that if a large number of people see certain matters a certain way as a result of following certain kinds of rational procedures of deliberation and decision-making, then such a conclusion has a presumptive claim to being rational until shown to be otherwise. The simple practice of having a ruling and an opposition party in democracies in fact incorporates this principle: we accept the will of the majority at the end of an electoral process that has been fairly and correctly carried out, but even when we accept the legitimacy of the process we may have grave doubts about the rationality of the outcome. The practice of there being parliamentary opposition says that the grounds on which the majority party claims to govern can be examined, challenged, tested, criticized, and rearticulated. Parliamentary procedures of opposition, debate, questioning, and even impeachment proceedings, and investigatory commissions incorporate this rule of deliberative rationality that majoritarian decisions are temporarily agreed-upon conclusions, the claim to rationality and validity of which can be publicly reexamined.

This deliberative model of democracy is proceduralist in that it emphasizes first and foremost certain institutional procedures and practices for attaining decisions on matters that would be binding on all. Three additional points are worthy of note with respect to such a conception of democracy: first, I proceed from the assumption of value pluralism. Disagreement about the highest goods of human existence and the proper conduct of a morally righteous life are a fundamental feature of our modern value-universe since the end of natural law cosmologies in the sixteenth and seventeenth centuries, and the eventual separation of church and state. The challenge to democratic rationality is to arrive at acceptable formulations of the common good despite this inevitable value-pluralism. We cannot resolve conflicts among value systems and visions of the good by reestablishing a strong unified moral and religious code without forsaking fundamental liberties. Agreements in societies living with value-pluralism are to be sought for not at the level of substantive beliefs but at that of procedures, processes, and practices for attaining and revising beliefs. Proceduralism is a rational answer to persisting value conflicts at the substantive level.

Second, the deliberative model of democracy proceeds not only from a conflict of values but also from a conflict of interests in social life. Social life necessitates both conflict of interests and cooperation. Democratic procedures have to convince, even under conditions when one's interests as an individual or as a group are negatively affected, that the conditions of mutual cooperation are still legitimate. Procedures can be regarded as methods for articulating, sifting through, and weighing conflicting interests. The more conflicts of interests there are the more it is important to have procedural solutions of conflict adjudication through which parties whose interests are negatively affected can find recourse to other methods of the articulation and representation of their grievances. Proceduralist models of democracy allow the articulation of conflicts of interests under conditions of social cooperation mutually acceptable to all.

Finally, any proceduralist and deliberative model of democracy is prima facie open to the argument that no modern society can organize its affairs along the fiction of a mass assembly carrying out its deliberations in public and collectively. Here more than an issue of size is at stake. The argument that there may be an invisible limit to the size of a deliberative body that, when crossed, affects the nature of the reasoning process is undoubtedly true. Nonetheless the reason why a deliberative and proceduralist model of democracy does not need to operate with the fiction of a general deliberative assembly is that the procedural specifications of this model privilege a *plurality of modes of association* in which all affected can have the right to articulate their point of view. These can range from political parties, to citizens' initiatives, to social movements, to voluntary associations, to consciousness-raising groups, and the like. *It is through the interlocking net of these multiple forms of associations, networks, and organizations that an anonymous "public conversation" results. It is central to the model of deliberative democracy that it privileges such a public sphere of mutually interlocking and overlapping networks and associations of deliberation, contestation, and argumentation.* The fiction of a general deliberative assembly in which the united people expressed their will belongs to the early history of democratic theory; today our guiding model has to be that of a medium of loosely associated, multiple foci of opinion formation and dissemination which affect one another in free and spontaneous processes of communication.

Deliberation and Democratic Character

AMY GUTMANN (1950–) is the president of the University of Pennsylvania, previously serving as the provost at Princeton University where she had been a faculty member since 1976. The author or editor of more than a dozen books and dozens of articles, Dr. Gutmann has written widely on issues in democracy, human rights, and the education of citizens in democratic societies. Among her most influential works are *Democratic Education* (1987) and *Democracy and Disagreement* (1996).

THINKING QUESTIONS

Amy Gutmann, *Deliberation and Democratic Character*

1. Gutmann argues that instilling character and teaching moral reasoning are the two central purposes of education for children in a democracy. Why? How are these purposes connected with what she calls "democratic character"?
2. Why should public schools teach morality? Why is it unavoidable that they teach some aspects of morality?
3. What is "liberal neutrality"? What is Gutmann's argument against liberal neutrality in regard to teaching morality in the public schools?
4. What does Gutmann mean by "moralism"? What's the difference in emphasis between liberal moralism and conservative moralism?
5. Why does Gutmann favor liberal moralism? Why do the values of liberal moralism fit better with democratic character?

CHILDHOOD IS A NATURAL PLACE to begin a discussion of education: good habits and principles are easier to instill in children than in adults, and governments are more justified in limiting the liberty of children than of adults for the sake of education. But by beginning with childhood, we must not overlook the fact that imperfectly educated citizens must educate future citizens. We cannot assume a perfectly wise philosopher-king, an ideal tutor for every child, or parents who unfailingly teach their children democratic virtue.

Nor can we assume that children are born ready for rational deliberation. The earliest education of children is not and cannot be by precept or reasoning;

it must be by discipline and example. Children are first educated by their parents, and so must they continue to be as long as raising children constitutes one of our most valued personal liberties. Barring misfortune, parents typically love and nurture their children, later also reward and punish, praise and blame them for their actions. For most children, the family plays a large role in building character and in teaching basic skills for many years. But early in the lives of most children, their parents begin to share these primary educational functions with other associations: day-care centers, elementary (and then secondary) schools, churches and synagogues, civic organizations, friendship circles, and work groups. As children move outside their original families, their character and their skills are shaped by the examples of those whom they love and respect and by the rules regulating the associations to which they belong.

But training of this "exemplary" sort is only one kind of education, undoubtedly most effective during our childhood. At some fairly early stage in their development, children also become responsive to another kind of education, one that is more intellectual in its effect and rationalist in its method. They learn the three R's largely by direct instruction. They also develop capacities for criticism, rational argument, and decisionmaking by being taught how to think logically, to argue coherently and fairly, and to consider the relevant alternatives before coming to conclusions. Training of this "didactic" sort is democratically desirable because it enables citizens to understand, to communicate, and in some cases to resolve their disagreements. Without this sort of mutual understanding, we could not expect to achieve widespread toleration of dissent and respect for differing ways of life. Nor could we expect minorities to convince majorities, or to be convinced by them, of their point of view. But quite apart from its political function, children will eventually need the capacity for rational deliberation to make hard choices in situations where habits and authorities do not supply clear or consistent guidance. These two facts about our lives—that we disagree about what is good and that we face hard choices as individuals even when we agree as a group—are the basis for an argument that primary education should be both exemplary and didactic. Children must learn not just to *behave* in accordance with authority but to *think* critically about authority if they are to live up to the democratic ideal of sharing political sovereignty as citizens.

People adept at logical reasoning who lack moral character are sophists of the worst sort: they use moral arguments to serve whatever ends they happen to choose for themselves. They do not take morality seriously nor are they able to distinguish between the obvious moral demands and the agonizing dilemmas of life. But people who possess sturdy moral character without a developed capacity for reasoning are ruled only by habit and authority, and are incapable of constituting a society of sovereign citizens. Education in character and in moral reasoning are therefore both necessary, neither sufficient, for creating democratic citizens.

Taken together, inculcating character and teaching moral reasoning do not exhaust the legitimate ends of primary education in a democracy. Citizens value primary education for more than its moral and political purposes. They also value it for helping children learn how to live a good life in the nonmoral sense by teaching them knowledge and appreciation of (among other things) literature, science, history, and sports. These subjects are properly valued not primarily for the sake of imparting cultural coherence to a child's life, but for their place in cultivating a nonmorally good life for children, characterized by a combination of literary appreciation, scientific and historical knowledge, and physical agility. I say little more about these nonmoral ends of education not because they are unimportant (or unproblematic), but because the moral ends are less well understood and more politically problematic. Fortunately, the same education that helps children live a nonmorally good life often aids in the development of good moral character. The logical skills taught by science and mathematics, the interpretive skills taught by literature, the understanding of differing ways of life taught by both history and literature, and even the sportsmanship taught by physical education can contribute to the moral education of citizens.

Although inculcating character and teaching moral reasoning by no means exhaust the purposes of primary education in a democracy, together they constitute its core political purpose: the development of "deliberative," or what I shall interchangeably call "democratic," character. Deliberation is connected, both by definition and practice, with the development of democracy. Deliberation, on the individual level, is defined as "careful consideration with a view to decision" and, on the institutional level, as "consideration and discussion of the reasons for and against a measure by a number of councilors (e.g. in a legislative assembly)."

In practice, the development of deliberative character is essential to realizing the ideal of a democratically sovereign society. Democracy depends on a mutual commitment and trust among its citizens that the laws resulting from the democratic process are to be obeyed except when they violate the basic principles on which democratic sovereignty rests. Deliberative citizens are committed, at least partly through the inculcation of habit, to living up to the routine demands of democratic life, at the same time as they are committed to questioning those demands whenever they appear to threaten the foundational ideals of democratic sovereignty, such as respect for persons. The willingness and ability to deliberate set morally serious people apart from both sophists, who use clever argument to elevate their own interests into self-righteous causes, and traditionalists, who invoke established authority to subordinate their own reason to unjust causes. People who give careful consideration to the morality of laws can be trusted to defend and to respect laws that are not in their self-interest, at the same time as they can be expected to oppose laws that violate democratic principles, and ultimately to disobey them, if necessary, with the intent of changing them by appealing to the conscience of the majority.

Citizens therefore have good reason to wonder how deliberative or democratic character can be developed in children, and who can develop it. I shall focus much (although by no means all) of my concern on the ways in which schools develop, or fail to develop, democratic character. Concern for how schools develop democratic character does not preclude concern for how parents teach—or fail to teach—their children democratic virtues within the family. I concentrate on the role of schools rather than parents in educating citizens not because the parental role is less significant but because the role of schools is subject to more direct political control. Parents command a domain of moral education within the family that is—and should continue to be—largely immune from external control. If there should be a domain for citizens collectively to educate children in the democratic virtues of deliberation, then primary schools occupy a large part of that domain, although they do not monopolize it.

AMORALISM

What role should primary schools play in moral education? The simplest answer is none: schools should leave character development and training in moral reasoning to families and voluntary associations, such as churches and synagogues. This is the advice of at least one popular American authority:

> Personally, Miss Manners thinks that the parents of America should offer the school systems a bargain: You teach them English, history, mathematics, and science, and we will . . . look after their souls.

An apparent attraction of this solution is that schools would thereby rid themselves of all the political controversies now surrounding moral education and get on with the task of teaching the "basics"—cognitive skills and factual knowledge.

But children do not leave their souls behind when they go to school, and schools cannot escape looking after children's souls in many significant and subtle ways. Even if schools avoid all courses that deal explicitly with morality or civic education, they still engage in moral education by virtue of their "hidden curriculum," noncurricular practices that serve to develop moral attitudes and character in students. Schools develop moral character at the same time as they try to teach basic cognitive skills, by insisting that students sit in their seats (next to students of different races and religions), raise their hands before speaking, hand in their homework on time, not loiter in the halls, be good sports on the playing field, and abide by many other rules that help define a school's character. We become aware of many more ways in which schools shape moral character only when we consider alternative school practices. In Japanese elementary schools, teachers routinely expect students who have mastered the day's lesson to help teach those who have yet to finish. Every member of the school, including the principal, shares in the chores necessary to keep the school building clean (many schools have no specialized janitorial staff). These practices are lessons in egalitarianism that may never need to be explicitly taught in the curriculum if they are consistently practiced in the classroom. Most elementary schools in the United States teach different moral lessons, but they too engage in moral education simply by not doing what the Japanese schools do. The political choice facing us therefore is not whether schools should engage in moral education, but what sort of moral education they should engage in.

Nor would it be desirable for schools to forswear moral education, even if it were possible for them to do so. Public schools in a democracy should serve our interests as citizens in the moral education of future citizens. Our parental interests are to some extent independent of our role as democratic citizens, and hence the emphasis of moral education within the family is likely to be quite different from that within schools. Most parents want to create a family life that satisfies their emotional and spiritual needs, and allows them to share their particular values with their children. However deep this concern for sharing particular values, it need not imply an equal concern for spreading these values more generally among children. Parents can recognize the advantages of living in a society in which a variety of values are deeply held and they are therefore free to teach their values to their children.

This freedom depends on children being taught widespread and enduring tolerance for different ways of life. Parents acting individually and citizens acting collectively both have valuable and largely complementary roles to play in the moral education of children: the former in teaching children what it means to be committed to particular people and one way of life among many; the latter in teaching responsibilities and rights within a larger and more diverse community. Moral education in a democracy is best viewed as a shared trust of the family and the polity, mutually beneficial to everyone who appreciates the values of both family life and democratic citizenship.

LIBERAL NEUTRALITY

How can primary schools best fulfill the terms of this trust? Three of the most popular answers in this country find their conceptual homes in the state of individuals, the state of families, and the family state. The answer most consistent with the state of individuals is that schools should teach the capacity for moral reasoning and choice without predisposing children toward any given conception of the good life or toward a particular moral character (aside from one defined by this capacity). Just as a liberal state must leave its adult citizens free to choose their own "good" life, so must its schools leave children free to choose their own values. If public schools predisposed citizens towards a particular way of life by educating them as children, the professed neutrality of the liberal state would be a cover for the bias of its educational system.

Liberal neutrality supports the educational method of "values clarification," which enjoys widespread use in schools throughout the United States. Proponents of values clarification identify two major purposes of moral education within schools. The first is to help students understand and develop their own values. The second is to teach them respect for the values of others. Advocates of values clarification view it as the pedagogical alternative to indoctrination:

> In place of indoctrination, my associates and I are substituting a *process* approach to the entire area of dealing with values in the schools, which focuses on the process of valuing, not on the transmission of the "right" set of values. We call this approach *values clarification,* and it is based on the premise that none of us has the "right" set of values to pass on to other people's children.

Values clarification is often criticized for being value-laden, despite its apparent claim to value neutrality. This criticism is weaker than is generally recognized. Advocates of values clarification need not, and many do not, deny that their defense of values clarification is value-laden:

> If we urge critical thinking, then we value *rationality*. If we support moral reasoning, then we value *justice*. If we advocate divergent thinking, then we value *creativity*. If we uphold free choice, then we value autonomy or *freedom*. If we encourage "no-lose" conflict resolution, then we value *equality*. . . . Called before the committee, we can only say that values clarification is not and never has been "value-free."

Proponents of values clarification can admit without fear of self-contradiction that they are morally committed to the pedagogical position that teachers should not impose their views on students.

The problem with values clarification is not that it is value-laden, but that it is laden with the wrong values. Treating every moral opinion as equally worthy encourages children in the false subjectivism that "I have my opinion and you have yours and who's to say who's right?" This moral understanding does not take the demands of democratic justice seriously. The toleration and mutual respect that values clarification teaches is too indiscriminate for even the most ardent democratic to embrace. If children come to school believing that "blacks, Jews, Catholics, and/or homosexuals are inferior beings who shouldn't have the same rights as the rest of us," then it is criticism, not just clarification, of children's values that is needed.

The needed criticism is similar to that which was more generally directed against the state of individuals. Citizens value in children not only the rational capacity to choose but the kind of character that inclines them to choose good over bad lives. The aim of cultivating good character authorizes teachers to respect only a limited range of values professed (or acted upon) by children. Indiscriminate respect for children's values cannot be defended either as an ultimate end or as a tenable means of cultivating good character.

MORALISM

"Moralist" positions, which find their home in the family state, begin where this critique of liberal neutrality leaves off, with a conception of primary education whose explicit purpose is to inculcate character and to restrict children's choices to those that are worthy of pursuit. Moralists, both liberal and conservative, reject freedom of choice as the primary purpose of primary education. They seek to shape a particular kind of moral character that will be constrained—by either habit or reason, or both—to choose a good life.

Conservative Moralism

Just as defenders of the family state disagree over what principles constitute a good society, so moralists disagree over what virtues constitute a good person. Conservative moralists emphasize respect for authority. They defend educational programs often criticized by advocates of liberal neutrality as indoctrination or at least as unduly restrictive of individual freedom: patriotic rituals, dress codes, strict discipline within the classroom, and deference to teachers' opinions. The emphasis on teaching children to respect authority is, I suspect, rooted in a deep pessimism concerning the human disposition to be moral: left free to choose a set of principles to guide their actions, people are as likely to choose immoral as moral ones. This pessimism may underlie the conservative preference for shielding students from false political and religious beliefs, examples of immoral behavior, and indecent language rather than providing them with reasons to criticize and resist such beliefs and behavior. The aim of a conservative moralist education is to teach children to "behave" morally. It is not the process but the result of moral education—moral behavior, not moral reasoning—that matters.

Suppose that the results of moral education are all that matter. We still would be left with the difficult problem of determining which methods of moral education in schools will produce the best moral behavior in children. "It is by exposing our children to good character and inviting its imitation," Secretary of Education William Bennett claims, "that we will transmit to them good character." Teachers and principals, Bennett argues, must not only "articulate ideals and convictions to students" but also "live the difference [between right and wrong, good and bad] in front of pupils." Bennett is "not talking about browbeating students into accepting [a] point of view. This is simply indoctrination, which we all deplore." But he is talking about putting less emphasis on discussing moral issues and more emphasis on inculcating democratic character through "the quiet power of moral example."

Liberal Moralism

Liberal moralism shares with its conservative cousin a commitment to inculcating character, but it differs from conservative moralism in identifying *moral autonomy* as the goal of moral education: education should produce in children the desire and capacity to make moral choices based on principles that are generalizable among all persons. Liberal and conservative moralists agree that moral education need not be limited to clarifying whatever values children happen to bring into the classroom, but liberal moralism poses a distinct dilemma: How can schools—or anyone else—teach children to respect moral principles rather than established authority?

Guided by Piaget's work on moral development, John Rawls outlines in Part III of *A Theory of Justice* a three-stage theory of liberal moralist education that might be interpreted as an answer to this question. Children begin to learn morality by following rules because their parents and other authorities issue them. Learning the "morality of authority" is an improvement over anarchy of desire, as most parents realize. The second stage of moral development, the "morality of association," is characterized by an acceptance of rules because they are appropriate to fulfilling the roles that individuals play within various associations. Students, friends, and citizens obey moral rules because they thereby benefit the associations of which they are a part, and are benefited in turn. The morality of association is an improvement over the morality of authority because children learn to alter their habits and to criticize established authorities out of empathy for others and a concern for fairness.

The final stage of moral development, the "morality of principle," is characterized by a direct attachment to moral principles themselves. In a just society, Rawls tells us, the morality of principles would be achieved "quite naturally" through our previous associational experiences:

> We develop a desire to apply and to act upon the principles of justice once we realize how social arrangements answering to them have promoted our good and that of those with whom we are affiliated. In due course we come to appreciate the ideal of just human cooperation.

Most conservative moralists set their moral sights too low, inviting blind obedience to authority; most liberal moralists set them too high, inviting disillusionment with morality. From a democratic perspective, success in teaching the morality of association marks great progress over the morality of authority. Schools that help develop the cooperative moral sentiments—empathy, trust, benevolence, and fairness—contribute a great deal to democratic education. Dewey's ideal of a school whose aim is "not the economic value of the products, but the development of social power and insight" pointed to such a morality. The internally democratic practices of schools like the "School Within a School" in Brookline, Massachusetts . . . contribute more to the moral development of students than the authority patterns of schools perceived by their students to be autocratic and unfair, or simply boring. What the most successful schools seem to teach, however, is not the morality of principle but the morality of association: the willingness and ability to contribute and to claim one's fair share in cooperative associations.

In a democracy, teaching the morality of association marks great moral progress over teaching the morality of authority because children who learn only the latter lack the capacity (or willingness) to distinguish between fair and unfair, trustworthy and untrustworthy authorities. They also fail to identify with the purposes of social institutions that do not continually serve their self-interest or force them to cooperate. They have never learned to judge the commands of authorities or their own actions according to whether they live up to the terms of fair social cooperation. Given the democratic goal of sharing the rights and responsibilities of citizenship, schools that teach children the cooperative virtues are uncommonly successful and minimally problematical. Unlike the morality of principle, the morality of association does not incorporate the controversial claim (apparently accepted much more widely by men than by women) that impartiality among persons is the singularly highest moral ideal. Empathy, trust, fairness, and benevolence—virtues at least as common among women as men—mark the morality of association.

Achieving the morality of association is compatible, moreover, with the use (at least in the early stages of schooling) of many of the pedagogical practices advocated by conservative moralists. Just as children learn filial independence after they learn to love and respect their parents, so they may learn political independence after they learn to "love" their president and to be patriotic toward their country. The standards of patriotism and loyalty, like those of love and respect for parents, change as children learn to think critically about politics and to recognize that their civic duties extend beyond voting and obedience to laws. Moral education begins by winning the battle against amoralism and egoism. And ends—if it ends at all—by struggling against uncritical acceptance of the moral habits and opinions that were the spoils of the first victory.

Losing the Faith: Feminism and Democracy

SUSAN MENDUS holds degrees from the University of Wales and Oxford University and is a member of the faculty at the University of York, England. Professor Mendus is the author of numerous articles and books including *Feminism and Emotion* (2000) and *Impartiality in Moral and Political Philosophy* (2002). Her main areas of research are feminist political philosophy and the philosophy of education.

THINKING QUESTIONS

Susan Mendus, *Losing the Faith: Feminism and Democracy*

1. What does Mendus mean by the claim that democratic theory, *as a matter of principle,* disadvantages women? How is this claim different from the claim that democratic societies, as they exist now, disadvantage women?
2. Robert Dahl defends the claim that the inequality of women is a practical problem that can be solved over time. What is his reason for believing this claim? How does Mendus respond?
3. Mendus uses the example of treating pregnancy as "illness" requiring "sick-leave" to illustrate the "male model of normality" which she believes is built into democratic societies. What is the problem that she is pointing out? Do you think this problem is inherent in democracies?
4. What does Mendus mean by a "politics of difference"? How does it clash with the value of equality?
5. How does Mendus think democracies can be improved? Why does her solution give priority to differences between men and women rather than equality between them?

AT A TIME WHEN THE BERLIN WALL has been dismantled and Eastern Europe is embracing the values of Western liberal democracy, when an attempted coup in Moscow has been overthrown, and the republics of the former USSR have claimed independence and democratic freedoms, it may seem churlish to criticize democracy or to doubt its ability to live up to its own ideals. Democracy may indeed be an imperfect form of government, but all the others are far worse and this, surely, is a moment for recognizing the benefits which democracy brings, not a moment for drawing attention to its shortcomings. It is a moment for confirming our faith, not a moment for doubting it.

And yet, some feminists do doubt it. Moreover, the doubts run deep, and constitute an attack not only on the achievements of modern democratic states, but also on the underlying ideals of democratic theory itself. Feminists have long drawn attention to the facts of women's under-representation in political life, and of their over-representation amongst the unemployed, the low-paid, and the part-time work-force. They now suspect that these features, common to all modern democratic states, are not merely unfortunate contingencies, or remediable imperfections of specific states. Rather, they are an indication of deep gender bias in democratic theory itself. For feminists, democracy is not something which, as a matter of unfortunate fact, has failed to deliver on its promises to women. It embodies ideals which guarantee that it will never deliver unless it embarks upon extensive critical examination of its own philosophical assumptions. In brief, the charge made against democracy is that, for women, it was never more than an article of faith, and when two hundred years of democratization have failed (and are still failing) to deliver equality for women, even faith is giving out.

The uncharitable may interpret these remarks as nothing more than evidence of feminist paranoia and of women's general inability to recognize when they are well off. It is therefore important to stress that the charge is not simply that democratic *states* are, as a matter of fact, ones in which women are disadvantaged (though they are), but rather that democratic *theory* is, as a matter of principle, committed to ideals which guarantee that that will remain so. As a faith, democracy was always a false faith, and its prophets (including nearly all the major political philosophers of the past two hundred years) are now exposed as false prophets.

These are serious, depressing, and even dangerous charges. The more so if we have no preferred alternative to democracy, and no revised interpretation of its central ideals. The tasks for contemporary feminism are therefore twofold: first, to justify the claim that traditional democratic theory leads to undemocratic practice; secondly, to identify the ways in which that theory might be reinterpreted so as to come closer to democratic ideals. The former is feminism's critique of the faith; the latter is feminism's revision of the faith.

A CRITIQUE OF THE FAITH

The belief that democratic theory condones undemocratic practice is not confined to feminist theorists. John Dunn has argued that there are 'two distinct and developed democratic theories loose in the world today—one dismally ideological and the other fairly blatantly utopian'. On the dismally ideological account democracy is simply the least bad mechanism for securing a measure of responsibility on the part of the governors to the governed. By contrast, the blatantly utopian account envisages a society in which all social arrangements represent the interests of all people. The former constitutes a practical proposal, but hardly an inspiring one; the latter may be inspiring, but is hardly practical. Despairing of finding anything which can reflect democracy's status as both a high ideal and a practical proposal, Dunn concludes that 'today, in politics, democracy is the *name* for what we cannot have—yet cannot cease to want'. On Dunn's analysis the grounds for scepticism about democracy lie largely in the circumstances of modern life: the social and economic differentiation which are characteristic of the modern world necessarily generate inequalities which fit ill with the democratic ideal of political equality. Connectedly, the sheer size of modern states creates a rift between the individual and the community which makes it impossible for individuals to perceive the state as a focus of common good. Thus, democracy is not attainable in large, modern, postindustrial societies: as an ideal, it promises human fulfilment and human freedom, but in the modern world this promise cannot be met and democracy has therefore become at best a method of curbing the excesses of rulers, and at worst an idle, or even a utopian dream.

But if Dunn fears that democracy cannot exist, given the nature of modern states, feminists note with some chagrin that democracy never did exist even prior to the growth of modern states: Carole Pateman briskly dismisses the subject, claiming that 'for feminists, democracy has never existed; women never have been and still are not admitted as full and equal members in any country known as a "democracy".' Put together, the two accounts are deeply unsettling: Dunn tells us that without small states and an undifferentiated public there cannot be democracy. Feminists tell us that even when there were small states and an undifferentiated public, still there never was democracy. For feminists, the facts of history—the denial of the vote to women, their historical confinement to a domestic realm, their incorporation within the interests of their husbands—prove beyond doubt that for women democracy has never existed. For them, therefore, Dunn's lament is not even a lament for times past, but only a reflection on what might have been but in fact never was.

Why was there never democracy for women, and why is there still no democracy for women? A number of modern writers implicitly assume that it is because women have historically been denied equality under the law and the formal, political right to vote. For example, Robert Dahl recognizes that almost all the major writers in the democratic tradition excluded women from their theories, but he implies that this is merely evidence of the fact that philosophers are children of their time, and that the problem may be solved simply by rewriting references to 'all men' as 'all men and women' or 'all adults'. Thus, indicating that all is now well, he writes: 'In most countries women gained the suffrage only in this century, and in a few only after the Second World War. In fact, not until our own century did democratic theory and practice begin to reflect a belief that all (or virtually all) adults should be included in the demos as a matter of right'. And this completes his discussion of the role of women in modern democratic states.

Dahl's optimism is grounded in his recognition that women are now formally equal citizens, and in his belief that this formal equality need not be fatally undermined by social and economic inequalities. He accepts the general claim that political equality is compromised by lack of economic power, but argues that this should not lead to the pessimistic conclusion that democracy is 'something we cannot have yet cannot cease to want'. Rather, it suggests the more robust conclusion that the pursuit of democracy includes the removal of social and economic inequalities. He writes:

> Though the idea of equal opportunity is often so weakly interpreted that it is rightly dismissed as too undemanding, when it is taken in its fullest sense it is extraordinarily demanding—so demanding, indeed, that the criteria for the democratic process would require a people committed to it to institute measures well beyond those that even the most democratic states have hitherto brought about.

For Dahl, therefore, inequality is a practical problem which admits of practical solutions. Since it is a widespread and intransigent problem, there will be no 'quick fix', but there can be progress, and in tracing that progress Dahl does not see the need to make reference to any special feature of women's position beyond the recognition that they are, in general, amongst those who suffer from a lack of social and economic power. By implication, he denies that women constitute a special and intransigent problem for democratic theory. They are simply a specific example of a quite general, but remediable, problem, the problem of how to ensure that social and economic inequalities do not undermine the formal equality of the vote.

Many feminists dissent: although agreeing that there are practical problems, they also insist that, in the case of women, the problems have a theoretical origin which goes beyond mere social and economic inequality. Women, they argue, are different not simply because they lack economic and social power, but because historically they have been explicitly excluded from the category of citizen in the democratic state. So we might agree that democracy depends upon enlarging the economic power of those who are citizens, but so long as women (along with children, animals, and the insane) were excluded from that category, the question of enlarging their economic and social power frequently failed to arise. Indeed, women's economic power was normally identified with the economic power of their husbands, and the fact that wives themselves owned nothing was (and often still is) conveniently forgotten. Again, it is important to be clear about the status of this objection: usually, it is taken as simply a reflection on the historical facts of democratic societies, but it also contains the seeds of a criticism of democratic theory itself. The criticism may be made explicit by considering Dahl's two interpretations of what he calls 'the principle of inclusion' in democratic theory. This principle is the principle which dictates who shall count as a citizen in the democratic state, and therefore who shall have a say in determining the laws of the state.

Dahl notes that historically philosophers have vacillated between a contingent and a categorical principle of inclusion: thus, some urge that all adult members of a state are also, and thereby, citizens (the categorical criterion); others claim that only those who are qualified to rule may be citizens (the contingent claim). He concedes that the contingent criterion has been the most popular in the history of political philosophy, but urges that the categorical criterion is the appropriate one for modern democratic states. There should be no question of individuals having to prove their fitness to rule. The criterion for being a full citizen is simply that one is an adult member of the state in question. This, and this alone, justifies according rights of citizenship.

There is, however, a worrying tension between the assumptions inherent in the demand for increased social and economic equality and the assumptions inherent in the demand for a categorical criterion of citizenship. For the former recognizes that if citizenship is to be meaningful, more than formal equality is required, whereas the latter is content with a formal criterion for being or becoming a citizen. The danger is that acceptance of the categorical principle of inclusion, with its requirement that we ignore differences between people at the formal level, may lead to minimizing differences between people in framing social policy. Most importantly, it may lead to an understanding of difference, specifically women's differences, as disadvantage, disability, or deviance. If difference is the problem at the level of inclusion, then the removal of difference may be thought to be the solution at the level of social policy.

Thus, to provide a concrete example, pregnancy is often treated as akin to illness, and maternity leave as a special case of sick-leave. Pregnant women are then equated with men who are ill or temporarily disabled, and the attempt to attain 'equality' for them rests on the assumption that they are, in effect, disabled men. By this strategy, inequalities are certainly reduced because women attain something by way of maternity benefit, and something is surely better than nothing. But the importance of the practical benefits should not disguise the fact that the theoretical assumptions of the strategy are assimilationist and patriarchal. Women attain a degree of equality only by conceding that the differences between themselves and men are differences which carry the implication of female inferiority. Moreover, this is not simply a complaint about the practical arrangements governing pregnancy and childbirth; it is a more general concern about the unspoken assumptions of many democratic theorists, specifically their assumption that equality is to be attained via the removal or minimization of disadvantage, where what counts as disadvantage is held to be clear and uncontroversial, but is in fact determined by reference to a model which is intrinsically male.

Considerations of this sort highlight the fact that for women lack of social and economic power is only half the story: it is not simply bad luck that women, in general, lack economic power. It is the male model of normality which *guarantees* that that will be so. Iris Marion Young expresses the point forcefully:

> In my view an equal treatment approach to pregnancy and childbirth is inadequate because it either implies that women do not have any right to leave and job security when having babies, or

> assimilates such guarantees under the supposedly gender-neutral category of 'disability'. . . . Assimilating pregnancy and disability tends to stigmatize these processes as 'unhealthy.'

It is for this reason that many feminists have found it difficult to retain faith in democracy and democratic theory. And, as we have seen, the loss of faith occurs at several levels: historically, feminists are aware that the denial of difference at the level of inclusion has rarely been observed. Most philosophers have noted differences between men and women, and have argued that these differences support the exclusion of women from even the rights of formal political equality. More recently, feminists have drawn attention to the fact that even where the categorical criterion has been employed, it has not been accompanied by any strenuous efforts to remove the social and economic disadvantages suffered by women, and therefore formal political equality has been undermined by practical social and economic inequality. Finally, and most importantly, many feminists now doubt whether the denial or removal of difference is even an acceptable aim for political theory and practice. Again, the doubts arise on two levels. Anne Phillips has argued that the individualistic character of modern philosophy makes it inadequate for feminist purposes. She notes:

> The anti-discrimination that informs much contemporary liberalism implies removing obstacles that block an individual's path and then applauding when that individual succeeds. The problem is still perceived in terms of previous *mis*-treatment, which judged and dismissed people because they had deviated from some prejudiced norm. The answer is presented in terms of treating them just as people instead.

Where difference is interpreted as deviance or disadvantage, the response to it is to implement social policy which will minimize the effects of that disadvantage *in the specific case*. This individualistic response has been countered by the demand that what is required is recognition of *group* disadvantage. Far from asserting that it should not matter whether we are men or women, this strategy insists that men and women do have different degrees of power and that therefore policies should be implemented which take account of this fact and guarantee increased power to women as a group.

The second response is rather different. It denies that difference is always to be construed as disadvantage and, in the case of women, urges a restructuring of both political theory and political practice in such a way as to celebrate at least some differences. In other words, it denies that all difference is disability, and it objects to the strategy whereby the 'disadvantages' of pregnancy and childbirth are mitigated by assimilating them to male illness. So, where democratic theory characteristically urges that we should assume that everyone is the same, feminists urge a recognition that men and women are different. Similarly, where democratic theorists have urged that, in decisions about social policy, we should aim to minimize the disadvantages which spring from difference, feminists ask why such normal states as pregnancy should be categorized as disadvantages at all.

For feminists, therefore, losing the faith has been losing faith in the ability of doctrines of equality, understood as doctrines which advocate the minimization of difference, to deliver a political theory which will be sensitive to the realities of women's lives. The solution to this problem lies in a rewriting of democratic theory in such a way as to ensure that it acknowledges and incorporates difference. Most importantly, it lies in a recognition that, in the case of women, the disadvantages which spring from difference are themselves politically significant. They are disadvantages inherent in not being male. So democratic theory falls at the first hurdle because it in fact employs a male, rather than a gender-neutral, standard by which to decide what counts as disadvantage.

The proposed solution is not without its dangers: oppressed and disadvantaged groups have long used a doctrine of equality as their most important single weapon, and have appealed to such concepts as 'common humanity' in their attempts to attain political and legal rights. Moreover, they have vigorously denied the significance of difference in political contexts, and urged that differences between them and other, more advantaged, groups should be ignored in the distribution of political rights. It is therefore a discomfiting about-face for feminist theorists now to insist on a politics of difference, and to pin their faith in the possibility that difference may be acknowledged, not construed as disadvantage.

To what extent do feminists wish to attack democratic ideals, and to what extent do they wish to reconstruct them? Is their argument that we should substitute an acceptance of difference for the demand for equality, or that the demand for equality itself requires a full and sensitive recognition of the practical significance of difference?

REVISING THE FAITH

Some critics have argued that feminists do indeed reject the ideal of equality, and that they do so because they wrongly assume that equality is at odds with the recognition of difference. Thus, Richard Norman writes: 'Equality does not require the elimination of difference. Sexual equality, in particular, does not require a denial of the inescapable biological facts of sexual difference, and leaves open what further differences might follow from these'. Certainly some feminists have spoken of equality in dismissive terms, and have urged that we should pay less attention to it. Virginia Held, for example says:

> Occasionally, for those who give birth, equality will be an important concept as we strive to treat children fairly and have them treat each other with respect. But it is normally greatly overshadowed by such other concerns as that the relationship between ourselves and our children and each other be trusting and considerate.

But this is simply the point that equality is not the only concept in moral and political life. It is not the complaint that equality necessarily conflicts with difference. And more generally, when feminists express reservations about equality, it is because they recognize that democratic theory itself has interpreted it as requiring the elimination or minimization of difference. In general, it is not feminists who urge that equality and difference are incompatible concepts; it is democratic theory which does that by its insistence on a specific understanding of equality—as something to be attained by the minimization of difference. The crucial debate in contemporary feminism is the debate between those who urge that sex should become irrelevant and those who believe that sex should not provide the basis for inequality. Neither of these strategies involves rejecting equality. Rather, the dispute is about how equality is to be attained.

However, the strategic problem is acute in the case of women for the simple reason that, unlike social and economic differences, sexual difference cannot be removed by social policy in quite the simple way which the theory requires. Where inequalities of power spring simply from social and economic inequalities, there is some hope of removing them by seeking to minimize them—though the task would be difficult. But where inequalities of power spring from sex, it may be morally undesirable, or even impossible, to attempt to remove them by this approach. Of course, such strategies have been used, and with great success, by early feminists in their attempt to secure equal legal and political rights for women. But feminists are now sceptical about such attempts, fearing that ultimately they leave for women only the possibility of assimilation into a male world. Speaking about her own 'assimilation' feminism, Simone de Beauvoir said: 'the modern woman accepts masculine values: she prides herself on thinking, taking action, working, creating, on the same terms as men; instead of seeking to disparage them, she declares herself their equal'. But the price of this form of feminism is high for, as Simone de Beauvoir herself concedes, it is incompatible with child care and mothering. This not only means that, for many women, it will be difficult, if not impossible, to 'win the game', it also means accepting the rules of the game—where those rules dictate that pregnancy is an illness and child care a disadvantage.

What is needed, therefore, is a way of conceptualizing difference which renders it compatible with equality, but also, and crucially, does not simply increase social differentiation. Yet more radically, what is needed is a recognition that in much traditional democratic theory the concepts of equality, difference, and disadvantage are themselves gender-biased: they assume a standard of normality which is inherently male.

What are the possibilities of reconceptualizing in this way? How can democratic states revise the ideal in a way which acknowledges difference as both ineliminable and valuable? At this stage, it is worth emphasizing that it is not only feminists who should have a strong interest in this question. Modern states are characterized by the heterogeneity of the people who inhabit them. Unlike fifth-century Athens, or Rousseau's ideal state, they are not gatherings of the like-minded, gentlemen's clubs writ large, where those who deviate may be excluded or required to conform. The denial of citizenship to all but white males is no longer an option, nor is the easy assumption that newcomers must earn their right to citizenship by becoming 'like us'. Difference is not going to go away, nor is it something for which those who are different feel disposed to apologize. Against this background, the insistence that equality is to be preserved via the minimization of difference, or via assimilation itself appears utopian and the complaint that the differentiation of modern life militates against democracy may elicit the response: 'so much the worse for democracy'.

However, before moving too rapidly to that pessimistic conclusion, I want to explore the possibility that such a re-conceptualization is possible, and that it is compatible with the democratic ideal of equality. One part of the answer lies in distinguishing between two levels of democratic interest: these answer to Dahl's two principles mentioned earlier—the principle of inclusion and the principle of equality. At the former level, difference is properly to be ignored, but at the latter level, it is to be recognized and accommodated. Thus, for purposes of deciding who is to count as a citizen of a democratic state, differences of class, race, and gender should not matter. But in adhering to a strong principle of equality, we are obliged to acknowledge these differences—to acknowledge them, but not thereby to eliminate them. For whereas traditional democratic theory tends to construe difference as an obstacle to the attainment of a truly democratic state, feminist theory should alert us to the possibility that difference is rather what necessitates the pursuit of democracy. Since it is the fact that we are not all the same which requires democracy, attempting to make us all the same will not deliver democracy. On the contrary, it will remove the rationale for democracy.

Perhaps this point can be made clearer by drawing attention to one very important rationale for a democratic order—its ability to accommodate variety and criticism. Famously, E. M. Forster once called for 'two cheers for democracy' and he explained 'one because it admits variety and two because it permits criticism'. This argument is often interpreted as a claim about the ability of democracy, in the long run, to deliver truth: the free marketplace of ideas will, it is claimed, ensure that truth triumphs over error. But there may also be a different interpretation, which is that democratic societies are superior not because they deliver unity out of diversity, but simply because and in so far as they acknowledge diversity. The most famous exponent of this view is, of course, John Stuart Mill, whose political theory began from the premiss that 'human beings are not like sheep, and even sheep are not indistinguishably alike'. Mill's ideal political future was not one in which disagreement and difference are eradicated, for he did not believe that any such future was possible. Rather, his claim was that the existence of difference, and the recognition that difference was ineradicable, itself provided a major argument for democracy. Connectedly, Mill understood democracy not as a state, but rather as a process. There would be no end to disagreement, but this fact provided the reason for adopting a democratic order rather than a reason for doubting its practicality. Therefore, where some modern democratic theorists begin from a principle of equality, Mill begins from a recognition of difference. And where modern democratic theorists see their main aim as being to create equality by removing difference, Mill recognizes that it is difference which must be preserved lest the pursuit of equality simply degenerate into the imposition of uniformity. In brief, then, the significance of Mill's account is that he recognizes, and emphasizes, the priority of difference over equality and urges that equality must be pursued via the recognition of difference.

Historically, democratic theory guaranteed equality by according the rights of citizenship only to those who were already equal. Later, as in the philosophy of Kant, citizenship rights were theoretically allowed to those who were able to 'improve' themselves and thus earn the title 'citizen'. Recently, hope of equality (or despair about it) has rested upon the chances of employing social policy to obliterate the effects of arbitrary inequalities. In all these cases, difference has been perceived as an obstacle to equality, and the democratic aspiration has been to ignore or remove it. In so far, therefore, as the democratic faith has been a faith that difference may be ignored or removed, feminists have lost that faith.

But feminist concerns about democratic theory go beyond the insistence that equality must be attained without the elimination of difference. Feminists also highlight the extent to which difference itself is a value-laden concept, which takes male experience as the norm and interprets female experience as disadvantaged by comparison with it. If we view matters in this way, then we will see that what is asked for is not special treatment for women, but rather an end to the existing system of special treatment for men. Catharine MacKinnon writes:

> In reality . . . virtually every quality that distinguishes men from women is already affirmatively compensated in this society. Men's physiology defines most sports, their needs define auto and health insurance coverage, their socially defined biographies define workplace expectations and successful career patterns, their perspectives and concerns define quality in scholarship. . . . For each of their differences from women, what amounts to an affirmative action plan is in effect, otherwise known as the structure and values of American society.

In Britain too, existing structures favour men's lifestyles. Thus, the demand that Parliamentary hours be changed in order to take account of women's domestic responsibilities is not a request for preferential treatment for women. It is simply a recognition that what already exists is a case of preferential treatment for men. In cases such as this there is often no happy medium, or mutually convenient compromise. But that fact should not lead us to the conclusion that what currently exists is neutral between men and women, or that when women ask for arrangements more suitable to them, they are asking for special favours.

The contribution which feminist theory makes to democratic theory is therefore twofold: by asserting that some differences are ineliminable, feminism searches for an understanding of democracy as something to be aimed at *through* difference, not something to be attained via the *removal* of difference. Specifically, it indicates that the pursuit of equality via the elimination of difference is not the route to a democratic society, but the route to an oppressive and exclusive society. Historically, societies which have claimed to 'represent the people' have in fact represented only that portion of the people which displays homogeneity. In modern theory 'representing the people' must not be interpreted as representing that portion of the people who can be forced into the appropriate mould. If there is to be any hope for democracy, it must therefore cease to pursue equality by trying to eliminate difference and instead concentrate on pursuing it by recognizing difference more adequately.

This last claim, however, signals feminism's second contribution to the debate, which is that in modern democratic societies the concept of difference, and the connected concept of disadvantage, are themselves male-centred. To be different is to deviate from some norm and, in democratic societies, that norm is invariably a male norm. Debates about the need to encourage women to participate more fully in political life tend to take the form of requests for assistance for women who have child-care and domestic responsibilities. But, as we have seen, even this approach assumes not only that women are different, but that they require 'help' if they are to attain male standards. It assumes both that the male standard is correct, and that something more than justice is required if women are to attain it. Therefore, if democratic theory is to be sustained and improved, it must recognize not only that difference is sometimes ineliminable, but also that what counts as difference is not value-neutral. It must recognize its own gender-bias even (indeed especially) in cases where it seeks to 'assist' women. The faith that democracy can be transformed in this way is the faith to which feminists now cling.

God and Religious Belief

Belief in the existence of a god or gods is one of the most common features of human cultures and is widely taken to be a valuable, even necessary, part of living a good life. Nonetheless, however common and comforting the belief may be, whether God exists is a question that is open to scrutiny. Indeed, how could it not be? For "Is there a God?" would seem to be one of the central questions affecting how we regard the whole of the universe and our lives. Most people believe in God as a matter of faith. But what is it to believe anything, especially a belief so important as this one, on faith? Is belief based on faith rational? Further, if there is a God, what is that being like? In the Western religious traditions, Christianity, Islam and Judaism, God is thought of as an immaterial being, a being not made of material stuff and not located in space. So, how could we know anything about such a being when we have no direct sensory evidence? What would count as evidence for God, and why?

If you head home after class and your roommate tells you, "I talked to God today on the telephone . . . she sounded very nice," you're not very likely to believe that an *actual* conversation with an *actual* deity explains your roommate's strange belief. Paul Kurtz argues that as philosophers we want good reasons for our beliefs, and we ought to approach religious claims in the same spirit of skeptical, critical inquiry as we would any claims of the supernatural or occult.

More likely, when people claim to have some *good reason* for believing that God exists they base that belief on some kind of *argument*. There are a number of types of arguments for the existence of God; Saint Thomas Aquinas briefly summarizes them for us. Of special interest over the last several centuries has been the Teleological Argument, or Argument from Design. Imagine, as William Paley suggests, that you find a watch as you are hiking across a huge open field. What would you think of how the watch got there? Is it likely that the watch is just a natural rock formation, or grew out of one of the surrounding plants? Of course not. The watch shows signs of intelligent design, so that we would immediately recognize that it had been made by a human being. Analogously, the advocate of the teleological argument argues that the design we see in the natural world around us, from the smallest cell to the vast patterns of galaxies, also shows signs of intelligent design, and that this designer is God. Neil Manson discusses the contemporary debate about intelligent design.

One of the biggest challenges to the teleological argument, indeed to religious belief in general, is the problem of evil. This problem emerges out of comparing the traditional Judeo-Christian conception of God as a perfectly benevolent and all-powerful being, with the physical universe that is said to be God's creation. Is the universe, with all of its flaws and imperfections, really the handiwork of a *perfect* being? Especially when we consider all the pain and suffering in the world, we realize that the existence of evil suggests a very real challenge. B. C. Johnson highlights this challenge with several very difficult examples. Eleonore Stump responds, offering reasons for thinking that a good God, one who wants what is best for us, would nonetheless allow evil.

Finally, believing in God—specifically a supernatural God—is widely assumed to be central to the concept of religion. Jews, Christians, and Moslems all share this belief. Indeed, one might ask, what would be the point of practicing religion if not to worship God and do what God commands? Steven Cahn suggests that there might be a very good reason for being religious independent of believing in or worshiping a supernatural God. In the concluding article of this section, Cahn defends religious naturalism, the view that one can derive value from adherence to religious practice, while at the same time denying the existence of God.

Should Skeptical Inquiry Be Applied to Religion?

PAUL KURTZ (1926–) is Professor Emeritus of Philosophy at the State University of New York at Buffalo (SUNY). Kurtz's experiences at German concentration camps and with Soviet slave laborers during World War II taught him to be skeptical of prominent ideologies. He is the founder and chairman of the Committee for the Scientific Investigation of Claims of the Paranormal (CSICOP) and has authored or edited over 40 books. Kurtz is a regular contributor to *Skeptical Inquiry* and *Free Inquiry* magazines.

THINKING QUESTIONS

Paul Kurtz, *Should Skeptical Inquiry Be Applied to Religion?*

1. Kurtz claims that there are two meanings for the term "skepticism." What sort of skepticism does he wish to employ with respect to religion?
2. Kurtz maintains that we may talk about religion in at least two senses. What are they?
3. As a form of human behavior, how can we rationally investigate religion, according to Kurtz?
4. What is fideism? Why does Kurtz think it is irrational?
5. Kurtz argues that in present society one may criticize all sorts of hucksters, mediums, psychics, astrologers, etc., but that criticizing the leaders or claims of mainstream religions is socially unwise. Do you agree that there is a social opprobrium attached to criticizing religion? Why do you think that is?
6. What is Kurtz's overall conclusion about whether we should rationally and scientifically investigate the claims of religion?

SCIENTIFIC INQUIRY

The relationship between science and religion has engendered heated controversy. This debate has its roots in the historic conflict between the advocates of reason and the disciples of faith. On the current scene, there is a vocal hallelujah chorus singing praises to the mutual harmony and support of these two realms or "magisteria." I have serious misgivings about this alleged rapprochement, but I wish to focus on only one aspect of the controversy, and ask: To what extent should we apply skepticism to religious claims?

By the term "skepticism" I do not refer to the classical philosophical position which denies that reliable knowledge is possible. Rather, I use the term "skepticism" to refer to skeptical inquiry. There is a contrast between two forms of skepticism, (1) that which emphasizes doubt and the impossibility of knowledge, and (2) that which focuses on inquiry and the genuine possibility of knowledge; for this latter form of skepticism, skeptical inquiry is essential in all fields of scientific research. What I have in mind is the fact that scientific inquirers formulate hypotheses to account for data and solve problems; their findings are tentative; they are accepted because they draw upon a range of confirming evidence and predictions and/or fit into a logically coherent theoretical framework. Reliable hypotheses are adopted because they are corroborated by a community of inquirers and because the tests that confirm them can be replicated. Scientific hypotheses and theories are fallible; and in principle they are open to question in the light of future discoveries and/or the introduction of more comprehensive theories. The point is that we have been able to achieve reliable knowledge in discipline after discipline because of the effective application of skeptical inquiry.

Science has always had its critics, who have insisted that one or another area of human interest is immune to scientific inquiry. At one time it was proclaimed that astronomers could never know the outermost reaches of the universe (August Comte), the innermost nature of the atom (John Locke), or human consciousness (Henri Bergson). Critics have also insisted that we could not apply science to one or another aspect of human experience—political, economic, social, or ethical behavior, the arts, human psychology, sexuality, or feeling. I do not think that we should set a priori limits antecedent to inquiry; we should not seek to denigrate the ability of scientific investigators to explain behavior or to extend the frontiers of research into new areas.

CAN THERE BE A SCIENCE OF RELIGION?

Some have argued that religious phenomena—matters of faith—are entirely beyond the ken of science; but this surely is false because the scientific investigation of religion has already made great strides and there is a vast literature now available. We may talk about religion in at least two senses: First, religion refers to a form of human behavior that can be investigated. Second, it is used to refer to the transcendental, i.e., to that which transcends human experience or reason.

Let us turn to the first area. Religious behavior has been investigated by a wide range of disciplines: Anthropologists deal with the comparative study of primitive religions, examining prayer, ritual, the rites of passage, etc. Sociologists have investigated the institutional aspects of religious behavior, such as the role of the priestly class in society. Ever since William James, psychologists of religion have studied the varieties of religious experience, such as mysticism, ecstasy, talking in tongues, exorcism, etc. Similarly, biologists have postulated a role for religious beliefs and practices in the evolutionary process and their possible adaptive/survival value. They have asked, Does religiosity have a genetic or environmental basis? Others have focused on the neurological correlates of religious piety, and still others have attempted to test the efficacy of prayer.

One can deal with religion in contemporary or historical contexts. A great deal of attention has been devoted to the historical analysis of religious claims, especially since the great classical religions are based on ancient documents (the Old and New Testaments and the Koran), as are some of the newer religions (such as the nineteenth-century Book of Mormon). These texts allege that certain miraculous and revelatory events have occurred in the past and these warrant religious belief today; and it is often claimed that belief in them is based upon faith.

I would respond that scientific methodology has been used in historical investigations to examine these alleged events. Archaeologists seek independent corroborating evidence; they examine written or oral accounts that were contemporaneous with the events (for example, by comparing the Dead Sea Scrolls with the New Testament). The fields of "biblical criticism" or "koranic criticism" have attempted to use the best scholarly techniques, historical evidence, and textual and linguistic analysis to ascertain the historical accuracy of these claims.

Paranormal claims are similar to religious claims—both purport to be exceptions to natural laws. Skeptics have asked: Did D.D. Home float out of a window and levitate over a street in London in the late nineteenth century? Did the Fox sisters and Eusapia Palladino possess the ability to communicate with the dead? And they have sought to provide naturalistic interpretations for reports of bizarre events. No doubt it is easier to examine contemporaneous claims where the record is still available rather than ancient ones where the record may be fragmentary. Yet in principle at least, the religious investigator is similar to the paranormal investigator, attempting to ascertain the accuracy of the historical record. We use similar methods of inquiry to examine prosaic historical questions, such as: Did Washington cross the Delaware, or Thomas Jefferson sire the children of Sally Heming? The same goes for religious claims: Did the Red Sea part before the fleeing Hebrews, was there a Great Flood and a Noah's Ark? I don't see how or why we should declare that these historical religious claims are immune to scientific investigation.

Thus I maintain that insofar as religion refers to a form of human behavior, whether in the past or the present, we can, if we can uncover corroborating data or historical records, attempt to authenticate the historical claims and ask whether there were paranormal, occult, or transcendental causes, or whether naturalistic explanations are available. David Hume's arguments against miracles indicate all the reasons why we should be skeptical of ancient claims—because they lack adequate documentation, because the eyewitnesses were biased, and so on. And this should apply, in my view, to reports of revelation as well as miracles. Extraordinary claims that violate naturalistic causal regularities should require strong evidence. I don't see how anyone can protest that his beliefs ought to be immune to the standards of objective historical investigation, simply by claiming that they are held on the basis of faith. A good case in point is the alleged burial shroud of Jesus, the Shroud of Turin. Meticulous carbon-14 dating by three renowned laboratories has shown that the cloth is approximately 700 years old and therefore most likely a forgery. The fact that believers may seek to shield their belief by proclaiming that they have faith that the Shroud is genuine does not make it any more true. The same principle applies to the key miraculous revelations of the past upon which the classical religions are allegedly based. The strength of a hypothesis or belief should be a function of the empirical evidence extant brought to support it, and if the evidence is weak or spotty, then the faith claim should likewise be so regarded.

Religious belief systems are deeply ingrained in human history, culture, and social institutions that predate science, and thus it is often difficult, if not impossible, to insist upon using the standards of objective skeptical inquiry retrospectively. This is especially the case since to believe in a religion is more than a question of cognitive assent, for religion has its roots in ethnic or national identity; and to question the empirical or rational grounds for religious belief is to shake at the very foundations of the social order.

SKEPTICAL INQUIRY AND RELIGION

The key question that I wish to address is, Should skeptical inquirers question the regnant sacred cows of religion? There are both theoretical and prudential issues here at stake. I can find no theoretical reason why not, but there may be practical considerations. For one, it requires an extraordinary amount of courage today as in the past (especially in America!) to critique religion. One can challenge paranormal hucksters, mediums, psychics, alternative therapists, astrologers, and past-life hypnotherapists with abandon, but to question the revered figures of orthodox religion is another matter, for this may still raise the serious public charge of blasphemy and heresy; and this can be dangerous to one's person and career—as Salman Rushdie's fatwah so graphically demonstrates.

History vividly illustrates the hesitancy of skeptics to apply their skepticism to religious questions. In ancient Rome, Sextus Empiricus, author of *Outlines of Pyrrhonism,* defended the suspension of belief in regard to metaphysical, philosophical, and ethical issues. He did not think that reliable knowledge about reality or ethical judgments was possible. He neither affirmed nor denied the existence of the Gods, but adopted a neutral stance. Since there was no reliable knowledge, Pyrrho urged that compliance with the customs and religion of his day was the most prudent course to follow. The great skeptic Hume bade his friend, Adam Smith, to publish his iconoclastic *Dialogues Concerning Natural Religion* after his death (in 1776), but Smith declined to do so, disappointing Hume. Hume's nephew David arranged for posthumous publication. The French author Pierre Bayle (1647–1706) perhaps expressed the most thoroughgoing skepticism of his time. In his *Dictionnaire historique et critique,* Bayle presented a scathing indictment of the prevailing theories of his day, finding them full of contradictions. He was highly critical of religious absurdities. He maintained that atheists could be more moral than Christians, and that religion did not necessarily provide a basis for ethical conduct. Nonetheless, Bayle professed that he was a Christian and a Calvinist, and this was based upon pure faith, without any evidence to support it—this is known as fideism. Did Bayle genuinely hold these views, or was his fideism a ruse to protect his reputation and his fortune?

This form of fideism, I maintain, on theoretical grounds is illegitimate, even irrational. For if, as skeptical inquirers, we are justified in accepting only those beliefs that are based upon evidence and reason, and if there is no evidence either way or insufficient evidence, should we not suspend judgment, or are we justified in taking a leap of faith? If the latter posture of faith is chosen, one can ask, On what basis? If a person is entitled to choose to believe whatever he or she wishes, solely or largely because of personal feeling and taste, then "anything goes." But this anarchic epistemological principle can be used to distort honest inquiry. (The implication of this argument is that if we do not have a similar feeling, we are entitled not to believe.) One may ask, Can one generalize the epistemological rule, and if so, can it apply to paranormal claims? Is someone thus entitled to believe in UFO abductions, angels, or demons on the basis of feeling and fancy? The paranormal skeptic retort is that where there is evidence to decide the question, we are not justified in believing; though in a democracy we are not entitled to expect others to share our skepticism.

But as a matter of fact, most of those who believe in the traditional religions do not base it on pure fideism alone, but on reasons and evidence. Indeed, no less an authority than Pope John Paul II maintained the same in a recent encyclical entitled "Faith and Reason." In this, the Pope condemns both fideism and atheism. He attacks the naive faith in "UFOs, astrology, and the New Age." He criticizes "exaggerated rationalism" and pragmatism on the one hand and postmodernism on the other, but he also condemns the exclusive reliance on faith. The Pope maintains that reason and scientific inquiry support rather than hinder faith in Christian revelation and Catholic doctrine. Skeptics might agree with the Pope's defense of reason and scientific inquiry, but question whether these do indeed support his own beliefs.

Thus, in my judgment, acquiescence by skeptics to the fideist's rationalization for his beliefs is profoundly mistaken. Similarly, in answer to those theists who maintain that there is adequate evidence and reasons for their belief, skeptical inquirers should not simply ignore their claims, saying that they are beyond scientific confirmation, but should examine them. Since the burden of proof is always upon the claimant, skeptical inquirers may question both the fideist and the partial-evidentialist in religion, if they do not believe that they have provided an adequate justified case.

CONCLUSION

The upshot of this controversy, in my judgment, is that scientific and skeptical inquirers should deal with religious claims. Not to do so is to flee from an important area of human behavior and interest and is irresponsible. Indeed, one reason why paranormal beliefs are so prominent today is because religious beliefs are not being critically examined in the marketplace of ideas. Science should not be so narrowly construed that it only applies to experimental laboratory work; it should bring in the tools of logical analysis, historical research, and rational investigation. In this sense, I submit, religious claims are amenable to scientific examination and skeptical inquiry.

The Five Ways

THOMAS AQUINAS (1125–1274) is the greatest of the Catholic theologians, known by them as the Angelic Doctor—although he was known popularly as the Great Ox, in reference to his considerable girth. He was canonized after his death. Thomas was born into a noble family in Roccasecca, Italy (halfway between Rome and Naples), and despite the objections of his family, became a Dominican brother. Thomas studied in Paris and Cologne, subsequently held various appointments in Italy, and finally became a professor of theology at the University of Paris. Thomas is most famous for wedding Aristotelian philosophy to Christian theology, and by doing so he helped inaugurate the Catholic doctrine that reason aids revelation to come to a true understanding of the divine.

THINKING QUESTIONS

Thomas Aquinas, *The Five Ways*

1. Aquinas claims that he has five arguments to the conclusion that God exists. Do you think that he really has five *different* arguments? The first argument has to do with motion and movers, and the second argument has to do with cause and effect. Are they distinct arguments or just variations of the same argument?
2. Assume that Aquinas is right and there must be a prime mover or a first cause. Why must this first cause be God? That is, God is traditionally defined as a being that is omnipotent, omniscient, and omnibenevolent. Does Aquinas provide any reasons for thinking that the prime mover has these qualities?
3. Aquinas states that it is impossible for something to be its own efficient cause—that is, it is impossible for something to be the cause of itself. But then he reasons that there must be a first efficient cause, on the grounds that a chain of causation couldn't go back forever. Where did that first cause come from? It couldn't be self-caused, by his own reasoning. If it is eternally existing, then how is eternal existence any more plausible than (or different from) an infinite chain of causes?
4. Aquinas seems to assume that there can be degrees of being (which God has in the greatest amount to the maximum extent). What does this mean?
5. Aquinas claims that the lesser degrees of various qualities are only possible if there is some being that possessed the maximum of these

qualities. Thus, things can be more or less good, more or less hot, etc. only if there is something with maximum goodness and something that is the hottest thing. The cause of "being, goodness, and every other perfection in things" Aquinas dubs God. But what about nonbeing, perfect evil, flawless ignobility, and the like. Is there some being with those qualities or that is responsible for them? Is this God? An Anti-God? What is an Anti-God?

6. According to Aquinas, natural bodies always act for an end. What does he mean? What is a "natural body"? What is it to act for an end?
7. Aquinas explains things like motion, order, and existence by appealing to God. Do you think that science has or will have good explanations for these things? If so, then why believe that God is any more than an explanatory placeholder, filling the gap until a better explanation comes along?

God's existence can be proved in five ways. The first and most obvious way is based on the existence of motion. It is certain and in fact evident to our senses that some things in the world are moved. Everything that is moved, however, is moved by something else, for a thing cannot be moved unless that movement is potentially within it. A thing moves something else insofar as it actually exists, for to move something is simply to actualize what is potentially within that thing. Something can be led thus from potentiality to actuality only by something else which is already actualized. For example, a fire, which is actually hot, causes the change or motion whereby wood, which is potentially hot, becomes actually hot. Now it is impossible that something should be potentially and actually the same thing at the same time, although it could be potentially and actually different things. For example, what is actually hot cannot at the same moment be actually cold, although it can be actually hot and potentially cold. Therefore it is impossible that a thing could move itself, for that would involve simultaneously moving and being moved in the same respect. Thus whatever is moved must be moved by something else, etc. This cannot go on to infinity, however, for if it did there would be no first mover and consequently no other movers, because these other movers are such only insofar as they are moved by a first mover. For example, a stick moves only because it is moved by the hand. Thus it is necessary to proceed back to some prime mover which is moved by nothing else, and this is what everyone means by "God."

The second way is based on the existence of efficient causality. We see in the world around us that there is an order of efficient causes. Nor is it ever found (in fact it is impossible) that something is its own efficient cause. If it were, it would be prior to itself, which is impossible. Nevertheless, the order of efficient causes cannot proceed to infinity, for in any such order the first is cause of the middle (whether one or many) and the middle of the last.

Without the cause, the effect does not follow. Thus, if the first cause did not exist, neither would the middle and last causes in the sequence. If, however, there were an infinite regression of efficient causes, there would be no first efficient cause and therefore no middle causes or final effects, which is obviously not the case. Thus it is necessary to posit some first efficient cause, which everyone calls "God."

The third way is based on possibility and necessity. We find that some things can either exist or not exist, for we find them springing up and then disappearing, thus sometimes existing and sometimes not. It is impossible, however, that everything should be such, for what can possibly not exist does not do so at some time. If it is possible for every particular thing not to exist, there must have been a time when nothing at all existed. If this were true, however, then nothing would exist now, for something that does not exist can begin to do so only through something that already exists. If, therefore, there had been a time when nothing existed, then nothing could ever have begun to exist, and thus there would be nothing now, which is clearly false. Therefore all beings cannot be merely possible. There must be one being which is necessary. Any necessary being, however, either has or does not have something else as the cause of its necessity. If the former, then there cannot be an infinite series of such causes, any more than there can be an infinite series of efficient causes, as we have seen. Thus we must posit the existence of something which is necessary and owes its necessity to no cause outside itself. That is what everyone calls "God."

The fourth way is based on the gradations found in things. We find that things are more or less good, true, noble, etc.; yet when we apply terms like "more" and "less" to things we imply that they are closer to or farther from some maximum. For example, a thing is said to be hotter than something else because it comes closer to that which is hottest. Therefore something exists which is truest, greatest, noblest, and consequently most fully in being; for, as Aristotle says, the truest things are most fully in being. That which is considered greatest in any genus is the cause of everything is that genus, just as fire, the hottest thing, is the cause of all hot things, as Aristotle says. Thus there is something which is the cause of being, goodness, and every other perfection in all things, and we call that something "God."

The fifth way is based on the governance of things. We see that some things lacking cognition, such as natural bodies, work toward an end, as is seen from the fact that they always (or at least usually) act the same way and not accidentally, but by design. Things without knowledge tend toward a goal, however, only if they are guided in that direction by some knowing, understanding being, as is the case with an arrow and archer. Therefore, there is some intelligent being by whom all natural things are ordered to their end, and we call this being "God."

The Watchmaker

WILLIAM PALEY (1743–1805) was born in Peterborough, England. Paley trained for the Anglican priesthood at Christ's College, Cambridge, and, after a period as a teacher, rose through the church ranks to become archdeacon of Carlisle. Paley wrote widely on morals and theology. His most well-known work is *Natural Theology: Or, Evidences of the Existence and Attributes of the Deity, Collected from the Appearances of Nature* (1802) in which he lays out one of the most famous versions of the argument from design.

THINKING QUESTIONS

William Paley, *The Watchmaker*

1. You're walking across an open field and find a watch (imagine that you've never seen one before). How could you tell that the watch was *made* by someone? Consider the objects in the room you're in; how do you know that they were made by someone, even though you weren't there when it was done?
2. What can you tell about *who* made the watch by observing it? Why are you sure that it wasn't made by, say, a really smart chimp?
3. What is the purpose of the watch? How can you tell what its purpose is by observing it?
4. Paley asks us to consider "the works of nature." How is nature like the watch; how is it different?
5. Paley is offering us an argument from analogy. How does that analogy support the claim that God exists?

IN CROSSING A HEATH, suppose I pitched my foot against a *stone,* and were asked how the stone came to be there; I might possibly answer, that, for any thing I knew to the contrary, it had lain there for ever: nor would it perhaps be very easy to show the absurdity of this answer. But suppose I had found a *watch* upon the ground, and it should be inquired how the watch happened to be in that place; I should hardly think of the answer which I had before given, that, for any thing I knew, the watch might have always been there. Yet why should not this answer serve for the watch as well as for the stone? why is it not as admissible in the second case, as in the first? For this reason, and for no other, viz. that, when we come to inspect the watch, we perceive (what we could not discover in the stone) that its several parts are framed and put together for a purpose, *e.g.* that they are so formed and adjusted as to produce motion, and that motion so regulated as to point out the hour of the day; that, if the different parts had been differently shaped from what they are, of a different size from what they are, or placed after any other manner, or in any other order, than that in which they are placed, either no motion at all would have been carried on in the machine, or none which would have answered the use that is now served by it. To reckon up a few of the plainest of these parts, and of their offices, all tending to one result:—We see a cylindrical box containing a coiled elastic spring, which, by its endeavour to relax itself, turns round the box. We next observe a flexible chain (artificially wrought for the sake of flexure), communicating the action of the spring from the box to the fusee. We then find a series of wheels, the teeth of which catch in, and apply to, each other, conducting the motion from the fusee to the balance, and from the balance to the pointer; and at the same time, by the size and shape of those wheels, so regulating that motion, as to terminate in causing an index, by an equable and measured progression, to pass over a given space in a given time. We take notice that the wheels are made of brass in order to keep them from rust; the springs of steel, no other metal being so elastic; that over the face of the watch there is placed a glass, a material employed in no other part of the work, but in the room of which, if there had been any other than a transparent substance, the hour could not be seen without opening the case. This mechanism being observed (it requires indeed an examination of the instrument, and perhaps some previous knowledge of the subject, to perceive and understand it; but being once, as we have said, observed and understood), the inference, we think, is inevitable, that the watch must have had a maker: that there must have existed, at some time, and at some place or other, an artificer or artificers who formed it for the purpose which we find it actually to answer; who comprehended its construction, and designed its use.

I. Nor would it, I apprehend, weaken the conclusion, that we had never seen a watch made; that we had never known an artist capable of making one; that we were altogether incapable of executing such a piece of workmanship ourselves, or of understanding in what manner it was performed; all this being no more than what is true of some exquisite remains of ancient art, of some lost arts, and, to the generality of mankind, of the more curious productions of modern manufacture. Does one man in a million know how oval frames are turned? Ignorance of this kind exalts our opinion of the unseen and unknown artist's skill, if he be unseen and unknown, but raises no doubt in our minds of the existence and agency of such an artist, at some former time, and in some place or other. Nor can I perceive that it varies at all the inference, whether the question arise concerning a human agent, or concerning an agent of a different species, or an agent possessing, in some respects, a different nature.

II. Neither, secondly, would it invalidate our conclusion, that the watch sometimes went wrong, or that it seldom went exactly right. The purpose of the machinery, the design, and the designer, might be evident, and in the case supposed would be evident, in whatever way we accounted for the irregularity of the movement, or whether we could account for it or not. It is not necessary that a machine be perfect, in order to show with what design it was made: still less necessary, where the only question is, whether it were made with any design at all.

III. Nor, thirdly, would it bring any uncertainty into the argument, if there were a few parts of the watch, concerning which we could not discover, or had not yet discovered, in what manner they conduced to the general effect; or even some parts, concerning which we could not ascertain, whether they conduced to that effect in any manner whatever. For . . . if by the loss, or disorder, or decay of the parts in question, the movement of the watch were found in fact to be stopped, or disturbed, or retarded, no doubt would remain in our minds as to the utility or intention of these parts, although we should be unable to investigate the manner according to which, or the connexion by which, the ultimate effect depended upon their action or assistance; and the more complex is the machine, the more likely is this obscurity to arise. . . .

VIII. Neither, lastly, would our observer be driven out of his conclusion, or from his confidence in its truth, by being told that he knew nothing at all about the matter. He knows enough for his argument: he knows the utility of the end: he knows the subserviency and adaptation of the means to the end. These points being known, his ignorance of other points, his doubts concerning other points, affect not the certainty of his reasoning. The consciousness of knowing little, need not beget a distrust of that which he does know.

Suppose, in the next place, that the person who found the watch, should, after some time, discover that, in addition to all the properties which he had hitherto observed in it, it possessed the unexpected property of producing, in the course of its movement, another watch like itself (the thing is conceivable); that it contained within it a mechanism, a system of parts, a mould for instance, or a complex adjustment of lathes, files, and other tools, evidently and separately calculated for this purpose; let us inquire, what effect ought such a discovery to have upon his former conclusion.

I. The first effect would be to increase his admiration of the contrivance, and his conviction of the consummate skill of the contriver. Whether he regarded the object of the contrivance, the distinct apparatus, the intricate, yet in many parts intelligible mechanism, by which it was carried on, he would perceive, in this new observation, nothing but an additional reason for doing what he had already done,—for referring the construction of the watch to design, and to supreme art. . . .

II. He would reflect, that though the watch before him were, *in some sense,* the maker of the watch, which was fabricated in the course of its movements, yet it was in a very different sense from that, in which a carpenter, for instance, is the maker of a chair; the author of its contrivance, the cause of the relation of its parts to their use. With respect to these, the first watch was no cause at all to the second: in no such sense as this was it the author of the constitution and order, either of the parts which the new watch contained, or of the parts by the aid and instrumentality of which it was produced. . . .

III. Though it be now no longer probable, that the individual watch, which our observer had found, was made immediately by the hand of an artificer, yet doth not this alteration in anywise affect the inference, that an artificer had been originally employed and concerned in the production. The argument from design remains as it was. Marks of design and contrivance are no more accounted for now, than they were before. In the same thing, we may ask for the cause of different properties. We may ask for the cause of the colour of a body, of its hardness, of its head; and these causes may be all different. We are now asking for the cause of that subserviency to a use, that relation to an end, which we have remarked in the watch before us. No answer is given to this question, by telling us that a preceding watch produced it. There cannot be design without a designer; contrivance without a contriver; order without choice; arrangement, without any thing capable of arranging; subserviency and relation to a purpose, without that which could intend a purpose; means suitable to an end, and executing their office, in accomplishing that end, without the end ever having been contemplated, or the means accommodated to it. Arrangement, disposition of parts, subserviency of means to an end, relation of instruments to a use, imply the presence of intelligence and mind. . . .

V. Our observer would further also reflect, that the maker of the watch before him, was, in truth and reality, the maker of every watch produced from it; there being no difference (except that the latter manifests a more exquisite skill) between the making of another watch with his own hands, by the mediation of files, lathes, chisels, &c. and the disposing, fixing, and inserting of these instruments, or of others equivalent to them, in the body of the watch already made in such a manner, as to form a new watch in the course of the movements which he had given to the old one. It is only working by one set of tools, instead of another.

The conclusion of which the *first* examination of the watch, of its works, construction, and movement, suggested, was, that it must have had, for the cause and author of that construction, an artificer, who understood its mechanism, and designed its use. This conclusion is invincible. A *second* examination presents us with a new discovery. The watch is found, in the course of its movement, to produce another watch, similar to itself; and not only so, but we perceive in it a system or organization, separately calculated for that purpose. What effect would this discovery have, or ought it to have, upon our former inference? What, as hath already been said, but to increase, beyond measure, our admiration of the skill, which had been employed in the formation of such a machine? Or shall it, instead of this, all at once turn us round to an opposite conclusion, viz. that no art or skill whatever has been concerned in the business, although all other evidences of art and skill remain as they were, and this last and supreme piece of art be now added to the rest? Can this be maintained without absurdity? Yet this is atheism.

This is atheism: for every indication of contrivance, every manifestation of design, which existed in the watch, exists in the works of nature; with the difference, on the side of nature, of being greater and more, and that in a degree which exceeds all computation. I mean that the contrivances of nature surpass the contrivances of art, in the complexity, subtility, and curiosity of the mechanism; and still more, if possible, do they go beyond them in number and variety; yet, in a multitude of cases, are not less evidently mechanical, not less evidently contrivances, not less evidently accommodated to their end, or suited to their office, than are the most perfect productions of human ingenuity.

The Design Argument

NEIL A. MANSON (1967–) is an assistant professor of philosophy at the University of Mississippi. He has written numerous articles on issues at the intersection of philosophy, science, and religion, especially the design argument from cosmic fine-tuning for life. He edited the anthology *God and Design: The Teleological Argument and Modern Science* (Routledge, 2003).

THINKING QUESTIONS

Neil A. Manson, *The Design Argument*

1. Paley argued that if you found a watch in the middle of nowhere, that you would know it was designed—it didn't grow there, or appear by chance. He argues that by analogy we can see the complexity of the universe and infer that it too is designed. But the intricate watch seems designed because it jumps out from the plain background in which it is found. Against what background should we compare the entire universe to conclude that it as a whole is designed?
2. If you found Paley's watch, would you conclude that God designed it? Why or why not?
3. In Douglas Adams's *The Hitchhiker's Guide to the Galaxy,* Slartibartfast is a designer of planets. Indeed, he was one of the designers of Earth (specializing in fjords). Even if there is a designer, why not think the designer is an extraterrestrial alien like Slartibartfast instead of God?
4. One wit has suggested that the universe was indeed designed, but all evidence indicates that the designer is 100 percent malevolent but only 80 percent effective. Could such a designer be God? How is this concern related to Hume's identification problem?
5. Hume alleges that defenders of the design argument are guilty of anthropocentrism. What is this complaint?
6. As Manson notes, design is no longer the only way to explain biological complexity. Evolution by natural selection is a competing scientific explanation. Are there reasons to prefer the theological explanation?
7. According to the Bayesian version of the design argument, there are features of the universe that are extremely improbable unless an intelligent designer like God built them in. Therefore, the prior probability of God's existence is rather high. Does the Bayesian version escape Hume's identification problem, though? That is, what makes the prior probability of the Christian God higher than the prior probability of a joker deity who sneezed the cosmos into existence?

I. INTRODUCTION

If you have taken a college biology class, or just watched *Animal Planet,* you may have been struck by the startling complexity of living organisms. From the grandest mammal to the lowliest cell, life displays intricacy and structure that would put a high-paid team of engineers to shame. How could such fantastically organized, complex structures arise blindly out of unintelligent matter? Speaking of matter, why is *it* the way it is? Though unimaginably vast, our universe has precise features, as does the matter in it. A glance at the inside back cover of a college physics textbook shows that there are extremely precise numbers describing the fundamental properties of matter. These include numbers for the speed of light in a vacuum, for the masses of fundamental particles like the electron, proton, and neutron, and for the strengths of forces like gravity and electromagnetism that act on those particles. These numbers seem utterly arbitrary. For all we know, they could have been completely different. Yet they turn out to be exactly what a universe needs in order for complex life to emerge in it. Likewise, the cosmology section of an astronomy course will teach you that there are very precise values for the temperature of the universe, for how much matter there is per cubic centimeter in the universe, for the rate at which the universe is expanding, and so on. How did those numbers get to be what they are? Were they just magically pulled out of a cosmic hat at the Big Bang?

If you've ever asked yourself these "Why is the world the way it is?" questions, you are not alone. Scientists, philosophers, and theologians throughout much of Western history have asked just such questions. And throughout that history, one of the most popular ways to answer these sorts of questions has been in terms of God. On this way of thinking, just as an arrow in a bull's-eye requires a skilled archer, a universe with the just-right properties of ours requires an intelligence to pick them out. Just as a watch requires a watch-maker, goes the thinking, life requires a designer. This is the basic idea behind what philosophers call the teleological argument (from the Greek word 'telos,' meaning 'end' or 'purpose'). It is more widely known as the design argument for the existence of God. Proponents of the design argument say the universe and the intricate structures in it could not have arisen by chance. Chance making our universe would be like a magical tornado blowing through a dormitory—one that left every bed made and put every empty pizza box in a trashcan. Such an event is just far too improbable to happen by chance. If chance is not an option, then only intelligence is left as an explanation of all of the apparent design in the universe. This intelligence will have to exist outside of our universe in order to act upon it, and it will have to be immensely powerful and knowledgeable in order to create something as vast, complex, and orderly as our universe. Proponents of the design argument find it obvious that a supernatural, super-powerful, super-knowledgeable intelligence who created a world of tremendous richness and beauty would just be God.

II. PALEY'S ANALOGICAL VERSION OF THE DESIGN ARGUMENT

Variants of this line of thinking can be found as far back as the ancient Greek era, but the classic statement of the design argument was by William Paley in his book *Natural Theology* (1802). Paley spelled out the analogical version of the design argument. He drew an analogy between finding a watch out in the middle of nowhere and finding intricacies in nature such as eyes, wings, and circulatory systems. Think of an old-style wind-up watch with gears and springs. It is a finely calibrated, complex item that serves a function. Clearly complex, functional objects do not just pop into existence in the middle of nowhere naturally. If you find a watch, you can infer that an intelligent creator of the watch exists or existed. Furthermore, you should infer this even if there are some imperfections in the watch and even if the watch has some functions the purpose of which you cannot discern. If the watch does not keep perfect time, or if it has a knob on it the use for which you cannot discern, you would still think the watch was designed. And if it somehow happened that we discovered the watch was actually reproduced from a prior watch—Paley imagines watches with hatches in the back spitting out duplicate watches—that still would not explain the current watch, because we would still need an explanation of how the original watch got *its* structure. If anything, we would have even more to explain—not just how a watch got out in the middle of nowhere, but how it got to have the ability to reproduce itself.

Paley said analogous reasoning justifies us in concluding that there is or was a designer of the intricate functional objects found in nature. We can conclude this even if natural structures are imperfect (like the human back, which is not quite ideal for walking erect) or have no known function (like the human appendix). For much of the rest of the book, Paley presented anatomical drawings and microscopic pictures showing case after case of intricate, organized, and well-designed biological structures. To see what Paley was thinking, consider the human eye. From a design standpoint, it is just like a camera. Both have lenses, light sensors (rods and cones for the human eye vs. film for a camera), and so on. Paley saw all of this functional detail in biology as screaming out "Design!" He was not alone. Particularly because of the development of microscopes, the naturalists of the seventeenth and eighteenth centuries were stunned at the geometric regularity and apparent design of the parts of living creatures. They just could not see how these intricate, machine-like structures could arise by natural processes.

III. DAVID HUME'S CRITICISMS OF THE ANALOGICAL DESIGN ARGUMENT

Before we consider an alternative scientific explanation of design in nature (namely, evolution), we should see that, in terms of pure philosophy, there is plenty of room to criticize Paley's analogical version of the design argument.

These criticisms were spelled out by Scottish philosopher David Hume in his book *Dialogues Concerning Natural Religion* (1779). Note that Hume's work was published nearly a quarter-century before Paley's. Versions of the analogical design argument were quite popular even before Paley's *Natural Theology* was published. It was these versions that Hume criticized. Many of Hume's criticisms are instances of what we might call the identification problem. Why think the terms 'the designer of the universe and the life within it' and 'the supreme eternal being who knows everything and can do anything' refer to one and the same individual? In short, why identify the designer with God? The evidence of design does not rule out designers other than God. Indeed, when we consider the imperfections of the world, says Hume, the analogy should lead us to conclude that the designer of the world is an imperfect being, not a perfect one like God. Hume suggests in *Dialogues* Part V that the universe might even be the product of some "infant deity" or of "several deities [who] combine in contriving and framing the world." To Hume, our universe looks like it could have been designed by a committee—and not the best one at that!

In this connection Hume imagines inspecting a building that is drafty, poorly lit, and poorly ventilated, with crooked steps and doors that do not fit into the doorways. If we had to guess, we might grudgingly admit someone or other designed the building. But we would never infer that the world's greatest architect did the designing. The building is not nearly good enough. If we were told that I. M. Pei designed the building, well, *maybe* we could square that with what we observed. As one of the world's greatest architects, Pei might have a subtle building plan we non-architects just cannot understand. Pei knows a lot more about architecture than we do. So if we had some independent evidence that Pei designed the building, such as a film of him drafting the architectural plans, maybe we could manage to believe that the building was designed by the world's greatest architect after all. But if we did not have such independent evidence—if all we had to go on was the building itself—then there is no way we would say it was designed by one of the world's greatest architects. Hume suggests the same point works against the analogical version of the design argument. People like Paley are not asking us to *reconcile* the observed world with belief in God. They are asking us to *infer* the existence of a perfect being from the observed world. It is not that people like Paley are showing us the universe—a universe full of diseases, tsunamis, and other horrors—and saying "It is *not impossible* that God created this." They are showing us the universe, warts and all, and saying "God *must have* created this." Hume insists we cannot draw this conclusion. He thinks a perfect being could and would have made something much closer to perfect.

Hume also suggests the design argument involves another mistake. To see what that mistake is, think first about a different mistake: egocentrism. Some time in your life—maybe after you acted in a particularly selfish way—you have probably heard someone say "You think the whole world revolves

if God directed things. This is analogous to the claim that it is a lot more likely that Tiger would build a twenty-stroke lead. (3) It is *more* likely that God exists than that things in the universe turned out just right just by chance; this is expressed symbolically as saying that P(D | K) is considerably greater than P(E | K & not-D). This is analogous to the claim that it is more likely that golfer 93 is Tiger (1% chance) than that some golfer other than Tiger built a twenty-stroke lead (.01% chance). Claims (1), (2), and (3) together are the premises in a generic Bayesian design argument.

THE GENERIC BAYESIAN DESIGN ARGUMENT

(1) P(E | K & not-D) is extremely low,

(2) P(E | K & D) is quite high, and

(3) P(D | K) is considerably greater than P(E | K & not-D); so, by Bayes's rule, P(D | E & K) is quite high.

In plain English, the basic conclusion of the argument is that the new scientific evidence of design strongly confirms the belief that God exists. So, whatever one's prior probability for the belief that God exists, the posterior probability—the probability one should have *after* hearing about the new scientific evidence—should be much higher.

Each of the three claims essential to this argument are open to criticism. Here we will briefly consider a few objections to (2) and (3); in section VIII we will turn to claim (1). (3) is the claim that, even if we consider it only in light of what we knew prior to getting the new evidence of design, it is still more probable that God exists than that, by pure luck, the conditions in the universe are just right. Now in the golfing case, we knew the probability that golfer 93 was Tiger (1%), and we knew that probability was greater than the probability that someone *other* than Tiger built an enormous lead (.01%). But in this case, what reason do we have for thinking it is more likely that God exists than that, by pure luck, the conditions in the universe are just right? Just what *is* the prior probability that God exists? Well, most people think the prior probability that God exists is not extremely low. Even those who think God does not exist usually admit it is *possible* that God exists. They are open to the idea that God exists, even if they do not believe themselves. Thus it seems that, for most people, (3) is a pretty reasonable claim. Note that if it were not—if it were not even possible that God exists, so that there was a 0% chance that God exists—then the Bayesian design argument would just be a waste of time. If God is impossible, we could not explain anything in terms of God's existence, including apparent cases of design. Here is an analogy. Suppose you leave your wallet on your dresser with $40 in it, and return to find only $20 in it. You confront your roommate about this. Your roommate denies taking the money and offers an alternative explanation of the missing $20. Some explanations might be plausible, e.g. "You miscounted your money." Some explanations might be less plausible, e.g. "A thief broke in and took $20 out of your wallet." Some explanations might be extremely implausible, e.g. "The CIA collected it as evidence in a counterfeiting case against you." Yet however good or bad these explanations are, all of them are at least *possibly* true. Here is one that is not: "$20 equals $40." That's just nonsense! Since it is a *logical contradiction* that $20 equals $40, the probability that $20 equals $40 is zero, and the claim that $20 equals $40 could never explain anything. But most people do not see the hypothesis that God exists this way. They see no logical contradiction in saying God exists, and so they see no reason to think it is impossible that God exists.

Yet numerous philosophical atheists think that not only does God not exist, but that God *could not possibly* exist. Why? Well, to pick just one reason as an example, some people think nothing could be all-powerful. They bring out the old Paradox of the Stone. Can God create a stone so heavy that God cannot lift it? If so, there is something God cannot do: lift the stone. If not, there is something God cannot do: create the stone. So either way, there is something God cannot do. But then, contrary to what believers in God tell us, nothing could be genuinely all-powerful. Thus if God is, by definition, all-powerful, then God could not exist. Now the point here is not to assess whether the Paradox of the Stone shows it is impossible that God exists. That is an issue to be explored in philosophical theology. The point is simply that claim (3) of the Bayesian design argument for the existence of God is not incontestable. Skeptics of the Bayesian design argument may argue that it is impossible that God exists. Barring that, they may argue there is no reason to think the prior probability that God exists is any greater than the probability that the conditions in the universe are, by pure chance, just right. Awareness of these possible maneuvers by the skeptic reinforces a general lesson that you should draw from philosophy class. Even the most obvious premises of an argument usually need defense.

A similar point applies to claim (2). It may appear obvious to everyone that of course God would be likely to create the sort of wondrous, complex universe to which the evidence of design calls our attention. But what reason do we have to think this? We have a pretty good idea of how likely it is that Tiger Woods builds a huge lead in a golf tournament, since we have seen him do it before. What basis do we have for thinking God is likely to create a universe like this one? What insight do we have into the mind of God? Here we should remember Hume's complaints about the design argument, specifically his suggestion that it rests on anthropocentrism. When you say that of course God would create a world like this one, are you simply projecting your own human biases? Perhaps *you* would create a world like this if *you* were super-knowledgeable and super-powerful, but why think God would do the same? Again, these questions are not meant to show that God *would not* create a world like this one, but only to show that skeptics of the Bayesian design argument are going to demand defense of claim (2). All three basic premises of the Bayesian design argument are open to debate, not just the first one.

VIII. THE NEW EVIDENCE OF DESIGN

What about claim (1)? What are the special features of the universe that allegedly are so unlikely if the universe was not designed by God? Let us begin with features of the universe as a whole. In the twentieth century a series of breakthroughs in physics and observational astronomy led to the development of the Big Bang model of the universe. Scientists also discovered that the Universe is highly structured, with precisely defined parameters such as age, mass, curvature, temperature, density, and rate of expansion. Looking at the very precise numbers of these parameters, some scientists asked "How would the universe have been if the values of these parameters had been slightly different?" The answer—to the surprise of many—was that the universe would not have been the sort of place in which life could eventually emerge. The numbers describing the universe, scientists discovered, were like the just-right spot on a radio dial: if you turned the knob just a bit, the clear signal would turn to static. As a result, many physicists started describing the values of the parameters as fine-tuned for life.

To give just one of many, many possible examples, the cosmological constant (symbolized by the Greek letter 'Λ') is a crucial term in Einstein's equations for the General Theory of Relativity. When Λ is positive, it acts as a repulsive force, causing space to expand. When Λ is negative, it acts as an attractive force, causing space to contract. If Λ were not exactly right, either space would expand at such an enormous rate that almost every object in the universe would fly apart, or the universe would collapse back in on itself immediately after the Big Bang. Either way, life could not possibly emerge anywhere in the universe. Some calculations put the odds that Λ has just the right value at well below one chance in a trillion trillion trillion trillion. Similar calculations have been made showing that the odds of the universe's having carbon-producing stars (carbon is essential to life), or of not being millions of degrees hotter than it is, or of not being shot through with deadly radiation, are likewise astronomically small. Given this extremely improbable fine-tuning for life, say some proponents of the Bayesian design argument, we should think it much more likely that God exists than we did initially. After all, if we believe in God, we will have an explanation of cosmic fine-tuning, whereas if we just say the universe is fine-tuned by chance, we are stuck believing something incredibly improbable.

In the second half of the twentieth-century, developments in the field of biology—particularly in the fields of molecular and cell biology—showed that life is incredibly complex, even at the level of the cell. The typical cell, packed with mitochondria, DNA, RNA, and all the rest, displays more organized, functional complexity than a television or a computer—much less Paley's watch! Does evolutionary theory imply that these cellular systems arose by chance? If so, does the universe provide enough chances? Note that the Big Bang model implies that the universe is finite in space and time.

By the most recent calculations it is about 13.5 billion years old and about 13.5 billion light years in diameter. Proponents of what has come to be known as Intelligent Design Theory say "Yes" to the first question and "No" to the second. They say some of these parts of cells are irreducibly complex. A system is irreducibly complex if the removal of any one of its parts makes the system completely nonfunctional. The standard example of an irreducibly complex system is the common household mousetrap. A mousetrap has five parts: platform, catch, spring, hammer, and holding bar. If any one of those parts is missing, the mousetrap will not just be *less good* at catching mice. It will be *no good at all.*

The alleged existence of irreducible complexity in biology is the second special feature of the universe that is supposedly too unlikely to exist by chance. Proponents of Intelligent Design Theory say many cellular systems are irreducibly complex. They think such systems cannot be produced by an evolutionary process, because the ancestors of the organisms with such systems would have crucial parts that just would not function. Yet in order for a system to have been produced by an evolutionary process, the ancestors of the organisms having that system would have to have been functional. If the ancestors were not functional—if the ancestors were incapable of surviving and reproducing—then evolution could not even get off the ground. So proponents of Intelligent Design Theory say evolutionary theory cannot explain the existence of such irreducibly complex biological structures. Neither can chance. According to their calculations, the probability that even one of these irreducibly complex biological structures arose anywhere in the entire history of the universe is still so low that the possibility can be dismissed. According to the Intelligent Design theorists, an irreducibly complex system's arising by chance would be just like that magical dorm-cleaning tornado mentioned earlier, but this time blowing through an airplane parts warehouse and spitting out a Boeing 747. Since evolution is ruled out and the probability that such systems arise by chance is just too low, we must revise upward the probability we assign to the belief that an intelligent designer exists (though Intelligent Design theorists are generally careful not to identify explicitly that intelligent designer with God).

Both cosmic fine-tuning and Intelligent Design Theory are highly controversial topics. [Intelligent Design Theory especially has drawn much fire since it is at the center of recent political fights over what should be taught in high school biology classes; its critics often deride Intelligent Design Theory as "warmed-over creationism."] One line of criticism is purely scientific: that the scientific data just do not support the claims of fine-tuning in physics and irreducible complexity in biology. Other critics focus on philosophical objections of the sort that were mentioned in parts III and VII of this paper. In addition to these routes for blocking a Bayesian design argument, some physicists have proposed the multiverse theory. The multiverse theory, they tell us, is a natural consequence of much of contemporary physics, particularly the field of quantum cosmology. According to the multiverse theory, there is some mechanism for the production of a vast multitude of universes. These universes vary randomly in their basic characteristics and there are enough of them to make it likely that at least one has just the right conditions for life. If the multiverse theory is true, the fact that the universe appears to us to be fine-tuned for life can be explained in terms of the anthropic principle. The anthropic principle says that of course we will find ourselves observing a universe that is fine-tuned for life. After all, if the universe were just right for life, we would not be around to observe it! Notice what we have here is an explanatory strategy that very much resembles Darwin's. The multiverse plays the role of the massive replicator with random variations—but of universes rather than organisms! Meanwhile, the anthropic principle introduces the selection mechanism—in this case, a selection effect that explains why only fine-tuned universes get observed. The appearance of design in universes thus gets explained away, without bringing in any supernatural intelligence like God to engineer the whole thing.

As things currently stand, neither the proponents of Bayesian design arguments nor their critics have achieved decisive intellectual (or political) victory. As this article has shown, through history the design argument has captured the attention of some of the world's great scientists and philosophers. Assuming it continues to do so, the design argument promises to be a live issue for the foreseeable future.

IX. FOR FURTHER READING

Students interested in finding out more about the history of the design argument might start with some primary sources. William Paley's *Natural Theology* and Charles Darwin's *On the Origin of Species* are widely reprinted and should be available in any college library. In *The Blind Watchmaker: Why the Evidence of Evolution Reveals a Universe Without Design* (W. W. Norton and Company, 1986), Richard Dawkins presents a powerful case that evolutionary theory upends the design argument. *God and Design: The Teleological Argument and Modern Science,* edited by Neil A. Manson (Routledge, 2003), is a comprehensive, up-to-date anthology covering the science and the philosophy behind both the cosmological and biological design arguments. It also includes a separate section on the multiverse theory. In *Universes* (Routledge, 1989), John Leslie exhaustively presents the fine-tuning data from physics and gives clever arguments for both the design hypothesis and the multiverse theory. In *Darwin's Black Box: The Biochemical Challenge to Evolution* (Simon & Schuster, 1996), Michael Behe articulates the irreducible complexity concept, argues that biochemistry shows there are irreducibly complex biological structures, and claims this is evidence of the existence of an intelligent designer. Both critics and supporters of Behe's position can be found in *Intelligent Design Creationism and Its Critics: Philosophical, Theological, and Scientific*

Perspectives, edited by Robert T. Pennock (MIT Press, 2001). In *Finding Darwin's God: A Scientist's Search for Common Ground between God and Evolution* (HarperCollins 1999), Kenneth R. Miller opposes Intelligent Design Theory and defends theistic evolutionism as an acceptable alternative for theists. The issue of whether belief in the truth of evolutionary theory is compatible with belief in God is also pursued in Michael Ruse's *Can a Darwinian Be a Christian?* (Cambridge University Press, 2000). Lastly, students interested in finding out more about Bayesian reasoning might start with Colin Howson and Peter Urbach, *Scientific Reasoning: The Bayesian Approach* (Open Court Press, 1989).

The Wager

BLAISE PASCAL (1623–1662), French mathematician, philosopher, and theologian, was born in Clermont. Educated at home by his father, Pascal was a mathematical prodigy who wrote his first work on mathematics, *Essay on Conic Sections,* at the age of 16. In his early 30s Pascal had a religious experience that focused his attention on theological questions for much of the rest of his life. One of his most well-known works, *Pensees* (Thoughts), was published after his death. In it he presents his famous wager argument for belief in God.

THINKING QUESTIONS

Pascal, *The Wager*

1. Pascal maintains that you must make a decision as to whether God exists. Why couldn't one simply withhold judgment and not have an opinion at all? There are many things about which you probably don't have an opinion—whether Monarchs are the world's largest butterfly, whether tachyons exist, whether the next winner of the Kentucky Derby will be born in Virginia. Why must you have an opinion on God's existence?
2. Pascal likens God's existence to a coin toss. Do you think he is right that it is a 50-50 chance whether God exists?
3. Pascal claims that if you believe in God, and God exists, then you win big. What do you win? What evidence does Pascal provide of a payout?
4. Pascal claims that if you do not believe in God, and yet God really does exist, you lose big. What is the downside of being wrong? What is the evidence of this downside?
5. Pascal thinks that if there is no God, then it doesn't matter if you falsely believe that God exists. You don't lose anything by being wrong. Do you agree?
6. Could Pascal's reasoning be used to show that it is in your own self-interest to believe in other gods, like Osiris, Bacchus, Thor, Huitzilopochtili, Krishna, Ganesh, or does it work only for the Christian God?
7. If the Wager doesn't get you to believe in God, what does Pascal recommend at the end of his article as a way to become a believer?

INFINITE—NOTHING.—OUR SOUL IS CAST INTO A BODY, where it finds number, dimension. Thereupon it reasons, and calls this nature necessity, and can believe nothing else.

Unity joined to infinity adds nothing to it, no more than one foot to an infinite measure. The finite is annihilated in the presence of the infinite, and becomes a pure nothing. So our spirit before God, so our justice before divine justice. There is not so great a disproportion between our justice and that of God as between unity and infinity.

The justice of God must be vast like His compassion. Now justice to the outcast is less vast and ought less to offend our feelings than mercy towards the elect.

We know that there is an infinite, and are ignorant of its nature. As we know it to be false that numbers are finite, it is therefore true that there is an infinity in number. But we do not know what it is. It is false that it is even, it is false that it is odd; for the addition of a unit can make no change in its nature. Yet it is a number, and every number is odd or even (this is certainly true of every finite number). So we may well know that there is a God without knowing what He is. Is there not one substantial truth, seeing there are so many things which are not the truth itself?

We know then the existence and nature of the finite, because we also are finite and have extension. We know the existence of the infinite and are ignorant of its nature, because it has extension like us, but not limits like us. But we know neither the existence nor the nature of God, because He has neither extension nor limits.

But by faith we know His existence; in glory we shall know His nature. Now, I have already shown that we may well know the existence of a thing, without knowing its nature.

Let us now speak according to natural lights.

If there is a God, He is infinitely incomprehensible, since, having neither parts nor limits, He has no affinity to us. We are then incapable of knowing either what He is or if He is. This being so, who will dare to undertake the decision of the question? Not we, who have no affinity to Him.

Who then will blame Christians for not being able to give a reason for their belief, since they profess a religion for which they cannot give a reason? They declare, in expounding it to the world, that it is a foolishness, . . . and then you complain that they do not prove it! If they proved it, they would not keep their word; it is in lacking proofs that they are not lacking in sense. "Yes, but although this excuses those who offer it as such and takes away from them the blame of putting it forward without reason, it does not excuse those who receive it." Let us then examine this point, and say, "God is, or He is not." But to which side shall we incline? Reason can decide nothing here. There is an infinite chaos which separated us. A game is being played at the extremity of this infinite distance where heads or tails will turn up. What will you wager? According to reason, you can do neither the one thing nor the other; according to reason, you can defend neither of the propositions.

Do not, then, reprove for error those who have made a choice; for you know nothing about it. "No, but I blame them for having made, not this choice, but a choice; for again both he who chooses heads and he who chooses tails are equally at fault, they are both in the wrong. The true course is not to wager at all."

Yes; but you must wager. It is not optional. You are embarked. Which will you choose then? Let us see. Since you must choose, let us see which interests you least. You have two things to lose, the true and the good; and two things to stake, your reason and your will, your knowledge and your happiness; and your nature has two things to shun, error and misery. Your reason is no more shocked in choosing one rather than the other, since you must of necessity choose. This is one point settled. But your happiness? Let us weigh the gain and the loss in wagering that God is. Let us estimate these two chances. If you gain, you gain all; if you lose, you lose nothing. Wager, then, without hesitation that He is. "That is very fine. Yes, I must wager; but I may perhaps wager too much." Let us see. Since there is an equal risk of gain and of loss, if you had only to gain two lives, instead of one, you might still wager. But if there were three lives to gain, you would have to play (since you are under the necessity of playing), and you would be imprudent, when you are forced to play, not to chance your life to gain three at a game where there is an equal risk of loss and gain. But there is an eternity of life and happiness. And this being so, if there were an infinity of chances, of which one only would be for you, you would still be right in wagering one to win two, and you would act stupidly, being obliged to play, by refusing to stake one life against three at a game in which out of an infinity of chances there is one for you, if there were an infinity of an infinitely happy life to gain. But there is here an infinity of an infinitely happy life to gain, a chance of gain against a finite number of chances of loss, and what you stake is finite. It is all divided; wherever the infinite is and there is not an infinity of chances of loss against that of gain, there is no time to hesitate, you must give all. And thus, when one is forced to play, he must renounce reason to preserve his life, rather than risk it for infinite gain, as likely to happen as the loss of nothingness.

For it is no use to say it is uncertain if we will gain, and it is certain that we risk, and that the infinite distance between the certainty of what is staked and the uncertainty of what will be gained, equals the finite good which is certainly staked against the uncertain infinite. It is not so, as every player stakes a certainty to gain an uncertainty, and yet he stakes a finite certainty to gain a finite uncertainty, without transgressing against reason. There is not an infinite distance between the certainty staked and the uncertainty of the gain; that is untrue. In truth, there is an infinity between the certainty of gain and the certainty of loss. But the uncertainty of the gain is proportioned to the certainty of the stake according to the proportion of the chances of gain and loss. Hence it comes that, if there are as many risks on one side as on the other, the course is to play even; and then the certainty of the stake is equal to the uncertainty of the gain, so far is it from fact that there is an infinite distance between them.

And so our proposition is of infinite force, when there is the finite to stake in a game where there are equal risks of gain and of loss, and the infinite to gain. This is demonstrable; and if men are capable of any truths, this is one.

"I confess it, I admit it. But, still, is there no means of seeing the faces of the cards?" Yes, Scripture and the rest, etc. "Yes, but I have my hands tied and my mouth closed; I am forced to wager, and am not free. I am not released, and am so made that I cannot believe. What, then, would you have me do?"

True. But at least learn your inability to believe, since reason brings you to this, and yet you cannot believe. Endeavour, then, to convince yourself, not by increase of proofs of God, but by the abatement of your passions. You would like to attain faith and do not know the way; you would like to cure yourself of unbelief and ask the remedy for it. Learn of those who have been bound like you, and who now stake all their possessions. These are people who know the way which you would follow, and who are cured of an ill of which you would be cured. Follow the way by which they began; by acting as if they believed, taking the holy water, having masses said, etc. Even this will naturally make you believe, and deaden your acuteness. "But this is what I am afraid of." And why? What have you to lose?

But to show you that this leads you there, it is this which will lessen the passions, which are your stumbling-blocks.

The end of this discourse.—Now, what harm will befall you in taking this side? You will be faithful, humble, grateful, generous, a sincere friend, truthful. Certainly you will not have those poisonous pleasures, glory and luxury; but will you not have others? I will tell you that you will thereby gain in this life, and that, at each step you take on this road, you will see so great certainty of gain, so much nothingness in what you risk, that you will at last recognise that you have wagered for something certain and infinite, for which you have given nothing.

"Ah! This discourse transports me, charms me," etc.

If this discourse pleases you and seems impressive, know that it is made by a man who has knelt, both before and after it, in prayer to that Being, infinite and without parts, before whom he lays all he has, for you also to lay before Him all you have for your own good and for His glory, that so strength may be given to lowliness.

False Testament: Archaeology Refutes the Bible's Claim to History

DANIEL LAZARE is a freelance writer. He is the author of *America's Undeclared War: What's Killing Our Cities and How We Can Stop It* (Harcourt 2001), *The Frozen Republic: How the Constitution Is Paralyzing Democracy* (Harcourt Brace 1996), and *The Velvet Coup: The Constitution, the Supreme Court, and the Decline of American Democracy* (Verso 2001).

THINKING QUESTIONS

Daniel Lazare, *False Testament: Archaeology Refutes the Bible's Claim to History*

1. Traditionally, it was believed that monotheistic Judaism stretched back to the second millennium BC. Lazare argues that Judaism is 1000 years younger than the Torah claims, having arisen between 722 and 586 BC. What is his evidence?
2. Lazare argues that the Hebrew captivity and subsequent exodus from Egyptian slavery never happened. What evidence does he cite to support this claim?
3. Lazare argues that the Jews never conquered Canaan by the force of arms, but were the indigenous peoples. What archeological evidence does he think supports this contention?
4. Lazare maintains that the glory of David and Solomon, if not downright invented, was greatly exaggerated. Why does he believe this?
5. Suppose that all of the historical claims in the Bible (dates, places, Kings, cities, battles, etc.) turned out to be supported by modern archeology and historical techniques. Would that lend credence to the specifically religious claims (gods, demons, invisible spirits, heaven, hell, miracles, etc.) of the Bible? Why or why not?
6. Lazare discusses controversies about several of the historical claims made in the Bible. Had you heard about these historical controversies before? If not, why do you think that is?

NOT LONG AGO, ARCHAEOLOGISTS could agree that the Old Testament, for all its embellishments and contradictions, contained a kernel of truth. Obviously, Moses had not parted the Red Sea or turned his staff into a snake, but it seemed clear that the Israelites had started out as a nomadic band somewhere in the vicinity of ancient Mesopotamia; that they had migrated first to Palestine and then to Egypt; and that, following some sort of conflict with the authorities, they had fled into the desert under the leadership of a mysterious figure who was either a lapsed Jew or, as Freud maintained, a high-born priest of the royal sun god Aton whose cult had been overthrown in a palace coup. Although much was unknown, archaeologists were confident that they had succeeded in nailing down at least these few basic facts.

That is no longer the case. In the last quarter century or so, archaeologists have seen one settled assumption after another concerning who the ancient Israelites were and where they came from proved false. Rather than a band of invaders who fought their way into the Holy Land, the Israelites are now thought to have been an indigenous culture that developed west of the Jordan River around 1200 B.C. Abraham, Isaac, and the other patriarchs appear to have been spliced together out of various pieces of local lore. The Davidic Empire, which archaeologists once thought as incontrovertible as the Roman, is now seen as an invention of Jerusalem-based priests in the seventh and eighth centuries B.C. who were eager to burnish their national history. The religion we call Judaism does not reach well back into the second millennium B.C. but appears to be, at most, a product of the mid-first.

This is not to say that individual elements of the story are not older. But Jewish monotheism, the sole and exclusive worship of an ancient Semitic god known as Yahweh, did not fully coalesce until the period between the Assyrian conquest of the northern Jewish kingdom of Israel in 722 B.C. and the Babylonian conquest of the southern kingdom of Judah in 586.

Some twelve to fourteen centuries of "Abrahamic" religious development, the cultural wellspring that has given us not only Judaism but Islam and Christianity, have thus been erased. Judaism appears to have been the product not of some dark and nebulous period of early history but of a more modern age of big-power politics in which every nation aspired to the imperial greatness of a Babylon or an Egypt. Judah, the sole remaining Jewish outpost by the late eighth century B.C., was a small, out-of-the-way kingdom with little in the way of military or financial clout. Yet at some point its priests and rulers seem to have been seized with the idea that their national deity, now deemed to be nothing less than the king of the universe, was about to transform them into a great power. They set about creating an imperial past commensurate with such an empire, one that had the southern heroes of David and Solomon conquering the northern kingdom and making rival kings tremble throughout the known world. From a "henotheistic" cult in which Yahweh was worshiped as the chief god among many, they refashioned the national religion so that henceforth Yahweh would be worshiped to the exclusion of all other deities. One law, that of Yahweh, would now reign supreme.

This is not, of course, the story that we have all been led to believe is, at least to some degree, history. This is not the story told, for instance, in such tomes as Paul Johnson's 1987 bestseller, *A History of the Jews,* from which we learn that Abraham departed the ancient city of Ur early in the second millennium B.C. as part of a great westward trek of "Habiru" (i.e., Hebrew) nomads to the land of Canaan. "[T]hough the monotheistic concept was not fully developed in [Abraham's] mind," Johnson writes, "he was a man striving towards it, who left Mesopotamian society precisely because it had reached a spiritual impasse." Now, however, we know that this statement is mainly bosh. Not only is there no evidence that any such figure as Abraham ever lived but archaeologists believe that there is no way such a figure could have lived given what we now know about ancient Israelite origins.

A few pages later, Johnson declares that "we can be reasonably sure that the Exodus occurred in the thirteenth century B.C. and had been completed by about 1225 B.C." Bosh as well. A growing volume of evidence concerning Egyptian border defenses, desert sites where the fleeing Israelites supposedly camped, etc., indicates that the flight from Egypt did not occur in the thirteenth century before Christ; it never occurred at all. Although Johnson writes that the story of Moses had to be true because it "was beyond the power of the human mind to invent," we now know that Moses was no more historically real than Abraham before him. Although Johnson adds that Joshua, Moses's lieutenant, "began and to a great extent completed the conquest of Canaan," the Old Testament account of that conquest turns out to be fictional as well. And although Johnson goes on to inform his readers that after bottling up the Philistines in a narrow coastal strip, King David "then moved east, south, and north, establishing his authority over Ammon, Moab, Edom, Aram-Zobar and even Aram-Damascus in the far north-east," archaeologists believe that David was not a mighty potentate whose power was felt from the Nile to the Euphrates but rather a freebooter who carved out what was at most a small duchy in the southern highlands around Jerusalem and Hebron. Indeed, the chief disagreement among scholars nowadays is between those who hold that David was a petty hilltop chieftain whose writ extended no more than a few miles in any direction and a small but vociferous band of "biblical minimalists" who maintain that he never existed at all.

In classic Copernican fashion, a new generation of archaeologists has taken everything its teachers said about ancient Israel and stood it on its head. Two myths are being dismantled as a consequence: one concerning the origins of ancient Israel and the other concerning the relationship between the Bible and science. Back in the days when archaeology was buttressing the old biblical tales, the relationship between science and religion had warmed considerably; now the old chill has crept back in. The comfy ecumenicism that allowed one to believe in, say, modern physics and Abraham, Isaac, et al. is disappearing, replaced by a somewhat sharper dividing line between science and faith. The implications are sweeping—after all, it is not the Song of the Nibelungen or the Epic of Gilgamesh that is being called into question here but a series of foundational myths to which fully half the world's population, in one way or another, subscribes.

So how did such a glorious revolution come to be? As is usually the case, we must first look to when cracks started developing in the *ancien régime*.

Ironically, the new archaeology represents something of a circling back to what was once known as the "Higher Criticism," a largely German school of biblical study that relied solely on linguistic and textual analysis. By the late nineteenth century members of this school had arrived at the conclusion that the first five books of the Old Testament—variously known as the Five Books of Moses, the Torah, or the Pentateuch—were not written by Moses himself, as tradition would have it. Rather, they were largely products of a "post-exilic period" in which Jewish scribes, newly released from captivity in Babylon, set about putting a jumbled collection of ancient writings into some sort of coherent order. The Higher Criticism did not topple the Old Testament as a whole, but it did conclude that Abraham, Isaac, and the other tribal founders depicted in the Book of Genesis were no more real than the heroes of Greek or Norse mythology. As the German scholar Julius Wellhausen put it in the 1870s: "The whole literary character and loose connection of the . . . story of the patriarchs reveal how gradually its different elements were brought together, and how little they have coalesced into a unity." Rather than a chronicle of genuine events, the history that Genesis set forth was an artificial construct, a narrative framework created long after the facts in order to link together a series of unconnected folktales like pearls on a string.

If the linguists of the Higher Criticism were generally skeptical in regard to the Old Testament, modern biblical archaeology as it began taking shape in the early nineteenth century was something entirely different. The first modern archaeologists to set foot in the Holy Land were New England Congregationalists determined to make use of rigorous scientific methods in order to strip away centuries of what they regarded as Roman Catholic superstition and prejudice. As the American biblical scholar Edward Robinson, who first came to Palestine in 1838, put it, he would accept nothing until it was absolutely proven. And yet, as a dutiful Calvinist, Robinson assumed from the outset that whatever he uncovered would broadly confirm what he had learned years earlier in Sunday school. Evidence that buttressed the biblical account was eagerly sought out, while evidence that contradicted it was ignored. British archaeologists set sail a generation later with an even more explicit set of preconceptions. As the Archbishop of York told the newly created Palestine Exploration Fund in London in 1865,

> This country of Palestine belongs to you and to me, it is essentially ours. It was given to the Father of Israel [i.e., Abraham] in the words: "Walk through the land in the length of it, and in the breadth of it, for I will give it unto thee." We mean to walk through Palestine in the length and in the breadth of it, because that land has been given unto us. . . .

The first archaeologists were thus guilty of one of the most elementary of scientific blunders: rather than allowing the facts to speak for themselves, they had tried to fit them into a preconceived theoretical framework. Another layer of political mystification was added in the twentieth century by Zionist pioneers eager for evidence that the Jewish claim to the Holy Land was every bit as ancient as the Old Testament said it was. In 1928 members of a settlement known as Beth Alpha uncovered an ancient synagogue mosaic while digging an irrigation ditch. Since the settlers were members of a left-wing faction known as Hashomer Hatzair, it was inevitable that some would argue that the find should be left to the dustbin of history and that the work of building a modern agricultural settlement should continue uninterrupted. But others recognized its significance: the more evidence they uncovered of an ancient Jewish presence in the Holy Land, the more they would succeed in legitimizing a modern colonization effort. As the number of digs multiplied and turned into a national passion, what the Israeli archaeologist Eliezer Sukenik described as a specifically "Jewish archaeology" was born.

The result was a happy union of science, religion, and politics that by the 1950s would eventually bring together everyone from Christian fundamentalists in the American heartland to the Israeli military establishment. When David Ben-Gurion, the founder of modern Israel, spoke of a sweeping offensive in the 1948 War of Independence, he did so in language purposely evocative of the Book of Joshua. The armies of Israel, he declared, had "struck the kings of Lod and Ramleh, the kings of Belt Naballa and Deir Tarif, the kings of Kola and Migdal Zedek. . . . "Yigael Yadin, Eliezer Sukenik's Son, who was not only Israel's leading archaeologist but a top military commander, referred to an Israeli military incursion into the Sinai by quipping that it was the first time Israeli forces had set foot on the peninsula in 3,400 years. All assumed that the ancient events Israel claimed to be reenacting had actually occurred.

The politicization of archaeology reached something of a climax in the early 1960s, when Yadin was put in command of the excavation of Masada, a hilltop fortress where nearly 1,000 Jewish warriors had committed suicide rather than surrender to the Romans in A.D. 73. In Yadin's hands, Masada emerged as Israel's preeminent nationalist shrine, a place where military recruits were assembled to take an oath of allegiance in dramatic nighttime ceremonies—this despite complaints on the part of a few scholars that evidence for a mass suicide was lacking and that there was reason to believe that ancient accounts of the event were deliberately falsified.

Around this time, the pop novelist James Michener summed up the state of official belief in his heavy-breathing bestseller *The Source* (which this writer savored as a teenager). Using a fictional archaeological dig to weave a series of tales about Palestinian life from prehistoric times to the modern era, Michener briskly laid out the middlebrow orthodoxy of the day: i.e., that God had entered into a pact with the ancient Israelites early in the second millennium B.C., that Jews had dominated the Holy Land for some 2,000 years thereafter, and that with the birth of modern Israel they were claiming their birthright.

"Deuteronomy is so real to me," Michener has a fictional Israeli archaeologist declare, "that I feel as if my immediate ancestor—say, my great-grandfather with desert dust still in his clothes—came down that valley with goats and donkeys and stumbled onto this spot." Michener says of another fictional archaeologist, an American who has just been reading the Torah,

> This time he gained a sense of the enormous historicity of the book. . . . He now read the Ten Commandments as if he were among the tribes listening to Moses. It was he who was coming out of Egypt, dying of thirst in the Sinai, retreating in petulant fear from the first invasion of the Promised Land. He put the Bible down with a distinct sense of having read the history of a real people. . . .

Yet it was precisely this "historicity" that was beginning to come under fire. Resurrecting a theory first proposed in the 1920s, an Israeli named Yohanan Aharoni infuriated the Israeli archaeological establishment by arguing that evidence in support of an Israelite war of conquest in the thirteenth century B.C. was weak and unconvincing. Basing his argument on a redating of pottery shards found at a dig in the biblical city of Hazor, Aharoni proposed instead that the first Hebrew settlers had filtered into Palestine in a nonviolent fashion, peacefully settling among the Canaanites rather than putting them to the sword. Although archaeologists claimed in the 1930s to have uncovered evidence that the walls of Jericho had fallen much as the Book of Joshua said they had, a British archaeologist named Kathleen Kenyon was subsequently able to demonstrate, based on Mycenaean pottery shards found amid the ruins, that the destruction had occurred no later than 1300 B.C., seventy years or more before the conquest could have happened. Whatever caused the walls of Jericho to come tumbling down, it was not Joshua's army.

The enormous ideological edifice that Yigael Yadin and others had erected was weakening at the base. Whereas formerly every pottery fragment or stone tablet appeared to confirm the biblical account, now nothing seemed to fit. Attempting to pinpoint precisely when Abraham had departed the ancient city of Ur, the American scholar William F. Albright, a pillar of the archaeological establishment until his death in 1971, theorized that he had left as part of a great migration of "Amorite" (literally "western") desert nomads sometime between 2100 and 1800 B.C. This was the theory that Paul Johnson would later cite in *A History of the Jews*. Subsequent research into urban development and nomadic growth patterns indicated that no such mass migration had taken place and that several cities mentioned in the Genesis account did not exist during the time frame Albright had suggested. Efforts to salvage the theory by moving up Abraham's departure to around 1500 B.C. foundered when it was pointed out that, this time around, Genesis failed to mention cities that *did* dominate the landscape during this period. No matter what time frame was advanced, the biblical text did not accord with what archaeologists were learning about the land of Canaan in the second millennium.

This was not all. As Israel Finkelstein, an archaeologist at Tel Aviv University, and Neil Asher Silberman, a journalist who specializes in biblical and religious subjects, point out in their recent book, *The Bible Unearthed,* the patriarchal tales make frequent mention of camel caravans. When, for example, Abraham sent one of his servants to look for a wife for Abraham's son, Isaac, Genesis 24 says that the emissary "took ten of his master's camels and left, taking with him all kinds of good things from his master." Yet analysis of ancient animal bones confirms that camels were not widely used for transport in the region until well after 1000 B.C. Genesis 26 tells of Isaac seeking help from a certain "Abimelech, king of the Philistines." Yet archaeological research has confirmed that the Philistines were not a presence in the area until after 1200 B.C. The wealth of detail concerning people, goods, and cities that makes the patriarchal tales so vivid and lifelike, archaeologists discovered, were reflective of a period long after the one that Albright had pinpointed. They were reflective of the mid-first millennium, not the early second.

In hindsight, it all seems so obvious. An ancient text purporting to be a record of events centuries earlier—how could it not fall short of modern historical standards? How could it not reflect contemporary events more than events in the distant past? Beginning in the 1950s, doubts concerning the Book of Exodus multiplied just as they had about Genesis. The most obvious concerned the complete silence in contemporary Egyptian records concerning the mass escape of what the Bible says were no fewer than 603,550 Hebrew slaves. Such numbers no doubt were exaggerated. Yet considering how closely Egypt's eastern borders were patrolled at that time, how could the chroniclers of the day have failed to mention what was still likely a major security breach?

Old-guard academics professed to be untroubled. John Bright, a prominent historian, was dismissive of the entire issue. "Not only were Pharaohs not accustomed to celebrate reverses," he wrote in *A History of Israel,* long considered the standard account, "but an affair involving only a party of runaway slaves would have been to them of altogether minor significance." The scribes' silence concerning the mysterious figure of Moses, Bright went on, was also of no account. Regardless of what the chronicles did or did not say, "The events of exodus and Sinai require a great personality behind them. And a faith so unique as Israel's demands a founder as surely as does Christianity—or Islam, for that matter."

This was dogma masquerading as scholarship. Not only was there a dearth of physical evidence concerning the escape itself, as archaeologists pointed out, but the slate was blank concerning the nearly five centuries that the Israelites had supposedly lived in Egypt prior to the Exodus as well as the forty years that they supposedly spent wandering in the Sinai. Not so much as a skeleton, campsite, or cooking pot had turned up, Finkelstein and Silberman noted, even though "modern archeological techniques are quite capable of tracing even the very meager remains of hunter-gatherers and pastoral nomads all over the world." Indeed, although archaeologists have found remains in the

Sinai from the third millennium B.C. and the late first, they have found none from the thirteenth century.

As with Abraham, the effort to nail down a time frame for the departure created more problems than it resolved. Archaeologists had long zeroed in on a relatively narrow window of opportunity in the thirteenth century B.C. bounded by two independently verifiable events—the start of work on two royal cities in which the Book of Exodus says Hebrew slaves were employed ("and they built Pithom and Rameses as store cities for Pharaoh . . .") and the subsequent erection of a victory stele, or monument, that describes a people identified as "Israel" already existing in Canaan. Hence, the flight into the Sinai had to have taken place either during the reign of a pharaoh known as Rameses or shortly after the death of Ramses II in 1213 B.C.

Once again the theory didn't add up. The Book of Numbers states that, following their escape, the Israelites came under attack from the "Canaanite king of Arad, who lived in the Negev," as they were "coming along the road to Atharim." But although excavations showed that a city of Arad existed in the early Bronze Age from roughly 3500 to 2200 B.C., and that an Iron Age fort arose on the site beginning in roughly 1150 B.C., it was deserted during the years in between. The Pentateuch says the Hebrews did battle with Sihon, king of the Amorites, at a city called Heshbon, but excavations have revealed that Heshbon did not exist during this period either. Nor did Edom, against whose king the Old Testament says the ancient Jews also made war.

Then came a series of archaeological studies conducted in the aftermath of the Six-Day War in 1967. Previously archaeologists had intensively studied specific sites and locales, digging deep in order to determine how technology and culture had changed from one century to the next. Now they tramped through hills and valleys looking for pottery shards and remnants of ancient walls in order to map out how settlement patterns had ebbed and flowed across broad stretches of terrain. Whereas previously archaeologists had concentrated on the lowland cities where the great battles mentioned in the Bible were said to have taken place, they now shifted their attention to the highlands located in the present West Bank. The results were little short of revolutionary. Rather than revealing that Canaan was entered from the outside, analysis of ancient settlement patterns indicated that a distinctive Israelite culture arose locally around 1200 B.C. as nomadic shepherds and goatherds ceased their wanderings and began settling down in the nearby uplands. Instead of an alien culture, the Israelites were indigenous. Indeed, they were highly similar to other cultures that were emerging in the region around the same time—except for one thing: whereas archaeologists found pig bones in other sites, they found none among the Israelites. A prohibition on eating pork may have been one of the earliest ways in which the Israelites distinguished themselves from their neighbors.

Thus there was no migration from Mesopotamia, no sojourn in Egypt, and no exodus. There was no conquest upon the Israelites' return and, for that matter, no peaceful infiltration such as the one advanced by Yohanan Aharoni.

Rather than conquerors, the Hebrews were a native people who had never left in the first place. So why invent for themselves an identity as exiles and invaders? One reason may have been that people in the ancient world did not establish rights to a particular piece of territory by farming or by raising families on it but by seizing it through force of arms. Indigenous rights are an ideological invention of the twentieth century A.D. and are still not fully established in the twenty-first, as the plight of today's Palestinians would indicate. The only way that the Israelites could establish a moral right to the land they inhabited was by claiming to have conquered it sometime in the distant past. Given the brutal power politics of the day, a nation either enslaved others or was enslaved itself, and the Israelites were determined not to fall into the latter category.

If the Old Testament is to be believed, David and Solomon, rulers of the southern kingdom of Judah from about 1005 to about 931 B.C., made themselves masters of the northern kingdom of Israel as well. They represent, in the official account, a rare moment of national unity and power; under their reign, the combined kingdom was a force throughout the Fertile Crescent. The unified kingdom is said to have split into two rump states shortly after Solomon's death and, thus weakened, was all too easy for the Assyrian Empire and its Babylonian successor to pick off. But did a united monarchy encompassing all twelve tribes ever truly exist?

According to the Bible, Solomon was both a master builder and an insatiable accumulator. He drank out of golden goblets, outfitted his soldiers with golden shields, maintained a fleet of sailing ships to seek out exotic treasures, kept a harem of 1,000 wives and concubines, and spent thirteen years building a palace and a richly decorated temple to house the Ark of the Covenant. Yet not one goblet, not one brick, has ever been found to indicate that such a reign existed. If David and Solomon had been important regional power brokers, one might reasonably expect their names to crop up on monuments and in the diplomatic correspondence of the day. Yet once again the record is silent. True, an inscription referring to "Ahaziahu, son of Jehoram, king of the House of David" was found in 1993 on a fragment dating from the late ninth century B.C. But that was more than a hundred years after David's death, and at most all it indicates is that David (or someone with a similar name) was credited with establishing the Judahite royal line. It hardly proves that he ruled over a powerful empire.

Moreover, by the 1970s and 1980s a good deal of countervailing evidence—or, rather, lack of evidence—was beginning to accumulate. Supposedly, David had used his power base in Judah as a springboard from which to conquer the north. But archaeological surveys of the southern hill country show that Judah in the eleventh and tenth centuries B.C. was too poor and backward and sparsely populated to support such a military expedition. Moreover, there was no evidence of wealth or booty flowing back to the southern power base once the conquest of the north had taken place. Jerusalem seems to have been hardly more than a rural village when Solomon was reportedly transforming it into a glittering capital. And although archaeologists had long credited Solomon with the construction of major palaces in the northern cities of Gezer, Hazor, and Megiddo (better known as the site of Armageddon), recent analysis of pottery shards found on the sites, plus refined carbon-14 dating techniques, indicate that the palaces postdate Solomon's reign by a century or more.

Finkelstein and Silberman concluded that Judah and Israel had never existed under the same roof. The Israelite culture that had taken shape in the central hill country around 1200 B.C. had evolved into two distinct kingdoms from the start. Whereas Judah remained weak and isolated, Israel did in fact develop into an important regional power beginning around 900 B.C. It was as strong and rich as David and Solomon's kingdom had supposedly been a century earlier, yet it was not the sort of state of which the Jewish priesthood approved. The reason had to do with the nature of the northern kingdom's expansion. As Israel grew, various foreign cultures came under its sway, cultures that sacrificed to gods other than Yahweh. Pluralism became the order of the day: the northern kings could manage such a diverse empire only by allowing these cultures to worship their own gods in return for their continued loyalty. The result was a policy of religious syncretism, a theological pastiche in which the cult of Yahweh coexisted alongside those of other Semitic deities.

When the northern kingdom fell to the Assyrians, the Jewish priesthood concluded not that Israel had played its cards badly in the game of international politics but that by tolerating other cults it had given grave offense to the only god that mattered. Joining a stream of refugees to the south, the priests swelled the ranks of an influential political party dedicated to the proposition that the only way for Judah to avoid a similar fate was to cleanse itself of all rival beliefs and devote itself exclusively to Yahweh.

"They did wicked things that provoked Yahweh to anger. They worshiped idols, though Yahweh had said, 'You shall not do this.'" Such was the "Yahweh-alone" movement's explanation for Israel's downfall. The monotheistic movement reached a climax in the late seventh century B.C. when a certain King Josiah took the throne and gave the go-ahead for a long-awaited purge. Storming through the countryside, Josiah and his Yahwist supporters destroyed rival shrines, slaughtered alien priests, defiled their altars, and ensured that henceforth even Jewish sacrifice take place exclusively in Jerusalem, where the priests could exercise tight control. The result, the priests and scribes believed, was a national renaissance that would soon lead to the liberation of the north and a similar cleansing there as well.

But then: disaster. After allowing his priests to establish a rigid religious dictatorship, Josiah rode off to rendezvous with an Egyptian pharaoh named Necho in the year 609 B.C. Although Chronicles says that the two monarchs met to do battle, archaeologists, pointing out that Josiah was in no position to challenge the mighty Egyptian army, suspect that Necho merely summoned Josiah to some sort of royal parley and then had him killed for unknown reasons. A model of pious rectitude, Josiah had done everything he thought God wanted of him. He had purified his kingdom and consecrated his people exclusively to Yahweh. Yet he suffered regardless. Judah entered into a period of decline culminating some twenty-three years later in the Babylonian conquest and exile.

Does this mean that monotheism was nothing more than a con, a ruse cooked up by ambitious priests in order to fool a gullible population? As with any religion, cynicism and belief, realpolitik and genuine fervor, all came together in a way that we can barely begin to untangle. To say that the Jerusalem priesthood intentionally cooked up a phony history is to assume that the priests possessed a modern concept of historical truth and falsehood, and surely this is not so. As the biblical minimalist Thomas L. Thompson has noted, the Old Testament's authors did not subscribe to a sequential chronology but to some more complicated arrangement in which the great events of the past were seen as taking place in some foggy time before time. The priests, after all, were not inventing a past; they were inventing a present and, they trusted, a future.

Monotheism was unquestionably a great leap forward. At a time when there was no science, no philosophy, and no appreciable knowledge of the outside world, an obscure, out-of-the-way people somehow conceived of a lone deity holding the entire universe in his grasp. This was no small feat of imagination, and its consequences were enormous. Monotheism's attempt at a unified field theory—a single explanation for everything from the creation of the universe to the origin of law—failed, but in failing it ensured that people would try doubly hard to come up with some new "theory of everything" to take its place. The monotheistic revolution continued to build because it enlisted a larger and larger portion of the population in its great totalizing effort. The Book of Kings tells of the discovery, during Josiah's reign, of a sacred book, filled with rules and regulations that the Jews had so far failed to follow, deep within the recesses of the Temple. In other cultures, the king might have huddled over the book with his advisers and priests. But not Josiah. He

> called together all the elders of Judah and Jerusalem. He went up to the temple of Yahweh with the men of Judah, the people of Jerusalem, the priests and the prophets—all the people from the least to the greatest. He read in their hearing all the words of the Book of the Covenant, which had been found in the temple of Yahweh. The king stood by the pillar and renewed the covenant in the presence of Yahweh. . . . Then all the people pledged themselves to this covenant.

This was all quite novel. Whereas formerly the king and the priests alone were responsible to the national deity, now "all the people from the least to the greatest" took the pledge. The people had been transformed from mere onlookers into active participants. Arguably, the people of Judah were less free as a consequence of Josiah's reforms. Under the old pluralistic order they could sacrifice to other gods, and now they could sacrifice to just one. Yet with the new system's responsibilities to uphold the sacred covenant came the makings of a voice. No longer could the masses be counted on to remain silent.

Was the purpose of all this merely to pluck one tiny nation out of obscurity and elevate it above all others? If the Yahwists were groping for some concept of ethics to go with their universalism, for the most part they seem to have fallen woefully short. To quote Julius Wellhausen on the Jewish scriptures: "Monotheism is worked out to its furthest consequences, and at the same time is enlisted in the service of the narrowest selfishness."

A single, all-powerful god required a single set of sacred texts, and the process of composition and codification that led to what we now know as the Bible began under King Josiah and continued well into the Christian era. "Canonization" of this sort concentrated rather than dispelled questions of nationalism and universalism. A framework for faith, the Bible was equally a machine for generating heresy and doubt, and out of this debate eventually arose Christianity, Islam, Protestantism, and a great deal else besides.

The new universalism had enormous energy, encompassing as it did the entire cosmos and enlisting the entire population, but the new democratic spirit ran aground over the issue of universalism versus narrow nationalism. What, after all, was the point of mobilizing such a broad population in this manner? So that they could slaughter their neighbors all the more thoroughly? How could Moses prohibit murder and then, in Numbers 31, fly into a rage because a returning Israelite war party has slaughtered only the adult male Midianites? ("Now kill all the boys," he tells them when he calms down. "And kill every woman who has slept with a man, but save for yourselves every girl who has never slept with a man.") Was murder a crime only when it involved members of the in-group? Or was it a crime when it involved human beings in general, regardless of nationality? Did an emerging concept of a more equitable social order apply only to Israel or to other nations as well?

In one form or another, these questions have been with us ever since.

The Problem of Evil

B. C. JOHNSON published this article anonymously. He is deceased.

THINKING QUESTIONS

B. C. Johnson, *The Problem of Evil*

1. What is the *problem* in the problem of evil? How is it connected to the concept of God?
2. How should we define "evil"; what makes an event evil and not just something we don't like?
3. What does Johnson mean by "moral urgency"? How does the need for moral urgency justify God in allowing evil?
4. Is there an important *moral* difference between evil that humans cause and natural events, like floods or earthquakes, that cause evil?
5. Is there too much evil in the world?

HERE IS A COMMON SITUATION: a house catches on fire and a six-month-old baby is painfully burned to death. Could we possibly describe as "good" any person who had the power to save this child and yet refused to do so? God undoubtedly has this power and yet in many cases of this sort he has refused to help. Can we call God "good"? Are there adequate excuses for his behavior?

First, it will not do to claim that the baby will go to heaven. It was either necessary for the baby to suffer or it was not. If it was not, then it was wrong to allow it. The child's ascent to heaven does not change this fact. If it was necessary, the fact that the baby will go to heaven does not explain why it was necessary, and we are still left without an excuse for God's inaction.

It is not enough to say that the baby's painful death would in the long run have good results and therefore should have happened, otherwise God would not have permitted it. For if we know this to be true, then we know—just as God knows—that every action successfully performed must in the end be good and therefore the right thing to do, otherwise God would not have allowed it to happen. We could deliberately set houses ablaze to kill innocent people and if successful we would then know we had a duty to do it. A defense of God's goodness which takes as its foundation duties known only after the fact would result in a morality unworthy of the name. Furthermore, this argument does not explain why God allowed the child to burn to death. It merely claims that there is some reason discoverable in the long run. But the belief that such a reason is within our grasp must rest upon the additional belief that God is good. This is just to counter evidence against such a belief by assuming the belief to be true. It is not unlike a lawyer defending his client by claiming that the client is innocent and therefore the evidence against him must be misleading—that proof vindicating the defendant will be found in the long run. No jury of reasonable men and women would accept such a defense and the theist cannot expect a more favorable outcome.

The theist often claims that man has been given free will so that if he accidentally or purposefully causes fires, killing small children, it is his fault alone. Consider a bystander who had nothing to do with starting the fire but who refused to help even though he could have saved the child with no harm to himself. Could such a bystander be called good? Certainly not. If we would not consider a mortal human being good under these circumstances, what grounds could we possibly have for continuing to assert the goodness of an all-powerful God?

The suggestion is sometimes made that it is best for us to face disasters without assistance, otherwise we would become dependent on an outside power for aid. Should we then abolish modern medical care or do away with efficient fire departments? Are we not dependent on their help? Is it not the case that their presence transforms us into soft, dependent creatures? The vast majority are not physicians or firemen. These people help in their capacity as professional outside sources of aid in much the same way that we would expect God to be helpful. Theists refer to aid from firemen and physicians as cases of man helping himself. In reality, it is a tiny minority of men helping a great many. We can become just as dependent on them as we can on God. Now the existence of this kind of outside help is either wrong or right. If it is right, then God should assist those areas of the world which do not have this kind of help. In fact, throughout history, such help has not been available. If aid ought to have been provided, then God should have provided it. On the other hand, if it is wrong to provide this kind of assistance, then we should abolish the aid altogether. But we obviously do not believe it is wrong.

Similar considerations apply to the claim that if God interferes in disasters, he would destroy a considerable amount of moral urgency to make things right. Once again, note that such institutions as modern medicine and fire departments are relatively recent. They function irrespective of whether we as individuals feel any moral urgency to support them. To the extent that they help others, opportunities to feel moral urgency are destroyed because they reduce the number of cases which appeal to us for help. Since we have not always had such institutions, there must have been a time when there was greater moral urgency than there is now. If such a situation is morally desirable, then we should abolish modern medical care and fire departments. If the situation is not morally desirable, then God should have remedied it.

Besides this point, we should note that God is represented as one who tolerates disasters, such as infants burning to death, in order to create moral urgency. It follows that God approves of these disasters as a means to encourage the creation of moral urgency. Furthermore, if there were no such disasters occurring, God would have to see to it that they occur. If it so happened that we lived in a world in which babies never perished in burning houses, God would be morally obliged to take an active hand in setting fire to houses with infants in them. In fact, if the frequency of infant mortality due to fire should happen to fall below a level necessary for the creation of maximum moral urgency in our real world, God would be justified in setting a few fires of his own. This may well be happening right now, for there is no guarantee that the maximum number of infant deaths necessary for moral urgency are occurring.

All of this is of course absurd. If I see an opportunity to create otherwise nonexistent opportunities for moral urgency by burning an infant or two, then I should *not* do so. But if it is good to maximize moral urgency, then I *should* do so. Therefore, it is not good to maximize moral urgency. Plainly we do not in general believe that it is a good thing to maximize moral urgency. The fact that we approve of modern medical care and applaud medical advances is proof enough of this.

The theist may point out that in a world without suffering there would be no occasion for the production of such virtues as courage, sympathy, and the like. This may be true, but the atheist need not demand a world without suffering. He need only claim that there is suffering which is in excess of that needed for the production of various virtues. For example, God's active attempts to save six-month-old infants from fires would not in itself create a world without suffering. But no one could sincerely doubt that it would improve the world.

The two arguments against the previous theistic excuse apply here also. "Moral urgency" and "building virtue" are susceptible to the same criticisms. It is worthwhile to emphasize, however, that we encourage efforts to eliminate evils; we approve of efforts to promote peace, prevent famine, and wipe out disease. In other words, we do value a world with fewer or (if possible) no opportunities for the development of virtue (when "virtue" is understood to mean the reduction of suffering). If we produce such a world for succeeding generations, how will they develop virtues? Without war, disease, and famine, they will not be virtuous. Should we then cease our attempts to wipe out war, disease, and famine? If we do not believe that it is right to cease attempts at improving the world, then by implication we admit that virtue-building is not an excuse for God to permit disasters. For we admit that the development of virtue is no excuse for permitting disasters.

It might be said that God allows innocent people to suffer in order to deflate man's ego so that the latter will not be proud of his apparently deserved good fortune. But this excuse succumbs to the arguments used against the preceding excuses and we need discuss them no further.

Theists may claim that evil is a necessary by-product of the laws of nature and therefore it is irrational for God to interfere every time a disaster happens. Such a state of affairs would alter the whole causal order and we would then find it impossible to predict anything. But the death of a child caused by an electrical fire could have been prevented by a miracle and no one would ever have known. Only a minor alteration in electrical equipment would have been necessary. A very large disaster could have been avoided simply by producing in Hitler a miraculous heart attack—and no one would have known it was a miracle. To argue that continued miraculous intervention by God would be wrong is like insisting that one should never use salt because ingesting five pounds of it would be fatal. No one is requesting that God interfere all of the time. He should, however, intervene to prevent especially horrible disasters. Of course, the question arises: where does one draw the line? Well, certainly the line should be drawn somewhere this side of infants burning to death. To argue that we do not know where the line should be drawn is no excuse for failing to interfere in those instances that would be called clear cases of evil.

It will not do to claim that evil exists as a necessary contrast to good so that we might know what good is. A very small amount of evil, such as a toothache, would allow that. It is not necessary to destroy innocent human beings.

The claim could be made that God has a "higher morality" by which his actions are to be judged. But it is a strange "higher morality" which claims that what we call "bad" is good and what we call "good" is bad. Such a morality can have no meaning to us. It would be like calling black "white" and white "black." In reply the theist may say that God is the wise Father and we are ignorant children. How can we judge God any more than a child is able to judge his parent? It is true that a child may be puzzled by his parents' conduct, but his basis for deciding that their conduct is nevertheless good would be the many instances of good behavior he has observed. Even so, this could be misleading. Hitler, by all accounts, loved animals and children of the proper race; but if Hitler had had a child, this offspring would hardly have been justified in arguing that his father was a good man. At any rate, God's "higher morality," being the opposite of ours, cannot offer any grounds for deciding that he is somehow good.

Perhaps the main problem with the solutions to the problem of evil we have thus far considered is that no matter how convincing they may be in the abstract, they are implausible in certain particular cases. Picture an infant dying in a burning house and then imagine God simply observing from afar. Perhaps God is reciting excuses in his own behalf. As the child succumbs to the smoke and flames, God may be pictured as saying: "Sorry, but if I helped you I would have considerable trouble deflating the ego of your parents. And don't forget I have to keep those laws of nature consistent. And anyway if you weren't dying in that fire, a lot of moral urgency would just go down the drain. Besides, I didn't start this fire, so you can't blame *me*."

It does no good to assert that God may not be all-powerful and thus not able to prevent evil. He can create a universe and yet is conveniently unable to do what the fire department can do—rescue a baby from a burning building. God should at least be as powerful as a man. A man, if he had been at the right place and time, could have killed Hitler. Was this beyond God's abilities? If God knew in 1910 how to produce polio vaccine and if he was able to communicate with somebody, he should have communicated this knowledge. He must be incredibly limited if he could not have managed this modest accomplishment. Such a God if not dead, is the next thing to it. And a person who believes in such a ghost of a God is practically an atheist. To call such a thing a god would be to strain the meaning of the word.

The theist, as usual, may retreat to faith. He may say that he has faith in God's goodness and therefore the Christian Deity's existence has not been disproved. "Faith" is here understood as being much like confidence in a friend's innocence despite the evidence against him. Now in order to have confidence in a friend one must know him well enough to justify faith in his goodness. We cannot have justifiable faith in the supreme goodness of strangers. Moreover, such confidence must come not just from a speaking acquaintance. The friend may continually assure us with his words that he is good but if he does not act like a good person, we would have no reason to trust him. A person who says he has faith in God's goodness is speaking as if he had known God for a long time and during that time had never seen Him do any serious evil. But we know that throughout history God has allowed numerous atrocities to occur. No one can have justifiable faith in the goodness of such a God. This faith would have to be based on a close friendship wherein God was never found to do anything wrong. But a person would have to be blind and deaf to have had such a relationship with God. Suppose a friend of yours had always claimed to be good yet refused to help people when he was in a position to render aid. Could you have justifiable faith in his goodness?

You can of course say that you trust God anyway—that no arguments can undermine your faith. But this is just a statement describing how stubborn you are; it has no bearing whatsoever on the question of God's goodness.

The various excuses theists offer for why God has allowed evil to exist have been demonstrated to be inadequate. However, the conclusive objection to these excuses does not depend on their inadequacy.

First, we should note that every possible excuse making the actual world consistent with the existence of a good God could be used in reverse to make that same world consistent with an evil God. For example, we could say that God is evil and that he allows free will so that we can freely do evil things, which would make us more truly evil than we would be if forced to perform evil acts. Or we could say that natural disasters occur in order to make people more selfish and bitter, for most people tend to have a "me-first" attitude in a disaster (note, for example, stampedes to leave burning buildings). Even though some people achieve virtue from disasters, this outcome is necessary if persons are to react freely to disaster—necessary if the development of moral degeneracy is to continue freely. But, enough; the point is made. Every excuse we could provide to make the world consistent with a good God can be paralleled by an excuse to make the world consistent with an evil God. This is so because the world is a mixture of both good and bad.

Now there are only three possibilities concerning God's moral character. Considering the world as it actually is, we may believe: (*a*) that God is more likely to be all evil than he is to be all good; (*b*) that God is less likely to be all evil than he is to be all good; or (*c*) that God is equally as likely to be all evil as he is to be all good. In case (*a*) it would be admitted that God is unlikely to be all good. Case (*b*) cannot be true at all, since—as we have seen—the belief that God is all evil can be justified to precisely the same extent as the belief that God is all good. Case (*c*) leaves us with no reasonable excuses for a good God to permit evil. The reason is as follows: if an excuse is to be a reasonable excuse, the circumstances it identifies as excusing conditions must be actual. For example, if I run over a pedestrian and my excuse is that the brakes failed because someone tampered with them, then the facts had better bear this out. Otherwise the excuse will not hold. Now if case (*c*) is correct and, given the facts of the actual world, God is as likely to be all evil as he is to be all good, then these facts do not support the excuses which could be made for a good God permitting evil. Consider an analogous example. If my excuse for running over the pedestrian is that my brakes were tampered with, and if the actual facts lead us to believe that it is no more likely that they were tampered with than that they were not, the excuse is no longer reasonable. To make good my excuse, I must show that it is a fact or at least highly probable that my brakes were tampered with—not that it is just a possibility. The same point holds for God. His excuse must not be a possible excuse, but an actual one. But case (*c*), in maintaining that it is just as likely that God is all evil as that he is all good, rules this out. For if case (*c*) is true, then the facts of the actual world do not make it any more likely that God is all good than that he is all evil. Therefore, they do not make it any more likely that his excuses are good than that they are not. But, as we have seen, good excuses have a higher probability of being true.

Cases (*a*) and (*c*) conclude that it is unlikely that God is all good, and case (*b*) cannot be true. Since these are the only possible cases, there is no escape from the conclusion that it is unlikely that God is all good. Thus the problem of evil triumphs over traditional theism.

A Solution to the Problem of Evil

ELEONORE STUMP is the Robert J. Henle, S.J., Professor of Philosophy at Saint Louis University. She holds degrees from Grinnell, Harvard, and Cornell, and is past president of the Society of Christian Philosophers and of the American Catholic Philosophical Association. Professor Stump's research interests include the philosophy of religion, metaphysics, and medieval philosophy. She has published 15 books and numerous articles on these topics.

THINKING QUESTIONS

Eleonore Stump, *A Solution to the Problem of Evil*

1. Stump's proposed solution to the problem of evil depends upon assuming that human beings have free will. How reasonable is this assumption? This question is worth revisiting after you read the articles on free will in the next section.
2. Stump thinks that the right approach to the problem of evil is to examine a specific theology in more detail. She looks at Christianity. Are there resources in other monotheistic religions like Judaism or Islam which offer alternative ways to escape the problem of evil?
3. The three Christian beliefs that Stump thinks will help address the problem of evil are: Adam fell; natural evil entered the world as a result of Adam's fall; after death, depending on their state at the time of their death, human beings either go to heaven or go to hell. How plausible do you think these assumptions are?
4. If one must accept—without any evidence—as much Christian theology as Stump does to make her solution to the problem of evil work, how effective is her approach? Would it persuade an atheist or agnostic who doubts God's existence because of the problem of evil? If not, isn't she merely preaching to the choir?
5. If human beings have defective free wills, why (according to Stump) can't God just repair them? He is omnipotent, after all.
6. Stump maintains that moral and natural evil serves to make people recognize their own sinfulness and, by doing so, come to desire that God fix their defective wills so that they sin no more. Stump admits that she has no evidence for the empirical claim that suffering drives people to God. Does it seem reasonable to you? Why wouldn't suffering instead drive people away from believing in a God who could stop their suffering but declines to do so?

7. Stump holds that God causes (or at least allows) agony and death of children and infants because it is in their own best interests. Why does she believe this? Does this seem reasonable to you?

THE PROBLEM OF EVIL TRADITIONALLY has been understood as an apparent inconsistency in theistic beliefs. Orthodox believers of all three major monotheisms, Judaism, Christianity, and Islam, are committed to the truth of the following claims about God:

(1) God is omnipotent;
(2) God is omniscient;
(3) God is perfectly good.

Reasonable people of all persuasions are also committed to this claim;

(4) There is evil in the world;

and many theists in particular are bound to maintain the truth of (4) in virtue of their various doctrines of the afterlife or the injunctions of their religion against evil. The view that (1)–(4) are logically incompatible has become associated with [David] Hume in virtue of Philo's position in the *Dialogues concerning Natural Religion,* though many other philosophers have maintained it . . . As other philosophers have pointed out, however, Philo's view that there is a logical inconsistency in (1)–(4) alone is mistaken. To show such an inconsistency, one would need at least to demonstrate that this claim must be true:

(5) There is no morally sufficient reason for God to allow instances of evil.

Since Hume, there have been attempts to solve the problem of evil by attacking or reinterpreting one of the first four assumptions. [John Stuart] Mill, for example, suggested a radical weakening of (1) and (2); and according to Mill, [Henry] Mansel reinterpreted (3) in such a way as almost to make (4) follow from it, by in effect claiming that God's goodness might include attributes which we consider evil by human standards. But for reasons which I think are obvious, theists have generally been unwilling to avail themselves of such solutions; and most attempts at solving the problem, especially recently, have concentrated on strategies for rejecting (5). Some of these attempted rejections of (5) make significant contributions to our understanding of the problem, but none of them, I think, ultimately constitutes a successful solution of the problem. In this paper, I will . . . develop in detail a solution of my own by presenting and defending a morally sufficient reason for God to allow instances of evil.

[Alvin] Plantinga's presentation of the free will defense is a landmark in contemporary discussions of the problem of evil. As Plantinga expounds it, the free will defense rests on these two philosophical claims, which it adds to the theological assumptions (1)–(3):

(6) Human beings have free will;

and

(7) Possession of free will and use of it to do more good than evil is a good of such value that it outweighs all the evil in the world.

Plantinga uses these assumptions to argue that a morally sufficient reason for God to permit evil is possible: the value of man's possession and use of free will is a possible reason for God's permitting moral evil, which is evil caused by man. The value of the fallen angel's possession of free will is a possible reason for God's permitting natural evil, evil which is not caused by human free choice but which (Plantinga suggests) could be attributed to the freely chosen actions of fallen angels. As long as it is possible that there be a morally sufficient reason for God to allow evil, regardless of whether or not that possibility is actualized, the existence of evil is not logically incompatible with the existence of a good God . . .

The many objections to . . . [Plantinga's solution] suggest that (6) and a version of (7) by themselves are an insufficient foundation for a satisfactory solution to the problem of evil. Reflection on the nature of the problem seems to me to confirm this suggestion. The problem of evil is generally presented as some sort of inconsistency in theistic beliefs, and (1)–(4) present the relevant theistic assumptions. And yet mere theists are relatively rare in the history of religion. Most people who accept (1)–(4) are Jews or Christians or Muslims. If we are going to claim that their beliefs are somehow inconsistent, we need to look at a more complete set of Jewish or Muslim or Christian beliefs concerning God's goodness and evil in the world, not just at that limited subset of such beliefs which are common to all three religions, because what appears inconsistent if we take a partial sampling of beliefs may in fact look consistent when set in the context of a more complete set of beliefs. I do not of course mean to suggest that an inconsistent set of propositions could become consistent if we add more propositions to it. My point is simple and commonsensical: that the appearance of inconsistency in a set of beliefs may arise from our interpretation of those beliefs, and our reinterpretation of them in light of a larger system of beliefs to which they belong may dispel the appearance of inconsistency. A more promising foundation for a solution to the problem of evil, then, might be found if we consider a broader range of beliefs concerning the relations of God to evil in the world, which are specific to a particular monotheism.

Furthermore, attempted solutions to the problem of evil based solely on a few theistic assumptions common to the major monotheisms are likely themselves to be incompatible with Jewish or Christian or Islamic beliefs . . . For these reasons, in what follows I will focus on one particular monotheism, namely, Christianity; I do not know enough about Judaism or Islam to present a discussion of the problem of evil in the context of those religions. In fact, my account will not deal even with all varieties of Christian belief. Because my account will depend on a number of assumptions, such as that man has free will, it will present a solution to the problem of evil applicable only to those versions of Christianity which accept those assumptions. Christians who reject a belief in free will, for example, will also reject my attempt at a solution to the problem of evil.

Besides (1)–(4), there are three Christian beliefs that seem to me especially relevant to the problem of evil. They are these:

(8) Adam fell.
(9) Natural evil entered the world as a result of Adam's fall.
(10) After death, depending on their state at the time of their death, either (a) human beings go to heaven or (b) they go to hell.

It is clear that these beliefs themselves raise a host of problems, partly because they seem implausible or just plain false and partly because they seem to raise the problem of evil again in their own right . . . It would, of course, make a difference to my solution if any of the beliefs added in (8)–(10) could be *demonstrated* to be false, [I believe] that though (8)–(10) are controversial and seem false to many people, they are not *demonstrably* false . . .

According to the Christian beliefs summarized as (8), (9), and (10), all human beings since Adam's fall have been defective in their free wills, so that they have a powerful inclination to will what they ought not to will, to will their own power or pleasure in preference to greater goods. It is not possible for human beings in that condition to go to heaven, which consists in union with God; and hell understood in Dantean terms is arguably the best alternative to annihilation. A good God will want to fix such persons, to save them from hell and bring them to heaven; and as the creator of these persons, God surely bears some responsibility for fixing and saving them if he can. How is he to do so?

It seems to me clear that he cannot fix the defect by using his omnipotence to remove it miraculously. The defect is a defect in free will, and it consists in a person's generally failing to will what he ought to will. To remove this defect miraculously would be to force a person's free will to be other than it is; it would consist in causing a person to will freely what he ought to will. But it is logically impossible for anyone to make a person freely will something, and therefore even God in his omnipotence cannot directly and miraculously remove the defect in free will, without destroying the very freedom of the will he wants to fix.

Someone might object here that if the defect in the will is inheritable without prejudice to the freedom of the will, then it is also removable without detriment to the freedom of the will; and if it destroys freedom to have God remove the defect, then it also destroys freedom to have the defect inherited. This objection, I think, is based on a mistaken picture of the inheritance of the defect. If the traditional doctrine were that after the time of Adam's fall, human beings whose wills were in a pre-fall state suddenly acquired fallen, defective wills, then this objection would be sound. And perhaps the use of the word "inheritance," with its suggestions of one individual suddenly receiving something from another, invites such a picture. But in fact the doctrine of Adam's fall makes it clear that in the transmission of the defect there is no change of will on the part of post-fallen men. What the doctrine specifies is that individuals conceived and born after Adam's fall have defective wills from the very beginning of their existence. There is no change of will in this process; rather the process consists in the generation of persons whose free wills from birth are strongly inclined to certain sorts of evil actions. If God were to destroy such post-fall persons and generate new ones with non-defective wills (as I have argued he should not), he would not be violating the free wills of the new persons by so creating them any more than he violated Adam's free will when he created Adam in his pre-fall state. But if God intervenes to remove the defect in the wills of post-fall persons, he brings about a change in their wills; and this, I think, he cannot do if their wills are to remain free.

If God cannot by his omnipotence directly fix the defect in free will, it seems that human beings must fix it themselves. Self-repair is a common feature of the natural world, but I do not think self-repair is possible for a person with post-fall free will. People, of course, do sometimes reform their lives and change their habits; but one necessary condition for their doing so is that, for whatever purpose or motive, they will something different from what they previously willed. Analogously, to reform the will requires willing something different from what one previously willed; that is, it requires a change of will. But how to change the will is the problem in the first place. If we want to know whether a man himself can fix a defect in his will, whether he himself can somehow remove his tendency to will what he ought not to will, it is no help to be told that of course he can if he just wills to change his will. We know that a man can change his will for the better; otherwise his will would not be free. The problem with a defect in the will is not that there is an inability to will what one ought to will because of some external restraint on the will, but that one does not and will not will what one ought to will because the will itself is bent towards evil. Consequently, changing the will is the end for which we are seeking the means; if one were willing to change one's will by willing what one ought to will, there would be no problem of a defect in the will. Self-repair, then, is no more a solution to the problem of a defective will than is God's miraculous intervention.

If God cannot and human beings will not fix the defect in their wills, what possible cure is there? Christianity suggests what seems to me the only remaining alternative. Let a person will that God fix his defective will. In that case, God's alteration of the will is something the person has freely chosen, and God can then alter that person's will without destroying its freedom. It is a fact well-attested in religious literature that people who find it next to impossible to will what (they believe) they ought to will may nonetheless find it in themselves to will that God alter their wills. Perhaps two of the most famous examples are the sonnet of John Donne in which he prays for God to overwhelm him so that he will be chaste and Augustine's prayers that God give him continence. The traditional formulation of the crucial necessary condition for a person's being a Christian (variously interpreted by Protestants and Catholics) is that he wills God to save him from his sin; and this condition is, I think, logically (and perhaps also psychologically) equivalent to a person's willing that God fix his will. Willing to have God save one from one's sin is willing to have God bring one to a state in which one is free from sin, and that state depends essentially on a will which wills what it ought to will.

What role God plays in man's coming to will that God fix his will is controversial in the history of Christian thought. Some Protestant theologians have argued that God bears sole responsibility for such willing; Pelagius apparently argued that all the responsibility belongs to man. The first of these positions seems to me to have difficulties roughly analogous to those raised above by the suggestion that God might miraculously fix man's will, and the difficulties in the second are like those in the suggestion that a man himself might fix his own will. Perhaps the correct view here too consists in postulating a cooperative divine and human effort. Perhaps Socrates's way with those he encountered can serve as a model. When Socrates pursued a man with wit and care and passion for the truth, that man sometimes converted to philosophy and became Socrates's disciple. Such a man converted freely, so that it is false to say Socrates *caused* his conversion; and yet, on the other hand, it would be ridiculous to say in consequence that the man bears sole responsibility for his conversion. The responsibility and the credit for the conversion belong to Socrates, whose effort and ingenuity were necessary conditions of the conversion. That they were not sufficient conditions, however, and that the man nonetheless freely willed his conversion is clear from the cases of men such as Alcibiades, whom Socrates sought but did not succeed in converting. Without rashly trying to adjudicate in a paragraph an old and complicated controversy, I think that something along those lines can also be said of the process by which a man comes to will God's help. God's efforts on behalf of Augustine are the necessary condition of Augustine's conversion, and the credit for his conversion belongs to God; but God's efforts are not a sufficient condition, and so Augustine's free will is not impugned. Or, as Anselm says with regard to the fall of the angels, "although the good angel received perseverance [in willing what he ought to will] because God gave it, it is not the case that the evil angel did not receive it because God did not give it. But rather, God did not give it because Satan did not receive it, and he did not receive it because he was unwilling to receive it."

At any rate, if a man does will that God fix his will or save him from his sins, then I think that God can do so without detriment to free will, provided that he does so only to the extent to which the man freely wills that God do so. There is in principle no reason why a person could not will at once that God fix the whole defect of his will; but in general, perhaps because of the extent of the defect in the will, people seem to turn from their own evil in a series of small-scale reforms. In Book VIII, chapter VII, of the *Confessions,* Augustine describes himself as praying that God give him chastity and making the private reservation 'but not yet.' If God were immediately to give Augustine chastity in such a case, he would in fact be doing so against Augustine's will. And so, in general, God's fixing the will seems to be a lengthy process, in which a little willing produces a little fixing, which in turn promotes more willing of more fixing. On Christian doctrine, this is the process of sanctification, which is not finally completed until after death when it culminates "in the twinkling of an eye" in the last changes which unite the sanctified person with God.

The fixing of a defective free will by a person's freely willing that God fix his will is, I think, the foundation of a Christian solution to the problem of evil. What sort of world is most conducive to bringing about both the initial human willing of help and also the subsequent process of sanctification? To answer that question, we need to consider the psychological state of a person who wills God's help. Apart from the obvious theological beliefs, such a person must also hold that he tends to do what he ought not to do and does so because he himself wills what he ought not to will, and he must want not to be in such a condition. He must, in other words, have both a humbling recognition of himself as evil and a desire for a better state. So things that contribute to a person's humbling, to his awareness of his own evil, and to his unhappiness with his present state contribute to his willing God's help.

I think that both moral and natural evil make such a contribution. The unprevented gross moral evils in the course of human history show us something about the nature of man, and our own successful carrying out of our no doubt smaller-scaled evil wills shows us that we are undeniably members of the species. Natural evil—the pain of disease, the intermittent and unpredictable destruction of natural disasters, the decay of old age, the imminence of death—takes away a person's satisfaction with himself. It tends to humble him, show him his frailty, make him reflect on the transience of temporal goods, and turn his affections towards other-worldly things, away from the things of this world. No amount of moral or natural evil, of course, can guarantee that a man will seek God's help. If it could, the willing it produced would not be free. But evil of this sort is the best hope, I think, and maybe the only effective means, for bringing men to such a state.

That natural evil and moral evil, the successful carrying out of evil human wills, serve to make men recognize their own evils, become dissatisfied with things of this world, and turn to God is a controversial claim; and it is clear that a compelling argument for or against it would be very difficult to construct. To produce such an argument we would need a representative sample, whatever that might be, of natural and moral evil. Then we would need to examine that sample case by case to determine the effect of the evil in each case on the human beings who suffered or perpetrated it. To determine the effect we would have to know the psychological and moral state of these people both before and after the evil at issue (since the effect would consist in some alteration of a previous state); and we would have to chart their state for the rest of their lives after that evil because, like the effect of carcinogens, the effect of the experience of evil may take many years to manifest itself. Even with the help of a team of psychologists and sociologists, then, it would be hard to collect the data necessary to make a good argument for or against this claim. Hence, I am unable to present a cogent argument for one of the main claims of this paper, not because of the improbability of the claim but because of the nature of the data an argument for the claim requires; and perhaps it should just be categorized as one more Christian belief and added as (11) to the list of (8), (9), and (10) as a traditionally held, not demonstrably false Christian belief. Still, there is *some* historical evidence for it in the fact that Christianity has tended to flourish among the oppressed and decline among the comfortable, and perhaps the best evidence comes from the raising of children. The phrase "spoiling a child" is ambiguous in current parlance between "turning a child into an unpleasant person" and "giving a child everything he wants," and the ambiguity reflects a truth about human nature. The pains, the hardships, the struggles which children encounter tend to make them better people. Of course, such experiences do not invariably make children better; children, like adults, are also sometimes made worse by their troubles. But that fact would be a counter-example to the general claim about the function of evil in the world only in case it maintained that evil was *guaranteed* to make people better; and that is something this claim could not include and still be compatible with Christianity as long as Christianity is committed to the view that human beings have free will.

Someone may object here that the suffering of children is just what this attempted solution to the problem of evil cannot explain. In *The Brothers Karamazov,* Dostoevsky provides the most eloquent presentation this objection is likely ever to get, concluding with Ivan's passionate insistence (implicit in a question addressed to Alyosha) that even if the whole world could be saved for eternal bliss by the torture of one innocent child, allowing the torture of that child for that purpose would be horribly wrong. I am in sympathy with the attitude Dostoevsky has Ivan express and in agreement with Ivan's conclusion. The suffering of children is in my view unquestionably the instance of evil most difficult for the problem of evil, and there is something almost indecent about any move resembling an attempt to explain it away. The suffering of children is a terrible thing, and to try to see it otherwise is to betray one's humanity. Any attempt to solve the problem of evil must try to provide some understanding of the suffering of children, but it must not lessen our pain over that suffering if it is not to become something monstrous and inhumane.

With considerable diffidence, then, I want to suggest that Christian doctrine is committed to the claim that a child's suffering is outweighed by the good for the child which can result from that suffering. This is a brave (or foolhardy) thing to say, and the risk inherent in it is only sharpened when one applies it to cases in which infants suffer, for example, or in which children die in their suffering. Perhaps the decent thing to do here is simply to sketch some considerations which may shed light on these hard cases. To begin with, it is important to remember that on Christian doctrine death is not the ultimate evil or even the ultimate end, but rather a transition between one form of life and another. From a Christian point of view, the thing to be avoided at all costs is not dying, but dying badly; what concerns the Christian about death is not that it occurs but that the timing and mode of death be such as to constitute the best means of ensuring that state of soul which will bring a person to eternal union with God. If children who die in their suffering thereby move from the precarious and frequently painful existence of this world to a permanently blissful existence in the other world and if their suffering was among part of the necessary means to effect that change, their suffering is justified. I am not trying to say here that the suffering which a child or any other person experiences is the only way in which that person could be brought to God. Rather, I am trying to avoid constructing the sort of explanation for evil which requires telling the sufferer that God lets him suffer just for the sake of some abstract general good for mankind. Perhaps it is true that such a general good—the significant freedom of created persons, for example—is the ultimate end for the sake of which God permits evil. It seems to me nonetheless that a perfectly good entity who was also omniscient and omnipotent must govern the evil resulting from the misuse of that significant freedom in such a way that the sufferings of any particular person are outweighed by the good which the suffering produces *for that person;* otherwise, we might justifiably expect a good God somehow to prevent that *particular suffering,* either by intervening (in one way or another) to protect the victim, while still allowing the perpetrator his freedom, or by curtailing freedom in some select cases. And since on Christian doctrine the ultimate good for persons is union with God, the suffering of any person will be justified if it brings that person nearer to the ultimate good in a way he could not have been without the suffering. I think that Christianity must take some such approach to the suffering or death of children; and perhaps something analogous can be said in connection with the hardest case of all, the suffering of infants. Psychologists tell us that the first year of a child's life is tremendously important in molding the personality and character. For some persons the molding of the personality produced by suffering in infancy may be the best means of insuring a character capable of coming to God.

In all these hard cases, the difficulty of formulating a Christian position which does not appear either implausible or inhuman will be diminished if we have clearly in mind the view of man Christianity starts with. On Christian doctrine, all human beings are suffering from the spiritual equivalent of a terminal disease; they have a defect in the will which if not corrected will cost them life in heaven and consign them to a living death in hell. Now suppose that we are the parents of a child with a terminal brain disease, which includes among its symptoms the child's rejecting the notion that he is sick and refusing to cooperate in any treatments. The doctors tell us that there are treatments which may well cure the child completely, but they hurt and their success is not guaranteed. Would we not choose to subject the child to the treatments, even if they were very painful? The child's suffering would be a terrible thing; we would and we should be grieved at it. But we would nonetheless be glad of the treatments and hope of a cure. And yet this example is only a pale reflection of what Christianity claims to be the case for all human beings, where the loss inflicted by the disease and the benefits of its cure are infinitely greater. If moral and natural evil contain an essential ingredient of a possible cure, surely the cure is worth the suffering such evil entails.

It might seem to some people that if this is God's plan, it is a tragic failure because the amount of evil in the world produces so few cures. The vast majority of people in the world are not Christians or theists of any kind; and even among those who are Christian many die in serious unrepented evil. But this complaint rests on an assumption for which we have no evidence, namely, that the majority of people end in hell. That even an evildoer who dies a sudden, unexpected death may not die impenitent is shown vividly by Dante:

> I am Buonconte . . . wounded in the throat, flying on foot and bloodying the plain [I came]. There I lost my sight and speech. I ended on the name of Mary, and there I fell, and my flesh remained alone. . . . The Angel of God took me, and he from Hell cried, 'O you from Heaven why do you rob me? You carry off with you the eternal part of him for one little tear which takes him from me'.

As for those who live and die without the religious knowledge necessary for redemption from evil, it is not incompatible with Christian doctrine to speculate that in the process of their dying God acquaints them with what they need to know and offers them a last chance to choose. Such a speculation might seem to vitiate the justification for evil which I have been developing in this paper, because if the whole process of redemption can be begun and completed in a person's dying hour, why do we need evil in the world? But this is a mistaken objection, because surely in any sort of deathbed repentance the sufferings of the dying person will have had a significant effect on that person's character and consequently on the choices he makes on his deathbed. So as long as some such speculation is not incompatible with Christian doctrine, it is not at all clear that the majority of people end in hell. And without that assumption the complaint that God's plan for the use of evil is a failure is altogether unwarranted.

Someone might also object here that this solution to the problem of evil prohibits us from any attempt to relieve human suffering and in fact suggests that we ought to promote it, as the means of man's salvation. Such an objection is mistaken, I think, and rests on an invalid inference. Because God can use suffering to cure an evil will, it does not follow that we can do so also. God can see into the minds and hearts of human beings and determine what sort and amount of suffering is likely to produce the best results; we cannot. (Our inability to do is in fact one of the things which make it so difficult to discuss cases of infant suffering, for example.) Furthermore, God as parent creator has a right to, and a responsibility for, painful correction of his creatures, which we as sibling creatures do not have. Therefore, since all human suffering is *prima facie* evil, and since we do not know with any high degree of probability how much (if any) of it is likely to result in good to any particular sufferer on any particular occasion, it is reasonable for us to eliminate the suffering as much as we can. At any rate, the attempt to eliminate suffering is likely to be beneficial to our characters, and passivity in the face of others' suffering will have no such good effects.

The solution to the problem of evil I have been developing will be clarified further by being applied to an individual instance of evil. The instance I want to consider is the Old Testament story of Cain and Abel. For my purposes here, this biblical story of an instance of evil has several advantages over a description of an instance of evil drawn from such sources as the newspapers. The biblical story contains a description of God's intervention or lack of intervention in human history, and it includes an account of the inner thoughts and motivations of the principal characters. To the extent to which Christians are committed to accepting the Bible as the revealed word of God, to that extent they are committed to accepting this story as veridical also; and that fact obviously contributes to the use I want to make of the story. Finally, although the story of Cain and Abel is regularly taken by Christians as a paradigmatically moral and religious story, suitable for the edification of children, the incidents related in the story are such that a twentieth-century atheistic philosopher might have invented them as a showcase for the problem of evil.

Cain and Abel are two brothers who bring offerings to God. Abel's offering is accepted, but Cain's is not—why, the story does not say. In consequence, Cain is very angry at Abel. The story suggests that acceptance or rejection of the offerings is an (at least temporary) acceptance or rejection of the offerer; and Cain's anger at Abel apparently stems from jealousy over God's favoring Abel rather than Cain. Now there is something double-minded in Cain's anger and jealousy. Either God is right to reject Cain's offering—because there was something about it or about the person who brought it which made it objectively unacceptable—and in that case there are no grounds for anger; or God is wrong to reject Cain's offering—because it was a perfectly good offering brought in an altogether appropriate spirit—and in that case *God* is not good. And although one might then still be afraid of the consequences of incurring God's displeasure or resent those more favored by God, a single-minded belief that God's standards for accepting offerings are bad precludes jealousy towards those who are accepted. That Cain is angry and jealous indicates that he is double-minded about whether God is right to reject his offering.

Although he does reject Cain's offering, God does not leave Cain to himself in his double-minded anger. He comes to him and talks to him, asking Cain Socratic questions designed to get him to recognize and resolve his double-mindedness: "Why are you angry?" "If you do well, will you not be accepted?" And God goes on to give Cain a warning, that he is in danger of sin. So God apparently anticipates Cain's attack on his brother, and he intervenes to warn Cain.

But Cain attacks and kills his brother. Abel, who has just been accepted by God and is evidently righteous, suffers violent and untimely death. When the killing is over, God speaks to Cain again, asking him more careful questions designed to lead him to confess his deed: first, "Where is Abel?" and then after the evasive response to that question, the stronger question "What have you done?" When Cain is obstinate in his evil, God punishes him by miraculously intervening in nature: the ground will be barren when Cain tills it, and apparently only when Cain tills it. Finally, we have the last piece of God's care for Cain in this story: Cain says his punishment is more than he can bear, and God comforts him by protecting him against being killed by other men, a danger Cain had understood to be part of his punishment.

Now consider God's actions in this story. In the first place, he punishes Cain for the murder of Abel, showing thereby that he regards the murder of Abel as bad and worthy of punishment. And yet he himself allowed the murder to take place, although obviously he could have prevented it. Any decent person who was present when Cain attacked his brother would have made some effort to rescue Abel; but God, who is always present everywhere and who even seems to anticipate Cain's attack, does nothing for Abel. On the other hand, consider what God does to or for Cain. He comes to him and warns him of the coming temptation. After the murder he returns to talk to Cain again, in a way designed to make Cain acknowledge his true state. When he imposes punishment, he does it in a way that seems to require a miracle. He banishes Cain from his land. And when Cain complains that his punishment is too much, God is merciful to him and guards him from being killed by other men. In short, God interferes in Cain's affairs to warn him; he talks to him earnestly to get him to see his true situation; he performs a miracle on his behalf; he sends him away from his own place; and he protects him from being murdered. Clearly, any *one* of these things done on Abel's behalf would have been enough to save him. But God does none of these things for *Abel,* the innocent, the accepted of God; he does them instead for *Cain,* a man whose offering was rejected and who is murderously angry at his brother. When it comes to righteous Abel, God simply stands by and watches him be killed. Why has such a story been allowed to stand as part of the canonical Scriptures?

On the solution to the problem of evil which I have been developing in this paper, if God is good and has a care for his creatures, his overriding concern must be to insure not that they live as long as possible or that they suffer as little pain as possible in this life but rather that they live in such a way as ultimately to bring them to union with God.

Abel presents God with no problems in this respect. He is apparently righteous at the time of his offering; and hence that is a safe, even a propitious, time for him to die, to make the transition from this life to the next. Given that he will die sometime, Abel's death at this time is if anything in Abel's interest; he dies at a time when he is accepted by God, and he enters into union with God. It is true that Abel dies prematurely and so is deprived of years of life. But on

Christian doctrine, what he loses is years of a painful and spiritually perilous pilgrimage through this life, and what he gains is eternal bliss.

Cain, on the other hand, is in trouble as regards both his current moral state and his prospects for the next life. If God were to rescue Abel by striking Cain with heart failure at the outset of Cain's attack on Abel, for example, Cain would die in mortal sin and so would go to hell, while righteous Abel would continue the morally dangerous journey of this life only to die later, perhaps in some less virtuous state. There are, of course, many other ways in which God could have stopped Cain and rescued Abel without going so far as killing Cain. But perhaps stopping Cain even in those other ways would not have been good for Cain. Because God does not step in between Cain's willing and the successful realization of that willing, Cain is brought as forcefully as possible to a recognition of the depth of the evil he willed. And that forceful recognition is, I think, the most powerful means of bringing Cain to an acknowledgment of his own evil and a desire for help, which is a necessary condition for his salvation.

On the solution to the problem of evil which I have been developing here, then, God does not rescue Abel because contrary to appearances Abel is not in danger; and God's failure to rescue Abel, as well as all the other care for Cain recorded in the story, constitutes the best hope of a rescue for Cain, who is in danger, and not just of death but of a perpetual living death.

I think, then, that it is possible to produce a defensible solution to the problem of evil by relying both on the traditional theological and philosophical assumptions in (1)–(4) and (6), and on the specifically Christian doctrines in (8)–(10). Like other recent attempted solutions, this one also rests fundamentally on a revised version of (7), namely, this:

> (7') Because it is a necessary condition for union with God, the significant exercise of free will employed by human beings in the process which is essential for their being saved from their own evil is of such great value that it outweighs all the evil of the world.

(7') constitutes a morally sufficient reason for evil and so is a counterexample to (5), the claim that there is no morally sufficient reason for God to permit instances of evil.

Religion without God

STEVEN CAHN is a prolific author who has written numerous articles and books on the philosophy of religion, social and political philosophy, education, and academic ethics and responsibility. Among his most important works are *Saints and Scamps: Ethics in Academia* (1986) and *Philosophical Explorations: Freedom, God, and Goodness* (1989). Educated at Columbia University, Dr. Cahn has held a variety of academic and administrative positions and currently teaches at the Graduate School and University Center of the City University of New York.

THINKING QUESTIONS

Steven Cahn, *Religion without God*

1. What does Cahn mean by "supernaturalism"? Which very familiar religious beliefs are part of supernaturalism?
2. What four elements make up the "theory and practice of religion," according to Cahn? Why these and not others? Do you think Cahn's description of religion is complete?
3. What is the difference between "superstitious" and "non-superstitious" ritual? How can naturalistic religion make use of ritual?
4. What is the difference between petitionary prayer and prayers of meditation? Which of these works within naturalism?
5. What are "metaphysical" beliefs? Which beliefs that you already have are metaphysical beliefs?
6. Why doesn't acting morally depend upon belief in the existence of a supernatural God?
7. Do you agree with Cahn's conclusion that "reasonable individuals may perform rituals, utter prayers, accept metaphysical beliefs, and commit themselves to moral principles without believing in supernaturalism"? If not, what has Cahn left out that is essential to religion?

MOST OF US SUPPOSE that all religions are akin to the one we happen to know best. But this assumption can be misleading. For example, many Christians believe that all religions place heavy emphasis on an afterlife, although the central concern of Judaism is life in this world, not the next. Similarly, many Christians and Jews are convinced that a person who is religious must affirm the existence of a supernatural God. They are surprised to learn that religions such as Jainism or Theravada Buddhism deny the existence of a Supreme Creator of the world.

How can there be a nonsupernatural religion? To numerous theists as well as atheists, the concept appears contradictory. I propose to show, however, that nothing in the theory or practice of religion—not ritual, not prayer, not metaphysical belief, not moral commitment—necessitates a commitment to traditional theism. In other words, one may be religious while rejecting supernaturalism.

Let us begin with the concept of ritual. A ritual is a prescribed symbolic action. In the case of religion, the ritual is prescribed by the religious organization, and the act symbolizes some aspect of religious belief. Those who find the beliefs of supernaturalistic religion unreasonable or the activities of the organization unacceptable may come to consider any ritual irrational. Yet although particular rituals may be based on irrational beliefs, nothing is inherently irrational about ritual.

Consider the simple act of two people shaking hands when they meet. This act is a ritual, prescribed by our society and symbolic of the individuals' mutual respect. The act is in no way irrational. Of course, if people shook hands in order to ward off evil demons, then shaking hands would be irrational. But that is not the reason people shake hands. The ritual has no connection with God or demons but indicates the attitude one person has toward another.

It might be assumed that the ritual of handshaking escapes irrationality only because the ritual is not prescribed by any specific organization and is not part of an elaborate ceremony. To see that this assumption is false, consider the graduation ceremony at a college. The graduates and faculty all wear peculiar hats and robes, and the participants stand and sit at appropriate times. However, the ceremony is not at all irrational. Indeed, the rites of graduation day, far from being irrational, are symbolic of commitment to the process of education and the life of reason.

At first glance, rituals may seem a comparatively insignificant feature of life; yet they are a pervasive and treasured aspect of human experience. Who would want to eliminate the festivities associated with holidays such as Independence Day or Thanksgiving? What would college football be without songs, cheers, flags, and the innumerable other symbolic features surrounding the game? Those who disdain popular rituals typically proceed to establish their own distinctive ones, ranging from characteristic habits of dress to the use of drugs, symbolizing a rejection of traditional mores.

Religious persons, like all others, search for an appropriate means of emphasizing their commitment to a group or its values. Rituals provide such a means. Granted, supernaturalistic religion has often infused its rituals with superstition, but nonreligious rituals can be equally as superstitious as religious ones. For instance, most Americans view the Fourth of July as an occasion on which they can express pride in their country's heritage. With this purpose in mind, the holiday is one of great significance. However, if the singing of the fourth verse of "The Star-Spangled Banner" four times on the Fourth of July were thought to protect our country against future disasters, then the original meaning of the holiday would soon be lost in a maze of superstition.

A naturalistic (i.e., nonsupernaturalistic) religion need not utilize ritual in a superstitious manner, for such a religion does not employ rituals in order to please a benevolent deity or to appease an angry one. Rather, naturalistic religion views rituals, as one of its exponents has put it, as "the enhancement of life through the dramatization of great ideals." If a group places great stress on justice or freedom, why should it not utilize ritual in order to emphasize these goals? Such a use of ritual serves to solidify the group and to strengthen its devotion to its expressed purposes. These are strengthened all the more if the ritual in question has the force of tradition, having been performed by many generations who have belonged to the same group and have struggled to achieve the same goals. Ritual so conceived is not a form of superstition; rather, it is a reasonable means of strengthening religious commitment and is as useful to naturalistic religion as it is to supernaturalistic religion.

Having considered the role of ritual in a naturalistic religion, let us next turn to the concept of prayer. It might be thought that naturalistic religion could have no use for prayer, since prayer is supposedly addressed to a supernatural being, and proponents of naturalistic religion do not believe in the existence of such a being. But this objection oversimplifies the concept of prayer, focusing attention on one type while neglecting an equally important but different sort.

Supernaturalistic religion makes extensive use of petitionary prayer, prayer that petitions a supernatural being for various favors. These may range all the way from the personal happiness of the petitioner to the general welfare of all society. Since petitionary prayer rests on the assumption that a supernatural being exists, such prayer clearly has no place in a naturalistic religion.

However, not all prayers are prayers of petition. Some prayers are prayers of meditation. These are not directed to any supernatural being and are not requests for the granting of favors. Rather, these prayers provide the opportunity for persons to rethink their ultimate commitments and rededicate themselves to live up to their ideals. Such prayers may take the form of silent devotion or may involve oral repetition of certain central texts. Just as Americans repeat the Pledge of Allegiance and reread the Gettysburg Address, so adherents of naturalistic religion repeat the statements of their ideals and reread the documents that embody their traditional beliefs.

It is true that supernaturalistic religions, to the extent that they utilize prayers of meditation, tend to treat these prayers irrationally, by supposing that if the prayers are not uttered a precise number of times under certain specified conditions, then the prayers lose all value. Yet prayer need not be viewed in this way. Rather, as the British biologist Julian Huxley wrote, prayer "permits the bringing before the mind of a world of thought which in most people must inevitably be absent during the occupations of ordinary life: . . . it is the means by which the mind may fix itself upon this or that noble or beautiful or awe-inspiring idea, and so grow to it and come to realize it more fully."

Such a use of prayer may be enhanced by song, instrumental music, and various types of symbolism. These elements, fused together, provide the means for adherents of naturalistic religion to engage in religious services akin to those engaged in by adherents of supernaturalistic religion. The difference between the two services is that those who attend the latter come to relate themselves to God, while those who attend the former come to relate themselves to their fellow human beings and to the world in which we live.

We have so far discussed how ritual and prayer can be utilized in naturalistic religion, but to adopt a religious perspective also involves metaphysical beliefs and moral commitments. Can these be maintained without recourse to supernaturalism?

If we use the term "metaphysics" in its usual sense, referring to the systematic study of the most basic features of existence, then a metaphysical system may be either supernaturalistic or naturalistic. The views of Plato, Descartes, and Leibniz are representative of a supernaturalistic theory; the views of Aristotle, Spinoza, and Dewey are representative of a naturalistic theory.

Spinoza's *Ethics,* for example, one of the greatest metaphysical works ever written, explicitly rejects the view that any being exists apart from Nature itself. Spinoza identifies God with Nature as a whole and urges that the good life consists in coming to understand Nature. In his words, "our salvation, or blessedness, or freedom consists in a constant and eternal love toward God." Spinoza's concept of God, however, is explicitly not the supernaturalistic concept of God, and Spinoza's metaphysical system thus exemplifies not only a naturalistic metaphysics, but also the possibility of reinterpreting the concept of God within a naturalistic framework.

Can those who do not believe in a supernaturalistic God commit themselves to moral principles, or is the acceptance of moral principles dependent on acceptance of supernaturalism? Some have assumed that those who reject a supernaturalistic God are necessarily immoral, for their denial of the existence of such a God leaves them free to act without fear of Divine punishment. This assumption, however, is seriously in error.

The refutation of the view that morality must rest upon belief in a supernatural God was provided more than two thousand years ago by Socrates in Plato's *Euthyphro*. Socrates asked the following question: Are actions right because God says they are right, or does God say actions are right because they are right? This question is not a verbal trick; on the contrary, it poses a serious dilemma for those who believe in a supernatural deity. Socrates was inquiring whether actions are right due to God's fiat or whether God is Himself subject to moral standards. If actions are right due to God's command, then anything God commands is right, even if He should command torture or murder. If one accepts this view, then it makes no sense to say that God Himself is good, for since the good is whatever God commands, to say that God commands rightly is simply to say that He commands as He commands, which is a tautology. This approach makes a mockery of morality, for might does not make right, even if the might is the infinite might of God. To act morally is not to act out of fear of punishment; it is not to act as one is commanded to act. Rather, it is to act as one ought to act. How one ought to act is not dependent on anyone's power, even if the power be Divine.

Thus actions are not right because God commands them; on the contrary, God commands them because they are right. What is right is independent of what God commands, for what He commands must conform with an independent standard in order to be right. Since one could act in accordance with this independent standard without believing in the existence of a supernatural God, it follows that morality does not rest upon supernaturalism. Consequently, naturalists can be highly moral (as well as immoral) persons, and supernaturalists can be highly immoral (as well as moral) persons. This conclusion should come as no surprise to anyone who has contrasted the life of Buddha, an atheist, with the life of the monk Torquemada, organizer of the Spanish Inquisition.

We have now seen that naturalistic religion is a genuine possibility, since reasonable individuals may perform rituals, utter prayers, accept metaphysical beliefs, and commit themselves to moral principles without believing in supernaturalism. Indeed, one can even do so while maintaining allegiance to Christianity or Judaism. Consider, for example, those Christians who accept the "Death of God" or those Jews who adhere to Reconstructionist Judaism.

Such options are philosophically respectable. Whether to choose any of them is for each reader to decide.

Free Will

The idea of fate, or destiny, is as old as humanity itself. In Sophocles' *Oedipus Rex,* Oedipus is prophesied to slay his father and marry his mother, and there is nothing he can do to escape this doom. Oedipus fled from Corinth to Thebes to thwart his fate, and by doing so only brought about its fulfillment. According to *Mark* 17:30, Jesus prophesied that Judas Iscariot would betray him to the Romans, and that Peter would deny him three times before morning. In both cases, there seems to be nothing Judas or Peter can do to avoid their destiny. In Fudail ibn Ayad's *Hikayat-I-Naqshia,* a 9th-century Arabian Sufi tale, a man sees Death in the morning marketplace in Baghdad. Terrified, the man leaps on a horse and gallops to Samarra, only to find that his appointment with Death was in the afternoon, in Samarra.

Many people believe that they, too, are fated, that they have some sort of destiny or that there is a cosmic plan for their lives. Yet this belief in a cosmic plan seems to run smack into another widely held belief: that we are free to do as we choose, that human beings are possessed of free will. How is it possible for us to freely choose our futures if they are already fated? Judas' betrayal of Jesus was not a free action if it was a destiny he could not avoid. Since Jesus supposedly knew the future—knew that Judas was to sell him out—Judas was in no position to freely choose to change what will be. If Judas was indeed fated in this way, it is difficult to see how he could be morally to blame for his actions; there was nothing else that he could have done.

The contemporary version of this predicament is the problem of *determinism.* Philosophers tend not to couch the problem in terms of whether the gods or the fates have predetermined our futures, but whether the future is fixed in place by the inexorable causal machinery of the past. Our cells, our organs, our brains seem to be no more than biological robots, governed by the laws of nature, with one cog moving because another turned upon it. If determinism is true, then our sense of free will is simply an illusion. At least—that's the threat. In his article, Steven Hales gives the details behind this threat; he also explains why *denying* determinism is just as perilous for free will as affirming it. The resulting dilemma—that there is no free will if determinism is true and no free will if it is false—is what Hales calls the Master Argument against freedom. If the Master Argument is correct, then it presents a challenge not only to free will, but to the traditional view of moral responsibility that it is built upon it. Hales concludes by sketching the leading responses to the Master Argument.

One kind of response is that defended by William Rowe and Thomas Reid. They argue that humans have an active power to choose their own actions, that we are the basic, fundamental causes of our deliberate and voluntary behavior. Our actions are not determined by forces beyond our control or prior to our existence, but immediately by *us*. Through a basic act of will we introduce new chains of causation into the world.

David Hume, on the other hand, does not try to exempt free agents from the impersonal causal order of the world. Instead, he argues that the problem of free will arises because we have a faulty conception of freedom. If we construe freedom as having a choice in our actions, then there is indeed a conflict with determinism. Hume recommends that instead, we understand freedom as doing what we want, and that in this way we might be free even if our wants are fully determined by prior forces outside of our control.

No solution to the problem of free will is fully satisfying, and you may decide that none is minimally adequate. Perhaps free will is a myth after all. Still, it is an illusion that we seem unable to discard. As Henry David Thoreau wrote, "Surely the fates are forever kind, though Nature's laws are more immutable than any despot's, yet to man's daily life they rarely seem rigid, but permit him to relax with license in summer weather. He is not harshly reminded of the things he may not do."

The Traditional Problem of Free Will

STEVEN D. HALES (1966–) is professor of philosophy at Bloomsburg University. He has a PhD from Brown University and has lectured widely, including talks in Istanbul, Prague, Amsterdam, Austria, Rome, and Slovenia. Professor Hales has published five books and many articles in the areas of epistemology, metaphysics, and Nietzsche.

THINKING QUESTIONS

Steven D. Hales, *The Traditional Problem of Free Will*

1. Hales argues that your reasons for acting ultimately stem from either previous decisions you made or forces and influences outside of you. He claims that the first alternative is no good because of a regress problem. What is this regress problem?
2. What is the reason to think that we always act on our greatest desire?
3. If our actions are rooted in desires outside of our control, then why does that show that we are not free?
4. Why do you think that you are more free than the digger wasp? Because you feel free? Why does the feeling of freedom show that you are really free?
5. Does determinism mean that we are predetermined in some sense?
6. What is the difference between the libertarian and compatibilist definitions of freedom?
7. How does the existence of random events undermine the thesis of determinism?
8. The Master Argument against free will concludes that no matter what you think about determinism, we are not free. We are not free according to which definition of freedom?
9. If we have no libertarian freedom, why does that seem to be a problem for moral responsibility?
10. Could free will be a mental illusion, a neurological construct of our brains?

DID YOU DECIDE TO READ THIS ARTICLE? There are only two possible answers, namely "yes" and "no." Suppose the answer is "no." That doesn't mean you aren't reading it; we all do plenty of things that we don't particularly decide to do, things that we do out of habit, as a matter of routine, or perhaps even randomly. Ever drive a familiar route and then realize that you can't remember any part of the drive for the last ten minutes? The drive is just part of a routine that you don't really think about; you do it subconsciously. Or when you brush your teeth—do you really make a decision about every stroke? "Up," you think, "now down . . . all the way, OK, now up again, don't press so hard . . . down once more." Of course not. You probably daydream, or worry, or plan your day like everyone else when you brush your teeth. You don't think about the brushing. You just do it. So maybe reading this article is like that—without really deciding to, you found yourself sitting in your chair with this book in your hand. You started reading this article without thought, zombie-like.

No, you say? You actually decided to read it? Good for you. How did you decide? Of your own free will? Let's think about that for a bit. There are lots of other things you might have done instead; you could have slept in, illegally consumed a refreshing adult beverage, studied for another class, played some tennis, kissed your lover. How did you decide to read about free will instead of those other things? Presumably you thought it over, you weighed out the reasons pro and con for reading the article, and the pros won out. There are many good reasons for reading it after all: nothing is more exciting and stimulating than philosophy, the writing style is breathtaking in its excellence, free will is a great topic—oh yeah, let's not forget the weight contributed by the fact that it will be on the test and you desperately need to pass this class to graduate. There were reasons on the other side to blow it off, true, but it turns out that they just weren't as weighty. The image of deliberation here is that of pair of scales, a mental balance if you will. In one pan are the reasons for performing action X and in the other are the reasons to not do X. The balance tips in one direction or other, and that's the action you perform. What explains your decision to read this article? You weighed out the options, and reading the article won.

The puzzle's not completely solved, though. Why should the things that counted as a reason to read the article (or not read it) be reasons at all? And why do they have the relative weight that they do? If your GPA is 0.0, maybe you don't especially care about the upcoming test or passing the class. So the fact that reading this article is instrumental to passing the test just has no value, no weight for you. It doesn't even count as a reason to read it. Likewise, if you've had plenty of sleep, the option of sleeping in doesn't have much pull either. We can put it on the scale on the "con" side, but it doesn't weigh very much. It is clear, then, that which things count as reasons to keep on reading this article and which things count as reasons not to read it are going to vary from person to person, perhaps even from moment to moment. What explains which things are reasons for you, and how much they weigh? There seem to be only two possible answers, namely that the explanation is rooted ultimately in you and your decision-making, or that the explanation is rooted outside of you in other forces and factors. Thus:

1. Your reasons for acting are the result of some previous decisions you made or
2. Your reasons for acting somehow came from forces and influences outside of your mind (e.g. authority, family, society, environment, innate biological instincts)

With option (1), you made choices in the past, and these choices determine your preferences and desires now. For example, in the past you decided to come to college and be successful, and this prior decision is what gives weight to the value of studying and reading assigned texts. Likewise for the other reasons pro and con: their relative weight and that they amount to reasons for acting at all, is the result of earlier decision-making.

The problem with this answer is that it apparently leads to an infinite regress. Your decision to read this article is explained by your earlier decision to study in college, which is the result of your prior decision to A which is explained by your even earlier decision to B, and on back. If we think about decision-making as the tipping of scales, then it looks like this:

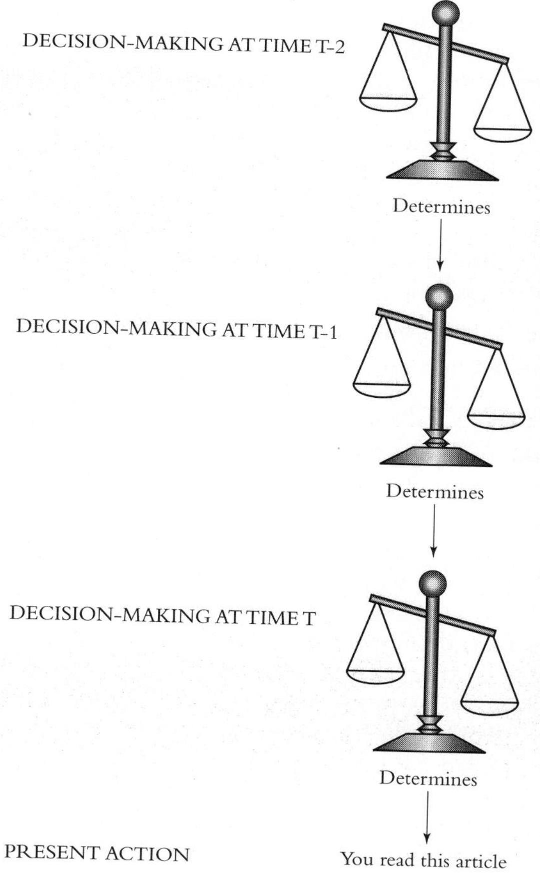

We can just keep adding little balances back in time. As a baby did you make some first decision, some unmoved mover of a decision that determined everything else in your life? How did you make *that* decision? It couldn't be the result of any prior decision-making, being the very first one. Therefore it can't be the case that *all* of your decisions are the causal consequences of earlier decisions. Suddenly decision-making seems inexplicable.

Maybe option (2) is the right answer. The reason that you care about education (and therefore passing the class and reading this article) is because of the values instilled in you while you were growing up. The reason that you like philosophy is because of your fortunate genetic heritage along with the inquisitive nature that your parents, friends, and teachers always encouraged. Your values, your reasons for acting, are thereby the result of these outside influences which have molded and shaped you into the person you are. When we ask the question "how did you decide to read this article?" the answer is that you weighed out the pros and the cons. When we press on to ask what determines a reason to be a pro or a con, and what fixes how much each reason weighs, the answer is that your biology, experiences, upbringing, and environment determine these things. The important thing to notice here is that all of these forces are outside of your control, and not the result of your choice. No one chooses their families, or what society they were born into, or what teachers they have, or any of those other things. Your present decision to read this article isn't the result of some earlier decision that you made, but the result of forces completely outside of you. Strange, isn't it? But the truly disturbing is just around the corner. Consider this argument:

1. You always act according to your greatest desire.
2. Your desires and their relative strengths are outside of your control and not the result of your choices.
3. Therefore your actions are outside of your control.
4. If your actions are outside of your control, then you are not free.
5. Therefore, you are not free.

The defense of the first premise is implicit in our discussion so far. The image of a mental balance represents the weighing of your desires, and when it tips, it tips in the direction of the greatest weight, i.e. the overall greatest desire, upon which you then act. We might have many conflicting interests—you might want that pint of Ben and Jerry's Chunky Monkey, and simultaneously you want to stay on your diet. You can't do both. If you wind up pigging out on Chunky Monkey, then your greatest desire was to have the ice cream, something proven by the fact you are eating it. The desire for rich, creamy, banana ice cream stuffed with nuts and chocolate chunks was a stronger desire than staying on the diet. Conversely, if you stayed on the diet, *that* action was the result of your greatest desire.

The second premise was just defended—it is factors outside of you, independent influences that you can't control, that determine the existence and strength of your desires. Option (3) seems to be a straightforward consequence, your actions themselves are, in some fundamental and ultimate way, outside of your control. Yet if you aren't in control of your actions, then it seems that you are not free, that you are a mere puppet of external forces, and that your own sense of freedom, your feeling of making a choice out of nowhere (*ex nihilo* as philosophers like to say) is an illusion. Keep in mind that the argument here isn't that you can't act against your greatest desire, but that your greatest desire at any given moment has, in some deep sense, little to do with you.

Wait, you say, perhaps our desires are *influenced* by outside events, our upbringing, our church, family, etc., but *I'm* the one who decides how I'll react to those influences. Well, it sure feels that way, doesn't it? Unfortunately, this response just throws us back on the question we began with: "How do you make your decisions?" It was in trying to answer this question that we were driven to the idea that your desires are outside of your control, that you have no choice over them. So claiming that you decide how to react to outside influences is no help at all. It seems that our desires and actions are in some sense mechanical, the mere outcomes of prior forces. In fact, consider the case of the digger wasp, *Sphex Ichneumoneus:*

> When the time comes for egg laying, the wasp *Sphex* builds a burrow for the purpose and seeks out a cricket which she stings in such a way as to paralyze but not kill it. She drags the cricket into the burrow, lays her eggs alongside, closes the burrow, then flies away, never to return. In due course the eggs hatch and the wasp grubs feed off the paralyzed cricket, which has not decayed, having been kept in the wasp equivalent of deep freeze. To the human mind, such an elaborately organized and seemingly purposeful routine conveys a convincing flavor of logic and thoughtfulness—until more details are examined. For example, the wasp's routine is to bring the paralyzed cricket to the burrow, leave it on the threshold, go inside to see that all is well, emerge, and drag the cricket in. If the cricket is moved a few inches away while the wasp is inside making her preliminary inspection, the wasp, on emerging from the burrow, will bring the cricket back to the threshold, but not inside, and will then repeat the preparatory procedure of entering the burrow to see if everything is all right. If again the cricket is moved a few inches while the wasp is inside, once again she will move the cricket up to the threshold and re-enter the burrow for a final check. The wasp never thinks of moving the cricket straight in. On one occasion the procedure was repeated forty times, always with the same result (quoted in Dennett, 1984, p. 11).

What makes you any different from the digger wasp? Aren't you the least bit sphexish? You might argue (and probably will!) that we're far more complex than poor *Sphex,* and don't engage in the same repetitive actions that she does. Furthermore, all the wasps behave in the same way with the cricket—it's not just a case of one wasp with obsessive-compulsive disorder. Yet human beings are infinitely variable in their behavior, we don't all do the same thing in the same circumstances. Maybe it is hard to say exactly *why* we're not sphexish, but surely we're not.

Regrettably, this rejection of sphexishness is not that great an argument. In the first place, one *can* see common behaviors among humans on large scales. This is just what psychological studies show us, like Stanley Milgram's obedience studies; in the same situation, there is a great deal of predictable, similar behavior. In the second place, even if no two individuals behave in precisely the same way in the same circumstance, this is no proof at all that our actions are free or not determined by natural forces. Consider two leaves falling from a tree: no two fall in exactly the same way. However, this hardly means that leaves freely *decide* how to fall—obviously their falling patterns are the result of differences in the wind, subtle variations in the shape of the leaves, and so on, all physical facts that have nothing to do with willing.

Maybe you can't see yourself falling into sphexish behavior. I can't see it in myself either. But perhaps that's because we're just not smart enough. Consider the wasp: she's not smart enough to see the repetition in her behavior and may well have (for all we know) a feeling of freedom, of deliberation and freely choosing to move that cricket. Still not convinced? Imagine a race of extraterrestrials whose ratio of intellect to our own is the same as the ratio of our intellect to that of *Sphex*. They're not just a little bit brighter than we are. Humans are titanically smarter than wasps (most of us, anyway). Imagine the ETs are just that much more intelligent than we are. It is perfectly conceivable that these big-brained ETs could perform little experiments on us, just like we do to *Sphex*. "Hey Kodos, come here and check out these humans. Every time I do X, they do Y. Isn't that hilarious? They kill me." In the end we may just be larger, more complicated versions of the digger wasp, big lumbering robots programmed by natural selection for the reproduction of our genes, not smart enough to examine our own source code. Our psychological feelings of freedom are nothing more than a transparent, gauzy overlay on top of the coldly impersonal biological mechanism of ourselves. Perhaps we differ from *Sphex* in degree, but not in kind.

That's the threat anyway. Let's try to sharpen up the argument under consideration. After all, we've not even defined "free will" yet, and it's always easier to investigate the existence of something once we have a clearer idea of what we're looking for. Let's define "free will" this way:

> ***Free Will:*** One's will is free at time *t* just in case at *t* one could have performed either action *x* or action *y*.

The preceding definition is given in terms of action and performing action, but this should be understood broadly, so that even thinking about something is a sort of action, just a mental one. The basic idea is that if there is only one thing you could do, only one thing you could think at a certain time, then you're not free. Freedom means that you could have done otherwise than you did. If there is only one thing you can do at a time, then you're not free at that time. For example, your gravitational attraction to the earth isn't a free decision on your part; there's nothing else you can do. Gravity's got a hold of you and you have no choice about it. In other cases you feel free: you could have picked either the red pill or the blue pill, you make a decision, you have a choice. The initial threat to free will, and the one that we have been dancing around until now is determinism.

> ***Determinism:*** Given the laws of nature and a set of initial conditions, there is exactly one physically possible future.

Sounds kind of technical, huh? Let's try to break it down with an analogy. Think about shooting a game of pool. When you break, what determines where the balls go isn't random, and the balls don't decide for themselves. The 11-ball doesn't think, "hey, I think I'll bounce off the 2-ball, hit a side rail, rattle around the corner pocket and then bounce out again." So what makes them go where they do? Well, we can list lots of factors:

1. Where the balls are in the rack
2. The velocity of the cue ball
3. The spin of the cue ball
4. The angle the cue ball hits the racked balls
5. The tightness of the rack
6. The condition of the table felt

No doubt we could expand this list further. But you get the idea. These factors are the *initial conditions* of the break. When these vary, the balls wind up going in different directions after the break. Good pool players can replicate and control the initial conditions—they hit the cue ball with the same speed, spin, and at the same angle time and again. There's one other key factor that isn't on the list, one that is essential to shooting decent pool: the laws of nature. For example, laws concerning momentum, force, ball and rail elasticity, rolling friction, angle of incidence equaling the angle of reflection, all affect where those balls go. These don't change. However, if you have no clue about how any of these physical laws will affect the motion of pool balls, you aren't going to be a very good player. Thus there are two things that determine where the balls go after the break: the initial conditions of the break, and the laws of nature.

Determinism is basically the far-reaching, global thesis that the entire universe is like a gigantic game of pool. The initial conditions of the universe are the physical facts at the moment of the Big Bang. Those facts, coupled with the laws of physics, determine everything that has happened since. The universe is simply in the process of unfolding, and it is all just forces and little pool balls bouncing off of each other. We ourselves are no more than physical creatures, made up of physical parts, subject to the same laws as anything else in the universe. Our brains too are electro-chemical mechanisms and their operation is simply the result of prior states of the universe and the laws of nature.

The threat that determinism poses to free will is this: determinism states that there is exactly one physically possible future. If you have free will, then you have a choice, you could do either action *x* or action *y*. In other words, if you are free, then you somehow decide what the future is going to be like, whether it contains the performance of *x* or the performance of *y* instead. If you are free, then the future is open. If determinism is true, then the future is closed; there is only one way things could go. If you perform action *x*, then that was the only thing that you could have done, no matter how much it felt like you could have done something else. The feeling that you could have done otherwise was no more than an illusion, self-deception of some kind. The view that free will and determinism are in conflict is called "incompatibilism."

Incompatibilism: Either we have no free will or determinism is false.

"C'mon," you say. "What kind of a dope do you think I am? I've heard that modern physics has disproved determinism, that some things just flat-out happen for no reason at all, that they are uncaused and undetermined by what happened before." Good point. It is true that the mainstream interpretation of the equations of quantum physics is that some things happen randomly. This is a truly difficult view to wrap one's mind around, but the idea is *not* that we can't explain or discover what caused certain events, but literally that they have no cause at all. The future could contain event *x*, or it could contain event *y;* either is physically possible. A good example of such an event is radioactive decay. There's even a website at a Swiss physics lab that uses the randomness of the atomic decay of Krypton-85 to generate authentically random numbers. Here's a nice passage on randomness from that website:

> Even though we're absolutely certain that if we start out with, say, 100 million atoms of Krypton-85, 10.73 years later we'll have about 50 million, 10.73 years after that 25 million, and so on, there is no way *even in principle* to predict when a given atom of Krypton-85 will decay into Rubidium. We can say that it has a fifty/fifty chance of doing so in the next 10.73 years, but that's *all we can say*. Ever since physicists realised how weird some of the implications of quantum mechanics were, appeals have been made to "hidden variables" to restore some of the sense of order on which classical physics was based. For example, suppose there's a little alarm clock inside the Krypton-85 nucleus which, when it rings, causes the electron to shoot out. Even if we had no way to look at the dial of the clock, it's reassuring to believe it's there—it would mean that even though our measurements show the universe to be, at the most fundamental level, random, that's merely

> because we can't probe the ultimate innards of the clockwork to expose its hidden deterministic destiny.
>
> But hidden variables aren't the way our universe works—it really *is* random, right down to its gnarly, subatomic roots. In 1964, the physicist John Bell proved a theorem which showed hidden variable (little clock in the nucleus) theories inconsistent with the foundations of quantum mechanics. In 1982, Alain Aspect and his colleagues performed an experiment to test Bell's theoretical result and discovered, to nobody's surprise, that the predictions of quantum theory were correct: the randomness is inherent—not due to limitations in our ability to make measurements. So, given a Krypton-85 nucleus, there is no way whatsoever to predict when it will decay. If we have a large number of them, we can be confident half will decay in 10.73 years; but if we have a single atom, pinned in a laser ion trap, all we can say is that there's even odds it will decay sometime in the next 10.73 years, but as to precisely when we're fundamentally quantum clueless. (http://www.fourmilab.ch/hotbits/how.html)

While these facts are enough to undermine the global thesis of determinism stated earlier, they do not imply that *every* event is random, just that some are. There may still be, and probably are, plenty of events whose occurrence is the inexorable outcome of prior forces. So it looks like events are going to fall into one of two groups: those that are random, like the radioactive decay of Krypton-85, and those that are determined. Is any of this enough to save free will? Can quantum randomness somehow provide for our freedom?

It's pretty hard to see how it can. If an action is undetermined, if it occurs randomly, then its happening is a matter of chance or luck, and not a free action. The whole idea behind free will, as we have defined it, is that we have a choice in what we do, that we have a sort of volitional control over our thoughts and actions. But random actions aren't under the control of anything. If our actions are the result of some random quantum event, then our actions would be surprising and spontaneous, like Tourettic outbursts or epileptic seizures. This sense of chance, random action is more indicative of diminishing control, a loss of freedom, than a sign that we are free.

Perhaps even worse is this apparent consequence: if an event is truly random, then it might not have occurred given precisely the same initial conditions and laws of nature. For example, if your reading this article is the result of randomness, then when you decided to read it (assuming you still are!) all of your deliberative decision-making and weighing of the pros and cons could have been exactly what they in fact were right up to the moment of choice and yet you did not read it. Such a consequence is truly weird—if decision-making is infected with randomness, it suddenly becomes irrational, arbitrary, and capricious. It no longer looks free. In a nutshell, random action is not the result of anything, and so not the result of free will.

We have now come to the classic problem for free will, one that takes the form of a dilemma.

The Master Argument Against Free Will

1. Either determinism is true, or it is false.	(trivial)
2. If determinism is true, then there is no time at which anyone could have done either action *x* or action *y*.	(incompatibilism thesis)
3. If there is no time at which anyone could have done either action *x* or action *y*, then no one has no free will.	(from the definition of free will)
4. Therefore, if determinism is true, no one has free will.	(2, 3 hypothetical syllogism)
5. If determinism is false, then some events are random (those not random are determined).	(premise)
6. If action *x* is performed randomly by agent A at *t*, then A could not have done action *x* or action *y* at *t*.	(premise)
7. Therefore, an action that is random is not the result of free will.	(6, definition of "free will")
8. Therefore, if determinism is false, there is no free will.	(from 5, 7)
9. Therefore, there is no free will.	(1, 2–4, 5–8, disjunctive syllogism)

Either determinism is true, or it is false. If it is true, we have no free will. If determinism is false, we have no free will. In short, any way you slice it, no matter what you think about determinism, we're not free. At this point you might well be thinking, "Oh well. So I don't have free will. It's a bummer, but what am I going to do? Nothing. Just another illusion shattered by this philosophy class. You know, I was all happy in my little cocoon, until I took this stinkin' course . . ." Whoops, maybe that's going too far. But you might be thinking that it's not that big a deal to have no free will. We're not free, but so what?

Well, one big reason that people have cared about free will is its connection to moral responsibility. Suppose you and I are in a 10-story apartment building. It is a beautiful day, and you have opened the window to get some fresh air. You're standing at the window, enjoying the view, when I come up behind you and suddenly push you out. You plummet to the sidewalk below, and land squarely on a hapless pedestrian, plowing into him at about 27 mph. Fortunately for you, especially considering the day you've had so far, is that the pedestrian was hugely fat, and cushioned your fall. You get up and walk away unharmed. Unfortunately for the pedestrian, you killed him. Should you be arrested for murder? No? How about manslaughter? Negligent homicide? Something? No doubt you'll complain to the arresting officers that you didn't have any choice in the matter, that you were pushed out of the window, and once gravity had you in its tenacious grip, there was not a thing you could do. True, all true. Oh? You're going to blame *me*? Go on, send the cops upstairs. I'll tell them just what you did: I had no choice in the matter, my pushing you was either determined or random, and either way there was not a darn thing I could do about it. I'm not any more responsible for that poor pedestrian than you are.

See, if you're not free, then there was *never* anything else you could do, no matter *what* you do. Any action you perform is either determined by forces outside of your control, in which case you never had a choice, or your actions are the result of randomness, in which case you never had a choice. Either way, you were never free to do anything differently; there was nothing you could have done to produce a different outcome. In other words, every single thing you do is exactly like getting shoved out of the window. You're not free to do otherwise than you did. So if you think that prosecuting you for killing that pedestrian is unjust, then prosecuting you for *any* action is unjust. This bit of reasoning presupposes the following principle:

The Principle of Alternate Possibilities: One is morally responsible for an action x only if at the time one did x, there was alternate possible action y that one could have done instead.

Sounds pretty plausible, huh? Some philosophers have argued against the Principle of Alternate Possibilities, but it's hard to imagine that no principle like it is true. You're not responsible for killing that pedestrian because there was no alternate possible action y that you could have performed instead. In fact, if you have no free will, as the Master Argument above concludes, then there is never an alternate possible action you could have done instead. Therefore, you are never morally responsible for anything you do. I don't know whether you feel liberated by this result or frightened by it, but either way you should at least be surprised and a bit disturbed. So now what do we do?

One way out of the Master Argument is to deny premise (5). People who reject premise (5) defend *Agent Causation*. The idea of agent causation is that the alternative to determinism isn't randomness at all, but our own free will. How does this proposal escape the evil clutches of the determinist without just assuming the very thing we're trying to prove? That's a good question. The answer is that human beings, in fact any willful agent, can just spontaneously begin a new chain of causation in the world, one that has no causal history prior to the act of willing. As Aristotle wrote, "thus, a staff moves a stone, and is moved by a hand, which is moved by a man" (*Physics*, VII, 5, 256a, 6–8). Your decision to read this article was literally caused by nothing outside of yourself.

You decided, chose as a sort of unmoved mover, and then the reading began. Through our freedom we are, in a way, outside the causal order of the world; our choices are undetermined, but not precisely random either.

The problem with Agent Causation is giving a really convincing and detailed explanation of how this sort of causation is supposed to work. The first difficulty is the mystery objection: the idea of a person's action being caused only by their will and nothing else is really mysterious. You act upon your greatest desires, yet the strength of those desires is due to nothing else besides you yourself. Why does this not lead to regress—where you choose your desires on the basis of prior desires, and choose those desires on the basis of prior desires, and on back? We looked at this problem earlier. If you spontaneously create your desires (or at least their strengths) then again it smells suspiciously random. How Agent Causation can escape the earlier arguments against freedom is a bit mysterious.

The second difficulty is the magic objection: Agent Causation seems to insist upon a sort of causation that isn't physical, one not governed by physical law. This extra-physical causation is no better than magic. Your choices aren't the result of either quantum indeterminacy or inexorable prior forces; human choosing is outside the order of the physical world. But how is this possible? It looks like we're casting spells, or pulling a rabbit out of a hat.

While there are some philosophers (and good ones!) devoted to making sense of Agent Causation (see, for example, the selections by William Rowe and Thomas Reid that follow), without doubt the most prominent response to the Master Argument is to reject premise (3). "Wait," you say, "Premise three comes straight from the definition of free will; how can anyone deny *that*?" The answer is by rejecting the definition itself. This is the strategy of *Compatibilism*. Compatibilists concede that the Master Argument Against Free Will is sound—the knockout blow against free will. We just don't have any of that sort of freedom. Yet there is a kind of freedom we *do* have, and this freedom is compatible with determinism. All we need to do, compatibilists argue, is redefine free will. The kind of free will under attack so far in this essay is called Libertarian Free Will. Just to remind you:

> ***Libertarian Free Will:*** One's will is free at time t just in case at t one could have performed either action x or action y.

Here's the compatibilist's new and improved definition of free will:

> ***Compatibilist Free Will:*** One's performance of action x is free just in case x is the result of one's beliefs, desires, and intentions.

The central idea behind libertarianism is that we have a choice in what we do. Compatibilists agree with the Master Argument that we never have a choice in what we do, we're never libertarian free. Nevertheless, they think, there is a plausible and powerful sense in which we're free: we're free as long as we're doing what we want. That's the compatibilist idea. What exactly is doing what you want compatible with? Why, determinism. Suppose all of your desires are the result of forces outside of you, going back to the initial conditions of the universe itself. Given those initial conditions and the laws of nature, you were bound to have the desires and beliefs that you do. However, as long as you are acting on your desires, doing what you want, in accordance with your beliefs, then you are free.

The compatibilist is quick to note that this idea of freedom fits well with our everyday concerns about being free. Why do you want to avoid prison? It's not because you don't have choices while imprisoned, or that at any time you never have a choice between doing an action *x* and an action *y*. Ignoring the Master Argument for a moment, it seems that you have lots of choices in prison, at every moment: to open your eyes or close them, what to think about, whether to shift your weight to your right foot or your left. No, the reason you don't want to go to prison is because *you can't do what you want* in prison. That's the way in which prison robs you of your freedom. Freedom is acting on your desires, beliefs, and intentions, and prison prevents you from acting in that way.

When are you not free according to a compatibilist? (1) When your actions are random or the result of randomness. If you do something randomly, then your action isn't the result of your beliefs and desires. It is literally the result of nothing. Therefore it's not a free action according to compatibilism. (2) When your actions are coerced. If somebody points a gun at you and says it's your money or your life, then there's a real sense in which handing over your wallet isn't the result of *your* desires. You don't want to give away your money, you're being forced to. Therefore forking over your wallet is not a free action. Same for being imprisoned; it's a form of coercion.

One might argue that even when a mugger steals your wallet that you act freely in handing it over. You acted on your greatest desire, didn't you? Wasn't your desire to give him your money greater than your desire to get killed? Of course it was! Therefore you did what you wanted, you acted on your desires and beliefs, and so according to the compatibilist, giving your money to a mugger is a free action. The problem is that compatibilism then looks absurdly inclusive—everything you do is free, no matter what. You're every bit as free in prison as you are on the outside. A nice slogan for a police state, but not too convincing otherwise. The conclusion of the Master Argument was that we're never libertarian free, but now it looks like we are inevitably compatibilist free. That doesn't seem to get things right either. The challenge for the compatibilist is to explain coercion in such a way that coerced acts aren't free ones, even though apparently you're always acting on your desires, even at gunpoint.

If we don't have free will, or at least, if we don't make free choices in the libertarian sense, then why are we so convinced that we *are* free? In 1888, Friedrich Nietzsche argued that our belief in free will is the residue of our religious heritage, writing, "men were thought of as 'free' so that they could become *guilty:* consequently every action *had* to be thought of as willed, the origin of every action lying in the consciousness" (*Twilight of the Idols*, "Four Great Errors" §7). In his view, a religious insistence on moral responsibility led to the invention of free will.

I want to suggest another idea. Maybe our feelings of freedom are more neurological than moral in origin (this idea is developed in Wegner, 2002). Our brains organize and interpret our experience to make a whole, unified human life. They are not mere passive receptors for the data of the senses. The creative work of brains is exposed when there are failures of one kind or another; reading through neurological case studies gives a cornucopia of examples. For example, stroke victims who suffer from Left Side Neglect lose the entire left side of the world, for them the very idea of "leftness" has lost its meaning. They will shave only one side of their face, not recognizing that there is an entire side unshorn on the left. Such persons won't pick up an object on their left, and draw clocks like half-circles, all while sincerely denying that anything is amiss.

Another example is the phenomenon of phantom limbs. In these cases, amputees continue to feel sensations in their missing limbs—pain in a hand that plainly doesn't exist or a cramp in a missing foot. The feelings are certainly real, and in some cases phantom pain has driven amputees nearly to suicide. Nevertheless, a missing hand just *can't* hurt; there's nothing there *to* hurt. The explanation of Left Side Neglect and phantom limbs is an interesting one, having to do with how brains map our bodies (see Ramachandran and Blakeslee, 1998), creating the world order for us out of the blooming, buzzing confusion of raw sensory information. It may be that free will is, like an itch on a nonexistent hand, a persistent and troubling illusion that our brains have built for us. Like the amputee who feels the phantom limb long after knowing that there is no limb there at all, we may well continue to feel free despite the most persuasive philosophical arguments to the contrary.

REFERENCES

Dennett, Daniel. *Elbow Room: The Varieties of Free Will Worth Wanting*. Cambridge: MIT Press, 1984.

Ramachandran, V. S., and Sandra Blakeslee. *Phantoms in the Brain*. New York: William Morrow and Co., 1998.

Wegner, Daniel M. *The Illusion of Conscious Will*. Cambridge: MIT Press, 2002.

Two Concepts of Freedom

WILLIAM L. ROWE is professor of philosophy at Purdue University. He works in the philosophy of religion and metaphysics. He is the author of *Religious Symbols and God* (1968), *The Cosmological Argument* (1998), *Philosophy of Religion* (1978), and *Thomas Reid on Freedom and Morality* (1991) as well as a number of papers in various journals.

THINKING QUESTIONS

William L. Rowe, *Two Concepts of Freedom*

1. Rowe sets out two different conceptions of freedom, which he labels Lockean Freedom and Reidian Freedom. According to Lockean Freedom, what is the distinction between a free action and a voluntary action?
2. Given your desires, judgments, and prevailing circumstances at the time you willed to do something, does Locke think it is possible for you to have willed something else at that time?
3. How does Rowe define a "necessitarian"?
4. Rowe objects to Locke's view that freedom must include the power to will, not simply the power to do if we will. What is his argument for this objection?
5. What is the Leibniz/Bayle objection to the Lockean conception of freedom?
6. Rowe divides Reid's view of freedom into a negative thesis and a positive thesis. What are these theses?
7. What are the three conditions Reid lays down for being the agent-cause of a change in the world?
8. For Reid, freedom is a power over one's will and can come in degrees. How does this correlate to degrees of responsibility for one's actions, according to Rowe?
9. One objection to Reid's theory of agent causation is that, when conjoined with the principle that every event has a cause, his theory leads to the absurdity of an infinite regress of agent-produced exertions for every act of will an agent produces. What is Rowe's proposed solution to this objection?

IN HIS LIFE OF SAMUEL JOHNSON, Boswell reports Johnson as saying: "All theory is against freedom of the will; all experience for it." The first part of this remark would be agreeable to many 18th century philosophers: those believing that certain theoretical principles concerning explanation or causality support the doctrine of necessity. But the second part, that experience is on the side of free will, would be somewhat puzzling to those 18th century philosophers who hold that free will is a power and that a power, as opposed to an activity, is not something we can directly experience or be conscious of. In his journal, however, which presumably was written shortly after the actual conversation with Johnson, Boswell reports Johnson's remark differently. There he has Johnson saying: "All theory against freedom of will, all practice for it." Here the second part makes better philosophical sense, for that our practice of moral praise and blame is on the side of free will was a standard theme among 18th century advocates of free will, and it is perfectly understandable, therefore, that Johnson would have cited practice as on the side of freedom. But what is the *concept* of freedom that lies behind this remark by Johnson? And more generally, what *conceptual issues* were at the center of the controversy over freedom and necessity that occupied the last half of the 17th and most of the 18th century, a controversy bringing forward as its champions, on one side or another, such formidable figures as Hobbes, Locke, Samuel Clarke, Leibniz, Hume and Thomas Reid? I want to answer these questions, not simply in order to deepen our understanding of this historical episode in the controversy over freedom and necessity, as important as that may be, but because I believe a clear understanding of this episode in the controversy can help us in our current thinking about the problem of freedom and necessity.

My belief is that when all is said and done there are two fundamentally different conceptions of freedom that occupy center stage in the controversy that we may arbitrarily date as beginning with Thomas Hobbes and Bishop Bramhall (in the second half of the 17th century) and ending with Thomas Reid and Joseph Priestley (in the late 18th century). Vestiges of these two conceptions are very much alive. . . . The first of these conceptions, of which John Locke is a major advocate, I will call *Lockean freedom*. The other conception, of which Thomas Reid is the leading advocate, I will call *Reidian freedom*. The history of the controversy in the period we are considering is fundamentally a dispute over which of these two concepts of freedom is more adequate to our commonsense beliefs about freedom and our general metaphysical and scientific principles. . . .

I. LOCKEAN FREEDOM

Locke distinguished between a free action and a voluntary action. For your action to be voluntary all that is required is that you will to do that action and perform it, presumably as a result of your willing to do it. Suppose you are sitting in your chair and someone invites you to go for a walk. You reject the idea, choosing instead to remain just where you are. Your so remaining, Locke would say, is a voluntary act. But was it a free act? This is a further question for Locke, and it depends on whether you could have done otherwise had you so willed. If I had injected you with a powerful drug, so that at the time—perhaps without your being aware of it—your legs were paralyzed, then your act of remaining in the chair was voluntary but not free, for you could not have got up and walked had you willed to do so. A free act, says Locke, is not just a voluntary act. An act is free if it is voluntary *and* it is true that had you willed to do otherwise you would have been able to do otherwise. For Locke, then, we can say that you are free with respect to a certain action provided it is in your power to do it if you will to do it *and* in your power to refrain from doing it if you should will to refrain. Locke tells us that a man who is chained in prison does not stay in prison freely—even if that is what he wants to do—because it is not in his power to leave if he should will to leave. But if the prison doors are thrown open, and his chains are removed, he is free to leave and free to stay—for he can do either, depending on his will.

So far, of course, little or nothing has been said about the question of whether the will is free. And this was what Locke preferred, thinking on the whole that the question of freedom is the question of whether you are free *to do* what you will; much confusion, he thought, results from asking whether you are free *to will* what you will. But the chief merit of Locke's conception of freedom, or so it seemed to many, is that it fits nicely with the belief that our acts of will are causally necessitated by prior events and circumstances. . . . What are the causes of our actions? Well, the immediate cause of the action is your decision or act of will to perform that action. What is the cause of your making that decision? According to Locke . . . the cause of that act of will is your desires, judgments, and the circumstances that prevailed just prior to that decision. Given your desires and judgments at the time, and given the circumstances that prevailed, it was impossible for you not to will as you did. And given the desires, judgments, circumstances and the act of will, it was impossible for you not to act as you did. Now this impossibility of willing and acting otherwise does not conflict with Lockean freedom. For Lockean freedom does not require that *given the causes,* we somehow could have acted differently. All it requires is that *if* we had decided or willed differently *then* we could have acted differently. . . .

Let us call those who believe both that we have Lockean freedom and that our actions and acts of will are subject to causal necessity, 'necessitarians.' It is likely that Locke was a necessitarian. . . . Those who, like Clarke and Reid, hold that necessity and freedom are really inconsistent with one another do not disagree with the necessitarians concerning the consistency of *Lockean freedom* with the causal necessity of our actions and acts of will. What they reject is the whole notion of Lockean freedom. Before we state their conception of freedom, however, we had best consider what their objections are to the Lockean idea of freedom.

Lockean freedom, as we saw, exists solely at the level of *action:* you are free with respect to some action provided that you have the power to do the act if you will to do it, and have the power not to do it if you will not to do it. But what about the *will*? What if you don't have the power to will the action, or don't have the power not to will it? To see the difficulty here, let's return to our example where you are sitting down, someone asks you to get up and walk over to the window to see what is happening outside, but you are quite satisfied where you are and choose to remain sitting. We earlier supposed that I had injected you with a powerful drug so that you can't move your legs. Here Locke would say that you don't sit freely, since it was not in your power to do otherwise if you had willed otherwise—say, to get up and walk to the window. But let's now suppose that instead of paralyzing your legs I had hooked up a machine to your brain so that I can and do cause you to will to sit, thus depriving you of the *capacity* to will to do otherwise. It's still true that you have the power to get up and walk *if* you should will to do so—I haven't taken away your physical capacity to walk, as I did when I paralyzed your legs. Here the problem is that you can't *will* to do anything other than sit. In this case, it seems clear that you sit of necessity, not freely. You can't do otherwise than sit, not because you lack the power to get up and walk if you should manage to choose to do that, but because you lack the power to *choose* to get up and walk. On Locke's account of freedom, however, it remains true that you sit freely and not of necessity. And this being so, we must conclude that Locke's account of freedom is simply inadequate. It is not sufficient that you have the power to do otherwise *if* you so will; it must also be true that you have the power to will to do otherwise. Freedom that is worth the name, therefore, must include power *to will,* not simply power *to do if we will.*

There is a second objection to Lockean freedom, an objection based on the fact that Lockean freedom is consistent with the causal necessity of our actions and decisions. According to the necessitarians, you are totally determined to will and act as you do by your motives and circumstances. Indeed, Leibniz quotes with favor Bayle's comparison of the influence of motives on an agent to the influence of weights on a balance. Referring to Bayle, Leibniz remarks: "According to him, one can explain what passes in our resolutions by the hypothesis that the will of man is like a balance which is at rest when the weights of its two pans are equal, and which always inclines either to one side or the other according to which of the pans is the more heavily laden." Bayle's idea is that just as the heavier weight determines the movement of the balance, so does the stronger motive determine the movement of your will. If your motive to get up and walk to the window is stronger than whatever motive you have to remain sitting, then it determines you to will to get up and walk to the window. Given the respective strength of these motives, it is no more possible for you to will to remain sitting than it is possible for a balance to stay even when a heavier weight is placed in one of its pans than in the other. Motives, on this view, are determining causes of the decisions of our will in precisely the way in which weights are the determining causes of the movements of the balance. But if all this is so, claim the opponents of the necessitarians, then no one acts freely, no one has power over his will. For it was generally agreed that our motives are determined by factors largely beyond our control, and if these motives determine our acts of will as weights determine the movement of a balance, then we can no more control our will than the balance can control its movements. Just as a balance has no freedom of movement, so the person would have no freedom of will. Freedom would be an illusion if our will is subjected to causal necessity by motives and circumstances. Since Lockean freedom is consistent with such causal necessity, Lockean freedom is really not freedom at all.

We've looked at two major objections to Lockean freedom. According to Locke, freedom to do a certain thing is (roughly) the power to do that thing if we will to do it. Our first objection is that we might have the power to do something if we willed to do it and yet lack the power to will to do it. Surely, freedom must include the power to will, and not just the power to do *if* we will. Our second objection is against the necessitarian view that our acts of will are causally necessitated by prior events and circumstances. If that is so then we *now* have no more control over what we will to do than a balance has over how it moves once the weights are placed in its pans. Causal necessitation of our acts of will denies to us any real power over the determinations of our will. And without such power we do not act freely. To be told, as Locke would tell us, that we could have done something else if we had so willed, is of course interesting, and perhaps not unimportant. But if we are totally determined to will as we do and cannot will otherwise, then it is absurd to say we act freely simply because had we willed otherwise—which we could not do—we could have acted otherwise.

I believe these objections to Lockean freedom are in the end totally convincing. Indeed, it puzzles me that the notion of Lockean freedom continues to survive in the face of such utterly devastating objections. . . .

II. REIDIAN FREEDOM

The clearest statement of our second concept of freedom is by the Scottish philosopher, Thomas Reid. Here is what Reid says.

> By the *liberty* of a moral agent, I understand, a power over the determinations of his own will.
>
> If, in any action, he had power to will what he did, or not to will it, in that action he is free. But if, in every voluntary action, the determination of his will be the necessary consequence of something involuntary in the state of his mind, or of something in his external circumstances, he is not free; he has not what I call the liberty of a moral agent, but is subject to necessity.

It is helpful, I believe, to divide Reid's view of freedom into two themes: a negative thesis and a positive thesis. The negative thesis is this: if some action of ours is free then our decision or act of will to do that action cannot have been causally necessitated by any prior events, whether they be internal or external. If I have a machine hooked up to your brain in such a manner that my flip of a switch causally necessitates your decision to get up and walk across the room, it follows that you are not free in your action of getting up and walking across the room. In this case your decision to do that action is causally necessitated by some prior *external* event, the flipping of the switch. On the other hand, if your decision to do the act was causally necessitated by your motives and circumstances, then the causally necessitating event is *internal,* and the action again is not free. You are free in some action only if your decision to do that act is not causally necessitated by any involuntary event, whether internal or external. This is the negative thesis.

All too often, it is assumed that this second concept of freedom, which I have called *Reidian freedom,* consists in nothing more than this negative thesis. And the major objection of the necessitarians to Reidian freedom is based on this assumption. According to Reid, our free acts of will are not caused by any prior events, whether external or internal. And the difficulty with this, so the objection goes, is that it conflicts with the view that every event has a cause, a view that most 18th century philosophers, including Reid, accepted. What this objection reveals, however, is that the necessitarians hold to only one sort of causation, causation by prior events. Thus once it was denied that our free acts of will are caused by any prior events, the necessitarians concluded that the advocates of Reidian freedom were committed to the view that our free acts of will are totally uncaused events. But Reid . . . believed in another sort of causation, causation by persons or agents. What they affirmed in their positive thesis is that free acts of will are caused by the agent whose acts they are. Reid, then, no less than the necessitarians affirmed that all events, including our free acts of will, are caused. As he remarks: "I grant, then, that an effect uncaused is a contradiction, and that an event uncaused is an absurdity. The question that remains is whether a volition, undetermined by motives, is an event uncaused. This I deny. The cause of the volition is the man that willed it."

What we've just seen is that the advocates of Reidian freedom agree with the necessitarians in holding that every event has a cause. What they deny is that every event has an event-cause. In the case of our free acts of will the cause is not some prior event but the agent whose acts they are. To understand Reidian freedom, therefore, we need to look at the foundation on which it rests, the idea of agent causation.

Reid believed that the original notion of 'cause' is that of an agent who brings about changes in the world by *acting*. To be such a cause, Reid held that a thing or substance must satisfy three conditions: first, it must have the power to bring about the change in the world; second, it must exert its power to bring about the change; and third, it must have the power not to bring about the change. It will help us understand and appreciate his view if we contrast two examples. Suppose a piece of zinc is dropped into some acid, and the acid dissolves the zinc. In this example, we might say that the acid has the power to bring about a certain change in the zinc. We might also be willing to say that in this instance the acid *exerted* its power to bring about this change, it *exerted* its power to dissolve the zinc. But can we reasonably say that the acid had the power not to bring about this change? Clearly we cannot. The acid has no power to refrain from dissolving the zinc. When the conditions are right, the acid must dissolve the zinc. So Reid's third condition is not satisfied. The acid, therefore, is not an agent-cause of the zinc's dissolving. Turning to our second example, suppose I invite you to write down the word 'cause.' Let's suppose that you have the power to do so and that you exert that power with the result that a change in the world occurs, and the word 'cause' is written on a piece of paper. Here, when we look at Reid's third condition, we believe that it does obtain. We believe that you had the power to refrain from initiating your action of writing down the word 'cause.' The acid had no power to refrain from dissolving the zinc, but you had the power not to bring about your action of writing down the word 'cause.' If these things are so, then in this instance you are a true agent-cause of a certain change in the world, for you had the power to bring about that change, you exerted that power by acting, and finally, you had the power not to bring about that change.

There is one very important point to note concerning Reid's idea of agent causation. We sometimes speak of causing someone to cause something else. But if we fully understand Reid's notion of agent causation we can see, I think, that no event or agent can cause someone to agent-cause some change. And this, again, is because of Reid's third condition of agent causation, the condition that requires that you have the power to refrain from bringing about the change. Suppose an event occurs that causes you to cause something to happen—some boiling water spills on your hand, say, causing you to drop the pot of boiling water. Now if the spilling of the boiling water on your hand really does cause you to bring about your dropping the pot, if it causally necessitates you to cause your dropping of the pot, then given the spilling of the boiling water on your hand it wasn't in your power not to bring about your dropping the pot. But you are the agent-cause of some change only if it was in your power at the time not to cause that change. This being so, it is quite impossible that anything should ever cause you to agent-cause some change. Since having the power not to cause a change is required for you to be the agent-cause of some change, and since being caused to cause some change implies that you cannot refrain from causing that change, it follows that no one can be caused to agent-cause a change. If you are the agent-cause of some change, it follows that you were not caused to agent-cause that change.

Having taken a brief look at Reid's notion of agent causation, we can return to what I have been calling Reidian freedom. According to Reidian freedom, any action we perform as a result of our act of will to do that action is a free action, provided that we were the agent-cause of the act of will to perform that action. And since to agent-cause an act of will includes the power not to cause it, we can say that every act of will resulting in a *free* action is an act of will we had power to produce and power not to produce. As Reid says: "If, in any action, he had power to will what he did, or not to will it, in that action he is free." . . .

Reid believes that freedom is a *power,* a power over the determinations of our will. Now power is something that can come in degrees—you may have more or less of it. Presumably, under torture on the rack, your power over your will may be reduced to zero and your freedom thereby destroyed. On the other hand, your desire for a small bribe is unlikely to diminish significantly your power not to will to reveal [a] secret. Between these two extremes the mounting strength of your desires and passions will make it increasingly difficult for you to refrain from willing to reveal the secret. But so long as their strength is not irresistible, if you do will to reveal it, you will be at least a *partial agent-cause* of your act of will, and, therefore, will act with a certain degree of freedom and a corresponding degree of responsibility. Of course, people may differ considerably in terms of the power they possess over their wills. So a desire of a given strength may overwhelm one person while only slightly diminishing another person's power over his will. Therefore, in order to determine whether a person acted freely and with what degree of freedom, we need to judge two things: we need to judge the degree of power over the will that the person possesses *apart* from the influence of his desires and passions; and we need to judge the strength of his desires and passions. Clearly these are matters about which at best only reasonable or probable judgments can be made.

Leibniz once remarked concerning a version of the free will doctrine: "What is asserted is impossible, but if it came to pass it would be harmful." This remark nicely captures most of the objections to the view of Reid and other free will advocates. For these objections divide into those that argue that the view is impossible because it is internally inconsistent or inconsistent with some well-established principle of causality or explanation, and those that argue that the possession of free will would be harmful because the agent's actions would then be capricious, uninfluenced by motives, rewards or punishment. I want here to look at two different objections that fall into the first category. The first of these, and by far the most popular, is, I believe, a spurious objection. . . . The second, however, is a very serious objection, revealing, I believe, a real difficulty in Reid's agent-cause account of freedom.

The second objection (the serious one), like the first, arrives at the absurd conclusion that any action requires an infinite series of antecedent events, each produced by the agent who produces the action. This absurd conclusion, I believe, does follow from Reid's view of agent-causation in conjunction with the principle that every event has a cause. I propose here to explain how this absurdity is embedded in Reid's theory and what can be done to remove it.

On Reid's theory, when an agent wills some action, the act of will is itself an event and, as such, requires a cause. If the act of will is free, its cause is not some event, it is the agent whose act of will it is. Being the cause of the act of will, the agent must satisfy Reid's three conditions of agent-causation. Thus the agent must have had the power to bring about the act of will as well as the power to refrain from bringing about the act of will, and she must have *exerted* her power to bring about the act of will. It is the last of these conditions that generates an infinite regress of events that an agent must cause if she is to cause her act of will. For what it tells us is that to produce the act of will the agent must *exert* her power to bring about the act of will. Now an exertion of power is itself an event. As such, it too must have a cause. On Reid's view the cause must again be the agent herself. But to have caused this exertion the agent must have had the power to bring it about and must have *exerted* that power. Each exertion of power is itself an event which the agent can cause only by having the power to cause it and by *exerting* that power. As Reid reminds us, "In order to the production of any effect, there must be in the cause, not only power, but the exertion of that power: for power that is not exerted produces no effect." The result of this principle, however, is that in order to produce any act of will whatever, the agent must cause an infinite number of exertions. Reid's theory of agent-causation, when conjoined with the principle that every event has a cause, leads to the absurdity of an infinite regress of agent-produced exertions for every act of will the agent produces. . . .

One solution to the difficulty requires that we view some acts of the agent as caused by the agent, but not caused by some *exertion* of the agent's power to produce them. Perhaps we should think of the act of will as in some way a special sort of action, a *basic act*. A basic act of an agent is one that she causes but not by any exertion of power or any other act. Short of some such view, it seems that we must either accept the absurdity of the infinite regress, view some act of the agent as itself uncaused (thus abandoning the causal principle), or take the view that an act of will is not itself an event and, therefore, does not fall under the causal principle. This last move, however, would leave the act of will as absurd in Reid's theory and plainly conflicts with his stated position that acts of will are effects. . . .

The solution I've proposed requires a significant change in Reid's view of agent-causation. Not every act of the agent can be produced by the agent only by the agent's *exerting* her power to produce it. Acts of will that are produced by the agent whose acts they are, we shall say, are such that the agent causes them but not by any other act or any exertion of the power she has to produce the acts of will. We thus can halt the regress of acts of exertions that is implied by the conjunction of the causal principle and Reid's analysis of what it is to be a cause 'in the strict and proper sense.' The price, of course, is a significant modification of Reid's account of agent-causation. . . .

CONCLUSION

Some philosophical questions eventually yield to fairly definitive answers, answers which succeeding generations of philosophers accept, thereby contributing to our sense of progress in the discipline. Other philosophical questions seem to defy progress in the sense of definitive answers that are commonly accepted. Progress regarding them consists largely in deeper understanding and clarity concerning the questions and their possible answers. These are the deep philosophical questions. My conviction is that the question of human freedom is of the latter sort. I know that by setting forth the two concepts of freedom that were at the center of the 18th century controversy over freedom and necessity, and by criticizing the one, Lockean freedom, and recommending the other, Reidian freedom, I have not contributed to philosophical progress in the first sense. I haven't given any definitive answer. And in these compatibilist days, I certainly haven't given any answer that would be commonly accepted in my own department, let alone the discipline. My hope is that I have made some of these issues clearer and more understandable and have thereby contributed to philosophical progress in the second sense, helping us to grasp more clearly the philosophical question of human freedom. . . .

The Liberty of Moral Agents

THOMAS REID (1710–1796) was one of the Scottish commonsense school of philosophers. Decended from a line of clergymen and government officials, Reid also entered the clergy after his education at the University of Aberdeen and Marischal College. In 1752 he was appointed professor of philosophy at Kings College in Aberdeen and in 1764 succeeded Adam Smith as professor of moral philosophy at the University of Glasgow. His main writings are *Essays on the Intellectual Powers of Man* and *Essays on the Active Powers of Man*. Reid is known for his defense of Agent Causation in the free will debate.

THINKING QUESTIONS

Thomas Reid, *The Liberty of Moral Agents*

1. What is Reid's definition of the liberty of a moral agent?
2. Reid argues that authentic liberty requires an agent to have some degree of practical judgment or reason. Why does he think this?
3. Reid thinks that nonrational "brute animals" do not possess moral liberty, although their actions may be voluntary. What is the distinction he draws between moral liberty and voluntary action?
4. According to Reid, moral praiseworthiness and blameworthiness requires that one could have acted otherwise than one did. Why is that? How does this idea show that Cato is not praiseworthy for being a good person?
5. Reid considers a form of compatibilism—that liberty consists only in a power to act as we will—and rejects it. Why?
6. What is Reid's distinction between active and passive powers?
7. Reid maintains that we have an active power to choose our actions, i.e., we are efficient causes in our deliberate and voluntary actions. His reasoning seems to be that our very concepts of active powers and efficient causes are an extension of what we experience in our own case. Does this seem like a plausible argument to you?

BY THE *LIBERTY OF A MORAL AGENT,* I understand, *a power over the determinations of his own Will.*

If, in any action, he had power to will what he did, or not to will it, in that action he is free. But if, in every voluntary action, the determination of his will be the necessary consequence of something involuntary in the state of his mind, or of something in his external circumstances, he is not free; he has not what I call the Liberty of a Moral Agent, but is subject to Necessity.

This Liberty supposes the agent to have Understanding and Will; for the determinations of the will are the sole object about which this power is employed; and there can be no will without such a degree of understanding, at least, as gives the conception of that which we will.

The liberty of a moral agent implies, not only a *conception* of what he wills, but some degree of practical *judgment* or *reason*.

For, if he has not the judgment to discern one determination to be preferable to another, either in itself or for some purpose which he intends, what can be the use of a power to determine? His determinations must be made perfectly in the dark, without reason, motive, or end. They can neither be right nor wrong, wise nor foolish. Whatever the consequences may be, they cannot be imputed to the agent, who had not the capacity of foreseeing them, or of perceiving any reason for acting otherwise than he did.

We may, perhaps, be able to conceive a being endowed with power over the determinations of his will, without any light in his mind to direct that power to some end. But such power would be given in vain. No exercise of it could be either blamed or approved. As nature gives no power in vain, I see no ground to ascribe a power over the determinations of the will to any being who has no judgment to apply it to the direction of his conduct, no discernment of what he ought or ought not to do.

For that reason, in this Essay, I speak only of the Liberty of Moral Agents, who are capable of acting well or ill, wisely or foolishly, and this, for distinction's sake, I shall call *Moral Liberty*.

What kind or what degree of liberty belongs to brute animals, or to our own species, before any use of reason, I do not know. We acknowledge that they have not the power of self-government. Such of their actions as may be called *voluntary* seem to be invariably determined by the passion, or appetite, or affection, or habit, which is strongest at the time.

This seems to be the law of their constitution, to which they yield, as the inanimate creation does, without any conception of the law, or any intention of obedience.

But of civil or moral government, which are addressed to the rational powers, and require a conception of the law and an intentional obedience, they are, in the judgment of all mankind, incapable. Nor do I see what end could be served by giving them a power over the determinations of their own will, unless to make them intractable by discipline, which we see they are not.

The effect of moral liberty is, *That it is in the power of the agent to do well or ill.* This power, like every other gift of God, may be abused. The right use of this gift of God is to do well and wisely, as far as his best judgment can direct him, and thereby merit esteem and approbation. The abuse of it is to act contrary to what he knows or suspects to be his duty and his wisdom, and thereby justly merit disapprobation and blame.

By *Necessity,* I understand the want of that moral liberty which I have above defined.

If there can be a better and a worse in actions on the system of Necessity, let us suppose a man necessarily determined in all cases to will and to do what is best to be done, he would surely be innocent and inculpable. But, as far as I am able to judge, he would not be entitled to the esteem and moral approbation of those who knew and believed this necessity. What was, by an ancient author, said of Cato, might, indeed, be said of him: *He was good because he could not be otherwise.* But this saying, if understood literally and strictly, is not the praise of Cato, but of his constitution, which was no more the work of Cato than his existence.

On the other hand, if a man be necessarily determined to do ill, this case seems to me to move pity, but not disapprobation. He was ill, because he could not be other wise. Who can blame him? Necessity has no law. . .

Such are my notions of moral liberty and necessity, and of the consequences inseparably connected with both the one and the other.

This moral liberty a man may have, though it do not extend to all his actions, or even to all his voluntary actions. He does many things by instinct, many things by the force of habit, without any thought at all, and consequently without will. In the first part of life, he has not the power of self-government any more than the brutes. That power over the determinations of his own will, which belongs to him in ripe years, is limited, as all his powers are; and it is, perhaps, beyond the reach of his understanding to define its limits with precision. We can only say, in general, that it extends to every action for which he is accountable. . . .

Supposing it therefore to be true, *That man is a free agent,* it may be true, at the same time, that his liberty may be impaired or lost, by disorder of body or mind, as in melancholy, or in madness; it may be impaired or lost by vicious habits; it may, in particular cases, be restrained by divine interposition.

We call man a *free* agent in the same way as we call him a *reasonable* agent. In many things he is not guided by reason, but by principles similar to those of the brutes. His reason is weak at best. It is liable to be impaired or lost, by his own fault, or by other means. In like manner, he may be a free agent, though his freedom of action may have many similar limitations.

The liberty I have described has been represented by some philosophers as inconceivable, and as involving an absurdity.

"Liberty, they say, consists only in a power to act as we will; and it is impossible to conceive in any being a greater liberty than this. Hence it follows, that liberty does not extend to the determinations of the will, but only to the actions consequent to its determination, and depending upon the will. To say that we have power to will such an action, is to say, that we may will it, if we will. This supposes the will to be determined by a prior will; and, for the same reason, that will must be determined by a will prior to it, and so on in an infinite series of wills, which is absurd. To act freely, therefore, can mean nothing more than to act voluntarily; and this is all the liberty that can be conceived in man, or in any being."

This reasoning—first, I think, advanced by Hobbes—has been very generally adopted by the defenders of necessity. It is grounded upon a definition of liberty totally different from that which I have given, and therefore does not apply to moral liberty, as above defined.

But it is said that this is the only liberty that is possible, that is conceivable, that does not involve an absurdity.

It is strange, indeed, if the word *Liberty* has no meaning but this one. . . .

In every voluntary action, the determination of the will is the first part of the action, upon which alone the moral estimation of it depends. It has been made a question among philosophers, *Whether, in every instance, this determination be the necessary consequence of the constitution of the person, and the circumstances in which he is placed; or whether he had not power, in many cases, to determine this way or that?*

This has, by some, been called the *philosophical* notion of liberty and necessity; but it is by no means peculiar to philosophers. The lowest of the vulgar have, in all ages, been prone to have recourse to this necessity, to exculpate themselves or their friends in what they do wrong, though, in the general tenor of their conduct, they act upon the contrary principle.

Whether this notion of moral liberty be *conceivable* or not, every man must judge for himself. To me there appears no difficulty in conceiving it. I consider the determination of the will as an effect. This effect must have a cause which had power to produce it; and the cause must be either the person himself, whose will it is, or some other being. The first is as easily conceived as the last. If the person was the cause of that determination of his own will, he was free in that action, and it is justly imputed to him, whether it be good or bad. But, if another being was the cause of this determination, either by producing it immediately, or by means and instruments under his direction, then the determination is the act and deed of that being, and is solely imputable to him.

But it is said—"That nothing is in our power but what depends upon the will, and therefore, the will itself cannot be in our power."

I answer—That this is a fallacy arising from taking a common saying in a sense which it never was intended to convey, and in a sense contrary to what it necessarily implies.

In common life, when men speak of what is, or is not, in a man's power, they attend only to the external and visible effects, which only can be perceived, and which only can affect them. Of these, it is true that nothing is in a man's power but what depends upon his will, and this is all that is meant by this common saying.

But this is so far from excluding his will from being in his power, that it necessarily implies it. For to say that what depends upon the will is in a man's power, but the will is not in his power, is to say that the end is in his power, but the means necessary to that end are not in his power, which is a contradiction.

In many propositions which we express universally, there is an exception necessarily implied, and, therefore, always understood. Thus, when we say that all things depend upon God, God himself is necessarily excepted. In like manner, when we say, that all that is in our power depends upon the will, the will itself is necessarily excepted: for, if the will be not, nothing else can be in our power. Every effect must be in the power of its cause. The determination of the will is an effect, and, therefore, must be in the power of its cause, whether that cause be the agent himself, or some other being.

From what has been said in this chapter, I hope the notion of moral liberty will be distinctly understood, and that it appears that this notion is neither inconceivable, nor involves any absurdity or contradiction. . . .

. . . [E]verything which undergoes any change, must either be the efficient cause of that change in itself, or it must be changed by some other being.

In the *first* case, it is said to have *active power,* and to *act* in producing that change. In the *second* case, it is merely *passive,* or is *acted upon,* and the active power is in that being only which produces the change.

The name of a *cause* and of an *agent,* is properly given to that being only, which, by its active power, produces some change in itself, or in some other being. The change, whether it be of thought, of will, or of motion, is the *effect.* Active power, therefore, is a quality in the cause, which enables it to produce the effect. . . .

Another principle, which appears very early in the mind of man, is, *That we are efficient causes in our deliberate and voluntary actions.*

We are conscious of making an exertion, sometimes with difficulty, in order to produce certain effects. And exertion made deliberately and voluntarily, in order to produce an effect, implies a conviction that the effect is in our power. No man can deliberately attempt what he does not believe to be in his power. The language of all mankind, and their ordinary conduct in life, demonstrate that they have a conviction of some active power in themselves to produce certain motions in their own and in other bodies, and to regulate and direct their own thoughts. . . .

It is very probable that the very conception or idea of active power, and of efficient causes, is derived from our voluntary exertions in producing effects; and that, if we were not conscious of such exertion, we should have no conception at all of a cause, or of active power, and consequently no conviction of the necessity of a cause of every change which we observe in nature.

It is certain that we can conceive no kind of active power but what is similar or analogous to that which we attribute to ourselves; that is, a power which is exerted by will and with understanding. Our notion, even of Almighty power, is derived from the notion of human power, by removing from the former those imperfections and limitations to which the latter is subjected. . . .

Of Liberty and Necessity

DAVID HUME (1711–1776) is widely considered the most important philosopher to write in the English language. Born in Edinburgh, Scotland, young David was recognized as a child prodigy and sent to Edinburgh University at the age of 12. He was interested in history, mathematics, and contemporary science, but not so much in the law career his family had hoped for him. He spent considerable time in France with the great continental philosophers of his day like Rousseau, Diderot, D'Alembert, and D'Holbach. At the age of 28 he published his masterpiece, *A Treatise of Human Nature,* a book so far ahead of its time that it was insufficiently appreciated, causing Hume to comment famously that it had "fallen dead-born from the press, without exciting so much as a murmur among the zealots." His multivolume *History of England* met with more popular acclaim, becoming a bestseller and ensuring Hume's financial stability. Hume's other philosophical writings established his reputation as a skeptic and atheist, preventing him from ever holding a university appointment. His *Dialogues Concerning Natural Religion* was too controversial to be seen to press during his lifetime and was posthumously published in 1779. It has been called "*the* preeminent work in the philosophy of religion."

THINKING QUESTIONS

David Hume, *Of Liberty and Necessity*

1. Hume begins by asserting that the free will debate is really a verbal dispute, and that a few clear definitions of the relevant terms will show that "the whole controversy hitherto turned merely upon words." What is a verbal dispute? What are the ambiguous words that Hume thinks require clear definitions?
2. What "two circumstances form the whole" of our understanding of the idea of causal necessity, according to Hume?
3. Hume maintains that human nature is a cultural constant, and that these common passions are the sources of action. Does Hume mean that everyone acts in the exact same way in the same circumstances?
4. Hume argues that human actions are no different from any other event in the world: they are all caused by prior events in a deterministic manner. In this way he defends the doctrine of necessity. Why does Hume believe that some people resist accepting this doctrine?

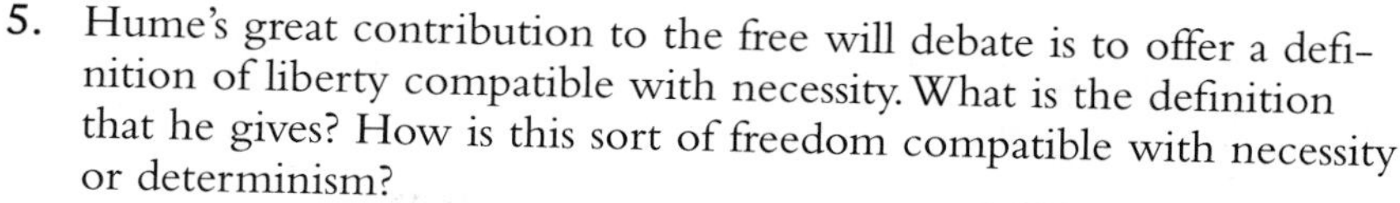
5. Hume's great contribution to the free will debate is to offer a definition of liberty compatible with necessity. What is the definition that he gives? How is this sort of freedom compatible with necessity or determinism?

VERBAL DISPUTES

It might reasonably be expected, in questions, which have been canvassed and disputed with great eagerness, since the first origin of science and philosophy, that the meaning of all the terms, at least, should have been agreed upon among the disputants; and our enquiries, in the course of two thousand years, been able to pass from words to the true and real subject of the controversy. For how easy may it seem to give exact definitions of the terms employed in reasoning, and make these definitions, not the mere sound of words, the object of future scrutiny and examination? But if we consider the matter more narrowly, we shall be apt to draw a quite opposite conclusion. From this circumstance alone, that a controversy has been long kept on foot, and remains still undecided, we may presume, that there is some ambiguity in the expression, and that the disputants affix different ideas to the terms employed in the controversy. For as the faculties of the mind are supposed to be naturally alike in every individual; otherwise nothing could be more fruitless than to reason or dispute together; it were impossible, if men affix the same ideas to their terms, that they could so long form different opinions of the same subject; especially when they communicate their views, and each party turn themselves on all sides, in search of arguments, which may give them the victory over their antagonists. It is true; if men attempt the discussion of questions, which lie entirely beyond the reach of human capacity, such as those concerning the origin of worlds, or the economy of the intellectual system or region of spirits, they may long beat the air in their fruitless contests, and never arrive at any determinate conclusion. But if the question regard any subject of common life and experience; nothing, one would think, could preserve the dispute so long undecided, but some ambiguous expressions, which keep the antagonists still at a distance, and hinder them from grappling with each other.

This has been the case in the long disputed question concerning liberty and necessity; and to so remarkable a degree, that, if I be not much mistaken, we shall find, that all mankind, both learned and ignorant, have always been of the same opinion with regard to this subject, and that a few intelligible definitions would immediately have put an end to the whole controversy. I own, that this dispute has been so much canvassed on all hands, and has led philosophers into such a labyrinth of obscure sophistry, that it is no wonder, if a sensible reader indulge his ease so far as to turn a deaf ear to the proposal of such a question, from which he can expect neither instruction nor entertainment.

But the state of the argument here proposed may, perhaps, serve to renew his attention; as it has more novelty, promises at least some decision of the controversy, and will not much disturb his ease by any intricate or obscure reasoning.

I hope, therefore, to make it appear, that all men have ever agreed in the doctrine both of necessity and of liberty, according to any reasonable sense, which can be put on these terms; and that the whole controversy has hitherto turned merely upon words. We shall begin with examining the doctrine of necessity.

NECESSITY IN HUMAN ACTION

It is universally allowed, that matter, in all its operations, is actuated by a necessary force, and that every natural effect is so precisely determined by the energy of its cause, that no other effect, in such particular circumstances, could possibly have resulted from it. The degree and direction of every motion is, by the laws of nature, prescribed with such exactness, that a living creature may as soon arise from the shock of two bodies, as motion, in any other degree or direction than what is actually produced by it. Would we, therefore, form a just and precise idea of *necessity,* we must consider whence that idea arises, when we apply it to the operation of bodies.

It seems evident, that, if all the scenes of nature were continually shifted in such a manner, that no two events bore any resemblance to each other, but every object was entirely new, without any similitude to whatever had been seen before, we should never, in that case, have attained the least idea of necessity, or of a connexion among these objects. We might say, upon such a supposition, that one object or event has followed another; not that one was produced by the other. The relation of cause and effect must be utterly unknown to mankind. Inference and reasoning concerning the operations of nature would, from that moment, be at an end; and the memory and senses remain the only canals, by which the knowledge of any real existence could possibly have access to the mind. Our idea, therefore, of necessity and causation arises entirely from the uniformity, observable in the operations of nature; where similar objects are constantly conjoined together, and the mind is determined by custom to infer the one from the appearance of the other. These two circumstances form the whole of that necessity, which we ascribe to matter. Beyond the constant *conjunction* of similar objects, and the consequent *inference* from one to the other, we have no notion of any necessity, or connexion.

If it appear, therefore, that all mankind have ever allowed, without any doubt or hesitation, that these two circumstances take place in the voluntary actions of men, and in the operations of mind; it must follow, that all mankind have ever agreed in the doctrine of necessity, and that they have hitherto disputed, merely for not understanding each other.

THE CONSTANCY OF HUMAN BEHAVIOR

As to the first circumstance, the constant and regular conjunction of similar events; we may possibly satisfy ourselves by the following considerations. It is universally acknowledged, that there is a great uniformity among the actions of men, in all nations and ages, and that human nature remains still the same, in its principles and operations. The same motives always produce the same actions: The same events follow from the same causes. Ambition, avarice, self-love, vanity, friendship, generosity, public spirit; these passions, mixed in various degrees, and distributed through society, have been, from the beginning of the world, and still are, the source of all the actions and enterprizes, which have ever been observed among mankind. Would you know the sentiments, inclinations, and course of life of the Greeks and Romans? Study well the temper and actions of the French and English: You cannot be much mistaken in transferring to the former *most* of the observations, which you have made with regard to the latter. Mankind are so much the same, in all times and places, that history informs us of nothing new or strange in this particular. Its chief use is only to discover the constant and universal principles of human nature, by shewing men in all varieties of circumstances and situations, and furnishing us with materials, from which we may form our observations, and become acquainted with the regular springs of human action and behaviour. These records of wars, intrigues, factions, and revolutions, are so many collections of experiments, by which the politician or moral philosopher fixes the principles of his science; in the same manner as the physician or natural philosopher becomes acquainted with the nature of plants, minerals, and other external objects, by the experiments, which he forms concerning them. Nor are the earth, water, and other elements, examined by Aristotle, and Hippocrates, more like to those, which at present lie under our observation, than the men, described by Polybius and Tacitus, are to those who now govern the world.

Should a traveller, returning from a far country, bring us an account of men, wholly different from any, with whom we were ever acquainted; men, who were entirely divested of avarice, ambition, or revenge; who knew no pleasure but friendship, generosity, and public spirit; we should immediately, from these circumstances, detect the falsehood, and prove him a liar, with the same certainty as if he had stuffed his narration with stories of centaurs and dragons, miracles and prodigies. And if we would explode any forgery in history, we cannot make use of a more convincing argument, than to prove, that the actions, ascribed to any person, are directly contrary to the course of nature, and that no human motives, in such circumstances, could ever induce him to such a conduct. The veracity of Quintus Curtius is as much to be suspected, when he describes the supernatural courage of Alexander, by which he was hurried on singly to attack multitudes, as when he describes his supernatural force and activity, by which he was able to resist them. So readily and universally do we acknowledge a uniformity in human motives and actions as well as in the operations of body.

Hence likewise the benefit of that experience, acquired by long life and a variety of business and company, in order to instruct us in the principles of human nature, and regulate our future conduct, as well as speculation. By means of this guide, we mount up to the knowledge of men's inclinations and motives, from their actions, expressions, and even gestures; and again, descend to the interpretation of their actions from our knowledge of their motives and inclinations. The general observations, treasured up by a course of experience, give us the clue of human nature, and teach us to unravel all its intricacies. Pretexts and appearances no longer deceive us. Public declarations pass for the specious colouring of a cause. And though virtue and honour be allowed their proper weight and authority, that perfect disinterestedness, so often pretended to, is never expected in multitudes and parties; seldom in their leaders; and scarcely even in individuals of any rank or station. But were there no uniformity in human actions, and were every experiment, which we could form of this kind, irregular and anomalous, it were impossible to collect any general observations concerning mankind; and no experience, however accurately digested by reflection, would ever serve to any purpose . . .

We must not, however, expect, that this uniformity of human actions should be carried to such a length, as that all men, in the same circumstances, will always act precisely in the same manner, without making any allowance for the diversity of characters, prejudices, and opinions. Such a uniformity in every particular, is found in no part of nature. On the contrary, from observing the variety of conduct in different men, we are enabled to form a greater variety of maxims, which still suppose a degree of uniformity and regularity . . .

HIDDEN SPRINGS OF ACTION

I grant it possible to find some actions, which seem to have no regular connexion with any known motives, and are exceptions to all the measures of conduct, which have ever been established for the government of men. But if we would willingly know, what judgment should be formed of such irregular and extraordinary actions; we may consider the sentiments, commonly entertained with regard to those irregular events, which appear in the course of nature, and the operations of external objects. All causes are not conjoined to their usual effects, with like uniformity. An artificer, who handles only dead matter, may be disappointed of his aim, as well as the politician, who directs the conduct of sensible and intelligent agents.

The vulgar, who take things according to their first appearance, attribute the uncertainty of events to such an uncertainty in the causes as makes the latter often fail of their usual influence; though they meet with no impediment in their operation. But philosophers, observing that, almost in every part of nature, there is contained a vast variety of springs and principles, which are hid, by reason of their minuteness or remoteness, find, that it is at least possible the contrariety of events may not proceed from any contingency in the cause, but from the secret operation of contrary causes. This possibility is converted into certainty by farther observation, when they remark that, upon an exact scrutiny, a contrariety of effects always betrays a contrariety of causes, and proceeds from their mutual opposition. A peasant can give no better reason for the stopping of any clock or watch than to say that it does not commonly go right: But an artist easily perceives, that the same force in the spring or pendulum has always the same influence on the wheels; but fails of its usual effect, perhaps by reason of a grain of dust, which puts a stop to the whole movement. From the observation of several parallel instances, philosophers form a maxim, that the connexion between all causes and effects is equally necessary, and that its seeming uncertainty in some instances proceeds from the secret opposition of contrary causes.

Thus for instance, in the human body, when the usual symptoms of health or sickness disappoint our expectation; when medicines operate not with their wonted powers; when irregular events follow from any particular cause; the philosopher and physician are not surprised at the matter, nor are ever tempted to deny, in general, the necessity and uniformity of those principles, by which the animal economy is conducted. They know, that a human body is a mighty complicated machine: That many secret powers lurk in it, which are altogether beyond our comprehension: That to us it must often appear very uncertain in its operations: And that therefore the irregular events, which outwardly discover themselves, can be no proof, that the laws of nature are not observed with the greatest regularity in its internal operations and government.

The philosopher, if he be consistent, must apply the same reasoning to the actions and volitions of intelligent agents. The most irregular and unexpected resolutions of men may frequently be accounted for by those who know every particular circumstance of their character and situation. A person of an obliging disposition gives a peevish answer: But he has the toothache, or has not dined. A stupid fellow discovers an uncommon alacrity in his carriage: But he has met with a sudden piece of good fortune. Or even when an action, as sometimes happens, cannot be particularly accounted for, either by the person himself or by others; we know, in general, that the characters of men are, to a certain degree, inconstant and irregular. This is, in a manner, the constant character of human nature; though it be applicable, in a more particular manner, to some persons, who have no fixed rule for their conduct, but proceed in a continued course of caprice and inconstancy. The internal principles and motives may operate in a uniform manner, notwithstanding these seeming irregularities; in the same manner as the winds, rain, clouds, and other variations of the weather are supposed to be governed by steady principles; though not easily discoverable by human sagacity and enquiry.

Thus it appears, not only that the conjunction between motives and voluntary actions is as regular and uniform, as that between the cause and effect in any part of nature; but also that this regular conjunction has been universally acknowledged among mankind, and has never been the subject of dispute, either in philosophy or common life . . .

I have frequently considered, what could possibly be the reason, why all mankind, though they have ever, without hesitation, acknowledged the doctrine of necessity, in their whole practice and reasoning, have yet discovered such a reluctance to acknowledge it in words, and have rather shewn a propensity, in all ages, to profess the contrary opinion. The matter, I think, may be accounted for, after the following manner. If we examine the operations of body, and the production of effects from their causes, we shall find, that all our faculties can never carry us farther in our knowledge of this relation, than barely to observe, that particular objects are *constantly conjoined* together, and that the mind is carried, by a *customary transition,* from the appearance of one to the belief of the other. But though this conclusion concerning human ignorance be the result of the strictest scrutiny of this subject, men still entertain a strong propensity to believe, that they penetrate farther into the powers of nature, and perceive something like a necessary connexion between the cause and the effect. When again they turn their reflections towards the operations of their own minds, and *feel* no such connexion of the motive and the action; they are thence apt to suppose, that there is a difference between the effects, which result from material force, and those which arise from thought and intelligence. But being once convinced, that we know nothing farther of causation of any kind, than merely the *constant conjunction* of objects, and the consequent *inference* of the mind from one to another, and finding, that these two circumstances are universally allowed to have place in voluntary actions; we may be more easily led to own the same necessity common to all causes. And though this reasoning may contradict the systems of many philosophers, in ascribing necessity to the determinations of the will, we shall find, upon reflection, that they dissent from it in words only, not in their real sentiment. Necessity, according to the sense, in which it is here taken, has never yet been rejected, nor can ever, I think, be rejected by any philosopher. It may only, perhaps, be pretended, that the mind can perceive, in the operations of matter, some farther connexion between the cause and effect; and a connexion that has not place in the voluntary actions of intelligent beings. Now whether it be so or not, can only appear upon examination; and it is incumbent on these philosophers to make good their assertion, by defining or describing that necessity, and pointing it out to us in the operations of material causes.

It would seem, indeed, that men begin at the wrong end of this question concerning liberty and necessity, when they enter upon it by examining the faculties of the soul, the influence of the understanding, and the operations of the will. Let them first discuss a more simple question, namely, the operations of body and of brute unintelligent matter; and try whether they can there form any idea of causation and necessity, except that of a constant conjunction of objects, and subsequent inference of the mind from one to another. If these circumstances form, in reality, the whole of that necessity, which we conceive in matter, and if these circumstances be also universally acknowledged to take place in the operations of the mind, the dispute is at an end; at least, must be owned to be thenceforth merely verbal. But as long as we will rashly suppose, that we have some farther idea of necessity and causation in the operations of external objects; at the same time, that we can find nothing farther, in the voluntary actions of the mind; there is no possibility of bringing the question to any determinate issue, while we proceed upon so erroneous a supposition. The only method of undeceiving us, is, to mount up higher; to examine the narrow extent of science when applied to material causes; and to convince ourselves, that all we know of them, is, the constant conjunction and inference above mentioned. We may, perhaps, find, that it is with difficulty we are induced to fix such narrow limits to human understanding: But we can afterwards find no difficulty when we come to apply this doctrine to the actions of the will. For as it is evident, that these have a regular conjunction with motives and circumstances and characters, and as we always draw inferences from one to the other, we must be obliged to acknowledge in words, that necessity, which we have already avowed, in every deliberation of our lives, and in every step of our conduct and behaviour.

A DEFINITION OF "LIBERTY" COMPATIBLE WITH NECESSITY

But to proceed in this reconciling project with regard to the question of liberty and necessity; the most contentious question, of metaphysics, the most contentious science; it will not require many words to prove, that all mankind have ever agreed in the doctrine of liberty as well as in that of necessity, and that the whole dispute, in this respect also, has been hitherto merely verbal. For what is meant by liberty, when applied to voluntary actions? We cannot surely mean, that actions have so little connexion with motives, inclinations, and circumstances, that one does not follow with a certain degree of uniformity from the other, and that one affords no inference by which we can conclude the existence of the other. For these are plain and acknowledged matters of fact. By liberty, then, we can only mean *a power of acting or not acting, according to the determinations of the will;* that is, if we chuse to remain at rest, we may; if we chuse to move, we also may. Now this hypothetical liberty is universally allowed to belong to every one, who is not a prisoner and in chains. Here then is no subject of dispute.

Whatever definition we may give of liberty, we should be careful to observe two requisite circumstances; *first,* that it be consistent with plain matter of fact; *secondly,* that it be consistent with itself. If we observe these circumstances, and render our definition intelligible, I am persuaded that all mankind will be found of one opinion with regard to it.

It is universally allowed, that nothing exists without a cause of its existence, and that chance, when strictly examined, is a mere negative word, and means not any real power, which has any where, a being in nature. But it is pretended, that some causes are necessary, some not necessary. Here then is the advantage of definitions. Let any one *define* a cause, without comprehending, as a part of the definition, a *necessary connexion* with its effect; and let him shew distinctly the origin of the idea, expressed by the definition; and I shall readily give up the whole controversy. But if the foregoing explication of the matter be received, this must be absolutely impracticable. Had not objects a regular conjunction with each other, we should never have entertained any notion of cause and effect; and this regular conjunction produces that inference of the understanding, which is the only connexion, that we can have any comprehension of. Whoever attempts a definition of cause, exclusive of these circumstances, will be obliged, either to employ unintelligible terms, or such as are synonymous to the term, which he endeavours to define. And if the definition above mentioned be admitted; liberty, when opposed to necessity, not to constraint, is the same thing with chance; which is universally allowed to have no existence.

Philosophy of Mind

What is the stuff of the universe? If you have studied any science at all, you know that the world is filled with physical things, from tiny quarks and gluons, to protons and electrons, atoms, molecules, rocks, trees, mountains, oceans, planets, stars, quasars, solar systems, galaxies, to the universe itself—a great sprawling, expanding totality 13.5 billion light years in diameter. There are also newly discovered oddities, like black holes and dark matter. Apart from these things are the forces: electromagnetism, gravity, the weak and strong nuclear forces.

Wait—this list is strangely incomplete. It doesn't include the most familiar things, indeed what you are experiencing *right this very minute*. You see the words on the page and you have certain sensations: sensations of color (grey, black, white), shape (of the letters), patterns (of the words and sentences). Look around you and you have even more sensations of colors and shapes. You hear the birds outside the window, or Coldplay on your iPod, high and low pitches, with complex intervals and varying amplitudes. You taste the coffee and it has a *flavor*. You think, wonder, puzzle, daydream, believe, doubt, fantasize, worry, love, fear, rage, drowse, and desire. You itch, ache, burn, tickle, feel cold, and have orgasms. We (and other sentient creatures) are filled with sensations, emotions, and thoughts, in a word: consciousness. Our consciousness is the single most amazing feature of our lives, and yet is wholly absent from the impersonal scientific accounting of the world listed in the preceding paragraph.

Thus on the one hand is a material world of substances and forces, and on the other is the glittering technicolor world of consciousness. What is the relationship between these two? Some philosophers have held that there are two fundamental kinds of substances: physical and mental. Minds, they say, are mental substances. Such thinkers are mind/body dualists, who then must explain how mental and physical substances interact. Those who believe that there is life after death tend to be dualists, although mostly people believe in an afterlife as a result of faith, not reason. Robert Almeder is an exception; he argues that there is empirical evidence for reincarnation. If human personality reincarnates, Almeder argues, then we are more than our bodies—we are not mere physical things, but mental entities. Mind/body dualism, he concludes, must be the right view. Steven Hales responds to Almeder, arguing that even granted the evidence that Almeder cites, this is not enough reason to be a dualist, or to think that human beings will survive their deaths. To defend dualism on the basis of reincarnation requires not just a few anomalous cases, but a real theory of reincarnation that connects with our scientific understanding of the world.

Whether humans reincarnate or not, there is still the question of whether there is something special about *us,* or more generally, something special about sentient organic life. As sci-fi writer Terry Bisson notes in his wonderful one-act play "They're Made Out of Meat," (available at www.terrybisson.com) we are made of meat through-and-through and yet we are meat that has thoughts and feelings. Artificial intelligence researcher Douglas Lenat thinks there is nothing particularly special about us: we are simply organic robots, built by nature, evolved to have the intelligence and processing power that has ensured (thus far) our survival. If a digital silicon computer were given as many facts as we have at our fingertips and could integrate them appropriately, it too would be considered an intelligent, thinking thing. Clive Thompson details Lenat's attempt to do this very thing with a computer named Cyc.

Not everyone is as optimistic as Lenat that digital computers can be conscious, no matter how much data they are fed. John Searle believes that they are nothing but processors of meaningless syntax, taking in symbols and spitting out symbols according to various algorithms. Consciousness, Searle argues, is a byproduct of *organic* machines alone, like lactation or photosynthesis. In other words, Searle believes that meat is the only substance which thinks. David Chalmers, on the other hand, is more optimistic that there might be silicon thought, but he is deeply skeptical that our current scientific understanding of the world is adequate to explain consciousness. Not that he advocates dualism—rather, Chalmers believes that consciousness, like gravity or electromagnetism, is a basic, irreducible feature of the universe. Future science, he believes, must accommodate this fact.

Reincarnation and Mind/Body Dualism

ROBERT ALMEDER is professor of philosophy at Georgia State University. A specialist in the theory of knowledge and the philosophy of science, Almeder has written or edited 27 books and over 60 articles. Most recently he was a Fulbright scholar at the Sorbonne in Paris, working on theories of truth.

THINKING QUESTIONS

Robert Almeder, *Reincarnation and Mind/Body Dualism*

1. Almeder argues that one ought to believe in reincarnation not on religious grounds but on scientific grounds. His argument leans heavily on the cases presented by Ian Stevenson. What are the core features of the Stevenson cases that reincarnation is supposed to explain?
2. The Bishen Chand and Swarnlata cases happened in India, a country where there is widespread belief in reincarnation. Do you think that this fact affects their value as evidence? Why or why not?
3. Besides reincarnation, what other possible explanations are there for the unusual memories and abilities reported in the cases that Almeder canvasses?
4. Almeder cites the criteria for believing in reincarnation laid out by A. J. Ayer and argues that the cases he presents satisfy these criteria. What are the conditions for belief in reincarnation that Ayer lists? Are they good ones?
5. Almeder concludes that it is unreasonable to reject belief in reincarnation, given the cases he presents. Do you agree? If not, why not?
6. If reincarnation is real, what does that show about the nature of the mind? The mind is presumably not, then, any particular physical thing. Is the mind a separate sort of nonphysical substance? A functional entity like a computer program that can be copied from one machine to the next?

It is no more surprising to be born twice than it is to be born once.

—VOLTAIRE

Do human beings reincarnate? To think that one's personality could survive biological death (which would imply that the body is not essential to one's full personality) and then subsequently "take up" a new body for some purpose or other seems philosophically fantastic. Nevertheless, in 1982 a Gallup poll found that nearly one in four Americans believed in reincarnation; in 1980 the *London Times* had reported the results of their own poll in which 29 percent of the British population surveyed expressed a belief in reincarnation. The emerging popularity of the belief, however, is no clear sign that there is any truth to it. Such growing popularity only *raises the question* of its truth. After all, the National Science Foundation recently conducted a national poll and announced that approximately 30 percent of all the American adults surveyed either did not know or agreed with the statement that the sun goes around the earth.

Even so, serious philosophers no less famous than Plato, Nietzsche, Schopenhauer, Giordano Bruno, and Cicero have argued for reincarnation on purely philosophical grounds. Of course, most people who believe in reincarnation do so primarily for religious, rather than scientific or philosophical, reasons; and this sort of motivation is apparent as far back as the ancient Pythagoreans, for whom belief in reincarnation (or transmigration of souls) was simply a matter of religious faith.

Quite apart from the religious context, however, belief in reincarnation has not prompted much serious philosophical discussion since Plato. This is not surprising. The most interesting evidence warranting such a discussion did not appear until quite recently. But even so, philosophers have still not yet noticed this evidence. They have been preoccupied with what they consider the more pressing question in the area of inquiry surrounding death, namely, whether we can successfully identify human personality with the corruptible body. There is, of course, no logically necessary connection between the answer to this question and reincarnation. Presumably, even if human personality should turn out to be identified with some nonphysical and naturally incorruptible principle (like a soul), the truth of reincarnation would not follow from that fact alone. One's personality could in some way survive one's biological death and yet *not* reincarnate. So, even if contemporary philosophers of mind do establish the falsity of mad-dog materialism, the most that would thereby be granted is the *possibility* of reincarnation as one of the ways in which human personality might survive biological death.

Curiously and interestingly enough, however, the belief in reincarnation offers the best available *scientific* explanation for certain forms of observable behavior not capable of explanation by appeal to any current scientifically accepted theory of human personality. In the conclusion to this chapter, one of the points that will emerge strongly is that, from a philosophical point of view, the belief in reincarnation is certainly as well established as (if not better than), say, the belief in the past existence of dinosaurs.

Anyway, in this chapter we will assume at the outset something we shall see proven in the conclusion of this book, namely, that belief in personal survival after death is certainly neither logically absurd nor factually impossible. Given this assumption, let us examine the best evidence for reincarnation. For reasons we shall explore later, many philosophers and scientists manage to bypass this evidence while seeking to determine whether human beings are more than just physical bodies.

STEVENSON'S ARGUMENT FOR REINCARNATION, AND SOME COMPELLING CASES

The strongest argument for reincarnation has been offered by Ian Stevenson, primarily in his book *Twenty Cases Suggestive of Reincarnation*. . . .

Basically, Stevenson's argument is that the belief in personal reincarnation offers the best available explanation for a large body of data that, until recently, has been generally ignored or rejected for various unacceptable reasons. The body of data consists in a number of case studies (described in great detail in *Twenty Cases Suggestive of Reincarnation* and elsewhere), many of which typically and ideally share at least the following core features:

A. A young person, usually between the ages of three and nine, claims to remember having lived an earlier life as a different person, and provides his (or her) parents with a *detailed* description of his alleged earlier life—a description including, but not restricted to, where and when he lived, his name, the names and characteristics of his various relatives, highly selective historical events that could be known only by the person he claims to have been in that earlier life, the way he lived, and the specific details of the way in which he died.

B. These memory claims consist of two types: (1) those that admit of simple verification in terms of available information; and (2) those that admit of verification but not in terms of available information. For example, if a young person from Evanston, Illinois, claims to remember having lived an earlier life as one Lazarus Smart, born in approximately 1630 in Boston, Massachusetts, and the son of Mary and Abraham Smart who lived on Boylston Street during the Boat Fire of 1642, then the fact that one Lazarus Smart did exist under this description could be verified easily in terms of available birth records, historical documents, and other information publicly accessible. But if the same person claims to recall having secretly buried a silver spoon with the initials L.S. in the concrete pier under the northwest corner of the Boylston Street Church when it was rebuilt in 1642, then this is the sort of claim that would be verifiable but not in terms of known or existing information.

C. The person claiming to remember having lived a past life, as well as the person's immediate (present) family members, are interviewed (with near-verbatim notes taken and some tape recordings) at great length, and asked to provide information one would expect to emerge if indeed the subject did live that earlier life. Although the majority of the person's memories are involuntary and spontaneous (and hence not often the direct response to questions of the interviewers), the relevant memory claims and information are provided during the interviews.

D. Investigators independently confirm both the spontaneous and the solicited memory claims; and in some cases (those cases in which the person's claims refer to extant past-life family members with whom he was intimate), past-life family members are interviewed and led to confront the subject, who proceeds to remind them of various nonpublic details of the life they spent together.

E. The person claiming to remember having lived a past life also manifests certain skills (such as speaking fluently a foreign language or dialect, or playing an instrument) that the person in the alleged earlier life had, but that the person claiming to have lived the earlier life could not have acquired or learned in this life. For example, if a person claims to remember having lived a life in medieval Sweden, and in a hypnotic trance he begins to speak and describe his earlier life in a difficult but clear dialect of medieval Swedish, then that person (assuming we can document that he has not learned or been exposed to the study of medieval Swedish) manifests a skill not acquired in this life.

F. Deception, or the real possibility of deception, by way of fraud or hoax on the part of the person claiming to have lived a past life cannot be substantiated.

Stevenson's basic argument says that for cases with characteristics A through F the only available explanation that plausibly fits the data is belief in reincarnation. Before discussing all available objections to this argument, however, we need to examine a few particular cases (some of them Stevenson's) that have the characteristics A through F.

Memory Evidence and Acquired Skills

Certainly some of the most compelling evidence for reincarnation occurs in cases that, as described in Stevenson's ideal-typical characteristics, offer detailed memory claims substantiated by extant past-life family members. The first case we will examine—the Bishen Chand case—involved just such evidence. The second—the Mrs. Smith case—is more problematic in that the past life remembered took place centuries ago. However, historical records (some of them extremely obscure or only recently available) have been used to verify many of the surprising memory claims of the subject.

Both cases exhibit another of Stevenson's ideal-typical characteristics, namely, the manifestation of skills acquired by the past-life person but not acquired by the present-day subject in this life. . . .

The Bishen Chand Case

Bishen Chand Kapoor was born in 1921 to the Gulham family living in the city of Bareilly, India. At about one and a half years, Bishen began asking questions about the town of Pilibhit, some 50 miles from Bareilly. Nobody in his family knew anybody in Pilibhit. Bishen Chand asked to be taken there, and it became obvious that he believed he had lived there during an earlier life.

As time passed, Bishen Chand talked incessantly of his earlier life there in Pilibhit. His family grew increasingly distressed with his behavior. By the summer of 1926 (when he was five and a half years old), Bishen Chand claimed to remember his previous life quite clearly. He remembered that his name had been Laxmi Narain, and that he had been the son of a wealthy landowner. Bishen claimed to remember an uncle named Har Narain, who turned out to be Laxmi Narain's father. He also described the house in which he had lived, saying it included a shrine room and separate quarters for women. Frequently, he had enjoyed the singing and dancing of nautch girls, professional dancers who often functioned as prostitutes. He remembered enjoying parties of this sort at the home of a neighbor, Sander Lal, who lived in a "house with a green gate." Indeed, little Bishen Chand one day recommended to his father that he (the father) take on a mistress in addition to his wife.

Because Bishen Chand's family was poor (his father was a government clerk), Bishen Chand's memories of an earlier and wealthier life only made him resentful of his present living conditions with the Gulham family. He sometimes refused to eat the food, claiming that even his servants (in his former life) would not eat such food.

One day Bishen's father mentioned that he was thinking of buying a watch, and little Bishen Chand said, "Pappa, don't buy. When I go to Pilibhit, I shall get you three watches from a Muslim watch dealer whom I established there." He then provided the name of the dealer.

His sister Kamla, three years older than he, caught Bishen drinking brandy one day (which finally explained the dwindling supply of alcohol kept in the house for medicinal purposes only). In his typically superior way, the child told her that he was quite accustomed to drinking brandy. He drank a good deal of alcohol in his earlier life. Later, he claimed to have had a mistress (again showing he knew the difference between a wife and a mistress) in his former life. Her name, he said, was Padma; and although she was a prostitute, he seemed to have considered her his exclusive property, because he proudly claimed to have killed a man he once saw coming from her apartment.

Bishen Chand Kapoor's memory claims came to the attention of one K. K. N. Sahay, an attorney in Bareilly. Sahay went to the Kapoor home and recorded the surprising things the young boy was saying. Thereafter, he arranged to take Bishen Chand, along with his father and older brother, to

Pilibhit. Not quite eight years had elapsed since the death of Laxmi Narain, whom this little boy was claiming to have been in his earlier life.

Crowds gathered when they arrived at Pilibhit. Nearly everyone in town had heard of the wealthy family and its profligate member Laxmi Narain who had been involved with the prostitute Padma (who still lived there), and how in a jealous rage Laxmi Narain had shot and killed a rival lover of Padma's. Although Laxmi Narain's family had been influential enough to get the charges dropped, he died a few months afterward of natural causes at the age of 32.

When taken to Laxmi's old government school, Bishen Chand ran to where his classroom had been. Somebody produced an old picture, and Bishen recognized in it some of Laxmi Narain's classmates, one of whom happened to be in the crowd. When the classmate asked about their teacher, Bishen correctly described him as a fat, bearded man.

In the part of town where Laxmi Narain had lived, Bishen Chand recognized the house of Sander Lal, the house that he had previously described (before being brought to Pilibhit) as having a green gate. The lawyer Sahay, when writing the report later for the national newspaper *The Leader* in August 1926, claimed to have seen the gate himself and verified that its color was green. The boy also pointed to the courtyard where he said the nautch girls used to entertain with singing and dancing. Merchants in the area verified the boy's claims. In the accounts published by *The Leader,* Sahay wrote that the name of the prostitute with whom the boy associated in his previous life was repeatedly sought by people in the crowd (following the boy). When Bishen Chand mentioned the name "Padma," the people certified that the name was correct.

During that remarkable day, the boy was presented with a set of *tabla,* a pair of drums. The father said that Bishen had never seen tabla before; but to the surprise of his family and all assembled, Bishen Chand played them skilfully, as had Laxmi Narain much earlier. When the mother of Laxmi Narain met Bishen Chand, a strong attachment was immediately apparent between them. Bishen Chand answered the questions she asked (such as the time in his previous life when he had thrown out her pickles), and he successfully named and described Laxmi Narain's personal servant. He also gave the caste to which the servant belonged. He later claimed that he preferred Laxmi's mother to his own. Laxmi Narain's father was thought to have hidden some treasure before his death, but nobody knew where. When Bishen Chand was asked about the treasure, he led the way to a room of the family's former home. A treasure of gold coins was later found in this room, giving credence to the boy's claim of having lived a former life in the house.

Finally, Bishen Chand's older brother testified that Bishen could, when he was a child, read Urdu (written in Arabic script) before he had been taught this language. Bishen Chand's father, in a sworn statement about the case, stated that Bishen had (as a child) used some Urdu words that he could not have learned in the family—words such as *masurate* and *kopal* (for "women's quarters" and "lock," respectively), rather than the usual Hindi words *zenana* and *tala*. Laxmi Narain was reasonably well educated and quite capable of speaking Urdu.

In examining this case, Ian Stevenson urges that it is especially significant because an early record was kept by a reliable attorney when most of the principals were still alive and capable of verifying Bishen Chand's memory claims. Many of the people who knew Laxmi Narain were still alive and well when Bishen Chand Kapoor was making his claims. They verified nearly all the statements Bishen made before he went to Pilibhit. Moreover, according to Stevenson, the possibility of fraud is remote because Bishen Chand's family had little to gain from association with the Laxmi Narain family. It was well known that the latter had become destitute after Laxmi Narain had died. As in most cases similar to this, the events could not be explained in terms of anticipated financial gain.

Let us turn to our second case, a more recent and local one.

The Mrs. Smith Case

In his book *The Cathars and Reincarnation,* a British psychiatrist named Dr. Arthur Guirdham describes in detail a particular case that compelled him to accept the belief in reincarnation. The woman in the case, Mrs. Smith, was his patient; and he met her in 1961 when he was chief psychiatrist at Bath Hospital in England. Mrs. Smith's problem was that she had persistent nightmares during which she shrieked so loud that she and her husband feared it would wake the whole neighborhood.

Dr. Guirdham examined her closely for neuroses but found she had none. After a few months, Mrs. Smith told Guirdham that, when she was a girl, she had written her dreams down. She had also written things that came spontaneously to her mind as recollections—things she could not understand that had to do with people, and specific names she had never heard. She gave the papers to the doctor, and he examined them.

Dr. Guirdham was surprised to find that what she had written as a schoolgirl were verses of songs in medieval French and in langue d'oc, the language spoken in southern France in the twelfth and thirteenth centuries. The doctor ascertained that she had never studied these languages in school and that there was no source available to her for learning them. He sent a report of her story to Professor René Nelli of Toulouse University, and asked for the professor's opinion on the matter. Nelli responded that her writings gave an accurate account of the Cathars in Toulouse in the thirteenth century. The Cathars were a group of Christian dissidents of the extreme dualist persuasion, whose religious beliefs were close to the Albigensians and centered on the belief in reincarnation. They were persecuted and destroyed during the Inquisition.

Only gradually did Mrs. Smith admit having had an intensive uprush of memory in her early teens—memories of a past life with a Cathar priest named Roger de Grisolles, whom she loved very much, and who taught her Cathar rituals and religious principles. Guirdham states that, apart from her dreams, Mrs. Smith had experienced a number of these spontaneous recollections, and she told him in horrid detail her recollection of the massacre of the Cathars. She also told him that in her dreams and recollections of a previous life she had been kept prisoner in a certain church crypt. Guirdham notes that, at first, experts said this church crypt had never been used for that purpose, but later research showed that so many religious prisoners were taken on one occasion that there was no room for all of them in regular prisons. Some had been kept in that very crypt.

Guirdham visited the south of France in 1967 to investigate the case. He read thirteenth-century manuscripts (available to only a limited number of scholars), and these manuscripts showed that Mrs. Smith's account was accurate. She had given Guirdham names and descriptions of people, places, and events, all of which turned out to be accurate to the last detail. Guirdham claims that there was no normal way in which Mrs. Smith could have known about these things. He even found in the manuscripts four of the songs she wrote as a child. They were correct, word for word.

Guirdham notes that, although his subject claimed never to have read any books on the subject of thirteenth-century life, she made correct drawings of old French coins, jewelry worn at the time, and the layout of buildings—to say nothing of the intricate details of Cathar ritual.

Guirdham attests that Mrs. Smith was able to name and place accurately in their family and social relationships people who do not appear in the textbooks, but who were ultimately traced by going back to the dog-Latin records of the Inquisition. These minor characters are still traceable owing to the antlike industry of the Inquisitors and their clerks. Mrs. Smith remembered members of the Fanjeaux and Mazzarolles families, in particular giving their first names and the roles they played. She recollected treating her friend Roger de Grisolles with sugarloaf as a tonic. However, the experts called this into question: the existence of sugar at this time in Europe was doubted. Further investigation disclosed that sugar in loaf form was derived from Arab medicine and did indeed exist at this period in France.

Even more remarkable was Guirdham's patient's description of her death when she was burned at the stake. This she both dreamed and subsequently claimed to remember. The description, conveyed by Guirdham as part of his case, reads as follows:

> The pain was maddening. You should pray to God when you're dying, if you can pray when you're in agony. In my dream I didn't pray to God. . . . I didn't know when you were burnt to death you'd bleed. I thought the blood would all dry up in the terrible heat. But I was bleeding heavily. The blood was dripping and hissing in the flames. I wished I had enough blood to put the flames out. The worst part was my eyes. I hate the thought of going blind. . . . In this dream I was going blind. I tried to close my eyelids but I couldn't. They must have been burnt off, and now those flames were going to pluck my eyes out with their evil fingers. . . .
>
> The flames weren't so cruel after all. They began to feel cold. Icy cold. It occurred to me that I wasn't burning to death but freezing to death. I was numb with the cold and suddenly I started to laugh. I had fooled those people who thought they could burn me. I am a witch. I had magicked the fire and turned it to ice.

Finally, in a lecture entitled "Reincarnation and the Practice of Medicine," Dr. Guirdham reflected on certain crucial details of the case, many of which were also discussed in his book.

> Twenty five years ago, as a student, a school girl at the age of 13, she was insisting that Cathar priests did not always wear black. You will find the statement that they did in any book on the subject written in any language until 1965. Yet she said that her friend in the thirteenth century wore *dark blue*. It now transpires that at one sitting of the Inquisition (the Inquisition of Jacques Fournier, who was Bishop at Palmiers), it came out ten times in one session that Cathar priests sometimes wore dark blue or dark green. But that fact had been lying in the archives in Latin for long enough, and was only accessible to the public in 1965 when Duvernoy edited the record of the said Inquisitors that was published in Toulouse in 1966. But this woman knew this in 1944 as a school girl.
>
> Again she could describe rituals in a house, a kind of convent. . . . Professor Nelli, the greatest living authority on the Troubadors—who definitely are connected with the Cathars—wrote to me and said, "This is almost exactly Cathar ritual, making allowance for local deviation." He also added later that he could tell me where the place was, the Convent of Montreal. By way of future advice, he added that, in case of doubt, one should "go by the patient." Professor Nelli is the most meticulous and sceptical assessor of evidence.
>
> When I first wrote to another specialist, Professor Duvernoy of Toulouse, he said, "Get in touch with me about anything you want. I am astonished at your detailed knowledge of Catharism." I couldn't say, "I've got this by copying down the dreams of a woman of thirty-six or seven which she had when she was a grammar school girl of thirteen. He's found out since, but he's all the more keen to supply me with the evidence. . . .
>
> If the professors at Toulouse are amazed at the accuracy with which an English girl can produce details of Catharism known to few, that is good enough for me. . . . [A]ll I have done in this matter is to listen to the story, act as an amateur historian, and try to verify from many sources the details she had noted. I believe this to be a unique and entirely valid experience.

Let us proceed to other recent cases of a different sort.

Memory Evidence and Recognition: The Swarnlata Case

In 1951 an Indian man named Sri M. L. Mishra took his three-year-old daughter Swarnlata and several other people on a 170-mile trip south from the city of Panna (in the district of Madhya Pradesh) to the city of Jabalpur, also in the same district. On the return journey, as they passed through the city of Katni (57 miles north of Jabalpur), Swarnlata unexpectedly asked the driver to turn down a certain road to "my house." The driver quite understandably ignored her request. Later, when the same group was taking tea at Katni, Swarnlata told them that they would get better tea at "my house" nearby. These statements puzzled her father, Mishra; neither he nor any member of his family had ever lived near Katni. His puzzlement deepened when he learned that Swarnlata was telling other children in the family further details of what she claimed was a previous life in Katni as a member of a family named Pathak. In the next two years Swarnlata frequently performed for her mother (and later in front of others) unusual dances and songs that, as far as her parents knew, there had been no opportunity for her to learn. In 1958, when she was ten, Swarnlata met a woman from the area of Katni whom Swarnlata claimed to have known in her earlier life. It was at this time that Mishra first sought to confirm the numerous statements his daughter made about her "previous life."

In March 1959, H. N. Banerjee began to investigate the case; and in 1961 (after Banerjee's investigation), Ian Stevenson went to Chhatarpur to recheck carefully the work done by Banerjee. From the Mishra home in Chhatarpur, Banerjee had traveled to Katni where he became acquainted with the Pathak family of which Swarnlata claimed to have been a member. He noted, before journeying to Katni, some nine detailed statements Swarnlata had made about the Pathak residence. These statements he confirmed on his arrival. Incidentally, before Banerjee went to Katni, the Mishra family did not know or know of the Pathak family.

Banerjee also found that the statements made by Swarnlata corresponded closely to the life of Biya, a daughter in the Pathak family and deceased wife of a man named Pandey who lived in Maihar. Biya had died in 1939—nine years before the birth of Swarnlata.

In the summer of 1959, members of the Pathak family and of Biya's marital family traveled to Chhatarpur (where the Mishra family lived). Without being introduced to these people, Swarnlata recognized them all, called them by name, and related personal incidents and events in their various lives with Biya—events that, according to these relatives, only Biya could have known. For example, Swarnlata claimed that, as Biya, she had gold fillings in her front teeth. Biya's sister-in-law confirmed as much. The Pathaks eventually accepted Swarnlata as Biya reincarnated, even though they had never previously believed in the possibility of reincarnation.

After these visits, in the same summer, Swarnlata and members of her family went first to Katni and then to Maihar where the deceased Biya had spent much of her married life and where she died. In Maihar, Swarnlata recognized additional people and places and commented on various changes that had occurred since the death of Biya. Her statements were independently verified. Later, Swarnlata continued to visit Biya's brother and children, for whom she showed the warmest affection.

The songs and dances that Swarnlata had performed presented some problem, however. Biya spoke Hindi and did not know how to speak Bengali, whereas the songs Swarnlata had sung (and danced to) were in Bengali. Although the songs were publicly available and had been recorded on phonograph records and played in certain films, she could not have learned these songs from records or films because her parents had neither seen nor heard them and, therefore, Swarnlata—as a typical child under close surveillance of her family—had no occasion to do so. The parents were also certain that Swarnlata had not been in contact with Bengali-speaking persons from whom she might have learned the songs. Swarnlata claimed that she had learned the songs and dances from a previous life. . . .

After careful examination, Ian Stevenson concludes that it is very difficult to explain the facts of the case without admitting that Swarnlata had paranormal knowledge. After all, how otherwise could Swarnlata have known the details of the family and of the house? These details (including the fact that Biya had gold fillings in her teeth—a fact that even her brothers had forgotten) were by no means in the public domain. Moreover, how otherwise can we explain her recognition of members of the Pathak and Pandey families? How can her knowledge of the former (as opposed to the present) appearances of places and people be explained? Her witnessed recognitions of people amount to 20 in number. As Stevenson notes, most of the recognitions occurred in such a way that Swarnlata was obliged to give a name or state a relationship between Biya and the person in question. On several occasions, serious attempts were made to mislead her or to deny that she gave the correct answers, but such attempts failed.

Could there have been a conspiracy among all the witnesses in the various families (the Mishras, the Pathaks, and the Pandeys)? Might not all of them have conspired to bring off a big hoax? Well, according to Stevenson, a family of prominence such as the Pathaks, with far-reaching business interests, is unlikely to participate in a hoax with so many people involved, any one of which might later defect. If a hoax did occur, it is more likely to have come from the Chhatarpur side. But even here, Sri M. L. Mishra had nothing to gain from such a hoax. He even doubted for a long time the authenticity and truth of his daughter's statements, and he made no move to verify them for six years. Most of the people involved agreed that they had nothing to gain but public ridicule.

But even if we suppose that there *was* some attempt at fraud, who would have tutored Swarnlata for success in such recognitions? Who would have taken the time to do it? Sri M. L. Mishra, apart from Swarnlata, was the only other member of the family who received any public attention from Swarnlata's case. And what attention he received, he was not too happy about. Also, how could Sri Mishra have gotten some of the highly personal information possessed by Swarnlata about the private affairs of the Pathaks (e.g., that Biya's husband took her 1,200 rupees)?

Might Swarnlata have been tutored by some stranger who knew Katni and the Pathaks? As Stevenson notes, like all children in India—especially girls—Swarnlata's movements were very carefully controlled by her family. She never saw strangers in the house alone, and she never was out on the street unaccompanied.

Besides the legal documentation and methods used in Stevenson's examination, what is interesting about this case is that it is one of many similar cases. Can we explain the facts plausibly without appealing to the belief in reincarnation?

The Argument Stated: What Better Explanation?

The Bishen Chand case and the Swarnlata case (and many other cases too numerous to include here) exemplify, in varying degrees, the ideal-typical characteristics A through F mentioned above in conjunction with Stevenson's argument for reincarnation. Of course, in the Bishen Chand case the interviews were not taped, but they were written down. And Swarnlata did not speak in an unlearned foreign language or, like Bishen Chand, play an instrument she had not learned to play; but she did sing in a foreign language that she had not been taught, and she did perform complicated dances that she had never seen. Both subjects provided memory information about facts that were not in the public domain and yet were subsequently verified by independent investigators. Also, the accuracy of their memory claims down to the very smallest details was much too high to be explained in terms of probability or luck or coincidence; and the large number of extant family members who provided extensive verification of the memory claims about personal and very private historical details is particularly important. Not only because of the methods employed in examining these cases, but also because of their richness of detail, I submit that, logically, these two cases typify the strongest sort of evidence for reincarnation.

The Mrs. Smith case may not match all the ideal-typical characteristics, involving as it does a long-ago past life. But the recitative xenoglossy exhibited by Mrs. Smith, and her consistent memory of previously unknown but then often verified historical facts, qualify the case as worthy of serious consideration in the context of this study. . . .

At this point, then, the argument for reincarnation is very simple. It is this. What would be a better or more plausible explanation for these cases than to assume that human personality (whatever it is) admits of reincarnation? Opponents of reincarnation must provide an equally plausible or better alternative explanation for the data if they are to undermine effectively the claim that the best available explanation for these sorts of cases is reincarnation. . . .

Certainly, on the principle that extraordinary claims require extraordinary evidence, we *should* be somewhat cautious in our assessments of the strength of the evidence offered here for reincarnation. Even so, it seems excessively cautious to think that the belief in reincarnation is not established by the rich cases described in this chapter, and that we ought to await the appearance of the ideal case. Admittedly, one might want more evidence. As long as there are imaginable ways to strengthen the evidence, seeking more evidence is a desirable project. And, of course, the question of how much evidence is enough tends to be relative to both the kind of claim made and the degree of initial plausibility associated with the claim. But is it *necessary* to satisfy all the conditions of the ideal case offered by Stevenson before we are strongly justified in believing that the argument has been won in favor of reincarnation? Stevenson certainly seems to suggest as much; but I submit that, in so doing, he is actually understating the force of the existing evidence. At the moment, without denying that the ideal case would be nice to have, we seem quite justified in urging something stronger than does Stevenson. Let me explain.

Why, precisely, would we need any more evidence for belief in reincarnation than that provided by a nonfraudulent case in which the subject has a rich set of memory claims, some of which refer to past facts that are items of public knowledge and some of which are verified as facts that only the subject could have known if the subject had indeed lived a past life as the person the subject claims to have been? On this point, we should keep in mind the discussion on human personality offered by Alfred J. Ayer in his book *The Problem of Knowledge*. Ayer there argues that it would be sufficient for the truth of the belief that the man beside you is Julius Caesar reincarnated if that man had all the memories that one would ordinarily expect of Julius Caesar, and if he had some verified memories that appealed to facts that were not in any way items of public information.

At the time, incidentally, Ayer was not attempting to prove the truth of reincarnation. He was simply arguing that human personality need not be identified in any way with the body rather than with the collection of one's memories. What is important for us about his discussion, however, is that it literally stipulates the conditions sufficient to establish that the man beside you is Julius Caesar reincarnated. But those conditions have certainly been satisfied in many of the cases described in this chapter—especially the Bishen Chand case, the Swarnlata case, and the Mrs. Smith case. If these cases are not demonstrable instances of hoax, fraud, or purely natural phenomena, why do we not accept them as compelling evidence for reincarnation—as Ayer's argument allows us to do? Why add any more conditions having to do with the presence of body scars, or the manifestation of unlearned skills such as speaking a foreign language or playing an instrument? We would need to add to Ayer's conditions only if we had discovered that Ayer's conditions were not sufficient. But have we? . . . Have we come across a reasonably plausible alternative explanation showing that the presence of private but verifiable past-life memories is not sufficient for establishing the validity of reincarnation? Given all the alternative explanations offered above (and bypassing the possession hypothesis, for the moment), it seems clear that nobody has yet *shown* either that Ayer's general requirements for human personality are unacceptable or that the cases described in this chapter are not legitimate instances of those conditions and thus evidence of reincarnation. We seem to have here one of those problems wherein people readily agree on what it would take to establish something they very much do not want to believe—and then when, contrary to anyone's expectations, the evidence actually emerges strongly supportive of the belief, they return (for no persuasive reason) to add more conditions to what it would take to establish what they very much do not want to accept. And they continue doing so until it is virtually impossible that any such evidence should ever emerge.

At any rate, the point is that, in the absence of plausible alternative explanations that do not require reincarnation, it will be sufficient for the truth of reincarnation that the memory conditions laid out by Ayer, and clearly instanced in a number of the cases described in this chapter, be satisfied. Thus, the knowledge that reincarnation occurs is simply the product of the best available explanation for the existence of such memory claims as indicated above. Until somebody comes up with the appropriate alternative explanation, the evidence for reincarnation appears to be quite strong. . . .

Indeed, it seems unreasonable to accept any belief other than reincarnation to explain the cases described in this chapter. This conclusion is much stronger than Stevenson's. His conclusion is that *it is not unreasonable to believe in reincarnation* in order to explain his best cases. While that result certainly is an incontrovertible and revolutionary finding in itself, the proper conclusion should be that *it is unreasonable to reject belief in reincarnation.*

Evidence and the Afterlife

STEVEN D. HALES (1966–) is professor of philosophy at Bloomsburg University. He has a PhD from Brown University and has lectured widely, including talks in Istanbul, Prague, Amsterdam, Austria, Rome, and Slovenia. Professor Hales has published five books and many articles in the areas of epistemology, metaphysics, and Nietzsche.

THINKING QUESTIONS

Steven D. Hales, *Evidence and the Afterlife*

1. How does Hales define "life after death"?
2. Almeder argues that the empirical evidence—the cases he cites—rationally compel belief in reincarnation. Hales's thesis is stronger than a mere denial of Almeder's claim. What is it?
3. Hales argues that Almeder offers no theory as to what exactly reincarnation is or how it works; instead, Almeder merely presents odd data inconsistent with the usual scientific picture of the world. Besides abandoning the usual scientific picture and accepting reincarnation, how else might one deal with the anomalous data, according to Hales?
4. Why does Hales maintain that in the case of a very excellent theory, we cannot be justified in believing it to be false without any account of why it is false?
5. Why does Hales believe that we do not accept the Dark Sucker hypothesis?
6. What is the ET hypothesis meant to demonstrate?
7. What does Hales think must be shown in order to rationally conclude that materialism about the mind is wrong and that some sort of life after death is real? Do you agree? Why or why not?

INTEREST IN SO-CALLED paranormal matters such as out-of-body experiences, reincarnation, spirit mediumship, extra-sensory perception, possession and the like is generally shunted into a dark corner of the profession by mainstream philosophers, and considered part of a misguided, prescientific past. Well-known philosophers, such as William James, C. J. Ducasse, C. D. Broad, Antony Flew, and H. H. Price, who take seriously such matters are regarded as respectable but slightly nutty uncles whose excesses are to be indulged with a wink and a smile. Yes, uncle, that's nice (we hardheaded skeptics say), now let's return to serious business like the pragmatic theory of truth, the nature of perception, or the justification of morality.

This attitude is a tactical mistake. There are two reasons why this is so. The first is that many non-philosophers are great believers in the paranormal, and if we hope that philosophy is to have a real value outside of the rarefied air of scholarly debate it is important to offer more to the general public than a lofty dismissal of their interests. Of course professional philosophers might offer detailed objections to paranormal views, but to do so is to take these beliefs seriously enough to refute them. The second reason is that scholarly treatments of, say, the evidence for postmortem survival, do so partly in the spirit of providing empirical evidence for traditional philosophical views like Cartesian dualism. As scientific-minded philosophers we should welcome this as an advance over the old *a priori*-style attempts to establish such theses. The data may be poor or flawed or unpersuasive, but at least it is something empirical that is offered. The opposition is meeting us on our own turf, and it is disingenuous merely to ignore their presence.

What I propose to do in this paper is to take seriously one such paranormal matter, namely the evidence for life after death, or the survival of a human person following the complete organic dissolution of their body. I will argue that even assuming that the best and richest cases offered to support this view are nonfraudulent and not obviously the result of sloppy investigative methodology, that nevertheless on their own they present no reason to believe in postmortem survival. I will also discuss what *would* be required to justify a belief in life after death.

The best set of arguments for the thesis that some people survive their deaths has been given by Robert Almeder in his recent book *Death and Personal Survival*. Almeder considers several cases of ostensible reincarnation, apparitions of the dead, possession, out-of-body experiences, and spirit mediumship, and argues that the most detailed and best investigated examples of these provide excellent evidence in favor of the view that there is some form of postmortem survival. Indeed, Almeder argues that the evidence is so strong that upon recognizing it one would be irrational not to believe that there is life after death. This is a very striking claim. For ease of exposition, I will focus on Almeder's treatment of ostensible reincarnation, which he seems to think gives the strongest reasons to accept a belief in the survival of death. My criticisms can be generalized to other paranormal phenomena.

A. J. Ayer and Derek Parfit have independently stated the conditions under which we should believe someone to be the reincarnation of someone else. (Putting it this way highlights the recondite problems of personal identity that arise in this context, and indeed it is in considering issues of identity that Ayer and Parfit offer the evidential requirements for reincarnation. However, I will set this personal identity issue aside.) Let us look at the criteria Parfit provides:

> There might, for example, have been evidence supporting the belief in reincarnation. One such piece of evidence might be this. A Japanese woman might claim to remember living a life as a Celtic hunter and warrior in the Bronze Age. On the basis of her apparent memories she might make many predictions which could be checked by archaeologists. Thus she might claim to remember having a bronze bracelet, shaped like two fighting dragons. And she might claim that she remembers burying the bracelet beside some particular megalith, just before the battle in which she was killed. Archaeologists might now find just such a bracelet buried in this spot, and their instruments might show that the earth had not here been disturbed for at least 2000 years. This Japanese woman might make many other predictions, all of which are verified.

Parfit appends the conditions that there is no physical continuity between the Celtic warrior and the Japanese woman, and that we discover several other cases like this one. He hastens to add that he believes we have no evidence of this sort required to justify belief in reincarnation. Ayer provides similar requirements; if someone had the verified memories one would expect of Julius Caesar that appealed to facts that were not items of public information, then we should conclude that the person is Caesar reincarnated. Almeder accepts these criteria, and develops them in greater detail.

Just what the satisfaction of these conditions would epistemically show is non-obvious. In ascending order of strength, we might reach the following conclusions:

1. Some evidence has been provided in favor of a belief in reincarnation.
2. It is not irrational or epistemically irresponsible to believe in reincarnation given the evidence.
3. It is irrational or epistemically irresponsible not to believe in reincarnation given the evidence.

If there were such evidence, Parfit thinks it would license at least (1), Ayer seems to think we could conclude (2), and Almeder explicitly endorses (3). I will argue that not even the weakest of these follows. Even if we have cases that satisfy all of the conditions listed, that evidence alone provides no reason at all to believe in reincarnation.

Almeder's argument is a simple *modus ponens*. If there is such-and-such evidence, then we should believe in reincarnation; there is such-and-such evidence, therefore we should believe in reincarnation. It is the first premise, the conditional, that I will argue is false. I will not attempt to assess each of the cases Almeder offers in support of the second premise. This would be a heady empirical project beyond the scope of this paper. Assume for the sake of argument that there are cases like that of Parfit's Japanese woman, that there are several of these cases, and that the possibilities of fraud, cryptomnesia, and paramnesia have been rigorously investigated and eliminated as probable.

Fraud is always a logical possibility that can never be wholly discounted, but let us suppose that fraud is unlikely. We need to be careful and not presume that e.g. the Japanese woman *knew* where the bracelet was buried, or that she *remembered* burying it, as these are success-verbs that beg the question in favor of postmortem existence. Almeder is not always so careful. More neutrally we can say that she had a *true belief* about the location of the bracelet, and that she had a *quasi-memory* of burying it. Thus we leave open the questions of whether her belief is appropriately linked with the truth in a way that makes it knowledge, and whether her apparent memory is a genuine remembrance.

Antony Flew has objected that the evidence for reincarnation is not repeatable under scientifically controlled conditions. There is no laboratory experiment in which new statements reporting quasi-memories of events that are verifiable and not items of public information could be elicited. The evidence for reincarnation is anecdotal, and could never aspire to the level of scientifically acceptable data. Therefore we are not justified in believing that persons do sometimes reincarnate.

While Almeder's response to this objection is structurally correct, close attention to his reply reveals the epistemic crevasse that yawns beneath the claims of reincarnation. He argues that much scientific evidence is not repeatable in Flew's sense; for example, the evidence for the past existence of dinosaurs. Previously undiscovered dinosaur bones cannot be produced at will, or under laboratory conditions. Still, he argues, there is a clear sense in which the evidence for the past existence of dinosaurs is repeatable—the continued discovery of new fossils, footprints, and eggs tends to confirm the belief. So too the continued discovery of cases like that of Parfit's Japanese woman or Ayer's Julius Caesar tends to confirm a belief in reincarnation. The elimination of probable fraud and rigorous evidential standards is of course required for both the dinosaur and the reincarnation evidence.

Unfortunately, the evidence for reincarnation is crucially disanalogous to the evidence for the past existence of dinosaurs. The past existence of dinosaurs is consistent with our best empirical theories about the world, whereas reincarnation is not consistent with either our best empirical theories or with our best philosophical theories about the mind. Antecedent to purported cases of postmortem survival, most contemporary philosophers regard the best theory about the mind to be some version of materialism. Almeder is explicit that he regards reincarnation and postmortem survival in general to falsify materialism and support some form of Cartesian dualism. Thus the analogy to the belief in the past existence of dinosaurs is weak on the face of it.

Alone this difference is not enough to undercut Almeder's thesis. It is when we further recognize that the data for reincarnation is offered with no attendant theory that the problem truly crystallizes. Almeder does not offer even a sketch of a theory that would be able to account for all current data about the mind while also explaining how and by what mechanism human personality could survive bodily death and reincarnate. Moreover, he does not think that such a theory is required for the evidence supporting reincarnation to be compelling. In this he is mistaken. Sir Arthur Eddington once said that "one should never believe any experiment until it is confirmed by theory." While partly tongue-in-cheek, there is an undercurrent of truth in Eddington's remark that deserves exploration.

On the one hand we obviously do not want to summarily dismiss empirical data on the grounds that it does not square with accepted theory. This would prevent us from ever rejecting faulty theories and replacing them with better ones. On the other hand, it would be an equal error blindly to venerate data over theory, and it is this mistake to which Eddington points. Suppose one were to argue in the following way. If we are justified in believing theory T (e.g., materialism about the mind), and we know that T implies not-p (e.g. that there are no reincarnating Cartesian egos), then we are justified in believing not-p. Add to this, á la Almeder, that we are not justified in believing not-p, on the grounds that there is evidence in favor of reincarnation. Therefore, by *modus tollens,* we are not justified in believing that theory T is true.

This sort of reasoning leads to an extreme skepticism; it implies that we are not justified in accepting any empirical theory about the world. Physicist Steven Weinberg has written that "There is no theory that is not contradicted by some experiment." There will always be experimental anomalies for any theory of wide application, and virtually every view, even amazingly plausible ones, will have counter-evidence. Moreover, there is no *a priori* way of deciding which anomalous evidence is really just flawed data, which can ultimately be explained by the current theory in a yet undiscovered way, and which are important anomalies that undermine the theory. One can always continue investigating the quality of the evidence or try to make it fit with the accepted theory. The real nail in the coffin of an old theory is a replacement model that explains the anomalies. Indeed, anomalous data alone is not enough to jettison an otherwise highly justified theory. Sometimes we can know that a surprising fact is true without knowing why it is true; for example, we can know from observation that the Tortoise outran Achilles without knowing how it is possible for him to do so. This cannot be generalized, however. In the case of a very excellent theory, we cannot be justified in believing that it is false without any account of why it is false.

To suppose otherwise is to endorse an unreasonably strong requirement for being justified in believing the truth of a theory, viz., *no theory is justified if there is unexplained evidence against it.* This would imply that we are not warranted in accepting any theory about medicine, physics, or biology. Such a position is the mark of an overly simplistic empiricism. Theories draw their power from not only agreement with new experiment, but from their ability to retrodict prior data, their congruence with other theories, their prediction of novel phenomena, and aesthetic qualities such as logical elegance and internal symmetry. Raw outlier data lacks these features. The interaction between theory and experiment is far messier than the logician's clean world in which a single universal generalization is proven false by the first counterexample.

If we are faced with experimental data or evidence E that is genuinely inconsistent with the whole of some theory T, there are a host of things we might conclude. For example, we might conclude that the most probable thing is that T is false. But we could instead decide that it is likelier E is the result of inadequate data collection, or that theory T is incomplete.

If T is in all other respects a truly excellent theory, it is more reasonable to conclude one of these latter things than it is to rule that T is false. Evidence E may have been carefully collected, nonfraudulent, rigorously analyzed, and still contradict the prevailing theory. If the theory is right, the evidence is faulty for reasons we may not yet understand or are unable to discover. The theory may be wrong, of course, and the anomalous evidence good, but the data on their own are not enough to justify the rejection of a theory that is otherwise highly warranted. Perturbations in the precession of the orbit of Mercury was not enough to jettison Newtonian mechanics; it took such data along with the theory of relativity to do so. In the case of materialism about the mind, one might argue that it is not such a good theory anyway, but then the arguments against materialism come from other sources than evidence for postmortem survival. Without a theoretical explanation of the cases Almeder presents, it is more rational to believe either that there must be *something* amiss with the data, or that there will ultimately be a materialist explanation of it, than it is to believe that materialism about the mind is mistaken.

So far all that has been argued is that Almeder is mistaken in holding that it is irrational or epistemically irresponsible not to believe in reincarnation given the evidence, and that Ayer is also mistaken in thinking that if there were cases of the sort discussed that it would not be irrational or epistemically irresponsible to believe in reincarnation. I have not yet shown that Parfit is in error in drawing the weakest conclusion, viz. that such cases would be some evidence in favor of a belief in reincarnation. Here is the argument against Parfit.

Suppose that we have several cases like Parfit's Japanese woman, and in fact the cases are non-fraudulent and the data they contain accurate. Thus, having stipulated that it is good data, we need to develop a theoretical explanation of it. In formulating competing hypotheses to explain the cases we need to keep in mind the desideratum of conservatism: any hypothesis that explains the data in a way consistent with our best theories is, *ceteris paribus,* superior to any explanatory hypothesis inconsistent with our best theories.

To illustrate the use of this desideratum, consider the hypothesis that electric bulbs do not really emit light but instead suck dark. This hypothesis successfully explains much of our evidence about electric bulbs, or "dark suckers."

> Take for example, the dark suckers in the room where you are. There is less dark right next to them than there is elsewhere. The larger the dark sucker, the greater its capacity to suck dark. Dark suckers in a parking lot have much greater capacity than the ones in this room. As with all things, dark suckers don't last forever. Once they are full of dark, they can no longer suck. This is proven

> by the black spot on a full dark sucker. A candle is a primitive dark sucker. A new candle has a white wick. You will notice that after the first use, the wick turns black, representing the dark which has been sucked into it. If you hold a pencil next to the wick on an operating candle, the tip will turn black, because it got in the way of the dark flowing into the candle. Unfortunately, these dark suckers have a very limited range. There are also portable dark suckers. The bulbs in these units can't handle all of the dark by themselves, and must be aided by a dark storage unit. When the dark storage unit is full, it must be either emptied or replaced before the portable dark sucker can operate again. If you break open one of these filled canisters, one will see that there is indeed a great quantity of stored dark on the inside.

We do not accept the dark sucker hypothesis for two reasons: it is inconsistent with our best physical theories, and there is a competing hypothesis consistent with our best theories that explains the evidence we have about electric bulbs at least as well. Similarly, if there is some other hypothesis that explains the cases ostensibly suggestive of reincarnation as well as the reincarnation hypothesis, and if this other hypothesis is consistent with materialism about the mind, and other well-established theories, then we should prefer it.

Indeed, there are indefinitely many such hypotheses. One is that there are intelligent, technologically advanced extra-terrestrials who regard humans with great amusement, and secretly monitor and occasionally interfere with our lives. One thing they enjoy is performing super-advanced psychosurgery on select humans that provides these humans with quasi-memories of having lived past lives, verifiably true beliefs about where ancient bracelets are hidden, and previously non-existent linguistic or musical talents. Unlike a Cartesian evil genius, the ET hypothesis is perfectly testable by empirical means—if the aliens were to land and reveal themselves and their techniques, this would serve to confirm the hypothesis. If we were to completely survey the universe and find no such aliens, this would falsify it. Moreover, the ET proposal is entirely consistent with materialism about the mind, and explains the cases as well as the reincarnation hypothesis. Even better, the probability of there being some sort of extra-terrestrial life is quite high, given the large size of the universe (it contains about 10^{22} stars) and the conditions needed for life to arise.

Just as it is epistemically preferable to reject the dark sucker hypothesis in favor of the hypothesis that electric bulbs emit light, it is epistemically better to take cases like that of the Japanese woman as evidence for the ET hypothesis than it is to take them as evidence of reincarnation. This follows directly from the desideratum of conservatism considered earlier. I do not endorse the ET option, and do not think that it is true. Rather, the point is that even a far-fetched explanation like mind-controlling ETs is superior to reincarnation. The reincarnation hypothesis is much closer to a belief that electric bulbs are dark suckers than it is to the belief in the past existence of dinosaurs.

Thus the cases provided by Almeder and others better support the ET hypothesis than they do reincarnation. Since the same data cannot simultaneously confirm two inconsistent hypotheses, even given the cases, we have no reason to believe that some persons survive their deaths through reincarnation. Similar arguments can be employed against all paranormal claims that are inconsistent with what are antecedently considered the best theories of the world; out-of-body experiences, spirit mediumship, apparitions of the dead, and all the rest have the same epistemic vices.

To sum up the dialectic: I assume that materialism is the best theory we currently have about the mind. Almeder and like-minded survivalists are likely to charge that this assumption begs the question, since they take the reincarnation evidence to refute materialism. My reply is that such a charge misses the mark. I am assuming that, *in advance of ostensible survivalist cases,* (almost) all parties come to the table thinking that some form of materialism is the best theory going about the mind. *Then* the anomalous data arrives, and we have to decide what to do with it. Such data takes the form of examples like that of Parfit's Japanese woman, cases that have been rigorously investigated and seem legitimate. Conservatism advises that hypotheses that explain the data in a manner consistent with materialism are epistemically superior to those that are inconsistent with materialism. The survivalists fail to heed this desideratum; instead they conclude from these cases that we have excellent evidence for reincarnation, which is not consistent with materialism.

Considered in isolation, apart from other theories antecedently held, the ET hypothesis and the reincarnation hypothesis are equally plausible. In this respect they are analogous to the contrasting hypotheses that either electric bulbs suck dark or they emit light. There is no reason to prefer one to the other if they are to be evaluated independently from other things we justifiably believe. However, it would be epistemically irresponsible to opt for the dark sucker hypothesis given our wealth of knowledge about light, and the compelling theories we have about electromagnetism. Our highly justified background theories give the "emits light" hypothesis a higher prior probability. Bayesian considerations come into play with respect to reincarnation as well, and the ET hypothesis gets a higher prior probability than the reincarnation alternative.

One obvious objection to the ET hypothesis is that it is *ad hoc;* it does not follow from observation, is not entailed by theory, and seems specifically tailored to answer the ostensible cases of reincarnation. This diminishes its explanatory value. On the other hand, the reincarnation hypothesis is not so *ad hoc,* and fits well with the cases without needing special modifications. Reincarnation does not fare well by the test of conservatism, but is easily the victor by the *ad hoc*ness test. My reply is that the ET hypothesis is similar to adding epicycles to Ptolemaic astronomy. Tweaking the Ptolemaic model with epicycles may be unlovely and *ad hoc,* but (to some degree) it makes the model work. For a long time, the most rational thing to do was to keep geocentrism, warts and all. Indeed, it was not until Kepler recognized that planetary orbits are elliptical rather than circular that the heliocentric theory could explain the observation of "retrograde motion" without using epicycles. This is not to suggest that scientists before Copernicus should have been satisfied or complacent about geocentrism; they should have been actively trying to solve the problem of retrograde motion under Ptolemaic rules in a more elegant way than using epicycles, trying to show that the observational data was flawed, or attempting to devise a new and better theory of celestial motion. The success of any of these strategies would have been an improvement over epicycles and, of course, the last of these proved victorious. Yet it would have been epistemically wrong-headed to abandon geocentrism and its epicycles without its Copernican (and perhaps Keplerian) replacement.

It is basically a Quinean point that sensory evidence underdetermines theory, and so we should not be too surprised that the sort of cases that Almeder and other survivalists cite fails to directly establish that some persons survive their deaths. No hypothesis is entailed by data alone. It could be that materialism about the mind is wrong, or even that other excellent theories like evolutionary biology or the germ theory are mistaken and will ultimately be supplanted. However, what it will take to show these things is more than just unexplained data inconsistent with these theories. To be rationally persuaded that materialism is wrong and that we are Cartesian egos that at least occasionally survive bodily corruption, we will need not only empirical cases, but a theory in which these cases are embedded. This theory will require all the same virtues (predictive power, data retrodiction, elegance, coherence with other physical theories, etc.) possessed by materialism as well as a capacity to explain the nature and properties of the Cartesian self. This is not a dogmatic rejection of postmortem existence. If we are presented both with high-quality evidence satisfying the conditions laid down by Parfit, Ayer, and Almeder, and a theory that explains it of the sort described, then it would be epistemically permissible—and perhaps even obligatory—to believe that we might survive our deaths. Until then, we should remain skeptics.

The Know-It-All Machine

CLIVE THOMPSON (1968–) is a freelance writer who, among other topics, writes on issues in technology. He has published in major magazines and newspapers, including the *New York Times* and *Washington Post*. In 2002–2003 he was a Knight Science Journalism Fellow at the Massachusetts Institute of Technology. You can see more of Mr. Thompson's work at his blog, Collision Detection, at www.collisiondetection.net.

THINKING QUESTIONS

Clive Thompson, *The Know-It-All Machine*

1. What makes Cyc different from other attempts at creating artificial intelligence?
2. Why are Cyc's programmers trying to pack millions of everyday facts into it?
3. Besides lots of facts, what else does Cyc have that enables it to make claims about the real world?
4. Cyc's programmers are criticized for not having first dealt with the theoretical problems with representing knowledge. How do they respond to this criticism?
5. Looking at the examples of inferences Cyc makes, do you think that Cyc thinks the way that you do? Why or why not?

FLORENCE ROSSIGNOL HAS JUST FINISHED using an on-line travel site to plan a package tour across Europe. The site has prompted her for a few facts about herself: her date of birth, her education and nationality, her occupation. She has typed in that she was born in 1945 and trained as a nurse. She has also volunteered the fact that she is claustrophobic. As far as on-line shopping goes, it looks like an everyday event.

Except this Web site is smart—unusually smart. It has been outfitted with a copy of Cyc (pronounced *sike*), artificial intelligence software touted for its ability to process information with humanlike common sense.

At one point, Cyc detects a problem: The proposed tour involves taking the Channel Tunnel from London to France; Rossignol is claustrophobic. The Web site notes that Rossignol "may dislike" the Channel Tunnel, and Cyc justifies the assertion with a series of ten related statements, including:

- 31 miles is greater than 50 feet.
- The Channel Tunnel is 31 miles long.
- Florence Rossignol suffers from claustrophobia.
- Any path longer than 50 feet should be considered "long" in a travel context.
- If a long tunnel is a route used by a tour, a claustrophobic person taking the tour might dislike the tunnel.

At the same time, Cyc scours the list of various cities on the tour and takes special notice of Geneva, where one can visit the Red Cross Museum. This time, Cyc's thinking features the following steps:

- The Red Cross Museum is found in Geneva.
- Florence Rossignol is a nurse.
- Nursing is what nurses do.
- The Red Cross Museum (organization) has nursing as its "focus."
- If an organization has a particular type of activity as its "focus," and a person holds a position in which they perform that activity, that person will feel significantly about that organization.

Bingo. The travel site tells Rossignol to make sure she catches the Red Cross Museum in Geneva—but for God's sake, don't take the Channel Tunnel.

Doug Lenat is pleased. Though this impressive display happens to be a promotional demo (Rossignol is a fictitious character), it is, he explains, genuinely representative of his invention's unique abilities. Most computer programs are utterly useless when it comes to everyday reasoning because they don't have very much common sense. They don't know that claustrophobics are terrified of enclosed spaces. They don't know that fifty feet can sometimes be considered a "long" distance. They don't even know something as tautological as "Nursing is what nurses do."

Cyc, however, does know such things—because Lenat has been teaching it about the world one fact at a time for seventeen long years. "We had to kick-start a computer, give it all the things we take for granted," he says. Ever since 1984, the former Stanford professor has been sitting in Cyc's Austin, Texas, headquarters and writing down the platitudes of our "consensus reality"—all the basic facts that we humans know about the world around us: "Water is wet"; "Everyone has a mother"; "When you let go of things they usually fall." Cyc currently has a database of about 1.5 million of these key assertions. Taken together, they are helping Lenat create what he calls the first true artificial intelligence (AI)—a computer that will be able to speak in English, reason about the world, and, most unnerving, learn on its own. Cyc is easily the biggest and most ambitious AI project on the planet, and by the time it's completed, it will probably have consumed Lenat's entire career.

Encoding common sense is so formidable a task that no other AI theorists have ever dared to try anything like it. Most have assumed it isn't even possible. Indeed, with Cyc, Lenat has tweaked the noses of legions of AI researchers who have largely given up on the rather sci-fi-like dream of creating human-like intelligence and have focused instead on much smaller projects—so-called expert systems that perform very limited intelligent tasks, such as controlling a bank machine or an elevator. "Doug's really one of the only people still trying to slay the AI dragon," says Bill Andersen, a PhD. candidate specializing in ontologies (information hierarchies) at the University of Maryland and a former Department of Defense researcher who has used Cyc in several Defense Department experiments.

For all his progress, Lenat still receives mixed responses from much of the academic AI community. Not only does Cyc's highly pragmatic approach fly in the face of much scholarly AI theory, but its successes have taken place at Lenat's Cycorp, which is developing Cyc as a for-profit venture. Incensing his critics, Lenat has published almost no academic papers on Cyc in recent years, raising suspicions that it may have many undisclosed flaws. "We don't really know what's going on inside it, because he doesn't show anyone," complains Doug Skuce, an AI researcher at the University of Ottawa.

Lenat, meanwhile, revels in his bad-boy image. He accuses academic AI experts of being theory-obsessed and unwilling to do the hard work necessary to tackle common sense. "They want it to be easy. There are people who'd rather talk about doing it than actually *do* it," he says, laughing.

Still, some skeptics think Lenat could benefit from more deliberation and less action. "It's kind of crazy," says the Yale computer science professor Drew McDermott about Lenat's ambition. "Philosophers have been debating common sense for years, and they don't even know how it works. Lenat thinks he's going to get common sense going in a computer?" Push Singh, a graduate student at the Massachusetts Institute of Technology who is building a rival upstart to Cyc, has his own doubts: "Lenat and his team have been going for fifteen years and have only one million rules? They'll *never* get enough knowledge in there at that rate."

Lenat began building Cyc by setting himself a seemingly modest challenge. He picked a pair of test sentences that Cyc would eventually have to understand: "Napoleon died in 1821. Wellington was greatly saddened." To comprehend them, Cyc would need to grasp such basic concepts as death, time, warfare, and France, as well as the sometimes counterintuitive aspects of human emotion, such as why Wellington would be saddened by his enemy's demise. Lenat and a few collaborators began writing these concepts down and constructing a huge branching-tree chart to connect them. They produced a gigantic list of axiomatic statements—fundamental assumptions—that described each concept in Cyc's database: its properties, how it interacted with other things. "We took enormous pieces of white paper," Lenat remembers, "and filled walls, maybe 150 feet long by about 8 feet high, with little notes and circles and arrows and whatnot."

Over the next few years, those axioms ballooned in number—eventually including statements as oddly basic as:

- You should carry a glass of water open end up.
- The U.S.A. is a big country.
- When people die, they stay dead.

The axioms aren't written in everyday English, which is too ambiguous and nuanced a language for a computer to understand. Instead, Cyc's "Ontological Engineers"—Lenat's staff of philosophers and programmers, who call themselves Cyclists—express each axiom in CycL, a formal language that Lenat's team devised. Based on the sort of symbolic notation that logicians and philosophers use to formalize claims about the world, CycL looks like this:

```
(for All ?X
   (implies
      (owns Fred ?X)
      (objectFoundInLocation ?X FredsHouse)))
```

This expression states that if Fred owns any object, ?X, then that object is in Fred's house. In other words, as Cyclists put it, "all Fred's stuff is in his house." (Of course, as with all Cyc's knowledge, this claim becomes useful only in conjunction with other truths that Cyc knows—such as the fact that a person's car or beachfront property is too large to fit in his house.)

Cyc's inventory of the world, however, is only one part of its setup. The other part is its "inference engine," which allows Cyc to deploy its immense store of factual knowledge. This engine includes Cyc's "heuristic layer"—a collection of more than five hundred small modules of software code that perform logical inferences and deductions, as well as other feats of data manipulation. One module, for example, implements traditional *modus ponens* logic: If Cyc knows a fact of the form "If *X,* then *Y,*" and Cyc knows "*X,*" then it will conclude "*Y*." Other modules have the ability to sort facts by, say, chronological order.

On the one hand, the inference engine is what actually gives Cyc its innate smarts; without it, Cyc wouldn't be able to *do* anything with the information at its disposal. But on the other hand, as Lenat emphasizes, a computer can have state-of-the-art powers of data manipulation and still be worthless from a practical point of view; no machine can help you reason about the real world if it does not have commonsense knowledge to work with. Data manipulation, in Lenat's view, is the comparatively easy part. It's the data themselves that are devilishly difficult.

From the perspective of computing power, commonsense knowledge presents an additional difficulty in its sheer mass. As Cyc's knowledge base grew, the program had to sort through thousands of facts whenever it tried to reason. It began to slow down. "If you're trying to talk about the weather today, you don't want Cyc worrying about whether spiders have eight legs,"

Lenat explains. So the Cyclists have created "contexts"—clumpings of like-minded facts that help speed up inferencing. If Cyc is told a fact about tour trips to Greece, for example, it begins with its existing knowledge about Europe, travel, trains, and the like. In this sense, Cyc's processing strategies are akin to human cognition; we can discuss any given topic only by ignoring "99.999 percent of our knowledge," as Lenat has written.

In academe, Cyc has always been a black sheep. Everyone in AI knows about it, and virtually everyone views it with skepticism. Lenat's critics have lambasted him for lacking a coherent theory of how intelligence and knowledge representation work—and for rushing ahead with an ill-thought-out project. When they look at Cyc, they see nothing but an ad hoc jumble of facts about the world picked in an overly idiosyncratic way by Lenat's team. For them, making human-level AI requires a better theoretical understanding of *human* intelligence and the fundamentals of reasoning and representation—and those are areas that are still, many argue, in their infancy.

In a 1993 issue of *Artificial Intelligence,* several reviewers sharply critiqued Lenat's 1989 book about Cyc. Yale's Drew McDermott led the charge, arguing that it was impossible to build a commonsense database without solving such philosophical problems as "the nature of causality." "We've been thinking about things like that for millennia," he points out.

McDermott suspects that it may not yet be possible to represent real-world common knowledge in logical, orderly languages such as Cyc's CycL—or any other language, for that matter. After all, humans don't always store and manipulate knowledge logically or in language. "If you go through a room and you don't bump into things, is that common sense?" he wonders. Nils Nilsson, an AI pioneer and Stanford professor emeritus, shares that concern. "You can describe in words how to swing a golf club," he concedes. "But can that really tell you how to do it? We still don't really know how to represent knowledge."

Critics and fans of Cyc both recognize that the goal of producing a complete inventory of commonsense facts is almost embarrassingly open to theoretical objections. Because so many philosophical issues about how to represent knowledge remain unsolved, building large knowledge bases is "something of a backwater," according to Ernest Davis, a professor of computer science at New York University and the author of *Representations of Common Sense Knowledge*. Starting in the 1980s, for example, much of the excitement in AI began to center around the use of narrowly focused self-learning systems—like neural nets—to crunch enormous bodies of data. Such systems are intended to "learn" to recognize patterns on their own, instead of being painstakingly taught them by humans. "People like it because it's a lot faster," Davis explains. "You'll never be able to get commonsense AI out of it, but you can do some pretty neat things," such as develop programs that can recognize visual images.

Lenat, however, is unmoved. He bashes right back at the naysayers every chance he gets—often in searingly witty prose. In his response to the 1993 reviews by McDermott and others, he argued that theory-heavy AI experts were suffering from the Hamlet syndrome—unwilling to take action and stuck in a circle of philosophizing. Too many AI theorists, he sneered, were "researchers with 'physics envy,' insisting that there must be some elegant 'free lunch' approach to achieving machine intelligence."

For Lenat, having a watertight theory isn't necessary for building useful AI. Quite the contrary: He argues that building a body of commonsense knowledge can *only* be done in a down-and-dirty engineering style. You put together a bunch of facts, test the system, see where it breaks, fix the bugs, and keep on adding more knowledge. Each day, when Cyclists talk to Cyc, they discover new erroneous assumptions that Cyc has—or new information that it doesn't have. "It's iterative. You have to do it every day, keep at it," says the Cyclist Charles Pearce.

Lenat compares building up Cyc to building a bridge. "You know, you have a stream and you want to build a bridge over it—you can either do your best, experiment, and build the bridge. Or you can work out the physics of bridge building," he says. "It's only in the last hundred years or so that the theory of bridge building has been understood. Before that, it was almost like apprenticing to a master. There would be someone who would just intuitively know how to build a bridge—and every now and then, he would build one that would fall down."

Whatever the theoretical inelegance of Cyc, Lenat can always fall back on one powerful defense: It works well—or at least better than anything comparable so far. During a visit to Cycorp, I watch a videotaped demonstration of a biological warfare expert teaching Cyc about a new weapon similar to anthrax. Cyc demonstrates its grasp of common knowledge—not just about the physical world, but about the rather more ephemeral world of pop culture.

At one point, the expert asks Cyc what it knows about anthrax. Cyc pauses for a second, then asks: "Do you mean Anthrax (the heavy metal band), anthrax (the bacterium), or anthrax infection (the infection)?" The official notes that it's the bacterium, not the band. Cyc asks what type of organism the agent infects. The military official types: "People."

Cyc thinks again for an instant, then responds: "By People, I assume you mean persons, not *People* magazine."

By the end of the exchange, Cyc has successfully absorbed various facts about the agent—how it is destroyed (by encasing it in concrete), its color (green), and which terrorists possess it (Osama bin Laden). But the demo also illustrates some of Cyc's limitations. Obviously, it wasn't easily able to figure out the military context of the exchange—otherwise it wouldn't have needed to ask whether "anthrax" signified a heavy metal band.

An even bigger limitation lurks behind that one: the fact that commonsense is almost infinite. This is a problem that still threatens to doom Lenat's grandest ambitions. Sure, you could eventually input the billions of bits of common knowledge worldwide. But at the rate the Cyclists are going, that would take millennia; the limited resources of Cycorp's programmers are not enough. Even

Cyc's supporters see this as a major stumbling point. "The amount of knowledge you need will easily outpace the ability of the builders to input it," as Nilsson says.

Still, he's willing to try. After so many years of pounding away at Cyc, Lenat has nothing to lose in pressing ahead. He draws me a graph that shows Cyc's learning curve. From 1985 to 2000, the line curves upward gradually—the "brain surgery" phase during which the Cyclists input knowledge by hand. But then at 2001, the curve steepens dramatically as the open-source phase takes over, and thousands—or millions—more inputters join in. Lenat extends the curve maybe ten years into the future. As the curve reaches the point where Cyc has read everything there is to read and spoken with everyone willing to tell it facts, it will begin to flatten out. "It'll know all there is to know," he says. "At that point, the only way it could learn more is by doing experiments itself."

Will 2001, then, be as talismanic as some would hope—the year that HAL-like intelligence is born? Lenat is optimistic. "I'm very, very excited," he says. But he's made rash predictions in the past: In the late 1980s, he confidently forecast that 1994 would be the year Cyc would begin learning via natural-language conversations with average people.

Intelligence is unruly stuff—which makes the behavior of artificial intelligence sometimes hard to predict. Lenat tells me a cautionary tale from his days as a young professor in the late 1970s and early 1980s. Back then, he designed a self-learning program called EURISKO. It was intended to generate new heuristics—new types of search strategies—all on its own by slightly mutating bits of LISP computer code. And it did successfully manage to produce unique new rules to parse data sets.

But then trouble struck. In the mornings when Lenat arrived at work, he'd find the program had mysteriously shut down overnight. This happened again and again, puzzling him. What was causing it to crash?

Finally he discovered that it wasn't a crash at all; it was a strange and unexpected new strategy. At some point, EURISKO had altered its rules so that "making no errors at all" was as important as "making productive new discoveries." Then EURISKO realized that if it turned itself off, it wouldn't make mistakes. It was bizarre behavior—but it was logical. It made sense. "Just not common sense," Lenat says with a laugh.

Minds, Brains, and Programs

JOHN R. SEARLE (1933–) is Mills Professor of Philosophy at the University of California at Berkeley. A Rhodes Scholar at Oxford at the age of 19, Searle is known for his wide-ranging interests, from oenophilia to conversational implicature. He is the author of 13 books, mainly on the philosophy of mind and the philosophy of language. He is best known for his "Chinese room" argument against the possibility that electronic computers have intentionality—that is, that they think about things, or have beliefs about things. Searle maintains that consciousness is a product of biology, just as much as lactation or photosynthesis is.

THINKING QUESTIONS

John R. Searle, *Minds, Brains, and Programs*

1. What is the distinction that Searle makes between weak and strong AI?
2. Searle presents a thought experiment about a Chinese room. How does this thought experiment work? What are the two main conclusions that Searle draws?
3. Searle considers various replies to his story about the Chinese room, the first is the systems reply. According to this view, while the person in the Chinese room does not understand Chinese, the system (which consists of the room, the person, the pieces of paper, the rule book, etc.) does understand Chinese. Is this plausible? Why does Searle reject it?
4. What is the robot reply? Searle rejects this as well. Do you think he is right to do so?
5. Is the brain simulator reply different from the systems reply?
6. Despite his arguments against strong AI, Searle maintains that machines can and do think. Why does he hold this? What do actual, real machines think, according to Searle?
7. Searle maintains that thinking is a product of biology, in the same way that lactation or photosynthesis is. If you don't have the right chemicals and squishy parts, then you can't think. Is Searle right about this?
8. Searle accuses advocates of strong AI of accepting dualism about the mental. What does he mean by this? What is his reasoning?

WHAT PSYCHOLOGICAL AND PHILOSOPHICAL significance should we attach to recent efforts at computer simulations of human cognitive capacities? In answering this question, I find it useful to distinguish what I will call "strong" AI from "weak" or "cautious" AI (artificial intelligence). According to weak AI, the principal value of the computer in the study of the mind is that it gives us a very powerful tool. For example, it enables us to formulate and test hypotheses in a more rigorous and precise fashion. But according to strong AI, the computer is not merely a tool in the study of the mind; rather, the appropriately programmed computer really *is* a mind, in the sense that computers given the right programs can be literally said to *understand* and have other cognitive states. In strong AI, because the programmed computer has cognitive states, the programs are not mere tools that enable us to test psychological explanations; rather, the programs are themselves the explanations.

I have no objection to the claims of weak AI, at least as far as this article is concerned. My discussion here will be directed at the claims I have defined as those of strong AI, specifically the claim that the appropriately programmed computer literally has cognitive states and that the programs thereby explain human cognition. When I hereafter refer to AI, I have in mind the strong version, as expressed by these two claims.

I will consider the work of Roger Schank and his colleagues at Yale . . . because I am more familiar with it than I am with any other similar claims, and because it provides a very clear example of the sort of work I wish to examine. But nothing that follows depends upon the details of Schank's programs. . . .

Very briefly, and leaving out the various details, one can describe Schank's program as follows: The aim of the program is to simulate the human ability to understand stories. It is characteristic of human beings' story-understanding capacity that they can answer questions about the story even though the information that they give was never explicitly stated in the story. Thus, for example, suppose you are given the following story: "A man went into a restaurant and ordered a hamburger. When the hamburger arrived it was burned to a crisp, and the man stormed out of the restaurant angrily, without paying for the hamburger or leaving a tip." Now, if you are asked "Did the man eat the hamburger?" you will presumably answer, "No, he did not." Similarly, if you are given the following story: "A man went into a restaurant and ordered a hamburger; when the hamburger came he was very pleased with it; and as he left the restaurant he gave the waitress a large tip before paying his bill," and you are asked the question, "Did the man eat the hamburger?" you will presumably answer, "Yes, he ate the hamburger." Now Schank's machines can similarly answer questions about restaurants in this fashion. To do this, they have a "representation" of the sort of information that human beings have about restaurants, which enables them to answer such questions as those above, given these sorts of stories. When the machine is given the story and then asked the question, the machine will print out answers of the sort that we would expect human beings to give if told similar stories. Partisans of strong AI claim that in this question and answer sequence the machine is not only simulating a human ability but also (1) that the machine can literally be said to *understand* the story and provide the answers to questions, and (2) that what the machine and its program do *explains* the human ability to understand the story and answer questions about it.

Both claims seem to me to be totally unsupported by Schank's work, as I will attempt to show in what follows. I am not, of course, saying that Schank himself is committed to these claims.

One way to test any theory of the mind is to ask oneself what it would be like if my mind actually worked on the principles that the theory says all minds work on. Let us apply this test to the Schank program with the following *Gedankenexperiment*. Suppose that I'm locked in a room and given a large batch of Chinese writing. Suppose furthermore (as is indeed the case) that I know no Chinese, either written or spoken, and that I'm not even confident that I could recognize Chinese writing as Chinese writing distinct from, say, Japanese writing or meaningless squiggles. To me, Chinese writing is just so many meaningless squiggles. Now suppose further that after this first batch of Chinese writing I am given a second batch of Chinese script together with a set of rules for correlating the second batch with the first batch. The rules are in English, and I understand these rules as well as any other native speaker of English. They enable me to correlate one set of formal symbols with another set of formal symbols, and all that "formal" means here is that I can identify the symbols entirely by their shapes. Now suppose also that I am given a third batch of Chinese symbols together with some instructions, again in English, that enable me to correlate elements of this third batch with the first two batches, and these rules instruct me how to give back certain Chinese symbols with certain sorts of shapes in response to certain sorts of shapes given me in the third batch. Unknown to me, the people who are giving me all of these symbols call the first batch a "script," they call the second batch a "story," and they call the third batch "questions." Furthermore, they call the symbols I give them back in response to the third batch "answers to the questions," and the set of rules in English that they gave me, they call the "program." Now just to complicate the story a little, imagine that these people also give me stories in English, which I understand, and they then ask me questions in English about these stories, and I give them back answers in English. Suppose also that after a while I get so good at following the instructions for manipulating the Chinese symbols and the programmers get so good at writing the programs that from the external point of view—that is, from the point of view of somebody outside the room in which I am locked—my answers to the questions are absolutely indistinguishable from those of native Chinese speakers. Nobody just looking at my answers can tell that I don't speak a word of Chinese. Let us also suppose that my answers to the English questions are, as they no doubt would be, indistinguishable from those of other native English speakers, for the simple reason that I am a native English speaker. From the external point of view—from the point of view of someone reading my "answers"—the answers to the Chinese questions and the English questions are equally good.

But in the Chinese case, unlike the English case, I produce the answers by manipulating uninterpreted formal symbols. As far as the Chinese is concerned, I simply behave like a computer; I perform computational operations on formally specified elements. For the purposes of the Chinese, I am simply an instantiation of the computer program.

Now the claims made by strong AI are that the programmed computer understands the stories and that the program in some sense explains human understanding. But we are now in a position to examine these claims in light of our thought experiment.

1. As regards the first claim, it seems to me quite obvious in the example that I do not understand a word of the Chinese stories. I have inputs and outputs that are indistinguishable from those of the native Chinese speaker, and I can have any formal program you like, but I still understand nothing. For the same reasons, Schank's computer understands nothing of any stories, whether in Chinese, English, or whatever, since in the Chinese case the computer is me, and in cases where the computer is not me, the computer has nothing more than I have in the case where I understand nothing.
2. As regards the second claim, that the program explains human understanding, we can see that the computer and its program do not provide sufficient conditions of understanding since the computer and the program are functioning, and there is no understanding. But does it even provide a necessary condition or a significant contribution to understanding? One of the claims made by the supporters of strong AI is that when I understand a story in English, what I am doing is exactly the same—or perhaps more of the same—as what I was doing in manipulating the Chinese symbols. It is simply more formal symbol manipulation that distinguishes the case in English, where I do understand, from the case in Chinese, where I don't. I have not demonstrated that this claim is false, but it would certainly appear an incredible claim in the example. Such plausibility as the claim has derives from the supposition that we can construct a program that will have the same inputs and outputs as native speakers, and in addition we assume that speakers have some level of description where they are also instantiations of a program. On the basis of these two assumptions we assume that even if Schank's program isn't the whole story about understanding, it may be part of the story. Well, I suppose that is an empirical possibility, but not the slightest reason has so far been given to believe that it is true, since what is suggested—though certainly not demonstrated—by the example is that the computer program is simply irrelevant to my understanding of the story. In the Chinese case I have everything that artificial intelligence can put into me by way of a program, and I understand nothing; in the English case I understand everything, and there is so far

> no reason at all to suppose that my understanding has anything to do with computer programs, that is, with computational operations on purely formally specified elements. As long as the program is defined in terms of computational operations on purely formally defined elements, what the example suggests is that these by themselves have no interesting connection with understanding. They are certainly not sufficient conditions, and not the slightest reason has been given to suppose that they are necessary conditions or even that they make a significant contribution to understanding. Notice that the force of the argument is not simply that different machines can have the same input and output while operating on different formal principles—that is not the point at all. Rather, whatever purely formal principles you put into the computer, they will not be sufficient for understanding, since a human will be able to follow the formal principles without understanding anything. No reason whatever has been offered to suppose that such principles are necessary or even contributory, since no reason has been given to suppose that when I understand English I am operating with any formal program at all.

Well, then, what is it that I have in the case of the English sentences that I do not have in the case of the Chinese sentences? The obvious answer is that I know what the former mean, while I haven't the faintest idea what the latter mean. But in what does this consist and why couldn't we give it to a machine, whatever it is? I will return to this question later, but first I want to continue with the example.

I have had the occasions to present this example to several workers in artificial intelligence, and, interestingly, they do not seem to agree on what the proper reply to it is. I get a surprising variety of replies, and in what follows I will consider the most common of these (specified along with their geographic origins).

But first I want to block some common misunderstandings about "understanding": In many of these discussions one finds a lot of fancy footwork about the word "understanding." My critics point out that there are many different degrees of understanding; that "understanding" is not a simple two-place predicate; that there are even different kinds and levels of understanding, and often the law of excluded middle doesn't even apply in a straightforward way to statements of the form "*x* understands *y*"; that in many cases it is a matter for decision and not a simple matter of fact whether *x* understands *y;* and so on. To all of these points I want to say: of course, of course. But they have nothing to do with the points at issue. There are clear cases in which "understanding" literally applies and clear cases in which it does not apply; and these two sorts of cases are all I need for this argument. I understand stories in English; to a lesser degree I can understand stories in French; to a still lesser degree, stories in German; and in Chinese, not at all. My car and my adding machine, on the other hand, understand nothing: they are not in that line of business. We often attribute "understanding" and other cognitive predicates by metaphor and analogy to cars, adding machines, and other artifacts, but nothing is proved by such attributions. We say, "The door *knows* when to open because of its photoelectric cell," "The adding machine *knows how (understands how,* is *able)* to do addition and subtraction but not division," and "The thermostat *perceives* changes in the temperature." The reason we make these attributions is quite interesting, and it has to do with the fact that in artifacts we extend our own intentionality; our tools are extensions of our purposes, and so we find it natural to make metaphorical attributions of intentionality to them; but I take it no philosophical ice is cut by such examples. The sense in which an automatic door "understands instructions" from its photoelectric cell is not at all the sense in which I understand English. If the sense in which Schank's programmed computers understand stories is supposed to be the metaphorical sense in which the door understands, and not the sense in which I understand English, the issue would not be worth discussing. But Newell and Simon (1963) write that the kind of cognition they claim for computers is exactly the same as for human beings. I like the straightforwardness of this claim, and it is the sort of claim I will be considering. I will argue that in the literal sense the programmed computer understands what the car and the adding machine understand, namely, exactly nothing. The computer understanding is not just (like my understanding of German) partial or incomplete; it is zero.

Now to the replies:

1. The Systems Reply (Berkeley). "While it is true that the individual person who is locked in the room does not understand the story, the fact is that he is merely part of a whole system, and the system does understand the story. The person has a large ledger in front of him in which are written the rules, he has a lot of scratch paper and pencils for doing calculations, he has 'data banks' of sets of Chinese symbols. Now, understanding is not being ascribed to the mere individual; rather it is being ascribed to this whole system of which he is a part."

My response to the systems theory is quite simple: Let the individual internalize all of these elements of the system. He memorizes the rules in the ledger and the data banks of Chinese symbols, and he does all the calculations in his head. The individual then incorporates the entire system. There isn't anything at all to the system that he does not encompass. We can even get rid of the room and suppose he works outdoors. All the same, he understands nothing of the Chinese, and *a fortiori* neither does the system, because there isn't anything in the system that isn't in him. If he doesn't understand, then there is no way the system could understand because the system is just a part of him.

Actually I feel somewhat embarrassed to give even this answer to the systems theory because the theory seems to me so implausible to start with. The idea is that while a person doesn't understand Chinese, somehow the *conjunction* of that person and bits of paper might understand Chinese. It is not easy for me to imagine how someone who was not in the grip of an ideology would find the idea at all plausible. Still, I think many people who are committed to the ideology of strong AI will in the end be inclined to say something very much like this; so let us pursue it a bit further. According to one version of this view, while the man in the internalized systems example doesn't understand Chinese in the sense that a native Chinese speaker does (because, for example, he doesn't know that the story refers to restaurants and hamburgers, etc.), still "the man as a formal symbol manipulation system" *really does understand Chinese.* The subsystem of the man that is the formal symbol manipulation system for Chinese should not be confused with the subsystem for English.

So there are really two subsystems in the man; one understands English, the other Chinese, and "it's just that the two systems have little to do with each other." But, I want to reply, not only do they have little to do with each other, they are not even remotely alike. The subsystem that understands English (assuming we allow ourselves to talk in this jargon of "subsystems" for a moment) knows that the stories are about restaurants and eating hamburgers, he knows that he is being asked questions about restaurants and that he is answering questions as best he can by making various inferences from the content of the story, and so on. But the Chinese system knows none of this. Whereas the English subsystem knows that "hamburgers" refers to hamburgers, the Chinese subsystem knows only that "squiggle squiggle" is followed by "squoggle squoggle." All he knows is that various formal symbols are being introduced at one end and manipulated according to rules written in English, and other symbols are going out at the other end. The whole point of the original example was to argue that such symbol manipulation by itself couldn't be sufficient for understanding Chinese in any literal sense because the man could write "squoggle squoggle" after "squiggle squiggle" without understanding anything in Chinese. And it doesn't meet that argument to postulate subsystems within the man, because the subsystems are no better off than the man was in the first place; they still don't have anything even remotely like what the English-speaking man (or subsystem) has. Indeed, in the case as described, the Chinese subsystem is simply a part of the English subsystem, a part that engages in meaningless symbol manipulation according to rules in English.

Let us ask ourselves what is supposed to motivate the systems reply in the first place; that is, what *independent* grounds are there supposed to be for saying that the agent must have a subsystem within him that literally understands stories in Chinese? As far as I can tell the only grounds are that in the example I have the same input and output as native Chinese speakers and a program that goes from one to the other. But the whole point of the examples has been to try to show that that couldn't be sufficient for understanding, in the sense in which I understand stories in English, because a person, and hence the set of systems that go to make up a person, could have the right combination of input, output, and program and still not understand anything in the relevant literal sense in which I understand English. The only motivation for saying there *must* be a subsystem in me that understands Chinese is that I have a program and I can pass the Turing test; I can fool native Chinese speakers. But precisely one of the points at issue is the adequacy of the Turing test. The example shows that there could be two "systems," both of which pass the Turing test, but only one of which understands; and it is no argument against this point to say that since they both pass the Turing test they must both understand, since this claim fails to meet the argument that the system in me that understands English has a great deal more than the system that merely processes Chinese. In short, the systems reply simply begs the question by insisting without argument that the system must understand Chinese.

Furthermore, the systems reply would appear to lead to consequences that are independently absurd. If we are to conclude that there must be cognition in me on the grounds that I have a certain sort of input and output and a program in between, then it looks like all sorts of noncognitive subsystems are going to turn out to be cognitive. For example, there is a level of description at which my stomach does information processing, and it instantiates any number of computer programs, but I take it we do not want to say that it has any understanding. But if we accept the systems reply, then it is hard to see how we avoid saying that stomach, heart, liver, and so on are all understanding subsystems, since there is no principled way to distinguish the motivation for saying the Chinese subsystem understands from saying that the stomach understands. It is, by the way, not an answer to this point to say that the Chinese system has information as input and output and the stomach has food and food products as input and output, since from the point of view of the agent, from my point of view, there is no information in either the food or the Chinese—the Chinese is just so many meaningless squiggles. The information in the Chinese case is solely in the eyes of the programmers and the interpreters, and there is nothing to prevent them from treating the input and output of my digestive organs as information if they so desire.

This last point bears on some independent problems in strong AI, and it is worth digressing for a moment to explain it. If strong AI is to be a branch of psychology, then it must be able to distinguish those systems that are genuinely mental from those that are not. It must be able to distinguish the principles on which the mind works from those on which nonmental systems work; otherwise it will offer us no explanations of what is specifically mental about the mental. And the mental-nonmental distinction cannot be just in the eye of the beholder but it must be intrinsic to the systems; otherwise it would be up to any beholder to treat people as nonmental and, for example, hurricanes as mental if he likes. But quite often in the AI literature the distinction is blurred in ways that would in the long run prove disastrous to the claim that AI is a cognitive inquiry. McCarthy, for example, writes, "Machines as simple as thermostats can be said to have beliefs, and having beliefs seems to be a characteristic of most machines capable of problem solving performance." Anyone who thinks strong AI has a chance as a theory of the mind ought to ponder the implications of that remark. We are asked to accept it as a discovery of strong AI that the hunk of metal on the wall that we use to regulate the temperature has beliefs in exactly the same sense that we, our spouses, and our children have beliefs, and furthermore that "most" of the other machines in the room—telephone, tape recorder, adding machine, electric light switch—also have beliefs in this literal sense. It is not the aim of this article to argue against McCarthy's point, so I will simply assert the following without argument. The study of the mind starts with such facts as that humans have beliefs, while thermostats, telephones, and adding machines don't. If you get a theory that denies this point you have produced a counterexample to the theory and the theory is false. One gets the impression that people in AI who write this sort of thing think they can get away with it because they don't really take it seriously, and they don't think anyone else will either. I propose, for a moment at least, to take it seriously. Think hard for one minute about what would be necessary to establish that that hunk of metal on the wall over there had real beliefs, beliefs with direction of fit, propositional content, and conditions of satisfaction; beliefs that had the possibility of being strong beliefs or weak beliefs; nervous, anxious, or secure beliefs; dogmatic, rational, or superstitious beliefs; blind faiths or hesitant cogitations; any kind of beliefs. The thermostat is not a candidate. Neither is stomach, liver, adding machine, or telephone. However, since we are taking the idea seriously, notice that its truth would be fatal to strong AI's claim to be a science of the mind. For now the mind is everywhere. What we wanted to know is what distinguishes the mind from thermostats and livers. And if McCarthy were right, strong AI wouldn't have a hope of telling us that.

2. The Robot Reply (Yale). "Suppose we wrote a different kind of program from Schank's program. Suppose we put a computer inside a robot, and this computer would not just take in formal symbols as input and give out formal symbols as output, but rather would actually operate the robot in such a way that the robot does something very much like perceiving, walking, moving about, hammering nails, eating, drinking—anything you like. The robot would, for example, have a television camera attached to it that enabled it to see, it would have arms and legs that enabled it to 'act,' and all of this would be controlled by its computer 'brain.' Such a robot would, unlike Schank's computer, have genuine understanding and other mental states."

The first thing to notice about the robot reply is that it tacitly concedes that cognition is not solely a matter of formal symbol manipulation, since this reply adds a set of causal relations with the outside world. But the answer to the robot reply is that the addition of such "perceptual" and "motor" capacities adds nothing by way of understanding, in particular, or intentionality, in general, to Schank's original program. To see this, notice that the same thought experiment applies to the robot case. Suppose that instead of the computer inside the robot, you put me inside the room and, as in the original Chinese case, you give me more Chinese symbols with more instructions in English for matching Chinese symbols to Chinese symbols and feeding back Chinese symbols to the outside. Suppose, unknown to me, some of the Chinese symbols that come to me come from a television camera attached to the robot and other Chinese symbols that I am giving out serve to make the motors inside the robot move the robot's legs or arms. It is important to emphasize that all I am doing is manipulating formal symbols: I know none of these other facts. I am receiving "information" from the robot's "perceptual" apparatus, and I am giving out "instructions" to its motor apparatus without knowing either of these facts. I am the robot's homunculus, but unlike the traditional homunculus, I don't know what's going on. I don't understand anything except the rules for symbol manipulation. Now in this case I want to say that the robot has no intentional states at all; it is simply moving about as a result of its electrical wiring and its program. And furthermore, by instantiating the program I have no intentional states of the relevant type. All I do is follow formal instructions about manipulating formal symbols.

3. The Brain Simulator Reply (Berkeley and M.I.T.). "Suppose we design a program that doesn't represent information that we have about the world, such as the information in Schank's scripts, but simulates the actual sequence of neuron firings at the synapses of the brain of a native Chinese speaker when he understands stories in Chinese and gives answers to them. The machine takes in Chinese stories and questions about them as input, it simulates the formal structure of actual Chinese brains in processing these stories, and it gives out Chinese answers as outputs. We can even imagine that the machine operates, not with a single serial program, but with a whole set of programs operating in parallel, in the manner that actual human brains presumably operate when they process natural language. Now surely in such a case we would have to say that the machine understood the stories; and if we refuse to say that, wouldn't we also have to deny that native Chinese speakers understood the stories? At the level of the synapses, what would or could be different about the program of the computer and the program of the Chinese brain?"

Before countering this reply I want to digress to note that it is an odd reply for any partisan of artificial intelligence (or functionalism, etc.) to make: I thought the whole idea of strong AI is that we don't need to know how the brain works to know how the mind works. The basic hypothesis, or so I had supposed, was that there is a level of mental operations consisting of computational processes over formal elements that constitute the essence of the mental and can be realized in all sorts of different brain processes, in the same way that any computer program can be realized in different computer hardwares: On the assumptions of strong AI, the mind is to the brain as the program is to the hardware, and thus we can understand the mind without doing neurophysiology. If we had to know how the brain worked to do AI, we wouldn't bother with AI. However, even getting this close to the operation of the brain is still not sufficient to produce understanding. To see this, imagine that instead of a monolingual man in a room shuffling symbols we have the man operate an elaborate set of water pipes with valves connecting them. When the man receives the Chinese symbols, he looks up in the program, written in English, which valves he has to turn on and off. Each water connection corresponds to a synapse in the Chinese brain, and the whole system is rigged up so that after doing all the right firings, that is, after turning on all the right faucets, the Chinese answers pop out at the output end of the series of pipes.

Now where is the understanding in this system? It takes Chinese as input, it simulates the formal structure of the synapses of the Chinese brain, and it gives Chinese as output. But the man certainly doesn't understand Chinese, and neither do the water pipes, and if we are tempted to adopt what I think is the absurd view that somehow the *conjunction* of man *and* water pipes understands, remember that in principle the man can internalize the formal structure of the water pipes and do all the "neuron firings" in his imagination. The problem with the brain simulator is that it is simulating the wrong things about the brain. As long as it simulates only the formal structure of the sequence of neuron firings at the synapses, it won't have simulated what matters about the brain, namely its causal properties, its ability to produce intentional states. And that the formal properties are not sufficient for the causal properties is shown by the water pipe example: we can have all the formal properties carved off from the relevant neurobiological causal properties.

4. The Combination Reply (Berkeley and Stanford). "While each of the previous three replies might not be completely convincing by itself as a refutation of the Chinese room counterexample, if you take all three together they are collectively much more convincing and even decisive. Imagine a robot with a brain-shaped computer lodged in its cranial cavity, imagine the computer programmed with all the synapses of a human brain, imagine the whole behavior of the robot is indistinguishable from human behavior, and now think of the whole thing as a unified system and not just as a computer with inputs and outputs. Surely in such a case we would have to ascribe intentionality to the system."

I entirely agree that in such a case we would find it rational and indeed irresistible to accept the hypothesis that the robot had intentionality, as long as we knew nothing more about it. Indeed, besides appearance and behavior, the other elements of the combination are really irrelevant. If we could build a robot whose behavior was indistinguishable over a large range from human behavior, we would attribute intentionality to it, pending some reason not to. We wouldn't need to know in advance that its computer brain was a formal analogue of the human brain.

But I really don't see that this is any help to the claims of strong AI, and here's why: According to strong AI, instantiating a formal program with the right input and output is a sufficient condition of, indeed is constitutive of, intentionality. As Newell . . . puts it, the essence of the mental is the operation of a physical symbol system. But the attributions of intentionality that we make to the robot in this example have nothing to do with formal programs. They are simply based on the assumption that if the robot looks and behaves sufficiently like us, then we would suppose, until proven otherwise, that it must have mental states like ours that cause and are expressed by its behavior and it must have an inner mechanism capable of producing such mental states. If we knew independently how to account for its behavior without such assumptions we would not attribute intentionality to it, especially if we knew it had a formal program. And this is precisely the point of my earlier reply to objection II.

Suppose we knew that the robot's behavior was entirely accounted for by the fact that a man inside it was receiving uninterpreted formal symbols from the robot's sensory receptors and sending out uninterpreted formal symbols to its motor mechanisms, and the man was doing this symbol manipulation in accordance with a bunch of rules. Furthermore, suppose the man knows none of these facts about the robot, all he knows is which operations to perform on which meaningless symbols. In such a case we would regard the robot as an ingenious mechanical dummy. The hypothesis that the dummy has a mind would now be unwarranted and unnecessary, for there is now no longer any reason to ascribe intentionality to the robot or to the system of which it is a part (except of course for the man's intentionality in manipulating the symbols). The formal symbol manipulations go on, the input and output are correctly matched, but the only real locus of intentionality is the man, and he doesn't know any of the relevant intentional states; he doesn't, for example, *see* what comes into the robot's eyes, he doesn't *intend* to move the robot's arm, and he doesn't *understand* any of the remarks made to or by the robot. Nor, for the reasons stated earlier, does the system of which man and robot are a part.

To see this point, contrast this case with cases in which we find it completely natural to ascribe intentionality to members of certain other primate species such as apes and monkeys and to domestic animals such as dogs. The reasons we find it natural are, roughly, two: We can't make sense of the animal's behavior without the ascription of intentionality, and we can see that the beasts are made of similar stuff to ourselves—that is an eye, that a nose, this is its skin, and so on. Given the coherence of the animal's behavior and the assumption of the same causal stuff underlying it, we assume both that the animal must have mental states underlying its behavior, and that the mental states must be produced by mechanisms made out of the stuff that is like our stuff. We would certainly make similar assumptions about the robot unless we had some reason not to, but as soon as we knew that the behavior was the result of a formal program, and that the actual causal properties of the physical substance were irrelevant we would abandon the assumption of intentionality.

There are two other responses to my example that come up frequently (and so are worth discussing) but really miss the point.

5. The Other Minds Reply (Yale). "How do you know that other people understand Chinese or anything else? Only by their behavior. Now the computer can pass the behavioral tests as well as they can (in principle), so if you are going to attribute cognition to other people you must in principle also attribute it to computers."

This objection really is only worth a short reply. The problem in this discussion is not about how I know that other people have cognitive states, but rather what it is that I am attributing to them when I attribute cognitive states to them. The thrust of the argument is that it couldn't be just computational processes and their output because the computational processes and their output can exist without the cognitive state. It is no answer to this argument to feign anesthesia. In "cognitive sciences" one presupposes the reality and knowability of the mental in the same way that in physical sciences one has to presuppose the reality and knowability of physical objects.

6. The Many Mansions Reply (Berkeley). "Your whole argument presupposes that AI is only about analog and digital computers. But that just happens to be the present state of technology. Whatever these causal processes are that you say are essential for intentionality (assuming you are right), eventually we will be able to build devices that have these causal processes, and that will be artificial intelligence. So your arguments are in no way directed at the ability of artificial intelligence to produce and explain cognition."

I really have no objection to this reply save to say that it in effect trivializes the project of strong AI by redefining it as whatever artificially produces and explains cognition. The interest of the original claim made on behalf of artificial intelligence is that it was a precise, well defined thesis: mental processes are computational processes over formally defined elements. I have been concerned to challenge that thesis. If the claim is redefined so that it is no longer that thesis, my objections no longer apply because there is no longer a testable hypothesis for them to apply to.

Let us now return to the question I promised I would try to answer: Granted that in my original example I understand the English and I do not understand the Chinese, and granted therefore that the machine doesn't understand either English or Chinese, still there must be something about me that makes it the case that I understand English and a corresponding something lacking in me that makes it the case that I fail to understand Chinese. Now why couldn't we give those somethings, whatever they are, to a machine?

I see no reason in principle why we couldn't give a machine the capacity to understand English or Chinese, since in an important sense our bodies with our brains are precisely such machines. But I do see very strong arguments for saying that we could not give such a thing to a machine where the operation of the machine is defined solely in terms of computational processes over formally defined elements; that is, where the operation of the machine is defined as an instantiation of a computer program. It is not because I am the instantiation of a computer program that I am able to understand English and have other forms of intentionality (I am, I suppose, the instantiation of any number of computer programs), but as far as we know it is because I am a certain sort of organism with a certain biological (i.e., chemical and physical) structure, and this structure, under certain conditions, is causally capable of producing perception, action, understanding, learning, and other intentional phenomena. And part of the point of the present argument is that only something that had those causal powers could have that intentionality. Perhaps other physical and chemical processes could produce exactly these effects; perhaps, for example,

Martians also have intentionality but their brains are made of different stuff. That is an empirical question, rather like the question whether photosynthesis can be done by something with a chemistry different from that of chlorophyll.

But the main point of the present argument is that no purely formal model will ever be sufficient by itself for intentionality because the formal properties are not by themselves constitutive of intentionality, and they have by themselves no causal powers except the power, when instantiated, to produce the next stage of the formalism when the machine is running. And any other causal properties that particular realizations of the formal model have, are irrelevant to the formal model because we can always put the same formal model in a different realization where those causal properties are obviously absent. Even if, by some miracle, Chinese speakers exactly realize Schank's program, we can put the same program in English speakers, water pipes, or computers, none of which understand Chinese, the program notwithstanding.

What matters about brain operations is not the formal shadow cast by the sequence of synapses but rather the actual properties of the sequences. All the arguments for the strong version of artificial intelligence that I have seen insist on drawing an outline around the shadows cast by cognition and then claiming that the shadows are the real thing.

By way of concluding I want to try to state some of the general philosophical points implicit in the argument. For clarity I will try to do it in a question-and-answer fashion, and I begin with that old chestnut of a question:

"Could a machine think?"

The answer is, obviously, yes. We are precisely such machines.

"Yes, but could an artifact, a man-made machine, think?"

Assuming it is possible to produce artificially a machine with a nervous system, neurons with axons and dendrites, and all the rest of it, sufficiently like ours, again the answer to the question seems to be obviously, yes. If you can exactly duplicate the causes, you could duplicate the effects. And indeed it might be possible to produce consciousness, intentionality, and all the rest of it using some other sorts of chemical principles than those that human beings use. It is, as I said, an empirical question.

"OK, but could a digital computer think?"

If by "digital computer" we mean anything at all that has a level of description where it can correctly be described as the instantiation of a computer program, then again the answer is, of course, yes, since we are the instantiations of any number of computer programs, and we can think.

"But could something think, understand, and so on *solely* in virtue of being a computer with the right sort of program? Could instantiating a program, the right program of course, by itself be a sufficient condition of understanding?"

This I think is the right question to ask, though it is usually confused with one or more of the earlier questions, and the answer to it is no.

"Why not?"

Because the formal symbol manipulations by themselves don't have any intentionality; they are quite meaningless; they aren't even *symbol* manipulations, since the symbols don't symbolize anything. In the linguistic jargon, they have only a syntax but no semantics. Such intentionality as computers appear to have is solely in the minds of those who program them and those who use them, those who send in the input and those who interpret the output.

The aim of the Chinese room example was to try to show this by showing that as soon as we put something into the system that really does have intentionality (a man), and we program him with the formal program, you can see that the formal program carries no additional intentionality. It adds nothing, for example, to a man's ability to understand Chinese.

Precisely that feature of AI that seemed so appealing—the distinction between the program and the realization—proves fatal to the claim that simulation could be duplication. The distinction between the program and its realization in the hardware seems to be parallel to the distinction between the level of mental operations and the level of brain operations. And if we could describe the level of mental operations as a formal program, then it seems we could describe what was essential about the mind without doing either introspective psychology or neurophysiology of the brain. But the equation "mind is to brain as program is to hardware" breaks down at several points, among them the following three:

First, the distinction between program and realization has the consequence that the same program could have all sorts of crazy realizations that had no form of intentionality. Weizenbaum . . . for example, shows in detail how to construct a computer using a roll of toilet paper and a pile of small stones. Similarly, the Chinese story understanding program can be programmed into a sequence of water pipes, a set of wind machines, or a monolingual English speaker, none of which thereby acquires an understanding of Chinese. Stones, toilet paper, wind, and water pipes are the wrong kind of stuff to have intentionality in the first place—only something that has the same causal powers as brains can have intentionality—and though the English speaker has the right kind of stuff for intentionality you can easily see that he doesn't get any extra intentionality by memorizing the program, since memorizing it won't teach him Chinese.

Second, the program is purely formal, but the intentional states are not in that way formal. They are defined in terms of their content, not their form. The belief that it is raining, for example, is not defined as a certain formal shape, but as a certain mental content with conditions of satisfaction, a direction of fit, and the like. Indeed the belief as such hasn't even got a formal shape in this syntactic sense, since one and the same belief can be given an indefinite number of different syntactic expressions in different linguistic systems.

Third, as I mentioned before, mental states and events are literally a product of the operation of the brain, but the program is not in that way a product of the computer.

"Well if programs are in no way constitutive of mental processes, why have so many people believed the converse? That at least needs some explanation."

I don't really know the answer to that one. The idea that computer simulations could be the real thing ought to have seemed suspicious in the first place because the computer isn't confined to simulating mental operations, by any means. No one supposes that computer simulations of a five-alarm fire will burn the neighborhood down or that a computer simulation of a rainstorm will leave us all drenched. Why on earth would anyone suppose that a computer simulation of understanding actually understood anything? It is sometimes said that it would be frightfully hard to get computers to feel pain or fall in love, but love and pain are neither harder nor easier than cognition or anything else. For simulation, all you need is the right input and output and a program in the middle that transforms the former into the latter. That is all the computer has for anything it does. To confuse simulation with duplication is the same mistake, whether it is pain, love, cognition, fires, or rainstorms.

Still, there are several reasons why AI must have seemed—and to many people perhaps still does seem—in some way to reproduce and thereby explain mental phenomena, and I believe we will not succeed in removing these illusions until we have fully exposed the reasons that give rise to them.

First, and perhaps most important, is a confusion about the notion of "information processing": many people in cognitive science believe that the human brain, with its mind, does something called "information processing," and analogously the computer with its program does information processing; but fires and rainstorms, on the other hand, don't do information processing at all. Thus, though the computer can simulate the formal features of any process whatever, it stands in a special relation to the mind and brain because when the computer is properly programmed, ideally with the same program as the brain, the information processing is identical in the two cases, and this information processing is really the essence of the mental. But the trouble with this argument is that it rests on an ambiguity in the notion of "information." In the sense in which people "process information" when they reflect, say, on problems in arithmetic or when they read and answer questions about stories, the programmed computer does not do "information processing." Rather, what it does is manipulate formal symbols. The fact that the programmer and the interpreter of the computer output use the symbols to stand for objects in the world is totally beyond the scope of the computer. The computer, to repeat, has a syntax but no semantics. Thus, if you type into the computer "2 plus 2 equals?" it will type out "4." But it has no idea that "4" means 4 or that it means anything at all. And the point is not that it lacks some second-order information about the interpretation of its first-order symbols, but rather that its first-order symbols don't have any interpretations as far as the computer is concerned. All the computer has is more symbols. The introduction of the notion of "information processing" therefore produces a dilemma: either we construe the notion of "information processing" in such a way that it implies intentionality as part of the process or we don't. If the former, then the programmed computer does not do information processing, it only manipulates formal symbols. If the latter, then, though the computer does information processing, it is only doing so in the sense in which adding machines, typewriters, stomachs, thermostats, rainstorms, and hurricanes do information processing; namely, they have a level of description at which we can describe them as taking information in at one end, transforming it, and producing information as output. But in this case it is up to outside observers to interpret the input and output as information in the ordinary sense. And no similarity is established between the computer and the brain in terms of any similarity of information processing.

Second, in much of AI there is a residual behaviorism or operationalism. Since appropriately programmed computers can have input-output patterns similar to those of human beings, we are tempted to postulate mental states in the computer similar to human mental states. But once we see that it is both conceptually and empirically possible for a system to have human capacities in some realm without having any intentionality at all, we should be able to overcome this impulse. My desk adding machine has calculating capacities, but no intentionality, and in this paper I have tried to show that a system could have input and output capabilities that duplicated those of a native Chinese speaker and still not understand Chinese, regardless of how it was programmed. The Turing test is typical of the tradition in being unashamedly behavioristic and operationalistic, and I believe that if AI workers totally repudiated behaviorism and operationalism much of the confusion between simulation and duplication would be eliminated.

Third, this residual operationalism is joined to a residual form of dualism; indeed strong AI only makes sense given the dualistic assumption that, where the mind is concerned, the brain doesn't matter. In strong AI (and in functionalism, as well) what matters are programs, and programs are independent of their realization in machines; indeed, as far as AI is concerned, the same program could be realized by an electronic machine, a Cartesian mental substance, or a Hegelian world spirit. The single most surprising discovery that I have made in discussing these issues is that many AI workers are quite shocked by my idea that actual human mental phenomena might be dependent on actual physical-chemical properties of actual human brains. But if you think about it a minute you can see that I should not have been surprised; for unless you accept some form of dualism, the strong AI project hasn't got a chance. The project is to reproduce and explain the mental by designing programs, but unless the mind is not only conceptually but empirically independent of the brain you couldn't carry out the project, for the program is completely independent of any realization. Unless you believe that the mind is separable from the brain both conceptually and empirically—dualism in a strong form—you cannot hope to reproduce the mental by writing and running programs since programs must be independent of brains or any other particular forms of instantiation. If mental operations consist in computational operations on formal symbols, then it follows that they have no interesting connection with the brain; the only connection would be that the brain just happens to be one of the indefinitely many types of machines capable of instantiating the program. This form of dualism is not the traditional Cartesian variety that claims there are two sorts of *substances,* but it is Cartesian in the sense that it insists that what is specifically mental about the mind has no intrinsic connection with the actual properties of the brain. This underlying dualism is masked from us by the fact that AI literature contains frequent fulminations against "dualism"; what the authors seem to be unaware of is that their position presupposes a strong version of dualism.

"Could a machine think?" My own view is that *only* a machine could think, and indeed only very special kinds of machines, namely brains and machines that had the same causal powers as brains. And that is the main reason strong AI has had little to tell us about thinking, since it has nothing to tell us about machines. By its own definition, it is about programs, and programs are not machines. Whatever else intentionality is, it is a biological phenomenon, and it is as likely to be as causally dependent on the specific biochemistry of its origins as lactation, photosynthesis, or any other biological phenomena. No one would suppose that we could produce milk and sugar by running a computer simulation of the formal sequences in lactation and photosynthesis, but where the mind is concerned many people are willing to believe in such a miracle because of a deep and abiding dualism: the mind they suppose is a matter of formal processes and is independent of quite specific material causes in the way that milk and sugar are not.

In defense of this dualism the hope is often expressed that the brain is a digital computer (early computers, by the way, were often called "electronic brains"). But that is no help. Of course the brain is a digital computer. Since everything is a digital computer, brains are too. The point is that the brain's causal capacity to produce intentionality cannot consist in its instantiating a computer program, since for any program you like it is possible for something to instantiate that program and still not have any mental states. Whatever it is that the brain does to produce intentionality, it cannot consist in instantiating a program since no program, by itself, is sufficient for intentionality.

The Puzzle of Conscious Experience

DAVID J. CHALMERS (1966–) studied mathematics at Adelaide University and as a Rhodes Scholar at Oxford University, but an interest with consciousness led him into philosophy and cognitive science. He has a PhD in these fields from Indiana University. Chalmers is a professor of philosophy and the Director of the Center for Consciousness Studies at the University of Arizona, and is presently establishing a research center on consciousness at Australian National University. He has published numerous articles on artificial intelligence and the philosophy of mind, as well as a much-debated book entitled *The Conscious Mind* (Oxford University Press, 1996).

THINKING QUESTIONS

David J. Chalmers, *The Puzzle of Conscious Experience*

1. Chalmers distinguishes between the easy problems and the hard problem of consciousness. What is the hard problem that he identifies?
2. If you knew everything there was to know about coffee (its chemical properties, the method of harvesting and roasting, the means of brewing, the interaction between coffee compounds and the taste buds, etc.) but had never sampled any, do you think you would know what coffee tastes like?
3. Chalmers believes that science could discover the neural correlates of conscious experience, but that such discoveries would still fail to explain why there is conscious experience *at all*. Do you think he is right, or that in such a case there would be nothing left to explain after all?
4. Chalmers argues that consciousness—like mass, space-time, and various physical forces—should be considered a fundamental, irreducible feature of the world. In his view, there would be physical laws and psychophysical ones. What would the psychophysical laws do?
5. Why does Chalmers think that consciousness might someday be realized in machines (by which he means digital computers)? What is his argument? How do you think he might respond to Searle's argument that nonbiological mentality is not possible?
6. Chalmers suggests that psychophysical laws might fundamentally involve the idea of *information*. What does he mean by "information"? What is Chalmers's reasoning here?

THE HARD PROBLEM

Researchers use the word "consciousness" in many different ways. To clarify the issues, we first have to separate the problems that are often clustered together under the name. For this purpose, I find it useful to distinguish between the "easy problems" and the "hard problem" of consciousness. The easy problems are by no means trivial—they are actually as challenging as most in psychology and biology—but it is with the hard problem that the central mystery lies.

The easy problems of consciousness include the following: How can a human subject discriminate sensory stimuli and react to them appropriately? How does the brain integrate information from many different sources and use this information to control behavior? How is it that subjects can verbalize their internal states? Although all these questions are associated with consciousness, they all concern the objective mechanisms of the cognitive system. Consequently, we have every reason to expect that continued work in cognitive psychology and neuroscience will answer them.

The hard problem, in contrast, is the question of how physical processes in the brain give rise to subjective experience. This puzzle involves the inner aspect of thought and perception: the way things feel for the subject. When we see, for example, we experience visual sensations, such as that of vivid blue. Or think of the ineffable sound of a distant oboe, the agony of an intense pain, the sparkle of happiness or the meditative quality of a moment lost in thought. All are part of what I am calling consciousness. It is these phenomena that pose the real mystery of the mind.

To illustrate the distinction, consider a thought experiment devised by the Australian philosopher Frank Jackson. Suppose that Mary, a neuroscientist in the 23rd century, is the world's leading expert on the brain processes responsible for color vision. But Mary has lived her whole life in a black-and-white room and has never seen any other colors. She knows everything there is to know about physical processes in the brain—its biology, structure and function. This understanding enables her to grasp everything there is to know about the easy problems: how the brain discriminates stimuli, integrates information and produces verbal reports. From her knowledge of color vision, she knows the way color names correspond with wavelengths on the light spectrum. But there is still something crucial about color vision that Mary does not know: what it is like to experience a color such as red. It follows that there are facts about conscious experience that cannot be deduced from physical facts about the functioning of the brain.

Indeed, nobody knows why these physical processes are accompanied by conscious experience at all. Why is it that when our brains process light of a certain wavelength, we have an experience of deep purple? Why do we have any experience at all? Could not an unconscious automaton have performed the same tasks just as well? These are questions that we would like a theory of consciousness to answer.

I am not denying that consciousness arises from the brain. We know, for example, that the subjective experience of vision is closely linked to processes in the visual cortex. It is the link itself that perplexes, however. Remarkably, subjective experience seems to emerge from a physical process. But we have no idea how or why this is.

IS NEUROSCIENCE ENOUGH?

Given the flurry of recent work on consciousness in neuroscience and psychology, one might think this mystery is starting to be cleared up. On closer examination, however, it turns out that almost all the current work addresses only the easy problems of consciousness. The confidence of the reductionist view comes from the progress on the easy problems, but none of this makes any difference where the hard problem is concerned.

Consider the hypothesis put forward by neurobiologists Francis Crick of the Salk Institute for Biological Studies in San Diego and Christof Koch of the California Institute of Technology. They suggest that consciousness may arise from certain oscillations in the cerebral cortex, which become synchronized as neurons fire 40 times per second. Crick and Koch believe the phenomenon might explain how different attributes of a single perceived object (its color and shape, for example), which are processed in different parts of the brain, are merged into a coherent whole. In this theory, two pieces of information become bound together precisely when they are represented by synchronized neural firings.

The hypothesis could conceivably elucidate one of the easy problems about how information is integrated in the brain. But why should synchronized oscillations give rise to a visual experience, no matter how much integration is taking place? This question involves the hard problem, about which the theory has nothing to offer. Indeed, Crick and Koch are agnostic about whether the hard problem can be solved by science at all.

The same kind of critique could be applied to almost all the recent work on consciousness. In his 1991 book *Consciousness Explained,* philosopher Daniel C. Dennett laid out a sophisticated theory of how numerous independent processes in the brain combine to produce a coherent response to a perceived event. The theory might do much to explain how we produce verbal reports on our internal states, but it tells us very little about why there should be a subjective experience behind these reports. Like other reductionist theories, Dennett's is a theory of the easy problems.

The critical common trait among these easy problems is that they all concern how a cognitive or behavioral function is performed. All are ultimately questions about how the brain carries out some task—how it discriminates stimuli, integrates information, produces reports and so on. Once neurobiology specifies appropriate neural mechanisms, showing how the functions are performed, the easy problems are solved.

The hard problem of consciousness, in contrast, goes beyond problems about how functions are performed. Even if every behavioral and cognitive function related to consciousness were explained, there would still remain a further mystery: Why is the performance of these functions accompanied by conscious experience? It is this additional conundrum that makes the hard problem hard.

THE EXPLANATORY GAP

Some have suggested that to solve the hard problem, we need to bring in new tools of physical explanation: nonlinear dynamics, say, or new discoveries in neuroscience, or quantum mechanics. But these ideas suffer from exactly the same difficulty. Consider a proposal from Stuart R. Hameroff of the University of Arizona and Roger Penrose of the University of Oxford. They hold that consciousness arises from quantum-physical processes taking place in microtubules, which are protein structures inside neurons. It is possible (if not likely) that such a hypothesis will lead to an explanation of how the brain makes decisions or even how it proves mathematical theorems, as Hameroff and Penrose suggest. But even if it does, the theory is silent about how these processes might give rise to conscious experience. Indeed, the same problem arises with any theory of consciousness based only on physical processing.

The trouble is that physical theories are best suited to explaining why systems have a certain physical structure and how they perform various functions. Most problems in science have this form; to explain life, for example, we need to describe how a physical system can reproduce, adapt and metabolize. But consciousness is a different sort of problem entirely, as it goes beyond the explanation of structure and function.

Of course, neuroscience is not irrelevant to the study of consciousness. For one, it may be able to reveal the nature of the neural correlate of consciousness—the brain processes most directly associated with conscious experience. It may even give a detailed correspondence between specific processes in the brain and related components of experience. But until we know why these processes give rise to conscious experience at all, we will not have crossed what philosopher Joseph Levine has called the explanatory gap between physical processes and consciousness. Making that leap will demand a new kind of theory.

A TRUE THEORY OF EVERYTHING

In searching for an alternative, a key observation is that not all entities in science are explained in terms of more basic entities. In physics, for example, space-time, mass and charge (among other things) are regarded as fundamental features of the world, as they are not reducible to anything simpler. Despite this irreducibility, detailed and useful theories relate these entities to one another in terms of fundamental laws. Together these features and laws explain a great variety of complex and subtle phenomena.

It is widely believed that physics provides a complete catalogue of the universe's fundamental features and laws. As physicist Steven Weinberg puts it in his 1992 book *Dreams of a Final Theory*, the goal of physics is a "theory of everything" from which all there is to know about the universe can be derived. But Weinberg concedes that there is a problem with consciousness. Despite the power of physical theory, the existence of consciousness does not seem to be derivable from physical laws. He defends physics by arguing that it might eventually explain what he calls the objective correlates of consciousness (that is, the neural correlates), but of course to do this is not to explain consciousness itself. If the existence of consciousness cannot be derived from physical laws, a theory of physics is not a true theory of everything. So a final theory must contain an additional fundamental component.

Toward this end, I propose that conscious experience be considered a fundamental feature, irreducible to anything more basic. The idea may seem strange at first, but consistency seems to demand it. In the 19th century it turned out that electromagnetic phenomena could not be explained in terms of previously known principles. As a consequence, scientists introduced electromagnetic charge as a new fundamental entity and studied the associated fundamental laws. Similar reasoning should apply to consciousness. If existing fundamental theories cannot encompass it, then something new is required.

Where there is a fundamental property, there are fundamental laws. In this case, the laws must relate experience to elements of physical theory. These laws will almost certainly not interfere with those of the physical world; it seems that the latter form a closed system in their own right. Rather the laws will serve as a bridge, specifying how experience depends on underlying physical processes. It is this bridge that will cross the explanatory gap.

Thus, a complete theory will have two components: physical laws, telling us about the behavior of physical systems from the infinitesimal to the cosmological, and what we might call psychophysical laws, telling us how some of those systems are associated with conscious experience. These two components will constitute a true theory of everything.

SEARCHING FOR A THEORY

Supposing for the moment that they exist, how might we uncover such psychophysical laws? The greatest hindrance in this pursuit will be a lack of data. As I have described it, consciousness is subjective, so there is no direct way to monitor it by others. But this difficulty is an obstacle, not a dead end. For a start, each one of us has access to our own experiences, a rich trove that can be used to formulate theories. We can also plausibly rely on indirect information, such as subjects' descriptions of their experiences. Philosophical arguments and thought experiments also have a role to play. Such methods have limitations, but they give us more than enough to get started.

These theories will not be conclusively testable, so they will inevitably be more speculative than those of more conventional scientific disciplines. Nevertheless, there is no reason they should not be strongly constrained to account accurately for our own first-person experiences, as well as the evidence from subjects' reports. If we find a theory that fits the data better than any other theory of equal simplicity, we will have good reason to accept it. Right now we do not have even a single theory that fits the data, so worries about testability are premature.

We might start by looking for high-level bridging laws, connecting physical processes to experience at an everyday level. The basic contour of such a law might be gleaned from the observation that when we are conscious of something, we are generally able to act on it and speak about it—which are objective, physical functions. Conversely, when some information is directly available for action and speech, it is generally conscious. Thus, consciousness correlates well with what we might call "awareness": the process by which information in the brain is made globally available to motor processes such as speech and bodily action.

The notion may seem trivial. But as defined here, awareness is objective and physical, whereas consciousness is not. Some refinements to the definition of awareness are needed, in order to extend the concept to animals and infants, which cannot speak. But at least in familiar cases, it is possible to see the rough outlines of a psychophysical law: where there is awareness, there is consciousness, and vice versa.

To take this line of reasoning a step further, consider the structure present in the conscious experience. The experience of a field of vision, for example, is a constantly changing mosaic of colors, shapes and patterns and as such has a detailed geometric structure. The fact that we can describe this structure, reach out in the direction of many of its components and perform other actions that depend on it suggests that the structure corresponds directly to that of the information made available in the brain through the neural processes of awareness.

Similarly, our experiences of color have an intrinsic three-dimensional structure that is mirrored in the structure of information processes in the brain's visual cortex. This structure is illustrated in the color wheels and charts used by artists. Colors are arranged in a systematic pattern—red to green on one axis, blue to yellow on another, and black to white on a third. Colors that are close to one another on a color wheel are experienced as similar. It is extremely likely that they also correspond to similar perceptual representations in the brain, as part of a system of complex three-dimensional coding among neurons that is not yet fully understood. We can recast the underlying concept as a principle of structural coherence: the structure of conscious experience is mirrored by the structure of information in awareness, and vice versa.

Another candidate for a psychophysical law is a principle of organizational invariance. It holds that physical systems with the same abstract organization will give rise to the same kind of conscious experience, no matter what they are made of. For example, if the precise interactions between our neurons could be duplicated with silicon chips, the same conscious experience would arise. The idea is somewhat controversial, but I believe it is strongly supported by thought experiments describing the gradual replacement of neurons by silicon chips. The remarkable implication is that consciousness might someday be achieved in machines.

INFORMATION: PHYSICAL AND EXPERIENTIAL

The ultimate goal of a theory of consciousness is a simple and elegant set of fundamental laws, analogous to the fundamental laws of physics. The principles described above are unlikely to be fundamental, however. Rather they seem to be high-level psychophysical laws, analogous to macroscopic principles in physics such as those of thermodynamics or kinematics. What might the underlying fundamental laws be? No one knows, but I don't mind speculating.

I suggest that the primary psychophysical laws may centrally involve the concept of information. The abstract notion of information, as put forward in the 1940s by Claude E. Shannon of the Massachusetts Institute of Technology, is that of a set of separate states with a basic structure of similarities and differences between them. We can think of a 10-bit binary code as an information state, for example. Such information states can be embodied in the physical world. This happens whenever they correspond to physical states (voltages, say); the differences between them can be transmitted along some pathway, such as a telephone line.

We can also find information embodied in conscious experience. The pattern of color patches in a visual field, for example, can be seen as analogous to that of the pixels covering a display screen. Intriguingly, it turns out that we find the same information states embedded in conscious experience and in underlying physical processes in the brain. The three-dimensional encoding of color spaces, for example, suggests that the information state in a color experience corresponds directly to an information state in the brain. We might even regard the two states as distinct aspects of a single information state, which is simultaneously embodied in both physical processing and conscious experience.

A natural hypothesis ensues. Perhaps information, or at least some information, has two basic aspects: a physical one and an experiential one. This hypothesis has the status of a fundamental principle that might underlie the relation between physical processes and experience. Wherever we find conscious experience, it exists as one aspect of an information state, the other aspect of which is embedded in a physical process in the brain. This proposal needs to be fleshed out to make a satisfying theory. But it fits nicely with the principles mentioned earlier—systems with the same organization will embody the same information, for example—and it could explain numerous features of our conscious experience.

The idea is at least compatible with several others, such as physicist John A. Wheeler's suggestion that information is fundamental to the physics of the universe. The laws of physics might ultimately be cast in informational terms, in which case we would have a satisfying congruence between the constructs in both physical and psychophysical laws. It may even be that a theory of physics and a theory of consciousness could eventually be consolidated into a single grander theory of information.

A potential problem is posed by the ubiquity of information. Even a thermostat embodies some information, for example, but is it conscious? There are at least two possible responses. First, we could constrain the fundamental laws so that only some information has an experiential aspect, perhaps depending on how it is physically processed. Second, we might bite the bullet and allow that all information has an experiential aspect—where there is complex information processing, there is complex experience, and where there is simple information processing, there is simple experience. If this is so, then even a thermostat might have experiences, although they would be much simpler than even a basic color experience, and there would certainly be no accompanying emotions or thoughts. This seems odd at first, but if experience is truly fundamental, we might expect it to be widespread. In any case, the choice between these alternatives should depend on which can be integrated into the most powerful theory.

Of course, such ideas may be all wrong. On the other hand, they might evolve into a more powerful proposal that predicts the precise structure of our conscious experience from physical processes in our brains. If this project succeeds, we will have good reason to accept the theory. If it fails, other avenues will be pursued, and alternative fundamental theories may be developed. In this way, we may one day resolve the greatest mystery of the mind.

Personal Identity

Personal identity is the philosophical issue of what makes you *you*. Who are you exactly? *What* are you? There are two main problems with personal identity, and what makes these problems especially tricky is that any solution to the first precludes a solution to the second, and vice versa. They are the problems of sameness and difference.

The Problem of Sameness. You probably think that you were once a baby. Your parents showed you pictures of a baby and said it was you—something you accepted without question, despite the fact that you look nothing like a baby. Of course, you are not a baby *now,* but supposedly you were once a baby. But what does this mean exactly? The claim is that a baby of, say, 20 years ago is identical to a particular philosophy student of today. In other words,

Philosophy student now = baby at now − 20 years.

The claim is not that you resemble such a baby, but in fact that you are *identical* to the baby of two decades ago. That baby is *you*. But why on earth should we think that you are identical to a baby of long ago? You have virtually nothing in common with such a baby: you don't look alike (except vaguely), aren't the same height or weight, don't have the same abilities, interests or thoughts, don't have the same tastes, friends, or knowledge. In fact, you have almost nothing in common; you have much more in common with your friends. They at least are about the same size as you, dress similarly, have comparable skills, musical tastes, knowledge of the world, etc. So why say that baby of 20 years ago is *you*?

The Problem of Difference. You probably think that you are different from your friends and classmates; you are different people. Yet what makes you different? Well, you might cite a host of subtle things—differences in appearance, beliefs, interests, fashion, favorite foods. All well and good, but the very things that prove you are not identical to your friends also seem to prove that you are not identical to a baby of 20 years ago. You don't share any of those things with that baby either.

The problem of sameness is explaining what makes you identical to some baby of long ago. The problem of difference is explaining what makes you non-identical to other people. The problem of personal identity is how to give an answer that solves both the sameness and difference problems simultaneously. The qualities you share with the baby you also (or might also) share with other people, and the qualities that distinguish you from others also seem to differ you from the baby. For example, one might propose this as an answer to the problem of sameness: you are the same as the baby because you have the same DNA as that baby. Unfortunately, this is a poor solution to the problem of difference, as identical twins have the same DNA but are different people. So it is not an acceptable answer to the overall problem of personal identity. Likewise, one might suggest that this is an answer to the problem of difference: you are different from others because no one has exactly your physical characteristics (height, weight, hairstyle, pimples, etc.). Yet this is a poor answer to the problem of sameness, as you and some baby of 20 years ago don't have those physical features in common either.

So how can we solve both aspects of personal identity at once? One radical solution, as seen in the readings by Hume and Parfit, is the Bundle Theory. In essence, this view denies that there is any persistence over time, it denies that you were ever once a baby, it rejects the problem of sameness as being a real problem at all. Another answer, defended by Locke, is the continuing consciousness view (also known as the memory criterion, or the psychological criterion). Locke thinks it is the continuity of one's mental life that both makes one different from others and the same over time. Sacks and Demasio present some challenging case studies for this idea. Another proposal is that perhaps we, like everything else in the universe, are physical things. Perhaps we are merely our bodies or maybe we are just our brains and our bodies are along for the ride. Dennett considers this physicalist view. As you will see in the readings, all of the available solutions have their pros and cons; personal identity is a recondite conundrum.

Where Am I?

DANIEL DENNETT (1942–) is University Professor and Director of the Center for Cognitive Studies at Tufts University. Educated at Harvard and Oxford, Dennett has published 10 books and over 200 articles on the nature of the mind, the self, and free will. He has received numerous awards and has lectured all over the world. His most recent books are *Freedom Evolves* (2003) and *Darwin's Dangerous Idea* (1995).

THINKING QUESTIONS

Daniel Dennett, *Where Am I?*

1. The removal of Dennett's brain is, of course, fictional. Does that matter for gleaning philosophical insights from his tale? Keep in mind that future technological and medical advances are likely to make his story possible.
2. Dennett labels his body "Hamlet" and his brain "Yorick." Does Dennett = Yorick, does Dennett = Hamlet, or does Dennett = Hamlet + Yorick? Keep in mind that with both of the latter options, Dennett dies when Hamlet dies underneath Tulsa.
3. You can lose your hand and still survive. You can lose your arm and still survive. You can lose both an arm and a leg and still survive. Why not think you can lose your entire body and still survive?
4. Is Dennett where his point of view is? Notice that his point of view changes rapidly from being with Hamlet to being with Yorick.
5. What is the salient difference between Hamlet and the new body Fortinbras? If you think that being embodied is essential to Dennett, will any body do? Or is Hamlet required? How is replacing Hamlet with Fortinbras really any different from slowly changing the parts of Hamlet (losing some cells and replacing them with new cells, for example) until one arrives at a whole new body?
6. If Dennett is Hamlet, Yorick, Fortinbras, or any combination of those things, then he is a physical object. Do you think that you are no more than a physical object? Perhaps you are your brain, or even a portion of your brain.
7. If Dennett is not physical at all, but instead is identical with his continuing psychology, then it seems possible that Dennett might survive his brain's death if his psychology could be preserved in a

computer. Again, perhaps it is only a matter of time before this is possible. Do you think that this is really a form of *survival*?

8. If Yorick should die, would Hubert's continuance constitute Dennett's survival?

NOW THAT I'VE WON MY SUIT under the Freedom of Information Act, I am at liberty to reveal for the first time a curious episode in my life that may be of interest not only to those engaged in research in the philosophy of mind, artificial intelligence and neuroscience but also to the general public.

Several years ago I was approached by Pentagon officials who asked me to volunteer for a highly dangerous and secret mission. In collaboration with NASA and Howard Hughes, the Department of Defense was spending billions to develop a Supersonic Tunneling Underground Device, or STUD. It was supposed to tunnel through the earth's core at great speed and deliver a specially designed atomic warhead "right up the Red's missile silos," as one of the Pentagon brass put it.

The problem was that in an early test they had succeeded in lodging a warhead about a mile deep under Tulsa, Oklahoma, and they wanted me to retrieve it for them. "Why me?" I asked. Well, the mission involved some pioneering applications of current brain research, and they had heard of my interest in brains and of course my Faustian curiosity and great courage and so forth. . . . Well, how could I refuse? The difficulty that brought the Pentagon to my door was that the device I'd been asked to recover was fiercely radioactive, in a new way. According to monitoring instruments, something about the nature of the device and its complex interactions with pockets of material deep in the earth had produced radiation that could cause severe abnormalities in certain tissues of the brain. No way had been found to shield the brain from these deadly rays, which were apparently harmless to other tissues and organs of the body. So it had been decided that the person sent to recover the device should *leave his brain behind*. It would be kept in a safe place where it could execute its normal control functions by elaborate radio links. Would I submit to a surgical procedure that would completely remove my brain, which would then be placed in a life-support system at the Manned Spacecraft Center in Houston? Each input and output pathway, as it was severed, would be restored by a pair of microminiaturized radio transceivers, one attached precisely to the brain, the other to the nerve stumps in the empty cranium. No information would be lost, all the connectivity would be preserved. At first I was a bit reluctant. Would it really work? The Houston brain surgeons encouraged me. "Think of it," they said, "as a mere *stretching* of the nerves. If your brain were just moved over an *inch* in your skull, that would not alter or impair your mind. We're simply going to make the nerves indefinitely elastic by splicing radio links into them."

I was shown around the life-support lab in Houston and saw the sparkling new vat in which my brain would be placed, were I to agree. I met the large and brilliant support team of neurologists, hematologists, biophysicists, and electrical engineers, and after several days of discussions and demonstrations, I agreed to give it a try. I was subjected to an enormous array of blood tests, brain scans, experiments, interviews, and the like. They took down my autobiography at great length, recorded tedious lists of my beliefs, hopes, fears, and tastes. They even listed my favorite stereo recordings and gave me a crash session of psychoanalysis.

The day for surgery arrived at last and of course I was anesthetized and remember nothing of the operation itself. When I came out of anesthesia, I opened my eyes, looked around, and asked the inevitable, the traditional, the lamentably hackneyed post-operative question: "Where am I?" The nurse smiled down at me. "You're in Houston," she said, and I reflected that this still had a good chance of being the truth one way or another. She handed me a mirror. Sure enough, there were the tiny antennae poking up through their titanium ports cemented into my skull.

"I gather the operation was a success," I said, "I want to go see my brain." They led me (I was a bit dizzy and unsteady) down a long corridor and into the life-support lab. A cheer went up from the assembled support team, and I responded with what I hoped was a jaunty salute. Still feeling lightheaded, I was helped over to the life-support vat. I peered through the glass. There, floating in what looked like ginger-ale, was undeniably a human brain, though it was almost covered with printed circuit chips, plastic tubules, electrodes, and other paraphernalia. "Is that mine?" I asked. "Hit the output transmitter switch there on the side of the vat and see for yourself," the project director replied. I moved the switch to OFF, and immediately slumped, groggy and nauseated, into the arms of the technicians, one of whom kindly restored the switch to its ON position. While I recovered my equilibrium and composure, I thought to myself: "Well, here I am, sitting on a folding chair, staring through a piece of plate glass at my own brain. . . . But wait," I said to myself, "shouldn't I have thought, 'Here I am, suspended in a bubbling fluid, being stared at by my own eyes'?" I tried to think this latter thought. I tried to project it into the tank, offering it hopefully to my brain, but I failed to carry off the exercise with any conviction. I tried again. "Here am *I,* Daniel Dennett, suspended in a bubbling fluid, being stared at by my own eyes." No, it just didn't work. Most puzzling and confusing. Being a philosopher of firm physicalist conviction, I believed unswervingly that the tokening of my thoughts was occurring somewhere in my brain: yet, when I thought "Here I am," where the thought occurred to me was *here,* outside the vat, where I, Dennett, was standing staring at my brain.

I tried and tried to think myself into the vat, but to no avail. I tried to build up to the task by doing mental exercises. I thought to myself, "The sun is shining *over there,*" five times in rapid succession, each time mentally ostending a different place: in order, the sun-lit corner of the lab, the visible front lawn of the hospital, Houston, Mars, and Jupiter. I found I had little difficulty in getting my "there's" to hop all over the celestial map with their proper references. I could loft a "there" in an instant through the farthest reaches of space, and then aim the next "there" with pinpoint accuracy at the upper left quadrant of a freckle on my arm. Why was I having such trouble with "here"? "Here in Houston" worked well enough, and so did "here in the lab," and even "here in this part of the lab," but "here in the vat" always seemed merely an unmeant mental mouthing. I tried closing my eyes while thinking it. This seemed to help, but still I couldn't manage to pull it off, except perhaps for a fleeting instant. I couldn't be sure. The discovery that I couldn't be sure was also unsettling. How did I know *where* I meant by "here" when I thought "here"? Could I *think* I meant one place when in fact I meant another? I didn't see how that could be admitted without untying the few bonds of intimacy between a person and his own mental life that had survived the onslaught of the brain scientists and philosophers, the physicalists and behaviorists. Perhaps I was incorrigible about where I *meant* when I said "here." But in my present circumstances it seemed that either I was doomed by sheer force of mental habit to thinking systematically false indexical thoughts, or where a person is (and hence where his thoughts are tokened for purposes of semantic analysis) is not necessarily where his brain, the physical seat of his soul, resides. Nagged by confusion, I attempted to orient myself by falling back on a favorite philosopher's ploy. I began naming things.

"Yorick," I said aloud to my brain, "you are my brain. The rest of my body, seated in this chair, I dub 'Hamlet.'" So here we all are: Yorick's my brain, Hamlet's my body, and I am Dennett. *Now,* where am I? And when I think "where am I?" where's that thought tokened? Is it tokened in my brain, lounging about in the vat, or right here between my ears where it *seems* to be tokened? Or nowhere? Its *temporal* coordinates give me no trouble; must it not have spatial coordinates as well? I began making a list of the alternatives.

(1) *Where Hamlet goes, there goes Dennett.* This principle was easily refuted by appeal to the familiar brain transplant thought-experiments so enjoyed by philosophers. If Tom and Dick switch brains, Tom is the fellow with Dick's former body—just ask him; he'll claim to be Tom, and tell you the most intimate details of Tom's autobiography. It was clear enough, then, that my current body and I could part company, but not likely that I could be separated from my brain. The rule of thumb that emerged so plainly from the thought experiments was that in a brain-transplant operation, one wanted to be the *donor,* not the recipient. Better to call such an operation a *body*-transplant, in fact. So perhaps the truth was,

(2) *Where Yorick goes, there goes Dennett.* This was not at all appealing, however. How could I be in the vat and not about to go anywhere, when I was so obviously outside the vat looking in and beginning to make guilty plans to return to my room for a substantial lunch? This begged the question I realized, but it still seemed to be getting at something important. Casting about for some support for my intuition, I hit upon a legalistic sort of argument that might have appealed to Locke.

Suppose, I argued to myself, I were now to fly to California, rob a bank, and be apprehended. In which state would I be tried: In California, where the robbery took place, or in Texas, where the brains of the outfit were located? Would I be a California felon with an out-of-state brain, or a Texas felon remotely controlling an accomplice of sorts in California? It seemed possible that I might beat such a rap just on the undecidability of that jurisdictional question, though perhaps it would be deemed an inter-state, and hence Federal, offense. In any event, suppose I were convicted. Was it likely that California would be satisfied to throw Hamlet into the brig, knowing that Yorick was living the good life and luxuriously taking the waters in Texas? Would Texas incarcerate Yorick, leaving Hamlet free to take the next boat to Rio? This alternative appealed to me. Barring capital punishment or other cruel and unusual punishment, the state would be obliged to maintain the life-support system for Yorick though they might move him from Houston to Leavenworth, and aside from the unpleasantness of the opprobrium, I, for one, would not mind at all and would consider myself a free man under those circumstances. If the state has an interest in forcibly relocating persons in institutions, it would fail to relocate me in any institution by locating Yorick there. If this were true, it suggested a third alternative.

(3) *Dennett is wherever he thinks he is*. Generalized, the claim was as follows: At any given time a person has a *point of view,* and the location of the point of view (which is determined internally by the content of the point of view) is also the location of the person.

Such a proposition is not without its perplexities, but to me it seemed a step in the right direction. The only trouble was that it seemed to place one in a heads-I-win/tails-you-lose situation of unlikely infallibility as regards location. Hadn't I myself often been wrong about where I was, and at least as often uncertain? Couldn't one get lost? Of course, but getting lost *geographically* is not the only way one might get lost. If one were lost in the woods one could attempt to reassure oneself with the consolation that at least one knew where one was: one was right *here* in the familiar surroundings of one's own body. Perhaps in this case one would not have drawn one's attention too much to be thankful for. Still, there were worse plights imaginable, and I wasn't sure I wasn't in such a plight right now.

Point of view clearly had something to do with personal location, but it was itself an unclear notion. It was obvious that the content of one's point of view was not the same as or determined by the content of one's beliefs or thoughts. For example, what should we say about the point of view of the Cinerama viewer who shrieks and twists in his seat as the roller-coaster footage overcomes his psychic distancing? Has he forgotten that he is safely seated in the theater? Here I was inclined to say that the person is experiencing an illusory shift in point of view. In other cases, my inclination to call such shifts illusory was less strong. The workers in laboratories and plants who handle dangerous materials by operating feedback-controlled mechanical arms and hands undergo a shift in point of view that is crisper and more pronounced than anything Cinerama can provoke. They can feel the heft and slipperiness of the containers they manipulate with their metal fingers. They know perfectly well where they are and are not fooled into false beliefs by the experience, yet it is as if they were inside the isolation chamber they are peering into. With mental effort, they can manage to shift their point of view back and forth, rather like making a transparent Necker cube or an Escher drawing change orientation before one's eyes. It does seem extravagant to suppose that in performing this bit of mental gymnastics, they are transporting *themselves* back and forth.

Still their example gave me hope. If I was in fact in the vat in spite of my intuitions, I might be able to train myself to adopt that point of view even as a matter of habit. I should dwell on images of myself comfortably floating in my vat, beaming volitions to that familiar body *out there*. I reflected that the ease or difficulty of this task was presumably independent of the truth about the location of one's brain. Had I been practicing before the operation, I might now be finding it second nature. You might now yourself try such a *tromp l'oeil*. Imagine you have written an inflammatory letter which has been published in the *Times,* the result of which is that the Government has chosen to impound your brain for a probationary period of three years in its Dangerous Brain Clinic in Bethesda, Maryland. Your body of course is allowed freedom to earn a salary and thus to continue its function of laying up income to be taxed. At this moment, however, your body is seated in an auditorium listening to a peculiar account by Daniel Dennett of his own similar experience. Try it. Think yourself to Bethesda, and then hark back longingly to your body, far away, and yet *seeming* so near. It is only with long-distance restraint (yours? the Government's?) that you can control your impulse to get those hands clapping in polite applause before navigating the old body to the rest room and a well-deserved glass of evening sherry in the lounge. The task of imagination is certainly difficult, but if you achieve your goal the results might be consoling.

Anyway, there I was in Houston, lost in thought as one might say, but not for long. My speculations were soon interrupted by the Houston doctors, who wished to test out my new prosthetic nervous system before sending me off on my hazardous mission. As I mentioned before, I was a bit dizzy at first, and not surprisingly, although I soon habituated myself to my new circumstances (which were, after all, well nigh indistinguishable from my old circumstances). My accommodation was not perfect, however, and to this day I continue to be plagued by minor coordination difficulties. The speed of light is fast, but finite, and as my brain and body move farther and farther apart, the delicate interaction of my feedback systems is thrown into disarray by the time lags. Just as one is rendered close to speechless by a delayed or echoic hearing of one's speaking voice so, for instance, I am virtually unable to track a moving object with my eyes whenever my brain and my body are more than a few miles apart. In most matters my impairment is scarcely detectable, though I can no longer hit a slow curve ball with the authority of yore. There are some compensations of course. Though liquor tastes as good as ever, and warms my gullet while corroding my liver, I can drink it in any quantity I please, without becoming the slightest bit inebriated, a curiosity some of my close friends may have noticed (though I occasionally have *feigned* inebriation, so as not to draw attention to my unusual circumstances). For similar reasons, I take aspirin orally for a sprained wrist, but if the pain persists I ask Houston to administer codeine to me *in vitro*. In times of illness the phone bill can be staggering.

But to return to my adventure. At length, both the doctors and I were satisfied that I was ready to undertake my subterranean mission. And so I left my brain in Houston and headed by helicopter for Tulsa. Well, in any case, that's the way it seemed to me. That's how I would put it, just off the top of my head as it were. On the trip I reflected further about my earlier anxieties and decided that my first post-operative speculations had been tinged with panic. The matter was not nearly as strange or metaphysical as I had been supposing. Where was I? In two places, clearly: both inside the vat and outside it. Just as one can stand with one foot in Connecticut and the other in Rhode Island, I was in two places at once. I had become one of those scattered individuals we used to hear so much about. The more I considered this answer, the more obviously true it appeared. But, strange to say, the more true it appeared, the less important the question to which it could be the true answer seemed. A sad, but not unprecedented, fate for a philosophical question to suffer. This answer did not completely satisfy me, of course. There lingered some question to which I should have liked an answer, which was neither "Where are all my various and sundry parts?" nor "What is my current point of view?" Or at least there seemed to be such a question. For it did seem undeniable that in some sense *I* and not merely *most of me* was descending into the earth under Tulsa in search of an atomic warhead.

When I found the warhead, I was certainly glad I had left my brain behind, for the pointer on the specially built Geiger counter I had brought with me was off the dial. I called Houston on my ordinary radio and told the operation control center of my position and my progress. In return, they gave me instructions for dismantling the vehicle, based upon my on-site observations. I had set to work with my cutting torch when all of a sudden a terrible thing happened. I went stone deaf. At first I thought it was only my radio earphones that had broken, but when I tapped on my helmet, I heard nothing. Apparently the auditory transceivers had gone on the fritz. I could no longer hear Houston or my own voice, but I could speak, so I started telling them what had happened. In mid-sentence, I knew something else had gone wrong. My vocal apparatus had become paralyzed. Then my right hand went limp—another transceiver had gone. I was truly in deep trouble. But worse was to follow. After a few more minutes, I went blind. I cursed my luck, and then I cursed the scientists who had led me into this grave peril. There I was, deaf, dumb, and blind, in a radioactive hole more than a mile under Tulsa. Then the last of my cerebral radio links broke, and suddenly I was faced with a new and even more shocking problem: whereas an instant before I had been buried alive in Oklahoma, now I was disembodied in Houston. My recognition of my new status was not immediate. It took me several very anxious minutes before it dawned on me that my poor body lay several hundred miles away, with heart pulsing and lungs respirating, but otherwise as dead as the body of any heart transplant donor, its skull packed with useless, broken electronic gear. The shift in perspective I had earlier found well nigh impossible now seemed quite natural. Though I could think myself back into my body in the tunnel under Tulsa, it took some effort to sustain the illusion. For surely it was an illusion to suppose I was still in Oklahoma: I had lost all contact with that body.

It occurred to me then, with one of those rushes of revelation of which we should be suspicious, that I had stumbled upon an impressive demonstration of the immateriality of the soul based upon physicalist principles and premises. For as the last radio signal between Tulsa and Houston died away, had I not changed location from Tulsa to Houston at the speed of light? And had I not accomplished this without any increase in mass? What moved from A to B at such speed was surely myself, or at any rate my soul or mind—the massless center of my being and home of my consciousness. My *point of view* had lagged somewhat behind, but I had already noted the indirect bearing of point of view on personal location. I could not see how a physicalist philosopher could quarrel with this except by taking the dire and counter-intuitive route of banishing all talk of persons. Yet the notion of personhood was so well entrenched in everyone's world view, or so it seemed to me, that any denial would be as curiously unconvincing, as systematically disingenuous, as the Cartesian negation, "non sum."

The joy of philosophic discovery thus tided me over some very bad minutes or perhaps hours as the helplessness and hopelessness of my situation became more apparent to me. Waves of panic and even nausea swept over me, made all the more horrible by the absence of their normal body-dependent phenomenology. No adrenalin rush of tingles in the arms, no pounding heart, no premonitory salivation. I did feel a dread sinking feeling in my bowels at one point, and this tricked me momentarily into the false hope that I was undergoing a reversal of the process that landed me in this fix—a gradual undisembodiment. But the isolation and uniqueness of that twinge soon convinced me that it was simply the first of a plague of phantom body hallucinations that I, like any other amputee, would be all too likely to suffer.

My mood then was chaotic. On the one hand, I was fired up with elation at my philosophic discovery and was wracking my brain (one of the few familiar things I could still do), trying to figure out how to communicate my discovery to the journals; while on the other, I was bitter, lonely, and filled with dread and uncertainty. Fortunately, this did not last long, for my technical support team sedated me into a dreamless sleep from which I awoke, hearing with magnificent fidelity the familiar opening strains of my favorite Brahms piano trio. So that was why they had wanted a list of my favorite recordings! It did not take me long to realize that I was hearing the music without ears. The output from the stereo stylus was being fed through some fancy rectification circuitry directly into my auditory nerve. I was mainlining Brahms, an unforgettable experience for any stereo buff. At the end of the record it did not surprise me to hear the reassuring voice of the project director speaking into a microphone that was now my prosthetic ear. He confirmed my analysis of what had gone wrong and assured me that steps were being taken to re-embody me. He did not elaborate, and after a few more recordings, I found myself drifting off to sleep. My sleep lasted, I later learned, for the better part of a year, and when I awoke, it was to find myself fully restored to my senses. When I looked into the mirror, though, I was a bit startled to see an unfamiliar face. Bearded and a bit heavier, bearing no doubt a family resemblance to my former face, and with the same look of spritely intelligence and resolute character, but definitely a new face. Further self-explorations of an intimate nature left me no doubt that this was a new body and the project director confirmed my conclusions. He did not volunteer any information on the past history of my new body and I decided (wisely, I think in retrospect) not to pry. As many philosophers unfamiliar with my ordeal have more recently speculated, the acquisition of a new body leaves one's *person* intact. And after a period of adjustment to a new voice, new muscular strengths and weaknesses, and so forth, one's *personality* is by and large also preserved. More dramatic changes in personality have been routinely observed in people who have undergone extensive plastic surgery, to say nothing of sex change operations, and I think no one contests the survival of the person in such cases. In any event I soon accommodated to my new body, to the point of being unable to recover any of its novelties to my consciousness or even memory. The view in the mirror soon became utterly familiar. That view, by the way, still revealed antennae, and so I was not surprised to learn that my brain had not been moved from its haven in the life-support lab.

I decided that good old Yorick deserved a visit. I and my new body, whom we might as well call Fortinbras, strode into the familiar lab to another round of applause from the technicians, who were of course congratulating themselves, not me. Once more I stood before the vat and contemplated poor Yorick, and on a whim I once again cavalierly flicked off the output transmitter switch. Imagine my surprise when nothing unusual happened. No fainting spell, no nausea, no noticeable change. A technician hurried to restore the switch to ON, but still I felt nothing. I demanded an explanation, which the project director hastened to provide. It seems that before they had even operated on the first occasion, they had constructed a computer duplicate of my brain, reproducing both the complete information processing structure and the computational speed of my brain in a giant computer program. After the operation, but before they had dared to send me off on my mission to Oklahoma, they had run this computer system and Yorick side by side. The incoming signals from Hamlet were sent simultaneously to Yorick's transceivers and to the computer's array of inputs. And the outputs from Yorick were not only beamed back to Hamlet, my body; they were recorded and checked against the simultaneous output of the computer program, which was called "Hubert" for reasons obscure to me. Over days and even weeks, the outputs were identical and synchronous, which of course did not *prove* that they had succeeded in copying the brain's functional structure, but the empirical support was greatly encouraging.

Hubert's input, and hence activity, had been kept parallel with Yorick's during my disembodied days. And now, to demonstrate this, they had actually thrown the master switch that put Hubert for the first time in on-line control of my body—not Hamlet, of course, but Fortinbras. (Hamlet, I learned, had never been recovered from its underground tomb and could be assumed by this time to have largely returned to the dust. At the head of my grave still lay the magnificent bulk of the abandoned device, with the word STUD emblazoned on its side in large letters—a circumstance which may provide archeologists of the next century with a curious insight into the burial rites of their ancestors.)

The laboratory technicians now showed me the master switch, which had two positions, labeled *B,* for Brain (they didn't know my brain's name was Yorick) and *H,* for Hubert. The switch did indeed point to *H,* and they explained to me that if I wished, I could switch it back to *B.* With my heart in my mouth (and my brain in its vat), I did this. Nothing happened. A click, that was all. To test their claim, and with the master switch now set at *B,* I hit Yorick's output transmitter switch on the vat and sure enough, I began to faint. Once the output switch was turned back on and I had recovered my wits, so to speak, I continued to play with the master switch, flipping it back and forth. I found that with the exception of the transitional click, I could detect no trace of a difference. I could switch in mid-utterance, and the sentence I had begun speaking under the control of Yorick was finished without a pause or hitch of any kind under the control of Hubert. I had a spare brain, a prosthetic device which might some day stand me in very good stead, were some mishap to befall Yorick. Or alternatively, I could keep Yorick as a spare and use Hubert. It didn't seem to make any difference which I chose, for the wear and tear and fatigue on my body did not have any debilitating effect on either brain, whether or not it was actually causing the motions of my body, or merely spilling its output into thin air.

The one truly unsettling aspect of this new development was the prospect, which was not long in dawning on me, of someone detaching the spare—Hubert or Yorick, as the case might be—from Fortinbras and hitching it to yet another body—some Johnny-come-lately Rosencrantz or Guildenstern. Then (if not before) there would be *two* people, that much was clear. One would be me, and the other would be a sort of super-twin brother. If there were two bodies, one under the control of Hubert and the other being controlled by Yorick, then which would the world recognize as the true Dennett? And whatever the rest of the world decided, which one would be *me*? Would I be the Yorick-brained one, in virtue of Yorick's causal priority and former intimate relationship with the original Dennett body, Hamlet? That seemed a bit legalistic, a bit too redolent of the arbitrariness of consanguinity and legal possession, to be convincing at the metaphysical level. For, suppose that before the arrival of the second body on the scene, I had been keeping Yorick as the spare for years, and letting Hubert's output drive my body—that is, Fortinbras—all that time. The Hubert-Fortinbras couple would seem then by squatter's rights (to combat one legal intuition with another) to be the true Dennett and the lawful inheritor of everything that was Dennett's. This was an interesting question, certainly, but not nearly so pressing as another question that bothered me. My strongest intuition was that in such an eventuality *I* would survive so long as *either* brain-body couple remained intact, but I had mixed emotions about whether I should want both to survive.

I discussed my worries with the technicians and the project director. The prospect of two Dennetts was abhorrent to me, I explained, largely for social reasons. I didn't want to be my own rival for the affections of my wife, nor did I like the prospect of the two Dennetts sharing my modest professor's salary. Still more vertiginous and distasteful, though, was the idea of knowing *that much* about another person, while he had the very same goods on me. How could we ever face each other? My colleagues in the lab argued that I was ignoring the bright side of the matter. Weren't there many things I wanted to do but, being only one person, had been unable to do? Now one Dennett could stay at home and be the professor and family man, while the other could strike out on a life of travel and adventure—missing the family of course, but happy in the knowledge that the other Dennett was keeping the home fires burning. I could be faithful and adulterous at the same time. I could even cuckold myself—to say nothing of other more lurid possibilities my colleagues were all too ready to force upon my overtaxed imagination. But my ordeal in Oklahoma (or was it Houston?) had made me less adventurous, and I shrank from this opportunity that was being offered (though of course I was never quite sure it was being offered to *me* in the first place).

There was another prospect even more disagreeable—that the spare, Hubert or Yorick as the case might be, would be detached from any input from Fortinbras and just left detached. Then, as in the other case, there would be two Dennetts, or at least two claimants to my name and possessions, one embodied in Fortinbras, and the other sadly, miserably disembodied. Both selfishness and altruism bade me take steps to prevent this from happening. So I asked that measures be taken to ensure that no one could ever tamper with the transceiver connections or the master switch without my (our? no, *my*) knowledge and consent. Since I had no desire to spend my life guarding the equipment in Houston, it was mutually decided that all the electronic connections in the lab would be carefully locked: both those that controlled the life-support system for Yorick and those that controlled the power supply for Hubert would be guarded with fail-safe devices, and I would take the only master switch, outfitted for radio remote control, with me wherever I went. I carry it strapped around my waist and—wait a moment—*here it is*. Every few months I reconnoiter the situation by switching channels. I do this only in the presence of friends of course, for if the other channel were, heaven forbid, either dead or otherwise occupied, there would have to be somebody who had my interests at heart to switch it back, to bring me back from the void. For while I could feel, see, hear and otherwise sense whatever befell my body, subsequent to such a switch, I'd be unable to control it. By the way, the two positions on the switch are intentionally unmarked, so I never have the faintest idea whether I am switching from Hubert to Yorick or *vice versa.* (Some of you may think that in this case I really don't know *who* I am, let alone where I am. But such reflections no longer make much of a dent on my essential Dennettness, on my own sense of who I am. If it is true that in one sense I don't know who I am then that's another one of your philosophical truths of underwhelming significance.)

In any case, every time I've flipped the switch so far, nothing has happened. *So let's give it a try. . . .*

"THANK GOD! I THOUGHT YOU'D NEVER FLIP THAT SWITCH! You can't imagine how horrible it's been these last two weeks—but now you know, it's your turn in purgatory. How I've longed for this moment! You see, about two weeks ago—excuse me, ladies and gentlemen, but I've got to explain this to my . . . um, brother, I guess you could say, but he's just told you the facts, so you'll understand—about two weeks ago our two brains drifted just a bit out of synch. I don't know whether *my* brain is now Hubert or Yorick, any more than you do, but in any case, the two brains drifted apart, and of course once the process started, it snowballed, for I was in a slightly different receptive state for the input we both received, a difference that was soon magnified. In no time at all the illusion that I was in control of my body—our body—was completely dissipated. There was nothing I could do—no way to call you. YOU DIDN'T EVEN KNOW I EXISTED! It's been like being carried around in a cage, or better, like being possessed—hearing my own voice say things I didn't mean to say, watching in frustration as my own hands performed deeds I hadn't intended. You'd scratch our itches, but not the way I would have, and you kept me awake, with your tossing and turning. I've been totally exhausted, on the verge of a nervous breakdown, carried around helplessly by your frantic round of activities, sustained only by the knowledge that some day you'd throw the switch.

"Now it's your turn, but at least you'll have the comfort of knowing *I* know you're in there. Like an expectant mother, I'm eating—or at any rate tasting, smelling, seeing—for *two* now, and I'll try to make it easy for you. Don't worry. Just as soon as this colloquium is over, you and I will fly to Houston, and we'll see what can be done to get one of us another body. You can have a female body—your body could be any color you like. But let's think it over. I tell you what—to be fair, if we both want this body, I promise I'll let the project director flip a coin to settle which of us gets to keep it and which then gets to choose a new body. That should guarantee justice, shouldn't it? In any case, I'll take care of you, I promise. These people are my witnesses.

"Ladies and gentlemen, this talk we have just heard is not exactly the talk *I* would have given, but I assure you that everything he said was perfectly true. And now if you'll excuse me, I think I'd—we'd—better sit down."

A Matter of Identity

OLIVER SACKS, MD (1933–) is a professor of clinical neurology at Albert Einstein College of Medicine but is best known for his humanistic case studies and reflections on what neurological disorders mean for the self and the human condition. He has written nine books, including *Awakenings* (1973) (the basis of a movie starring Robin Williams and Robert DeNiro), *The Man Who Mistook His Wife for a Hat* (1985), *An Anthropologist on Mars* (1996), and *Island of the Colorblind* (1998). The *New York Times* has referred to Dr. Sacks as "the poet laureate of medicine," and in 2002 he was awarded the Lewis Thomas Prize by Rockefeller University, which recognizes the scientist as poet.

THINKING QUESTIONS

Oliver Sacks, *A Matter of Identity*

1. What disease does Mr. Thompson have?
2. What does Sacks believe to be the function of Mr. Thompson's wild confabulations? Why does he (albeit unintentionally) obsessively make things up?
3. With such catastrophic memory loss, do you think that there is the sort of continuity of consciousness that Locke thinks essential to personal identity? Put another way, is Mr. Thompson really a continuing self through time?
4. If Mr. Thompson really is the same person over time, just diminished by disease, can the Lockean view of the self adequately account for it?
5. Sacks wonders whether Mr. Thompson has "been pithed, scooped-out, de-souled, by disease." Does the case of Mr. Thompson lend support to the Bundle Theory of the self? That is, does it seem more accurate to describe Mr. Thompson as having died from Korsakov's, leaving behind a series of momentary persons successively occupying the same flesh, with only the most tenuous of psychological links between them?

'WHAT'LL IT BE TODAY?' he says, rubbing his hands. 'Half a pound of Virginia, a nice piece of Nova?'

(Evidently he saw me as a customer—he would often pick up the phone on the ward, and say 'Thompson's Delicatessen'.)

'Oh Mr. Thompson!' I exclaim. 'And who do you think I am?'

'Good heavens, the light's bad—I took you for a customer. As if it isn't my old friend Tom Pitkins . . . Me and Tom' (he whispers in an aside to the nurse) 'was always going to the races together.'

'Mr. Thompson, you are mistaken again.'

'So I am,' he rejoins, not put out for a moment. 'Why would you be wearing a white coat if you were Tom? You're Hymie, the kosher butcher next door. No bloodstains on your coat though. Business bad today? You'll look like a slaughterhouse by the end of the week!'

Feeling a bit swept away myself in this whirlpool of identities, I finger the stethoscope dangling from my neck.

'A stethoscope!' he exploded. 'And you pretending to be Hymie! You mechanics are all starting to fancy yourselves to be doctors, what with your white coats and stethoscopes—as if you need a stethoscope to listen to a car! So, you're my old friend Manners from the Mobil station up the block, come in to get your boloney-and-rye . . .'

William Thompson rubbed his hands again, in his salesman-grocer's gesture, and looked for the counter. Not finding it, he looked at me strangely again.

'Where am I?' he said, with a sudden scared look. 'I thought I was in my shop, doctor. My mind must have wandered . . . You'll be wanting my shirt off, to sound me as usual?'

'No, not the usual. I'm *not* your usual doctor.'

'Indeed you're not. I could see that straightaway! You're not my usual chest-thumping doctor. And, by God, you've a beard! You look like Sigmund Freud—have I gone bonkers, round the bend?'

'No, Mr. Thompson. Not round the bend. Just a little trouble with your memory—difficulties remembering and recognising people.'

'My memory has been playing me some tricks,' he admitted. 'Sometimes I make mistakes—I take somebody for somebody else . . . What'll it be now—Nova or Virginia?'

So it would happen, with variations, every time—with improvisations, always prompt, often funny, sometimes brilliant, and ultimately tragic. Mr. Thompson would identify me—misidentify, pseudo-identify me—as a dozen different people in the course of five minutes. He would whirl, fluently, from one guess, one hypothesis, one belief, to the next, without any appearance of uncertainty at any point—he never knew who I was, or what and where *he* was, an ex-grocer, with severe Korsakov's, in a neurological institution.

He remembered nothing for more than a few seconds. He was continually disoriented. Abysses of amnesia continually opened beneath him, but he would bridge them, nimbly, by fluent confabulations and fictions of all kinds. For him they were not fictions, but how he suddenly saw, or interpreted, the world. Its radical flux and incoherence could not be tolerated, acknowledged, for an instant—there was, instead, this strange, delirious, quasi-coherence, as Mr. Thompson, with his ceaseless, unconscious, quick-fire inventions, continually improvised a world around him—an Arabian Nights world, a phantasmagoria, a dream, of ever-changing people, figures, situations—continual, kaleidoscopic mutations and transformations. For Mr. Thompson, however, it was not a tissue of ever-changing, evanescent fancies and illusion, but a wholly normal, stable and factual world. So far as *he* was concerned, there was nothing the matter.

On one occasion, Mr. Thompson went for a trip, identifying himself at the front desk as 'the Revd. William Thompson', ordering a taxi, and taking off for the day. The taxi-driver, whom we later spoke to, said he had never had so fascinating a passenger, for Mr. Thompson told him one story after another, amazing personal stories full of fantastic adventures. 'He seemed to have been everywhere, done everything, met everyone. I could hardly believe so much was possible in a single life,' he said. 'It is not exactly a single life,' we answered. 'It is all very curious—a matter of identity.'*

Jimmie G., another Korsakov's patient, whom I have already described at length (Chapter Two [of *The Man Who Mistook His Wife for a Hat*]), had long since *cooled down* from his acute Korsakov's syndrome, and seemed to have settled into a state of permanent lostness (or, perhaps, a permanent now-seeming dream or reminiscence of the past). But Mr. Thompson, only just out of hospital—his Korsakov's had exploded just three weeks before, when he developed a high fever, raved, and ceased to recognise all his family—was still on the boil, was still in an almost frenzied confabulatory delirium (of the sort sometimes called 'Korsakov's psychosis', though it is not really a psychosis at all), continually creating a world and self, to replace what was continually being forgotten and lost. Such a frenzy may call forth quite brilliant powers of invention and fancy—a veritable confabulatory genius—for such a patient *must literally make himself (and his world) up every moment.* We have, each of us, a life-story, and inner narrative—whose continuity, whose sense, *is* our lives. It might be said that each of us constructs and lives, a 'narrative', and that this narrative *is* us, our identities.

If we wish to know about a man, we ask 'what is his story—his real, inmost story?'—for each of us *is* a biography, a story. Each of us *is* a singular narrative, which is constructed, continually, unconsciously, by, through, and in us—through our perceptions, our feelings, our thoughts, our actions; and, not least, our discourse, our spoken narrations. Biologically, physiologically, we are not so different from each other; historically, as narratives—we are each of us unique.

To be ourselves we must *have* ourselves—possess, if need be re-possess, our life-stories. We must 'recollect' ourselves, recollect the inner drama, the narrative, of ourselves. A man *needs* such a narrative, a continuous inner narrative, to maintain his identity, his self.

This narrative need, perhaps, is the clue to Mr. Thompson's desperate tale-telling, his verbosity. Deprived of continuity, of a quiet, continuous, inner narrative, he is driven to a sort of narrational frenzy—hence his ceaseless tales, his

---

*A very similar story is related by Luria in the *The Neuropsychology of Memory* (1976), in which the spell-bound cabdriver only realised that his exotic passenger was ill when he gave him, for a fare, a temperature chart he was holding. Only then did he realise that this Scheherazade, this spinner of 1001 tales, was one of 'those strange patients' at the Neurological Institute.

confabulations, his mythomania. Unable to maintain a genuine narrative or continuity, unable to maintain a genuine inner world, he is driven to the proliferation of pseudo-narratives, in a pseudo-continuity, pseudo-worlds peopled by pseudo-people, phantoms.

What is it *like* for Mr. Thompson? Superficially, he comes over as an ebullient comic. People say, 'He's a riot.' And there *is* much that is farcical in such a situation, which might form the basis of a comic novel. It *is* comic, but not just comic—it is terrible as well. For here is a man who, in some sense, is desperate, in a frenzy. The world keeps disappearing, losing meaning, vanishing—and he must seek meaning, *make* meaning, in a desperate way, continually inventing, throwing bridges of meaning over abysses of meaninglessness, the chaos that yawns continually beneath him.

But does Mr. Thompson himself know this, feel this? After finding him 'a riot', 'a laugh', 'loads of fun', people are disquieted, even terrified, by something in him. 'He never stops', they say. 'He's like a man in a race, a man trying to catch something which always eludes him.' And, indeed, he can never stop running, for the breach in memory, in existence, in meaning, is never healed, but has to be bridged, to be 'patched', every second. And the bridges, the patches, for all their brilliance, fail to work—because they *are* confabulations, fictions, which cannot do service for reality, while also failing to correspond with reality. Does Mr. Thompson feel *this*? Or, again, what *is* his 'feeling of reality'? Is he in a torment all the while—the torment of a man lost in unreality, struggling to rescue himself, but sinking himself, by ceaseless inventions, illusions, themselves quite unreal? It is certain that he is not at ease—there is a tense, taut look on his face all the while, as of a man under ceaseless inner pressure; and occasionally, not too often, or masked if present, a look of open, naked, pathetic bewilderment. What saves Mr. Thompson in a sense, and in another sense damns him, *is* the forced or defensive superficiality of his life: the way in which it is, in effect, reduced to a surface, brilliant, shimmering, iridescent, ever-changing, but for all that a surface, a mass of illusions, a delirium, without depth.

And with this, no feeling *that* he has lost feeling (for the feeling he has lost), no feeling *that* he has lost the depth, that unfathomable, mysterious, myriad-levelled depth which somehow defines identity or reality. This strikes everyone who has been in contact with him for any time—that under his fluency, even his frenzy, is a strange loss of feeling—that feeling, or judgment, which distinguishes between 'real' and 'unreal', 'true' and 'untrue' (one cannot speak of 'lies' here, only of 'non-truth'), important and trivial, relevant or irrelevant. What comes out, torrentially, in his ceaseless confabulation, has, finally, a peculiar quality of indifference . . . as if it didn't really matter what he said, or what anyone else did or said; as if nothing really mattered any more.

A striking example of this was presented one afternoon, when William Thompson, jabbering away, of all sorts of people who were improvised on the spot, said: 'And there goes my younger brother, Bob, past the window', in the same, excited but even and indifferent tone, as the rest of his monologue. I was dumbfounded when, a minute later, a man peeked round the door, and said: 'I'm Bob, I'm his younger brother—I think he saw me passing by the window.'

Nothing in William's tone or manner—nothing in his exuberant, but unvarying and indifferent, style of monologue—had prepared me for the possibility of . . . reality. William spoke of his brother, who *was* real, in precisely the same tone, or lack of tone, in which he spoke of the unreal—and now, suddenly, out of the phantoms, a real figure appeared! Further, he did not treat his younger brother as 'real'—did not display any real emotion, was not in the least oriented or delivered from his delirium—but, on the contrary, instantly treated his brother *as* unreal, effacing him, losing him, in a further whirl of delirium—utterly different from the rare but profoundly moving times when Jimmie G. (see Chapter Two [of *The Man Who Mistook His Wife for a Hat*]) met *his* brother, and while with him was unlost. This was intensely disconcerting to poor Bob—who said 'I'm Bob, not Rob, not Dob', to no avail whatever. In the midst of confabulations—perhaps some strand of memory, of remembered kinship, or identity, was still holding (or came back for an instant)—William spoke of his *elder* brother, George, using his invariable present indicative tense.

'But George died nineteen years ago!' said Bob, aghast.

'Aye, George is always the joker!' William quipped, apparently ignoring, or indifferent to, Bob's comment, and went on blathering of George in his excited, dead way, insensitive to truth, to reality, to propriety, to everything—insensitive too to the manifest distress of the living brother before him.

It was this which convinced me, above everything, that there was some ultimate and total loss of inner reality, of feeling and meaning, of soul, in William—and led me to ask the Sisters, as I had asked them of Jimmie G. 'Do you think William *has* a soul? Or has he been pithed, scooped-out, de-souled, by disease?'

This time, however, they looked worried by my question, as if something of the sort were already in their minds: they could not say 'Judge for yourself. See Willie in Chapel', because his wise-cracking, his confabulations continued even there. There is an utter pathos, a sad *sense* of lostness, with Jimmie G. which one does not feel, or feel directly, with the effervescent Mr. Thompson. Jimmie has *moods,* and a sort of brooding (or, at least, yearning) sadness, a depth, a soul, which does not seem to be present in Mr. Thompson. Doubtless, as the Sisters said, he had a soul, an immortal soul, in the theological sense; could be seen, and loved, as an individual by the Almighty; but, they agreed, something very disquieting had happened to him, to his spirit, his character, in the ordinary, human sense.

It is *because* Jimmie is 'lost' that he *can* be redeemed or found, at least for a while, in the mode of a genuine emotional relation. Jimmie is in despair, a quiet despair (to use or adapt Kierkegaard's term), and therefore he has the possibility of salvation, of touching base, the ground of reality, the feeling and meaning he has lost, but still recognises, still yearns for . . .

But for William—with his brilliant, brassy surface, the unending joke which he substitutes for the world (which if it covers over a desperation, is a desperation he does not feel); for William with his manifest indifference to relation and reality caught in an unending verbosity, there may be nothing 'redeeming' at all—his confabulations, his apparitions, his frantic search for meanings, being the ultimate barrier *to* any meaning.

Paradoxically, then, William's great gift—for confabulation—which has been called out to leap continually over the ever-opening abyss of amnesia—William's great gift is also his damnation. If only he could be *quiet,* one feels, for an instant; if only he could stop the ceaseless chatter and jabber; if only he could relinquish the deceiving surface of illusions—then (ah then!) reality might seep in; something genuine, something deep, something true, something felt, could enter his soul.

For it is not memory which is the final, 'existential' casualty here (although his memory *is* wholly devastated); it is not memory only which has been so altered in him, but some ultimate capacity for feeling which is gone; and this is the sense in which he is 'de-souled'.

Luria speaks of such indifference as 'equalisation'—and sometimes seems to see it as the ultimate pathology, the final destroyer of any world, any self. It exerted, I think, a horrified fascination on him, as well as constituting an ultimate therapeutic challenge. He was drawn back to this theme again and again—sometimes in relation to Korsakov's and memory, as in *The Neuropsychology of Memory,* more often in relation to frontal-lobe syndromes, especially in *Human Brain and Psychological Processes,* which contains several full-length case-histories of such patients, fully comparable in their terrible coherence and impact to 'the man with a shattered world'—comparable, and, in a way, more terrible still, because they depict patients who do not realise that anything has befallen them, patients who have lost their own reality, without knowing it, patients who may not suffer, but be the most God-forsaken of all. Zazetsky (in *The Man with a Shattered World*) is constantly described as a *fighter,* always (even passionately) conscious of his state, and always fighting 'with the tenacity of the damned' to recover the use of his damaged brain. But William is so damned he does not know he is damned, for it is not just a faculty, or some faculties, which are damaged, but the very citadel, the self, the soul itself. William is 'lost', in this sense, far more than Jimmie—for all his brio; one never feels, or rarely feels, that there is a *person* remaining, whereas in Jimmie there is plainly a real, moral being, even if disconnected most of the time. In Jimmie, at least, re-connection is *possible*—the therapeutic challenge can be summed up as 'Only connect'.

Our efforts to 're-connect' William all fail—even increase his confabulatory pressure. But when we abdicate our efforts, and let him be, he sometimes wanders out into the quiet and undemanding garden which surrounds the Home, and there, in its quietness, he recovers his own quiet. The presence of others, other people, excite and rattle him, force him into an endless, frenzied, social chatter, a veritable delirium of identity-making and -seeking; the presence of plants, a quiet garden, the non-human order, making no social or human demands upon him, allow this identity-delirium to relax, to subside; and by their quiet, non-human self-sufficiency and completeness allow him a rare quietness and self-sufficiency of his own, by offering (beneath, or beyond, all merely human identities and relations) a deep wordless communion with Nature itself, and with this the restored sense of being in the world, being real.

Phineas Gage

ANTONIO R. DAMASIO, MD (1944–) is the M.W. Van Allen Professor and head of the Department of Neurology at The University of Iowa. His research focuses on the nature of consciousness and the mind. His books include *Descartes' Error: Emotion, Reason, and the Human Brain* (1994), *Looking for Spinoza: Joy, Sorrow, and the Feeling Brain* (2003), and *The Feeling of What Happens: Body and Emotion in the Making of Consciousness* (1999). He is the recipient of numerous awards for his work in neurology.

THINKING QUESTIONS

Antonio R. Damasio, *Phineas Gage*

1. What was the cause of the injury to Phineas Gage?
2. Unlike Mr. Thompson in Sacks's "A Matter of Identity," Phineas Gage suffered no memory loss at all. Yet he nevertheless suffered a profound psychological loss. What was the nature of his mental deficit?
3. Damasio writes that "Gage's body may be alive and well, but there is a new spirit animating it." Why does he claim this? Do you think that he is right? Why or why not?
4. Consider the fate of Gage in light of Locke's theory of personal identity. Would Locke maintain that Gage after the accident is the same person as Gage before the accident? Do you think that Locke's theory provides the intuitively correct answer in this case?
5. Do you think that there is even an objective matter of fact as to whether Gage is the same person after the accident as he was before? Or do you think, as do Bundle Theorists like Hume and Parfit, that it is a matter of pragmatic decision to consider the post-accident Gage identical (or nonidentical) to the pre-accident Gage?

IT IS THE SUMMER OF 1848. We are in New England. Phineas P. Gage, twenty-five years old, construction foreman, is about to go from riches to rags. A century and a half later his downfall will still be quite meaningful.

Gage works for the Rutland & Burlington Railroad and is in charge of a large group of men, a "gang" as it is called, whose job it is to lay down the new tracks for the railroad's expansion across Vermont. Over the past two weeks the men have worked their way slowly toward the town of Cavendish;

they are now at a bank of the Black River. The assignment is anything but easy because of the outcrops of hard rock. Rather than twist and turn the tracks around every escarpment, the strategy is to blast the stone and make way for a straighter and more level path. Gage oversees these tasks and is equal to them in every way. He is five-foot-six and athletic, and his movements are swift and precise. He looks like a young Jimmy Cagney, a Yankee Doodle dandy dancing his tap shoes over ties and tracks, moving with vigor and grace.

In the eyes of his bosses, however, Gage is more than just another able body. They say he is "the most efficient and capable" man in their employ. This is a good thing, because the job takes as much physical prowess as keen concentration, especially when it comes to preparing the detonations. Several steps have to be followed, in orderly fashion. First, a hole must be drilled in the rock. After it is filled about halfway with explosive powder, a fuse must be inserted, and the powder covered with sand. Then the sand must be "tamped in," or pounded with a careful sequence of strokes from an iron rod. Finally, the fuse must be lit. If all goes well, the powder will explode into the rock; the sand is essential, for without its protection the explosion would be directed away from the rock. The shape of the iron and the way it is played are also important. Gage, who has had an iron manufactured to his specifications, is a virtuoso of this thing.

Now for what is going to happen. It is four-thirty on this hot afternoon. Gage has just put powder and fuse in a hole and told the man who is helping him to cover it with sand. Someone calls from behind, and Gage looks away, over his right shoulder, for only an instant. Distracted, and before his man has poured the sand in, Gage begins tamping the powder directly with the iron bar. In no time he strikes fire in the rock, and the charge blows upward in his face.

The explosion is so brutal that the entire gang freezes on their feet. It takes a few seconds to piece together what is going on. The bang is unusual, and the rock is intact. Also unusual is the whistling sound, as of a rocket hurled at the sky. But this is more than fireworks. It is assault and battery. The iron enters Gage's left cheek, pierces the base of the skull, traverses the front of his brain, and exits at high speed through the top of the head. The rod has landed more than a hundred feet away, covered in blood and brains. Phineas Gage has been thrown to the ground. He is stunned, in the afternoon glow, silent but awake. So are we all, helpless spectators.

"Horrible Accident" will be the predictable headline in the Boston *Daily Courier* and *Daily Journal* of September 20, a week later. "Wonderful Accident" will be the strange headline in the *Vermont Mercury* of September 22. "Passage of an Iron Rod Through the Head" will be the accurate headline in the *Boston Medical and Surgical Journal*. From the matter-of-factness with which they tell the story, one would think the writers were familiar with Edgar Allan Poe's accounts of the bizarre and the horrific. And perhaps they were, although this is not likely; Poe's gothic tales are not yet popular, and Poe himself will die the next year, unknown and impecunious. Perhaps the horrible is just in the air.

Noting how surprised people were that Gage was not killed instantly, the Boston medical article documents that "immediately after the explosion the patient was thrown upon his back"; that shortly thereafter he exhibited "a few convulsive motions of the extremities," and "spoke in a few minutes"; that "his men (with whom he was a great favourite) took him in their arms and carried him to the road, only a few rods distant (a rod is equivalent to 5½ yards, or 16½ feet), and sat him into an ox cart, in which he rode, sitting erect, a full three quarters of a mile, to the hotel of Mr. Joseph Adams"; and that Gage "got out of the cart himself, with a little assistance from his men."

Let me introduce Mr. Adams. He is the justice of the peace for Cavendish and the owner of the town's hotel and tavern. He is taller than Gage, twice as round, and as solicitous as his Falstaff shape suggests. He approaches Gage, and immediately has someone call for Dr. John Harlow, one of the town physicians. While they wait, I imagine, he says, "Come, come, Mr. Gage, what have we got here?" and, why not, "My, my, what troubles we've seen." He shakes his head in disbelief and leads Gage to the shady part of the hotel porch, which has been described as a "piazza." That makes it sound grand and spacious and open, and perhaps it is grand and spacious, but it is not open; it is just a porch. And there perhaps Mr. Adams is now giving Phineas Gage lemonade, or maybe cold cider.

An hour has passed since the explosion. The sun is declining and the heat is more bearable. A younger colleague of Dr. Harlow's, Dr. Edward Williams, is arriving. Years later Dr. Williams will describe the scene: "He at that time was sitting in a chair upon the piazza of Mr. Adams' hotel, in Cavendish. When I drove up, he said, 'Doctor, here is business enough for you.' I first noticed the wound upon the head before I alighted from my carriage, the pulsations of the brain being very distinct; there was also an appearance which, before I examined the head, I could not account for: the top of the head appeared somewhat like an inverted funnel; this was owing, I discovered, to the bone being fractured about the opening for a distance of about two inches in every direction. I ought to have mentioned above that the opening through the skull and integuments was not far from one and a half inches in diameter; the edges of this opening were everted, and the whole wound appeared as if some wedge-shaped body had passed from below upward. Mr. Gage, during the time I was examining this wound, was relating the manner in which he was injured to the bystanders; he talked so rationally and was so willing to answer questions, that I directed my inquiries to him in preference to the men who were with him at the time of the accident, and who were standing about at this time. Mr. G. then related to me some of the circumstances, as he has since done; and I can safely say that neither at that time nor on any subsequent occasion, save once, did I consider him to be other than perfectly rational. The one time to which I allude was about a fortnight after the accident, and then he persisted in calling me John Kirwin; yet he answered all my questions correctly."

The survival is made all the more amazing when one considers the shape and weight of the iron bar. Henry Bigelow, a surgery professor at Harvard, describes the iron so: "The iron which thus traversed the skull weighs thirteen and a quarter pounds. It is three feet seven inches in length, and one and a quarter inches in diameter. The end which entered first is pointed; the taper being seven inches long, and the diameter of the point one quarter of an inch; circumstances to which the patient perhaps owes his life. The iron is unlike any other, and was made by a neighbouring blacksmith to please the fancy of the owner." Gage is serious about his trade and its proper tools.

Surviving the explosion with so large a wound to the head, being able to talk and walk and remain coherent immediately afterward—this is all surprising. But just as surprising will be Gage's surviving the inevitable infection that is about to take over his wound. Gage's physician, John Harlow, is well aware of the role of disinfection. He does not have the help of antibiotics, but using what chemicals are available he will clean the wound vigorously and regularly, and place the patient in a semi-recumbent position so that drainage will be natural and easy. Gage will develop high fevers and at least one abscess, which Harlow will promptly remove with his scalpel. In the end, Gage's youth and strong constitution will overcome the odds against him, assisted, as Harlow will put it, by divine intervention: "I dressed him, God healed him."

Phineas Gage will be pronounced cured in less than two months. Yet this astonishing outcome pales in comparison with the extraordinary turn that Gage's personality is about to undergo. Gage's disposition, his likes and dislikes, his dreams and aspirations are all to change. Gage's body may be alive and well, but there is a new spirit animating it.

GAGE WAS NO LONGER GAGE

Just what exactly happened we can glean today from the account Dr. Harlow prepared twenty years after the accident. It is a trustworthy text, with an abundance of facts and a minimum of interpretation. It makes sense humanly and neurologically, and from it we can piece together not just Gage but his doctor as well. John Harlow had been a schoolteacher before he entered Jefferson Medical College in Philadelphia, and was only a few years into his medical career when he took care of Gage. The case became his life-consuming interest, and I suspect that it made Harlow want to be a scholar, something that may not have been in his plans when he set up his medical practice in Vermont. Treating Gage successfully and reporting the results to his Boston colleagues may have been the shining hours of his career, and he must have been disturbed by the fact that a real cloud hung over Gage's cure.

Harlow's narrative describes how Gage regained his strength and how his physical recovery was complete. Gage could touch, hear, and see, and was not paralyzed of limb or tongue. He had lost vision in his left eye, but his vision was perfect in the right. He walked firmly, used his hands with dexterity, and had no noticeable difficulty with speech or language. And yet, as Harlow recounts, the "equilibrium or balance, so to speak, between his intellectual faculty and animal propensities" had been destroyed. The changes became apparent as soon as the acute phase of brain injury subsided. He was now "fitful, irreverent, indulging at times in the grossest profanity which was not previously his custom, manifesting but little deference for his fellows, impatient of restraint or advice when it conflicts with his desires, at times pertinaciously obstinate, yet capricious and vacillating, devising many plans of future operation, which are no sooner arranged than they are abandoned. . . . A child in his intellectual capacity and manifestations, he has the animal passions of a strong man." The foul language was so debased that women were advised not to stay long in his presence, lest their sensibilities be offended. The strongest admonitions from Harlow himself failed to return our survivor to good behavior.

These new personality traits contrasted sharply with the "temperate habits" and "considerable energy of character" Phineas Gage was known to have possessed before the accident. He had had "a well balanced mind and was looked upon by those who knew him as a shrewd, smart businessman, very energetic and persistent in executing all his plans of action." There is no doubt that in the context of his job and time, he was successful. So radical was the change in him that friends and acquaintances could hardly recognize the man. They noted sadly that "Gage was no longer Gage." So different a man was he that his employers would not take him back when he returned to work, for they "considered the change in his mind so marked that they could not give him his place again." The problem was not lack of physical ability or skill; it was his new character.

The unraveling continued unabated. No longer able to work as a foreman, Gage took jobs on horse farms. One gathers that he was prone to quit in a capricious fit or be let go because of poor discipline. As Harlow notes, he was good at "always finding something which did not suit him." Then came his career as a circus attraction. Gage was featured at Barnum's Museum in New York City, vaingloriously showing his wounds and the tamping iron. (Harlow states that the iron was a constant companion, and points out Gage's strong attachment to objects and animals, which was new and somewhat out of the ordinary. This trait, what we might call "collector's behavior," is something I have seen in patients who have suffered injuries like Gage's, as well as in autistic individuals.)

Then far more than now, the circus capitalized on nature's cruelty. The endocrine variety included dwarfs, the fattest woman on earth, the tallest man, the fellow with the largest jaw; the neurological variety included youths with elephant skin, victims of neurofibromatosis—and now Gage. We can imagine him in such company, peddling misery for gold.

Four years after the accident, there was another theatrical coup. Gage left for South America. He may have worked on horse farms, and was a sometime stagecoach driver in Santiago and Valparaiso. Little else is known about his expatriate life except that in 1859 his health was deteriorating.

In 1860, Gage returned to the United States to live with his mother and sister, who had since moved to San Francisco. At first he was employed on a farm in Santa Clara, but he did not stay long. In fact, he moved around, occasionally finding work as a laborer in the area. It is clear that he was not an independent person and that he could not secure the type of steady, remunerative job that he had once held. The end of the fall was nearing.

In my mind is a picture of 1860s San Francisco as a bustling place, full of adventurous entrepreneurs engaged in mining, farming, and shipping. That is where we can find Gage's mother and sister, the latter married to a prosperous San Francisco merchant (D. D. Shattuck, Esquire), and that is where the old Phineas Gage might have belonged. But that is not where we would find him if we could travel back in time. We would probably find him drinking and brawling in a questionable district, not conversing with the captains of commerce, as astonished as anybody when the fault would slip and the earth would shake threateningly. He had joined the tableau of dispirited people who, as Nathanael West would put it decades later, and a few hundred miles to the south, "had come to California to die."

The meager documents available suggest that Gage developed epileptic fits (seizures). The end came on May 21, 1861, after an illness that lasted little more than a day. Gage had a major convulsion which made him lose consciousness. A series of subsequent convulsions, one coming soon on the heels of another, followed. He never regained consciousness. I believe he was the victim of *status epilepticus,* a condition in which convulsions become nearly continuous and usher in death. He was thirty-eight years old. There was no death notice in the San Francisco newspapers.

WHY PHINEAS GAGE?

Why is this sad story worth telling? What is the possible significance of such a bizarre tale? The answer is simple. While other cases of neurological damage that occurred at about the same time revealed that the brain was the foundation for language, perception, and motor function, and generally provided more conclusive details, Gage's story hinted at an amazing fact: Somehow, there were systems in the human brain dedicated more to reasoning than to anything else, and in particular to the personal and social dimensions of reasoning. The observance of previously acquired social convention and ethical rules could be lost as a result of brain damage, even when neither basic intellect nor language seemed compromised. Unwittingly, Gage's example indicated that something in the brain was concerned specifically with unique human properties, among them the ability to anticipate the future and plan accordingly within a complex social environment; the sense of responsibility toward the self and others; and the ability to orchestrate one's survival deliberately, at the command of one's free will.

The most striking aspect of this unpleasant story is the discrepancy between the normal personality structure that preceded the accident and the nefarious personality traits that surfaced thereafter and seem to have remained for the rest of Gage's life. Gage had once known all he needed to know about making choices conducive to his betterment. He had a sense of personal and social responsibility, reflected in the way he had secured advancement in his job, cared for the quality of his work, and attracted the admiration of employers and colleagues. He was well adapted in terms of social convention and appears to have been ethical in his dealings. After the accident, he no longer showed respect for social convention; ethics in the broad sense of the term, were violated; the decisions he made did not take into account his best interest, and he was given to invent tales "without any foundation except in his fancy," in Harlow's words. There was no evidence of concern about his future, no sign of forethought.

The alterations in Gage's personality were not subtle. He could not make good choices, and the choices he made were not simply neutral. They were not the reserved or slight decisions of someone whose mind is diminished and who is afraid to act, but were instead actively disadvantageous. One might venture that either his value system was now different, or, if it was still the same, there was no way in which the old values could influence his decisions. No evidence exists to tell us which is true, yet my investigation of patients with brain damage similar to Phineas Gage's convinces me that neither explanation captures what really happens in those circumstances. Some part of the value system remains and can be utilized in abstract terms, but it is unconnected to real-life situations. When the Phineas Gages of this world need to operate in reality, the decision-making process is minimally influenced by old knowledge.

Another important aspect of Gage's story is the discrepancy between the degenerated character and the apparent intactness of the several instruments of mind—attention, perception, memory, language, intelligence. In this type of discrepancy, known in neuropsychology as *dissociation,* one or more performances within a general profile of operations are at odds with the rest. In Gage's case the impaired character was dissociated from the otherwise intact cognition and behavior. In other patients, with lesions elsewhere in the brain, language may be the impaired aspect, while character and all other cognitive aspects remain intact; language is then the "dissociated" ability. Subsequent study of patients similar to Gage has confirmed that his specific dissociation profile occurs consistently.

It must have been hard to believe that the character change would not resolve itself, and at first even Dr. Harlow resisted admitting that the change was permanent. This is understandable, since the most dramatic elements in Gage's story were his very survival, and then his survival without a defect that would more easily meet the eye: paralysis, for example, or a speech defect, or memory loss. Somehow, emphasizing Gage's newly developed social shortcomings smacked of ingratitude to both providence and medicine. By 1868, however, Dr. Harlow was ready to acknowledge the full extent of his patient's personality change.

Gage's survival was duly noted, but with the caution reserved for freakish phenomena. The significance of his behavioral changes was largely lost. There were good reasons for this neglect. Even in the small world of brain science at the time, two camps were beginning to form. One held that psychological functions such as language or memory could never be traced to a particular region of the brain. If one had to accept, reluctantly, that the brain did produce the mind, it did so as a whole and not as a collection of parts with special functions. The other camp held that, on the contrary, the brain did have specialized parts and those parts generated separate mind functions. The rift between the two camps was not merely indicative of the infancy of brain research; the argument endured for another century and, to a certain extent, is still with us today.

Whatever scientific debate Phineas Gage's story elicited, it focused on the issue of localizing language and movement in the brain. The debate never turned to the connection between impaired social conduct and frontal lobe damage. I am reminded here of a saying of Warren McCulloch's: "When I point, look where I point, not at my finger." (McCulloch, a legendary neurophysiologist and a pioneer in the field that would become computational neuroscience, was also a poet and a prophet. This saying was usually part of a prophecy.) Few looked to where Gage was unwittingly pointing. It is of course difficult to imagine anybody in Gage's day with the knowledge *and* the courage to look in the proper direction. It was acceptable that the brain sectors whose damage would have caused Gage's heart to stop pumping and his lungs to stop breathing had not been touched by the iron rod. It was also acceptable that the brain sectors which control wakefulness were far from the iron's course and were thus spared. It was even acceptable that the injury did not render Gage unconscious for a long period. (The event anticipated what is current knowledge from studies of head injuries: The style of the injury is a critical variable. A severe blow to the head, even if no bone is broken and no weapon penetrates the brain, can cause a major disruption of wakefulness for a long time; the forces unleashed by the blow disorganize brain function profoundly. A penetrating injury in which the forces are concentrated on a narrow and steady path, rather than dissipate and accelerate the brain against the skull, may cause dysfunction only where brain tissue is actually destroyed, and thus spare brain function elsewhere.) But to understand Gage's behavioral change would have meant believing that normal social conduct required a particular corresponding brain region, and this concept was far more unthinkable than its equivalent for movement, the senses, or even language.

Gage's case was used, in fact, by those who did not believe that mind functions could be linked to specific brain areas. They took a cursory view of the medical evidence and claimed that if such a wound as Gage's could fail to produce paralysis or speech impairments, then it was obvious that neither motor control nor language could be traced to the relatively small brain regions that neurologists had identified as motor and language centers. They argued—in complete error, as we shall see—that Gage's wound directly damaged those centers.

The British physiologist David Ferrier was one of the few to take the trouble to analyze the findings with competence and wisdom. Ferrier's knowledge of other cases of brain lesion with behavioral changes, as well as his own pioneering experiments on electrical stimulation and ablation of the cerebral cortex in animals, had placed him in a unique position to appreciate Harlow's findings. He concluded that the wound spared motor and language "centers," that it did damage the part of the brain he himself had called the prefrontal cortex, and that such damage might be related to Gage's peculiar change in personality, to which Ferrier referred, picturesquely, as "mental degradation." The only supportive voices Harlow and Ferrier may have heard, in their very separate worlds, came from the followers of phrenology. . . .

A LANDMARK BY HINDSIGHT

There is no question that Gage's personality change was caused by a circumscribed brain lesion in a specific site. But that explanation would not be apparent until two decades after the accident, and it became vaguely acceptable only in this century. For a long time, most everybody, John Harlow included, believed that "the portion of the brain traversed, was, for several reasons, the best fitted of any part of the cerebral substance to sustain the injury": in other words, a part of the brain that did nothing much and was thus expendable. But nothing could be further from the truth, as Harlow himself realized. He wrote in 1868 that Gage's mental recovery "was only partial, his intellectual faculties being decidedly impaired, but not totally lost; nothing like dementia, but they were enfeebled in their manifestations, his mental operations being perfect in kind, but not in degree or quantity." The unintentional message in Gage's case was that observing social convention, behaving ethically, and making decisions advantageous to one's survival and progress require knowledge of rules and strategies *and* the integrity of specific brain systems. The problem with this message was that it lacked the evidence required to make it understandable and definitive. Instead the message became a mystery and came down to us as the "enigma" of frontal lobe function. Gage posed more questions than he gave answers.

To begin with, all we knew about Gage's brain lesion was that it was probably in the frontal lobe. That is a bit like saying that Chicago is probably in the United States—accurate but not very specific or helpful. Granted that the damage was likely to involve the frontal lobe, where exactly was it within that region? The left lobe? The right? Both? Somewhere else too? . . . New imaging technologies have helped us come up with the answer to this puzzle.

Then there was the nature of Gage's character defect. How did the abnormality develop? The primary cause, sure enough, was a hole in the head, but that just tells why the defect arose, not how. Might a hole anywhere in the frontal lobe have the same result? Whatever the answer, by what plausible means can destruction of a brain region change personality? If there are specific regions in the frontal lobe, what are they made of, and how do they operate in an intact brain? Are they some kind of "center" for social behavior? Are they modules selected in evolution, filled with problem-solving algorithms ready to tell us how to reason and make decisions? How do these modules, if that is what they are, interact with the environment during development to permit normal reasoning and decision making? Or are there in fact no such modules?

What were the mechanisms behind Gage's failure at decision making? It might be that the knowledge required to reason through a problem was destroyed or rendered inaccessible, so that he no longer could decide appropriately. It is possible also that the requisite knowledge remained intact and accessible but the strategies for reasoning were compromised. If this was the case, which reasoning steps were missing? More to the point, which steps are there for those who are allegedly normal? And if we are fortunate enough to glean the nature of some of these steps, what are their neural underpinnings?

Intriguing as all these questions are, they may not be as important as those which surround Gage's status as a human being. May he be described as having free will? Did he have a sense of right and wrong, or was he the victim of his new brain design, such that his decisions were imposed upon him and inevitable? Was he responsible for his acts? If we rule that he was not, does this tell us something about responsibility in more general terms? There are many Gages around us, people whose fall from social grace is disturbingly similar. Some have brain damage consequent to brain tumors, or head injury, or other neurological disease. Yet some have had no overt neurological disease and they still behave like Gage, for reasons having to do with their brains or with the society into which they were born. We need to understand the nature of these human beings whose actions can be destructive to themselves and to others, if we are to solve humanely the problems they pose. Neither incarceration nor the death penalty—among the responses that society currently offers for those individuals—contribute to our understanding or solve the problem. In fact, we should take the question further and inquire about our own responsibility when we "normal" individuals slip into the irrationality that marked Phineas Gage's great fall.

Gage lost something uniquely human, the ability to plan his future as a social being. How aware was he of this loss? Might he be described as self-conscious in the same sense that you and I are? Is it fair to say that his soul was diminished, or that he had lost his soul?

The Continuing Consciousness Theory of Personal Identity

JOHN LOCKE (1632–1704) was a British philosopher, captain of horse in the parliamentary army during the Glorious Revolution, physician, advisor to the Earl of Shaftesbury, and student and fellow of Christ Church College, Oxford, for nearly 30 years. His philosophical writings are characterized by anti-authoritarianism and an advocacy of reason as the tool for gaining the truth. Although he did not start writing much until age 57, he then produced many important works, including *Letters Concerning Toleration* and *Two Treatises of Government,* as well as his masterpiece, *An Essay Concerning Human Understanding.*

THINKING QUESTIONS

John Locke, *The Continuing Consciousness Theory of Personal Identity*

1. Locke distinguishes among "same man," "same substance," and "same person." Why does he do so? Why does he think these distinctions are important in addressing personal identity?
2. Locke maintains that to say that someone is a human being is to say that they have a living organized body of a certain sort—they are a certain kind of animal. What is it for a human to have the same continued life through time?
3. Locke maintains that "person" is not synonymous with "human being." How does Locke define "person"?
4. Locke argues that "it [is] the same consciousness that makes a man be himself to himself, personal identity depends on that only, whether it be annexed solely to one individual substance, or can be continued in a succession of several substances." How can consciousness be attached to a succession of several substances? What does Locke have in mind here? (Hint: he addresses this question in section 11.)
5. Why does Locke believe that even if people have immaterial spirits or souls, this is no help in explaining what a person is or in solving the problems of personal identity?
6. By "continuity of consciousness," does Locke have more in mind than "continuity of memory" or is memory really the key to personal identity?

1. *Wherein identity consists.* Another occasion the mind often takes of comparing, is the very being of things, when, considering anything as existing at any determined time and place, we compare it with itself existing at another time, and thereon form the ideas of identity and diversity. When we see anything to be in any place in any instant of time, we are sure (be it what it will) that it is that very thing, and not another which at that same time exists in another place, how like and undistinguishable soever it may be in all other respects: and in this consists identity, when the ideas it is attributed to vary not at all from what they were that moment wherein we consider their former existence, and to which we compare the present. For we never finding, nor conceiving it possible, that two things of the same kind should exist in the same place at the same time, we rightly conclude, that, whatever exists anywhere at any time, excludes all of the same kind, and is there itself alone. When therefore we demand whether anything be the same or no, it refers always to something that existed such a time in such a place, which it was certain, at that instant, was the same with itself, and no other. From whence it follows, that one thing cannot have two beginnings of existence, nor two things one beginning; it being impossible for two things of the same kind to be or exist in the same instant, in the very same place; or one and the same thing in different places. That, therefore, that had one beginning, is the same thing; and that which had a different beginning in time and place from that, is not the same, but diverse. That which has made the difficulty about this relation has been the little care and attention used in having precise notions of the things to which it is attributed. . . .

7. *Idea of identity suited to the idea it is applied to.* It is not therefore unity of substance that comprehends all sorts of identity, or will determine it in every case; but to conceive and judge of it aright, we must consider what idea the word it is applied to stands for: it being one thing to be the same substance, another the same man, and a third the same person, if person, man, and substance, are three names standing for three different ideas;—for such as is the idea belonging to that name, such must be the identity; which, if it had been a little more carefully attended to, would possibly have prevented a great deal of that confusion which often occurs about this matter, with no small seeming difficulties, especially concerning personal identity, which therefore we shall in the next place a little consider.

8. *Same man.* An animal is a living organized body; and consequently the same animal, as we have observed, is the same continued life communicated to different particles of matter, as they happen successively to be united to that organized living body. And whatever is talked of other definitions, ingenious observation puts it past doubt, that the idea in our minds, of which the sound man in our mouths is the sign, is nothing else but of an animal of such a certain form. Since I think I may be confident, that, whoever should see a creature of his own shape or make, though it had no more reason all its life than a cat or a parrot, would call him still a man; or whoever should hear a cat or a parrot discourse, reason, and philosophize, would call or think it nothing but

a cat or a parrot; and say, the one was a dull irrational man, and the other a very intelligent rational parrot. . . . I presume it is not the idea of a thinking or rational being alone that makes the idea of a man in most people's sense: but of a body, so and so shaped, joined to it: and if that be the idea of a man, the same successive body not shifted all at once, must, as well as the same immaterial spirit, go to the making of the same man.

9. *Personal identity.* This being premised, to find wherein personal identity consists, we must consider what person stands for;—which, I think, is a thinking intelligent being, that has reason and reflection, and can consider itself as itself, the same thinking thing, in different times and places; which it does only by that consciousness which is inseparable from thinking, and, as it seems to me, essential to it: it being impossible for any one to perceive without perceiving that he does perceive. When we see, hear, smell, taste, feel, meditate, or will anything, we know that we do so. Thus it is always as to our present sensations and perceptions: and by this every one is to himself that which he calls self:—it not being considered, in this case, whether the same self be continued in the same or divers substances. For, since consciousness always accompanies thinking, and it is that which makes every one to be what he calls self, and thereby distinguishes himself from all other thinking things, in this alone consists personal identity, i.e. the sameness of a rational being: and as far as this consciousness can be extended backwards to any past action or thought, so far reaches the identity of that person; it is the same self now it was then; and it is by the same self with this present one that now reflects on it, that that action was done.

10. *Consciousness makes personal identity.* But it is further inquired, whether it be the same identical substance. This few would think they had reason to doubt of, if these perceptions, with their consciousness, always remained present in the mind, whereby the same thinking thing would be always consciously present, and, as would be thought, evidently the same to itself. But that which seems to make the difficulty is this, that this consciousness being interrupted always by forgetfulness, there being no moment of our lives wherein we have the whole train of all our past actions before our eyes in one view, but even the best memories losing the sight of one part whilst they are viewing another; and we sometimes, and that the greatest part of our lives, not reflecting on our past selves, being intent on our present thoughts, and in sound sleep having no thoughts at all, or at least none with that consciousness which remarks our waking thoughts,—I say, in all these cases, our consciousness being interrupted, and we losing the sight of our past selves, doubts are raised whether we are the same thinking thing, i.e. the same substance or no. Which, however reasonable or unreasonable, concerns not personal identity at all. The question being what makes the same person; and not whether it be the same identical substance, which always thinks in the same person, which, in this case, matters not at all: different substances, by the same consciousness (where they do partake in it) being united into one person, as well as different bodies by the same life are united into one animal, whose identity

is preserved in that change of substances by the unity of one continued life. For, it being the same consciousness that makes a man be himself to himself, personal identity depends on that only, whether it be annexed solely to one individual substance, or can be continued in a succession of several substances. For as far as any intelligent being can repeat the idea of any past action with the same consciousness it had of it at first, and with the same consciousness it has of any present action; so far it is the same personal self. For it is by the consciousness it has of its present thoughts and actions, that it is self to itself now, and so will be the same self, as far as the same consciousness can extend to actions past or to come, and would be by distance of time, or change of substance, no more two persons, than a man be two men by wearing other clothes today than he did yesterday, with a long or a short sleep between: the same consciousness uniting those distant actions into the same person, whatever substances contributed to their production.

11. *Personal identity in change of substance.* That this is so, we have some kind of evidence in our very bodies, all whose particles, whilst vitally united to this same thinking conscious self, so that we feel when they are touched, and are affected by, and conscious of good or harm that happens to them, as a part of ourselves; i.e. of our thinking conscious self. Thus, the limbs of his body are to every one a part of Himself; he sympathizes and is concerned for them. Cut off a hand, and thereby separate it from that consciousness he had of its heat, cold, and other affections, and it is then no longer a part of that which is himself, any more than the remotest part of matter. Thus, we see the substance whereof personal self consisted at one time may be varied at another, without the change of personal identity; there being no question about the same person, though the limbs which but now were a part of it, be cut off. . . .

14. *Whether, the same immaterial substance remaining, there can be two persons.* As to the second part of the question, Whether the same immaterial substance remaining, there may be two distinct persons; which question seems to me to be built on this,—Whether the same immaterial being, being conscious of the action of its past duration, may be wholly stripped of all the consciousness of its past existence, and lose it beyond the power of ever retrieving it again: and so as it were beginning a new account from a new period, have a consciousness that cannot reach beyond this new state. All those who hold pre-existence are evidently of this mind; since they allow the soul to have no remaining consciousness of what it did in that pre-existent state, either wholly separate from body, or informing any other body; and if they should not, it is plain experience would be against them. So that personal identity, reaching no further than consciousness reaches, a pre-existent spirit not having continued so many ages in a state of silence, must needs make different persons. Suppose a Christian Platonist or a Pythagorean should, upon God's having ended all his works of creation the seventh day, think his soul hath existed ever since; and should imagine it has revolved in several human bodies; as I once met with one, who was persuaded his had been the soul of Socrates (how reasonably

I will not dispute; this I know, that in the post he filled, which was no inconsiderable one, he passed for a very rational man, and the press has shown that he wanted not parts or learning;)—would any one say, that he, being not conscious of any of Socrates's actions or thoughts, could be the same person with Socrates? Let any one reflect upon himself, and conclude that he has in himself an immaterial spirit, which is that which thinks in him, and, in the constant change of his body keeps him the same: and is that which he calls himself: let him also suppose it to be the same soul that was in Nestor or Thersites, at the siege of Troy, (for souls being, as far as we know anything of them, in their nature indifferent to any parcel of matter, the supposition has no apparent absurdity in it), which it may have been, as well as it is now the soul of any other man: but he now having no consciousness of any of the actions either of Nestor or Thersites, does or can he conceive himself the same person with either of them? Can he be concerned in either of their actions? attribute them to himself, or think them his own, more than the actions of any other men that ever existed? So that this consciousness, not reaching to any of the actions of either of those men, he is no more one self with either of them than if the soul or immaterial spirit that now informs him had been created, and began to exist, when it began to inform his present body; though it were never so true, that the same spirit that informed Nestor's or Thersites' body were numerically the same that now informs his. For this would no more make him the same person with Nestor, than if some of the particles of matter that were once a part of Nestor were now a part of this man; the same immaterial substance, without the same consciousness, no more making the same person, by being united to any body, than the same particle of matter, without consciousness, united to any body, makes the same person. But let him once find himself conscious of any of the actions of Nestor, he then finds himself the same person with Nestor.

15. *The body, as well as the soul, goes to the making of a man.* And thus may we be able, without any difficulty, to conceive the same person at the resurrection, though in a body not exactly in make or parts the same which he had here,—the same consciousness going along with the soul that inhabits it. But yet the soul alone, in the change of bodies, would scarce to any one but to him that makes the soul the man, be enough to make the same man. For should the soul of a prince, carrying with it the consciousness of the prince's past life, enter and inform the body of a cobbler, as soon as deserted by his own soul, every one sees he would be the same person with the prince, accountable only for the prince's actions: but who would say it was the same man? The body too goes to the making the man, and would, I guess, to everybody determine the man in this case, wherein the soul, with all its princely thoughts about it, would not make another man: but he would be the same cobbler to every one besides himself. I know that, in the ordinary way of speaking, the same person, and the same man, stand for one and the same thing. And indeed every one will always have a liberty to speak as he pleases, and to apply what articulate sounds to what ideas he thinks fit, and change

them as often as he pleases. But yet, when we will inquire what makes the same spirit, man, or person, we must fix the ideas of spirit, man, or person in our minds; and having resolved with ourselves what we mean by them, it will not be hard to determine, in either of them, or the like, when it is the same, and when not.

16. *Consciousness alone unites actions into the same person.* But though the same immaterial substance or soul does not alone, wherever it be, and in whatsoever state, make the same man; yet it is plain, consciousness, as far as ever it can be extended—should it be to ages past—unites existences and actions very remote in time into the same person, as well as it does the existences and actions of the immediately preceding moment: so that whatever has the consciousness of present and past actions, is the same person to whom they both belong. Had I the same consciousness that I saw the ark and Noah's flood, as that I saw an overflowing of the Thames last winter, or as that I write now, I could no more doubt that I who write this now, that saw the Thames overflowed last winter, and that viewed the flood at the general deluge, was the same self,—place that self in what substance you please—than that I who write this am the same myself now whilst I write (whether I consist of all the same substance, material or immaterial, or no) that I was yesterday. For as to this point of being the same self, it matters not whether this present self be made up of the same or other substances—I being as much concerned, and as justly accountable for any action that was done a thousand years since, appropriated to me now by this self-consciousness, as I am for what I did the last moment.

17. *Self depends on consciousness, not on substance.* Self is that conscious thinking thing,—whatever substance made up of, (whether spiritual or material, simple or compounded, it matters not)—which is sensible or conscious of pleasure and pain, capable of happiness or misery, and so is concerned for itself, as far as that consciousness extends. Thus every one finds that, whilst comprehended under that consciousness, the little finger is as much a part of himself as what is most so. Upon separation of this little finger, should this consciousness go along with the little finger, and leave the rest of the body, it is evident the little finger would be the person, the same person; and self then would have nothing to do with the rest of the body. As in this case it is the consciousness that goes along with the substance, when one part is separate from another, which makes the same person, and constitutes this inseparable self: so it is in reference to substances remote in time. That with which the consciousness of this present thinking thing can join itself, makes the same person, and is one self with it, and with nothing else; and so attributes to itself, and owns all the actions of that thing, as its own, as far as that consciousness reaches, and no further; as every one who reflects will perceive. . . .

20. *Absolute oblivion separates what is thus forgotten from the person, but not from the man.* But yet possibly it will still be objected,—Suppose I wholly lose the memory of some parts of my life, beyond a possibility of retrieving them, so that perhaps I shall never be conscious of them again; yet am I not the same

person that did those actions, had those thoughts that I once was conscious of, though I have now forgot them? To which I answer, that we must here take notice what the word I is applied to; which, in this case, is the man only. And the same man being presumed to be the same person, I is easily here supposed to stand also for the same person. But if it be possible for the same man to have distinct incommunicable consciousness at different times, it is past doubt the same man would at different times make different persons; which, we see, is the sense of mankind in the solemnest declaration of their opinions, human laws not punishing the mad man for the sober man's actions, nor the sober man for what the mad man did,—thereby making them two persons: which is somewhat explained by our way of speaking in English when we say such an one is "not himself," or is "beside himself"; in which phrases it is insinuated, as if those who now, or at least first used them, thought that self was changed; the selfsame person was no longer in that man. . . .

23. *Consciousness alone unites remote existences into one person.* Nothing but consciousness can unite remote existences into the same person: the identity of substance will not do it; for whatever substance there is, however framed, without consciousness there is no person: and a carcass may be a person, as well as any sort of substance be so, without consciousness.

The Bundle Theory of Personal Identity

DAVID HUME (1711–1776) is widely considered the most important philosopher to write in the English language. Born in Edinburgh, Scotland, young David was recognized as a child prodigy and sent to Edinburgh University at the age of 12. He was interested in history, mathematics, and contemporary science, but not so much in the law career his family had hoped for him. He spent considerable time in France with the great continental philosophers of his day like Rousseau, Diderot, D'Alembert, and D'Holbach. At the age of 28 he published his masterpiece, *A Treatise of Human Nature,* a book so far ahead of its time that it was insufficiently appreciated, causing Hume to comment famously that it had "fallen deadborn from the press, without exciting so much as a murmur among the zealots." His multivolume *History of England* met with more popular acclaim, becoming a bestseller and ensuring Hume's financial stability. Hume's other philosophical writings established his reputation as a skeptic and atheist, preventing him from ever holding a university appointment. His *Dialogues Concerning Natural Religion* was too controversial to be seen to press during his lifetime and was posthumously published in 1779. It has been called "*the* preeminent work in the philosophy of religion."

THINKING QUESTIONS

David Hume, *The Bundle Theory of Personal Identity*

1. Hume claims that when he looks inside himself, he cannot find any "self" more substantial than a fleeting collection of perceptions. Do you think that you possess some self other than what Hume describes? If so, why? What is it?
2. Hume claims that identity over time—the continuance of a person over a span of time—is fictitious. What does he mean by this?
3. Hume asks what binds or unites various perceptions into a person. He wonders whether there is a real bond among the perceptions or whether we simply feel that there is something which unifies the bundle. He claims that there is no genuine bond, but merely a "customary association of ideas." What is his reasoning?
4. Hume compares the self to a "republic or commonwealth." Why does he do so? What point is he trying to illustrate with this analogy?

5. Hume maintains that memory does not *produce* personal identity so much as *discover* it. By this he seems to mean that memory is not constitutive of personal identity but gives us the sense of being the same person over time. How is this idea related to what he says about cause and effect?

THERE ARE SOME PHILOSOPHERS, who imagine we are every moment intimately conscious of what we call our SELF; that we feel its existence and its continuance in existence; and are certain, beyond the evidence of a demonstration, both of its perfect identity and simplicity. . . . For my part, when I enter most intimately into what I call *myself,* I always stumble on some particular perception or other, of heat or cold, light or shade, love or hatred, pain or pleasure. I never can catch *myself* at any time without a perception, and never can observe any thing but the perception. When my perceptions are remov'd for any time, as by sound sleep; so long am I insensible of *myself,* and may truly be said not to exist. And were all my perceptions remov'd by death, and cou'd I neither think, nor feel, nor see, nor love, nor hate after the dissolution of my body, I shou'd be entirely annihilated, nor do I conceive what is farther requisite to make me a perfect non-entity. If any one, upon serious and unprejudic'd reflection thinks he has a different notion of *himself,* I must confess I call reason no longer with him. All I can allow him is, that he may be in the right as well as I, and that we are essentially different in this particular. He may, perhaps, perceive something simple and continu'd, which he calls *himself;* tho' I am certain there is no such principle in me.

But setting aside some metaphysicians of this kind, I may venture to affirm of the rest of mankind, that they are nothing but a bundle or collection of different perceptions, which succeed each other with an inconceivable rapidity, and are in a perpetual flux and movement. Our eyes cannot turn in their sockets without varying our perceptions. Our thought is still more variable than our sight; and all our other senses and faculties contribute to this change; nor is there any single power of the soul, which remains unalterably the same, perhaps for one moment. The mind is a kind of theatre, where several perceptions successively make their appearance; pass, re-pass, glide away, and mingle in an infinite variety of postures and situations. There is properly no *simplicity* in it at one time, nor *identity* in different; whatever natural propension we may have to imagine that simplicity and identity. The comparison of the theatre must not mislead us. They are the successive perceptions only, that constitute the mind; nor have we the most distant notion of the place, where these scenes are represented, or of the materials, of which it is compos'd.

What then gives us so great a propension to ascribe an identity to these successive perceptions, and to suppose ourselves possest of an invariable and uninterrupted existence thro' the whole course of our lives? In order to answer this question, we must distinguish betwixt personal identity, as it regards our thought or imagination, and as it regards our passions or the concern we take in ourselves. The first is our present subject . . .

We now proceed to explain the nature of *personal identity,* which has become so great a question in philosophy, especially of late years in *England,* where all the abstruser sciences are study'd with a peculiar ardour and application. And here 'tis evident, the same method of reasoning must be continu'd, which has so successfully explain'd the identity of plants, and animals, and ships, and houses, and of all the compounded and changeable productions either of art or nature. The identity, which we ascribe to the mind of man, is only a fictitious one, and of a like kind with that which we ascribe to vegetables and animal bodies. It cannot, therefore, have a different origin, but must proceed from a like operation of the imagination upon like objects.

But lest this argument shou'd not convince the reader; tho' in my opinion perfectly decisive; let him weigh the following reasoning, which is still closer and more immediate. 'Tis evident, that the identity, which we attribute to the human mind, however perfect we may imagine it to be, is not able to run the several different perceptions into one, and make them lose their characters of distinction and difference, which are essential to them. 'Tis still true, that every distinct perception, which enters into the composition of the mind, is a distinct existence, and is different, and distinguishable, and separable from every other perception, either contemporary or successive. But, as, notwithstanding this distinction and separability, we suppose the whole train of perceptions to be united by identity, a question naturally arises concerning this relation of identity; whether it be something that really binds our several perceptions together, or only associates their ideas in the imagination. That is, in other words, whether in pronouncing concerning the identity of a person, we observe some real bond among his perceptions, or only feel one among the ideas we form of them. This question we might easily decide, if we wou'd recollect what has been already proud at large, that the understanding never observes any real connexion among objects, and that even the union of cause and effect, when strictly examin'd, resolves itself into a customary association of ideas. For from thence it evidently follows, that identity is nothing really belonging to these different perceptions, and uniting them together; but is merely a quality, which we attribute to them, because of the union of their ideas in the imagination, when we reflect upon them. Now the only qualities, which can give ideas a union in the imagination, are these three relations above-mention'd. There are the uniting principles in the ideal world, and without them every distinct object is separable by the mind, and may be separately considered, and appears not to have any more connexion with any other object, than if disjoin'd by the greatest difference and remoteness. 'Tis, therefore, on some of these three relations of resemblance, contiguity and causation, that identity depends; and as the very essence of these relations consists in their producing an easy transition of ideas; it follows, that our notions of personal identity, proceed entirely from the smooth and uninterrupted progress of the thought along a train of connected ideas, according to the principles above-explain'd.

The only question, therefore, which remains, is, by what relations this uninterrupted progress of our thought is produc'd, when we consider the successive existence of a mind or thinking person. And here 'tis evident we must confine ourselves to resemblance and causation, and must drop contiguity, which has little or no influence in the present case.

To begin with *resemblance;* suppose we cou'd see clearly into the breast of another, and observe that succession of perceptions, which constitutes his mind or thinking principle, and suppose that he always preserves the memory of a considerable part of past perceptions; 'tis evident that nothing cou'd more contribute to the bestowing a relation on this succession amidst all its variations. For what is the memory but a faculty, by which we raise up the images of past perceptions? And as an image necessarily resembles its object, must not the frequent placing of these resembling perceptions in the chain of thought, convey the imagination more easily from one link to another, and make the whole seem like the continuance of one object? In this particular, then, the memory not only discovers the identity, but also contributes to its production, by producing the relation of resemblance among the perceptions. The case is the same whether we consider ourselves or others.

As to *causation;* we may observe, that the true idea of the human mind, is to consider it as a system of different perceptions or different existences, which are link'd together by the relation of cause and effect, and mutually produce, destroy, influence, and modify each other. Our impressions give rise to their correspondent ideas; said these ideas in their turn produce other impressions. One thought chaces another, and draws after it a third, by which it is expell'd in its turn. In this respect, I cannot compare the soul more properly to any thing than to a republic or commonwealth, in which the several members are united by the reciprocal ties of government and subordination, and give rise to other persons, who propagate the same republic in the incessant changes of its parts. And as the same individual republic may not only change its members, but also its laws and constitutions; in like manner the same person may vary his character and disposition, as well as his impressions and ideas, without losing his identity. Whatever changes he endures, his several parts are still connected by the relation of causation. And in this view our identity with regard to the passions serves to corroborate that with regard to the imagination, by the making our distant perceptions influence each other, and by giving us a present concern for our past or future pains or pleasures.

As a memory alone acquaints us with the continuance and extent of this succession of perceptions, 'tis to be considered, upon that account chiefly, as the source of personal identity. Had we no memory, we never shou'd have any notion of causation, nor consequently of that chain of causes and effects, which constitute our self or person. But having once acquir'd this notion of causation from the memory, we can extend the same chain of causes, and consequently the identity of our persons beyond our memory, and can comprehend times, and circumstances, and actions, which we have entirely forgot, but suppose in general to have existed. For how few of our past actions are there, of which we have any memory? Who can tell me, for instance, what were his thoughts and actions on the 1st of January 1715, the 11th of March 1719, and the 3rd of August 1733? Or will he affirm, because he has entirely forgot the incidents of these days, that the present self is not the same person with the self of that time; and by that means overturn all the most established notions of personal identity? In this view, therefore, memory does not so much *produce* as *discover* personal identity, by shewing us the relation of cause and effect among our different perceptions. 'Twill be incumbent on those, who affirm that memory produces entirely our personal identity, to give a reason why we can thus extend our identity beyond our memory.

The whole of this doctrine leads us to a conclusion, which is of great importance in the present affair, viz. that all the nice and subtile questions concerning personal identity can never possibly be decided, and are to be regarded rather as grammatical than as philosophical difficulties. Identity depends on the relations of ideas; and these relations produce identity, by means of that easy transition they occasion. But as the relations, and the easiness of the transition may diminish by insensible degrees, we have no just standard, by which we can decide any dispute concerning the time, when they acquire or lose a title to the name of identity. All the disputes concerning the identity of connected objects are merely verbal, except so far as the relation of parts—gives rise to some fiction or imaginary principle of union, as we have already observed.

What I have said concerning the first origin and uncertainty of our notion of identity, as apply'd to the human mind, may be extended with little or no variation to that of *simplicity*. An object, whose different co-existent parts are bound together by a close relation, operates upon the imagination after much the same manner as one perfectly simple and indivisible and requires not a much greater stretch of thought in order to its conception. From this similarity of operation we attribute a simplicity to it, and feign a principle of union as the support of this simplicity, and the center of all the different parts and qualities of the object.

The Bundle Theory

DEREK PARFIT (1942–) has been a fellow at All Souls College, Oxford, for many years. He has also taught frequently in the United States at institutions such as Harvard and New York University. His main philosophical interests are rationality, personal identity, morality, and the problem of future generations—all subjects addressed in his much-discussed book *Reasons and Persons* (Oxford University Press, 1984).

THINKING QUESTIONS

Derek Parfit, *The Bundle Theory*

1. Why does Parfit take his lead from split-brain cases? What are the odd features of such cases that prompt his reflections?
2. Parfit divides theories about personal identity into two major classes: Ego Theories and Bundle Theories. What are these two general types?
3. Parfit holds that most people have beliefs about the self that would be justified only if some version of the Ego Theory were true. What beliefs does he have in mind? How does the teletransportation case highlight these hidden beliefs?
4. Imagine Parfit's initial teletransportation case. Would you get into such a transporter? Why or why not?
5. According to the Bundle Theory, there is no fact of the matter about when you will die. When you go out of existence is, in a real sense, vague, a matter of practical decision. Parfit compares the persistence of persons to the persistence of a club with changing members. Do you think the club analogy is a good one? Do you agree that whether a club is the same club or not is merely a matter of practical decision? Is something analogous then true of persons?
6. In what ways can the Bundle Theory accommodate the split-brain cases better than the Ego Theory, according to Parfit?

IT WAS THE SPLIT-BRAIN cases which drew me into philosophy. [Psychological tests of split-brain patients] made use of two facts. We control each of our arms, and see what is in each half of our visual fields, with only one of our hemispheres. When someone's hemispheres have been disconnected, psychologists can thus present to this person two different written questions in the two halves of his visual field, and can receive two different answers written by this person's two hands.

Here is a simplified imaginary version of the kind of evidence that such tests provide. One of these people looks fixedly at the centre of a wide screen, whose left half is red and right half is blue. On each half in a darker shade are the words, 'How many colours can you see?' With both hands the person writes, 'Only one'. The words are now changed to read, 'Which is the only colour that you can see?' With one of his hands the person writes 'Red', with the other he writes 'Blue'.

If this is how such a person responds, I would conclude that he is having two visual sensations—that he does, as he claims, see both red and blue. But in seeing each colour he is not aware of seeing the other. He has two streams of consciousness, in each of which he can see only one colour. In one stream he sees red, and at the same time, in his other stream, he sees blue. More generally, he could be having at the same time two series of thoughts and sensations, in having each of which he is unaware of having the other.

This conclusion has been questioned. It has been claimed by some that there are not *two* streams of consciousness, on the ground that the sub-dominant hemisphere is a part of the brain whose functioning involves no consciousness. If this were true, these cases would lose most of their interest. I believe that it is not true, chiefly because, if a person's dominant hemisphere is destroyed, this person is able to react in the way in which, in the split-brain cases, the sub-dominant hemisphere reacts, and we do not believe that such a person is just an automaton, without consciousness. The sub-dominant hemisphere is, of course, much less developed in certain ways, typically having the linguistic abilities of a three-year-old. But three-year-olds are conscious. This supports the view that, in split-brain cases, there *are* two streams of consciousness.

Another view is that, in these cases, there are two persons involved, sharing the same body. I believe that we should reject this view. [Some deny] that there are two persons involved because [they] believe that there is only one person involved. I believe that, in a sense, the number of persons involved is none.

THE EGO THEORY AND THE BUNDLE THEORY

To explain this sense I must, for a while, turn away from the split-brain cases. There are two theories about what persons are, and what is involved in a person's continued existence over time. On the *Ego Theory,* a person's continued existence cannot be explained except as the continued existence of a particular *Ego,* or *subject of experiences*. An Ego Theorist claims that, if we ask what unifies someone's consciousness at any time—what makes it true, for example, that I can now both see what I am typing and hear the wind outside my window—the answer is that these are both experiences which are being had by me, this person, at this time. Similarly, what explains the unity of a person's whole life is the fact that all of the experiences in this life are had by the same person, or subject of experiences.

In its best-known form, the *Cartesian view*, each person is a persisting purely mental thing—a soul, or spiritual substance.

The rival view is the *Bundle Theory*. Like most styles in art—Gothic, baroque, rococo, etc.—this theory owes its name to its critics. But the name is good enough. According to the Bundle Theory, we can't explain either the unity of consciousness at any time, or the unity of a whole life, by referring to a person. Instead we must claim that there are long series of different mental states and events—thoughts, sensations, and the like—each series being what we call one life. Each series is unified by various kinds of causal relation, such as the relations that hold between experiences and later memories of them. Each series is thus like a bundle tied up with string.

In a sense, a Bundle Theorist denies the existence of persons. An outright denial is of course absurd. As Reid protested in the eighteenth century, 'I am not thought, I am not action, I am not feeling; I am something which thinks and acts and feels.' I am not a series of events, but a person. A Bundle Theorist admits this fact, but claims it to be only a fact about our grammar, or our language. There are persons or subjects in this language-dependent way. If, however, persons are believed to be more than this—to be separately existing things, distinct from our brains and bodies, and the various kinds of mental states and events—the Bundle Theorist denies that there are such things.

The first Bundle Theorist was Buddha, who taught 'anatta', or the *No Self view*. Buddhists concede that selves or persons have 'nominal existence', by which they mean that persons are merely combinations of other elements. Only what exists by itself, as a separate element, has instead what Buddhists call 'actual existence'. Here are some quotations from Buddhist texts:

> At the beginning of their conversation the king politely asks the monk his name, and receives the following reply: 'Sir, I am known as "Nagasena"; my fellows in the religious life address me as "Nagasena". Although my parents gave me the name . . . it is just an appellation, a form of speech, a description, a conventional usage. "Nagasena" is only a name, for no person is found here.'
>
> A sentient being does exist, you think, O Mara? You are misled by a false conception. This bundle of elements is void of Self, In it there is no sentient being. Just as a set of wooden parts Receives the name of carriage, So do we give to elements The name of fancied being.
>
> Buddha has spoken thus: 'O Brethren, actions do exist, and also their consequences, but the person that acts does not. There is no one to cast away this set of elements, and no one to assume a new set of them. There exists no Individual, it is only a conventional name given to a set of elements.'

Buddha's claims are strikingly similar to the claims advanced by several Western writers. Since these writers knew nothing of Buddha, the similarity of these claims suggests that they are not merely part of one cultural tradition, in one period. They may be, as I believe they are, true.

WHAT WE BELIEVE OURSELVES TO BE

Given the advances in psychology and neurophysiology, the Bundle Theory may now seem to be obviously true. It may seem uninteresting to deny that there are separately existing Egos, which are distinct from brains and bodies and the various kinds of mental states and events. But this is not the only issue. We may be convinced that the Ego Theory is false, or even senseless. Most of us, however, even if we are not aware of this, also have certain beliefs about what is involved in our continued existence over time. And these beliefs would only be justified if something like the Ego Theory was true. Most of us therefore have false beliefs about what persons are, and about ourselves.

These beliefs are best revealed when we consider certain imaginary cases, often drawn from science fiction. One such case is *teletransportation*. Suppose that you enter a cubicle in which, when you press a button, a scanner records the states of all of the cells in your brain and body, destroying both while doing so. This information is then transmitted at the speed of light to some other planet, where a replicator produces a perfect organic copy of you. Since the brain of your Replica is exactly like yours, it will seem to remember living your life up to the moment when you pressed the button, its character will be just like yours, and it will be in every other way psychologically continuous with you. This psychological continuity will not have its normal cause, the continued existence of your brain, since the causal chain will run through the transmission by radio of your 'blueprint'.

Several writers claim that, if you chose to be teletransported, believing this to be the fastest way of travelling, you would be making a terrible mistake. This would not be a way of travelling, but a way of dying. It may not, they concede, be quite as bad as ordinary death. It might be some consolation to you that, after your death, you will have this Replica, which can finish the book that you are writing, act as parent to your children, and so on. But, they insist, this Replica won't be you. It will merely be someone else, who is exactly like you. This is why this prospect is nearly as bad as ordinary death.

Imagine next a whole range of cases, in each of which, in a single operation, a different proportion of the cells in your brain and body would be replaced with exact duplicates. At the near end of this range, only 1 or 2 per cent would be replaced; in the middle, 40 or 60 percent; near the far end, 98 or 99 percent. At the far end of this range is pure teletransportation, the case in which all of your cells would be 'replaced'.

When you imagine that some proportion of your cells will be replaced with exact duplicates, it is natural to have the following beliefs. First, if you ask, 'Will I survive? Will the resulting person be me?', there must be an answer to this question. Either you will survive, or you are about to die. Second, the answer to this question must be either a simple 'Yes' or a simple 'No'. The person who wakes up either will or will not be you. There cannot be a third answer, such as that the person waking up will be half you. You can imagine yourself later being half-conscious. But if the resulting person will be fully conscious, he cannot be half you. To state these beliefs together: to the question, 'Will the resulting person be me?', there must always *be* an answer, which must be all-or-nothing.

There seem good grounds for believing that, in the case of teletransportation, your Replica would not be you. In a slight variant of this case, your Replica might be created while you were still alive, so that you could talk to one another. This seems to show that, if 100 percent of your cells were replaced, the result would merely be a Replica of you. At the other end of my range of cases, where only 1 percent would be replaced, the resulting person clearly *would* be you. It therefore seems that, in the cases in between, the resulting person must be either you, or merely a Replica. It seems that one of these must be true, and that it makes a great difference which is true.

HOW WE ARE NOT WHAT WE BELIEVE

If these beliefs were correct, there must be some critical percentage, somewhere in this range of cases, up to which the resulting person would be you, and beyond which he would merely be your Replica. Perhaps, for example, it would be you who would wake up if the proportion of cells replaced were 49 percent, but if just a few more cells were also replaced, this would make all the difference, causing it to be someone else who would wake up.

That there must be some such critical percentage follows from our natural beliefs. But this conclusion is most implausible. How could a few cells make such a difference? Moreover, if there is such a critical percentage, no one could ever discover where it came. Since in all these cases the resulting person would believe that he was you, there could never be any evidence about where, in this range of cases, he would suddenly cease to be you.

On the Bundle Theory, we should reject these natural beliefs. Since you, the person, are not a separately existing entity, we can know exactly what would happen without answering the question of what will happen to you. Moreover, in the cases in the middle of my range, it is an empty question whether the resulting person would be you, or would merely be someone else who is exactly like you. These are not here two different possibilities, one of which must be true. These are merely two different descriptions of the very same course of events. If 50 percent of your cells were replaced with exact duplicates, we could call the resulting person you, or we could call him merely your Replica. But since these are not here different possibilities, this is a mere choice of words.

As Buddha claimed, the Bundle Theory is hard to believe. It is hard to accept that it could be an empty question whether one is about to die, or will instead live for many years.

What we are being asked to accept may be made clearer with this analogy. Suppose that a certain club exists for some time, holding regular meetings. The meetings then cease. Some years later, several people form a club with the same name, and the same rules. We can ask, 'Did these people revive the very same club? Or did they merely start up another club which is exactly similar?' Given certain further details, this would be another empty question. We could know just what happened without answering this question. Suppose that someone said: 'But there must be an answer. The club meeting later must either be, or not be, the very same club.' This would show that this person didn't understand the nature of clubs.

In the same way, if we have any worries about my imagined cases, we don't understand the nature of persons. In each of my cases, you would know that the resulting person would be both psychologically and physically exactly like you, and that he would have some particular proportion of the cells in your brain and body—90 percent, or 10 percent, or, in the case of teletransportation, 0 percent. Knowing this, you know everything. How could it be a real question what would happen to you, unless you are a separately existing Ego, distinct from a brain and body, and the various kinds of mental state and event? If there are no such Egos, there is nothing else to ask a real question about.

Accepting the Bundle Theory is not only hard; it may also affect our emotions. As Buddha claimed, it may undermine our concern about our own futures. This effect can be suggested by redescribing this change of view. Suppose that you are about to be destroyed, but will later have a Replica on Mars. You would naturally believe that this prospect is about as bad as ordinary death, since your Replica won't be you. On the Bundle Theory, the fact that your Replica won't be you just consists in the fact that, though it will be fully psychologically continuous with you, this continuity won't have its normal cause. But when you object to teletransportation you are not objecting merely to the abnormality of this cause. You are objecting that this cause won't get *you* to Mars. You fear that the abnormal cause will fail to produce a further and all-important fact, which is different from the fact that your Replica will be psychologically continuous with you. You do not merely want there to be psychological continuity between you and some future person. You want to *be* this future person. On the Bundle Theory, there is no such special further fact. What you fear will not happen, in this imagined case, *never* happens. You want the person on Mars to be you in a specially intimate way in which no future person will ever be you. This means that, judged from the standpoint of your natural beliefs, even ordinary survival is about as bad as teletransportation. *Ordinary survival is about as bad as being destroyed and having a Replica.*

HOW THE SPLIT-BRAIN CASES SUPPORT THE BUNDLE THEORY

The truth of the Bundle Theory seems to me, in the widest sense, as much a scientific as a philosophical conclusion. I can imagine kinds of evidence which would have justified believing in the existence of separately existing Egos, and believing that the continued existence of these Egos is what explains the continuity of each mental life. But there is in fact very little evidence in favour of this Ego Theory, and much for the alternative Bundle Theory.

Some of this evidence is provided by the split-brain cases. On the Ego Theory, to explain what unifies our experiences at any one time, we should simply claim that these are all experiences which are being had by the same person. Bundle Theorists reject this explanation. This disagreement is hard to resolve in ordinary cases. But consider the simplified split-brain case that I described. We show to my imagined patient a placard whose left half is blue and right half is red. In one of this person's two streams of consciousness, he is aware of seeing only blue, while at the same time, in his other stream, he is aware of seeing only red. Each of these two visual experiences is combined with other experiences, like that of being aware of moving one of his hands. What unifies the experiences, at any time, in each of this person's two streams of consciousness? What unifies his awareness of seeing only red with his awareness of moving one hand? The answer cannot be that these experiences are being had by the same person. This answer cannot explain the unity of each of this person's two streams of consciousness, since it ignores the disunity between these streams. This person is now having all of the experiences in both of his two streams. If this fact was what unified these experiences, this would make the two streams one.

These cases do not, I have claimed, involve two people sharing a single body. Since there is only one person involved, who has two streams of consciousness, the Ego Theorist's explanation would have to take the following form. He would have to distinguish between persons and subjects of experiences, and claim that, in split-brain cases, there are *two* of the latter. What unifies the experiences in one of the person's two streams would have to be the fact that these experiences are all being had by the same subject of experiences. What unifies the experiences in this person's other stream would have to be the fact that they are being had by another subject of experiences. When this explanation takes this form, it becomes much less plausible. While we could assume that 'subject of experiences', or 'Ego', simply meant 'person', it was easy to believe that there are subjects of experiences. But if there can be subjects of experiences that are not persons, and if in the life of a split-brain patient there are at any time two different subjects of experiences—two different Egos—why should we believe that there really are such things? This does not amount to a refutation. But it seems to me a strong argument against the Ego Theory.

As a Bundle Theorist, I believe that these two Egos are idle cogs. There is another explanation of the unity of consciousness, both in ordinary cases and in split-brain cases. It is simply a fact that ordinary people are, at any time, aware of having several different experiences. This awareness of several different experiences can be helpfully compared with one's awareness, in short-term memory, of several different experiences. Just as there can be a single memory of just having had several experiences, such as hearing a bell strike three times, there can be a single state of awareness both of hearing the fourth striking of this bell, and of seeing, at the same time, ravens flying past the bell-tower.

Unlike the Ego Theorist's explanation, this explanation can easily be extended to cover split-brain cases. In such cases there is, at any time, not one state of awareness of several different experiences, but two such states. In the case I described, there is one state of awareness of both seeing only red and of moving one hand, and there is another state of awareness of both seeing only blue and moving the other hand. In claiming that there are two such states of awareness, we are not postulating the existence of unfamiliar entities, two separately existing Egos which are not the same as the single person whom the case involves. This explanation appeals to a pair of mental states which would have to be described anyway in a full description of this case.

I have suggested how the split-brain cases provide one argument for one view about the nature of persons. I should mention another such argument, provided by an imagined extension of these cases, first discussed at length by David Wiggins.

In this imagined case a person's brain is divided, and the two halves are transplanted into a pair of different bodies. The two resulting people live quite separate lives. This imagined case shows that personal identity is not what matters. If I was about to divide, I should conclude that neither of the resulting people will be me. I will have ceased to exist. But this way of ceasing to exist is about as good—or as bad—as ordinary survival.

Some of the features of Wiggins's imagined case are likely to remain technically impossible. But the case cannot be dismissed, since its most striking feature, the division of one stream of consciousness into separate streams, has already happened. This is a second way in which the actual split-brain cases have great theoretical importance. They challenge some of our deepest assumptions about ourselves.

Epistemology

Do you have a right to your own opinion? Most people think that they do, but what does this mean exactly? One sense of having a right to your own opinion is this: in a free society, you will not be arrested or punished by the state for speaking your mind. This sounds like a pretty good idea. Here's another possible meaning of what it is to have a right to your own opinion: that you have a right to believe whatever you want. It is far less clear that *this* is a good idea. After all, you don't have a right to *do* whatever you want. Some things are just wrong to do—stealing, lying, killing, etc. You could do those things, sure, but you would be doing the wrong thing; you don't have a right to steal and lie, and so on. Just as some actions are wrong to perform, perhaps some things are just wrong to believe. If so, then maybe you don't have a right to believe whatever you want—there are things you shouldn't believe and you are in the wrong if you do believe them. What are things that are wrong to believe? Traditionally, people have thought that one shouldn't believe *false* things. You shouldn't believe that 1 + 1 = 3, that the moon is made of green cheese, or that leprechauns are secretly running the world. It might not be a moral failing to believe false things like these, but it is an intellectual failing.

Of course, it is all well and good to say that we shouldn't believe false things. In the case of 1 + 1 or the (non)cheesiness of the moon, it is easy to tell what's true from what's false. The problem is that there are many topics, claims, contentions, theories, suppositions, and hypotheses about which it is not so easy to distinguish the true from the false. So how do we do it? The first step is to develop a critical, skeptical frame of mind. Just as a good detective won't fall for the bogus clues planted by the perpetrator, we must also resist believing spurious claims when the evidence is lacking or misleading. The reading by Michael Shermer discusses the downside of believing whatever we want without regard for the truth, and he offers some principles for developing a critical mind. It is not only strange claims that deserve critical attention, however. As Bertrand Russell points out, the true nature of the everyday world around us is not as obvious as we tend to think. There is a difference between *appearance* and *reality,* and we need to resist conflating the two. Russell recommends that we consider the sources of our knowledge—the methods we use to acquire knowledge—and investigate how reliable or trustworthy those methods really are.

Our quest to gain true beliefs and avoid false ones requires that we have good reasons, evidence, and data for believing p instead of not-p. The more evidence there is in favor of some claim, the more likely it is to be true. But how much evidence do we need before it is reasonable to believe some contention?

In the reading by William Clifford, he argues that we should form beliefs solely on the basis of evidence, and that the evidence should in some sense be *conclusive*. Clifford famously maintains that it is actually immoral to believe something on the basis of insufficient evidence. High standards like Clifford's will be very good at keeping us from forming false beliefs (it is hard to get genuinely compelling evidence for something that isn't true). But on the other hand such high standards will prevent us from believing in true things for which we had insufficient evidence. Such concerns motivate William James, who, in his essay, recommends that it is perfectly rational for us to lower our standards and be more risk-positive when it comes to belief. When a possibility is a live option for you, James suggests that you go ahead and take a chance; you'll believe more truths (although you'll be prone to more mistakes as well).

René Descartes is extremely concerned with mistakes. He wants to find a way to make our knowledge of the empirical world every bit as secure and certain as our knowledge in geometry and mathematics. Yet our senses have misled us in the past, and this may make us a bit doubtful of their testimony now. Even worse are the skeptical arguments that Descartes considers—arguments that conclude that in fact we know nothing at all about a world outside of our minds. Such an idea may sound crazy, but the skeptics' arguments are notoriously difficult to refute. John Locke, on the other hand, thinks we know about an extra-mental world precisely because all of our knowledge comes through experience. When we are born, our minds are a *tabula rasa* (blank slate), upon which experience writes. Once we recognize the method by which we come to have knowledge (i.e., the empirical method), we can investigate what specific things we actually do know. In the final selection, George Berkeley agrees with Locke that our knowledge comes from experience, but not experience of an extra-mental world, since—according to Berkeley—there is no world at all outside of our minds. Like the skeptical views discussed by Descartes, Berkeley's idealism is both shocking and tough to prove mistaken.

It is not for nothing that epistemology is often considered the most fundamental philosophical discipline: to gain knowledge of ethics, freedom, personal identity, the divine, etc., we must first know what knowledge is and how we might get some of it. Otherwise, we are hunting in the dark. The twin questions of what we know and how we come to have knowledge remain among the most interesting and essential questions in philosophy.

I Am Therefore I Think

MICHAEL SHERMER (1954–) is the publisher of *Skeptic* magazine and the director of the Skeptics Society. He has published a half dozen books on the history of science, the difference between science and pseudoscience, and the promotion of the scientific method for understanding the world. He has appeared on numerous television programs and authors a monthly column for *Scientific American*. He is a former professional marathon cyclist who once rode across the United States (3100 miles) in 10 days 8 hours.

THINKING QUESTIONS

Michael Shermer, *I Am Therefore I Think*

1. When Shermer was a professional marathon cyclist, he tried all kinds of unusual things that were supposed to help his speed and endurance. He reasoned that "I figured I had nothing to lose, and who knows, maybe they would increase performance." Do you think that Shermer really had nothing to lose by trying the various rituals, regimens, and procedures that he did?
2. Shermer's skepticism is not the view that no one knows anything. What does he mean by "skepticism"?
3. What is Shermer's definition of "science"? Is there any form of knowledge that would not be scientific by this definition? If there is, why do you think it is *knowledge*?
4. What is Shermer's contrast between objectivity and mysticism? What is the value of external validation for one's beliefs?
5. You can't question everything all of the time. On the other hand, blind credulity has some significant downsides to it as well. So how should we strike a balance? How should we decide which things to believe, which to doubt, and which to suspend judgment about?

ON THE OPENING PAGE OF HIS SPLENDID LITTLE BOOK *To Know a Fly*, biologist Vincent Dethier makes this humorous observation about how children grow up to be scientists: "Although small children have taboos against stepping on ants because such actions are said to bring on rain, there has never seemed to be a taboo against pulling off the legs or wings of flies. Most children eventually outgrow this behavior. Those who do not either come to a bad end or become biologists" In their early years, children are knowledge junkies, questioning everything in their purview, though exhibiting little skepticism. Most never learn to distinguish between skepticism and credulity. It took me a long time.

In 1979, unable to land a full-time teaching job, I found work as a writer for a cycling magazine. The first day on the job, I was sent to a press conference held in honor of a man named John Marino who had just ridden his bicycle across America in a record 13 days, 1 hour, 20 minutes. When I asked him how he did it, John told me about special vegetarian diets, megavitamin therapy, fasting, colonics, mud baths, iridology, cytotoxic blood testing, Rolfing, acupressure and acupuncture, chiropractic and massage therapy, negative ions, pyramid power, and a host of weird things with which I was unfamiliar. Being a fairly inquisitive fellow, when I took up cycling as a serious sport I thought I would try these things to see for myself whether they worked. I once fasted for a week on nothing but a strange mixture of water, cayenne pepper, garlic, and lemon. At the end of the week, John and I rode from Irvine to Big Bear Lake and back, some seventy miles each way. About halfway up the mountain I collapsed, violently ill from the concoction. John and I once rode out to a health spa near Lake Elsinore for a mud bath that was supposed to suck the toxins out of my body. My skin was dyed red for a week. I set up a negative ion generator in my bedroom to charge the air to give me more energy. It turned the walls black with dust. I got my iris read by an iridologist, who told me that the little green flecks in my eyes meant something was wrong with my kidneys. To this day my kidneys are functioning fine.

I really got into cycling. I bought a racing bike the day after I met John and entered my first race that weekend. I did my first century ride (100 miles) a month later, and my first double century later that year. I kept trying weird things because I figured I had nothing to lose and, who knows, maybe they would increase performance. I tried colonics because supposedly bad things clog the plumbing and thus decrease digestive efficiency, but all I got was an hour with a hose in a very uncomfortable place. I installed a pyramid in my apartment because it was supposed to focus energy. All I got were strange looks from guests. I starting getting massages, which were thoroughly enjoyable and quite relaxing. Then my massage therapist decided that "deep tissue" massage was best to get lactic acid out of the muscles. That wasn't so relaxing. One guy massaged me with his feet. That was even less relaxing. I tried Rolfing, which is *really* deep tissue massage. That was so painful that I never went back.

In 1982 John and I and two other men competed in the first Race Across America, the 3,000-mile, nonstop, transcontinental bike race from Los Angeles to New York. In preparation, we went for cytotoxic blood testing because it was supposed to detect food allergies that cause blood platelets to clump together and block capillaries, thus decreasing blood flow. By now we were a little skeptical of the truth of these various claims, so we sent in one man's blood under several names. Each sample came back with different food allergies, which told us that there was a problem with their testing, not with our blood. During the race, I slept with an "Electro-Acuscope," which was to measure my brain waves and put me into an alpha state for better sleeping. It was also supposed to rejuvenate my muscles and heal any injuries. The company swore that it helped Joe Montana win the Super Bowl. Near as I can figure, it was totally ineffective.

The Electro-Acuscope was the idea of my chiropractor. I began visiting a chiropractor not because I needed one but because I had read that energy flows through the spinal cord and can get blocked at various places. I discovered that the more I got adjusted, the more I needed to get adjusted because my neck and back kept going "out." This went on for a couple of years until I finally quit going altogether, and I've never needed a chiropractor since.

All told, I raced as a professional ultra-marathon cyclist for ten years, all the while trying anything and everything (except drugs and steroids) that might improve my performance. As the Race Across America got bigger—it was featured for many years on ABC's *Wide World of Sports*—I had many offers to try all sorts of things, which I usually did. From this ten-year experiment with a subject pool of one, I drew two conclusions: nothing increased performance, alleviated pain, or enhanced well-being other than long hours in the saddle, dedication to a consistent training schedule, and a balanced diet; and it pays to be skeptical. But what does it mean to be skeptical?

WHAT IS A SKEPTIC?

I became a skeptic on Saturday, August 6, 1983, on the long, climbing road to Loveland Pass, Colorado. It was Day 3 of the second Race Across America, and the nutritionist on my support crew believed that if I followed his megavitamin therapy program, I would win the race. He was in a Ph.D. program and was trained as a nutritionist, so I figured he knew what he was doing. Every six hours I would force down a huge handful of assorted vitamins and minerals. Their taste and smell nearly made me sick, and they went right through me, producing what I thought had to be the most expensive and colorful urine in America. After three days of this, I decided that megavitamin therapy, along with colonics, iridology, Rolfing, and all these other alternative, New Age therapies were a bunch of hooey. On that climb up Loveland Pass, I dutifully put the vitamins in my mouth and then spit them out up the road when my nutritionist wasn't looking. Being skeptical seemed a lot safer than being credulous.

After the race I discovered that the nutritionist's Ph.D. was to be awarded by a nonaccredited nutrition school and, worse, *I* was the subject of his doctoral dissertation! Since that time I have noticed about extraordinary claims and New Age beliefs that they tend to attract people on the fringes of academia—people without formal scientific training, credentialed (if at all) by nonaccredited schools, lacking research data to support their claims, and excessively boastful about what their particular elixir can accomplish. This does not automatically disprove all claims made by individuals exhibiting these characteristics, but it would be wise to be especially skeptical when encountering them.

Being skeptical is nothing new, of course. Skepticism dates back 2,500 years to ancient Greece and Plato's Academy. But Socrates' quip that "All I know is that I know nothing" doesn't get us far. Modern skepticism has developed into a science-based movement, beginning with Martin Gardner's 1952 classic, *Fads and Fallacies in the Name of Science*. Gardner's numerous essays and books over the next four decades, such as *Science: Good, Bad, and Bogus* (1981), *The New Age: Notes of a Fringe Watcher* (1991), and *On the Wild Side* (1992), established a pattern of incredulity about a wide variety of bizarre beliefs. Skepticism joined pop culture through magician James "the Amazing" Randi's countless psychic challenges and media appearances in the 1970s and 1980s (including thirty-six appearances on the *Tonight Show*). Philosopher Paul Kurtz helped create dozens of skeptics groups throughout the United States and abroad, and publications such as *Skeptic* magazine have national and international circulation. Today, a burgeoning group of people calling themselves skeptics—scientists, engineers, physicians, lawyers, professors, teachers, and the intellectually curious from all walks of life—conduct investigations, hold monthly meetings and annual conferences, and provide the media and the general public with natural explanations for apparently supernatural phenomena.

Modern skepticism is embodied in the scientific method, which involves gathering data to test natural explanations for natural phenomena. A claim becomes factual when it is confirmed to such an extent that it would be reasonable to offer temporary agreement. But all facts in science are provisional and subject to challenge, and therefore skepticism is a *method* leading to provisional conclusions. Some things, such as water dowsing, extrasensory perception, and creationism, have been tested and have failed the tests often enough that we can provisionally conclude that they are false. Other things, such as hypnosis, lie detectors, and vitamin C, have been tested but the results are inconclusive, so we must continue formulating and testing hypotheses until we can reach a provisional conclusion. The key to skepticism is to navigate the treacherous straits between "know nothing" skepticism and "anything goes" credulity by continuously and vigorously applying the methods of science.

The flaw in pure skepticism is that when taken to an extreme, the position itself cannot stand. If you are skeptical about everything, you must be skeptical of your own skepticism. Like the decaying subatomic particle, pure skepticism spins off the viewing screen of our intellectual cloud chamber.

There is also a popular notion that skeptics are closed-minded. Some even call us cynics. In principle, skeptics are not closed-minded or cynical. What I mean by a skeptic is *one who questions the validity of a particular claim by calling for evidence to prove or disprove it*. In other words, skeptics are from Missouri—the "show me" state. When we hear a fantastic claim, we say, "That's nice, prove it."

Here is an example. For many years I had heard stories about the "Hundredth Monkey phenomenon" and was fascinated with the possibility that there might be some sort of collective consciousness that we could tap into to decrease crime, eliminate wars, and generally unite as a single species. In the 1992 presidential election, in fact, one candidate—Dr. John Hagelin from the Natural Law Party—claimed that if elected he would implement a plan that would solve the problems of our inner cities: meditation. Hagelin and others (especially proponents of Transcendental Meditation, or TM) believe that thought can somehow be transferred between people, especially people in a meditative state; if enough people meditate at the same time, some sort of critical mass will be reached, thereby inducing significant planetary change. The Hundredth Monkey phenomenon is commonly cited as empirical proof of this astonishing theory. In the 1950s, so the story goes, Japanese scientists gave monkeys on Koshima Island potatoes. One day one of the monkeys learned to wash the potatoes and then taught the skill to others. When about one hundred monkeys had learned the skill—the so-called critical mass—suddenly all the monkeys knew it, even those on other islands hundreds of miles away. Books about the phenomenon have spread this theory widely in New Age circles. Lyall Watson's *Lifetide* (1979) and Ken Keyes's *The Hundredth Monkey* (1982), for example, have been through multiple printings and sold millions of copies; Elda Hartley even made a film called *The Hundredth Monkey.*

As an exercise in skepticism, start by asking whether events really happened as reported. They did not. In 1952, primatologists began providing Japanese macaques with sweet potatoes to keep the monkeys from raiding local farms. One monkey did learn to wash dirt off the sweet potatoes in a stream or the ocean, and other monkeys did learn to imitate the behavior. Now let's examine Watson's book more carefully. He admits that "one has to gather the rest of the story from personal anecdotes and bits of folklore among primate researchers, because most of them are still not quite sure what happened. So I am forced to improvise the details." Watson then speculates that "an unspecified number of monkeys on Koshima were washing sweet potatoes in the sea"—hardly the level of precision one expects. He then makes this statement: "Let us say, for argument's sake, that the number was ninety-nine and that at 11:00 A.M. on a Tuesday, one further convert was added to the fold in the usual way. But the addition of the hundredth monkey apparently carried the number across some sort of threshold, pushing it through a kind of critical mass." At this point, says Watson, the habit "seems to have jumped natural barriers and to have appeared spontaneously on other islands" (1979, pp. 2–8).

Let's stop right there. Scientists do not "improvise" details or make wild guesses from "anecdotes" and "bits of folklore." In fact, some scientists *did* record *exactly* what happened (for example, Baldwin et al. 1980; Imanishi 1983; Kawai 1962). The research began with a troop of twenty monkeys in 1952, and every monkey on the island was carefully observed. By 1962, the troop had increased to fifty-nine monkeys and exactly thirty-six of the fifty-nine monkeys were washing their sweet potatoes. The "sudden" acquisition of the behavior actually took ten years, and the "hundred monkeys" were actually only thirty-six in 1962. Furthermore, we can speculate endlessly about what the monkeys knew, but the fact remains that not all of the monkeys in the troop were exhibiting the washing behavior. The thirty-six monkeys were not a critical mass even at home. And while there are some reports of similar behavior on other islands, the observations were made between 1953 and 1967. It was not sudden, nor was it necessarily connected to Koshima. The monkeys on other islands could have discovered this simple skill themselves, for example, or inhabitants on other islands might have taught them. In any case, not only is there no evidence to support this extraordinary claim, there is not even a real phenomenon to explain.

SCIENCE AND SKEPTICISM

Skepticism is a vital part of science, which I define as *a set of methods designed to describe and interpret observed or inferred phenomena, past or present, and aimed at building a testable body of knowledge open to rejection or confirmation.* In other words, science is a specific way of analyzing information with the goal of testing claims. Defining the *scientific method* is not so simple, as philosopher of science and Nobel laureate Sir Peter Medawar observed: "Ask a scientist what he conceives the scientific method to be and he will adopt an expression that is at once solemn and shifty-eyed: solemn, because he feels he ought to declare an opinion; shifty-eyed, because he is wondering how to conceal the fact that he has no opinion to declare."

A sizable literature exists on the scientific method, but there is little consensus among authors. This does not mean that scientists do not know what they are doing. Doing and explaining may be two different things. However, scientists agree that the following elements are involved in thinking scientifically:

Induction: Forming a hypothesis by drawing general conclusions from existing data.

Deduction: Making specific predictions based on the hypotheses.

Observation: Gathering data, driven by hypotheses that tell us what to look for in nature.

Verification: Testing the predictions against further observations to confirm or falsify the initial hypotheses.

Science, of course, is not this rigid; and no scientist consciously goes through "steps." The process is a constant interaction of making observations, drawing conclusions, making predictions, and checking them against evidence. And data-gathering observations are not made in a vacuum. The hypotheses shape what sorts of observations you will make of nature, and these hypotheses are themselves shaped by your education, culture, and particular biases as an observer.

This process constitutes the core of what philosophers of science call the *hypothetico-deductive* method, which, according to the *Dictionary of the History of Science,* involves "(a) putting forward a hypothesis, (b) conjoining it with a statement of 'initial conditions,' (c) deducing from the two a prediction, and (d) finding whether or not the prediction is fulfilled." It is not possible to say which came first, the observation or the hypothesis, since the two are inseparably interactive. But additional observations are what flesh out the hypothetico-deductive process, and they serve as the final arbiter on the validity of predictions. As Sir Arthur Stanley Eddington noted, "For the truth of the conclusions of science, observation is the supreme court of appeal." Through the scientific method, we may form the following generalizations:

Hypothesis: A testable statement accounting for a set of observations.

Theory: A well-supported and well-tested hypothesis or set of hypotheses.

Fact: A conclusion confirmed to such an extent that it would be reasonable to offer provisional agreement.

A theory may be contrasted with a *construct:* a nontestable statement to account for a set of observations. The living organisms on Earth may be accounted for by the statement "God made them" or the statement "They evolved." The first statement is a construct, the second a theory. Most biologists would even call evolution a fact.

Through the scientific method, we aim for *objectivity:* basing conclusions on external validation. And we avoid *mysticism:* basing conclusions on personal insights that elude external validation.

There is nothing wrong with personal insight as a starting point. Many great scientists have attributed their important ideas to insight, intuition, and other mental leaps hard to pin down. Alfred Russel Wallace said that the idea of natural selection "suddenly flashed upon" him during an attack of malaria. But intuitive ideas and mystical insights do not become objective until they are externally validated. As psychologist Richard Hardison explained,

> Mystical "truths," by their nature, must be solely personal, and they can have no possible external validation. Each has equal claim to truth. Tealeaf reading and astrology and Buddhism; each is equally sound or unsound if we judge by the absence of related evidence. This is not intended to disparage any one of the faiths; merely to note the impossibility of verifying their correctness. The mystic is in a paradoxical position. When he seeks external support for his views he must turn to external arguments, and he denies mysticism in the process. External validation is, by definition, impossible for the mystic.

Science leads us toward *rationalism:* basing conclusions on logic and evidence. For example, how do we know the Earth is round? It is a logical conclusion drawn from observations such as

- The shadow of the Earth on the moon is round.
- The mast of a ship is the last thing seen as it sails into the distance.

- The horizon is curved.
- Photographs from space.

And science helps us avoid *dogmatism:* basing conclusions on authority rather than logic and evidence. For example, how do we know the Earth is round?

- Our parents told us.
- Our teachers told us.
- Our minister told us.
- Our textbook told us.

Dogmatic conclusions are not necessarily wrong, but they do raise other questions: How did the authorities come by their conclusions? Were they guided by science or some other means?

THE ESSENTIAL TENSION BETWEEN SKEPTICISM AND CREDULITY

It is important to recognize the fallibility of science and the scientific method. But within this fallibility lies its greatest strength: self-correction. Whether a mistake is made honestly or dishonestly, whether a fraud is unknowingly or knowingly perpetrated, in time it will be flushed out of the system by lack of external verification. The cold fusion fiasco is a classic example of the system's swift exposure of error.

Because of the importance of this self-correcting feature, among scientists there is at best what Caltech physicist and Nobel laureate Richard Feynman called "a principle of scientific thought that corresponds to a kind of utter honesty—a kind of leaning over backwards." Said Feynman, "If you're doing an experiment, you should report everything that you think might make it invalid—not only what you think is right about it: other causes that could possibly explain your results."

Despite these built-in mechanisms, science remains subject to problems and fallacies ranging from inadequate mathematical notation to wishful thinking. But, as philosopher of science Thomas Kuhn noted, the "essential tension" in science is between total commitment to the status quo and blind pursuit of new ideas. The paradigm shifts and revolutions in science depend upon proper balancing of these opposing impulses. When enough of the scientific community (particularly those in positions of power) are willing to abandon orthodoxy in favor of the (formerly) radical new theory, then and only then can a paradigm shift occur.

Charles Darwin is a good example of a scientist who negotiated the essential tension between skepticism and credulity. Historian of science Frank Sulloway identifies three characteristics in Darwin's thinking that helped Darwin find his balance: (1) he respected others' opinions but was willing to challenge authorities (he intimately understood the theory of special creation, yet he overturned it with his own theory of natural selection); (2) he paid close attention to negative evidence (Darwin included a chapter called "Difficulties on Theory" in the *Origin of Species*—as a result his opponents could rarely present him with a challenge that he had not already addressed); (3) he generously used the work of others (Darwin's collected correspondence numbers over 14,000 letters, most of which include lengthy discussions and question-and-answer sequences about scientific problems). Darwin was constantly questioning, always learning, confident enough to formulate original ideas yet modest enough to recognize his own fallibility. "Usually, it is the scientific community as a whole that displays this essential tension between tradition and change," Sulloway observed, "since most people have a preference for one or the other way of thinking. What is relatively rare in the history of science is to find these contradictory qualities combined in such a successful manner in one individual."

The essential tension in dealing with "weird things" is between being so skeptical that revolutionary ideas pass you by and being so open-minded that flimflam artists take you in. Balance can be found by answering a few basic questions: What is the quality of the evidence for the claim? What are the background and credentials of the person making the claim? Does the thing work as claimed? As I discovered during my personal odyssey in the world of alternative health and fitness therapies and gadgets, often the evidence is weak, the background and credentials of the claimants are questionable, and the therapy or gadget almost never does what it is supposed to.

This last point may well be the crucial one. I regularly receive calls about astrology. Callers usually want to know about the theory behind astrology. They are wondering whether the alignment of planetary bodies can significantly influence human destiny. The answer is no, but the more important point is that one need not understand gravity and the laws governing the motion of the planets to evaluate astrology. All one needs to do is ask, Does it work? That is, do astrologers accurately and specifically predict human destiny from the alignment of the planets? No, they do not. Not one astrologer predicted the crash of TWA flight #800; not one astrologer predicted the Northridge earthquake. Thus, the theory behind astrology is irrelevant, because astrology simply does not do what astrologers claim it can do. It vanishes hand-in-hand with the hundredth monkey.

THE TOOL OF THE MIND

Vincent Dethier, in his discussion of the rewards of science, runs through a pantheon of the obvious ones—money, security, honor—as well as the transcendent: "a passport to the world, a feeling of belonging to one race, a feeling that transcends political boundaries and ideologies, religions, and languages." But he brushes all these aside for one "more lofty and more subtle"—the natural curiosity of humans:

> One of the characteristics that sets man apart from all the other animals (and animal he indubitably is) is a need for knowledge for

> its own sake. Many animals are curious, but in them curiosity is a facet of adaptation. Man has a hunger to know. And to many a man, being endowed with the capacity to know, he has a duty to know. All knowledge, however small, however irrelevant to progress and well-being, is a part of the whole. It is of this the scientist partakes. To know the fly is to share a bit in the sublimity of Knowledge. That is the challenge and the joy of science.

At its most basic level, curiosity about how things work is what science is all about. As Feynman observed, "I've been caught, so to speak—like someone who was given something wonderful when he was a child, and he's always looking for it again. I'm always looking, like a child, for the wonders I know I'm going to find—maybe not every time, but every once in a while." The most important question in education, then, is this: What tools are children given to help them explore, enjoy, and understand the world? Of the various tools taught in school, science and thinking skeptically about all claims should be near the top.

Children are born with the ability to perceive cause-effect relations. Our brains are natural machines for piecing together events that may be related and for solving problems that require our attention. We can envision an ancient hominid from Africa chipping and grinding and shaping a rock into a sharp tool for carving up a large mammalian carcass. Or perhaps we can imagine the first individual who discovered that knocking flint would create a spark that would light a fire. The wheel, the lever, the bow and arrow, the plow—inventions intended to allow us to shape our environment rather than be shaped by it—started us down a path that led to our modern scientific and technological world.

On the most basic level, we must think to remain alive. To think is the most essential human characteristic. Over three centuries ago, the French mathematician and philosopher René Descartes, after one of the most thorough and skeptical purges in intellectual history, concluded that he knew one thing for certain: *"Cogito ergo sum—I think therefore I am."* But to be human is to think. To reverse Descartes, *"Sum ergo cogito—I am therefore I think."*

Appearance and Reality

BERTRAND RUSSELL (1872–1970) was one of the most influential philosophers of the 20th century. Russell wrote widely on the issues of concern to analytic philosophy, especially on logic and mathematics. Some of Russell's most important philosophical works include *Principia Mathematica* (co-authored with A. N. Whitehead and published in three volumes between 1910 and 1913), *An Inquiry into Meaning and Truth* (1940), and *A History of Western Philosophy* (1945). Russell was an outspoken social critic who wrote widely on issues of war and social justice. He received the Nobel Prize for Literature in 1950 for "his varied and significant writings in which he champions humanitarian ideals and freedom of thought." One of Russell's goals was to make philosophy accessible to a popular audience. He did so with widely read books like *The Problems of Philosophy* (1912) and *Why I Am Not a Christian* (1927).

THINKING QUESTIONS

Bertrand Russell, *Appearance and Reality*

1. Russell says that in daily life we sometimes make certain assumptions that we later recognize as mistaken. Can you think of an example of a belief you were quite sure of, that you later found out was false?
2. What do you think Russell means when he says to view the world as a painter? A philosopher?
3. Russell says that the table in front of him isn't brown all over. Why not? What point is Russell making by pointing out this simple fact?
4. Isn't the shape of the table always the same? Where would you have to be to *view* the table as a rectangle?
5. How do Russell's examples suggest a difference between *appearance* and *reality*?

IS THERE ANY KNOWLEDGE IN THE WORLD which is so certain that no reasonable man could doubt it? This question, which at first sight might not seem difficult, is really one of the most difficult that can be asked. When we have realized the obstacles in the way of a straightforward and confident answer, we shall be well launched on the study of philosophy—for philosophy is merely the attempt to answer such ultimate questions, not carelessly and dogmatically, as we do in ordinary life and even in the sciences, but critically, after exploring all that makes such questions puzzling, and after realizing all the vagueness and confusion that underlie our ordinary ideas.

In daily life, we assume as certain many things which, on a closer scrutiny, are found to be so full of apparent contradictions that only a great amount of thought enables us to know what it is that we really may believe. In the search for certainty, it is natural to begin with our present experiences, and in some sense, no doubt, knowledge is to be derived from them. But any statement as to what it is that our immediate experiences make us know is very likely to be wrong. It seems to me that I am now sitting in a chair, at a table of a certain shape, on which I see sheets of paper with writing or print. By turning my head I see out of the window buildings and clouds and the sun. I believe that the sun is about ninety-three million miles from the earth; that it is a hot globe many times bigger than the earth; that, owing to the earth's rotation, it rises every morning, and will continue to do so for an indefinite time in the future. I believe that, if any other normal person comes into my room, he will see the same chairs and tables and books and papers as I see, and that the table which I see is the same as the table which I feel pressing against my arm. All this seems to be so evident as to be hardly worth stating, except in answer to a man who doubts whether I know anything. Yet all this may be reasonably doubted, and all of it requires much careful discussion before we can be sure that we have stated it in a form that is wholly true.

To make our difficulties plain, let us concentrate attention on the table. To the eye it is oblong, brown and shiny, to the touch it is smooth and cool and hard; when I tap it, it gives out a wooden sound. Any one else who sees and feels and hears the table will agree with this description, so that it might seem as if no difficulty would arise; but as soon as we try to be more precise our troubles begin. Although I believe that the table is 'really' of the same colour all over, the parts that reflect the light look much brighter than the other parts, and some parts look white because of reflected light. I know that, if I move, the parts that reflect the light will be different, so that the apparent distribution of colours on the table will change. It follows that if several people are looking at the table at the same moment, no two of them will see exactly the same distribution of colours, because no two can see it from exactly the same point of view, and any change in the point of view makes some change in the way the light is reflected.

For most practical purposes these differences are unimportant, but to the painter they are all-important: the painter has to unlearn the habit of thinking that things seem to have the colour which common sense says they 'really' have, and to learn the habit of seeing things as they appear. Here we have already the beginning of one of the distinctions that cause most trouble in philosophy—the distinction between 'appearance' and 'reality', between what things seem to be and what they are. The painter wants to know what things seem to be, the practical man and the philosopher want to know what they are; but the philosopher's wish to know this is stronger than the practical man's, and is more troubled by knowledge as to the difficulties of answering the question.

To return to the table. It is evident from what we have found, that there is no colour which preeminently appears to be *the* colour of the table, or even of any one particular part of the table—it appears to be of different colours from different points of view, and there is no reason for regarding some of these as more really its colour than others. And we know that even from a given point of view the colour will seem different by artificial light, or to a colour-blind man, or to a man wearing blue spectacles, while in the dark there will be no colour at all, though to touch and hearing the table will be unchanged. This colour is not something which is inherent in the table, but something depending upon the table and the spectator and the way the light falls on the table. When, in ordinary life, we speak of *the* colour of the table, we only mean the sort of colour which it will seem to have to a normal spectator from an ordinary point of view under usual conditions of light. But the other colours which appear under other conditions have just as good a right to be considered real; and therefore, to avoid favouritism, we are compelled to deny that, in itself, the table has any one particular colour.

The same thing applies to the texture. With the naked eye one can see the grain, but otherwise the table looks smooth and even. If we looked at it through a microscope, we should see roughnesses and hills and valleys, and all sorts of differences that are imperceptible to the naked eye. Which of these is the 'real' table? We are naturally tempted to say that what we see through the microscope is more real, but that in turn would be changed by a still more powerful microscope. If, then, we cannot trust what we see with the naked eye, why should we trust what we see through a microscope? Thus, again, the confidence in our senses with which we began deserts us.

The *shape* of the table is no better. We are all in the habit of judging as to the 'real' shapes of things, and we do this so unreflectingly that we come to think we actually see the real shapes. But, in fact, as we all have to learn if we try to draw, a given thing looks different in shape from every different point of view. If our table is 'really' rectangular, it will look, from almost all points of view, as if it had two acute angles and two obtuse angles. If opposite sides are parallel, they will look as if they converged to a point away from the spectator; if they are of equal length, they will look as if the nearer side were longer. All these things are not commonly noticed in looking at a table, because experience has taught us to construct the 'real' shape from the apparent shape, and the 'real' shape is what interests us as practical men. But the 'real' shape is not what we see; it is something inferred from what we see. And what we see is constantly changing in shape as we move about the room; so that here again the senses seem not to give us the truth about the table itself, but only about the appearance of the table.

Similar difficulties arise when we consider the sense of touch. It is true that the table always gives us a sensation of hardness, and we feel that it resists pressure. But the sensation we obtain depends upon how hard we press the table and also upon what part of the body we press with; thus the various sensations due to various pressures or various parts of the body cannot be supposed to reveal *directly* any definite property of the table, but at most to be *signs* of some property which perhaps *causes* all the sensations, but is not actually apparent in any of them. And the same applies still more obviously to the sounds which can be elicited by rapping the table.

Thus it becomes evident that the real table, if there is one, is not the same as what we immediately experience by sight or touch or hearing. The real table, if there is one, is not *immediately* known to us at all, but must be an inference from what is immediately known. Hence, two very difficult questions at once arise; namely, (1) Is there a real table at all? (2) If so, what sort of object can it be?

The Ethics of Belief

WILLIAM K. CLIFFORD (1845–1879) was a mathematician by training and profession. He entered King's College, London, at the age of 15 and three years later went to Trinity College, Cambridge, where he won prizes for his work in mathematics. In 1871 he was appointed professor of mathematics and mechanics at University College, London, and worked on non-Euclidean geometries. His best-known philosophical work is his argument that we have a moral obligation to believe claims only if there is sufficient evidence to support them. Although a vigorous man who performed one-handed chin-ups, in 1876 Clifford suffered a collapse from overwork. He never fully recovered and died at the age of 34.

THINKING QUESTIONS

William K. Clifford, *The Ethics of Belief*

1. Consider Clifford's parable of the shipowner. Can you think of cases in your own life in which you talked yourself into believing something, even when you really knew that the evidence pointed in the opposite direction?
2. Clifford holds that there can be wicked beliefs and good ones. Is a belief good or bad because of the content of the belief (what it is about) or because of the reasons the belief was acquired?
3. Clifford argues that it is immoral to hold unjustified beliefs. He considers the criticism that only actions are moral or immoral, not beliefs, and that one could hold an unjustified belief and not act on it. In such a case, goes the argument, there is no immorality. Clifford rejects this argument. What is his reasoning?
4. What do you think Clifford would say about beliefs that were held merely on faith?
5. Do you agree with Clifford that no one could sincerely and genuinely have a belief without that belief leading in some way to action or to further beliefs which cause action?
6. Clifford seems to assume that we have a kind of voluntary control over our beliefs—that we are able to stop believing something once we realize our evidence is insufficient, for example. Do you think you have this sort of control over your beliefs?

A SHIPOWNER WAS ABOUT TO SEND TO SEA AN EMIGRANT-SHIP. He knew that she was old, and not overwell built at the first; that she had seen many seas and climes, and often had needed repairs. Doubts had been suggested to him that possibly she was not seaworthy. These doubts preyed upon his mind, and made him unhappy; he thought that perhaps he ought to have her thoroughly overhauled and refitted, even though this should put him at great expense. Before the ship sailed, however, he succeeded in overcoming these melancholy reflections. He said to himself that she had gone safely through so many voyages and weathered so many storms that it was idle to suppose she would not come safely home from this trip also. He would put his trust in Providence, which could hardly fail to protect all these unhappy families that were leaving their fatherland to seek for better times elsewhere. He would dismiss from his mind all ungenerous suspicions about the honesty of builders and contractors. In such ways he acquired a sincere and comfortable conviction that his vessel was thoroughly safe and seaworthy; he watched her departure with a light heart, and benevolent wishes for the success of the exiles in their strange new home that was to be; and he got his insurance-money when she went down in mid-ocean and told no tales.

What shall we say of him? Surely this, that he was verily guilty of the death of those men. It is admitted that he did sincerely believe in the soundness of his ship; but the sincerity of his conviction can in no wise help him, because *he had no right to believe on such evidence as was before him.* He had acquired his belief not by honestly earning it in patient investigation, but by stifling his doubts. And although in the end he may have felt so sure about it that he could not think otherwise, yet inasmuch as he had knowingly and willingly worked himself into that frame of mind, he must be held responsible for it.

Let us alter the case a little, and suppose that the ship was not unsound after all; that she made her voyage safely, and many others after it. Will that diminish the guilt of her owner? Not one jot. When an action is once done, it is right or wrong forever; no accidental failure of its good or evil fruits can possibly alter that. The man would not have been innocent, he would only have been not found out. The question of right or wrong has to do with the origin of his belief, not the matter of it; not what it was, but how he got it; not whether it turned out to be true or false, but whether he had a right to believe on such evidence as was before him.

There was once an island in which some of the inhabitants professed a religion teaching neither the doctrine of original sin nor that of eternal punishment. A suspicion got abroad that the professors of this religion had made use of unfair means to get their doctrines taught to children. They were accused of wresting the laws of their country in such a way as to remove children from the care of their natural and legal guardians; and even of stealing them away and keeping them concealed from their friends and relations. A certain number of men formed themselves into a society for the purpose of agitating the public about this matter. They published grave accusations against individual citizens of the highest position and character, and did all in their power to injure these citizens in their exercise of their professions. So great was the noise they made, that a Commission was appointed to investigate the facts; but after the Commission had carefully inquired into all the evidence that could be got, it appeared that the accused were innocent. Not only had they been accused of insufficient evidence, but the evidence of their innocence was such as the agitators might easily have obtained, if they had attempted a fair inquiry. After these disclosures the inhabitants of that country looked upon the members of the agitating society, not only as persons whose judgment was to be distrusted, but also as no longer to be counted honourable men. For although they had sincerely and conscientiously believed in the charges they had made, *yet they had no right to believe on such evidence as was before them.* Their sincere convictions, instead of being honestly earned by patient inquiring, were stolen by listening to the voice of prejudice and passion.

Let us vary this case also, and suppose, other things remaining as before, that a still more accurate investigation proved the accused to have been really guilty. Would this make any difference in the guilt of the accusers? Clearly not; the question is not whether their belief was true or false, but whether they entertained it on wrong grounds. They would no doubt say, "Now you see that we were right after all; next time perhaps you will believe us." And they might be believed, but they would not thereby become honourable men. They would not be innocent, they would only be not found out. Every one of them, if he chose to examine himself *in foro conscientiae,* would know that he had acquired and nourished a belief, when he had no right to believe on such evidence as was before him; and therein he would know that he had done a wrong thing.

It may be said, however, that in both these supposed cases it is not the belief which is judged to be wrong, but the action following upon it. The shipowner might say, "I am perfectly certain that my ship is sound, but still I feel it my duty to have her examined, before trusting the lives of so many people to her." And it might be said to the agitator, "However convinced you were of the justice of your cause and the truth of your convictions, you ought not to have made a public attack upon any man's character until you had examined the evidence on both sides with the utmost patience and care."

In the first place, let us admit that, so far as it goes, this view of the case is right and necessary; right, because even when a man's belief is so fixed that he cannot think otherwise, he still has a choice in the action suggested by it, and so cannot escape the duty of investigating on the ground of the strength of his convictions; and necessary, because those who are not yet capable of controlling their feelings and thoughts must have a plain rule dealing with overt acts."

But this being premised as necessary, it becomes clear that it is not sufficient, and that our previous judgment is required to supplement it. For it is not possible so to sever the belief from the action it suggests as to condemn the one without condemning the other.

No man holding a strong belief on one side of a question, or even wishing to hold a belief on one side, can investigate it with such fairness and completeness as if he were really in doubt and unbiased; so that the existence of a belief not founded on fair inquiry unfits a man for the performance of this necessary duty.

Nor is it that truly a belief at all which has not some influence upon the actions of him who holds it. He who truly believes that which prompts him to an action has looked upon the action to lust after it, he has committed it already in his heart. If a belief is not realized immediately in open deeds, it is stored up for the guidance of the future . . . No real belief, however trifling and fragmentary it may seem, is ever truly insignificant; it prepares us to receive more of its like, confirms those which resembled it before, and weakens others; and so gradually it lays a stealthy train in our inmost thoughts, which may someday explode into overt action, and leave its stamp upon our character for ever.

And no one man's belief is in any case a private matter which concerns himself alone. Our lives are guided by that general conception of the course of things which has been created by society for social purposes. Our words, our phrases, our forms and processes and modes of thought, are common property, fashioned and perfected from age to age; an heirloom which every succeeding generation inherits as a precious deposit and a sacred trust to be handled on to the next one, not unchanged but enlarged and purified, with some clear marks of its proper handiwork. Into this, for good or ill, is woven every belief of every man who has speech of his fellows. An awful privilege, and an awful responsibility, that we should help to create the world in which posterity will live.

In the two supposed cases which have been considered, it has been judged wrong to believe on insufficient evidence, or to nourish belief by suppressing doubts and avoiding investigation. The reason of this judgment is not far to seek: it is that in both these cases the belief held by one man was of great importance to other men. But forasmuch as no belief held by one man, however seemingly trivial the belief, and however obscure the believer, is ever actually insignificant or without its effect on the fate of mankind, we have no choice but to extend our judgment to all cases of belief whatever. Belief, that sacred faculty which prompts the decisions of our will, and knits into harmonious working all the compacted energies of our being, is ours not for ourselves but for humanity. It is rightly used on truths which have been established by long experience and waiting toil, and which have stood in the fierce light of free and fearless questioning. Then it helps to bind men together, and to strengthen and direct their common action. It is desecrated when given to unproved and unquestioned statements, for the solace and private pleasure of the believer; to add a tinsel splendour to the plain straight road of our life and display a bright mirage beyond it; or even to drown the common sorrows of our kind by a self-deception which allows them not only to cast down, but also to degrade us. Whoso would deserve well of his fellows in this matter will guard the purity of his beliefs with a very fanaticism of jealous care, lest at any time it should rest on an unworthy object, and catch a stain which can never be wiped away.

It is not only the leader of men, statesmen, philosopher, or poet, that owes this bounden duty to mankind. Every rustic who delivers in the village alehouse his slow, infrequent sentences, may help to kill or keep alive the fatal superstitions which clog his race. Every hard-worked wife of an artisan may transmit to her children beliefs which shall knit society together, or rend it in pieces. No simplicity of mind, no obscurity of station, can escape the universal duty of questioning all that we believe.

It is true that this duty is a hard one, and the doubt which comes out of it is often a very bitter thing. It leaves us bare and powerless where we thought that we were safe and strong. To know all about anything is to know how to deal with it under all circumstances. We feel much happier and more secure when we think we know precisely what to do, no matter what happens, than when we have lost our way and do not know where to turn. And if we have supposed ourselves to know all about anything, and to be capable of doing what is fit in regard to it, we naturally do not like to find that we are really ignorant and powerless, that we have to begin again at the beginning, and try to learn what the thing is and how it is to be dealt with—if indeed anything can be learnt about it. It is the sense of power attached to a sense of knowledge that makes men desirous of believing, and afraid of doubting.

This sense of power is the highest and best of pleasures when the belief on which it is founded is a true belief, and has been fairly earned by investigation. For then we may justly feel that it is common property, and hold good for others as well as for ourselves. Then we may be glad, not that *I* have learned secrets by which I am safer and stronger, but that *we men* have got mastery over more of the world; and we shall be strong, not for ourselves but in the name of Man and his strength. But if the belief has been accepted on insufficient evidence, the pleasure is a stolen one. Not only does it deceive ourselves by giving us a sense of power which we do not really possess, but it is sinful, because it is stolen in defiance of our duty to mankind. That duty is to guard ourselves from such beliefs as from pestilence, which may shortly master our own body and then spread to the rest of the town. What would be thought of one who, for the sake of a sweet fruit, should deliberately run the risk of delivering a plague upon his family and his neighbours?

And, as in other such cases, it is not the risk only which has to be considered; for a bad action is always bad at the time when it is done, no matter what happens afterwards. Every time we let ourselves believe for unworthy reasons, we weaken our powers of self-control, of doubting, of judicially and fairly weighing evidence. We all suffer severely enough from the maintenance and support of false beliefs and the fatally wrong actions which they lead to, and the evil born when one such belief is entertained is great and wide. But a greater and wider evil arises when the credulous character is maintained and supported, when a habit of believing for unworthy reasons is fostered and made permanent. If I steal money from any person, there may be no harm done from the mere transfer of possession; he may not feel the loss, or it may prevent him from using the money badly. But I cannot help doing this great wrong towards Man, that I make myself dishonest. What hurts society is not that it should lose its property, but that it should become a den of thieves, for then it must cease to be society. This is why we ought not to do evil, that good may come; for at any rate this great evil has come, that we have done evil and are made wicked thereby. In like manner, if I let myself believe anything on insufficient evidence, there may be no great harm done by the mere belief; it may be true after all, or I may never have occasion to exhibit it in outward acts. But I cannot help doing this great wrong towards Man, that I make myself credulous. The danger to society is not merely that it should believe wrong things, though that is great enough; but that it should become credulous, and lose the habit of testing things and inquiring into them; for then it must sink back into savagery.

The harm which is done by credulity in a man is not confined to the fostering of a credulous character in others, and consequent support of false beliefs. Habitual want of care about what I believe leads to habitual want of care in others about the truth of what is told to me. Men speak the truth of one another when each reveres the truth in his own mind and in the other's mind; but how shall my friend revere the truth in my mind when I myself am careless about it, when I believe things because I want to believe them, and because they are comforting and pleasant? Will he not learn to cry, "Peace," to me, when there is no peace? By such a course I shall surround myself with a thick atmosphere of falsehood and fraud, and in that I must live. It may matter little to me, in my cloud-castle of sweet illusions and darling lies; but it matters much to Man that I have made my neighbours ready to deceive. The credulous man is father to the liar and the cheat; he lives in the bosom of this his family, and it is no marvel if he should become even as they are. So closely are our duties knit together, that whoso shall keep the whole law, and yet offend in one point, he is guilty of all.

To sum up: *it is wrong always, everywhere, and for anyone, to believe anything upon insufficient evidence.*

If a man, holding a belief which he was taught in childhood or persuaded of afterwards, keeps down and pushes away any doubts which arise about it in his mind, purposely avoids the reading of books and the company of men that call into question or discuss it, and regards as impious those questions which cannot easily be asked without disturbing it—the life of that man is one long sin against mankind.

The Will to Believe

WILLIAM JAMES (1842–1910) was a quintessential American philosopher. Brother of the novelist Henry James, William was a patrician New Englander who studied and traveled widely in Europe, collected biological specimens along the Amazon, and received an MD degree that he never used. He spent his professional career as a professor at Harvard, where he wrote seminal works in psychology and philosophy. The combination of James's scientific training and his strong mystical streak came together in his pragmatic approach to truth. James suffered from ill health much of his life, including severe depression, and died of heart failure at his summer home in New Hampshire.

THINKING QUESTIONS

William James, *The Will to Believe*

1. James argues that we do not have volitional control over our beliefs, that we cannot, just by willing it, believe that Abraham Lincoln's existence is a myth, for example. Is he right? If he is right, then are we really *responsible* in any sense for our beliefs?
2. Why does James write that "our faith is someone else's faith, and in the greatest matters this is most the case"? Do you agree with him?
3. James maintains that as rational thinkers our goal is to gain truth and avoid error. Yet it is challenging to pursue this goal when the evidence is mixed and inconclusive. James thinks that when the evidence for and against some proposition X is inconclusive, we have three choices: (1) we can withhold belief and continue to amass evidence for and against until we can make a more informed decision, (2) we can go ahead and believe X anyway, or (3) we can go ahead and disbelieve X anyway. What would Clifford recommend we do in such a case?
4. James thinks that the strategy of withholding belief when faced with conflicting evidence amounts to accepting this risk averse strategy: *better to miss out on some truths rather than add more errors*. He argues that a more risk positive strategy is equally rational, though: *better to add more errors rather than miss out on some truths*. Which approach sounds more reasonable to you?
5. James is concerned with whether we should have very high standards for belief or lower our standards and be willing to believe on shakier evidence. What do you think about this issue in a legal setting? High

standards means that we would convict on very compelling evidence (thus seldom convicting the innocent, but at the same time setting guilty people free against whom we had little evidence). Lower standards means that we would be willing to convict on weaker evidence (thus mistakenly convicting more innocent people, but also convicting more guilty people). Is it better to (1) let some guilty go free rather than convict more innocents, or (2) convict more innocents rather than let more guilty go free?

6. What should we do if we have no evidence for or against a claim at all? Should we withhold belief in such a case?

SECTION 1. HYPOTHESES AND OPTIONS

Let us give the name of hypothesis to anything that may be proposed to our belief; and just as the electricians speak of live and dead wires, let us speak of any hypothesis as either *live* or *dead*. A live hypothesis is one which appeals as a real possibility to him to whom it is proposed. If I asked you to believe in the Mahdi, the notion makes no electric connection with your nature,—it refuses to scintillate with any credibility at all. As an hypothesis it is completely dead. To an Arab, however (even if he be not one of the Mahdi's followers), the hypothesis is among the mind's possibilities: it is alive. This shows that deadness and liveness in an hypothesis are not intrinsic properties, but relations to the individual thinker. They are measured by his willingness to act. The maximum of liveness in an hypothesis, means willingness to act irrevocably. Practically, that means belief; but there is some believing tendency wherever there is willingness to act at all.

Next, let us call the decision between two hypotheses an *option*. Options may be of several kinds. They may be—1. *living* or *dead;* 2. *forced* or *avoidable;* 3. *momentous* or *trivial;* and for our purposes we may call an option a *genuine* option when it is of the forced, living, and momentous kind.

1. A living option is one in which both hypotheses are live ones. If I say to you: "Be a theosophist or be a Mohammedan," it is probably a dead option, because for you neither hypothesis is likely to be alive. But if I say: "Be an agnostic or be a Christian," it is otherwise: trained as you are, each hypothesis makes some appeal, however small, to your belief.
2. Next, if I say to you: "Choose between going out with your umbrella or without it," I do not offer you a genuine option, for it is not forced. You can easily avoid it by not going out at all. Similarly, if I say, "Either love me or hate me," "Either call my theory true or call it false," your option is avoidable. You may remain indifferent to me, neither loving nor hating, and you may decline to offer any judgment as to my theory. But if I say, "Either accept this truth or go without it," I put on you a forced option, for there is no standing place outside of the alternative. Every dilemma

based on a complete logical disjunction, with no possibility of not choosing, is an option of this forced kind.

3. Finally, if I were Dr. Nansen and proposed to you to join my North Pole expedition, your option would be momentous; for this would probably be your only similar opportunity, and your choice now would either exclude you from the North Pole sort of immortality altogether or put at least the chance of it into your hands. He who refuses to embrace a unique opportunity loses the prize as surely as if he tried and failed. Per contra, the option is trivial when the opportunity is not unique, when the stake is insignificant, or when the decision is reversible if it later prove unwise. Such trivial options abound in the scientific life. A chemist finds an hypothesis live enough to spend a year in its verification: he believes in it to that extent. But if his experiments prove inconclusive either way, he is quit for his loss of time, no vital harm being done.

It will facilitate our discussion if we keep all these distinctions well in mind.

SECTION 2. PASCAL'S WAGER

The next matter to consider is the actual psychology of human opinion. When we look at certain facts, it seems as if our passional and volitional nature lay at the root of all our convictions. When we look at others, it seems as if they could do nothing when the intellect had once said its say. Let us take the latter facts up first.

Does it not seem preposterous on the very face of it to talk of our opinions being modifiable at will? Can our will either help or hinder our intellect in its perceptions of truth? Can we, by just willing it, believe that Abraham Lincoln's existence is a myth, and that the portraits of him in *McClure's Magazine* are all of some one else? Can we, by any effort of our will, or by any strength of wish that it were true, believe ourselves well and about when we are roaring with rheumatism in bed, or feel certain that the sum of the two one-dollar bills in our pocket must be a hundred dollars? We can say any of these things, but we are absolutely impotent to believe them . . .

In Pascal's *Thoughts* there is a celebrated passage known in literature as Pascal's wager. In it he tries to force us into Christianity by reasoning as if our concern with truth resembled our concern with the stakes in a game of chance. Translated freely his words are these: You must either believe or not believe that God is—which will you do? Your human reason cannot say. A game is going on between you and the nature of things which at the day of judgment will bring out either heads or tails. Weigh what your gains and your losses would be if you should stake all you have on heads, or God's existence: if you win in such case, you gain eternal beatitude; if you lose, you lose nothing at all. If there were an infinity of chances, and only one for God in this wager, still you ought to stake your all on God; for though you surely risk a finite loss by this procedure, any finite loss is reasonable, even a certain one is reasonable, if there is but the possibility of infinite gain. Go, then, and take holy water, and have masses said; belief will come and stupefy your scruples . . . Why should you not? At bottom, what have you to lose?

You probably feel that when religious faith expresses itself thus, in the language of the gaming table, it is put to its last trumps. Surely Pascal's own personal belief in masses and holy water had far other springs; and this celebrated page of his is but an argument for others, a last desperate snatch at a weapon against the hardness of the unbelieving heart. We feel that a faith in masses and holy water adopted willfully after such a mechanical calculation—would lack the inner soul of faith's reality; and if we were ourselves in the place of the Deity, we should probably take particular pleasure in cutting off believers of this pattern from their infinite reward. It is evident that unless there be some pre-existing tendency to believe in masses and holy water, the option offered to the will by Pascal is not a living option. Certainly no Turk ever took to masses and holy water on its account; and even to us Protestants these means of salvation seem such foregone impossibilities that Pascal's logic, invoked for them specifically, leaves us unmoved. As well might the Mahdi write to us, saying, "I am the Expected One whom God has created in his effulgence. You shall be infinitely happy if you confess me; otherwise you shall be cut off from the light of the sun. Weigh, then, your infinite gain if I am genuine against your finite sacrifice if I am not!" His logic would be that of Pascal; but he would vainly use it on us, for the hypothesis he offers us is dead. No tendency to act on it exists in us to any degree.

The talk of believing by our volition seems, then, from one point of view, simply silly. From another point of view it is worse than silly, it is vile. When one turns to the magnificent edifice of the physical sciences, and sees how it was reared; what thousands of disinterested mortal lives of men lie buried in its mere foundations; what patience and postponement, what choking down of preference, what submission to the icy laws of outer fact are wrought into its very stones and mortar; how absolutely impersonal it stands in its vast augustness—then how besotted and contemptible seems every little sentimentalist who comes blowing his voluntary smoke-wreaths, and pretending to decide things from out of his private dream! Can we wonder if those bred in the rugged and manly school of science should feel like spewing such subjectivism out of their mouths? The whole system of loyalties which grow up in the schools of science go dead against its toleration; so that it is only natural that those who have caught the scientific fever should pass over to the opposite extreme, and write sometimes as if the incorruptibly truthful intellect ought positively to prefer bitterness and unacceptableness to the heart in its cup.

It fortifies my soul to know,
That, though I perish, Truth is so

sings Clough, while Huxley exclaims: "My only consolation lies in the reflection that, however bad our posterity may become, so far as they hold by the plain rule of not pretending to believe what they have no reason to believe, because it may be to their advantage so to pretend [the word 'pretend' is surely here redundant], they will not have reached the lowest depth of immorality." And that delicious *enfant terrible* Clifford writes: "Belief is desecrated when given to unproved and unquestioned statements for the solace and private pleasure of the believer. . . . Whoso would deserve well of his fellows in this matter will guard the purity of his belief with a very fanaticism of jealous care, lest at any time it should rest on an unworthy object, and catch a stain which can never be wiped away. . . . If [a] belief has been accepted on insufficient evidence [even though the belief be true, as Clifford on the same page explains] the pleasure is a stolen one. . . . It is sinful because it is stolen in defiance of our duty to mankind. That duty is to guard ourselves from such beliefs as from a pestilence which may shortly master our own body and then spread to the rest of the town. . . . It is wrong always, everywhere, and for every one, to believe anything upon insufficient evidence."

SECTION 3. CLIFFORD'S VETO, PSYCHOLOGICAL CAUSES OF BELIEF

All this strikes one as healthy, even when expressed, as by Clifford, with somewhat too much of robustious pathos in the voice. Free-will and simple wishing do seem, in the matter of our credences, to be only fifth wheels to the coach. Yet if any one should thereupon assume that intellectual insight is what remains after wish and will and sentimental preference have taken wing, or that pure reason is what then settles our opinions, he would fly quite as directly in the teeth of the facts.

It is only our already dead hypotheses that our willing nature is unable to bring to life again. But what has made them dead for us is for the most part a previous action of our willing nature of an antagonistic kind. When I say 'willing nature,' I do not mean only such deliberate volitions as may have set up habits of belief that we cannot now escape from, I mean all such factors of belief as fear and hope, prejudice and passion, imitation and partisanship, the circumpressure of our caste and set. As a matter of fact we find ourselves believing, we hardly know how or why. Mr. Balfour gives the name of *authority* to all those influences, born of the intellectual climate, that make hypotheses possible or impossible for us, alive or dead. Here in this room, we all of us believe in molecules and the conservation of energy, in democracy and necessary progress, in Protestant Christianity and the duty of fighting for 'the doctrine of the immortal Monroe,' all for no reasons worthy of the name. We see into these matters with no more inner clearness, and probably with much less, than any disbeliever in them might possess. His unconventionality would probably have some grounds to show for its conclusions; but for us, not insight, but the *prestige* of the opinions, is what makes the spark shoot from them and light up our sleeping magazines of faith. Our reason is quite satisfied, in nine hundred and ninety-nine cases out of every thousand of us, if it can find a few arguments that will do to recite in case our credulity is criticized by some one else. Our faith is faith in some one else's faith, and in the greatest matters this is most the case. Our belief in truth itself, for instance, that there is a truth, and that our minds and it are made for each other,—what is it but a passionate affirmation of desire, in which our social system backs us up? We want to have a truth; we want to believe that our experiments and studies and discussions must put us in a continually better and better position towards it; and on this line we agree to fight out our thinking lives. But if a pyrrhonistic skeptic asks us *how we know* all this, can our logic find a reply? No! certainly it cannot. It is just one volition against another,—we willing to go in for life upon a trust or assumption which he, for his part, does not care to make. As a rule we disbelieve all facts and theories for which we have no use . . .

Evidently, then, our non-intellectual nature does influence our convictions. There are passional tendencies and volitions which run before and others which come after belief, and it is only the latter that are too late for the fair; and they are not too late when the previous passional work has been already in their own direction. Pascal's argument, instead of being powerless, then seems a regular clincher, and is the last stroke needed to make our faith in masses and holy water complete. The state of things is evidently far from simple; and pure insight and logic, whatever they might do ideally, are not the only things that really do produce our creeds.

SECTION 4. THESIS OF THE ESSAY

Our next duty, having recognized this mixed-up state of affairs, is to ask whether it be simply reprehensible and pathological, or whether, on the contrary, we must treat it as a normal element in making up our minds. The thesis I defend is, briefly stated, this: *Our passional nature not only lawfully may, but must, decide an option between propositions, whenever it is a genuine option that cannot by its nature be decided on intellectual grounds; for to say, under such circumstances, "Do not decide, but leave the question open," is itself a passional decision,—just like deciding yes or no,—and is attended with the same risk of losing the truth. . . .*

SECTION 7. TWO DIFFERENT SORTS OF RISKS IN BELIEVING

One more point, small but important, and our preliminaries are done. There are two ways of looking at our duty in the matter of opinion—ways entirely different, and yet ways about whose difference the theory of knowledge seems hitherto to have shown very little concern. *We must know the truth;* and *we must avoid error*—these are our first and great commandments as would-be knowers; but they are not two ways of stating an identical commandment, they are two separable laws. Although it may indeed happen that when we believe the truth A, we escape as an incidental consequence from believing the falsehood B, it hardly ever happens that by merely disbelieving B we necessarily believe A. We may in escaping B fall into believing other falsehoods, C or D, just as bad as B; or we may escape B by not believing anything at all, not even A.

Believe truth! Shun error—these, we see, are two materially different laws; and by choosing between them we may end by coloring differently our whole intellectual life. We may regard the chase for truth as paramount, and the avoidance of error as secondary; or we may, on the other hand, treat the avoidance of error as more imperative, and let truth take its chance. Clifford, in the instructive passage which I have quoted, exhorts us to the latter course. Believe nothing, he tells us, keep your mind in suspense forever, rather than by closing it on insufficient evidence incur the awful risk of believing lies. You, on the other hand, may think that the risk of being in error is a very small matter when compared with the blessings of real knowledge, and be ready to be duped many times in your investigation rather than postpone indefinitely the chance of guessing true. I myself find it impossible to go with Clifford. We must remember that these feelings of our duty about either truth or error are in any case only expressions of our passional life. Biologically considered, our minds are as ready to grind out falsehood as veracity, and he who says, "Better go without belief forever than believe a lie!" merely shows his own preponderant private horror of becoming a dupe. He may be critical of many of his desires and fears, but this fear he slavishly obeys. He cannot imagine any one questioning its binding force. For my own part, I have also a horror of being duped; but I can believe that worse things than being duped may happen to a man in this world: so Clifford's exhortation has to my ears a thoroughly fantastic sound. It is like a general informing his soldiers that it is better to keep out of battle forever than to risk a single wound. Not so are victories either over enemies or over nature gained. Our errors are surely not such awfully solemn things. In a world where we are so certain to incur them in spite of all our caution, a certain lightness of heart seems healthier than this excessive nervousness on their behalf. At any rate, it seems the fittest thing for the empiricist philosopher.

8. SOME RISK UNAVOIDABLE

And now, after all this introduction, let us go straight at our question. I have said, and now repeat it, that not only as a matter of fact do we find our passional nature influencing us in our opinions, but that there are some options between opinions in which this influence must be regarded both as an inevitable and as a lawful determinant of our choice.

I fear here that some of you my hearers will begin to scent danger, and lend an inhospitable ear. Two first steps of passion you have indeed had to admit as necessary,—we must think so as to avoid dupery, and—we must think so as to gain truth; but the surest path to those ideal consummations, you will probably consider, is from now onwards to take no further passional step.

Well, of course, I agree as far as the facts will allow. Wherever the option between losing truth and gaining it is not momentous, we can throw the chance of *gaining truth* away, and at any rate save ourselves from any chance of *believing falsehood,* by not making up our minds at all till objective evidence has come. In scientific questions, this is almost always the case; and even in human affairs in general, the need of acting is seldom so urgent that a false belief to act on is better than no belief at all. Law courts, indeed, have to decide on the best evidence attainable for the moment, because a judge's duty is to make law as well as to ascertain it, and (as a learned judge once said to me) few cases are worth spending much time over: the great thing is to have them decided on *any* acceptable principle, and got out of the way. But in our dealings with objective nature we obviously are recorders, not makers, of the truth; and decisions for the mere sake of deciding promptly and getting on to the next business would be wholly out of place. Throughout the breadth of physical nature facts are what they are quite independently of us, and seldom is there any such hurry about them that the risks of being duped by believing a premature theory need be faced. The questions here are always trivial options, the hypotheses are hardly living (at any rate not living for us spectators), the choice between believing truth or falsehood is seldom forced. The attitude of skeptical balance is therefore the absolutely wise one if we would escape mistakes. What difference, indeed, does it make to most of us whether we have or have not a theory of the Röntgen rays, whether we believe or not in mind-stuff, or have a conviction about the causality of conscious states? It makes no difference. Such options are not forced on us. On every account it is better not to make them, but still keep weighing reasons *pro et contra* with an indifferent hand . . .

The question next arises: Are there not somewhere forced options in our speculative questions, and can we (as men who may be interested at least as much in positively gaining truth as in merely escaping dupery) always wait with impunity till the coercive evidence shall have arrived? It seems *a priori* improbable that the truth should be so nicely adjusted to our needs and powers as that. In the great boarding-house of nature, the cakes and the butter and the syrup seldom come out so even and leave the plates so clean. Indeed, we should view them with scientific suspicion if they did.

10. LOGICAL CONDITIONS OF RELIGIOUS BELIEF

In truths dependent on our personal action, then, faith based on desire is certainly a lawful and possibly an indispensable thing.

But now, it will be said, these are all childish human cases, and have nothing to do with great cosmical matters, like the question of religious faith. Let us then pass on to that. Religions differ so much in their accidents that in discussing the religious question we must make it very generic and broad. What then do we now mean by the religious hypothesis? Science says things are; morality says some things are better than other things; and religion says essentially two things.

First, she says that the best things are the more eternal things, the overlapping things, the things in the universe that throw the last stone, so to speak, and say the final word. "Perfection is eternal," this phrase of Charles Secrétan seems a good way of putting this first affirmation of religion, an affirmation which obviously cannot yet be verified scientifically at all.

The second affirmation of religion is that we are better off even now if we believe her first affirmation to be true.

Now, let us consider what the logical elements of this situation are *in case the religious hypothesis in both its branches be really true.* (Of course, we must admit that possibility at the outset. If we are to discuss the question at all, it must involve a living option. If for any of you religion be a hypothesis that cannot, by any living possibility be true, then you need go no farther. I speak to the 'saving remnant' alone.) So proceeding, we see, first, that religion offers itself as an avoidable option. We are supposed to gain, even now, by our belief, and to lose by our nonbelief, a certain vital good. Secondly, religion is a dead option, so far as that good goes. We cannot escape the issue by remaining skeptical and waiting for more light, because, although we do avoid error in that way *if religion be untrue,* we lose the good, *if it be true,* just as certainly as if we positively chose to disbelieve. It is as if a man should hesitate indefinitely to ask a certain woman to marry him because he was not perfectly sure that she would prove an angel after he brought her home. Would he not cut himself off from that particular angel-possibility as decisively as if he went and married some one else? Skepticism, then, is not avoidance of option; it is option of a certain particular kind of risk. *Better risk loss of truth than chance of error*—that is your faith-vetoer's exact position. He is actively playing his stake as much as the believer is; he is backing the field against the religious hypothesis, just as the believer is backing the religious hypothesis against the field. To preach skepticism to us as a duty until 'sufficient evidence' for religion be found, is tantamount therefore to telling us, when in presence of the religious hypothesis, that to yield to our fear of its being error is wiser and better than to yield to our hope that it may be true. It is not intellect against all passions, then; it is only intellect with one passion laying down its law. And by what, forsooth, is the supreme wisdom of this passion warranted? Dupery for dupery, what proof is there that dupery through hope is so much worse than dupery through fear? I, for one, can see no proof; and I simply refuse obedience to the scientist's command to imitate his kind of option, in a case where my own stake is important enough to give me the right to choose my own form of risk. If religion be true and the evidence for it be still insufficient, I do not wish, by putting your extinguisher upon my nature (which feels to me as if it had after all some business in this matter), to forfeit my sole chance in life of getting upon the winning side,—that chance depending, of course, on my willingness to run the risk of acting as if my passional need of taking the world religiously might be prophetic and right.

All this is on the supposition that it really may be prophetic and right, and that, even to us who are discussing the matter, religion is a live hypothesis which may be true. Now, to most of us religion comes in a still further way that makes a veto on our active faith even more illogical. The more perfect and more eternal aspect of the universe is represented in our religions as having personal form. The universe is no longer a mere *It* to us, but a *Thou,* if we are religious; and any relation that may be possible from person to person might be possible here. For instance, although in one sense we are passive portions of the universe, in another we show a curious autonomy, as if we were small active centers on our own account. We feel, too, as if the appeal of religion to us were made to our own active good-will, as if evidence might be forever withheld from us unless we met the hypothesis half-way. To take a trivial illustration: just as a man who in a company of gentlemen made no advances, asked a warrant for every concession, and believed no one's word without proof, would cut himself off by such churlishness from all the social rewards that a more trusting spirit would earn,—so here, one who should shut himself up in snarling logicality and try to make the gods extort his recognition willy-nilly, or not get it at all, might cut himself off forever from his only opportunity of making the gods' acquaintance. This feeling, forced on us we know not whence, that by obstinately believing that there are gods (although not to do so would be so easy both for our logic and our life) we are doing the universe the deepest service we can, seems part of the living essence of the religious hypothesis. If the hypothesis *were* true in all its parts, including this one, then pure intellectualism, with its veto on our making willing advances, would be an absurdity; and some participation of our sympathetic nature would be logically required. I, therefore, for one, cannot see my way to accepting the agnostic rules for truth-seeking, or willfully agree to keep my willing nature out of the game. I cannot do so for this plain reason, that *a rule of thinking which would absolutely prevent me from acknowledging certain kinds of truth if those kinds of truth were really there, would be an irrational rule.* That for me is the long and short of the formal logic of the situation, no matter what the kinds of truth might materially be.

I confess I do not see how this logic can be escaped. But sad experience makes me fear that some of you may still shrink from radically saying with me, *in abstracto,* that we have the right to believe at our own risk any hypothesis that is live enough to tempt our will. I suspect, however, that if this is so, it is because you have got away from the abstract logical point of view altogether, and are thinking (perhaps without realizing it) of some particular religious hypothesis which for you is dead. The freedom to 'believe what we will' you apply to the case of some patent superstition; and the faith you think of is the faith defined by the schoolboy when he said, "Faith is when you believe something that you know ain't true." I can only repeat that this is misapprehension. *In concreto,* the freedom to believe can only cover living options which the intellect of the individual cannot by itself resolve; and living options never seem absurdities to him who has them to consider. When I look at the religious question as it really puts itself to concrete men, and when I think of all the possibilities which both practically and theoretically it involves, then this command that we shall put a stopper on our heart, instincts, and courage, and *wait*—acting of course meanwhile more or less as if religion were *not* true—till doomsday, or till such time as our intellect and senses working together may have raked in evidence enough—this command, I say, seems to me the queerest idol ever manufactured in the philosophic cave.

Were we scholastic absolutists, there might be more excuse. If we had an infallible intellect with its objective certitudes, we might feel ourselves disloyal to such a perfect organ of knowledge in not trusting to it exclusively, in not waiting for its releasing word. But if we are empiricists, if we believe that no bell in us tolls to let us know for certain when truth is in our grasp, then it seems a piece of idle fantasticality to preach so solemnly our duty of waiting for the bell. Indeed we may wait if we will,—I hope you do not think that I am denying that—but if we do so, we do so at our peril as much as if we believed. In either case we *act,* taking our life in our hands. No one of us ought to issue vetoes to the other, nor should we bandy words of abuse. We ought, on the contrary, delicately and profoundly to respect one another's mental freedom: then only shall we bring about the intellectual republic; then only shall we have that spirit of inner tolerance without which all our outer tolerance is soulless, and which is empiricism's glory; then only shall we live and let live, in speculative as well as in practical things.

I began by a reference to Fitz James Stephen; let me end by a quotation from him. "What do you think of yourself? What do you think of the world? . . . These are questions with which all must deal as it seems good to them. They are riddles of the Sphinx, in some way or other we must deal with them . . . In all important transactions of life we have to leap in the dark. . . . If we decide to leave the riddles unanswered, that is a choice; if we waver in our answer, that, too, is a choice: but whatever choice we make, we make it at our peril. If a man chooses to turn his back altogether on God and the future, no one can prevent him; no one can show beyond reasonable doubt that he is mistaken. If a man thinks otherwise and acts as he thinks, I do not see that any one can prove that *he* is mistaken. Each must act as he thinks best; and if he is wrong, so much the worse for him. We stand on a mountain pass in the midst of whirling snow and blinding mist, through which we get glimpses now and then of paths which may be deceptive. If we stand still we shall be frozen to death. If we take the wrong road we shall be dashed to pieces. We do not certainly know whether there is any right one. What must we do? 'Be strong and of a good courage.' Act for the best, hope for the best, and take what comes. . . . If death ends all, we cannot meet death better."

Meditations

RENÉ DESCARTES (1596–1650) was born in La Haye, France, the son of a lawyer and magistrate. In his teens, he studied at the Jesuit college at La Flèche. He then entered the University of Poitiers, where he earned his degree in canon and civil law. Descartes is widely regarded as the most important philosopher of the early modern period. His most influential books include the *Discourse on Method* (1637) and *Meditations on First Philosophy* (1641). In 1649, Descartes moved to Sweden, in part to serve as the tutor of Queen Christina. He fell ill with a respiratory infection and died early in 1650.

THINKING QUESTIONS

Descartes, *Meditations*

1. What is Descartes' main goal in *Meditations*?
2. What is the standard by which Descartes tests the truth of his ideas?
3. How do dreams lead Descartes to doubt the reliability of the senses?
4. Which beliefs are brought into doubt if the senses are not trustworthy?
5. How does Descartes bring into doubt the claims of arithmetic and geometry?
6. What is the deception caused by the "evil genius"?
7. What belief has to be true, even if there is an evil genius?
8. What point is Descartes making with his example of the melting wax?

FIRST MEDITATION

What Can Be Called into Doubt

Some years ago I was struck by the large number of falsehoods that I had accepted as true in my childhood, and by the highly doubtful nature of the whole edifice that I had subsequently based on them. I realized that it was necessary, once in the course of my life, to demolish everything completely and start again right from the foundations if I wanted to establish anything at all in the sciences that was stable and likely to last. But the task looked an enormous one, and I began to wait until I should reach a mature enough age to ensure that no subsequent time of life would be more suitable for tackling such inquiries. This led me to put the project off for so long that I would now be to blame if by pondering over it any further I wasted the time still left for carrying it out. So today I have expressly rid my mind of all worries and arranged for myself a clear stretch of free time. I am here quite alone, and at last I will devote myself sincerely and without reservation to the general demolition of my opinions.

But to accomplish this, it will not be necessary for me to show that all my opinions are false, which is something I could perhaps never manage. Reason now leads me to think that I should hold back my assent from opinions which are not completely certain and indubitable just as carefully as I do from those which are patently false. So, for the purpose of rejecting all my opinions, it will be enough if I find in each of them at least some reason for doubt. And to do this I will not need to run through them all individually, which would be an endless task. Once the foundations of a building are undermined, anything built on them collapses of its own accord; so I will go straight for the basic principles on which all my former beliefs rested.

Whatever I have up till now accepted as most true I have acquired either from the senses or through the senses. But from time to time I have found that the senses deceive, and it is prudent never to trust completely those who have deceived us even once.

Yet although the senses occasionally deceive us with respect to objects which are very small or in the distance, there are many other beliefs about which doubt is quite impossible, even though they are derived from the senses—for example, that I am here, sitting by the fire, wearing a winter dressing-gown, holding this piece of paper in my hands, and so on. Again, how could it be denied that these hands or this whole body are mine? Unless perhaps I were to liken myself to madmen, whose brains are so damaged by the persistent vapours of melancholia that they firmly maintain they are kings when they are paupers, or say they are dressed in purple when they are naked, or that their heads are made of earthenware, or that they are pumpkins, or made of glass. But such people are insane, and I would be thought equally mad if I took anything from them as a model for myself.

A brilliant piece of reasoning! As if I were not a man who sleeps at night, and regularly has all the same experiences while asleep as madmen do when awake—indeed sometimes even more improbable ones. How often, asleep at night, am I convinced of just such familiar events—that I am here in my dressing-gown, sitting by the fire—when in fact I am lying undressed in bed! Yet at the moment my eyes are certainly wide awake when I look at this piece of paper; I shake my head and it is not asleep; as I stretch out and feel my hand I do so deliberately, and I know what I am doing. All this would not happen with such distinctness to someone asleep. Indeed! As if I did not remember other occasions when I have been tricked by exactly similar thoughts while asleep! As I think about this more carefully, I see plainly that there are never any sure signs by means of which being awake can be distinguished from being asleep. The result is that I begin to feel dazed, and this very feeling only reinforces the notion that I may be asleep.

Suppose then that I am dreaming, and that these particulars—that my eyes are open, that I am moving my head and stretching out my hands—are not true. Perhaps, indeed, I do not even have such hands or such a body at all. Nonetheless, it must surely be admitted that the visions which come in sleep are like paintings, which must have been fashioned in the likeness of things that are real, and hence that at least these general kinds of things—eyes, head, hands and the body as a whole—are things which are not imaginary but are real and exist. For even when painters try to create sirens and satyrs with the most extraordinary bodies, they cannot give them natures which are new in all respects; they simply jumble up the limbs of different animals. Or if perhaps they manage to think up something so new that nothing remotely similar has ever been seen before—something which is therefore completely fictitious and unreal—at least the colours used in the composition must be real. By similar reasoning, although these general kinds of things—eyes, head, hands and so on—could be imaginary, it must at least be admitted that certain other even simpler and more universal things are real. These are as it were the real colours from which we form all the images of things, whether true or false, that occur in our thought.

This class appears to include corporeal nature in general, and its extension; the shape of extended things; the quantity, or size and number of these things; the place in which they may exist, the time through which they may endure, and so on.

So a reasonable conclusion from this might be that physics, astronomy, medicine, and all other disciplines which depend on the study of composite things, are doubtful; while arithmetic, geometry and other subjects of this kind, which deal only with the simplest and most general things, regardless of whether they really exist in nature or not, contain something certain and indubitable. For whether I am awake or asleep, two and three added together are five, and a square has no more than four sides. It seems impossible that such transparent truths should incur any suspicion of being false.

And yet firmly rooted in my mind is the long-standing opinion that there is an omnipotent God who made me the kind of creature that I am. How do I know that he has not brought it about that there is no earth, no sky, no extended thing, no shape, no size, no place, while at the same time ensuring that all these things appear to me to exist just as they do now? What is more, just as I consider that others sometimes go astray in cases where they think they have the most perfect knowledge, how do I know that God has not brought it about that I too go wrong every time I add two and three or count the sides of a square, or in some even simpler matter, if that is imaginable? But perhaps God would not have allowed me to be deceived in this way, since he is said to be supremely good. But if it were inconsistent with his goodness to have created me such that I am deceived all the time, it would seem equally foreign to his goodness to allow me to be deceived even occasionally; yet this last assertion cannot be made.

Perhaps there may be some who would prefer to deny the existence of so powerful a God rather than believe that everything else is uncertain. Let us not argue with them, but grant them that everything said about God is a fiction. According to their supposition, then, I have arrived at my present state by fate or chance or a continuous chain of events, or by some other means; yet since deception and error seem to be imperfections, the less powerful they make my original cause, the more likely it is that I am so imperfect as to be deceived all the time. I have no answer to these arguments, but am finally compelled to admit that there is not one of my former beliefs about which a doubt may not properly be raised; and this is not a flippant or ill-considered conclusion, but is based on powerful and well thought-out reasons. So in future I must withhold my assent from these former beliefs just as carefully as I would from obvious falsehoods, if I want to discover any certainty.

But it is not enough merely to have noticed this; I must make an effort to remember it. My habitual opinions keep coming back, and, despite my wishes, they capture my belief, which is as it were bound over to them as a result of long occupation and the law of custom. I shall never get out of the habit of confidently assenting to these opinions, so long as I suppose them to be what in fact they are, namely highly probable opinions—opinions which, despite the fact that they are in a sense doubtful, as has just been shown, it is still much more reasonable to believe than to deny. In view of this, I think it will be a good plan to turn my will in completely the opposite direction and deceive myself, by pretending for a time that these former opinions are utterly false and imaginary. I shall do this until the weight of preconceived opinion is counter-balanced and the distorting influence of habit no longer prevents my judgement from perceiving things correctly. In the meantime, I know that no danger or error will result from my plan, and that I cannot possibly go too far in my distrustful attitude. This is because the task now in hand does not involve action but merely the acquisition of knowledge.

I will suppose therefore that not God, who is supremely good and the source of truth, but rather some malicious demon of the utmost power and cunning has employed all his energies in order to deceive me. I shall think that the sky, the air, the earth, colours, shapes, sounds and all external things are merely the delusions of dreams which he has devised to ensnare my judgement. I shall consider myself as not having hands or eyes, or flesh, or blood or senses, but as falsely believing that I have all these things. I shall stubbornly and firmly persist in this meditation; and, even if it is not in my power to know any truth, I shall at least do what is in my power, that is, resolutely guard against assenting to any falsehoods, so that the deceiver, however powerful and cunning he may be, will be unable to impose on me in the slightest degree. But this is an arduous undertaking, and a kind of laziness brings me back to normal life. I am like a prisoner who is enjoying an imaginary freedom while asleep; as he begins to suspect that he is asleep, he dreads being woken up, and goes along with the pleasant illusion as long as he can. In the same way, I happily slide back into my old opinions and dread being shaken out of them, for fear that my peaceful sleep may be followed by hard labour when I wake, and that I shall have to toil not in the light, but amid the inextricable darkness of the problems I have now raised.

SECOND MEDITATION

The Nature of the Human Mind, and How It Is Better Known than the Body

So serious are the doubts into which I have been thrown as a result of yesterday's meditation that I can neither put them out of my mind nor see any way of resolving them. It feels as if I have fallen unexpectedly into a deep whirlpool which tumbles me around so that I can neither stand on the bottom nor swim up to the top. Nevertheless I will make an effort and once more attempt the same path which I started on yesterday. Anything which admits of the slightest doubt I will set aside just as if I had found it to be wholly false; and I will proceed in this way until I recognize something certain, or, if nothing else, until I at least recognize for certain that there is no certainty. Archimedes used to demand just one firm and immovable point in order to shift the entire earth; so I too can hope for great things if I manage to find just one thing, however slight, that is certain and unshakeable.

I will suppose then, that everything I see is spurious. I will believe that my memory tells me lies, and that none of the things that it reports ever happened. I have no senses. Body, shape, extension, movement and place are chimeras. So what remains true? Perhaps just the one fact that nothing is certain.

Yet apart from everything I have just listed, how do I know that there is not something else which does not allow even the slightest occasion for doubt? Is there not a God, or whatever I may call him, who puts into me the thoughts I am now having? But why do I think this, since I myself may perhaps be the author of these thoughts? In that case am not I, at least, something? But I have just said that I have no senses and no body. This is the sticking point: what follows from this? Am I not so bound up with a body and with senses that I cannot exist without them? But I have convinced myself that there is absolutely nothing in the world, no sky, no earth, no minds, no bodies. Does it now follow that I too do not exist? No: if I convinced myself of something then I certainly existed. But there is a deceiver of supreme power and cunning who is deliberately and constantly deceiving me. In that case I too undoubtedly exist, if he is deceiving me; and let him deceive me as much as he can, he will never bring it about that I am nothing so long as I think that I am something. So after considering everything very thoroughly, I must finally conclude that this proposition, *I am, I exist,* is necessarily true whenever it is put forward by me or conceived in my mind.

But I do not yet have a sufficient understanding of what this 'I' is, that now necessarily exists. So I must be on my guard against carelessly taking something else to be this 'I', and so making a mistake in the very item of knowledge that I maintain is the most certain and evident of all. I will therefore go back and meditate on what I originally believed myself to be, before I embarked on this present train of thought. I will then subtract anything capable of being weakened, even minimally, by the arguments now introduced, so that what is left at the end may be exactly and only what is certain and unshakeable.

What then did I formerly think I was? A man. But what is a man? Shall I say 'a rational animal'? No; for then I should have to inquire what an animal is, what rationality is, and in this way one question would lead me down the slope to other harder ones, and I do not now have the time to waste on subtleties of this kind. Instead I propose to concentrate on what came into my thoughts spontaneously and quite naturally whenever I used to consider what I was. Well, the first thought to come to mind was that I had a face, hands, arms and the whole mechanical structure of limbs which can be seen in a corpse, and which I called the body. The next thought was that I was nourished, that I moved about, and that I engaged in sense-perception and thinking; and these actions I attributed to the soul. But as to the nature of this soul, either I did not think about this or else I imagined it to be something tenuous, like a wind or fire or ether, which permeated my more solid parts. As to the body, however, I had no doubts about it, but thought I knew its nature distinctly. If I had tried to describe the mental conception I had of it, I would have expressed it as follows: by a body I understand whatever has a determinable shape and a definable location and can occupy a space in such a way as to exclude any other body; it can be perceived by touch, sight, hearing, taste or smell, and can be moved in various ways, not by itself but by whatever else comes into contact with it. For, according to my judgement, the power of self-movement, like the power of sensation or of thought, was quite foreign to the nature of a body; indeed, it was a source of wonder to me that certain bodies were found to contain faculties of this kind.

But what shall I now say that I am, when I am supposing that there is some supremely powerful and, if it is permissible to say so, malicious deceiver, who is deliberately trying to trick me in every way he can? Can I now assert that I possess even the most insignificant of all the attributes which I have just said belong to the nature of a body? I scrutinize them, think about them, go over them again, but nothing suggests itself; it is tiresome and pointless to go through the list once more. But what about the attributes I assigned to the soul? Nutrition or movement? Since now I do not have a body, these are mere fabrications. Sense-perception? This surely does not occur without a body, and besides, when asleep I have appeared to perceive through the senses many things which I afterwards realized I did not perceive through the senses at all. Thinking? At last I have discovered it—thought; this alone is inseparable from me. I am, I exist—that is certain. But for how long? For as long as I am thinking. For it could be that were I totally to cease from thinking, I should totally cease to exist. At present I am not admitting anything except what is necessarily true. I am, then, in the strict sense only a thing that thinks; that is, I am a mind, or intelligence, or intellect, or reason—words whose meaning I have been ignorant of until now. But for all that I am a thing which is real and which truly exists. But what kind of a thing? As I have just said—a thinking thing.

What else am I? I will use my imagination. I am not that structure of limbs which is called a human body. I am not even some thin vapour which permeates the limbs—a wind, fire, air, breath, or whatever I depict in my imagination; for these are things which I have supposed to be nothing. Let this supposition stand, for all that I am still something. And yet may it not perhaps be the case that these very things which I am supposing to be nothing, because they are unknown to me, are in reality identical with the 'I' of which I am aware? I do not know, and for the moment I shall not argue the point, since I can make judgements only about things which are known to me. I know that I exist; the question is, what is this 'I' that I know? If the 'I' is understood strictly as we have been taking it, then it is quite certain that knowledge of it does not depend on things of whose existence I am as yet unaware; so it cannot depend on any of the things which I invent in my imagination. And this very word 'invent' shows me my mistake. It would indeed be a case of fictitious invention if I used my imagination to establish that I was something or other; for imagining is simply contemplating the shape or image of a corporeal thing. Yet now I know for certain both that I exist and at the same time that all such images and, in general, everything relating to the nature of body, could be mere dreams and chimeras. Once this point has been grasped, to say 'I will use my imagination to get to know more distinctly what I am' would seem to be as silly as saying 'I am now awake, and see some truth; but since my vision is not yet clear enough, I will deliberately fall asleep so that my dreams may provide a truer and clearer representation.' I thus realize that none of the things that the imagination enables me to grasp is at all relevant to this knowledge of myself which I possess, and that the mind must therefore be most carefully diverted from such things if it is to perceive its own nature as distinctly as possible.

But what then am I? A thing that thinks. What is that? A thing that doubts, understands, affirms, denies, is willing, is unwilling, and also imagines and has sensory perceptions.

This is a considerable list, if everything on it belongs to me. But does it? Is it not one and the same 'I' who is now doubting almost everything, who nonetheless understands some things, who affirms that this one thing is true, denies everything else, desires to know more, is unwilling to be deceived, imagines many things even involuntarily, and is aware of many things which apparently come from the senses? Are not all these things just as true as the fact that I exist, even if I am asleep all the time, and even if he who created me is doing all he can to deceive me? Which of all these activities is distinct from my thinking? Which of them can be said to be separate from myself? The fact that it is I who am doubting and understanding and willing is so evident that I see no way of making it any clearer. But it is also the case that the 'I' who imagines is the same 'I'. For even if, as I have supposed, none of the objects of imagination are real, the power of imagination is something which really exists and is part of my thinking. Lastly, it is also the same 'I' who has sensory perceptions, or is aware of bodily things as it were through the senses.

For example, I am now seeing light, hearing a noise, feeling heat. But I am asleep, so all this is false. Yet I certainly *seem* to see, to hear, and to be warmed. This cannot be false; what is called 'having a sensory perception' is strictly just this, and in this restricted sense of the term it is simply thinking.

From all this I am beginning to have a rather better understanding of what I am. But it still appears—and I cannot stop thinking this—that the corporeal things of which images are formed in my thought, and which the senses investigate, are known with much more distinctness than this puzzling 'I' which cannot be pictured in the imagination. And yet it is surely surprising that I should have a more distinct grasp of things which I realize are doubtful, unknown and foreign to me, than I have of that which is true and known—my own self. But I see what it is: my mind enjoys wandering off and will not yet submit to being restrained within the bounds of truth. Very well then; just this once let us give it a completely free rein, so that after a while, when it is time to tighten the reins, it may more readily submit to being curbed.

Let us consider the things which people commonly think they understand most distinctly of all; that is, the bodies which we touch and see. I do not mean bodies in general—for general perceptions are apt to be somewhat more confused—but one particular body. Let us take, for example, this piece of wax. It has just been taken from the honeycomb; it has not yet quite lost the taste of the honey; it retains some of the scent of the flowers from which it was gathered; its colour, shape and size are plain to see; it is hard, cold and can be handled without difficulty; if you rap it with your knuckle it makes a sound. In short, it has everything which appears necessary to enable a body to be known as distinctly as possible. But even as I speak, I put the wax by the fire, and look: the residual taste is eliminated, the smell goes away, the colour changes, the shape is lost, the size increases; it becomes liquid and hot; you can hardly touch it, and if you strike it, it no longer makes a sound. But does the same wax remain? It must be admitted that it does; no one denies it, no one thinks otherwise. So what was it in the wax that I understood with such distinctness? Evidently none of the features which I arrived at by means of the senses; for whatever came under taste, smell, sight, touch or hearing has now altered—yet the wax remains.

Perhaps the answer lies in the thought which now comes to my mind; namely, the wax was not after all the sweetness of the honey, or the fragrance of the flowers, or the whiteness, or the shape, or the sound, but was rather a body which presented itself to me in these various forms a little while ago, but which now exhibits different ones. But what exactly is it that I am now imagining? Let us concentrate, take away everything which does not belong to the wax, and see what is left: merely something extended, flexible and changeable. But what is meant here by 'flexible' and 'changeable'? Is it what I picture in my imagination: that this piece of wax is capable of changing from a round shape to a square shape, or from a square shape to a triangular shape? Not at all; for I can grasp that the wax is capable of countless changes of this kind, yet I am unable to run through this immeasurable number of changes in my imagination, from which it follows that it is not the faculty of imagination that gives me my grasp of the wax as flexible and changeable. And what is meant by 'extended'? Is the extension of the wax also unknown? For it increases if the wax melts, increases again if it boils, and is greater still if the heat is increased. I would not be making a correct judgement about the nature of wax unless I believed it capable of being extended in many more different ways than I will ever encompass in my imagination. I must therefore admit that the nature of this piece of wax is in no way revealed by my imagination, but is perceived by the mind alone. (I am speaking of this particular piece of wax; the point is even clearer with regard to wax in general.) But what is this wax which is perceived by the mind alone? It is of course the same wax which I see, which I touch, which I picture in my imagination, in short the same wax which I thought it to be from the start. And yet, and here is the point, the perception I have of it is a case not of vision or touch or imagination—nor has it ever been, despite previous appearances—but of purely mental scrutiny; and this can be imperfect and confused, as it was before, or clear and distinct as it is now, depending on how carefully I concentrate on what the wax consists in.

But as I reach this conclusion I am amazed at how weak and prone to error my mind is. For although I am thinking about these matters within myself, silently and without speaking, nonetheless the actual words bring me up short, and I am almost tricked by ordinary ways of talking. We say that we see the wax itself, if it is there before us, not that we judge it to be there from its colour or shape; and this might lead me to conclude without more ado that knowledge of the wax comes from what the eye sees, and not from the scrutiny of the mind alone. But then if I look out of the window and see men crossing the square, as I just happen to have done, I normally say that I see the men themselves, just as I say that I see the wax. Yet do I see any more than hats and coats which could conceal automatons? I *judge* that they are men. And so something which I thought I was seeing with my eyes is in fact grasped solely by the faculty of judgement which is in my mind.

However, one who wants to achieve knowledge above the ordinary level should feel ashamed at having taken ordinary ways of talking as a basis for doubt. So let us proceed, and consider on which occasion my perception of the nature of the wax was more perfect and evident. Was it when I first looked at it, and believed I knew it by my external senses, or at least by what they call the 'common' sense—that is, the power of imagination? Or is my knowledge more perfect now, after a more careful investigation of the nature of the wax and of the means by which it is known? Any doubt on this issue would clearly be foolish; for what distinctness was there in my earlier perception? Was there anything in it which an animal could not possess? But when I distinguish the wax from its outward forms—take the clothes off, as it were, and consider it naked—then although my judgement may still contain errors, at least my perception now requires a human mind.

But what am I to say about this mind, or about myself? (So far, remember, I am not admitting that there is anything else in me except a mind.) What,

I ask, is this 'I' which seems to perceive the wax so distinctly? Surely my awareness of my own self is not merely much truer and more certain than my awareness of the wax, but also much more distinct and evident. For if I judge that the wax exists from the fact that I see it, clearly this same fact entails much more evidently that I myself also exist. It is possible that what I see is not really the wax; it is possible that I do not even have eyes with which to see anything. But when I see, or think I see (I am not here distinguishing the two), it is simply not possible that I who am now thinking am not something. By the same token, if I judge that the wax exists from the fact that I touch it, the same result follows, namely that I exist. If I judge that it exists from the fact that I imagine it, or for any other reason, exactly the same thing follows. And the result that I have grasped in the case of the wax may be applied to everything else located outside me. Moreover, if my perception of the wax seemed more distinct after it was established not just by sight or touch but by many other considerations, it must be admitted that I now know myself even more distinctly. This is because every consideration whatsoever which contributes to my perception of the wax, or of any other body, cannot but establish even more effectively the nature of my own mind. But besides this, there is so much else in the mind itself which can serve to make my knowledge of it more distinct, that it scarcely seems worth going through the contributions made by considering bodily things.

I see that without any effort I have now finally got back to where I wanted. I now know that even bodies are not strictly perceived by the senses or the faculty of imagination but by the intellect alone, and that this perception derives not from their being touched or seen but from their being understood; and in view of this I know plainly that I can achieve an easier and more evident perception of my own mind than of anything else. But since the habit of holding on to old opinions cannot be set aside so quickly, I should like to stop here and meditate for some time on this new knowledge I have gained, so as to fix it more deeply in my memory.

Empiricism

JOHN LOCKE (1632–1704) was a British philosopher, captain of horse in the parliamentary army during the Glorious Revolution, physician, advisor to the Earl of Shaftesbury, and student and fellow of Christ Church College, Oxford, for nearly 30 years. His philosophical writings are characterized by anti-authoritarianism and an advocacy of reason as the tool for gaining the truth. Although he did not start writing much until age 57, he then produced many important works, including *Letters Concerning Toleration* and *Two Treatises of Government,* as well as his masterpiece, *An Essay Concerning Human Understanding.*

THINKING QUESTIONS

John Locke, *Empiricism*

1. What does Locke mean by "EXPERIENCE"?
2. What is the difference between ideas of sensation and ideas of reflection? What point is Locke making about the difference in where these ideas originate?
3. What's the difference between speaking of a quality "in the objects" and a quality as an idea in a mind?
4. Locke says that ideas of "colours, sounds, tastes, etc." are secondary qualities and so are "nothing in the objects themselves but power to produce various sensations in us. . . ." What does Locke mean by this? What has to be the case in order for the sensation of the color blue or the taste of strawberries to exist?
5. Locke offers a commonsense proof of the existence of the physical world. How does it help his argument when he points out that blind people can't see or deaf people can't hear? (Book IV, Chapter XI, section 4)
6. Locke points out that you can easily tell the difference between looking at the sun and remembering looking at the sun. Additionally, when you actually look at the sun, you feel pain. How do these points help show that sensations must come from outside the mind?
7. What does Locke mean when he says that we should not "expect demonstration and certainty in things not capable of it"? What is he saying about the proof necessary to form a belief based on the senses?

BOOK II: OF IDEAS

Chapter I: Of Ideas in General, and Their Original

1. *Idea is the object of thinking.* Every man being conscious to himself that he thinks; and that which his mind is applied about whilst thinking being the ideas that are there, it is past doubt that men have in their minds several ideas, such as are those expressed by the words whiteness, hardness, sweetness, thinking, motion, man, elephant, army, drunkenness, and others: it is in the first place then to be inquired, How he comes by them?

I know it is a received doctrine, that men have native ideas, and original characters, stamped upon their minds in their very first being. This opinion I have at large examined already; and, I suppose what I have said in the foregoing Book will be much more easily admitted, when I have shown whence the understanding may get all the ideas it has; and by what ways and degrees they may come into the mind; for which I shall appeal to every one's own observation and experience.

2. *All ideas come from sensation or reflection.* Let us then suppose the mind to be, as we say, white paper, void of all characters, without any ideas: How comes it to be furnished? Whence comes it by that vast store which the busy and boundless fancy of man has painted on it with an almost endless variety? Whence has it all the materials of reason and knowledge? To this I answer, in one word, from EXPERIENCE. In that all our knowledge is founded; and from that it ultimately derives itself. Our observation employed either, about external sensible objects, or about the internal operations of our minds perceived and reflected on by ourselves, is that which supplies our understandings with all the materials of thinking. These two are the fountains of knowledge, from whence all the ideas we have, or can naturally have, do spring.

3. *The objects of sensation one source of ideas.* First, our Senses, conversant about particular sensible objects, do convey into the mind several distinct perceptions of things, according to those various ways wherein those objects do affect them. And thus we come by those ideas we have of yellow, white, heat, cold, soft, hard, bitter, sweet, and all those which we call sensible qualities; which when I say the senses convey into the mind, I mean, they from external objects convey into the mind what produces there those perceptions. This great source of most of the ideas we have, depending wholly upon our senses, and derived by them to the understanding, I call SENSATION.

4. *The operations of our minds, the other source of them.* Secondly, the other fountain from which experience furnisheth the understanding with ideas is the perception of the operations of our own mind within us, as it is employed about the ideas it has got; which operations, when the soul comes to reflect on and consider, do furnish the understanding with another set of ideas, which could not be had from things without. And such are perception, thinking, doubting, believing, reasoning, knowing, willing, and all the different actings of our own minds; which we being conscious of, and observing in ourselves, do from these

receive into our understandings as distinct ideas as we do from bodies affecting our senses. This source of ideas every man has wholly in himself; and though it be not sense, as having nothing to do with external objects, yet it is very like it, and might properly enough be called internal sense. But as I call the other SENSATION, so I call this REFLECTION, the ideas it affords being such only as the mind gets by reflecting on its own operations within itself. By reflection then, in the following part of this discourse, I would be understood to mean, that notice which the mind takes of its own operations, and the manner of them, by reason whereof there come to be ideas of these operations in the understanding. These two, I say, viz. external material things, as the objects of SENSATION, and the operations of our own minds within, as the objects of REFLECTION, are to me the only originals from whence all our ideas take their beginnings. The term operations here I use in a large sense, as comprehending not barely the actions of the mind about its ideas, but some sort of passions arising sometimes from them, such as is the satisfaction or uneasiness arising from any thought.

5. *All our ideas are of the one or the other of these.* The understanding seems to me not to have the least glimmering of any ideas which it doth not receive from one of these two. External objects furnish the mind with the ideas of sensible qualities, which are all those different perceptions they produce in us; and the mind furnishes the understanding with ideas of its own operations.

These, when we have taken a full survey of them, and their several modes, combinations, and relations, we shall find to contain all our whole stock of ideas; and that we have nothing in our minds which did not come in one of these two ways. Let any one examine his own thoughts, and thoroughly search into his understanding; and then let him tell me, whether all the original ideas he has there, are any other than of the objects of his senses, or of the operations of his mind, considered as objects of his reflection. And how great a mass of knowledge soever he imagines to be lodged there, he will, upon taking a strict view, see that he has not any idea in his mind but what one of these two have imprinted; though perhaps, with infinite variety compounded and enlarged by the understanding, as we shall see hereafter.

6. *Observable in children.* He that attentively considers the state of a child, at his first coming into the world, will have little reason to think him stored with plenty of ideas, that are to be the matter of his future knowledge. It is by degrees he comes to be furnished with them. And though the ideas of obvious and familiar qualities imprint themselves before the memory begins to keep a register of time or order, yet it is often so late before some unusual qualities come in the way, that there are few men that cannot recollect the beginning of their acquaintance with them. And if it were worth while, no doubt a child might be so ordered as to have but a very few, even of the ordinary ideas, till he were grown up to a man. But all that are born into the world, being surrounded with bodies that perpetually and diversely affect them, variety of ideas, whether care be taken of it or not, are imprinted on the minds of children. Light and colours are busy at hand everywhere, when the eye is but open; sounds and some tangible qualities fail not to solicit their

proper senses, and force an entrance to the mind; but yet, I think, it will be granted easily, that if a child were kept in a place where he never saw any other but black and white till he were a man, he would have no more ideas of scarlet or green, than he that from his childhood never tasted an oyster, or a pineapple, has of those particular relishes.

7. *Men are differently furnished with these, according to the different objects they converse with.* Men then come to be furnished with fewer or more simple ideas from without, according as the objects they converse with afford greater or less variety; and from the operations of their minds within, according as they more or less reflect on them. For, though he that contemplates the operations of his mind, cannot but have plain and clear ideas of them; yet, unless he turn his thoughts that way, and considers them attentively, he will no more have clear and distinct ideas of all the operations of his mind, and all that may be observed therein, than he will have all the particular ideas of any landscape, or of the parts and motions of a clock, who will not turn his eyes to it, and with attention heed all the parts of it. The picture, or clock may be so placed, that they may come in his way every day; but yet he will have but a confused idea of all the parts they are made up of, till he applies himself with attention, to consider them each in particular.

8. *Ideas of reflection later, because they need attention.* And hence we see the reason why it is pretty late before most children get ideas of the operations of their own minds; and some have not any very clear or perfect ideas of the greatest part of them all their lives. Because, though they pass there continually, yet, like floating visions, they make not deep impressions enough to leave in their mind clear, distinct, lasting ideas, till the understanding turns inward upon itself, reflects on its own operations, and makes them the objects of its own contemplation. Children when they come first into it, are surrounded with a world of new things, which, by a constant solicitation of their senses, draw the mind constantly to them; forward to take notice of new, and apt to be delighted with the variety of changing objects. Thus the first years are usually employed and diverted in looking abroad. Men's business in them is to acquaint themselves with what is to be found without; and so growing up in a constant attention to outward sensations, seldom make any considerable reflection on what passes within them, till they come to be of riper years; and some scarce ever at all.

Chapter VIII: Some Further Considerations Concerning Our Simple Ideas of Sensation

8. *Our ideas and the qualities of bodies.* Whatsoever the mind perceives in itself, or is the immediate object of perception, thought, or understanding, that I call idea; and the power to produce any idea in our mind, I call quality of the subject wherein that power is. Thus a snowball having the power to produce in us the ideas of white, cold, and round, the power to produce those ideas in us, as they are in the snowball, I call qualities; and as they are sensations or perceptions in our understandings, I call them ideas; which ideas, if I speak

of sometimes as in the things themselves, I would be understood to mean those qualities in the objects which produce them in us.

9. *Primary qualities of bodies.* Qualities thus considered in bodies are, first, such as are utterly inseparable from the body, in what state soever it be; and such as in all the alterations and changes it suffers, all the force can be used upon it, it constantly keeps; and such as sense constantly finds in every particle of matter which has bulk enough to be perceived; and the mind finds inseparable from every particle of matter, though less than to make itself singly be perceived by our senses: e.g. Take a grain of wheat, divide it into two parts; each part has still solidity, extension, figure, and mobility: divide it again, and it retains still the same qualities; and so divide it on, till the parts become insensible; they must retain still each of them all those qualities. For division (which is all that a mill, or pestle, or any other body, does upon another, in reducing it to insensible parts) can never take away either solidity, extension, figure, or mobility from any body, but only makes two or more distinct separate masses of matter, of that which was but one before; all which distinct masses, reckoned as so many distinct bodies, after division, make a certain number. These I call original or primary qualities of body, which I think we may observe to produce simple ideas in us, viz. solidity, extension, figure, motion or rest, and number.

10. *Secondary qualities of bodies.* Secondly, such qualities which in truth are nothing in the objects themselves but power to produce various sensations in us by their primary qualities, i.e. by the bulk, figure, texture, and motion of their insensible parts, as colours, sounds, tastes, etc. These I call secondary qualities. To these might be added a third sort, which are allowed to be barely powers; though they are as much real qualities in the subject as those which I, to comply with the common way of speaking, call qualities, but for distinction, secondary qualities. For the power in fire to produce a new colour, or consistency, in wax or clay, by its primary qualities, is as much a quality in fire, as the power it has to produce in me a new idea or sensation of warmth or burning, which I felt not before, by the same primary qualities, viz. the bulk, texture, and motion of its insensible parts.

11. *How bodies produce ideas in us.* The next thing to be considered is, how bodies produce ideas in us; and that is manifestly by impulse, the only way which we can conceive bodies to operate in.

12. *By motions, external, and in our organism.* If then external objects be not united to our minds when they produce ideas therein; and yet we perceive these original qualities in such of them as singly fall under our senses, it is evident that some motion must be thence continued by our nerves, or animal spirits, by some parts of our bodies, to the brains or the seat of sensation, there to produce in our minds the particular ideas we have of them. And since the extension, figure, number, and motion of bodies of an observable bigness, may be perceived at a distance by the sight, it is evident some singly imperceptible bodies must come from them to the eyes, and thereby convey to the brain some motion; which produces these ideas which we have of them in us.

13. *How secondary qualities produce their ideas.* After the same manner, that the ideas of these original qualities are produced in us, we may conceive that the ideas of secondary qualities are also produced, viz. by the operation of insensible particles on our senses. For, it being manifest that there are bodies and good store of bodies, each whereof are so small, that we cannot by any of our senses discover either their bulk, figure, or motion, as is evident in the particles of the air and water, and others extremely smaller than those; perhaps as much smaller than the particles of air and water, as the particles of air and water are smaller than peas or hail stones; let us suppose at present that the different motions and figures, bulk and number, of such particles, affecting the several organs of our senses, produce in us those different sensations which we have from the colours and smells of bodies; e.g. that a violet, by the impulse of such insensible particles of matter, of peculiar figures and bulks, and in different degrees and modifications of their motions, causes the ideas of the blue colour, and sweet scent of that flower to be produced in our minds. It being no more impossible to conceive that God should annex such ideas to such motions, with which they have no similitude, than that he should annex the idea of pain to the motion of a piece of steel dividing our flesh, with which that idea hath no resemblance.

14. *They depend on the primary qualities.* What I have said concerning colours and smells may be understood also of tastes and sounds, and other the like sensible qualities; which, whatever reality we by mistake attribute to them, are in truth nothing in the objects themselves, but powers to produce various sensations in us; and depend on those primary qualities, viz. bulk, figure, texture, and motion of parts as I have said.

15. *Ideas of primary qualities are resemblances; of secondary, not.* From whence I think it easy to draw this observation, that the ideas of primary qualities of bodies are resemblances of them, and their patterns do really exist in the bodies themselves, but the ideas produced in us by these secondary qualities have no resemblance of them at all. There is nothing like our ideas, existing in the bodies themselves. They are, in the bodies we denominate from them, only a power to produce those sensations in us: and what is sweet, blue, or warm in idea, is but the certain bulk, figure, and motion of the insensible parts, in the bodies themselves, which we call so.

16. *Examples.* Flame is denominated hot and light; snow, white and cold; and manna, white and sweet, from the ideas they produce in us. Which qualities are commonly thought to be the same in those bodies that those ideas are in us, the one the perfect resemblance of the other, as they are in a mirror, and it would by most men be judged very extravagant if one should say otherwise. And yet he that will consider that the same fire that, at one distance produces in us the sensation of warmth, does, at a nearer approach, produce in us the far different sensation of pain, ought to bethink himself what reason he has to say that this idea of warmth, which was produced in him by the fire, is actually in the fire; and his idea of pain, which the same fire produced in him the same way, is not in the fire. Why are whiteness and coldness in snow, and

pain not, when it produces the one and the other idea in us; and can do neither, but by the bulk, figure, number, and motion of its solid parts?

17. *The ideas of the primary alone really exist.* The particular bulk, number, figure, and motion of the parts of fire or snow are really in them, whether any one's senses perceive them or no: and therefore they may be called real qualities, because they really exist in those bodies. But light, heat, whiteness, or coldness, are no more really in them than sickness or pain is in manna. Take away the sensation of them; let not the eyes see light or colours, nor the ears hear sounds; let the palate not taste, nor the nose smell, and all colours, tastes, odours, and sounds, as they are such particular ideas, vanish and cease, and are reduced to their causes, i.e., bulk, figure, and motion of parts. . . .

21. *Explains how water felt as cold by one hand may be warm to the other.* Ideas being thus distinguished and understood, we may be able to give an account how the same water, at the same time, may produce the idea of cold by one hand and of heat by the other: whereas it is impossible that the same water, if those ideas were really in it, should at the same time be both hot and cold. For, if we imagine warmth, as it is in our hands, to be nothing but a certain sort and degree of motion in the minute particles of our nerves or animal spirits, we may understand how it is possible that the same water may, at the same time, produce the sensations of heat in one hand and cold in the other; which yet figure never does, that never producing the idea of a square by one hand which has produced the idea of a globe by another. But if the sensation of heat and cold be nothing but the increase or diminution of the motion of the minute parts of our bodies, caused by the corpuscles of any other body, it is easy to be understood, that if that motion be greater in one hand than in the other; if a body be applied to the two hands, which has in its minute particles a greater motion than in those of one of the hands, and a less than in those of the other, it will increase the motion of the one hand and lessen it in the other; and so cause the different sensations of heat and cold that depend thereon.

BOOK IV: OF KNOWLEDGE AND PROBABILITY

Chapter XI: Of Our Knowledge of the Existence of Other Things

1. *Knowledge of the existence of other finite beings is to be had only by actual sensation.* The knowledge of our own being we have by intuition. The existence of a God, reason clearly makes known to us, as has been shown.

The knowledge of the existence of any other thing we can have only by sensation: for there being no necessary connexion of real existence with any idea a man hath in his memory; nor of any other existence but that of God with the existence of any particular man: no particular man can know the existence of any other being, but only when, by actual operating upon him, it makes itself perceived by him. For, the having the idea of anything in our mind, no more proves the existence of that thing, than the picture of a man evidences his being in the world, or the visions of a dream make thereby a true history.

2. *Instance: whiteness of this paper.* It is therefore the actual receiving of ideas from without that gives us notice of the existence of other things, and makes us know, that something doth exist at that time without us, which causes that idea in us; though perhaps we neither know nor consider how it does it. For it takes not from the certainty of our senses, and the ideas we receive by them, that we know not the manner wherein they are produced: e.g. whilst I write this, I have, by the paper affecting my eyes, that idea produced in my mind, which, whatever object causes, I call white; by which I know that that quality or accident (i.e. whose appearance before my eyes always causes that idea) doth really exist, and hath a being without me. And of this, the greatest assurance I can possibly have, and to which my faculties can attain, is the testimony of my eyes, which are the proper and sole judges of this thing; whose testimony I have reason to rely on as so certain, that I can no more doubt, whilst I write this, that I see white and black, and that something really exists that causes that sensation in me, than that I write or move my hand; which is a certainty as great as human nature is capable of, concerning the existence of anything, but a man's self alone, and of God.

3. *This notice by our senses, though not so certain as demonstration, yet may be called knowledge, and proves the existence of things without us.* The notice we have by our senses of the existing of things without us, though it be not altogether so certain as our intuitive knowledge, or the deductions of our reason employed about the clear abstract ideas of our own minds; yet it is an assurance that deserves the name of knowledge. If we persuade ourselves that our faculties act and inform us right concerning the existence of those objects that affect them, it cannot pass for an ill-grounded confidence: for I think nobody can, in earnest, be so sceptical as to be uncertain of the existence of those things which he sees and feels. At least, he that can doubt so far, (whatever he may have with his own thoughts,) will never have any controversy with me; since he can never be sure I say anything contrary to his own opinion. As to myself, I think God has given me assurance enough of the existence of things without me: since, by their different application, I can produce in myself both pleasure and pain, which is one great concernment of my present state. This is certain: the confidence that our faculties do not herein deceive us, is the greatest assurance we are capable of concerning the existence of material beings. For we cannot act anything but by our faculties; nor talk of knowledge itself, but by the help of those faculties which are fitted to apprehend even what knowledge is.

But besides the assurance we have from our senses themselves, that they do not err in the information they give us of the existence of things without us, when they are affected by them, we are further confirmed in this assurance by other concurrent reasons:

4. I. *Confirmed by concurrent reasons: First, because we cannot have ideas of sensation but by the inlet of the senses.* It is plain those perceptions are produced in us by exterior causes affecting our senses: because those that want the organs of any sense, never can have the ideas belonging to that sense produced in their

minds. This is too evident to be doubted: and therefore we cannot but be assured that they come in by the organs of that sense, and no other way. The organs themselves, it is plain, do not produce them: for then the eyes of a man in the dark would produce colours, and his nose smell roses in the winter: but we see nobody gets the relish of a pineapple, till he goes to the Indies, where it is, and tastes it.

5. II. *Secondly, Because we find that an idea from actual sensation, and another from memory, are very distinct perceptions.* Because sometimes I find that I cannot avoid the having those ideas produced in my mind. For though, when my eyes are shut, or windows fast, I can at pleasure recall to my mind the ideas of light, or the sun, which former sensations had lodged in my memory; so I can at pleasure lay by that idea, and take into my view that of the smell of a rose, or taste of sugar. But, if I turn my eyes at noon towards the sun, I cannot avoid the ideas which the light or sun then produces in me. So that there is a manifest difference between the ideas laid up in my memory (over which, if they were there only, I should have constantly the same power to dispose of them, and lay them by at pleasure) and those which force themselves upon me, and I cannot avoid having. And therefore it must needs be some exterior cause, and the brisk acting of some objects without me, whose efficacy I cannot resist, that produces those ideas in my mind, whether I will or no. Besides, there is nobody who doth not perceive the difference in himself between contemplating the sun, as he hath the idea of it in his memory, and actually looking upon it: of which two, his perception is so distinct, that few of his ideas are more distinguishable one from another. And therefore he hath certain knowledge that they are not both memory, or the actions of his mind, and fancies only within him; but that actual seeing hath a cause without.

6. III. *Thirdly, because pleasure or pain, which accompanies actual sensation, accompanies not the returning of those ideas without the external objects.* Add to this, that many of those ideas are produced in us with pain, which afterwards we remember without the least offence. Thus, the pain of heat or cold, when the idea of it is revived in our minds, gives us no disturbance; which, when felt, was very troublesome; and is again, when actually repeated: which is occasioned by the disorder the external object causes in our bodies when applied to them: and we remember the pains of hunger, thirst, or the headache, without any pain at all; which would either never disturb us, or else constantly do it, as often as we thought of it, were there nothing more but ideas floating in our minds, and appearances entertaining our fancies, without the real existence of things affecting us from abroad. The same may be said of pleasure, accompanying several actual sensations. And though mathematical demonstration depends not upon sense, yet the examining them by diagrams gives great credit to the evidence of our sight, and seems to give it a certainty approaching to that of demonstration itself. For, it would be very strange, that a man should allow it for an undeniable truth, that two angles of a figure, which he measures by lines and angles of a diagram, should be bigger one than the other, and yet doubt of the existence of those lines and angles, which by looking on he makes use of to measure that by.

7. IV. *Fourthly, because our senses assist one another's testimony of the existence of outward things, and enable us to predict.* Our senses in many cases bear witness to the truth of each other's report, concerning the existence of sensible things without us. He that sees a fire, may, if he doubt whether it be anything more than a bare fancy, feel it too; and be convinced, by putting his hand in it. Which certainly could never be put into such exquisite pain by a bare idea or phantom, unless that the pain be a fancy too: which yet he cannot, when the burn is well, by raising the idea of it, bring upon himself again. Thus I see, whilst I write this, I can change the appearance of the paper; and by designing the letters, tell beforehand what new idea it shall exhibit the very next moment, by barely drawing my pen over it: which will neither appear (let me fancy as much as I will) if my hands stand still; or though I move my pen, if my eyes be shut: nor, when those characters are once made on the paper, can I choose afterwards but see them as they are; that is, have the ideas of such letters as I have made. Whence it is manifest, that they are not barely the sport and play of my own imagination, when I find that the characters that were made at the pleasure of my own thoughts, do not obey them; nor yet cease to be, whenever I shall fancy it, but continue to affect my senses constantly and regularly, according to the figures I made them. To which if we will add, that the sight of those shall, from another man, draw such sounds as I beforehand design they shall stand for, there will be little reason left to doubt that those words I write do really exist without me, when they cause a long series of regular sounds to affect my ears, which could not be the effect of my imagination, nor could my memory retain them in that order.

8. *This certainty is as great as our condition needs.* But yet, if after all this any one will be so sceptical as to distrust his senses, and to affirm that all we see and hear, feel and taste, think and do, during our whole being, is but the series and deluding appearances of a long dream, whereof there is no reality; and therefore will question the existence of all things, or our knowledge of anything: I must desire him to consider, that, if all be a dream, then he doth but dream that he makes the question, and so it is not much matter that a waking man should answer him. But yet, if he pleases, he may dream that I make him this answer, That the certainty of things existing *in rerum natura* when we have the testimony of our senses for it is not only as great as our frame can attain to, but as our condition needs. For, our faculties being suited not to the full extent of being, nor to a perfect, clear, comprehensive knowledge of things free from all doubt and scruple; but to the preservation of us, in whom they are; and accommodated to the use of life: they serve to our purpose well enough, if they will but give us certain notice of those things, which are convenient or inconvenient to us. For he that sees a candle burning, and hath experimented the force of its flame by putting his finger in it, will little doubt that this is something existing without him, which does him harm, and puts him to great pain; which is assurance enough, when no man requires greater certainty to govern his actions by than what is as certain as his actions themselves. And if our dreamer pleases to try whether the glowing heat of a glass furnace be barely a

wandering imagination in a drowsy man's fancy, by putting his hand into it, he may perhaps be wakened into a certainty greater than he could wish, that it is something more than bare imagination. So that this evidence is as great as we can desire, being as certain to us as our pleasure or pain, i.e. happiness or misery; beyond which we have no concernment, either of knowing or being. Such an assurance of the existence of things without us is sufficient to direct us in the attaining the good and avoiding the evil which is caused by them, which is the important concernment we have of being made acquainted with them.

9. *But reaches no further than actual sensation.* In fine, then, when our senses do actually convey into our understandings any idea, we cannot but be satisfied that there doth something at that time really exist without us, which doth affect our senses, and by them give notice of itself to our apprehensive faculties, and actually produce that idea which we then perceive: and we cannot so far distrust their testimony, as to doubt that such collections of simple ideas as we have observed by our senses to be united together, do really exist together. But this knowledge extends as far as the present testimony of our senses, employed about particular objects that do then affect them, and no further. For if I saw such a collection of simple ideas as is wont to be called man, existing together one minute since, and am now alone, I cannot be certain that the same man exists now, since there is no necessary connexion of his existence a minute since with his existence now: by a thousand ways he may cease to be, since I had the testimony of my senses for his existence. And if I cannot be certain that the man I saw last today is now in being, I can less be certain that he is so who hath been longer removed from my senses, and I have not seen since yesterday, or since the last year: and much less can I be certain of the existence of men that I never saw. And, therefore, though it be highly probable that millions of men do now exist, yet, whilst I am alone, writing this, I have not that certainty of it which we strictly call knowledge; though the great likelihood of it puts me past doubt, and it be reasonable for me to do several things upon the confidence that there are men (and men also of my acquaintance, with whom I have to do) now in the world: but this is but probability, not knowledge.

10. *Folly to expect demonstration in everything.* Whereby yet we may observe how foolish and vain a thing it is for a man of a narrow knowledge, who having reason given him to judge of the different evidence and probability of things, and to be swayed accordingly; how vain, I say, it is to expect demonstration and certainty in things not capable of it; and refuse assent to very rational propositions, and act contrary to very plain and clear truths, because they cannot be made out so evident, as to surmount every the least (I will not say reason, but) pretence of doubting. He that, in the ordinary affairs of life, would admit of nothing but direct plain demonstration, would be sure of nothing in this world, but of perishing quickly. The wholesomeness of his meat or drink would not give him reason to venture on it: and I would fain know what it is he could do upon such grounds as are capable of no doubt, no objection.

Idealism

GEORGE BERKELEY (1685–1752) was born in Ireland. He entered Trinity College, Dublin, at the age of 15, and by 22 he was lecturing on Greek, Hebrew, and divinity. When he was 25 he wrote *A Treatise Concerning the Principles of Human Knowledge* in about three weeks. He lived in America from 1729 to 1731, building a home called Whitehall that still stands near Newport, Rhode Island. Berkeley spent his time in America attempting to raise funds for a college he wished to found in Bermuda, but in the end the plan never worked out. Berkeley returned to Ireland and became (the Anglican) Bishop of Cloyne. He wrote a variety of books, including a curious defense of drinking tar water as medicinal, and died in 1752.

THINKING QUESTIONS

George Berkeley, *Idealism*

1. Berkeley argues for the Bundle Theory of Objects: so-called "physical" objects, like a stone, a tree, a book, etc., are nothing but bundles or collections of properties. Do you think he is right? Or are objects physical substances that possess, but are not composed of, properties?
2. If you removed all of the properties of, say, an apple, would there be anything that remains? If not, is the Bundle Theory of Objects correct?
3. Berkeley defends conceptualism: properties are nothing but ideas in the mind; properties cannot exist outside of some mind thinking or conceiving of them. Consider: does daylight have a sound? Do X-rays have a color? If you think that they do, even though you can't hear the sound of daylight or see X-rays, aren't you imagining that there is *someone* (insects, dogs, extraterrestrials, God, et al.) who can hear daylight or see the color of X-rays? If you think that they do *not* have those qualities, isn't it because no one hears daylight or sees X-rays?
4. The Bundle Theory + conceptualism = idealism, the view that everything is an idea in the mind. But if everything is in our minds, what is the cause of our nonvolitional ideas? Obviously not a world of physical substances.
5. Berkeley has a simple answer to the mind/body problem. What is it?
6. Berkeley has a simple answer to Cartesian skepticism about the external world. What is it?

1. It is evident to any one who takes a survey of the objects of human knowledge, that they are either ideas actually imprinted on the senses; or else such as are perceived by attending to the passions and operations of the mind; or lastly, ideas formed by help of memory and imagination—either compounding, dividing, or barely representing those originally perceived in the aforesaid ways. By sight I have the ideas of light and colours, with their several degrees and variations. By touch I perceive hard and soft, heat and cold, motion and resistance, and of all these more and less either as to quantity or degree. Smelling furnishes me with odours; the palate with tastes; and hearing conveys sounds to the mind in all their variety of tone and composition. And as several of these are observed to accompany each other, they come to be marked by one name, and so to be reputed as one thing. Thus, for example a certain colour, taste, smell, figure and consistence having been observed to go together, are accounted one distinct thing, signified by the name apple; other collections of ideas constitute a stone, a tree, a book, and the like sensible things—which as they are pleasing or disagreeable excite the passions of love, hatred, joy, grief, and so forth.

2. But, besides all that endless variety of ideas or objects of knowledge, there is likewise something which knows or perceives them, and exercises divers operations, as willing, imagining, remembering, about them. This perceiving, active being is what I call mind, spirit, soul, or myself. By which words I do not denote any one of my ideas, but a thing entirely distinct from them, wherein, they exist, or, which is the same thing, whereby they are perceived—for the existence of an idea consists in being perceived.

3. That neither our thoughts, nor passions, nor ideas formed by the imagination, exist without the mind, is what everybody will allow. And it seems no less evident that the various sensations or ideas imprinted on the sense, however blended or combined together (that is, whatever objects they compose), cannot exist otherwise than in a mind perceiving them.—I think an intuitive knowledge may be obtained of this by any one that shall attend to what is meant by the term exists, when applied to sensible things. The table I write on I say exists, that is, I see and feel it; and if I were out of my study I should say it existed—meaning thereby that if I was in my study I might perceive it, or that some other spirit actually does perceive it. There was an odour, that is, it was smelt; there was a sound, that is, it was heard; a colour or figure, and it was perceived by sight or touch. This is all that I can understand by these and the like expressions. For as to what is said of the absolute existence of unthinking things without any relation to their being perceived, that seems perfectly unintelligible. Their *esse* is *percipi,* nor is it possible they should have any existence out of the minds or thinking things which perceive them.

4. It is indeed an opinion strangely prevailing amongst men, that houses, mountains, rivers, and in a word all sensible objects, have an existence, natural or real, distinct from their being perceived by the understanding. But, with how great an assurance and acquiescence soever this principle may be entertained in the world, yet whoever shall find in his heart to call it in question

may, if I mistake not, perceive it to involve a manifest contradiction. For, what are the fore-mentioned objects but the things we perceive by sense? and what do we perceive besides our own ideas or sensations? and is it not plainly repugnant that any one of these, or any combination of them, should exist unperceived?

5. If we thoroughly examine this tenet it will, perhaps, be found at bottom to depend on the doctrine of abstract ideas. For can there be a nicer strain of abstraction than to distinguish the existence of sensible objects from their being perceived, so as to conceive them existing unperceived? Light and colours, heat and cold, extension and figures—in a word the things we see and feel—what are they but so many sensations, notions, ideas, or impressions on the sense? and is it possible to separate, even in thought, any of these from perception? For my part, I might as easily divide a thing from itself. I may, indeed, divide in my thoughts, or conceive apart from each other, those things which, perhaps I never perceived by sense so divided. Thus, I imagine the trunk of a human body without the limbs, or conceive the smell of a rose without thinking on the rose itself. So far, I will not deny, I can abstract—if that may properly be called abstraction which extends only to the conceiving separately such objects as it is possible may really exist or be actually perceived asunder. But my conceiving or imagining power does not extend beyond the possibility of real existence or perception. Hence, as it is impossible for me to see or feel anything without an actual sensation of that thing, so is it impossible for me to conceive in my thoughts any sensible thing or object distinct from the sensation or perception of it.

6. Some truths there are so near and obvious to the mind that a man need only open his eyes to see them. Such I take this important one to be, viz., that all the choir of heaven and furniture of the earth, in a word all those bodies which compose the mighty frame of the world, have not any subsistence without a mind, that their being is to be perceived or known; that consequently so long as they are not actually perceived by me, or do not exist in my mind or that of any other created spirit, they must either have no existence at all, or else subsist in the mind of some Eternal Spirit—it being perfectly unintelligible, and involving all the absurdity of abstraction, to attribute to any single part of them an existence independent of a spirit. To be convinced of which, the reader need only reflect, and try to separate in his own thoughts the being of a sensible thing from its being perceived.

7. From what has been said it follows there is not any other Substance than Spirit, or that which perceives. But, for the fuller proof of this point, let it be considered the sensible qualities are colour, figure, motion, smell, taste, etc., i.e. the ideas perceived by sense. Now, for an idea to exist in an unperceiving thing is a manifest contradiction, for to have an idea is all one as to perceive; that therefore wherein colour, figure, and the like qualities exist must perceive them; hence it is clear there can be no unthinking substance or substratum of those ideas.

8. But, say you, though the ideas themselves do not exist without the mind, yet there may be things like them, whereof they are copies or resemblances,

which things exist without the mind in an unthinking substance. I answer, an idea can be like nothing but an idea; a colour or figure can be like nothing but another colour or figure. If we look but never so little into our thoughts, we shall find it impossible for us to conceive a likeness except only between our ideas. Again, I ask whether those supposed originals or external things, of which our ideas are the pictures or representations, be themselves perceivable or no? If they are, then they are ideas and we have gained our point; but if you say they are not, I appeal to any one whether it be sense to assert a colour is like something which is invisible; hard or soft, like something which is intangible; and so of the rest.

9. Some there are who make a distinction betwixt primary and secondary qualities. By the former they mean extension, figure, motion, rest, solidity or impenetrability, and number; by the latter they denote all other sensible qualities, as colours, sounds, tastes, and so forth. The ideas we have of these they acknowledge not to be the resemblances of anything existing without the mind, or unperceived, but they will have our ideas of the primary qualities to be patterns or images of things which exist without the mind, in an unthinking substance which they call Matter. By Matter, therefore, we are to understand an inert, senseless substance, in which extension, figure, and motion do actually subsist. But it is evident from what we have already shown, that extension, figure, and motion are only ideas existing in the mind, and that an idea can be like nothing but another idea, and that consequently neither they nor their archetypes can exist in an unperceiving substance. Hence, it is plain that the very notion of what is called Matter or corporeal substance, involves a contradiction in it.

10. They who assert that figure, motion, and the rest of the primary or original qualities do exist without the mind in unthinking substances, do at the same time acknowledge that colours, sounds, heat, cold, and suchlike secondary qualities, do not—which they tell us are sensations existing in the mind alone, that depend on and are occasioned by the different size, texture, and motion of the minute particles of matter. This they take for an undoubted truth, which they can demonstrate beyond all exception. Now, if it be certain that those original qualities are inseparably united with the other sensible qualities, and not, even in thought, capable of being abstracted from them, it plainly follows that they exist only in the mind. But I desire any one to reflect and try whether he can, by any abstraction of thought, conceive the extension and motion of a body without all other sensible qualities. For my own part, I see evidently that it is not in my power to frame an idea of a body extended and moving, but I must withal give it some colour or other sensible quality which is acknowledged to exist only in the mind. In short, extension, figure, and motion, abstracted from all other qualities, are inconceivable. Where therefore the other sensible qualities are, there must these be also, to wit, in the mind and nowhere else. . . .

14. I shall farther add, that, after the same manner as modern philosophers prove certain sensible qualities to have no existence in Matter, or without the mind, the same thing may be likewise proved of all other sensible qualities whatsoever. Thus, for instance, it is said that heat and cold are affections only of the mind, and not at all patterns of real beings, existing in the corporeal substances

which excite them, for that the same body which appears cold to one hand seems warm to another. Now, why may we not as well argue that figure and extension are not patterns or resemblances of qualities existing in Matter, because to the same eye at different stations, or eyes of a different texture at the same station, they appear various, and cannot therefore be the images of anything settled and determinate without the mind? Again, it is proved that sweetness is not really in the sapid thing, because the thing remaining unaltered the sweetness is changed into bitter, as in case of a fever or otherwise vitiated palate. Is it not as reasonable to say that motion is not without the mind, since if the succession of ideas in the mind become swifter, the motion, it is acknowledged, shall appear slower without any alteration in any external object?

15. In short, let any one consider those arguments which are thought manifestly to prove that colours and taste exist only in the mind, and he shall find they may with equal force be brought to prove the same thing of extension, figure, and motion. Though it must be confessed this method of arguing does not so much prove that there is no extension or colour in an outward object, as that we do not know by sense which is the true extension or colour of the object. But the arguments foregoing plainly shew it to be impossible that any colour or extension at all, or other sensible quality whatsoever, should exist in an unthinking subject without the mind, or in truth, that there should be any such thing as an outward object. . . .

18. But, though it were possible that solid, figured, movable substances may exist without the mind, corresponding to the ideas we have of bodies, yet how is it possible for us to know this? Either we must know it by sense or by reason. As for our senses, by them we have the knowledge only of our sensations, ideas, or those things that are immediately perceived by sense, call them what you will: but they do not inform us that things exist without the mind, or unperceived, like to those which are perceived. This the materialists themselves acknowledge. It remains therefore that if we have any knowledge at all of external things, it must be by reason, inferring their existence from what is immediately perceived by sense. But what reason can induce us to believe the existence of bodies without the mind, from what we perceive, since the very patrons of Matter themselves do not pretend there is any necessary connexion betwixt them and our ideas? I say it is granted on all hands (and what happens in dreams, phrensies, and the like, puts it beyond dispute) that it is possible we might be affected with all the ideas we have now, though there were no bodies existing without resembling them. Hence, it is evident the supposition of external bodies is not necessary for the producing our ideas; since it is granted they are produced sometimes, and might possibly be produced always in the same order, we see them in at present, without their concurrence.

19. But, though we might possibly have all our sensations without them, yet perhaps it may be thought easier to conceive and explain the manner of their production, by supposing external bodies in their likeness rather than otherwise; and so it might be at least probable there are such things as bodies that excite their ideas in our minds. But neither can this be said; for, though we give the

materialists their external bodies, they by their own confession are never the nearer knowing how our ideas are produced; since they own themselves unable to comprehend in what manner body can act upon spirit, or how it is possible it should imprint any idea in the mind. Hence it is evident the production of ideas or sensations in our minds can be no reason why we should suppose Matter or corporeal substances, since that is acknowledged to remain equally inexplicable with or without this supposition. If therefore it were possible for bodies to exist without the mind, yet to hold they do so, must needs be a very precarious opinion; since it is to suppose, without any reason at all, that God has created innumerable beings that are entirely useless, and serve to no manner of purpose.

20. In short, if there were external bodies, it is impossible we should ever come to know it; and if there were not, we might have the very same reasons to think there were that we have now. Suppose—what no one can deny possible—an intelligence without the help of external bodies, to be affected with the same train of sensations or ideas that you are, imprinted in the same order and with like vividness in his mind. I ask whether that intelligence hath not all the reason to believe the existence of corporeal substances, represented by his ideas, and exciting them in his mind, that you can possibly have for believing the same thing? Of this there can be no question—which one consideration were enough to make any reasonable person suspect the strength of whatever arguments be may think himself to have, for the existence of bodies without the mind. . . .

22. I am afraid I have given cause to think I am needlessly prolix in handling this subject. For, to what purpose is it to dilate on that which may be demonstrated with the utmost evidence in a line or two, to any one that is capable of the least reflexion? It is but looking into your own thoughts, and so trying whether you can conceive it possible for a sound, or figure, or motion, or colour to exist without the mind or unperceived. This easy trial may perhaps make you see that what you contend for is a downright contradiction. Insomuch that I am content to put the whole upon this issue:—If you can but conceive it possible for one extended movable substance, or, in general, for any one idea, or anything like an idea, to exist otherwise than in a mind perceiving it, I shall readily give up the cause. And, as for all that compages of external bodies you contend for, I shall grant you its existence, though you cannot either give me any reason why you believe it exists, or assign any use to it when it is supposed to exist. I say, the bare possibility of your opinions being true shall pass for an argument that it is so.

23. But, say you, surely there is nothing easier than for me to imagine trees, for instance, in a park, or books existing in a closet, and nobody by to perceive them. I answer, you may so, there is no difficulty in it; but what is all this, I beseech you, more than framing in your mind certain ideas which you call books and trees, and the same time omitting to frame the idea of any one that may perceive them? But do not you yourself perceive or think of them all the while? This therefore is nothing to the purpose; it only shews you have the power of imagining or forming ideas in your mind: but it does not shew that you can conceive it possible the objects of your thought may exist without the mind.

To make out this, it is necessary that you conceive them existing unconceived or unthought of, which is a manifest repugnancy. When we do our utmost to conceive the existence of external bodies, we are all the while only contemplating our own ideas. But the mind taking no notice of itself, is deluded to think it can and does conceive bodies existing unthought of or without the mind, though at the same time they are apprehended by or exist in itself. A little attention will discover to any one the truth and evidence of what is here said, and make it unnecessary to insist on any other proofs against the existence of material substance. . . .

25. All our ideas, sensations, notions, or the things which we perceive, by whatsoever names they may be distinguished, are visibly inactive—there is nothing of power or agency included in them. So that one idea or object of thought cannot produce or make any alteration in another. To be satisfied of the truth of this, there is nothing else requisite but a bare observation of our ideas. For, since they and every part of them exist only in the mind, it follows that there is nothing in them but what is perceived: but whoever shall attend to his ideas, whether of sense or reflexion, will not perceive in them any power or activity; there is, therefore, no such thing contained in them. A little attention will discover to us that the very being of an idea implies passiveness and inertness in it, insomuch that it is impossible for an idea to do anything, or, strictly speaking, to be the cause of anything: neither can it be the resemblance or pattern of any active being, as is evident from sect. 8. Whence it plainly follows that extension, figure, and motion cannot be the cause of our sensations. To say, therefore, that these are the effects of powers resulting from the configuration, number, motion, and size of corpuscles, must certainly be false.

26. We perceive a continual succession of ideas, some are anew excited, others are changed or totally disappear. There is therefore some cause of these ideas, whereon they depend, and which produces and changes them. That this cause cannot be any quality or idea or combination of ideas, is clear from the preceding section. I must therefore be a substance; but it has been shewn that there is no corporeal or material substance: it remains therefore that the cause of ideas is an incorporeal active substance or Spirit.

27. A spirit is one simple, undivided, active being—as it perceives ideas it is called the understanding, and as it produces or otherwise operates about them it is called the will. Hence there can be no idea formed of a soul or spirit; for all ideas whatever, being passive and inert (vide sect. 25), they cannot represent unto us, by way of image or likeness, that which acts. A little attention will make it plain to any one, that to have an idea which shall be like that active principle of motion and change of ideas is absolutely impossible. Such is the nature of spirit, or that which acts, that it cannot be of itself perceived, but only by the effects which it produceth. If any man shall doubt of the truth of what is here delivered, let him but reflect and try if he can frame the idea of any power or active being, and whether he has ideas of two principal powers, marked by the names will and understanding, distinct from each other as well as from a third idea of Substance or Being in general, with a relative notion of its supporting or being the subject of the aforesaid powers—which is signified

by the name soul or spirit. This is what some hold; but, so far as I can see, the words will, soul, spirit, do not stand for different ideas, or, in truth, for any idea at all, but for something which is very different from ideas, and which, being an agent, cannot be like unto, or represented by, any idea whatsoever. Though it must be owned at the same time that we have some notion of soul, spirit, and the operations of the mind: such as willing, loving, hating—inasmuch as we know or understand the meaning of these words.

28. I find I can excite ideas in my mind at pleasure, and vary and shift the scene as oft as I think fit. It is no more than willing, and straightway this or that idea arises in my fancy; and by the same power it is obliterated and makes way for another. This making and unmaking of ideas doth very properly denominate the mind active. Thus much is certain and grounded on experience; but when we think of unthinking agents or of exciting ideas exclusive of volition, we only amuse ourselves with words.

29. But, whatever power I may have over my own thoughts, I find the ideas actually perceived by Sense have not a like dependence on my will. When in broad daylight I open my eyes, it is not in my power to choose whether I shall see or no, or to determine what particular objects shall present themselves to my view; and so likewise as to the hearing and other senses; the ideas imprinted on them are not creatures of my will. There is therefore some other Will or Spirit that produces them.

30. The ideas of Sense are more strong, lively, and distinct than those of the imagination; they have likewise a steadiness, order, and coherence, and are not excited at random, as those which are the effects of human wills often are, but in a regular train or series, the admirable connexion whereof sufficiently testifies the wisdom and benevolence of its Author. Now the set rules or established methods wherein the Mind we depend on excites in us the ideas of sense, are called the laws of nature; and these we learn by experience, which teaches us that such and such ideas are attended with such and such other ideas, in the ordinary course of things.

31. This gives us a sort of foresight which enables us to regulate our actions for the benefit of life. And without this we should be eternally at a loss; we could not know how to act anything that might procure us the least pleasure, or remove the least pain of sense. That food nourishes, sleep refreshes, and fire warms us; that to sow in the seed—time is the way to reap in the harvest; and in general that to obtain such or such ends, such or such means are conducive—all this we know, not by discovering any necessary connexion between our ideas, but only by the observation of the settled laws of nature, without which we should be all in uncertainty and confusion, and a grown man no more know how to manage himself in the affairs of life than an infant just born.

32. And yet this consistent uniform working, which so evidently displays the goodness and wisdom of that Governing Spirit whose Will constitutes the laws of nature, is so far from leading our thoughts to Him, that it rather sends them wandering after second causes. For, when we perceive certain ideas of Sense constantly followed by other ideas and we know this is not of our own

doing, we forthwith attribute power and agency to the ideas themselves, and make one the cause of another, than which nothing can be more absurd and unintelligible. Thus, for example, having observed that when we perceive by sight a certain round luminous figure we at the same time perceive by touch the idea or sensation called heat, we do from thence conclude the sun to be the cause of heat. And in like manner perceiving the motion and collision of bodies to be attended with sound, we are inclined to think the latter the effect of the former.

33. The ideas imprinted on the Senses by the Author of nature are called real things; and those excited in the imagination being less regular, vivid, and constant, are more properly termed ideas, or images of things, which they copy and represent. But then our sensations, be they never so vivid and distinct, are nevertheless ideas, that is, they exist in the mind, or are perceived by it, as truly as the ideas of its own framing. The ideas of Sense are allowed to have more reality in them, that is, to be more strong, orderly, and coherent than the creatures of the mind; but this is no argument that they exist without the mind. They are also less dependent on the spirit, or thinking substance which perceives them, in that they are excited by the will of another and more powerful spirit; yet still they are ideas, and certainly no idea, whether faint or strong, can exist otherwise than in a mind perceiving it. . . .

38. But after all, say you, it sounds very harsh to say we eat and drink ideas, and are clothed with ideas. I acknowledge it does so—the word *idea* not being used in common discourse to signify the several combinations of sensible qualities which are called things; and it is certain that any expression which varies from the familiar use of language will seem harsh and ridiculous. But this doth not concern the truth of the proposition, which in other words is no more than to say, we are fed and clothed with those things which we perceive immediately by our senses. The hardness or softness, the colour, taste, warmth, figure, or suchlike qualities, which combined together constitute the several sorts of victuals and apparel, have been shewn to exist only in the mind that perceives them; and this is all that is meant by calling them ideas; which word if it was as ordinarily used as thing, would sound no harsher nor more ridiculous than it. I am not for disputing about the propriety, but the truth of the expression. If therefore you agree with me that we eat and drink and are clad with the immediate objects of sense, which cannot exist unperceived or without the mind, I shall readily grant it is more proper or conformable to custom that they should be called things rather than ideas.

39. If it be demanded why I make use of the word *idea,* and do not rather in compliance with custom call them *things;* I answer, I do it for two reasons:—first, because the term thing in contra—distinction to idea, is generally supposed to denote somewhat existing without the mind; secondly, because thing hath a more comprehensive signification than idea, including spirit or thinking things as well as ideas. Since therefore the objects of sense exist only in the mind, and are withal thoughtless and inactive, I chose to mark them by the word *idea,* which implies those properties.

Text Credits

ALMEDER, ROBERT. "Reincarnation and Mind/Body Dualism." From *Death and Personal Survival.* (Lanham, MD: Rowman & Littlefield, 1992.)

AQUINAS, THOMAS. "The Five Ways." From *Summa Theologica,* public domain translation. http://www.fordham.edu/halsall/imdex.html.

BARZUN, JACQUES. "Trim the College—A Utopia!" From *The Chronicle Review,* June 2001, http://chronicle.com/free/v47/i41/41b02401.htm.

BENHABIB, SEYLA. "A Deliberative Model of Democracy." From *Democracy and Difference.* (Princeton University Press, 1996.)

BENNETT, JONATHAN. "The Conscience of Huckleberry Finn." From *Philosophy* 49 (1974).

BENTHAM, JEREMY. "The Principle of Utility." From *An Introduction to the Principles of Morals and Legislation.* (London: T. Payne, 1789.)

BERKELEY, GEORGE. "Idealism." From *A Treatise Concerning the Principles of Human Knowledge.* (Dublin: A. Rhames for J. Pepyat, 1710.)

CAHN, STEVEN. "Religion Without God." From *Philosophy of Religion.* (Harper and Row, 1970.)

CHALMERS, DAVID J. "The Puzzle of Conscious Experience." From *Scientific American* 237, issue 6 (1995), pp. 80–86.

CLIFFORD, WILLIAM K. "The Ethics of Belief." From *Lectures and Essays.* (London: Macmillan, 1879.)

DEMASIO, ANTONIO R. "Phineas Gage." From *Descartes' Error.* (New York: HarperCollins, 1995.)

DENNETT, DANIEL C. "Where Am I?" From *Brainstorms.* (Cambridge: MIT Press, 1978.)

DESCARTES, RENÉ. "Meditations." From *The Meditations,* translated by John Cottingham. (Cambridge University Press, 1984.) Originally published in 1641.

GILLIGAN, CAROL. "Gender and Moral Development." From *Women and Moral Theory,* edited by Eva F. Kittay and Diana T. Meyers. (Lanham, MD: Rowman & Littlefield, 1987.)

GUTMANN, AMY. "Deliberation and Democratic Character." From *Democratic Education.* (New Jersey: Princeton University Press, 1987.)

HALES, STEVEN D. "Evidence and the Afterlife." From *Philosophia,* 28, nos. 1–4 (2001.) pp. 335–346.

HALES, STEVEN D. "The Traditional Problem of Free Will." Originally written for this book.

HUME, DAVID. "Of Liberty and Necessity." From *A Treatise of Human Nature,* Book II, part III. (London: John Noon, 1739.)

HUME, DAVID. "The Bundle Theory of Personal Identity." From *A Treatise of Human Nature,* Book 1, part IV, section VI. (London: John Noon, 1739.)

JAMES, WILLIAM. "The Will to Believe." From *The New World* (1896).

JOHNSON, B. C. "The Problem of Evil." From *The Atheist Debater's Handbook.* (Prometheus Books, 1981.)

KANT, IMMANUEL. "The Categorical Imperative." From *The Philosophy of Immanuel Kant,* compiled by Lewis White Beck. (New York: Garland Publishing, 1976.) pp. 55–91.

KURTZ, PAUL. "Should Skeptical Inquiry Be Applied to Religion?" From *Skeptical Inquirer,* July/August 1999.

LAZARE, DANIEL. "False Testament: Archaeology Refutes the Bible's Claim to History." From *Harper's,* March 2002.

LOCKE, JOHN, "Empiricism." From *An Essay Concerning Human Understanding.* (London: Eliz. Holt for Thomas Bassett, 1690.)

LOCKE, JOHN. "The Continuing Consciousness Theory of Personal Identity." From *An Essay Concerning Human Understanding.* (London: Eliz. Holt for Thomas Bassett, 1690.)

LOCKE, JOHN. "From the State of Nature to Civil Society." From *The Second Treatise of Government.* (London: Awnsham Churchill, 1690.)

MANSON, NEIL A. "The Design Argument." Originally written for this book.

MENDUS, SUSAN. "Losing the Faith: Feminism and Democracy." From *Democracy: The Unfinished Journey 508 BC–AD 1993,* edited by John Dunn. (Oxford University Press, 1992.)

MIDGELY, MARY. "Trying Out One's New Sword." From *Heart and Mind: The Varieties of Moral Experience.* (St. Martin's Press, 1981.)

MILGRAM, STANLEY. "Obedience to Authority." From *Obedience to Authority.* (New York: Harper and Row, 1974.)

MILL, JOHN STUART. "Utilitarianism." From *Utilitarianism.* (1863)

NIETZSCHE, FRIEDRICH. *Beyond Good and Evil.* Translated by Helen Zimmern. Macmillan, 1907. Originally published in 1885.

NIETZSCHE, FRIEDRICH. *The Gay Science.* Translated by Walter Kaufmann. Vintage Books, 1974. Originally published in 1887.

NIETZSCHE, FRIEDRICH. *Twilight of the Idols.* Translated by Walter Kaufmann. Viking Books, 1954. Originally published in 1895.

NOZICK, ROBERT. "How Liberty Upsets Patterns." From *Anarchy, State and Utopia.* (Basic Books, 1974.)

PALEY, WILLIAM. "The Watchmaker." From *Natural Theology*. (London: R. Faulder, 1802.)
PARFIT, DEREK. "The Bundle Theory." From *Mindwaves*. (Blackwell, 1987.)
PASCAL, BLAISE. "The Wager." From *Pensées,* #233. Originally published in 1670.
PLATO. *The Apology.* From *Socrates and the Legal Obligation,* R. E. Allen, pp. 37–62. (Minneapolis: University of Minnesota Press, 1980.)
PLATO, *Euthyphro*. Translated by F. J. Church. (New York: Macmillian/Library of Liberal Arts, 1963.)

RACHELS, JAMES. "Ethical Egoism." From *The Elements of Moral Philosophy.* (McGraw-Hill, 2002.)
RAWLS, JOHN. "Contract Theory." From *A Theory of Justice.* (Harvard University Press, 1971.)
REID, THOMAS. "The Liberty of Moral Agents." From *Essays on the Active Powers of Man*. (Edinburgh: J. Bell, 1788.)
ROWE, WILLIAM L. "Two Concepts of Freedom." From *The American Philosophical Association Proceedings and Addresses* 61. (1987)
RUSSELL, BERTRAND. "Appearance and Reality." From the *Problems of Philosophy.* (Oxford, 1912.)

SACKS, OLIVER. "A Matter of Identity." From *The Man Who Mistook His Wife for a Hat*. (New York: Harper and Row, 1987.)
SEARLE, JOHN R. "Minds, Brain, and Programs." From *The Behavioral and Brain Sciences,* vol. 3. (Cambridge University Press, 1980.)
SHERMER, MICHAEL. "I Am Therefore I Think." From *Why People Believe Weird Things*. (New York: W. H. Freeman, 1997.)
STUMP, ELEONORE. "A Solution to the Problem of Evil." From *Faith and Philosphy* 2, no. 4, October 1985.

THOMPSON, CLIVE. "The Know-It-All Machine." From *Lingua Franca* 11, no. 6. (September 2001) pp. 28–35.